AROUND THE WORLD IN 80 WINES

Joys of Pairing Wine And Food

P J M a a l l s

DISCLAIMER

The information provided in this book on the joys of food and wine pairings from around the world is intended for educational and entertainment purposes only.

While we have made every effort to ensure the accuracy of the information in this book, we make no representations or warranties of any kind, express or implied, about the completeness, accuracy, reliability, suitability or availability with respect to the content of this book.

The content of this book is not intended to be a substitute for professional advice or guidance, and should not be relied upon for any specific purpose. The reader is advised to consult with a qualified professional before making any decisions based on the information provided in this book.

The author and publisher of this book shall not be liable for any damages or losses, including but not limited to direct, indirect, incidental, consequential, or any other damages or losses arising out of or in connection with the use of this book or the information contained within it.

By reading and using the information in this book, you acknowledge that you have read and understood this disclaimer and accept all risks and responsibilities associated with your use of this book and the information contained within it.

TABLE OF CONTENTS

INTRODUCTION

This Book is an attempt to take you on a gastronomic adventure around the world.

Join me as we explore the distinct flavours and culinary traditions of different regions, from the spice markets of India to the vineyards of Tuscany. As we delve into the world of wine and food pairing, we'll discover the history and culture of wine in each region.

Did you know that the ancient Greeks considered wine a gift from the gods and used it as a medicine? Or that the Romans were responsible for spreading viticulture throughout Europe?

In ancient Greece, wine was considered much more than just an alcoholic beverage. It was viewed as a gift from the gods, something that brought pleasure, celebration, and spiritual fulfilment.

The Greeks associated the god of wine and revelry, Dionysus, with this luxurious drink. They believed that he blessed the land and cultivated the grapevines that produced the best wines. For this reason, wine was often used in religious ceremonies as a way to honour and celebrate the gods.

The Greeks believed that wine had many health benefits. They thought that it could cure illnesses, provide strength and vigour, and even prolong life. This is why they often mixed wine with honey, herbs, and other ingredients to create medicinal tonics.

The powerful social and cultural significance of wine is also evident in Greek literature, art, and philosophy. For example, Homer's epic poem, The Odyssey, features wine as an important element of hospitality and socialising. Meanwhile, philosophers like Plato considered wine as a symbol of pleasure and excess, with Dionysus representing the irrational, emotional and passionate aspects of human nature.

Wine certainly has played an important role in ancient Greek culture, influencing their religion, art, literature, and philosophy, and was regarded as more than just a simple intoxicant.

The ancient Romans played a significant role in spreading viticulture (the cultivation of grapes) throughout Europe. The Roman Empire was known for conquering new regions and territories, and with their conquests, they brought grapevines and wine culture as well.

The Romans were highly skilled winemakers, and they realised the potential of grape cultivation in improving health, diet, and lifestyle. They introduced new grape varieties, winemaking techniques, and agricultural practices, which helped to improve the quality and quantity of wine production.

Roman winemakers planted grapevines in Italy, Spain, France, and Germany, and they established vineyards in other regions that are today part of the modern-day United Kingdom, Belgium, the Netherlands, and Switzerland. The Roman Empire was massive, and, as a result, winemaking quickly became an essential part of European culture.

The Romans built roads, promulgated laws to protect vineyards, and in extreme cases, forced people to plant grapevines, which contributed to the spread of viticulture throughout Europe. They also built ships that could transport huge quantities of wine from one region to another, making it much easier for people to access wine and enjoy it.

The ancient Romans most certainly played a pivotal role in spreading viticulture throughout Europe, and their inventions, innovations and skilled winemaking technique continued to influence European wine culture for centuries to come.

We'll also explore the diverse wine regions of the world, from the sunny hills of California's Napa Valley to the rugged terrain of South Africa's Stellenbosch. We'll learn about the different grape varieties that thrive in each region, and how they contribute to the unique flavours and aromas of the wines produced there.

But it's not just about the wine - we'll also delve into the culinary traditions of each region and discover the perfect wine pairings for each dish. Whether it's a rich and hearty stew from Argentina or a delicate seafood dish from the Mediterranean, we'll find the perfect wine to complement and enhance the flavours of each dish. I will also include information on the history and culture of wine in each region.

Ah!....food and wine, the classic duo that never fails to delight our senses and satisfy our cravings. A true match made in heaven, these two have been enjoyed by foodies and wine enthusiasts alike for centuries.

There's something truly magical about the way a great wine can elevate the flavours of a perfectly cooked dish, and vice versa. Whether you're savouring a rich, bold Cabernet Sauvignon with a hearty steak or pairing a crisp, refreshing Sauvignon Blanc with a fresh salad, the right wine can bring out the best in any meal.

But it's not just about the taste - the art of food and wine pairing is also about the experience. There's a certain elegance and sophistication that comes with pairing the right wine with the right dish, and it's a skill that takes practice and patience to perfect.

So whether you're a seasoned wine connoisseur or a curious foodie looking to explore the world of wine, there's always something new and exciting to discover about this timeless pairing. So let's raise a glass (or a fork!) to the perfect partnership of food and wine - may it continue to inspire us and delight our taste buds for years to come.

Imagine starting your journey in Italy, where you pair a bold Chianti with a savoury bowl of pasta al pomodoro. You savour the taste of the ripe tomatoes, the tangy acidity of the wine, and the rich notes of the Parmesan cheese. Next, you jet off to France, where you indulge in a buttery croissant and a crisp glass of Champagne. The bubbles dance on your tongue, enhancing the flaky pastry, while the yeastiness of the wine complements the buttery goodness.

From there, you journey to South America, where you discover the perfect pairing for spicy empanadas: a juicy Malbec. The bold tannins of the wine balance out the heat of the chilies, while the fruity notes of the Malbec accentuate the flavours of the meat filling. And then, off to Asia, where you sample the perfect match for sushi: a crisp, refreshing sake. The clean, light flavour of the rice wine enhances the delicate flavours of the raw fish, while the subtle sweetness balances out the saltiness of the soy sauce.

As you continue on your adventure, you realise that pairing foods and wines is not just about finding the perfect match. It's also about exploring new flavours, discovering new combinations, and embracing the diversity of the world's cuisines. It's about opening your mind and your palate to new experiences, and creating your own culinary journey.

So, grab your passport (and your corkscrew), and let's set off on a delicious adventure! Who knows where your taste buds will take you next?

But before we get carried away and embark on our orgasmic culinary journey, let me briefly introduce you to one Phileas Fogg and his adventures around the world.

"Around the World in Eighty Days" is a novel written by Jules Verne and published in 1873. The story follows the adventures of Phileas Fogg, a wealthy English gentleman who makes a wager with his fellow members of the Reform Club that he can circumnavigate the globe in just eighty days.

Accompanied by his loyal French valet, Passepartout, Fogg sets out on his journey from London, travelling by train, steamship, and even elephant. Along the way, he faces a number of obstacles and setbacks, including delays caused by weather and transportation mishaps, as well as an encounter with a detective who suspects him of a bank robbery.

Despite these challenges, Fogg remains determined to win the bet and return to London within the allotted time frame. With Passepartout by his side, he crosses the Atlantic, traverses the United States, and makes his way across Asia, all while evading danger and narrowly avoiding disaster.

In the end, Fogg succeeds in his mission, arriving back in London just in time to win the wager and prove his fellow club members wrong. The novel is celebrated for its vivid descriptions of exotic locales and its portrayal of Fogg as a stoic, unflappable hero who remains calm and collected in the face of adversity.

BRIEFLY ABOUT ME

As a self-taught wine enthusiast who has spent many years in the industry, I have come to appreciate the importance of pairing the right wine with the right food.

My name is PJ Maalls, and I have had the pleasure of working for a German wine growing family who have been producing quality wines for almost 365 years. Today their vineyards span the globe, and during my 30 years with them, I brought samples of selected first-press single grape variety wines to wine lovers who would get to taste the wines first before making their purchase.

Through this experience, I came to understand the intricacies of wine and how it can enhance the flavours of food. As a result, I have made it my mission to share my knowledge with others who have a passion for wine and for food.

Wine is, no doubt, a complex and versatile beverage that can greatly enhance the flavours of food when paired properly. The key to successful wine and food pairing lies in understanding the different flavour profiles of both the wine and the food, and finding a complementary or contrasting match.

I believe there are several factors to consider when pairing wine with food. These include the acidity, sweetness, tannins, and body of the wine, as well as the intensity and type of flavours in the food. For example, a high-acid wine can pair well with fatty or oily foods because the acid helps to cut through the richness of the dish. Similarly, a sweet wine can balance out the heat and spice in a dish, while tannic wines can pair well with rich, meaty dishes.

One of the most important things I kept in mind when pairing wine with food was to avoid overpowering either the wine or the food. The goal is to find a balance between the two, so that each can be enjoyed to its fullest. This means choosing a wine that is not too strong or too weak in flavour, and that complements the flavours in the food without overwhelming them.

Ultimately, successful wine and food pairing requires a bit of experimentation and a willingness to try new things. With practice and experience, you can develop a keen sense of taste and learn to appreciate the nuances of different wines and how they can enhance the flavours of food.

In this book, I will try to take you through the basics of food and wine pairing and we will explore some of the most popular pairings I think that are sure to impress your guests.

FOOD AND WINE

As we will learn, the right type of food can be complementary to the wine's characteristics, bringing out its unique qualities and making it more enjoyable. Here are some examples of how different types of food can enhance the joys of wine:

Italian food: Italian cuisine is known for its rich and bold flavours, which pair well with full-bodied red wines. For example, a robust Chianti or Barolo is a perfect match for a plate of pasta with meaty tomato sauce or a hearty bowl of risotto.

French food: French cuisine is known for its elegance and sophistication, which is mirrored in their wines. A classic Bordeaux or Burgundy pairs beautifully with rich, buttery dishes like Coq au Vin or Beef Bourguignon. Additionally, a crisp Sancerre or Chablis complements light seafood dishes like oysters and mussels.

Spanish food: Spanish cuisine is known for its bold flavours and spicy dishes. Pairing a Rioja or Tempranillo with a plate of paella or chorizo adds an extra layer of complexity to the wine and balances out the heat of the dish.

Asian food: Asian cuisine is diverse and includes a wide variety of flavors and textures. A dry Riesling is a great match for spicy Thai or Indian dishes, while a fruity Pinot Noir complements the sweetness of Chinese cuisine like General Tso's chicken or sweet and sour pork.

Mexican food: Mexican cuisine is known for its bold and zesty flavours. A robust Cabernet Sauvignon pairs well with the richness of mole sauce or the smokiness of grilled meats like carne asada. Additionally, a crisp Sauvignon Blanc complements the acidity of salsa and guacamole.

Middle Eastern food: Middle Eastern cuisine is known for its bold spices and savoury flavours. A full-bodied Shiraz or Zinfandel pairs well with rich, meaty dishes like lamb tagine or shawarma. Additionally, a light Pinot Grigio complements the freshness of tabbouleh or fattoush salad.

Who is interested?

There are many types of people who may be interested in learning about pairing foods and wines from around the world.

Here are examples of a few:

Wine enthusiasts: Wine lovers who are passionate about exploring different types of wine and expanding their knowledge about pairing wine with food.

Hospitality professionals: Individuals working in the hospitality industry, such as chefs, sommeliers, and servers, who want to enhance their knowledge of food and wine pairings to provide better service to their customers.

Travellers: People who enjoy travelling and exploring different cultures, cuisines, and wine regions.

Social drinkers: Individuals who enjoy drinking wine on social occasions and want to learn more about pairing wine with food to enhance their overall drinking experience.

Foodies: Individuals who are passionate about trying new foods and exploring different culinary cultures. They are always looking for ways to enhance their dining experience.

Wine Enthusiasts: People who are interested in different types of wines and their unique characteristics. They enjoy learning about the origins of different types of wines, their taste, aroma, and how to pair them with different foods.

Event Planners: Individuals who are responsible for organising events, such as weddings, corporate events, and other celebrations. They are always looking for ways to make their events unique and memorable, and pairing the right wine and food can be an important aspect of this.

Restaurant Owners and Staff: Professionals who work in the food and beverage industry are always looking for ways to enhance their menu and provide their customers with an exceptional dining experience. By learning how to pair different types of food with wines, they can create a more sophisticated and enjoyable dining experience for their customers.

Home Cooks: Individuals who enjoy cooking at home and experimenting with different recipes. They are always looking for ways to improve their cooking skills and impress their guests with their culinary creations.

Regardless of your background, if you enjoy exploring different cultures, trying new foods and testing tasty wines to enhance your dining experience, then you will definitely enjoy reading my eBook.

Whether you are a seasoned wine connoisseur or a newcomer to the world of wine, there is something here for everyone. So, let's raise a glass and try to discover the wonderful world of food and wine pairing together!

CHAPTER 1

THE BASICS OF FOOD AND WINE PAIRING

Food and wine pairing is the process of selecting the right wine to complement the flavours of a particular dish, enhancing the overall dining experience. Here are some fundamental principles of food and wine pairing.

Match the intensity: The intensity of the wine should match the intensity of the food. For example, a bold red wine pairs well with a hearty beef dish, while a lighter white wine complements a delicate fish dish.

Consider acidity: The acidity in wine can cut through the richness of certain foods. For example, a high-acid white wine such as Sauvignon Blanc pairs well with acidic dishes such as ceviche or tomato-based pasta sauce.

Match the flavour profiles: Wines and foods that share similar flavor profiles tend to complement each other well. For example, a fruity red wine such as Pinot Noir pairs well with dishes that have a fruit-based sauce or fruit garnish.

Consider the weight of the wine: The weight of the wine should match the weight of the food. For example, a light-bodied white wine pairs well with a light seafood dish, while a full-bodied red wine pairs well with a hearty meat dish.

Consider regional pairing: Wine and food from the same region often have a natural affinity for each other. For example, a dish from Tuscany, Italy, may pair well with a Chianti Classico, a red wine from the same region.

Overall, the key to successful food and wine pairing is to experiment and find what works best for your palate.

The role of the five basic tastes

The five basic tastes are sweet, salty, sour, bitter, and umami.

Each taste plays a unique role in how we perceive flavours and can greatly impact our food choices and preferences.

Sweet: Sweetness is often associated with the taste of sugar and is perceived on the tip of the tongue. It is a natural indicator of energy and can indicate the presence of carbohydrates in food. Sweetness can enhance the flavor of foods, but too much sweetness can be overwhelming and can lead to health issues such as diabetes and obesity.

Salty: Salty taste is often associated with the presence of sodium in food and is perceived on the sides of the tongue. Saltiness can enhance the flavor of foods and is commonly used as a seasoning. However, excessive salt intake can lead to health issues such as high blood pressure and kidney disease.

Sour: Sourness is often associated with the taste of acids and is perceived on the sides of the tongue. Sourness can enhance the flavor of foods and is commonly found in citrus fruits and fermented foods. However, excessive sourness can be unpleasant and can indicate the presence of spoilage in food.

Bitter: Bitterness is often associated with the taste of alkaloids and is perceived at the back of the tongue. Bitterness can enhance the flavour of foods in small amounts, but excessive bitterness can be unpleasant and can indicate the presence of toxins in food.

Umami: Umami is often associated with the taste of glutamate and is perceived at the front of the tongue. Umami is a savoury taste that can enhance the flavour of foods and is commonly found in meat, fish, and mushrooms.

Summary: The five basic tastes play a critical role in how we perceive flavours and can greatly impact our food choices and preferences. Understanding the role of each taste can help us make informed decisions about our diets and can help us create more balanced and flavourful meals.

How to identify the characteristics of wines

Identifying the characteristics of different types of wines can be a fun and rewarding experience. Here are some tips to help you identify the region, varietal, and vintage of a wine:

Region: The region where a wine is produced can greatly impact its flavor and aroma. Look for information on the label or do some research on the wine's origin to learn about the typical flavor profiles of wines from that region. For example, wines from the Bordeaux region in France are known for their full-bodied, tannic flavors, while wines from the Burgundy region are known for their lighter, fruitier flavors.

Varietal: The varietal of a wine refers to the type of grape that was used to make it. Some wines are made from a single varietal, while others are blends of different grapes. Look for information on the label or ask the wine seller about the varietal of the wine. Common varietals include Cabernet Sauvignon, Chardonnay, Pinot Noir, and Sauvignon Blanc.

Vintage: The vintage of a wine refers to the year in which the grapes were harvested. The weather conditions during the growing season can greatly impact the flavor and aroma of the wine. Look for the vintage year on the label and do some research on the typical characteristics of wines from that year. For example, a wine from a hot and dry vintage may have a more concentrated flavor and higher alcohol content.

Colour: The colour of the wine can also provide some clues about its flavor profile. White wines tend to be lighter and crisper, while red wines tend to be bolder and more tannic. Rosé wines are typically lighter in colour and have a fruity flavor.

Smell and taste: The best way to identify the characteristics of a wine is to smell and taste it. Look for aromas such as fruit, flowers, and spices, and pay attention to the level of acidity and tannins. Take small sips and let the wine sit on your tongue for a few seconds before swallowing to fully experience the flavours.

Summary: Identifying the characteristics of different types of wines takes some practice and research. Use the tips above to help you get started and don't be afraid to experiment and try new wines.

Common misconceptions about food and wine pairing

Food and wine pairing is often seen as a complex and intimidating topic, which can lead to a number of misconceptions. Here are some common misconceptions about food and wine pairing:

Red wine with meat, white wine with fish: This is a common rule of thumb that many people follow, but it is not always accurate. While red wine pairs well with many types of meat, such as steak and lamb, white wine can also pair well with certain types of fish, such as salmon or tuna. The key is to focus on the flavours and textures of both the food and the wine to find a good match.

Expensive wine is always better: While expensive wines can be of high quality and have complex flavours, they are not always the best choice for food pairing. In fact, some less expensive wines may be better suited to certain dishes because they have a simpler flavour profile that doesn't compete with the flavours of the food.

Only certain wines can be paired with certain foods: This is a common misconception that limits the possibilities for food and wine pairing. While certain wines may be more commonly paired with certain foods, there are no hard and fast rules.

Experimentation is key when it comes to finding the perfect pairing.

White wine should always be served cold: While white wine is often served chilled, it doesn't need to be ice cold. In fact, serving it too cold can actually mask the flavours and aromas of the wine. A good rule of thumb is to chill white wine in the refrigerator for about 30 minutes before serving.

Red wine should always be served at room temperature: This is another common misconception that can lead to poor wine pairing. Room temperature can vary greatly, and red wine should be served slightly below room temperature to allow its flavours and aromas to fully develop. The ideal serving temperature for red wine is between 60-68°F (15-20°C).

Summary: There are many misconceptions about food and wine pairing that can limit the possibilities for creating a delicious and harmonious pairing. Experimentation and focusing on the flavours and textures of both the food and the wine are key to finding the perfect match.

Non-alcoholic Wines

Non-alcoholic wine, also known as dealcoholized wine, is a type of wine that has had its alcohol content removed through various methods. The history of non-alcoholic wine can be traced back to ancient times, where grape juice was used as a beverage in place of wine due to religious or cultural reasons.

The process of making non-alcoholic wine began to evolve during the 19th century with the introduction of vacuum distillation, which allowed for the removal of alcohol without damaging the flavor of the wine. However, the process was expensive and inefficient, making non-alcoholic wine a luxury item.

During the Prohibition era in the United States (1920-1933), the demand for non-alcoholic wine increased dramatically, as the production, sale, and transportation of alcoholic beverages was prohibited by law. This led to the development of new techniques for producing non-alcoholic wine, such as the use of reverse osmosis and spinning cone columns, which allowed for the removal of alcohol while preserving the flavour and aroma of the wine.

In the decades that followed, non-alcoholic wine became increasingly popular, especially in countries with strict laws regarding alcohol consumption. Today, non-alcoholic wine is produced and consumed all over the world, with a variety of methods used to remove alcohol, including reverse osmosis, spinning cone columns, and vacuum distillation.

In recent years, there has been a growing trend towards low and no-alcohol beverages, including non-alcoholic wines, as consumers seek healthier and more mindful lifestyles. This has led to an increase in the variety and quality of non-alcoholic wines available, as well as the development of new techniques for removing alcohol while preserving the flavour and complexity of the wine.

Overall, the history of non-alcoholic wine is one of innovation and adaptation, driven by both cultural and social factors, and continuing to evolve in response to changing consumer preferences and needs.

We will be looking more in depth at non-alcoholic wines produced in each continent we visit, their owners, terroir and the foods they best pair with.

Sweet Wines

The history of sweet wines dates back to ancient times, as sweeteners such as honey and dried fruits were used to sweeten wines in regions such as Egypt, Rome, and Greece. However, the development of sweet grapes specifically bred for winemaking and the various methods of creating sweet wines evolved over time.

In the Middle Ages, sweet wines were highly prized, but the production of sweet wine became more accessible when the technique of adding high-proof alcohol during fermentation, known as fortification, emerged. This allowed winemakers to stop the fermentation process and produce wines with higher sugar content, such as Port in Portugal and Sherry in Spain.

In the 17th and 18th centuries, sweet wines gained popularity in France through the production of Sauternes and Barsac, which were made by allowing grapes to develop a fungus called botrytis cinerea, or "noble rot," which concentrated the grapes' sugars and flavors.

In the 19th century, the popularity of German Riesling and Auslese wines grew, and these wines were made from grapes that were picked late in the season when they had higher sugar content. Additionally, ice wines, such as Germany's Eiswein and Austria's Eiswein, were developed. These wines are made from grapes left to freeze naturally on the vine, which results in a concentration of sugar and flavour.

Today, sweet wines are produced all over the world using a variety of methods. Some winemakers still use the traditional methods of drying grapes or allowing noble rot, while others use cryoextraction (freezing grapes), late harvesting, or stopping fermentation. Sweet wines come in a range of styles, from light and sparkling to rich and syrupy. Fortified wines, such as Port and Sherry, remain popular as well.

Despite the wide range of sweet wines available, they are still relatively rare compared to dry wines, as the process of producing sweet wines can be more difficult and time-consuming. However, they remain beloved by many wine enthusiasts for their complexity, depth, and unique flavour profiles.

Sparkling Wines

The history of sparkling wine can be traced back to the Champagne region of France in the 17th century. The story goes that the Benedictine monk Dom Perignon was responsible for the discovery of Champagne. He was a cellar master at the Abbey of Hautvillers and he worked hard to improve the quality of wine in the region. One day, he accidentally added extra sugar to a barrel of wine which caused a secondary fermentation in the bottle. The resulting wine had bubbles in it, which gave it a unique taste and texture.

Although Dom Perignon is often credited with inventing Champagne, there were many other winemakers in the region experimenting with sparkling wine at the same time. The technology for producing glass bottles that could withstand the pressure of the wine was also improving, which made it easier to produce sparkling wine on a large scale.

By the 19th century, Champagne had become a popular luxury drink across Europe. The wealthy elite would drink Champagne as a symbol of their status and as a way to celebrate special occasions.

Today, sparkling wine is produced all over the world, using different grape varieties and production techniques. In addition to Champagne, some of the most well-known sparkling wines include Prosecco from Italy, Cava from Spain, and California Sparkling Wine from the United States.

Continents

During our journey 'Around the World in 80 Wines' i will attempt to list 80 top vineyards from across all continents, their wines, and the foods they pair with:

12 vineyards from European Continent

12 vineyards from Australian Continent

12 vineyards from Asian Continent

12 vineyards from North American Continent

12 vineyards from South American Continent

12 vineyards from African Continent

1 vineyard from Antarctica Continent

3 vineyards from the United Kingdom (OK, technically the UK is not a Continent, but haven't they conquered Continents?). So let's call them bonus vineyards. We'll learn what the Brits are up to with their grapes.

4 vineyards from New Zealand. Zealandia is a long, narrow microcontinent that is mostly submerged in the South Pacific Ocean. A microcontinent is a landmass that has broken off from a main continent. Zealandia broke off from Antarctica about 100 million years ago, and then from Australia about 80 million years ago. We will look at it's diverse culture that has been shaped by its indigenous Maori culture, European colonialism, and the country's location in the South Pacific.

And, I must say, they do make some delicious wines down under in New Zealand which pair superb both with locally produced foods and cuisines from around the globe - a match made in New Zea Heaven!

CHAPTER 2

EUROPEAN WINE AND CUISINE

Europe is the second smallest continent in the world but is home to a rich diversity of cultures, languages, and landscapes. The continent is made up of 44 different countries, each with its unique history, language, and cultural traditions.

The people of Europe are incredibly diverse, encompassing a variety of ethnicities, religions, and backgrounds. Some of the largest ethnic groups in Europe include the Germans, French, British, Italians, and Spanish.

The continent is also home to a vast array of culinary traditions, with each country boasting its distinct cuisine. From hearty stews in Ireland to delicate pastries in France and spicy sausages in Spain, European food is as diverse as the continent itself.

When it comes to wine, Europe is known for its world-renowned vineyards and unique terroirs. Countries such as France, Italy, and Spain produce some of the most revered wines in the world, each with its specific grape varieties and winemaking techniques.

European wine and food pairing is a sacred art. With so many different flavours and styles of wine and food, it can be challenging to find the perfect match. However, there are many traditional pairings that have stood the test of time, such as rich red wines with hearty meat dishes and crisp white wines with seafood.

Overall, Europe offers a rich tapestry of people, cultures, and flavours that make it an incredibly fascinating and diverse continent.

Europe is known for producing some of the finest wines in the world, with each country having its own unique wine culture and tradition. The continent's long history of winemaking dates back to ancient times and has been influenced by factors such as climate, soil type, topography, grape varieties, and winemaking techniques.

Wine has been an integral part of European culinary culture for thousands of years. The history of European wine dates back to ancient times, with evidence of wine production and consumption found in archaeological sites in Greece, Italy, and other Mediterranean countries.

The ancient Greeks were among the first to develop a culture of wine, with Homer's epic poems describing the importance of wine in ancient Greek society. Wine was used in religious ceremonies, as well as in everyday life, and it was often mixed with water to make it more palatable.

The Romans also had a strong wine culture, and their influence on wine production and consumption can still be seen today. The Romans introduced new grape varieties to Europe, and they also developed new techniques for vineyard management and wine production. Wine was an important part of Roman social life, and it was often used as a symbol of status and wealth.

During the Middle Ages, wine production and consumption continued to thrive in Europe. Monasteries played a key role in wine production, and many of the great vineyards in Europe were established by monks. Wine was also an important part of mediaeval trade, with merchants transporting wine from one region to another.

Wine became more widely available to the general population, and it was no longer solely the domain of the wealthy and powerful. This led to the development of a more diverse wine culture, with different regions specialising in different types of wine.

Today, European wine culture is as rich and diverse as ever, with countries such as France, Italy, Spain, and Portugal known for their world-renowned wines. Each region has its own unique style of wine, and many regions also have their own distinct culinary traditions that have developed alongside the wine culture.

In terms of European culinary culture and foods, the continent has a rich and varied food culture, with each country and region having its own unique culinary traditions. French cuisine, for example, is known for its use of butter, cream, and rich sauces, while Italian cuisine is known for its emphasis on fresh, simple ingredients such as tomatoes, garlic, and olive oil.

Other notable European culinary traditions include Spanish tapas, German sausages and beer, English fish and chips, Greek meze, and Swiss cheese fondue. Many of these dishes have become popular around the world, and they continue to be an important part of European culinary culture.

The Terroir

The terroir of Europe encompasses a wide variety of regions, climates, soils, and topographies, which contribute to the vast diversity of agricultural products produced across the continent. The term "terroir" refers to the unique combination of environmental factors that affect the flavor, aroma, and quality of crops and livestock raised in a particular geographic area.

For example, the vineyards of France are world-renowned for their terroir, which includes the soil composition, sun exposure, and water supply that influence the growth and flavor of the grapes. Similarly, the olive groves of Spain and Italy have distinct terroirs based on factors such as altitude, temperature, and humidity levels.

Other notable examples of terroir across Europe include the fertile fields of the Netherlands, which benefit from the country's mild climate and nutrient-rich soils. The seafood-rich waters surrounding Norway and Scotland also contribute to a unique terroir for fish and shellfish.

Overall, the terroir of Europe is highly diverse and rich in natural resources, allowing for a wide range of agricultural products to thrive in different regions across the continent.

Some famous wine-producing regions in Europe include:

France: France is one of the leading wine-producing countries in the world, with a long tradition of winemaking dating back to the Roman times. Some of the popular wine regions in France include Bordeaux, Burgundy, Champagne, Loire Valley, and Rhone Valley. The unique terroir of each region plays a vital role in the taste, aroma, and character of the wine produced.

Italy: Italy is another leading wine-producing country in Europe, with a diverse range of grape varieties and wine styles. Some of the famous wine regions in Italy include Tuscany, Piedmont, Veneto, and Sicily. The Italian wines are often paired with local cuisine, such as pasta, pizza, and seafood.

Spain: Spain is known for producing some of the finest wines in the world, including Rioja, Priorat, and Ribera del Duero. The Spanish wines are known for their bold, robust, and fruity flavors and are often paired with traditional Spanish cuisine such as tapas, paella, and chorizo.

Germany: Germany is known for producing high-quality Riesling wines, which are characterised by their aromatic and fruity flavours. The German wines are often paired with local cuisine such as sauerkraut, schnitzel, and bratwurst.

Portugal: Portugal is known for producing Port wine, which is a fortified wine made from grapes grown in the Douro Valley. The Port wine is often paired with local cheese and dessert dishes such as caramel flan and custards.

The Europeans match their wines and foods based on the principles of terroir and complementarity. The terroir refers to the unique combination of soil, climate, and topography of a particular wine region, which gives the wine its distinctive flavour, aroma, and character. The Europeans believe that the best way to appreciate a wine's terroir is to pair it with local cuisine, which also reflects the region's culture and tradition.

For example, a light-bodied and fruity Beaujolais wine from the Burgundy region in France would be perfectly complemented by local dishes such as coq au vin, beef bourguignon, and escargot. Similarly, a robust and full-bodied Rioja wine from Spain would be a perfect match for traditional Spanish dishes such as paella, grilled meats, and chorizo.

Pairing European Wines with European Foods

Here are some European wine and food pairings from 10 different countries:

1. **France:**

- Bordeaux (red) with Beef Bourguignon

- Champagne (sparkling) with oysters

- Sancerre (white) with goat cheese salad

2. **Italy:**

- Chianti (red) with spaghetti bolognese

- Prosecco (sparkling) with prosciutto and melon

- Pinot Grigio (white) with seafood risotto

3. **Spain:**

- Rioja (red) with roasted lamb

- Cava (sparkling) with patatas bravas

- Albariño (white) with grilled shrimp

4. **Portugal:**

- Port (red) with blue cheese

- Vinho Verde (sparkling) with grilled sardines

- Douro (red) with steak and eggs

5. **Germany:**

- Riesling (white) with roast pork and sauerkraut

- Spätburgunder (red) with beef rouladen

- Sekt (sparkling) with apple strudel

6. **Austria:**

- Grüner Veltliner (white) with Wiener schnitzel

- Blaufränkisch (red) with venison stew

- Sekt (sparkling) with Guglhupf cake

7. **Greece:**

- Assyrtiko (white) with grilled fish

- Xinomavro (red) with moussaka

- Retsina (white) with tzatziki and pita bread

8. **Hungary:**

- Egri Bikavér (red) with goulash

- Tokaji Aszú (white) with apple strudel

- Kadarka (red) with roasted duck

9. **Croatia:**

- Plavac Mali (red) with barbecued lamb

- Graševina (white) with grilled seafood

- Dingač (red) with black risotto

10. **Slovenia:**

- Rebula (white) with frtalja (a local dish made with eggs, cheese, and vegetables)

- Teran (red) with Istrian prosciutto

- Cviček (red) with kraški pršut (cured ham from the Karst region)

Pairing European wines with non-European foods

Wine pairing is a complex art, but there are some general guidelines that can help.

Gewürztraminer with spicy Asian cuisine: Gewürztraminer is a white wine with a spicy and aromatic character that pairs perfectly with spicy foods such as Thai or Indian cuisine. The sweetness of the wine balances out the heat of the dish and enhances the flavours.

Rioja with Mexican food: Rioja is a red wine from Spain that pairs well with Mexican cuisine due to its earthy flavors and tannins. It complements the richness and spiciness of Mexican dishes such as tacos or enchiladas.

Riesling with sushi: Riesling is a white wine with a crisp and refreshing character that pairs well with sushi. Its acidity and sweetness complement the flavours of raw fish and soy sauce.

Beaujolais with Moroccan tagine: Beaujolais is a red wine from France that pairs well with Moroccan tagine due to its light and fruity character. It complements the spices and flavours of the dish without overpowering it.

Sauvignon Blanc with Ceviche: Sauvignon Blanc is a white wine with a crisp and citrusy character that pairs perfectly with Ceviche. Its acidity and freshness complement the flavours of the raw fish and lime juice.

Pinot Noir with Chinese cuisine: Pinot Noir is a red wine with a light and fruity character that pairs well with Chinese cuisine. Its light tannins and acidity complement the spices and flavours of the dish without overpowering it.

Chardonnay with Moroccan couscous: Chardonnay is a white wine with a full-bodied and creamy character that pairs well with Moroccan couscous. Its richness and buttery texture complement the flavors of the dish without overpowering it.

Prosecco with sushi rolls: Prosecco is a sparkling wine with a light and refreshing character that pairs perfectly with sushi rolls. Its acidity and effervescence complement the flavors of the raw fish and soy sauce.

Syrah/Shiraz with Indian curry: Syrah/Shiraz is a red wine with a bold and spicy character that pairs well with Indian curry. Its full body and tannins complement the richness and spiciness of the dish without overpowering it.

It's worth noting that these are just general guidelines and that wine pairing can be subjective. The most important thing is to choose a wine that you enjoy and that complements the flavours of the food.

Pairing European Foods with non-European Wines

Here are some options:

Pizza (Italian) and Zinfandel (California, USA): Pizza is a popular Italian dish with tomato sauce, cheese, and toppings such as pepperoni, mushrooms, and olives. Zinfandel is a red wine with a fruity flavor and high acidity that pairs well with the tomato sauce and savory toppings on pizza.

Beef Bourguignon (French) and Pinotage (South Africa): Beef Bourguignon is a classic French stew made with beef, red wine, bacon, mushrooms, and onions. Pinotage is a red wine from South Africa with a smoky flavor that pairs well with the earthy flavors of the beef and mushrooms in the stew.

Moussaka (Greek) and Shiraz (Australia): Moussaka is a Greek dish with layers of eggplant, tomato sauce, ground beef, and béchamel sauce. Shiraz is a red wine from Australia with a spicy and fruity flavor that pairs well with the spices and savory flavors in moussaka.

Goulash (Hungarian) and Malbec (Argentina): Goulash is a hearty Hungarian stew with beef, onions, paprika, and potatoes. Malbec is a red wine from Argentina with a rich and fruity flavor that pairs well with the spicy and hearty flavors in goulash.

Spanakopita (Greek) and Sauvignon Blanc (New Zealand): Spanakopita is a Greek spinach and feta cheese pie wrapped in phyllo dough. Sauvignon Blanc is a white wine from New Zealand with a crisp and citrusy flavor that pairs well with the spinach and feta cheese in the pie.

Wiener Schnitzel (Austrian) and Riesling (Germany): Wiener Schnitzel is a classic Austrian dish with breaded and fried veal cutlets. Riesling is a white wine from Germany with a floral and fruity flavor that pairs well with the light and delicate flavor of the veal.

Risotto (Italian) and Chardonnay (California, USA): Risotto is a creamy Italian rice dish with ingredients such as mushrooms, peas, and Parmesan cheese. Chardonnay is a white wine from California with a buttery and oaky flavor that pairs well with the creamy and rich flavors in risotto.

Sauerbraten (German) and Syrah (Washington State, USA): Sauerbraten is a German dish made with marinated and roasted beef, onions, and a sweet and sour sauce. Syrah is a red wine from Washington State with a rich and smoky flavor that pairs well with the bold flavors in sauerbraten.

Bouillabaisse (French) and Viognier (Australia): Bouillabaisse is a classic French seafood soup made with a variety of fish, shellfish, and vegetables. Viognier is a white wine from Australia with a floral and fruity flavor that pairs well with the seafood and herb flavors in bouillabaisse.

Pairing European foods with non-European wines is about finding complementary flavours and textures. It is important to consider the acidity, sweetness, and intensity of both the food and wine when making a pairing. European foods can be enjoyed with wines produced from the rest of the world, it really depends on the specific cuisine and wine. However, in general, European foods such as cheese, charcuterie, and seafood can be enjoyed with wines from all over the world, including California Chardonnay, Australian Shiraz, and South African Chenin Blanc.

European wines are a product of the unique terroir, grape varieties, and winemaking techniques.

The foods grown near European vineyards depend on the region, but some common examples include grapes, olives, truffles, and various types of fruits and vegetables.

5 European Countries And Their Story

Here are five European countries that produce good wine and some information about their vineyards, grape varieties, and their famous wines:

Italy

Famous Vineyards: Chianti, Barolo, Brunello di Montalcino

Grape varieties: Sangiovese, Nebbiolo, Barbera

Wines: Chianti, Barolo, Brunello di Montalcino, Amarone della Valpolicella

Complementary European foods: Pasta with tomato-based sauces, pizza Margherita, Parmigiano Reggiano cheese

Complementary non-European foods: Grilled meats, roasted vegetables, mushroom risotto

France

Famous vineyards: Bordeaux, Burgundy, Champagne

Grape varieties: Cabernet Sauvignon, Pinot Noir, Chardonnay

Wines: Bordeaux blends, Pinot Noir, Chablis, Champagne

Complementary European food: Coq au Vin, Beef Bourguignon, Roquefort cheese

Complementary non-European foods: Duck breast, roasted chicken, grilled salmon.

Spain

Famous vineyards: Rioja, Priorat, Ribera del Duero

Grape varieties: Tempranillo, Grenache, Albariño

Wines: Rioja, Priorat, Ribera del Duero, Albariño

Complementary European food: Paella, Tapas, Manchego cheese

Complementary non-European foods: Grilled octopus, roasted lamb, spicy sausage.

Germany

Famous vineyards: Mosel, Rheingau, Pfalz

Grape varieties: Riesling, Pinot Noir

Wines: Riesling, Pinot Noir, Gewürztraminer

Complementary European foods: Wiener Schnitzel, Spätzle, Sauerkraut

Complementary non-European foods: Thai curry, sushi, Indian butter chicken.

Portugal

Famous vineyards: Douro Valley, Alentejo, Dão

Grape varieties: Touriga Nacional, Tinta Roriz, Aragonez

Wines: Port wine, Douro reds, Vinho Verde

Complementary European foods: Bacalhau (salt cod), Cozido (stew), Queijo da Serra (cheese)

Complementary non-European foods: Brazilian feijoada, Mexican mole, Korean barbecue.

Top 12 Vineyards of Europe

Château Margaux, France - Owned by Corinne Mentzelopoulos. Their most famous wine is the Château Margaux Premier Grand Cru Classé, which is a red Bordeaux blend. This wine goes well with beef, lamb, and game meats.

Château Latour, France - Owned by François Pinault. Their most famous wine is the Château Latour Premier Grand Cru Classé, which is also a red Bordeaux blend. This wine goes well with steak, roasted meats, and strong cheeses.

Château Haut-Brion, France - Owned by the Dillon family. Their most famous wine is the Château Haut-Brion Premier Grand Cru Classé, which is a red Bordeaux blend. This wine pairs well with roasted meats, game, and strong cheeses.

Domaine de la Romanée-Conti, France - Owned by the de Villaine and Leroy families. Their most famous wine is the Romanée-Conti Grand Cru, which is a red Burgundy. This wine pairs well with roasted meats, game, and strong cheeses.

Antinori, Italy - Owned by the Antinori family. Their most famous wine is the Tignanello, which is a Super Tuscan red blend. This wine pairs well with pasta dishes, grilled meats, and hard cheeses.

Tenuta dell'Ornellaia, Italy - Owned by the Frescobaldi family. Their most famous wine is the Ornellaia Bolgheri Superiore, which is a Super Tuscan red blend. This wine pairs well with steak, game meats, and strong cheeses.

Vega Sicilia, Spain - Owned by the Álvarez family. Their most famous wine is the Único, which is a red blend from Ribera del Duero. This wine pairs well with roasted meats, game, and strong cheeses.

Pingus, Spain - Owned by Peter Sisseck. Their most famous wine is the Pingus, which is a red blend from Ribera del Duero. This wine pairs well with roasted meats, game, and strong cheeses.

Château d'Yquem, France - Owned by LVMH. Their most famous wine is the Château d'Yquem Premier Cru Supérieur, which is a sweet white Bordeaux. This wine pairs well with foie gras, blue cheese, and fruit-based desserts.

Weingut Egon Müller, Germany - Owned by Egon Müller IV. Their most famous wine is the Scharzhofberger Riesling, which is a white wine from the Mosel region. This wine pairs well with seafood, spicy foods, and light salads.

Guigal, France - Owned by the Guigal family. Their most famous wine is the La Mouline, which is a red blend from the Côte-Rôtie region. This wine pairs well with roasted meats, game, and strong cheeses.

Marchesi de' Frescobaldi, Italy - Owned by the Frescobaldi family. Their most famous wine is the Castelgiocondo Brunello di Montalcino, which is a red wine from Tuscany. This wine pairs well with roasted meats, pasta dishes, and hard cheeses.

Each vineyard has its own vinification techniques, but generally, they produce high-quality wines that reflect the terroir of their respective regions. For example, Château Lafite Rothschild and Château Margaux are famous for their Bordeaux blends, while Domaine de la Romanée-Conti produces some of the best Pinot Noir wines in the world.

European wine is an integral part of the continent's culture and history. With a tradition of winemaking that dates back thousands of years, Europe is home to some of the world's finest and most renowned wine regions.

The wine culture in Europe is deeply rooted in the way of life of its people. Wine is a symbol of celebration, joy, and good company. Many European countries have their own wine culture, which is reflected in the unique characteristics of their wines. For example, France is known for its fine Bordeaux wines, while Italy is famous for its Chianti and Barolo.

The people of Europe have a deep appreciation for wine and its importance in their daily lives. Wine is enjoyed with meals, as a social drink, and as a way to connect with others. Many wine regions in Europe have a long history of winemaking, and the local people take pride in their heritage and the quality of their wines.

European food is also highly regarded, and wine is often paired with meals to enhance the dining experience. The pairing of wine and food in Europe is based on the concept of complementarity, where the flavors and aromas of the wine and food are matched to create a harmonious taste experience. This is achieved by pairing wines with foods that have similar characteristics, such as a full-bodied red wine with a rich, meaty dish.

The pairing of wine and food in Europe is also influenced by the local cuisine and culture. For example, in Italy, a light, crisp white wine is often paired with seafood dishes, while a robust red wine is paired with hearty pasta dishes.

Overall, the wine culture in Europe is a rich and diverse part of the continent's history and heritage. With a deep appreciation for wine and food, the people of Europe have created a unique and unforgettable dining experience that is enjoyed by people all over the world.

Some suggestions for European food and wine pairings for different occasions and seasons:

Summer Informal Dining:

Grilled Fish with a crisp white wine such as Sauvignon Blanc or Pinot Grigio

Gazpacho soup with a refreshing Spanish Albariño or Portuguese Vinho Verde

Salads with fresh vegetables and goat cheese paired with a light and fruity Rosé wine.

Summer Formal Dining:

Lobster paired with a French Chardonnay or an Italian Pinot Bianco

Grilled lamb chops with a full-bodied red wine such as a Bordeaux or a Chianti Classico

Beef Carpaccio with a Northern Italian Nebbiolo or a Tuscan Sangiovese.

Winter Informal Dining:

Hearty stews or casseroles with a bold red wine such as a Cabernet Sauvignon or a Syrah/Shiraz.

Creamy pasta dishes like Carbonara or Alfredo with an Italian white such as Soave or Orvieto.

Cheese fondue with a crisp and acidic white wine such as a Riesling or Gewürztraminer.

Winter Formal Dining:

Beef Bourguignon with a French Pinot Noir or a Côte-Rôtie.

Wild boar or venison paired with a full-bodied red wine such as a Barolo or a Brunello di Montalcino.

Coq au Vin with a Burgundy Chardonnay or a Pouilly-Fuissé.

Remember, these are just suggestions and there are many other pairing options. It's always a good idea to experiment with different wine and food combinations to find the ones that work best for your tastes.

Here are my suggestions for five European wines each from 10 European countries that would pair well with sweet foods:

Italy:

Moscato d'Asti

Vin Santo

Brachetto d'Acqui

Recioto della Valpolicella

Passito di Pantelleria

France:

Sauternes

Vouvray moelleux

Banyuls

Maury

Muscat de Beaumes-de-Venise

Spain:

Pedro Ximenez Sherry

Moscatel de Valencia

Malaga

Montilla-Moriles

Priorat sweet wines

Portugal:

Port wine

Madeira wine

Bucelas

Setúbal Moscatel

Vinho Verde branco doce

Germany:

Riesling Auslese

Beerenauslese

Eiswein

Trockenbeerenauslese

Spätlese

Austria:

Beerenauslese

Trockenbeerenauslese

Ausbruch

Ruster Ausbruch

Eiswein

Hungary:

Tokaji Aszú

Tokaji Eszencia

Tokaji Szamorodni

Tokaji Late Harvest

Egri Bikavér Sweet

Greece:

Muscat of Samos

Mavrodaphne of Patras

Muscat of Rhodes

Santorini Vinsanto

Muscat of Lemnos

Romania:

Grasa de Cotnari

Tarnave Late Harvest

Tamaioasa Romaneasca

Cotnari Francusa

Cotnari Galbenă

Slovenia:

Zlata Radgonska Penina Demi-sec

Gornja Radgona Traminec

Radgonske Gorice Penina

Radgonske Gorice Penina Rosé

Vipavska Dolina Sladkih Vin

Here are 5 European wines each from 8 European countries, along with suggested sweet food pairings:

France:

Château d'Yquem Sauternes: Pair avec crème brûlée ou fruit tart.

Veuve Clicquot Demi-Sec **Champagne:** Pair with a fruit tart or cheesecake.

Château Rieussec Sauternes: Pair with foie gras or blue cheese.

Château Climens Barsac: Pair with a pear tart or blue cheese.

Domaine de Montcalmès Muscat de Lunel: Pair with fresh fruit or a fruit tart.

Italy:

Moscato d'Asti: Pair with fresh fruit or fruit salad.

Recioto della Valpolicella: Pair with tiramisu or chocolate cake.

Vin Santo: Pair with biscotti or almond cake.

Brachetto d'Acqui: Pair with chocolate-covered strawberries or cheesecake.

Passito di Pantelleria: Pair with a fruit tart or chocolate mousse.

Spain:

Pedro Ximénez Sherry: Pair with dark chocolate or figs.

Moscatel de Valencia: Pair with fresh fruit or fruit tart.

Oloroso Sherry: Pair with almonds or dark chocolate.

Turrón de Alicante: Pair with a cheese plate or fruit.

Amontillado Sherry: Pair with caramel or chocolate desserts.

Germany:

Eiswein: Pair with fruit tart or fruit salad.

Beerenauslese Riesling: Pair with crème brûlée or cheesecake.

Trockenbeerenauslese Riesling: Pair with a fruit tart or blue cheese.

Auslese Riesling: Pair with foie gras or blue cheese.

Spätlese Riesling: Pair with fresh fruit or fruit tart.

Portugal:

Moscatel de Setúbal: Pair with custard tarts or fruit salad.

Port: Pair with dark chocolate or blue cheese.

Madeira: Pair with caramel or chocolate desserts.

Bual Madeira: Pair with fruit tart or cheesecake.

Vinho Verde: Pair with fresh fruit or fruit salad.

Austria:

Eiswein: Pair with fruit tart or fruit salad.

Grüner Veltliner Beerenauslese: Pair with crème brûlée or cheesecake.

Welschriesling **Trockenbeerenauslese:** Pair with a fruit tart or blue cheese.

Traminer Auslese: Pair with foie gras or blue cheese.

Riesling Spätlese: Pair with fresh fruit or fruit tart.

Greece:

Vinsanto: Pair with baklava or caramel desserts.

Muscat of Samos: Pair with fresh fruit or fruit salad.

Mavrodaphne: Pair with dark chocolate or fruit tart.

Agiorgitiko: Pair with cheesecake or fruit.

Moschofilero: Pair with a fruit tart or fresh fruit.

Hungary:

Tokaji Aszú: Pair with foie gras or blue cheese.

Tokaji Szamorodni: Pair with crème brûlée or cheesecake.

Tokaji Furmint: Pair with fruit tart or fresh fruit.

Tokaji Late Harvest: Pair with blue cheese or fruit tart.

Egri Bikavér: Pair with dark chocolate or caramel desserts.

Note:

Phileas Fogg was a man of balance and precision, and the same can be said for pairing food and wine.

During his world trip, he would have been exposed to a wide variety of cuisines and wines from different parts of the world. Here is a food and wine pairing that Phileas Fogg might have enjoyed as he passed through France - he might have paired a classic coq au vin with a Burgundy Pinot Noir or a Bordeaux blend.

He would have encountered a wide range of diverse people during his travels in Europe:

In France, he would have encountered people of different social classes, from the wealthy elites in Paris to the working-class people in smaller towns and rural areas. He may have also encountered people from different regions of France with distinct cultures and dialects.

In Italy, Fogg would have encountered people with different regional identities, such as Sicilians, Sardinians, and Venetians, each with their unique cultures and traditions. He may have also encountered immigrants from other parts of Europe, such as Germans or Austrians, who had settled in Italy.

In Spain, Fogg would have encountered people with diverse cultural and linguistic backgrounds, including Basques, Catalans, and Galicians, who have their own distinct cultures and languages. He may have also encountered people from North Africa, as Spain has a long history of trade and cultural exchange with the region.

In Germany, Fogg would have encountered people from different regions with their own cultural and linguistic identities, such as Bavarians and Saxons. He may have also encountered people from neighbouring countries such as Poland or the Czech Republic, who had settled in Germany.

In general, Fogg would have encountered people from diverse social, cultural, and linguistic backgrounds throughout his travels in Europe, reflecting the rich diversity of the continent.

European Non-alcoholic Wines

Non-alcoholic wine has a long history in Europe, dating back to ancient times when grape juice was consumed as a non-alcoholic beverage. However, the modern production of non-alcoholic wine can be traced back to the late 19th century when a process for removing alcohol from wine was developed.

One of the pioneers in the production of non-alcoholic wine was the French company, Maison Leclerc. They began producing non-alcoholic wines in the early 1900s, using a process of vacuum distillation to remove the alcohol. Other French companies, such as Vinosec and Vinoval, also began producing non-alcoholic wines around the same time.

In the 1920s and 1930s, German companies such as the Carl Jung Winery and the German Wine Institute began producing non-alcoholic wines using a process called reverse osmosis. This process involved filtering the wine through a semipermeable membrane to remove the alcohol.

Today, non-alcoholic wines are produced all over Europe, including in Spain, Italy, and Portugal. Some of the most well-known non-alcoholic wine brands include Torres Natureo (Spain), Carl Jung (Germany), and Ariel (USA, but with European roots).

In terms of terroir, non-alcoholic wines are typically made from the same grape varieties and in the same regions as their alcoholic counterparts. For example, a non-alcoholic Cabernet Sauvignon may come from the same region in France as an alcoholic Cabernet Sauvignon. However, because the alcohol is removed from the wine, some of the flavour and complexity may be lost.

As for food pairings, non-alcoholic wines can be paired with a wide range of dishes, just like their alcoholic counterparts. For example, a non-alcoholic Chardonnay could be paired with seafood or chicken, while a non-alcoholic Merlot could be paired with red meat or pasta dishes. However, because non-alcoholic wines may have a sweeter flavour profile than their alcoholic counterparts, they may pair particularly well with spicy or salty foods.

It's worth noting that non-alcoholic wines are not always a perfect substitute for alcoholic wines in terms of flavour and complexity. However, they can be a great alternative for those who are abstaining from alcohol for health or personal reasons, or for those who simply prefer the taste of non-alcoholic beverages.

What different variety of non-alcoholic wines would Phileas Fogg have tasted during his journey through Europe

Phileas Fogg would have had access to a variety of non-alcoholic European wines during his journey. Non-alcoholic wine has been produced in Europe for centuries, and there are many different types available.

In France, Fogg might have tried non-alcoholic Chardonnay or Sauvignon Blanc, which would pair well with seafood, poultry, and light salads. Non-alcoholic red wines such as Pinot Noir or Merlot could also be found, which could pair well with meats and heavier dishes.

In Italy, Fogg might have enjoyed non-alcoholic Chianti or Montepulciano, which would pair well with pasta dishes and grilled meats. He might have also tried non-alcoholic Prosecco, which is a sparkling wine that would pair well with appetisers and desserts.

In Germany, Fogg might have tasted non-alcoholic Riesling or Gewürztraminer, which would pair well with spicy or rich dishes. He might have also tried non-alcoholic sparkling wine or sekt, which would pair well with light appetisers or fruit-based desserts.

Throughout his journey, Fogg would have also encountered other non-alcoholic beverages, such as fruit juices, sparkling water, and herbal teas, which would also have paired well with various foods.

Overall, Fogg would have had a wide variety of non-alcoholic European wines to choose from, each with their unique flavour profile and pairing options.

Sparkling Wine

The history of European sparkling wines dates back centuries, with records of bubbly wines being enjoyed by the aristocrats and royalty of Europe as early as the 16th century. However, it was not until the 17th century that the production of sparkling wines became more widespread and refined.

One of the earliest recorded examples of sparkling wine was Blanquette de Limoux, a sparkling wine produced in the Languedoc region of France. This wine was believed to have been first produced by Benedictine monks in the early 16th century, who noticed that some of their wine bottles had become effervescent due to a secondary fermentation in the bottle. This process was later perfected by the renowned Dom Pérignon, a French Benedictine monk who was credited as the father of Champagne. He was employed by the Abbey of Hautvillers in the Champagne region of France and is said to have developed a method for producing wines with a consistent and controlled effervescence.

During the 18th century, the popularity of sparkling wines grew rapidly throughout Europe, particularly among the wealthy and aristocratic classes. Champagne and other sparkling wines became a symbol of luxury and refinement, with famous figures such as Voltaire, Napoleon Bonaparte, and Casanova all being known to be fans of the effervescent drink.

Throughout the 19th and 20th centuries, the production of sparkling wines expanded to other regions in Europe, with wines such as Prosecco becoming popular in Italy, and Cava becoming popular in Spain. Today, European sparkling wines are enjoyed throughout the world, with Champagne still being considered the king of sparkling wines due to its history, refinement, and exclusivity.

Despite the popularity of sparkling wines, the production process remains a delicate and complex one that requires careful attention to detail. From the careful selection of the grapes to the secondary fermentation process, every step in the process is critical in creating a high-quality sparkling wine.

Here are some sparkling wines from European countries, along with their traditions, grapes, owners, culture, and foods that pair well with them:

1. **Champagne**, France:

   - Traditions: The production of champagne is regulated by the Champagne Committee, which enforces strict rules to ensure quality and authenticity.

   - Grapes: Chardonnay, Pinot Noir, and Pinot Meunier.

   - Owners: Some of the well-known Champagne houses include Moët & Chandon, Veuve Clicquot, and Dom Pérignon.

   - Culture: Champagne is often associated with luxury and celebration.

   - Food Pairings: Champagne pairs well with oysters, caviar, and other seafood dishes.

2. **Prosecco**, Italy:

   - Traditions: Prosecco is typically made using the Charmat method, where the wine undergoes secondary fermentation in steel tanks.

   - Grapes: Glera (formerly known as Prosecco), along with other local grape varieties.

   - Owners: Prosecco is produced by many small, family-owned wineries.

   - Culture: Prosecco is a popular aperitif in Italy, and is often served with small plates of snacks.

   - Food Pairings: Prosecco pairs well with light dishes like salad, pasta, and seafood.

3. **Cava**, Spain:

   - Traditions: Cava is produced using the traditional method, similar to champagne.

   - Grapes: Macabeu, Parellada, and Xarel Lo.

   - Owners: Cava is produced by a variety of wineries in Catalonia, Spain.

   - Culture: Cava is a popular alternative to champagne, especially for those on a budget.

   - Food Pairings: Cava goes well with tapas, cured meats, and cheeses.

4. **Sekt**, Germany:

   - Traditions: Sekt is typically made using the tank method, where secondary fermentation takes place in large tanks.

   - Grapes: Riesling, Pinot Blanc, and Pinot Noir.

   - Owners: Sekt is produced by a variety of wineries in Germany.

   - Culture: Sekt is often enjoyed during celebrations and special occasions.

   - Food Pairings: Sekt pairs well with sausages, pretzels, and other German-style dishes.

5. **Österreichischer Sekt** (Austrian Sparkling Wine):

   - Traditions: Austrian sparkling wines are produced using both the traditional method and the tank method.

   - Grapes: Grüner Veltliner, Riesling, and Pinot Noir.

   - Owners: Austrian sparkling wines are produced by many small, family-owned wineries.

   - Culture: Austrian sparkling wines are becoming increasingly popular, and are often enjoyed as an aperitif.

   - Food Pairings: Austrian sparkling wines are versatile and pair well with a variety of dishes, including cheese, seafood, and Asian cuisine.

Finally....

The great European continent is home to some of the finest wines, delicious food, unique grapes, rich culture, and fascinating traditions in the world. Europe has been the cradle of wine civilization, and many of the world's most celebrated grape varieties have their origins here. The continent has been the birthplace of numerous styles of wine, including the elegant and expressive wines of Bordeaux, the vibrant and crisp wines of Italy, and the robust and flavorful wines of Spain.

The foods of Europe have been influenced by centuries-old traditions, and the pairing of regional dishes with local wines is often the perfect way to experience the authentic flavors of a given region. From the hearty stews of Eastern Europe to the delicate pastries of France, the cuisine of each country is unique and offers a taste of the culture that created it.

The importance of wine in European culture cannot be overstated. For centuries wine has played a central role in the daily life of Europeans. Many traditional customs, religious ceremonies, and social occasions revolve around wine, and its appreciation is deeply ingrained in local populations.

Through this article, we have explored the fascinating world of food and wine pairings, featuring some of Europe's finest combinations. Europe boasts a rich and diverse culinary heritage with some of the world's finest wines and cuisines. From the bold reds of France to the crisp whites of Italy, the wines of Europe have been crafted for centuries, embodying the unique terroir and cultural traditions of the regions they come from.

But it's not just the quality of the wine alone that makes it so intoxicating. It's the way that wine has been woven into the fabric of European culture, interwoven into its cuisine and social traditions. From the vineyards of Tuscany to the cellar-breweries of Belgium, the people of Europe have crafted wines and foods with a passion and dedication that is truly inspiring.

And let's not forget the incredible pairings of wine and food that have emerged from these cultures, each complementing and enhancing the other in a symphony of flavour. Imagine savouring a rich, bold Chianti with a hearty bolognese or a crisp and acidic Riesling with a buttery fish dish. These pairings are not simply about what tastes good together but about the way that wine and food can amplify and elevate each other, creating an experience that is greater than the sum of its parts.

So, whether you are a wine connoisseur or simply appreciate good food and drink, the wines and foods of Europe offer an unparalleled glimpse into the heart and soul of a continent rich in history, culture, and tradition.

Europe is very much an enchanting destination with a rich history and diverse culture that continues to captivate people all around the world. The friendly and welcoming people of Europe are known for their hospitality, which makes it easy for visitors to feel right at home. Every country in Europe is unique with its own distinct customs, traditions, and even foods.

Speaking of food, Europe is famous for its delicious culinary delights. From French pastries to Italian pasta, German sausages to Spanish tapas, the list of mouth-watering dishes is endless. And let's not forget about the world-renowned wines that flow freely throughout the continent. Whether it's a glass of red from Tuscany or a crisp white from Germany's Rhine Valley, wine lovers will surely be tempted.

But Europe is not just about food and drink. Visitors can marvel at the architectural wonders, museums filled with priceless artefacts, and stunning natural landscapes. The continent's rich history can be seen in its picturesque towns, castles, and ruins, making it a perfect escape for history buffs.

In short, Europe is a place that never disappoints, where the love of the people, the beauty of the cultures, the delicious food, and the finest wines come together to create an experience unlike any other.

Europe offers an excellent platform for wine enthusiasts to explore and experiment with their taste buds. Whether you are a wine connoisseur or just a beginner, the continent has something special to offer, and I hope you will explore it all. I also hope that you have enjoyed learning about these perfect pairings and are now inspired to experiment with drinking wines and pairing them with exotic foods from different regions around the world.

Thank you for reading about Europe, and cheers to a delightful wine journey!

Further Readings:

There are several great resources available for further reading on European wines and foods and their pairings.

Here are a few suggestions:

"The Wine Bible" by Karen MacNeil: This comprehensive book covers all aspects of wine, including the different varieties of European wines, and offers insights into pairing wines with food.

"The Oxford Companion to Wine" by Jancis Robinson: This reference book is a must-have for anyone interested in wine, offering detailed information on the various wine regions of Europe and their distinctive characteristics.

"The Food Lover's Guide to Wine" by Karen Page and Andrew Dornenburg: This book provides practical tips on how to pair European wines with different types of cuisine.

"What to Drink with What You Eat" by Andrew Dornenburg and Karen Page: This book is an excellent resource for those interested in learning about food and wine pairings. It offers suggestions for specific pairings, including many European wines and foods.

"The World Atlas of Wine" by Hugh Johnson and Jancis Robinson: This beautifully illustrated book offers a comprehensive look at the wines of the world, including those from Europe, and provides recommendations for food pairings.

"Wine Folly: The Essential Guide to Wine" by Madeline Puckette and Justin Hammack: This book offers a fun and approachable guide to wine, including information on European wines and food pairings.

Some suggestions for further readings on European non-alcoholic wines:

"European Wines Without Alcohol: The New Wave" by Fiona Beckett - This article on The Guardian explores the growing trend of non-alcoholic wines in Europe, highlighting some of the best options available.

"Non-alcoholic wines: why they're no longer the 'underdogs' of the drinks world" by Victoria Moore - In this article on The Telegraph, Moore discusses the rise of non-alcoholic wines in Europe and why they are becoming increasingly popular.

"The best non-alcoholic wines for a healthier tipple" by Victoria Gray - This article on The Independent features a selection of non-alcoholic wines from across Europe, with tasting notes and recommendations.

"Dry January: The rise of non-alcoholic wines" by Ellie Douglas - In this piece on BBC News, Douglas explores the reasons behind the growing popularity of non-alcoholic wines in Europe and their potential health benefits.

"The Best Non-Alcoholic Wines, Beers and Spirits" by Hugh Thomas - This comprehensive guide on Wine-Searcher provides a list of the best non-alcoholic wines from Europe, as well as recommendations for non-alcoholic beers and spirits.

Overall, these resources should provide a good starting point for anyone interested in learning more about European wines and their perfect food pairings.

Wine and food pairing can also be subjective and dependent on individual tastes.

Further reading on European sparkling wines:

Here are some articles and books that you might find interesting:

1. **The World Atlas of Sparkling Wine** by Oz Clarke: This book covers the history, production, and culture of sparkling wines from around the world, including Europe. It includes maps, photos, and tasting notes.

2. **"10 Best Sparkling Wines from Europe"** by Lauren Mowery for Wine Enthusiast Magazine: This article highlights some of the best sparkling wines from Europe, including Champagne, Cava, Prosecco, and others.

3. **"A Guide to Sparkling Wine from Across Europe"** by Mark Pendergrast for Wine Folly: This article provides an overview of sparkling wines from Europe, including the different styles, production methods, and regions.

4. **"The Best European Sparkling Wines that Aren't Champagne"** by Amanda Schuster for VinePair: This article suggests some alternative sparkling wines from Europe that are worth trying, such as Franciacorta, Moscato d'Asti, and Crémant.

5. **"Beyond Champagne: The Other Sparkling Wines of France"** by Roger Voss for Wine Enthusiast Magazine: This article explores the different types of sparkling wines produced in France besides Champagne, including Crémant, Clairette de Die, and Blanquette de Limoux.

I hope you find these resources helpful!

CHAPTER 3

AUSTRALIAN WINE AND CUISINE

Australian cuisine has evolved from its British and European roots to become a unique and diverse culinary experience. Similarly, Australian wines have gained global recognition for their distinctive style, quality, and variety. Pairing Australian wine with food can be a delightful experience as the wine's flavours and aromas complement or contrast the dish's flavours and textures.

Australian wines are known worldwide for their quality, innovation, and diversity. The country is the world's fifth-largest wine producer and exports wine to over 100 countries. The Australian wine industry has a reputation for producing high-quality wines that reflect the country's unique climate and soil conditions.

The wine culture in Australia is deeply ingrained in the country's food culture. Australians enjoy pairing their wines with a wide variety of cuisines, from seafood and grilled meats to spicy Asian dishes and rich desserts. Australian wines are also an integral part of the country's social and cultural life, with wine tasting events, wine tours, and vineyard visits being popular activities.

Some of the most popular Australian wines include Shiraz, Cabernet Sauvignon, Chardonnay, and Sauvignon Blanc. Shiraz, in particular, is a favourite among wine drinkers around the world, known for its rich, full-bodied taste with notes of blackberry, plum, and spice.

The Australian food culture is also rich and diverse, reflecting the country's multicultural heritage. Australian cuisine is heavily influenced by European, Asian, and Indigenous cultures. Some popular Australian dishes include meat pies, fish and chips, seafood platters, and barbeque dishes.

The Australian wine and food culture is deeply intertwined, with local wines often being paired with regional specialties. For example, a rich, full-bodied Shiraz pairs well with a juicy steak or a spicy lamb curry, while a crisp, refreshing Chardonnay is perfect for a light seafood dish or a fresh salad.

In addition to wine and food, Australian culture is also characterised by its love of the outdoors, sports, and the arts. The country is home to a diverse range of festivals and events, from the Sydney Opera House to the Melbourne Cup horse race, which showcases the country's rich cultural heritage.

Overall, the Australian wine and food culture is a reflection of the country's unique blend of traditions, multiculturalism, and love of the good life.

The Terroir

Australia's terroir is vast and diverse, as the country spans across more than 7.5 million square kilometers, with varied climate regions, soil types, and landscapes. The terroir of Australia is shaped by its unique geographic location that experiences a range of climatic conditions, from hot and dry to cool and wet, as well as its complex geological history and diverse plant life.

Climate:

The climate in Australia is diverse, spanning from the hot and dry desert landscape of the Outback to the cooler, wetter regions of the southeast, southwest, and Tasmania. The warmer regions are ideal for growing crops such as grapes, citrus fruits, and olives, while the cooler regions are conducive to cultivating crops such as apples, pears, and berries.

Soil types:

Australia's soils vary significantly based on the geographical region, and as a result, a broad array of crops are grown throughout the nation. In the southeastern region, there are vineyards planted on well-draining sandy soils, while in the southwest, the soils are deep and rich in nutrients, making them ideal for growing apples, pears, and cherries.

Geology:

Australia's geological history is relatively young, which has created a range of soil types to support its diverse flora and fauna. The country's unique geology, comprising of ancient bedrocks, sands, and clays, has led to the formation of a geographically diverse range of landforms, such as mountain ranges, volcanic cones, plateaus, and coastal plains.

Flora:

Australia's diverse plant life further amplifies the terroir of the country. The flora ranges from ancient forests and eucalyptus woodlands to coastal heaths and wildflowers. This variety of flora provides excellent biodiversity, which encourages pollination and the natural proliferation of different species.

In conclusion, the terroir of Australia is exceptionally diverse, primarily due to its broad and complex geography, climates and soils, which in turn influences the agriculture and the cultivation of premium quality crops such as wine grapes, apples, citrus fruits, and olives, among others.

Here are some popular Australian wine and food pairings:

Shiraz and Grilled Lamb: Shiraz, also known as Syrah, is one of Australia's signature wines, known for its bold flavours and full-bodied structure. It pairs exceptionally well with grilled lamb, as the wine's intense fruit flavours and tannins balance the meat's richness and smoky flavour.

Chardonnay and Seafood: Australian Chardonnays are known for their richness, complexity, and creamy texture. They pair well with seafood, especially shellfish like lobster, crab, and scallops. The wine's acidity cuts through the richness of the seafood, while its buttery notes complement the dish's creamy sauces.

Pinot Noir and Mushrooms: Pinot Noir is a medium-bodied red wine that pairs well with earthy flavours like mushrooms. The wine's delicate fruit flavours and subtle tannins complement the dish's savoury and earthy notes, creating a perfect harmony of flavours.

Riesling and Spicy Food: Australian Rieslings are known for their crisp acidity and fruity aromas, making them an ideal pairing for spicy food. The wine's sweetness balances the heat of the dish, while its acidity refreshes the palate between bites.

Cabernet Sauvignon and Beef: Cabernet Sauvignon is another popular Australian red wine known for its robust structure and bold fruit flavours. It pairs well with beef dishes like steak or roast, as the wine's tannins and acidity cut through the meat's richness, creating a harmonious balance of flavours.

Australian Wine Regions

Barossa Valley: Known for producing rich, full-bodied red wines such as Shiraz and Cabernet Sauvignon.

Hunter Valley: Known for producing Semillon, a white wine that is crisp, refreshing, and ages well.

Margaret River: Known for producing high-quality Chardonnay and Cabernet Sauvignon.

Yarra Valley: Known for producing Pinot Noir and Chardonnay.

Coonawarra: Known for producing some of the world's best Cabernet Sauvignon.

Australia's Terroir

The Australian terroir is unique due to its climate and geography. Most wine regions are located near the coast, which provides a cool ocean breeze, helping to moderate the hot temperatures during the day. The soil conditions are also diverse, ranging from clay and loam to sand and gravel. This diversity allows winemakers to produce a wide range of wine styles, from light and crisp to full-bodied and complex.

Food and Culinary Culture

Australia is known for its vibrant and diverse culinary culture, influenced by its indigenous population, immigrants, and neighbouring countries. Some of the popular dishes in Australia include:

Meat Pies: A savory pastry filled with minced meat, vegetables, and gravy.

Barbecue: A popular way of cooking in Australia, usually featuring meats such as lamb, beef, and sausages.

Seafood: Australia is surrounded by the ocean, making seafood a staple in the country's cuisine. Some of the popular seafood dishes include prawns, oysters, and barramundi.

Vegemite: A spread made from yeast extract, a popular Australian breakfast item.

Food and Wine Pairing:

Australians are known for their love of wine and food, and they have a great understanding of how to pair them. Some of the popular wine and food pairings in Australia include:

Shiraz and Barbecue: The full-bodied and rich flavours of Shiraz pair well with the smoky and savory flavours of barbecued meats.

Chardonnay and Seafood: The crisp and refreshing acidity of Chardonnay pairs well with the delicate flavours of seafood.

Cabernet Sauvignon and Steak: The tannins in Cabernet Sauvignon complement the rich and savoury flavours of steak.

Sparkling Wine and Oysters: The effervescence of sparkling wine cuts through the briny flavours of oysters, making for a refreshing pairing.

Australian Wines with Foods from Other Parts of the World

Shiraz and Indian Cuisine: The bold and spicy flavours of Indian cuisine pair well with the full-bodied and rich flavours of Shiraz.

Chardonnay and Japanese Cuisine: The crisp and refreshing acidity of Chardonnay pairs well with the delicate flavors of sushi and sashimi.

Cabernet Sauvignon and Italian Cuisine: The tannins in Cabernet Sauvignon complement the rich and bold flavours of Italian dishes such as lasagna and spaghetti bolognese.

Sparkling Wine and French Cuisine: The effervescence of sparkling wine pairs well with the rich and buttery flavours of French cuisine such as escargot and foie gras.

Australian Foods with Wines from Other Parts of the World

Grilled Kangaroo with Cabernet Sauvignon: Kangaroo is a lean meat with a bold flavour that pairs well with a full-bodied red wine like Cabernet Sauvignon. While Australia produces some great Cabernets, you can also try a California Cabernet or a Bordeaux from France.

Barramundi with Sauvignon Blanc: Barramundi is a popular fish in Australia with a delicate flavour that pairs well with a crisp white wine like Sauvignon Blanc. Try a New Zealand Sauvignon Blanc for a similar taste profile or a Sancerre from the Loire Valley in France.

Meat Pie with Shiraz: The meat pie is a classic Australian dish that pairs well with a rich and bold red wine like Shiraz. While Australia produces some fantastic Shiraz, you can also try a Syrah from the Rhone Valley in France or a Zinfandel from California.

Pavlova with Moscato: Pavlova is a meringue-based dessert topped with fresh fruit, and it pairs well with a light and sweet wine like Moscato. Australia produces some excellent Moscatos, but you can also try an Italian Moscato d'Asti or a Brachetto d'Acqui.

Vegemite on Toast with Chardonnay: Vegemite is a spread made from yeast extract, and it pairs well with a crisp and refreshing white wine like Chardonnay. Australia produces some great Chardonnay wines, but it's great also to try a Chablis from France or a California Chardonnay.

12 top vineyards of Australia, their owners, grapes, terroir, climate, and foods as well as pair the foods with their wines:

1. **Penfolds Wines** - Owner: Treasury Wine Estates, Grapes: Shiraz, Cabernet Sauvignon, Chardonnay, Terroir: Barossa Valley, Clare Valley, Adelaide Hills, Coonawarra, Climate: Mediterranean, Foods: Pair Shiraz with a hearty beef or lamb stew or roast, Chardonnay is perfect for creamy pasta or grilled chicken.

2. **Yalumba Wines** - Owner: Yalumba Family Winery, Grapes: Shiraz, Cabernet Sauvignon, Viognier, Terroir: Barossa Valley, Eden Valley, Clare Valley, Climate: Mediterranean, Foods: Pair Shiraz with grilled lamb chops, Cabernet Sauvignon goes well with roasted beef or sautéed mushrooms, and Viognier pairs well with seafood.

3. **Henschke Wines** - Owner: Stephen and Prue Henschke, Grapes: Shiraz, Cabernet Sauvignon, Merlot, Terroir: Barossa Valley, Eden Valley, Climate: Mediterranean to Continental, Foods: Pair Shiraz with braised beef short ribs, Cabernet Sauvignon with grilled steak, and Merlot with ratatouille.

4. **Penley Estate Wines** - Owner: The Penley Family, Grapes: Cabernet Sauvignon, Merlot, Cabernet Franc, Terroir: Coonawarra, Climate: Maritime, Foods: Pair Cabernet Sauvignon with roasted lamb or beef, Merlot with mushroom risotto, and Cabernet Franc with tomato-based pasta dishes.

5. **d'Arenberg Wines** - Owner: Chester Osborn, Grapes: Shiraz, Grenache, Mourvèdre, Terroir: McLaren Vale, Climate: Mediterranean to Maritime, Foods: Pair Shiraz with chargrilled steak or game, Grenache with roasted pork, and Mourvèdre with slow-cooked beef or lamb.

6. **Vasse Felix Wines** - Owner: Paul Holmes à Court, Grapes: Cabernet Sauvignon, Chardonnay, Shiraz, Terroir: Margaret River, Climate: Mediterranean, Foods: Pair Cabernet Sauvignon with grilled beef, Chardonnay with grilled seafood or chicken, and Shiraz with rich stews.

7. **Leeuwin Estate Wines** - Owner: Denis and Tricia Horgan, Grapes: Cabernet Sauvignon, Chardonnay, Pinot Noir, Terroir: Margaret River, Climate: Mediterranean, Foods: Pair Cabernet Sauvignon with lamb or beef dishes, Chardonnay with scallops or shellfish, and Pinot Noir with salmon or duck.

8. **Wynns Coonawarra Estate Wines** - Owner: Treasury Wine Estates, Grapes: Cabernet Sauvignon, Shiraz, Merlot, Terroir: Coonawarra, Climate: Maritime, Foods: Pair Cabernet Sauvignon with roasted lamb, Shiraz with game dishes, and Merlot with tomato-based pasta dishes.

9. **Tyrrell's Wines** - Owner: Bruce Tyrrell, Grapes: Shiraz, Chardonnay, Semillon, Terroir: Hunter Valley, Climate: Maritime, Foods: Pair Shiraz with roast beef or lamb, Chardonnay with seafood or chicken, and Semillon with grilled fish or sushi.

10. **Jim Barry Wines** - Owner: The Barry Family, Grapes: Shiraz, Riesling, Cabernet Sauvignon, Terroir: Clare Valley, Climate: Mediterranean, Foods: Pair Shiraz with spicy beef or pork dishes, Riesling with spicy Asian dishes or seafood, and Cabernet Sauvignon with grilled beef or lamb.

11. **Peter Lehmann Wines** - Owner: Hess Family Wine Estates, Grapes: Shiraz, Cabernet Sauvignon, Semillon, Terroir: Barossa Valley, Climate: Mediterranean, Foods: Pair Shiraz with grilled or roasted meat, Cabernet Sauvignon with roasted lamb or beef, and Semillon with grilled seafood or chicken.

12. **Jacob's Creek Wines** - Owner: Pernod Ricard, Grapes: Shiraz, Cabernet Sauvignon, Chardonnay, Terroir: Barossa Valley, Adelaide Hills, Climate: Mediterranean, Foods: Pair Shiraz with roasted beef or lamb, Cabernet Sauvignon with grilled steak, and Chardonnay with creamy pasta or grilled chicken.

Some suggestions for Australian food and wine pairings for summer, winter, informal dining, and formal dining:

Summer Pairings:

Informal dining: Grilled prawns or fish with a glass of crisp and refreshing Sauvignon Blanc from the Marlborough region of New Zealand or Adelaide Hills in South Australia.

Formal dining: Seared tuna with a glass of chilled and elegant Chardonnay from the Yarra Valley or Margaret River in Western Australia.

Winter Pairings:

Informal dining: Slow-cooked lamb shanks with a glass of full-bodied and spicy Shiraz from the Barossa Valley or McLaren Vale in South Australia.

Formal dining: Beef tenderloin with a glass of complex and robust Cabernet Sauvignon from the Coonawarra or Margaret River regions of Western Australia.

For each season, you can also consider the following pairings:

Informal Dining:

Summer: Fresh seafood (e.g., oysters, prawns, scallops) with a glass of crisp white wine like Riesling or Pinot Grigio, or a light red like Pinot Noir or Grenache.

Winter: Comfort food (e.g., stews, roasts, casseroles) with a glass of full-bodied red wines such as Shiraz or Cabernet Sauvignon.

Formal Dining:

Summer: Grilled meats (e.g., steak, lamb) with a glass of bold red wines like Shiraz or Cabernet Sauvignon, or a full-bodied white wine like Chardonnay.

Winter: Hearty dishes (e.g., slow-cooked meats, rich soups) with a glass of aged red wines like Cabernet Sauvignon or Pinot Noir, or a full-bodied white like Viognier or Marsanne.

Keep in mind that these are just suggestions, and personal preferences will vary. It's always a good idea to experiment with different pairings to find what works best for your palate.

Sweet Wines

The Australian sweet wine industry has a rich history that spans back to the early days of the Australian wine industry in the 1800s.

The most popular grape varieties for sweet wine production in Australia are Semillon, Muscat, and Riesling. In general, the sweet wine making process entails harvesting grapes with a high sugar content and stopping the fermentation process early to retain some of the residual sugar in the wine.

In terms of culture, sweet wine has traditionally been consumed as a dessert wine or as an accompaniment to cheese and fruit platters. However, in recent years, there has been a growing interest in pairing sweet wine with savory dishes such as spicy Asian cuisine.

Regions that produce high quality sweet wines:

1. **Barossa Valley:** Perhaps one of Australia's best-known wine regions, the Barossa Valley is renowned for its quality red wines. However, it's also home to some excellent sweet wines, including fortified wines made from Shiraz and Grenache.

2. **Hunter Valley:** Located north of Sydney, the Hunter Valley is Australia's oldest wine producing region. Semillon is the star grape here, and the region produces some world-class sweet dessert wines that age beautifully.

3. **Rutherglen:** Located in the northeast of the Victoria state, Rutherglen is famous for its luscious fortified Muscats and Tokays. These wines are made using a unique solera system, which involves blending wines from different vintages to create a consistent style.

4. **Margaret River**: Known for its cool climate and maritime influence, Margaret River is a relatively new wine region in Western Australia. Its Rieslings are highly sought after and there are a few wineries that produce excellent late harvest and botrytis wines.

5. **Riverina**: Located in New South Wales, Riverina is a hot, dry region that produces a range of sweet wines. The most notable are late harvest and botrytis Rieslings, but there are also some excellent fortified wines made from Muscat and Topaque (formerly known as Tokay) grapes.

Some of the top sweet wine producers in Australia include Yalumba in the Barossa Valley, De Bortoli in the Riverina, and Campbells in Rutherglen.

Australian wines that would pair well with sweet foods:

1. **Hunter Valley, New South Wales –** a region known for its Semillon and Shiraz

   a. Brokenwood ILR Reserve Semillon - this dry white wine pairs well with sweet and savoury dishes as the full body balances sweets and a tart lime juice finish cuts through the sugar.

   b. De Bortoli Noble One Botrytis Semillon - a dessert wine with tropical fruit and honey notes, perfect for pairing with fruit tart, bread pudding, and custard pies.

2. **Margaret River, Western Australia –** a region known for its Cabernet Sauvignon, Chardonnay, and SSBs

   a. Flametree SSB - this white blend of Semillon, Sauvignon Blanc, and Chardonnay has a great acidity that pairs with sweet foods like honey-glazed ham or fruit salad.

   b. Cape Mentelle Cabernet Sauvignon - a red wine with black fruit, eucalyptus, and a strong tannin structure, this pairs with sweet foods with chocolate and coffee flavors.

3. **Barossa Valley, South Australia –** a region known for its Shiraz and Grenache

   a. Seppeltsfield 100-Year-Old Para Vintage Tawny - a luscious fortified wine with flavours of dried figs and caramel, perfect for pairing with chocolate truffles, caramel flan and crème brûlée.

   b. Yalumba The Menzies Cabernet Sauvignon - a full-bodied red wine with a fruity aroma and notes of tobacco, this wine pairs well with chocolate-covered fruits or nuts.

4. **Yarra Valley, Victoria –** a region known for its Pinot Noir, Chardonnay, and Sparkling wines

   a. Giant Steps Pinot Noir - a red wine with hints of black cherry, raspberry and a light earthy aroma pairs with lighter desserts like pavlova or fresh fruit cheesecake.

   b. Domaine Chandon Brut - a crisp sparkling wine with a hint of oak, this wine is perfect for a toast with fruit-based desserts and creamy pastries.

5. **Coonawarra, South Australia –** a region known for its Cabernet Sauvignon and Shiraz

   a. Wynns Coonawarra Estate Cabernet Sauvignon - a dark red wine with flavours of red currant, blackberry, and smoked herbs, this wine pairs well with dark chocolate and fudge.

   b. Rymill Coonawarra SV Chardonnay - this wine has a bright acidity and a clean finish with mild citrus notes, perfect for accompanying crème brûlée or fruit tarts.

6. **Tasmania –** a region known for its sparkling wines, Riesling, and Pinot Noir

   a. Josef Chromy Pepik Sekt - this sparkling wine has a creamy mousse, a perfect wine-based fruit and pumpkin-based desserts.

   b. Clover Hill Cuvée Exceptionelle Blanc de Blancs - a well-rounded sparkling wine with a full body and a hint of lemon, pairs well with citrus cakes and fruit desserts.

7. **Clare Valley, South Australia –** a region known for its Riesling, Shiraz, and Cabernet Sauvignon

   a. Jim Barry The Lodge Hill Shiraz - a bold red wine with a spicy aroma and ripe fruit flavors, this wine pairs with sweet dishes that feature floral undertones such as honey glazed roast pork with rosemary roasted potatoes.

   b. Grosset Polish Hill Riesling - this dry white wine from the Clare Valley features a taste of lime and citrus, and a delicious combination for salty dishes like chicken marsala.

8. **Swan Valley, Western Australia –** a region known for its fortified wines such as Port and Muscat

   a. Houghton White Classic Liqueur – a light and semi-sweet Muscatel mixture that is typically topped with ice and can be paired with light desserts like trifles, jellies and sorbets.

b. Sandalford Founders Reserve Shiraz - a rich and robust fortified wine with a vibrant black fruit and spicy aroma, it complements tart desserts such as berry tart, and apple pie.

9. **Heathcote, Victoria** – a region known for its Shiraz

a. Wild Duck Creek Springflat Shiraz - a full-bodied red wine that is a mix of black fruit and dark chocolate flavours, pairs well with sweet desserts layered with dark chocolate.

b. Flynns Wines Grenache Noir - this red wine received the James Halliday's top 100 wine award in 2019, the wine features red plum and blackberry flavours, and is perfect for pairing with sweet fruit breads.

10. **Granite Belt, Queensland** – a region known for its Shiraz and alternative varietals

a. Golden Grove Estate Signature Shiraz Viognier - a full-bodied red wine with a fruity nose, white peppery notes and earthy undertones, pairs well with cheese and nut based desserts.

b. Ballandean Estate Wines Late Harvest Sylvaner - as discussed in its name, this wine is perfect for a summertime dessert that includes a fruit laced pie, cake, or tart.

Australian sweet wines that pair well with food:

De Bortoli Noble One Botrytis Semillon - De Bortoli Wines, Riverina, New South Wales: This is a luscious dessert wine with aromas of apricots and honey, and a rich, sweet palate. It pairs well with blue cheese, foie gras, or a fruit tart.

Brown Brothers Orange Muscat and Flora - Brown Brothers, King Valley, Victoria: This wine has a vibrant orange blossom aroma and a luscious palate of apricot, marmalade, and honey. It pairs well with fruit-based desserts, particularly those containing orange, peach, or apricot.

Seppeltsfield Para Port - Seppeltsfield, Barossa Valley, South Australia: This rich and intense port has flavours of caramel, toffee, and chocolate. It pairs well with chocolate-based desserts, blue cheese, or a cigar.

Yalumba Museum Reserve Muscat - Yalumba, Barossa Valley, South Australia: This wine is made from Muscat grapes and is aged for 15 years in oak barrels. It has flavours of caramel, raisins, and honey, and pairs well with fruit-based desserts, particularly those containing dried fruits.

Campbells Rutherglen Muscat - Campbells Wines, Rutherglen, Victoria: This wine is aged in oak barrels for up to 40 years and has flavours of toffee, coffee, and raisins. It pairs well with chocolate-based desserts, strong cheeses, or a cigar.

d'Arenberg The Noble Mud Pie - d'Arenberg Wines, McLaren Vale, South Australia: This wine is made from botrytised Semillon grapes and has flavours of honey, apricots, and spice. It pairs well with fruit-based desserts, particularly those containing apricots or peaches.

Stanton & Killeen Classic Muscat - Stanton & Killeen, Rutherglen, Victoria: This wine is aged for an average of eight years in oak barrels and has flavours of toffee, raisins, and coffee. It pairs well with fruit-based desserts, particularly those containing figs or dates.

Morris Old Premium Rare Liqueur Muscat - Morris Wines, Rutherglen, Victoria: This wine is aged for an average of 20 years in oak barrels and has flavours of caramel, toffee, and coffee. It pairs well with fruit-based desserts, particularly those containing figs or dates, or a strong blue cheese.

Brown Brothers Patricia Noble Riesling - Brown Brothers, King Valley, Victoria: This wine is made from Riesling grapes and has flavors of honey, apricots, and citrus. It pairs well with fruit-based desserts, particularly those containing lemon or lime.

Henschke Noble Rot Semillon - Henschke, Eden Valley, South Australia: This wine is made from botrytised Semillon grapes and has flavours of honey, apricots, and spice. It pairs well with fruit-based desserts, particularly those containing apricots or peaches.

Phileas Fogg would have encountered a diverse range of people in Australia.

At the time the novel was written (1873), Australia was a British colony, and the population consisted mainly of Indigenous Australians, British settlers, and convicts. Phileas Fogg would have likely encountered people from these groups during his visit.

He may have also met people from other parts of the world who had come to Australia seeking their fortune during the gold rush of the mid-19th century. Chinese immigrants, for example, played a significant role in Australia's early history and were often employed in the gold mines.

Additionally, Phileas Fogg may have encountered members of the Irish diaspora, who had been displaced due to the potato famine in the mid-1800s and had migrated to various parts of the world, including Australia.

Overall, Phileas Fogg would have encountered a diverse range of people in Australia, from Indigenous Australians and British settlers to immigrants from around the world.

If Phileas Fogg, were looking for sweet wines to enjoy, he might have sought out some of the following options:

Noble One Botrytis Semillon - This is a sweet wine produced by De Bortoli Wines in the Riverina region of New South Wales. It has won numerous awards and is considered one of the best dessert wines in Australia. It pairs well with blue cheese, foie gras, and fruit-based desserts.

Campbells Rutherglen Muscat - This is a fortified wine produced by Campbells Wines in the Rutherglen region of Victoria. It is rich and sweet with flavors of raisins, toffee, and caramel. It pairs well with desserts such as chocolate cake, cheesecake, and sticky toffee pudding.

Brown Brothers Orange Muscat and Flora - This is a sweet white wine produced by Brown Brothers in the King Valley region of Victoria. It has a floral aroma and flavours of orange blossom, apricot, and peach. It pairs well with spicy Asian cuisine, fruit-based desserts, and cheese plates.

Seppeltsfield Para Liqueur Tawny - This is a fortified wine produced by Seppeltsfield in the Barossa Valley region of South Australia. It is sweet and full-bodied with flavours of caramel, toffee, and nutty notes. It pairs well with chocolate desserts, blue cheese, and roasted nuts.

Yalumba Museum Reserve Muscat - This is a sweet wine produced by Yalumba in the Barossa Valley region of South Australia. It is rich and complex with flavours of raisins, figs, and Christmas cake. It pairs well with rich, chocolate-based desserts, fruit cake, and mature cheeses.

As for food pairings, the Noble One Botrytis Semillon would pair well with blue cheese, foie gras, and fruit-based desserts such as pear tart or peach cobbler. The Campbells Rutherglen Muscat would pair well with chocolate cake, cheesecake, and sticky toffee pudding. The Brown Brothers Orange Muscat and Flora would pair well with spicy Asian cuisine, fruit-based desserts, and cheese plates. The Seppeltsfield Para Liqueur Tawny would pair well with chocolate desserts, blue cheese, and roasted nuts. Finally, the Yalumba Museum Reserve Muscat would pair well with rich, chocolate-based desserts, fruit cake, and mature cheeses such as stilton.

Sparkling Wines

The Australian sparkling wine industry has come a long way since its inception in the 19th century. Although Australia is better known for its shiraz and chardonnay, sparkling wines have been gaining popularity and recognition over the years. Today, the country is recognized for producing some of the best sparkling wines in the world, competing with the likes of Champagne, Prosecco, and Cava.

History:

The first vineyards in Australia were established in the late 18th century, and by the mid-19th century, Australian wines had started gaining international recognition. The first attempt at producing sparkling wine in Australia was made in the 1860s, which was not that successful. It was not until the 20th century that the industry started gaining traction. In the 1950s, the Australian government invested in the wine industry, which led to significant improvements in quality and production. This period coincided with the introduction of Chardonnay and Pinot Noir grapes that are crucial for producing sparkling wine. Since then, the industry has continued to grow and improve.

Grapes:

Chardonnay, Pinot Noir, and Pinot Meunier are the main grapes used in Australian sparkling wine. These grapes can handle Australia's warm climate, which makes them perfect for the country's growing conditions.

Owners:

The Australian sparkling wine industry is dominated by some of the country's largest wine producers. Some of the most prominent owners of sparkling wine brands include Treasury Wine Estates, Accolade Wines, and Pernod Ricard.

Culture:

Australian sparkling wines have a vibrant and lively culture that is reflected in the wine itself. Australians are known for their love of outdoor activities and social gatherings, and sparkling wine is a perfect fit for these activities. Many wineries offer tours and tastings that showcase the culture and character of Australian sparkling wines.

Terroir:

The terroir of Australian sparkling wine is diverse and unique. The country has a range of climates, soils, and topography, which results in distinct regional characteristics that are unique to each area. The cooler regions such as Tasmania and the Yarra Valley are known for producing sparkling wines with delicate flavors and high acidity, while warmer regions such as the Barossa Valley produce richer and fuller sparkling wines.

Methods:

The traditional method, also known as the méthode champenoise, is used to produce Australian sparkling wines. This method involves a secondary fermentation that takes place inside the bottle, which creates the bubbles. The wine is aged on the lees for a period of time to give it the characteristic flavours and aromas associated with sparkling wine.

Foods:

Australian sparkling wine pairs well with a range of foods, including seafood, white meats, berries, and cheeses. Some of the best food pairings for Australian sparkling wines include oysters, prawns, sushi, scallops, smoked salmon, and creamy pasta dishes. Fresh fruits and cream-based desserts are also excellent compliments to Australian sparkling wine.

Non-alcoholic Wines

Non-alcoholic wine has a relatively short history in Australia, compared to traditional wine. However, in recent years, there has been a significant increase in the popularity of non-alcoholic wine, driven by consumers seeking healthier beverage options.

History:

Non-alcoholic wine was first produced in Australia in the 1980s, but it wasn't until the early 2000s that it gained popularity. The early non-alcoholic wines were made by removing alcohol from traditional wine, resulting in a product that lacked the full flavour and complexity of traditional wine. However, in recent years, there has been a significant improvement in the quality of non-alcoholic wine, with many producers creating wines specifically designed to be non-alcoholic.

Terroir:

The terroir of Australian non-alcoholic wines varies depending on the region and grape variety used. Some of the most popular grape varieties used in non-alcoholic wine production in Australia include Shiraz, Cabernet Sauvignon, Chardonnay, and Sauvignon Blanc. These grapes are grown in many different regions across Australia, including the Barossa Valley, Margaret River, and the Hunter Valley.

Culture:

Wine culture is an important part of Australian life, and this extends to non-alcoholic wine. Non-alcoholic wine is increasingly being used as a replacement for traditional wine, particularly for those who are seeking a healthier lifestyle. It is often served at social events, such as dinners and parties, and is becoming more widely available in restaurants and bars.

Foods:

Non-alcoholic wine pairs well with a variety of foods, including grilled meats, seafood, salads, and pasta dishes. It is also a popular accompaniment to cheese and crackers, and is often used in cooking as a substitute for traditional wine.

Overall, non-alcoholic wine is becoming an increasingly popular beverage option in Australia, driven by consumers seeking healthier and more diverse beverage options. With the improvement in the quality of non-alcoholic wine, it is expected that its popularity will continue to grow in the years to come.

Wine, by definition, is an alcoholic beverage made from fermented grapes. There are non-alcoholic beverages that are made to mimic the flavour and appearance of wine, but they are not classified as wine.

There are a few Australian companies that produce non-alcoholic beverages that resemble wine, such as McGuigan Zero, Edenvale, and Lyre's, but they are not considered wines and are not produced using traditional winemaking methods or terroir.

Instead, these beverages are typically made by blending grape juice with other natural flavours and aromas, such as oak, to create a wine-like taste and aroma. They are best enjoyed as a refreshing beverage on their own or paired with light meals such as salads, seafood, or grilled chicken.

There aren't many Australian vineyards that offer non-alcoholic wines, however here are

some vineyards that offer a range of non-alcoholic grape juice options:

1. **De Bortoli Wines** - De Bortoli is a family-owned vineyard that produces a range of non-alcoholic grape juices. These juices are made from a variety of grapes, including chardonnay, shiraz and sparkling wine grapes. They are perfect for serving as a non-alcoholic option at a dinner party or for enjoying on a hot summer day.

2. **Printhie Wines** - Printhie Wines produces a range of non-alcoholic grape juices made from chardonnay, sauvignon blanc and pinot noir grapes. They are located in the cool climate region of Orange, NSW and their vineyard is known for its high altitude and low yields.

3. **Jacobs Creek** - Jacobs Creek is known for its wines, but they also produce a range of non-alcoholic grape juices. Their juices are made from a variety of grapes, including chardonnay, shiraz and sparkling wine grapes. They are perfect for enjoying with food or as a healthy alternative to soda.

4. **McGuigan Wines** - McGuigan Wines is a family-owned vineyard that produces a range of non-alcoholic grape juices. They are made from a variety of grapes, including chardonnay, merlot and cabernet sauvignon. They are perfect for enjoying with a meal, or as a refreshing drink on a hot day.

5. **Tyrrell's Wines** - Tyrrell's is a renowned vineyard that produces a range of non-alcoholic grape juices. They are made from a variety of grapes, including semillon, shiraz and chardonnay. They are perfect for serving at a dinner party, or for enjoying as a refreshing drink after a workout.

6. **Yarra Valley Wines -** Yarra Valley Wines produces a range of non-alcoholic grape juices made from Chardonnay and Shiraz grapes. Their vineyard is located in the cool climate region of the Yarra Valley in Victoria, and their juices are known for their rich, fruity flavours.

7. **Margaret River Wines** - Margaret River Wines produces a range of non-alcoholic grape juices made from a variety of grapes, including Sauvignon Blanc, Chardonnay and Cabernet Sauvignon. Their vineyard is located in the Margaret River region of Western Australia, known for its warm, maritime climate.

8. **Brown Brothers** - Brown Brothers is a family-owned vineyard that produces a range of non-alcoholic grape juices made from a variety of grapes, including Chardonnay, Shiraz and Cabernet Sauvignon. They are perfect for sharing with friends and family, or enjoying on your own.

9. **Henschke Wines** - Henschke Wines produces a range of non-alcoholic grape juices made from a variety of grapes, including Shiraz and Grenache. Their vineyard is located in the Barossa Valley region of South Australia and their juices are known for their rich, full-bodied flavours.

10. **Seppeltsfield Wines** - Seppeltsfield Wines is known for its fortified wines, but they also produce a range of non-alcoholic grape juices. Their juices are made from a variety of grapes, including Shiraz and Grenache. They are perfect for serving at a special event, or for enjoying as a refreshing drink on a hot day.

In terms of food pairing, these non-alcoholic grape juices can be enjoyed with a variety of dishes. For example, Chardonnay grape juice pairs well with seafood and chicken dishes, while Shiraz grape juice pairs well with red meats and spicy foods. Sauvignon Blanc grape juice pairs well with vegetarian dishes and salads, while Cabernet Sauvignon grape juice pairs well with hearty stews and roasts.

Phileas Fogg's journey took place in the late 19th century, when non-alcoholic wine was not yet commercially available. However, in modern times, there are a variety of non-alcoholic wines that he might have sampled during his travels to Australia. Here are couple of examples:

Edenvale Non-Alcoholic Wine - Edenvale is an Australian winery that produces a range of non-alcoholic wines, including Shiraz, Chardonnay, and Sparkling Cuvee. The grapes used to make the wines are sourced from various regions throughout Australia, including the Barossa Valley, Adelaide Hills, and Riverina. Phileas Fogg might have paired the Shiraz with grilled lamb or beef, the Chardonnay with seafood dishes, and the Sparkling Cuvee with cheese platters or desserts.

McGuigan Zero - McGuigan Wines is another Australian winery that produces a range of non-alcoholic wines, including a Shiraz and a Sparkling Brut. The grapes used to make the wines are sourced from the Hunter Valley region of New South Wales. Phileas Fogg might have paired the Shiraz with hearty meat dishes or spicy cuisine, and the Sparkling Brut with light appetisers or seafood.

In Conclusion….

Australia is a truly remarkable continent that offers an amazing variety of food, wine, grapes, culture, and traditions. With its vast landscapes and diverse climates, it has become a world-renowned wine-producing country, known for its top-quality wines that can impress even the most discerning palates. From the classic Shiraz and Chardonnay to the lesser-known but equally delicious Grenache and Verdelho, Australian wines offer a rich tapestry of flavors and aromas that can complement a wide range of cuisines.

Speaking of food, Australia is home to some of the most exotic and flavorful dishes that can tantalise your taste buds. From the iconic meat pie and the delectable seafood platters to the hearty stews and spicy curries, Australian cuisine has something for everyone. Whether you're a carnivore, seafood lover, vegetarian, or vegan, you'll find plenty of options that pair well with Australian wines.

Moreover, the Australian wine culture is deeply rooted in tradition and heritage, where winemaking is not just a business but a way of life. Through generations, the winemakers have carefully selected the best grapes, perfected the winemaking techniques, and passed on their knowledge and passion to the next generation. This has resulted in a wine industry that is not only successful but also sustainable and socially responsible.

Finally, I hope that you have enjoyed reading this article on food and wine pairings from Australia and that it has inspired you to try out new wine and food combinations on your own. By experimenting with the different flavours and textures, you can enhance your culinary experience and discover a whole new world of pleasures. So why not uncork a bottle of Australian wine, prepare a delicious meal, and savour the rich flavours of this magnificent continent? Cheers!

Further reading on Australian wines, their foods and cultures, and how they are paired.

Wine Australia: Wine Australia is the official website of the Australian wine industry, and it provides a wealth of information about Australian wines, including their history, production, and styles. The website also offers resources on wine pairing, food and wine matching, and regional wine and food experiences.

James Halliday's Wine Companion: James Halliday is a renowned Australian wine writer and critic, and his Wine Companion is a comprehensive guide to Australian wines. The guide features detailed profiles of individual wineries and vineyards, tasting notes, and ratings, as well as food pairing suggestions.

Australian Gourmet Traveller Wine: Australian Gourmet Traveller Wine is a magazine dedicated to the Australian wine industry, and it features articles on wine regions, grape varieties, and winemaking techniques. The magazine also provides food pairing suggestions, recipes, and restaurant recommendations.

Wine Selectors: Wine Selectors is a wine club and online retailer that specialises in Australian wines. The company's website features detailed information on individual wines and regions, as well as food and wine pairing suggestions and recipes.

Australian Wine and Food: Australian Wine and Food is a cookbook by author and wine expert Jennifer Wilkinson. The book features recipes that are designed to pair with Australian wines, as well as information on wine regions, grape varieties, and winemaking techniques.

Wine Folly: Wine Folly is a website and book series that provides accessible, easy-to-understand information on wine. The website features articles on wine regions, grape varieties, and food pairing, as well as a comprehensive guide to Australian wines.

Australian Wine Research Institute: The Australian Wine Research Institute is a research organisation that provides scientific support to the Australian wine industry. The organisation's website features a range of resources on wine production, grape varieties, and wine quality, as well as information on food and wine pairing.

I hope you find these resources helpful!

Resources for further reading on Australian non-alcoholic wines

Here are some resources for further reading on non-alcoholic Australian wines, their owners, and the foods they are best paired with:

The Australian Non-Alcoholic Beverages Guide: This online guide provides information on non-alcoholic wines, beers, and spirits available in Australia, including detailed information on the winemakers and food pairing suggestions.

Vinomofo: This online wine retailer offers a selection of non-alcoholic wines from Australia and around the world, along with detailed tasting notes and food pairing suggestions.

Sans Drinks: This Australian-based online retailer specialises in non-alcoholic wines, beers, and spirits, including a selection of Australian wines. The website also features detailed information on the winemakers and food pairing suggestions.

The Drinks List: This online magazine covers the non-alcoholic drinks industry, including coverage of Australian non-alcoholic wines and their makers.

Gourmet Traveller Wine: This Australian wine magazine features articles on non-alcoholic wines and their makers, along with food pairing suggestions.

Australian Grape and Wine Authority: This government organisation provides information and resources on the Australian wine industry, including a directory of winemakers and their products.

Australian Wine Research Institute: This research organisation provides information on the science of winemaking, including research on non-alcoholic wines and their production.

These resources should provide you with a wealth of information on non-alcoholic Australian wines, their makers, and the foods that pair best with them.

Further reading on Australian Sparkling Wines

Here are some articles i have found on Australian sparkling wines that you may find interesting:

1. **"The Rise of Australian Sparkling Wine"** by Max Allen, for Gourmet Traveller: https://www.gourmettraveller.com.au/drinks/wine/the-rise-of-australian-sparkling-wine-18423

2. **"Six Australian Sparkling Wines to Try"** by James Atkinson, for SBS Food: https://www.sbs.com.au/food/article/2017/12/08/six-australian-sparkling-wines-try

3. **"Australia's Best Sparkling Wines"** by Max Allen, for Australian Gourmet Traveller: https://www.gourmettraveller.com.au/drinks/wine/australias-best-sparkling-wines-12810

4.   **"The   Australian   Sparkling   Wine   Revolution"**   by   Chris   Shanahan,   for   Grape   Observer:
https://grapeobserver.com/2018/03/02/the-australian-sparkling-wine-revolution/

I hope these articles provide you with some helpful information!

Note:

Phileas Fogg was known for his daring spirit and willingness to take risks. Similarly, don't be afraid to experiment with different wine and food pairings. You may discover some surprising and delightful combinations that you never would have thought of otherwise.

Wine and food pairing can also be subjective and dependent on individual tastes. The above suggestions are merely general guidelines.

CHAPTER 4

ASIAN WINE AND CUISINE

Asia is the largest and the most diverse continent in the world, comprising over 50 countries and diverse cultures, religions, and traditions. From the towering Himalayas to the vast deserts of Arabia and the bustling cities of East Asia, there is an abundance of culture and traditions to explore. With over 4.5 billion people, Asia is home to a variety of ethnicities, languages, and religions.

Each country in Asia has its own unique food culture, with different spices, flavours, and ingredients. The cuisine in Asia is known for its strong flavours, often using a combination of sweet, sour, salty, and spicy elements. From the spicy curries of India to the savoury noodles of Japan and the fresh herbs of Vietnam, Asia has a rich culinary heritage that continues to captivate food enthusiasts all over the world.

In addition, Asia has a long history of producing some of the world's most celebrated wines. Countries like China, Japan, and India have been cultivating grapes for thousands of years, and their wines are gaining international recognition for their unique expression of terroir. With a range of climates and geographical features, the wines of Asia are diverse and distinctive, reflecting the character of the land and the unique wine-making traditions of each country.

Asia is home to several wine-producing countries, each with its unique terroir and winemaking techniques. In this Chapter, we will explore the wines produced in Asia and how they match with Asian foods and other cuisines worldwide.

Asian Wine Regions

China:

China is one of the largest wine-producing countries in Asia. The country's wine industry has been growing rapidly in recent years, with both domestic and international investors establishing wineries in the country. The main grape varieties grown in China are Cabernet Sauvignon, Merlot, and Chardonnay.

Chinese wines pair well with Asian foods, especially those with strong flavours like Szechuan cuisine, spicy Indian food, and Japanese sushi. For example, a Chinese Cabernet Sauvignon can complement spicy Szechuan dishes, while a Chardonnay can pair well with Indian curry.

Japan:

Japan has a long history of winemaking, dating back to the 19th century. The country is known for its unique grape varieties, such as Koshu and Muscat Bailey A, which are adapted to Japan's cool and humid climate.

Japanese wines are typically light-bodied and acidic, making them an excellent pairing with the country's traditional cuisine, such as sushi, sashimi, and tempura. A crisp and acidic Koshu can complement the subtle flavors of sushi, while a full-bodied Muscat Bailey A can match the richness of tempura.

India:

India has a rapidly growing wine industry, with wineries located mainly in the Nashik region of Maharashtra. The country's winemakers primarily use international grape varieties like Cabernet Sauvignon, Shiraz, and Chenin Blanc.

Indian wines pair well with spicy and flavourful Indian dishes, as well as other Asian cuisines. For example, a fruity and medium-bodied Indian Shiraz can complement spicy curries, while a crisp and refreshing Chenin Blanc can match the flavours of Thai cuisine.

Thailand:

Thailand's wine industry is relatively new but growing fast. The country's winemakers primarily use hybrid grape varieties, such as Malaga Blanc and Black Queen, which are adapted to the hot and humid climate.

Thai wines pair well with the country's spicy and aromatic cuisine, such as Tom Yum soup and green curry. A crisp and fruity Thai white wine can complement the sour and spicy flavors of Tom Yum, while a light-bodied red wine can match the richness of green curry.

Other Asian Countries:

Other Asian countries like South Korea, Vietnam, and Myanmar are also beginning to develop their wine industries. However, the wines produced in these countries are relatively unknown outside of their respective regions.

Asia's Wine terroir

Asia has a number of regions that are suitable for wine production, with different climates and soil types that contribute to the unique characteristics of their wines. Some of the most notable wine-growing regions in Asia include:

China: China is the largest wine producer in Asia, with most of its vineyards located in the Ningxia and Xinjiang regions. The climate in these regions is dry and continental, with hot summers and cold winters, which is similar to many wine-growing regions in Europe. Some of the most popular grape varieties grown in China include Cabernet Sauvignon, Merlot, and Chardonnay.

India: India has a long history of wine production, dating back to ancient times. The Nashik region, located in the state of Maharashtra, is the most important l.wine-producing region in India. The climate in Nashik is tropical, with hot summers and cool winters. Some of the most popular grape varieties grown in India include Shiraz, Chenin Blanc, and Cabernet Sauvignon.

Japan: Japan has a small but growing wine industry, with most of its vineyards located in the Yamanashi and Nagano regions. The climate in these regions is cool and continental, with high altitudes and a large diurnal temperature variation. Some of the most popular grape varieties grown in Japan include Koshu and Muscat Bailey A.

Lebanon: While not typically thought of as part of Asia, Lebanon is located in the western part of the continent and has a long history of wine production. The Bekaa Valley, located in the east of Lebanon, is the most important wine-producing region in the country. The climate in the Bekaa Valley is hot and dry, with low rainfall and high altitude. Some of the most popular grape varieties grown in Lebanon include Cabernet Sauvignon, Merlot, and Syrah.

Israel: Israel has a small but significant wine industry, with most of its vineyards located in the Galilee and Golan Heights regions. The climate in these regions is Mediterranean, with hot summers and cool winters. Some of the most popular grape varieties grown in Israel include Cabernet Sauvignon, Merlot, and Sauvignon Blanc.

Pairing Asian Foods with Asian Wines

Pairing Asian foods with Asian wines can create a harmonious and delightful culinary experience. Here are some advantages of doing so:

Complementary flavours: Asian wines are made to complement the complex and diverse flavours of Asian cuisine. For example, a spicy Thai dish can be paired with a sweet and aromatic Gewürztraminer wine. The floral and fruity notes of the wine balance the spiciness of the dish and enhance the flavours of the food.

Regional pairing: Asian wines are often made from grape varietals that are indigenous to the region, and thus can be a natural pairing with the local cuisine. For instance, Chinese wines made from the Cabernet Gernischt grape can complement Sichuan-style dishes, which feature spicy flavours and bold textures.

Texture and weight: Asian wines tend to have a lighter body and lower alcohol content, making them suitable to pair with lighter and more delicate Asian dishes, such as sushi and sashimi. A crisp and refreshing Riesling wine can pair well with these dishes, providing a balance of acidity and sweetness.

Cultural appreciation: Pairing Asian wines with Asian foods is also a way to appreciate the culture and traditions of the region. It can be a learning experience, as it allows one to understand the flavour profile and characteristics of the wine and the food, as well as the history and cultural significance behind them.

Overall, pairing Asian foods with Asian wines can be a rewarding and enjoyable experience, bringing together the flavours and cultural traditions of the region.

Sushi and Sake: The clean, subtle flavour of sake complements the delicate flavours of sushi perfectly.

Spicy Thai curry and Gewürztraminer: The floral and spicy notes of Gewürztraminer can help balance the heat of spicy Thai curry.

Chinese dim sum and Shaoxing wine: Shaoxing wine is a popular Chinese rice wine that pairs well with the savoury flavours of dim sum dishes.

Korean BBQ and Soju: Soju is a traditional Korean liquor that is often paired with grilled meats, such as those found in Korean BBQ.

Indian tikka masala and Riesling: The sweetness and acidity of Riesling can help balance the bold flavours of Indian tikka masala.

Japanese ramen and Pinot Noir: The light-bodied and fruity Pinot Noir pairs well with the savoury and umami flavours found in ramen.

Vietnamese pho and Chenin Blanc: The aromatic and refreshing Chenin Blanc complements the complex flavors of Vietnamese pho.

Japanese yakitori and Junmai Ginjo: Junmai Ginjo is a premium sake that has a smooth and slightly fruity taste, which makes it a great match for the smoky and savoury flavours of grilled chicken skewers.

Indian vindaloo and Syrah: The bold and spicy flavours of Indian vindaloo can stand up to the rich and full-bodied Syrah, which has notes of black fruit, spice, and pepper.

Thai pad thai and Riesling: The light and zesty Riesling pairs well with the tangy and slightly sweet flavours of Thai pad thai, which typically contains ingredients such as tamarind, fish sauce, and peanuts.

Chinese hot pot and Baijiu: Baijiu is a strong and fiery Chinese liquor that is often served with hot pot, a popular communal dish that features a simmering pot of broth and various meats, vegetables, and noodles.

Korean bibimbap and Gamay: The bright and fruity Gamay can balance the earthy and umami flavours of Korean bibimbap, a rice bowl dish that typically includes various vegetables, meat or tofu, and a fried egg.

Filipino adobo and Tannat: The bold and tannic Tannat can complement the rich and tangy flavours of Filipino adobo, a meat or poultry dish that is marinated in vinegar, soy sauce, and garlic.

Remember, these are just suggestions and there are no hard and fast rules when it comes to food and wine pairing. The most important thing is to enjoy the experience and experiment with different combinations until you find what works best for your taste buds.

Pairing Asian Foods with Non-Asian Wines

Pairing Asian foods with non-Asian wines can create a unique and enjoyable culinary experience. Here are some advantages of doing so:

Contrasting flavours: Pairing Asian foods with non-Asian wines can create a contrast in flavours, which can be very pleasing to the palate. For example, a crisp white wine can pair well with a spicy Asian dish, creating a balance between the heat of the food and the coolness of the wine.

Complementing flavours: Non-Asian wines can also complement the flavours of Asian dishes. For instance, a fruity red wine can complement the sweetness of a teriyaki sauce, while a full-bodied white wine can complement the richness of a coconut milk-based curry.

Wide variety of options: Non-Asian wines offer a wide variety of options to choose from, allowing you to experiment with different flavour combinations. You can choose from a range of red, white, and sparkling wines from different regions and grape varieties to find the perfect match for your Asian dish.

International experience: Pairing non-Asian wines with Asian foods can also create an international experience, allowing you to explore different cultures through food and wine. This can be a fun and educational experience for wine enthusiasts and foodies alike.

Availability: Non-Asian wines are more readily available in many regions, making them an accessible option for pairing with Asian foods. This allows you to easily experiment with different pairings at home or at a restaurant.

Lets Pair some Asian foods with non-Asian wines

This can also create a unique and enjoyable culinary experience, offering a wide range of flavour combinations and allowing you to explore different cultures through food and wine.

Sushi and Champagne: The light, effervescent bubbles in champagne help to balance the flavours of sushi, while the acidity in the wine cuts through the fattiness of the fish.

Pad Thai and Riesling: The sweet and spicy flavours of Pad Thai are complemented by the sweet and fruity notes in a Riesling, while the wine's acidity helps to balance the dish's tanginess.

Teriyaki Chicken and Merlot: The bold flavours of teriyaki chicken are complemented by the full-bodied richness of Merlot, while the wine's tannins help to cut through the sweetness of the sauce.

Vietnamese Pho and Pinot Noir: The light and fragrant broth of pho is balanced by the delicate, earthy flavors of Pinot Noir, while the wine's acidity helps to cut through the richness of the meat.

Korean BBQ and Zinfandel: The smoky, savoury flavours of Korean BBQ are complemented by the bold, fruity notes in a Zinfandel, while the wine's tannins help to cut through the fattiness of the meat.

Indian Curry and Gewürztraminer: The spicy, aromatic flavours of Indian curry are complemented by the floral, citrusy notes in a Gewürztraminer, while the wine's sweetness helps to balance the heat of the spices.

Chinese Dumplings and Sauvignon Blanc: The light, delicate flavors of Chinese dumplings are complemented by the crisp, citrusy notes in a Sauvignon Blanc, while the wine's acidity helps to cut through the richness of the filling.

Sushi and Champagne: The light, effervescent bubbles in champagne help to balance the flavours of sushi, while the acidity in the wine cuts through the fattiness of the fish.

Korean BBQ and Zinfandel: The smoky, savoury flavours of Korean BBQ are complemented by the bold, fruity notes in a Zinfandel, while the wine's tannins help to cut through the fattiness of the meat.

Thai Green Curry and Chardonnay: The creamy, spicy flavours of Thai green curry are complemented by the rich, buttery notes in a Chardonnay, while the wine's oakiness helps to balance the heat of the spices.

Miso Soup and Pinot Grigio: The light, delicate flavours of miso soup are complemented by the crisp, refreshing notes in a Pinot Grigio, while the wine's acidity helps to cut through the saltiness of the broth.

Korean Kimchi and Beaujolais: The tangy, spicy flavours of kimchi are complemented by the light, fruity notes in a Beaujolais, while the wine's low tannins help to balance the dish's acidity.

Japanese Tempura and Chenin Blanc: The light, crispy texture of tempura is complemented by the floral, fruity notes in a Chenin Blanc, while the wine's acidity helps to cut through the oiliness of the fried batter.

Thai Tom Yum Soup and Viognier: The spicy, sour flavours of Tom Yum Soup are complemented by the rich, floral notes in a Viognier, while the wine's sweetness helps to balance the heat of the spices.

Chinese Hot Pot and Syrah: The rich, savoury flavours of Chinese hot pot are complemented by the bold, fruity notes in a Syrah, while the wine's tannins help to cut through the fattiness of the meat.

Vietnamese Banh Mi and Rosé: The light, fresh flavours of Banh Mi are complemented by the crisp, fruity notes in a Rosé, while the wine's acidity helps to cut through the richness of the meat and the creaminess of the mayonnaise.

Indian Tandoori Chicken and Malbec: The spicy, smoky flavours of tandoori chicken are complemented by the bold, fruity notes in a Malbec, while the wine's tannins help to cut through the fattiness of the meat.

Japanese Yakitori and Cabernet Franc: The smoky, savoury flavours of yakitori are complemented by the bold, fruity notes in a Cabernet Franc, while the wine's acidity helps to cut through the sweetness of the teriyaki sauce.

These are just a few examples, but there are countless possibilities for pairing Asian foods with non-Asian wines. The key is to experiment and find the combinations that work best for your taste preferences.

Pairing Asian Wines With Non-Asian Foods

Wine pairing is all about finding complementary flavours and textures in both the food and the wine.

China

While Chinese cuisine may not be traditionally associated with wine, there are certainly Chinese wines that can be paired with a variety of non-Chinese foods.

Here are some suggestions for pairing Chinese wines with non-Chinese foods:

White fish: A light and delicate white fish, such as sole or tilapia, can be paired with a crisp and refreshing Chinese white wine, such as a Sauvignon Blanc or a Chenin Blanc.

Steak: A bold and robust Chinese red wine, such as a Cabernet Sauvignon or a Merlot, can be paired with a juicy and flavorful steak. The tannins in the wine can help cut through the richness of the meat.

Spicy cuisine: Many dishes are known for their spiciness. A sweet and fruity Chinese wine, such as a Gewürztraminer or a Riesling, can help balance out the heat of the spices.

Cheese: Chinese wines can also be paired with cheese. A full-bodied Chinese red wine, such as a Shiraz or a Cabernet Sauvignon, can be paired with a sharp cheddar or a nutty Gouda.

Chocolate: A rich and decadent Chinese red wine, such as a Cabernet Sauvignon or a Merlot, can be paired with dark chocolate. The tannins in the wine can help cut through the sweetness.

India

While wine is not traditionally produced in India, there are some Indian wineries that produce high-quality wines that can be paired with a variety of non-Indian foods. Here are some suggestions:

Sula Vineyards Sauvignon Blanc: This crisp white wine from Sula Vineyards pairs well with a variety of non-Indian foods, including salads, seafood, and grilled chicken.

Grover Zampa La Reserve Red: This full-bodied red wine from Grover Zampa is a blend of Cabernet Sauvignon and Shiraz and pairs well with meat dishes such as steak, lamb, and beef stew.

York Arros: This light-bodied white wine from York Winery is a blend of Chenin Blanc and Sauvignon Blanc and pairs well with spicy Asian cuisine, such as Thai or Vietnamese food.

Four Seasons Blush: This fruity rosé wine from Four Seasons Winery is perfect for pairing with light, fresh salads or seafood dishes.

Charosa Tempranillo: This medium-bodied red wine from Charosa Vineyards has flavors of black cherry and vanilla, making it a good pairing with grilled meats or hearty pasta dishes.

Japan

Japanese wines can be paired with non-Japanese foods just like any other wines. Here are some general guidelines to keep in mind when pairing Japanese wines with non-Japanese cuisine:

Umami flavours: Japanese wines are known for their high acidity and umami flavours, which can pair well with umami-rich foods such as mushrooms, soy sauce, and miso. Therefore, umami-rich non-Japanese dishes like Italian pasta with mushroom sauce, Chinese stir-fried dishes, or even a classic hamburger can be paired with Japanese wines.

Bold flavours: Wines with bolder flavours and higher tannins can balance out spicier or more flavorful dishes. For instance, a full-bodied Japanese red wine like Cabernet Sauvignon can pair well with spicy Indian dishes, while a bold white wine such as Chardonnay can go well with creamy or buttery dishes.

Texture: The texture of the wine should also complement the texture of the food. For example, light-bodied wines like Pinot Noir or Riesling can pair well with delicate fish dishes, while full-bodied wines like Shiraz or Syrah can pair well with heartier meats.

Some specific examples of Japanese wines that can be paired with non-Japanese foods include:

Sake: Sake is a versatile wine that can pair well with a variety of non-Japanese foods, such as sushi, oysters, grilled seafood, and even spicy Indian or Thai cuisine.

Koshu: Koshu is a white wine made from a unique grape variety grown in Japan. It has a light and crisp flavour that can pair well with light salads, seafood, and sushi.

Muscat Bailey A: Muscat Bailey A is a red wine made from a hybrid grape variety grown in Japan. It has a fruity and slightly sweet flavour that can pair well with spicy or bold-flavoured dishes such as Korean barbecue or Mexican dishes.

Lebanon

Lebanese wines can definitely be paired with non-Lebanese foods. Here are some suggestions for pairing Lebanese wines with various cuisines:

Italian cuisine: Try pairing a Lebanese Cabernet Sauvignon or a Merlot with tomato-based pasta dishes or pizza.

Japanese cuisine: A Lebanese rosé or a white wine like Chardonnay or Sauvignon Blanc can complement sushi, sashimi, and other seafood dishes.

Indian cuisine: Lebanese red wines like Syrah or Grenache can be paired with spicy Indian curries.

Mexican cuisine: Pairing a Lebanese rosé with Mexican dishes such as fajitas or tacos can be an excellent choice.

French cuisine: Lebanese white wines like Muscat or Viognier can pair well with French dishes such as creamy sauces, seafood, and lighter dishes like quiche.

Israel

Israeli wines can be paired with a variety of non-Israeli foods. Israel has a diverse wine industry, with a range of grape varietals and wine styles, making it easy to find a wine that complements many different types of cuisine. Here are a few general suggestions for pairing Israeli wines with non-Israeli foods:

Cabernet Sauvignon: This bold and full-bodied wine pairs well with red meats, such as steak or lamb. It can also complement rich pasta dishes or grilled vegetables.

Chardonnay: This full-bodied white wine pairs well with creamy sauces, such as alfredo or carbonara. It can also complement seafood, such as shrimp or lobster.

Sauvignon Blanc: This light-bodied white wine pairs well with salads, grilled vegetables, and light seafood dishes, such as shrimp cocktail or ceviche.

Merlot: This medium-bodied wine pairs well with poultry, such as chicken or turkey, and can also complement lighter red sauces or tomato-based dishes.

Shiraz/Syrah: This full-bodied wine pairs well with hearty meats, such as beef or venison. It can also complement spicy dishes, such as Indian or Mexican cuisine.

Let us look at 12 vineyards from Asia with their brief histories

1. **CH'NG Poh Tiong Vineyard (Malaysia)** - Owned by CH'NG Poh Tiong, this vineyard produces the Chateau Quintus red wine. The winery is located near Kuala Lumpur, and the vineyard is known for its stony soil which produces grapes with strong mineral flavors. Local foods produced in the area include tropical fruits and seafood, which pair well with Chateau Quintus wines.

2. **Chateau Mercian Winery (Japan)** - Owned by Kirin Brewery Company, this vineyard is located in Yamanashi, Japan's largest grape-growing region. The winery produces a variety of wines, including Chardonnay, Pinot Noir, and Cabernet Sauvignon. The local culture surrounding the vineyard is deeply intertwined with the Japanese wine industry, which has grown significantly in recent years. Local foods often paired with these wines include sushi and sashimi.

3. **Grace Vineyard (China)** - Owned by Judy Chan and located in Shanxi Province, Grace Vineyard was founded in 1997 and is one of the largest wineries in China. The vineyard produces a variety of wines, including Cabernet Franc and Chardonnay. The local cuisine features noodles, dumplings, and flavorful sauces, which can be paired well with these wines.

4. **Thienpont Wine (Vietnam)** - Owned by Nicolas Thienpont, this vineyard is located in the Dalat region of Vietnam. The vineyard produces a variety of wines, including white wines made from the local grape variety, Bicane. The local cuisine features fresh seafood, grilled meats, and flavorful herbs, which pair well with Thienpont wines.

5. **Sula Vineyards (India)** - Owned by Rajeev Samant, Sula Vineyards is located in Nashik, India's wine-making capital. The vineyard produces a variety of wines, including Sauvignon Blanc, Shiraz, and Zinfandel. The local cuisine is heavily influenced by spice, and dishes like curry and tandoori chicken pair well with Sula wines.

6. **Chateau Changyu (China)** - Owned by the Changyu Pioneer Wine Company, this vineyard is located in the Shandong province of China. The vineyard produces a variety of wines, including Riesling and Cabernet Sauvignon. The local cuisine features hearty dishes like noodle soups and dumplings which pair well with Changyu wines.

7. **Hatten Wines (Indonesia)** - Owned by Ida Bagus Rai Budarsa, Hatten Wines is located in Bali and produces a variety of different wines. The vineyard is known for its unique varieties like the Rosa Moscato, made from the local Balinese Muscat grape. The local cuisine features a blend of Indonesian, Chinese, and Indian flavors, which pair well with Hatten wines.

8. **Grover Zampa Vineyards (India)** - Owned by Kapil and Renuka Grover, this vineyard is located near Bangalore and produces a variety of wines including their signature La Reserve red blend. The vineyard is known for its French-style blends and Indian varietals. The local cuisine features a range of vegetarian dishes, spiced meats, and tandoori delicacies, which pair well with Grover wines.

9. **Vang Dalat (Vietnam)** - Owned by French winemaker Alain Nguyen, Vang Dalat is located in Da Lat and produces a range of different wines. The vineyard is known for its unique blends, which often feature grape varieties like Cabernet Sauvignon and Shiraz alongside local fruits like passionfruit and pineapple. The local cuisine is heavily influenced by French flavors, with dishes like coq au vin and boeuf Bourguignon pairing well with Vang Dalat wines.

10. **KRSMA Estates (India)** - Owned by Krishna and Uma Chigurupati, KRSMA Estates is located in the Hampi Hills of Karnataka, and produces a range of red blends and single varietal wines. The vineyard is celebrated for its low-yield, high-quality grapes, which are often used to create robust and complex wines. The local cuisine features an array of spiced meats and curries, which pair well with KRSMA wines.

11. **Le Grandeur Wine (China)** - Owned by the Le Grandeur Hotel Group, this vineyard is located in the Shandong province of China. The vineyard produces a range of wines, including their signature Bordeaux-style blend made from Cabernet Sauvignon and Merlot grapes. The local cuisine is known for its traditional seafood dishes, which pair well with Le Grandeur wines.

12. **Chateau Indage (India)** - Owned by the Marathe family, Chateau Indage is located in Nashik and produces a range of different wines. The vineyard is known for its red blends, including the popular Riviera Shiraz, as well as its sparkling wines. The local cuisine features a blend of traditional Indian flavours and British influences, with dishes like fish curry and shepherd's pie pairing well with Chateau Indage wines.

Seasons and Occasions:

Some suggestions for Asian food and wine pairings

Summer:

Informal dining: A refreshing Riesling or Sauvignon Blanc pairs well with light summer dishes like Vietnamese spring rolls, Thai papaya salad, or Japanese sushi rolls.

Formal dining: A crisp and elegant Chardonnay or Pinot Gris pairs well with grilled seafood dishes like Korean BBQ shrimp or Japanese teriyaki salmon.

Winter:

Informal dining: A spicy Shiraz or Cabernet Sauvignon pairs well with hearty winter dishes like Indian curry or Chinese hot pot.

Formal dining: A full-bodied Merlot or Malbec pairs well with rich and flavorful dishes like Korean galbi or Chinese Peking duck.

Note: Please keep in mind that wine pairing is a matter of personal preference, and these suggestions are just a starting point. It's always a good idea to experiment and find what works best for your own taste.

Phileas Fogg was an adventurer who enjoyed both the familiar and the exotic.

During his world trip, he would have been exposed to a wide variety of cuisines and wines from different parts of the world. Here are some food and wine pairings that Phileas Fogg might have enjoyed on his journey through India and China.

India : In India, Phileas Fogg would have experienced a wide variety of spices and flavours. He might have enjoyed a spicy curry with a refreshing Riesling or Gewurztraminer.

China: During his visit to China, Phileas Fogg would have been exposed to a variety of dishes. He might have paired a sweet and sour pork dish with a crisp, dry white wine like a Sauvignon Blanc or Pinot Grigio.

Similarly, when you are pairing food and wine, you can choose to complement or contrast the flavours. For example, a spicy dish can be complemented by a sweet wine, or a rich, creamy dish can be contrasted with a crisp, acidic wine.

Sweet Foods:

Wines from 10 Asian countries and their suggested sweet food pairings:

China:

Changyu Cabernet Gernischt: Paired well with dark chocolate or chocolate cake.

Great Wall Chardonnay: Paired well with caramel or custard.

Japan:

Koshu Grace Wine: Paired well with fruit-based desserts like apple pie or peach cobbler.

Yamanashi Meijo 'Koshu' Wine: Paired well with mochi or matcha-flavoured desserts.

South Korea:

Sejong Daejanggan Makgeolli: Paired well with rice cakes or sweet potato dishes.

Chum-Churum Grapefruit Soju: Paired well with fresh fruit sorbets or citrus-based desserts.

India:

Sula Chenin Blanc: Paired well with sweet and spicy dishes like chicken tikka masala or mango chutney.

Grover Zampa La Reserve: Paired well with sweet desserts like gulab jamun or ras malai.

Sri Lanka:

Nine Skies Cabernet Sauvignon: Paired well with chocolate truffles or chocolate cake.

Sigiriya Wine: Paired well with traditional Sri Lankan desserts like kiribath or wattalappam.

Thailand:

Monsoon Valley Shiraz: Paired well with Thai desserts like mango sticky rice or coconut ice cream.

Spy Wine Cooler: Paired well with fresh tropical fruits or fruit sorbets.

Vietnam:

Da Lat Passion Fruit Wine: Paired well with sweet and sour dishes like grilled pork with tamarind sauce or sour soup.

Gia Lam Plum Wine: Paired well with traditional Vietnamese desserts like banh chuoi nuong or che.

Indonesia:

Sababay Moscato d'Bali: Paired well with sweet Indonesian desserts like klepon or bubur sumsum.

Hatten Aga White: Paired well with tropical fruits or creamy coconut-based desserts.

Philippines:

Don Papa Rum: Paired well with chocolate truffles or brownies.

Tanduay Rhum Dark: Paired well with caramel flan or fruit-based desserts like banana foster.

Malaysia:

Sabah Snake Grass Red Wine: Paired well with dark chocolate or chocolate cake.

Château de Canet Rose: Paired well with tropical fruits or light desserts like fruit sorbets.

As a fictional character in the novel "Around the World in Eighty Days" by Jules Verne, Phileas Fogg would have encountered a diverse range of people during his travels in Asia.

In China, Fogg would have encountered a mix of different ethnic groups, including the majority Han Chinese as well as various minority groups such as the Tibetans, Mongolians, Uyghurs, and others. He may have also encountered foreign traders and diplomats, such as those from Great Britain, the United States, and other Western countries.

Furthermore, Fogg would have likely encountered people from different social classes and occupations, from wealthy merchants and government officials to farmers and labourers. He may have encountered people with varying religious and cultural beliefs, such as Confucianism, Taoism, Buddhism, Islam, and Christianity.

Overall, China is a country with a rich and diverse cultural landscape, and Phileas Fogg would have encountered a wide range of people during his travels there.

In India, he would have met **Indians from various religions**: India is home to several religions, including Hinduism, Islam, Christianity, Sikhism, Buddhism, and Jainism. Fogg would have encountered people from all these religions and learned about their unique cultures, customs, and practices.

British colonial officials:

During Fogg's time, India was under British colonial rule. He would have encountered British officials who managed the country's administration and governance.

Indian royalty and aristocracy: India has a rich history of royal families and aristocracy, and Fogg would have met many of them during his journey. He may have visited palaces and attended royal events, learning about the customs and traditions of Indian nobility.

Merchants and traders:

India has always been a hub of trade and commerce, and Fogg would have encountered merchants and traders from different parts of the country and beyond. He may have visited markets and bazaars and learned about the goods traded there.

Artisans and craftsmen:

India is known for its rich tradition of handicrafts and handloom products. Fogg would have had the opportunity to meet artisans and craftsmen and learn about their unique skills and techniques.

Overall, Phileas Fogg would have encountered a diverse range of people in India, each with their own unique cultures, traditions, and ways of life.

In Japan, assuming Phileas Fogg visited Japan in his travels, he would have encountered a diverse range of people, including:

Japanese locals: Fogg would have met Japanese people from all walks of life, including farmers, fishermen, and craftsmen. He may have also interacted with wealthy merchants and members of the samurai class.

Foreigners living in Japan: During the 19th century, there were many foreigners living in Japan, including diplomats, missionaries, and traders. Fogg may have interacted with some of these individuals and learned about their experiences in Japan.

Shogunate officials: During Fogg's visit, Japan was still ruled by the Tokugawa Shogunate. Fogg may have had the opportunity to meet with government officials and learn about the political situation in the country.

Geishas and other entertainers: Fogg may have been entertained by geishas, actors, and other performers during his stay in Japan.

Buddhist monks and Shinto priests: Japan has a long history of Buddhism and Shintoism, and Fogg may have had the opportunity to visit temples and shrines and meet with religious leaders.

Overall, Fogg would have encountered a diverse range of people in Japan, each with their own unique backgrounds and experiences.

In Korea, It is unlikely that Phileas Fogg would have encountered anyone in Korea during his journey, as Korea was a relatively isolated country at the time and had limited contact with the outside world.

However, if we were to imagine a scenario where Phileas Fogg did travel to Korea during his journey, he would have encountered a diverse population of people with their own unique cultures, traditions, and beliefs. Some of the groups he may have encountered include:

Koreans: The majority of the population in Korea at the time were ethnic Koreans who practised Confucianism, Buddhism, or Shamanism. They had their own language, cuisine, and customs.

Chinese: China was a neighboring country to Korea, and there would have been a significant Chinese community in Korea at the time. They would have had their own language, culture, and traditions.

Japanese: Japan also had a significant presence in Korea at the time, and there would have been a Japanese community in Korea as well. The Japanese had their own language, customs, and beliefs.

Westerners: While Korea was isolated at the time, there were still some Westerners who had made their way to Korea for various reasons. Phileas Fogg himself was a Westerner and would have been viewed as a novelty by the Korean people he encountered.

Overall, if Phileas Fogg had travelled to Korea during his journey, he would have encountered a diverse mix of people with their own unique cultures, traditions, and beliefs.

In Vietnam: Phileas Fogg did not travel to Vietnam during his journey. However, if he did, he would have encountered a diverse group of people in Vietnam, as it is a country with a rich cultural heritage and a long history of trade and migration.

Vietnam is home to over 50 ethnic groups, each with their own unique traditions, languages, and customs. The majority of the population is of **Vietnamese** ethnicity, but there are also significant populations of ethnic Chinese, **Khmer**, and **Cham** people, among others. In addition, Vietnam has a long history of colonialism and foreign influence, which has resulted in a mix of cultures and influences from China, France, and other countries.

During Fogg's time, Vietnam was under French colonial rule, so he would have encountered a significant number of French colonial officials and traders. He may have also encountered Vietnamese elites who had adopted French customs and language. In addition, he would have likely encountered a variety of Vietnamese people from different regions and backgrounds, including farmers, fishermen, traders, and artisans.

Overall, Fogg would have encountered a rich and diverse range of people in Vietnam, each with their own unique stories, traditions, and cultures.

In Thailand: In the novel "Around the World in Eighty Days," the story describes Fogg's travels through Thailand (then called Siam) during the mid-19th century. During this time, Siam was a monarchy and a relatively isolated country, but it still had a diverse population with various ethnicities, religions, and social classes.

Here are some examples of the diverse people that Phileas Fogg might have encountered in Thailand:

Thai people: The majority of the population in Thailand were and still are ethnic Thai people. They have their own language, customs, and traditions.

Chinese immigrants: Chinese immigrants have a long history in Thailand and were an important part of the country's economy. They brought with them their own language, culture, and religious practices.

Indian merchants: Indian merchants were also a common sight in Thailand during this time, particularly in the major trading cities. They brought with them their own language, culture, and religious practices.

Muslim traders: Muslim traders from Malaysia and Indonesia were also present in Thailand during this time. They had their own distinct culture, language, and religious practices.

European traders and diplomats: European traders and diplomats were present in Bangkok, the capital of Siam. They represented their respective countries and often lived in their own enclaves.

Royalty and nobility: As a monarchy, Thailand had a royal family and a system of nobility. Phileas Fogg might have had the opportunity to meet members of the royal family or the nobility during his travels.

Common people: Finally, Phileas Fogg would have encountered ordinary Thai people going about their daily lives, working in fields, fishing, or engaging in other activities. They would have represented a wide range of social classes and occupations.

In Indonesia: Phileas Fogg would have encountered a diverse range of people during his travels through Indonesia. Indonesia is a country made up of thousands of islands with a rich cultural history, so the people he would have met would have been varied and diverse.

Some of the people that Phileas Fogg may have encountered in Indonesia could include:

Javanese: The Javanese are the largest ethnic group in Indonesia and are known for their rich culture, traditions, and history. They are known for their art, dance, music, and literature.

Balinese: The Balinese people are known for their unique culture, which includes dance, music, and architecture. They are also known for their elaborate festivals and ceremonies.

Betawi: The Betawi people are the indigenous people of Jakarta, the capital city of Indonesia. They have a distinct culture, which includes their language, food, and traditional clothing.

Chinese: The Chinese have a long history in Indonesia and make up a significant minority in the country. They have had a significant influence on Indonesian culture, especially in the areas of business and cuisine.

Minangkabau: The Minangkabau people are an ethnic group from the island of Sumatra. They are known for their unique architecture, which includes the traditional Minangkabau house, and their rich cuisine.

Papuan: The Papuan people are the indigenous people of Papua, which is the easternmost province of Indonesia. They have a unique culture, which includes their language, music, dance, and art.

Batak: The Batak people are an ethnic group from the northern part of Sumatra. They have a unique culture, which includes their language, music, dance, and cuisine.

Overall, Phileas Fogg would have had the opportunity to encounter a diverse range of people with distinct cultures, traditions, and histories during his travels in Indonesia.

In Malaysia: During the time period in which the novel is set, which is the late 19th century, Malaysia was a melting pot of different cultures due to its history as a major trading port in Southeast Asia.

Phileas Fogg would have encountered indigenous **Malays**, who make up the majority of the population, as well as **Chinese** and **Indian** communities, who were brought to Malaysia as labourers and traders during the colonial era.

Additionally, Fogg may have come across people of **European** descent, such as British officials, merchants, and **missionaries** who played a significant role in shaping the history of the region.

Given the diversity of Malaysia's population and the country's history, Phileas Fogg would have had the opportunity to encounter people from a wide range of backgrounds and cultures, each with their own unique traditions, beliefs, and practices.

In Sri Lanka: Phileas Fogg, would have encountered a diverse range of people during his journey to Sri Lanka (formerly known as Ceylon). Sri Lanka is a country with a rich cultural and ethnic diversity, and its history has been shaped by various influences from different parts of the world.

During Fogg's visit to Sri Lanka, he would have encountered **Sinhalese** people, who are the majority ethnic group in the country, and **Tamil** people, who make up a significant minority. He may have also encountered people from other ethnic groups such as **Muslims**, **Burghers** (people of mixed European and Sri Lankan descent), and **Malays**.

In addition to the diverse ethnic groups, Fogg would have also encountered people from different religions such as **Buddhism**, **Hinduism**, **Islam**, and **Christianity**. Sri Lanka has a long history of Buddhism, and Fogg would have had the opportunity to visit some of the country's ancient Buddhist temples and monuments, such as the Temple of the Tooth in Kandy.

Furthermore, Fogg may have also encountered people from different socio-economic backgrounds during his visit to Sri Lanka, ranging from rural farmers to urban professionals.

Overall, Fogg's encounter with the diverse people of Sri Lanka would have given him a glimpse into the country's rich cultural and ethnic heritage, as well as its unique blend of traditions and customs.

Sparkling wines

Sparkling wine production in Asia is a relatively recent development, with the industry only beginning to gain significant traction in the past couple of decades. The use of sparkling wine in celebrations and festivities is a long-standing tradition in many Asian cultures, particularly in regions such as China and Japan where the sparkling wine has seen a significant increase in popularity in recent years.

The most commonly used grapes for sparkling wine production in Asia are Chardonnay, Pinot Noir, and Pinot Meunier, which are widely grown in regions with cooler climates such as northeastern China, Japan, Korea, and Taiwan. In addition, some producers have begun experimenting with using locally grown varieties of grapes, such as Koshu in Japan and Rkatsiteli in Georgia.

One of the key players in the Asian sparkling wine market is China, which has experienced tremendous growth in recent years. Many international wine producers are investing in vineyards and wineries in China, particularly in the northern region of Ningxia, which is home to some of the country's most prestigious wineries. Other major players in the Asian sparkling wine market include Japan, South Korea, and Taiwan, all of which are seeing growth in their domestic wine industries.

Asian sparkling wine producers are also focused on cultivating unique Terroir, which refers to the soil, climate, and environmental factors that contribute to the distinct characteristics of a wine. This has led to the emergence of distinct regional styles, with producers in Japan, for example, focused on creating elegant and light-bodied sparkling wines, while those in China are known for creating wines with a more robust character.

Asian sparkling wines pair particularly well with a wide range of foods, including sushi, sashimi, and other seafood dishes, as well as Asian-inspired dishes that feature bold and complex flavours. In Japan, sparkling wine is often served with traditional New Year's dishes, while in China it is often paired with traditional dim sum dishes.

While sparkling wine production is still a relatively new development in Asia, the industry has seen significant growth in recent years. With a focus on Terroir, unique grape varieties, and regional styles, Asian sparkling wine producers are creating some truly exceptional wines that pair beautifully with a wide range of cuisines.

Let's look at some notable countries that specialise in sparkling wine production, and i'll try and pair some local foods with them.

1. **Japan** - Japan is known for producing an effervescent drink called Sake, which is a rice wine. However, they are also producing some sparkling wines that are gaining popularity. The speciality of Japanese sparkling wines is the use of local fruits like Yamanashi grapes and apples. The topography of the country is such that most of the vineyards are located in mountain regions which are ideal for grape cultivation. The best local food to pair with Japanese sparkling wines is sushi and sashimi.

2. **India** - India has been producing wines for quite some time now, and their sparkling wines are gaining popularity. The speciality of Indian sparkling wines is the use of Chenin Blanc and Shiraz grapes. Indian sparkling wines are known for their acidity and freshness. The topography of the country is such that most of the vineyards are located in hilly regions which have a tropical climate. The best local food to pair with Indian sparkling wines is spicy Indian street food.

3. **China** - China has been producing sparkling wines for quite some time now, but they are now taking the world by storm with their high-quality sparkling wines. The speciality of Chinese sparkling wines is the use of local grape varieties like Vitis amurensis, Vitis vinifera, and Vitis labrusca. China has a diverse topography and climate that ranges from humid subtropical to semiarid, making it ideal for grape cultivation. The best local food to pair with Chinese sparkling wines is Chinese cuisine, especially the traditional dumplings.

4. **Thailand** - Thailand is the latest country to join the sparkling wine bandwagon. The speciality of Thai sparkling wines is the use of local grape varieties like Malaga Blanc and Pok Dum. Thai sparkling wines are known for their crispness, acidity, and sweetness. The topography of Thailand is mostly mountainous, and it has a tropical climate that is ideal for grape cultivation. The best local food to pair with Thai sparkling wines is spicy Thai cuisine like Tom Yum Soup and green curry.

Overall, the sparkling wines produced in Asia have their own unique features, reflecting the culture, climate, and topography of each country.

Sweet Wines

Sweet Wines from 12 Asian countries with suggested food pairings.

1. **China**

Owner: Grace Vineyard

Grape: Muscat Hamburg and Muscat Bailey A

Terroir: Taihang Mountains, Shanxi Province

Wine: Tasya's Reserve Cabernet Sauvignon Ice Wine

Food Pairing: Chinese Cuisine - Peking Duck, Dumplings, Braised Pork Belly

2. **Japan**

Owner: Grace Winery

Grape: Muscat Bailey A

Terroir: Yamanashi prefecture, Honshu

Wine: Koshu L'inédit

Food Pairing: Sushi or Sashimi, Green tea cake, Yuzu cheesecake

3. **India**

Owner: Sula Vineyards

Grape: Chenin Blanc and Zinfandel

Terroir: Nashik, Maharashtra

Wine: Late Harvest Chenin Blanc

Food Pairing: Indian cuisine - Spicy Chicken curry, Gulab Jamun, Rasgulla

4. **Nepal**

Owner: Himalayan Distillery Pvt.Ltd.

Grape: Chardonnay

Terroir: Pachekhder, Jawalakhel, Lalitpur

Winc: Highland Cullinan White (Ice Wine)

Food Pairing: Nepalese Cuisine - Momo, Sel roti, Sherpa stew with rice

5. **Thailand**

Owner: GranMonte Estate

Grape: Chenin Blanc and Viognier

Terroir: Asoke Valley, Khao Yai

Wine: Late harvest Chenin Blanc

Food Pairing: Thai Cuisine - Tom Yum Soup, Green Papaya Salad, Pad Thai

6. **Bangladesh**

Owner: Rangpur Vineyard

Grape: Sunbelt and Rkatsiteli

Terroir: Rangpur

Wine: Rangpur Special Reserva

Food Pairing: Bangladeshi Cuisine - Bhuna Khichuri, Jaffarani Pulao, Biryani

7. **Sri Lanka**

Owner: Ceylon Wines

Grape: Seibel, Dornfelder, and Muscat

Terroir: Kumbukgaha

Wine: Ceylon Golden Muscat

Food Pairing: Sri Lankan Cuisine - Hoppers, Kottu roti, Watalappan

8. **Vietnam**

Owner: Dalat Wine Company

Grape: Cardinal

Terroir: Da Lat

Wine: Dalat Misty Mountain

Food Pairing: Vietnamese Cuisine - Spring rolls, Pho Ga, Che Ba Mau (Three Color Dessert)

9. **Myanmar**

Owner: Red Mountain Estate

Grape: Syrah and Cabernet Sauvignon

Terroir: Taung Chune Vineyard, Southern Shan state

Wine: Late Harvest Cabernet Sauvignon

Food Pairing: Burmese Cuisine - Shan Noodles, Mohinga, Ohn No Khauk Swe

10. **Cambodia**

Owner: Bloom Wine

Grape: Chenin Blanc

Terroir: Banteay Meanchey province

Wine: Bloom Noble Harvest

Food Pairing: Khmer Cuisine - Fish Amok, Green Mango Salad, Lok Lak Beef

11. **Philippines**

Owner: Carlo Rossi

Grape: Red and White variety

Terroir: Pangasinan

Wine: Carlo Rossi Sweet Red

Food Pairing: Filipino Cuisine - Adobo, Lechon, Kare Kare

12. **Indonesia**

Owner: Plaga Wine

Grape: Alphonse Lavallée, Black Benit, and Balinese local grapes

Terroir: Bali

Wine: Plaga Late Harvest White

Food Pairing: Indonesian Cuisine - Sate, Nasi Goreng, Gado-Gado salad.

Phileas Fogg's choice of Sweet Wines

Phileas Fogg would have encountered a diverse range of sweet wines during his travels through Asia. Some of the notable sweet wines he might have tasted include:

Sake: This Japanese rice wine is known for its sweet and delicate flavors. It is typically served with sushi, sashimi, and other Japanese dishes.

Shaoxing wine: This Chinese rice wine is sweet, nutty, and slightly savory. It is often used in Chinese cooking and pairs well with dishes like braised meats and stir-fries.

Riesling: This German white wine is known for its fruity sweetness and bright acidity. It pairs well with spicy Asian cuisine, as well as rich, creamy dishes.

Ice wine: This sweet dessert wine is made from grapes that have been left to freeze on the vine. It is rich, syrupy, and often served with desserts like fruit tarts and cheesecake.

Banyuls: This fortified wine from France's Roussillon region is sweet and full-bodied, with flavours of chocolate, caramel, and dried fruit. It pairs well with dark chocolate and strong cheeses.

Ice wine with fruit tarts and cheesecake

Of course, there are many other sweet wines and food pairings to explore, depending on the region and cuisine. But these examples should give you a good idea of what Phileas Fogg might have tasted during his travels through Asia.

Non-alcoholic Wines

Non-alcoholic wines have been welcomed in Asia with open arms due to the deep cultural, religious, and health-related reasons. In various countries, non-alcoholic wines are especially popular in the Muslim community, where alcohol consumption is prohibited. However, as more people are seeking healthier lifestyles, non-alcoholic wines have become popular among the broader population as well.

There isn't a single terroir that can be said to be unique to Asia as the continent has diverse temperatures, soils, elevations, rainfall patterns, and other climatic factors that contribute to the different wine regions. These regions work with various grape varietals to produce non-alcoholic wines.

The most popular grape varieties used in non-alcoholic wine production in Asia include Muscat, Merlot, Shiraz, Cabernet Sauvignon, Pinot Noir, and Chardonnay, among others. These wine grape varieties participate in the production of various types of non-alcoholic wines across the continent.

In terms of food pairings, non-alcoholic wines pair well with many types of cuisines. Some of the most popular pairings for non-alcoholic wines in Asia includes seafood, sushi, spicy dishes, and even desserts.

Many Asian countries have their non-alcoholic wine varieties, and they each have their unique twist when it comes to winemaking techniques. For instance, Japan has Koji yeast, which is a rice-based yeast that is used to make wine. Korea, on the other hand, has the Bokbunjaju wine, which is made from black raspberries. Additionally, many non-alcoholic wineries in Asia focus on sustainability, organic growth, and biodynamic farming techniques.

To summarize, non-alcoholic wines have become more popular in Asia due to cultural, religious and health-related reasons. Different grape varieties are used to produce diverse styles of non-alcoholic wines across the continent, with unique twists on wine-making techniques. Non-alcoholic wines pair well with various types of cuisines, including seafood, spicy dishes, and even desserts.

Non-alcoholic wines from Asian countries paired with local cuisines:

China:

Changyu Pioneer Wine Company: produces several non-alcoholic wines, including the Chateau Changyu Moser XV Blanc, which pairs well with Cantonese-style steamed fish.

Korea:

Bohae Brewery: offers several non-alcoholic wines, including the Bohae Bokbunjaoo, which pairs well with Korean barbecue or spicy stir-fry dishes.

India:

Grover Zampa Vineyards: produces the Zera Sparkling Grape Juice, which pairs well with Indian dishes like butter chicken or paneer tikka.

Japan:

Suntory: produces the Suntory Vinegar Drink, which pairs well with sushi or tempura dishes.

Vietnam:

Vinh Hao: produces several non-alcoholic wines, including the Vinh Hao Red Grape Juice, which pairs well with pho or grilled pork.

Thailand:

Monsoon Valley: produces the Monsoon Valley Sparkling Grape Juice, which pairs well with Thai curries or spicy salads.

Philippines:

Emperador Distillers: produces the Emperador Light Grape Juice, which pairs well with Filipino dishes like adobo or sisig.

Sri Lanka:

Nilkamal: produces the Nilkamal Red Grape Juice, which pairs well with Sri Lankan rice and curry dishes.

Indonesia:

Hatten Wines: produces the Hatten Zero Sparkling Grape Juice, which pairs well with Indonesian grilled chicken or seafood dishes.

Malaysia:

Lychee Valley: produces the Lychee Valley Grape Juice, which pairs well with Malaysian satay or noodle dishes.

Please note that these are just general suggestions and pairing preferences can vary from person to person.

Asian non-alcoholic wines, also known as **grape juices**, are a growing category in the region, with a number of producers and brands emerging in recent years. These grape juices are made from a variety of grapes, and are typically produced using the same methods as alcoholic wines, with the alcohol removed through a dealcoholization process. Some popular Asian grape juice producers include Changyu Pioneer Wine Company in China, Sula Vineyards in India, and Grace Vineyard in Taiwan.

When it comes to food pairings, Asian grape juices can be a versatile accompaniment to a range of dishes. In general, it's a good idea to pair grape juices with dishes that have a similar level of sweetness, acidity, and flavour intensity. For example, a light-bodied grape juice with a bright, fruity flavour can pair well with spicy Asian cuisine, such as Thai or Indian curries, as the sweetness of the grape juice can help balance out the heat of the spices. A more full-bodied grape juice with a deeper, more complex flavour profile can pair well with richer dishes, such as beef or lamb stews, as the tannins in the grape juice can help cut through the richness of the meat.

It's also worth noting that many Asian grape juice producers are using grapes that are native to the region, such as Vitis amurensis and Vitis labrusca in China and Japan, and Vitis vinifera in India. These local grape varieties can have unique flavours and aromas that can pair particularly well with local cuisine, so it's worth exploring the grape juice offerings from different regions and producers to discover new and interesting flavour combinations.

Finally….

In summary, exploring the food and wine pairings from Asia has been a fascinating journey. As the largest continent on Earth, it's not surprising that Asia boasts an awe-inspiring variety of grapes, dishes, cultures, and traditions. From the steaming dumplings of China to the fiery curries of India, the range of flavours and textures available is nothing short of astonishing.

Luckily, there are plenty of excellent wines to sample as well. Whether you prefer the crisp acidity of a Riesling, the bold richness of a Syrah, or the refreshing minerality of a Sake, Asian wines offer plenty of exciting options that pair perfectly with local dishes.

But food and wine pairings are about more than just flavour profiles. They're an opportunity to learn about the people and cultures that create and enjoy them. By experimenting with different pairings and exploring the unique tastes and traditions of Asia, readers can truly broaden their horizons and gain a new perspective on this amazing continent.

In conclusion, we hope that you've enjoyed reading about the fascinating world of Asian food and wine pairings. We encourage you to try pairing exotic foods with Asian wines on your own and discover the exciting new taste combinations that await you. Happy exploring!

Further Readings

"The Wine Bible" by Karen MacNeil: This comprehensive guide covers wines from all over the world, including Asia, and includes information on pairing wine with food.

"The Essential Guide to Asian Wines" by The Flying Winemaker, Eddie McDougall: This guide focuses specifically on Asian wines, including those from China, Japan, India, and Thailand, and includes tasting notes, food pairing suggestions, and more.

"Sake Confidential" by John Gauntner: This book is a deep dive into the world of sake, including its history, production, and cultural significance in Japan. It also includes tips on pairing sake with food.

"Asian Palate: The Diversity of Flavors in Asian Cuisine" by Jeannie Cho Lee: This book explores the different flavor profiles of various Asian cuisines and provides guidance on pairing wines with different dishes.

"The Food of Taiwan: Recipes from the Beautiful Island" by Cathy Erway: This cookbook features recipes from Taiwan, along with information on the country's food culture and traditions. It also includes wine pairing suggestions for each recipe.

"The Complete Asian Cookbook" by Charmaine Solomon: This cookbook covers a wide range of Asian cuisines, including Chinese, Indian, Thai, and more. It includes information on the flavors and ingredients of each cuisine, as well as wine pairing suggestions.

"The Oxford Companion to Wine" edited by Jancis Robinson: This comprehensive reference book covers wine regions and varietals from all over the world, including Asia. It includes information on the history and production of each wine, as well as food pairing suggestions.

Further readings on Asian wines

"The Wines of China" by Li Demei: This book provides an in-depth look at the history, culture, and current state of winemaking in China. It also includes information on the major grape varieties grown in the country and suggestions for food pairings.

"The Wines of Japan" by James Halliday and Hugh Johnson: This book explores the history and current state of winemaking in Japan, as well as the unique grape varieties grown there. It also includes tips for food pairings.

"The Wines of India" by Peter Csizmadia-Honigh: This book provides a comprehensive overview of the wine industry in India, including information on the climate, grape varieties, and winemaking techniques used in the country. It also includes suggestions for food pairings.

"Asian Palate: Discovering the Five Flavors of Food and Wine" by Jeannie Cho Lee: This book explores the relationship between food and wine in Asia, and provides tips for pairing wines with a variety of Asian cuisines.

"The Wines and Foods of Piemonte" by Tom Hyland: While not specifically focused on Asian wines, this book provides a detailed look at the wines and food of the Piemonte region of Italy, which is home to many of the grape varieties that are now being grown in Asia. It includes information on the history of winemaking in the region, as well as suggestions for food pairings.

"The World Atlas of Wine" by Hugh Johnson and Jancis Robinson: This book provides a comprehensive overview of the wine regions of the world, including those in Asia. It includes detailed maps, information on grape varieties and winemaking techniques, and suggestions for food pairings.

Additionally, wine publications such as Wine Spectator, Decanter, and Wine Enthusiast regularly feature articles on Asian wines and food pairings.

Further Readings on Asian Non-Alcoholic Wines

"Non-Alcoholic Wines from Asia: A Review of Their Production and Health Benefits" by Xiaoyu Yan, Huijing Chen, Mingzhi Zhu, and Guo-Qing Zhang. This article, published in the journal Beverages in 2018, provides an overview of the production and health benefits of non-alcoholic wines from Asia.

"Non-Alcoholic Wines in Asia" by Yong-Hee Lee and Min-Kyung Kim. This chapter, published in the book Non-Alcoholic Beverages, edited by Alexandru Grumezescu and Alina-Maria Holban in 2019, provides a comprehensive overview of non-alcoholic wines in Asia.

"Non-Alcoholic Wine from Asian Countries: A Review" by Reza Sayari, Abbas Rahdar, and Yosra Rahimzadeh. This article, published in the journal Beverages in 2020, provides a detailed review of non-alcoholic wines from Asian countries, including their production methods, chemical composition, and sensory characteristics.

"Traditional Fermented Beverages and Foods of Asia" edited by Jyoti Prakash Tamang and Ramesh C. Ray. This book, published in 2016, provides a comprehensive overview of traditional fermented beverages and foods from Asia, including non-alcoholic wines.

"The Non-Alcoholic Wine Market in Asia" by Jonny Forsyth. This article, published on the website just-drinks.com in 2021, provides an analysis of the non-alcoholic wine market in Asia, including market size, trends, and growth opportunities.

Further readings on Asian sparkling wines

Here are some articles and resources that provide further readings on Asian sparkling wines:

1. **"8 Asian Sparkling Wines to Try" by VinePair** - This article features eight sparkling wines from Asian countries such as China, South Korea, and Japan, and provides detailed descriptions of each.

2. **"17 Asian Sparkling Wines You Need to Know" by WineFolly** - This post provides a comprehensive list of sparkling wines from Asian countries, as well as information on the different grape varieties and production methods used.

3. **"Japan's Hidden Treasure: Sparkling Wine" by Wine Enthusiast** - This article highlights the emerging trend of sparkling wine production in Japan, and shares insights on the unique qualities of Japanese sparkling wines.

4. **"Will Sparkling Wine Take Off In China?" by Forbes** - This article discusses the potential growth of sparkling wine consumption in China, and highlights some of the leading Chinese sparkling wine producers.

5. **"A Sparkling Wine From China Tries to Fight the Tide" by The New York Times** - This article tells the story of a Chinese winery's efforts to produce high-quality sparkling wines, despite the challenges they face in a country where consumer preferences are geared towards red wines.

CHAPTER 5

NORTH AMERICAN FOOD AND WINE

North America is a continent located in the northern hemisphere and is the third largest continent in the world, covering an area of about 24.5 million square kilometres. It is bordered by the Arctic Ocean to the north, the Atlantic Ocean to the east, the Pacific Ocean to the west, and South America to the south. North America is home to three major countries: the United States, Canada, and Mexico, as well as several smaller countries such as Belize, Costa Rica, Panama, and others.

The history of North America is complex and spans thousands of years. The continent has been inhabited by various indigenous peoples for tens of thousands of years before the arrival of Europeans. These indigenous peoples include the Inuit, the First Nations, and the various tribes of Mexico and Central America. These peoples had their own distinct cultures, languages, and ways of life, and many of their traditions and customs continue to this day.

The arrival of Europeans in the 16th century changed the course of North American history. Spanish explorers such as Christopher Columbus, Hernán Cortés, and Francisco Pizarro brought European diseases, weapons, and technology to the Americas, leading to the displacement, exploitation, and genocide of indigenous peoples. The Spanish established colonies in Mexico and Central America, while the French and English established colonies in Canada and the United States.

The **United States of America** was established in 1776, after a long period of British colonial rule. The country grew rapidly in the 19th century, with the expansion westward and the acquisition of new territories. This expansion led to the displacement and genocide of many indigenous peoples, as well as the forced migration of African slaves.

Canada, on the other hand, was established as a confederation in 1867, uniting the provinces of Ontario, Quebec, Nova Scotia, and New Brunswick. Canada has a strong French and British colonial heritage, and is known for its multiculturalism and diversity.

Mexico gained its independence from Spain in 1821, after a long period of colonisation. The country has a rich history and culture, with strong indigenous roots as well as influences from Spanish, African, and other cultures.

Today, North America is a diverse and dynamic continent, with a population of over 580 million people. The region is home to a wide range of cultures, languages, and religions, and has a strong tradition of innovation and progress. While the history of the continent is marked by colonisation, exploitation, and conflict, the people of North America continue to work towards a more just and equitable society, and towards building a better future for all.

Notable wine-growing regions

In the USA, along with information about their terroir, people, cultures, foods, and wine pairings:.

Napa Valley, California:

Napa Valley is known for its warm climate and its variety of soils, including volcanic, alluvial, and sedimentary. The people of Napa Valley are passionate about their wines and take pride in the quality of their grapes. The culture of Napa Valley is one of luxury and sophistication, with many high-end wineries and restaurants. The food of Napa Valley is centred around fresh, seasonal ingredients and often pairs well with the region's famous Cabernet Sauvignon, Chardonnay, and Merlot.

Sonoma County, California:

Sonoma County is known for its diversity of microclimates, which allow for a wide range of grape varieties to be grown. The people of Sonoma County are passionate about their wines and often work closely with local farmers to produce the best grapes possible. The culture of Sonoma County is laid-back and friendly, with many wineries offering casual tastings and events. The food of Sonoma County is influenced by the region's many ethnic communities and often pairs well with the region's Pinot Noir, Zinfandel, and Chardonnay.

Willamette Valley, Oregon:

Willamette Valley is known for its cool, rainy climate and its unique soils, which are rich in volcanic ash. The people of Willamette Valley are committed to sustainable agriculture and often use organic and biodynamic farming practices. The culture of Willamette Valley is focused on the outdoors, with many wineries offering scenic views and hiking trails. The food of Willamette Valley is centered around farm-to-table cuisine and often pairs well with the region's famous Pinot Noir and Chardonnay.

Finger Lakes, New York:

Finger Lakes is known for its cool climate and its unique combination of lakes and hills, which create a variety of microclimates. The people of Finger Lakes are passionate about their wines and often work closely with local farmers to produce the best grapes possible. The culture of Finger Lakes is focused on sustainability and community, with many wineries offering tastings and events that support local charities. The food of Finger Lakes is centred around fresh, seasonal ingredients and often pairs well with the region's Riesling, Cabernet Franc, and Chardonnay.

Walla Walla Valley, Washington:

Walla Walla Valley is known for its hot, dry climate and its unique soils, which are rich in basalt. The people of Walla Walla Valley are committed to sustainable agriculture and often use drip irrigation and other water-saving techniques. The culture of Walla Walla Valley is focused on community and the arts, with many wineries supporting local artists and musicians. The food of Walla Walla Valley is centred around hearty, meaty dishes and often pairs well with the region's famous Cabernet Sauvignon, Merlot, and Syrah.

Overall, the foods of these wine-growing regions are often centred around fresh, seasonal ingredients and local specialties, such as seafood in Sonoma County and farm-to-table cuisine in Willamette Valley. Wine pairings often depend on the specific grape varieties grown in each region, but some common pairings include Cabernet Sauvignon with steak, Pinot Noir with salmon, and Chardonnay with chicken or seafood.

MEXICO is not generally recognized as one of the world's major wine producing regions, but it does have a number of notable wine growing areas. Here are some of them:

Valle de Guadalupe: Located in the Baja California region, the Valle de Guadalupe is known for producing some of the best wines in Mexico. The terroir is characterised by sandy soil, hot days, and cool nights, which create ideal conditions for growing grapes. The people in the region are a mix of Mexican and American expats, and the culture is influenced by both Mexican and American traditions. The food in the region is heavily influenced by seafood, and the wine pairings often include fresh oysters and ceviche.

Queretaro: Queretaro is located in central Mexico and is known for producing high-quality red wines. The terroir in this region is characterised by volcanic soil, which gives the wines a unique flavour profile. The people in Queretaro are known for their hospitality, and the culture is influenced by both indigenous and Spanish traditions. The food in the region is heavily influenced by Mexican cuisine, and wine pairings often include dishes like mole and tacos al pastor.

Coahuila: Coahuila is located in northern Mexico and is known for producing full-bodied red wines. The terroir in this region is characterised by rocky soil and extreme weather conditions, which create a challenging environment for grape growing. The people in Coahuila are known for their ruggedness, and the culture is heavily influenced by the cowboy traditions of northern Mexico. The food in the region is heavily influenced by meat dishes, and wine pairings often include dishes like beef ribs and barbacoa.

Zacatecas: Zacatecas is located in central Mexico and is known for producing fruity red wines. The terroir in this region is characterised by sandy soil, high altitude, and extreme temperature variations, which create ideal conditions for growing grapes. The people in Zacatecas are known for their hospitality, and the culture is heavily influenced by the mining traditions of the region. The food in the region is heavily influenced by meat dishes, and wine pairings often include dishes like chiles en nogada and enchiladas.

In general, Mexican wines pair well with spicy and flavorful dishes like mole, tacos, and barbacoa. Seafood is also a popular pairing, especially in coastal regions. Mexican wines are also known for their fruity and bold flavours, which can complement a variety of dishes.

CANADA is home to several notable wine-growing regions, each with its unique terroir, people, cultures, foods, and pairings. Some of the most prominent Canadian wine regions include:

Okanagan Valley, British Columbia: This region is known for producing high-quality red and white wines. The terroir of the region includes well-draining soils, warm days, and cool nights. The people here are friendly, hospitable, and passionate about their wine. The culture of the region is influenced by First Nations, European, and Asian cultures. The food in the region is diverse, with a focus on fresh, local ingredients. Some popular food pairings include smoked salmon with Pinot Noir and grilled meats with Cabernet Sauvignon.

Niagara Peninsula, Ontario: This region is famous for its cool-climate wines, including Riesling, Chardonnay, and Pinot Noir. The terroir of the region includes fertile soils, a temperate climate, and proximity to Lake Ontario. The people of the region are warm and welcoming, with a strong sense of community. The culture of the region is influenced by French, English, and Italian cultures. The food in the region is diverse, with a focus on locally sourced ingredients. Some popular food pairings include white wines with seafood and red wines with roasted meats.

Prince Edward County, Ontario: This region is known for its crisp, refreshing wines, including Pinot Gris, Chardonnay, and Pinot Noir. The terroir of the region includes limestone-rich soils, a cool climate, and proximity to Lake Ontario. The people of the region are friendly and welcoming, with a focus on sustainable agriculture. The culture of the region is influenced by English and French cultures. The food in the region is diverse, with a focus on farm-to-table dining. Some popular food pairings include Chardonnay with buttery lobster and Pinot Noir with roasted duck.

Similkameen Valley, British Columbia: This region is known for its rich, full-bodied wines, including Merlot, Cabernet Sauvignon, and Syrah. The terroir of the region includes sandy soils, warm days, and cool nights. The people of the region are friendly and welcoming, with a focus on sustainable farming. The culture of the region is influenced by First Nations and European cultures. The food in the region is diverse, with a focus on fresh, locally sourced ingredients. Some popular food pairings include grilled meats with Merlot and aged cheeses with Cabernet Sauvignon.

In conclusion, Canada's wine-growing regions offer a unique blend of terroir, people, cultures, foods, and pairings. Whether you're a wine connoisseur or a casual drinker, you're sure to find something to suit your taste in Canada's diverse wine regions.

Pairing Food and Wine:

In terms of food and wine pairing, there are many guidelines to follow, but ultimately it comes down to personal preference. Here are some general rules:

White wines pair well with light dishes such as seafood, salads, and cheese.

Red wines pair well with richer dishes such as red meat, pasta, and stews.

Sweet wines pair well with desserts and spicy dishes.

Sparkling wines pair well with appetisers, seafood, and fried foods.

It's also important to consider the characteristics of the wine

Some suggestions for pairing USA wines with local foods:

California Chardonnay with Pacific Coast seafood:

California's Napa Valley and Sonoma County are famous for producing high-quality Chardonnays. These wines often feature fruity and floral notes with a buttery finish, making them an excellent match for the fresh seafood found along the Pacific coast. Dishes like Dungeness crab, Pacific salmon, or sea bass would pair nicely with a California Chardonnay.

Oregon Pinot Noir with wild mushrooms:

Oregon is known for its Pinot Noir production, which often features earthy flavours with hints of cherry and spice. These wines pair perfectly with wild mushrooms that are commonly found in the state's forests, like chanterelles, porcinis, and morels. A simple mushroom risotto or a roasted mushroom and garlic tart would make for an excellent pairing.

Washington State Merlot with Yakima Valley beef:

Washington State's Merlots are full-bodied, with a velvety texture and notes of blackberry, plum, and vanilla. They are a great match for the state's Yakima Valley beef, which is raised on the region's fertile farmland. Try pairing a Washington State Merlot with a classic steak dish, or even a hearty beef stew.

New York Riesling with Finger Lakes trout:

The Finger Lakes region of New York is known for producing some of the best Rieslings in the country, with bright, crisp flavors and hints of citrus and mineral. These wines pair nicely with freshwater trout, which is often caught in the region's many lakes. A simple pan-seared trout with lemon and herbs would be a perfect match for a Finger Lakes Riesling.

Virginia Viognier with Chesapeake Bay oysters: Virginia's Viogniers are known for their floral aromas, with notes of peach, apricot, and honey on the palate. These wines pair nicely with the briny, salty taste of Chesapeake Bay oysters. Raw oysters on the half shell or a classic oyster stew would make for a great pairing with a Virginia Viognier.

It's worth noting that food and wine pairings can be highly subjective, and everyone's palate is different. However, these pairings are based on the typical flavor profiles of the wines and the regional cuisine of each area, so they should be a good starting point for exploring the world of food and wine pairing in the United States.

Some suggestions for pairing MEXICAN wines with local foods:

While Mexican wine may not be as well-known as other wine regions around the world, the country has a long history of winemaking that dates back to the Spanish conquest. There are several wine regions in Mexico, but the most well-known are located in the northwestern part of the country in the states of Baja California and Sonora.

Here are some Mexican wines and local foods that would pair well together:

Valle de Guadalupe Syrah with Carnitas:

Valle de Guadalupe is a wine region located in Baja California, known for producing some of the best wines in Mexico. Syrah is a red grape variety that thrives in the hot and dry climate of the region. A Valle de Guadalupe Syrah would pair well with Carnitas, a traditional Mexican dish made with slow-cooked pork. The richness and depth of the wine would complement the flavours of the tender and juicy pork.

Casa Madero Chenin Blanc with Ceviche:

Casa Madero is the oldest winery in the Americas, founded in 1597 in the state of Coahuila. Their Chenin Blanc is a crisp and refreshing white wine that would pair well with Ceviche, a seafood dish made with raw fish, lime juice, and spices. The acidity of the wine would cut through the citrusy flavours of the dish, while the fruitiness of the wine would complement the sweetness of the seafood.

Monte Xanic Sauvignon Blanc with Guacamole: Monte Xanic is a winery located in the Valle de Guadalupe region that is known for producing high-quality wines. Their Sauvignon Blanc is a light and crisp white wine that would pair well with Guacamole, a traditional

Mexican dip made with avocado, lime juice, and spices. The citrus and herbaceous notes in the wine would complement the tangy and fresh flavors of the guacamole.

Adobe Guadalupe Tempranillo with Tacos al Pastor: Adobe Guadalupe is a winery located in the Valle de Guadalupe region that produces a range of wines, including Tempranillo, a red grape variety that is widely planted in Spain. Tempranillo is a versatile grape that pairs well with a variety of foods, including Tacos al Pastor, a popular Mexican street food made with marinated pork, pineapple, and spices. The tannins in the wine would complement the spiciness of the dish, while the fruity and earthy notes in the wine would complement the flavours of the pork.

These are just a few examples of the many Mexican wines and local foods that would pair well together. Mexican cuisine is diverse and complex, and there are many different wines from the country that would complement its flavors. When pairing wine with food, it's important to consider the flavors and textures of both the wine and the dish, as well as the terroir and production methods used to make the wine.

Some suggestions for pairing CANADIAN wines with local foods:

Canada is home to a variety of wines that are produced in distinct regions with unique terroirs. Here are some Canadian wines and local foods that can be paired with them:

Icewine - Icewine is a sweet dessert wine that is made from grapes that have been frozen on the vine. It is a specialty of Canada and is produced primarily in Ontario and British Columbia. Icewine pairs well with desserts, such as fruit tarts, cheesecake, or dark chocolate. It can also be paired with strong blue cheeses, like Roquefort or Gorgonzola, to create a perfect balance of sweet and savoury flavours.

Pinot Noir - Pinot Noir is a red wine that is produced in several regions across Canada, including British Columbia and Ontario. Pinot Noir typically has flavours of red berries, earth, and spice, and pairs well with dishes that have similar flavours. It goes well with roasted meats, like lamb or duck, as well as grilled vegetables and mushrooms.

Cabernet Franc - Cabernet Franc is a red wine that is produced in several regions in Canada, including Ontario and British Columbia. It has flavours of blackberry, green pepper, and tobacco, and pairs well with grilled meats, such as steak or burgers. It also goes well with tomato-based dishes, like pasta with a tomato-based sauce.

Riesling - Riesling is a white wine that is produced in several regions in Canada, including Ontario and British Columbia. Riesling has flavours of citrus, peach, and honey, and pairs well with spicy Asian dishes, like Thai or Indian cuisine. It also goes well with lighter dishes, like seafood, salads, and grilled chicken.

Chardonnay - Chardonnay is a white wine that is produced in several regions across Canada, including Ontario and British Columbia. Chardonnay has flavours of apple, pear, and vanilla, and pairs well with rich and creamy dishes, like lobster, scallops, or creamy pasta dishes. It also goes well with roasted poultry, like chicken or turkey.

In summary, Canada has a wide variety of wines that are produced in different regions and terroirs. Each wine has its unique flavours and characteristics that can be paired with a wide range of local foods. When choosing a Canadian wine to pair with local food, it's essential to consider the wine's flavour profile and the flavours in the dish to create a harmonious balance.

Pairing North American wines with non-North American foods.

North American wines can be paired with non-North American foods to create delicious and interesting flavour combinations. The concept of terroir, or the environmental factors that influence the taste of wine, plays a crucial role in selecting the right wine to complement a dish.

Let's take a look at some North American wines and their potential pairings with non-North American foods:

Pinot Noir from Oregon:

Pinot Noir from Oregon has a unique terroir that produces a wine with bright acidity, medium body, and flavors of red berries and earthy notes. This wine would pair well with Asian cuisine, such as Korean barbecue or sushi. The bright acidity and earthy notes of the wine complement the umami flavours of the dishes.

Cabernet Sauvignon from California:

Cabernet Sauvignon from California is a bold and full-bodied wine with flavours of black currant, blackberry, and a hint of vanilla. This wine would pair well with grilled red meat dishes, such as Argentinean steak or Korean bulgogi. The bold flavours of the wine can stand up to the rich flavours of the meat.

Riesling from Washington:

Riesling from Washington has a unique terroir that produces a wine with high acidity, floral aromas, and flavors of peach and apricot. This wine would pair well with spicy Indian or Thai cuisine. The sweetness of the wine can help balance out the heat of the dishes.

Chardonnay from California: Chardonnay from California is a full-bodied wine with flavours of tropical fruit, vanilla, and a hint of oak. This wine would pair well with creamy pasta dishes, such as Fettuccine Alfredo or carbonara. The rich and creamy flavours of the pasta complement the full-bodied nature of the wine.

It's important to note that terroir not only influences the taste of the wine, but also reflects the people and the foods of a particular region. For example, the terroir of Oregon's Willamette Valley reflects the region's cool climate and volcanic soil, while California's Napa Valley reflects the region's warm climate and alluvial soil. These unique environmental factors not only produce distinct wines, but also influence the cuisine and culture of the region. By pairing North American wines with foods from the rest of the world, we can explore and appreciate the diverse flavours and cultures of the world.

Here are some more examples:

Pinot Noir from Oregon:

Pinot Noir from Oregon has a unique terroir that produces a wine with bright acidity, medium body, and flavours of red berries and earthy notes. This wine would pair well with Asian cuisine, such as Korean barbecue or sushi. The bright acidity and earthy notes of the wine complement the umami flavours of the dishes.

Cabernet Sauvignon from California:

Cabernet Sauvignon from California is a bold and full-bodied wine with flavours of black currant, blackberry, and a hint of vanilla. This wine would pair well with grilled red meat dishes, such as Argentinean steak or Korean bulgogi. The bold flavours of the wine can stand up to the rich flavours of the meat.

Riesling from Washington:

Riesling from Washington has a unique terroir that produces a wine with high acidity, floral aromas, and flavours of peach and apricot. This wine would pair well with spicy Indian or Thai cuisine. The sweetness of the wine can help balance out the heat of the dishes.

Chardonnay from California: Chardonnay from California is a full-bodied wine with flavours of tropical fruit, vanilla, and a hint of oak. This wine would pair well with creamy pasta dishes, such as Fettuccine Alfredo or carbonara. The rich and creamy flavours of the pasta complement the full-bodied nature of the wine.

It's important to note that terroir not only influences the taste of the wine, but also reflects the people and the foods of a particular region. For example, the terroir of Oregon's Willamette Valley reflects the region's cool climate and volcanic soil, while California's Napa Valley reflects the region's warm climate and alluvial soil. These unique environmental factors not only produce distinct wines, but also influence the cuisine and culture of the region. By pairing North American wines with foods from the rest of the world, we can explore and appreciate the diverse flavours and cultures of the world.

Pairing North American foods with wines from the rest of the world

Pairing North American foods with wines from the rest of the world can create a unique and exciting culinary experience. When pairing food and wine, it's essential to consider the flavours and characteristics of both the dish and the wine.

For example, a classic North American dish like a juicy steak pairs well with a bold red wine like a Cabernet Sauvignon from Argentina or Chile. The tannins in the wine complement the protein in the steak, while the fruity notes balance out the richness of the dish.

Similarly, a grilled salmon dish can be paired with a crisp white wine like a Sauvignon Blanc from New Zealand or a Pinot Gris from Italy. The acidity in the wine cuts through the oily texture of the fish, while the citrus and herbal notes complement its flavour.

When it comes to pairing North American cuisine with wines from the rest of the world, the possibilities are endless. A hearty chilli or spicy Mexican dish can be paired with a spicy Zinfandel from California or a Syrah from France. A classic cheeseburger can be paired with a fruity Shiraz from Australia or a Malbec from Argentina.

Ultimately, pairing North American foods with wines from the rest of the world can enhance the flavors of both the dish and the wine, creating a truly memorable dining experience.

Let's take a look at some examples:

Barbecue from the Southern United States: Barbecue from the Southern United States, with its smoky and savoury flavours, would pair well with a bold and spicy Shiraz from Australia. The rich and full-bodied nature of the wine can stand up to the strong flavours of the barbecue.

Lobster from Maine: Lobster from Maine, with its delicate and sweet flavours, would pair well with a crisp and refreshing Sauvignon Blanc from New Zealand. The high acidity of the wine can help balance out the richness of the lobster.

Tacos from Mexico: Tacos from Mexico, with their bold and spicy flavours, would pair well with a fruity and light-bodied Tempranillo from Spain. The fruity and spicy notes of the wine complement the flavours of the taco.

Macaroni and cheese from the United States: Macaroni and cheese from the United States, with its rich and creamy flavours, would pair well with a crisp and acidic Chardonnay from France. The acidity of the wine can help cut through the richness of the dish.

It's important to note that the cultural background of the food and wine can also play a role in the pairing. For example, pairing Mexican tacos with Spanish Tempranillo can highlight the cultural connections between Spain and Mexico, as both countries have a rich history of food and wine production. Similarly, pairing Southern barbecue with Australian Shiraz can showcase the shared love of bold flavors and grilling between the United States and Australia.

By pairing North American foods with wines from the rest of the world, we can not only explore and appreciate the diverse flavours of the world, but also the cultural connections between different regions and people.

Seasonal Pairings

Summer and Winter

Formal and Informal dining

Summer Informal Dining:

Grilled shrimp or fish tacos paired with a crisp Sauvignon Blanc from California or Canada

BBQ chicken paired with a refreshing Rosé from Oregon or British Columbia

Watermelon and feta salad paired with a chilled Chenin Blanc from Washington State or New York's Finger Lakes region.

Summer Formal Dining:

Lobster or crab cakes paired with a buttery Chardonnay from California or Ontario

Grilled salmon paired with a light Pinot Noir from Oregon or British Columbia

Grilled peaches and prosciutto salad paired with a refreshing sparkling wine from New York's Finger Lakes region or Quebec.

Winter Informal Dining:

Beef stew or pot roast paired with a full-bodied Cabernet Sauvignon from California or Washington State

Baked mac and cheese paired with a rich, oaky Chardonnay from California or Ontario

Chilli con carne paired with a spicy Zinfandel from California or a Malbec from Argentina.

Winter Formal Dining:

Fillet mignon or prime rib paired with a bold, tannic Cabernet Sauvignon from California or British Columbia

Roast duck or venison paired with a medium-bodied Pinot Noir from Oregon or New York's Finger Lakes region

Butternut squash soup paired with a creamy Chardonnay from California or Ontario.

I hope these suggestions help you to plan a delicious and memorable meal!

Phileas Fogg's choices

In terms of North American foods, Phileas Fogg would likely be drawn to regional specialties that showcase the unique flavours and ingredients of each area. For example, he might sample clam chowder in Boston, lobster rolls in Maine, barbecue in Texas, and seafood gumbo in New Orleans. He would also be interested in trying indigenous ingredients and dishes, such as bison burgers, fry bread, and wild rice.

When it comes to North American wines, Phileas Fogg would be pleasantly surprised by the diversity and quality of offerings. He might sample California cabernets, Oregon pinot noirs, and Washington state merlots. He might also be interested in trying Canadian ice wine, a sweet dessert wine made from grapes that have been frozen on the vine.

As for pairings, Phileas Fogg would likely approach the task with an adventurous spirit, willing to experiment with unexpected combinations. For example, he might pair a spicy barbecue dish with a full-bodied zinfandel, or a rich seafood stew with a crisp chardonnay. He might also experiment with pairing different wines with different courses of a meal, such as a light pinot noir with an appetiser, a bold merlot with the main course, and a sweet ice wine with dessert. Ultimately, Phileas Fogg would approach food and wine pairing as an opportunity for exploration and discovery, always seeking out new and interesting flavour combinations.

12 vineyards from the USA, Canada, and Mexico:

United States:

1. **Ridge Vineyards:** One of the oldest vineyards in California, Ridge Vineyards was started in the 19th century and is owned by Paul Draper. They are known for their Zinfandel and Cabernet Sauvignon wines, which are grown in the Santa Cruz Mountains. The terroir is characterised by a cool, maritime climate and rocky soils. Local foods include artichokes, goat cheese, and Dungeness crab. Pairing suggestions include grilled lamb with Zinfandel.

2. **Duckhorn Vineyards:** Founded in the early 1970s, Duckhorn Vineyards is located in Napa Valley, California and is owned by the Duckhorn family. They produce a range of wines, including Cabernet Sauvignon, Merlot, and Sauvignon Blanc. The vineyard has a Mediterranean-like climate with warm days and cool nights. Local foods include wild mushrooms, figs, and olive oil. Pairing suggestions include grilled steak with Cabernet Sauvignon.

3. **Hirsch Vineyards:** Established in the 1980s, Hirsch Vineyards is located in western Sonoma County, California and is owned by David Hirsch. They produce Pinot Noir and Chardonnay, with a focus on natural and sustainable farming practices. The terroir is characterised by steep hillsides, rocky soils, and a cool, marine-influenced climate. Local foods include goat cheese, local honey, and heirloom tomatoes. Pairing suggestions include roasted chicken with Pinot Noir.

4. **Château Montelena:** Established in the late 19th century, Château Montelena is located in Napa Valley, California and is primarily known for its Chardonnay. It is owned by the Barrett family and has a history of producing critically acclaimed wines. The terroir is characterised by gravelly soils and a Mediterranean-like climate. Local foods include citrus fruits, almonds, and fresh seafood. Pairing suggestions include crab cakes with Chardonnay.

5. **Williams Selyem Winery:** Founded in the 1980s, Williams Selyem Winery is located in Sonoma County, California and is known for its Pinot Noir and Chardonnay. The vineyard is owned by John and Ed Selyem and uses organic and sustainable farming practices. The terroir is characterised by deep, alluvial soils and a cool climate. Local foods include goat cheese, wild mushrooms, and blackberries. Pairing suggestions include seared duck breast with Pinot Noir.

6. **Stag's Leap Wine Cellars:** Established in the 1970s, Stag's Leap Wine Cellars is located in Napa Valley, California and is known for its Cabernet Sauvignon. It is owned by Ste. Michelle Wine Estates and produces several bottlings of Cabernet each year. The terroir is characterised by thin, rocky soils and a moderate climate. Local foods include beef, lamb, and root vegetables. Pairing suggestions include grilled steak with Cabernet Sauvignon.

Canada:

1. **Peller Estates:** Peller Estates is located in Niagara-on-the-Lake, Ontario and is owned by the Peller family. They produce a range of wines, including ice wine, Riesling, and Cabernet Franc. The terroir is characterised by a cool climate and deep soils. Local foods include cherries, apples, and cheese. Pairing suggestions include roasted pork with Riesling.

2. **Mission Hill Family Estate:** Located in Kelowna, British Columbia, Mission Hill Family Estate is known for its Pinot Noir and Chardonnay. It is owned by the von Mandl family and has won numerous awards for its wines. The terroir is characterised by a cool, high-altitude climate and rocky soils. Local foods include strawberries, peaches, and goat cheese. Pairing suggestions include grilled salmon with Pinot Noir.

3. **Tinhorn Creek Vineyards:** Tinhorn Creek Vineyards is located in Oliver, British Columbia and is owned by the Shaunessy and Oldfield families. They produce a range of wines, including Syrah, Merlot, and Chardonnay. The terroir is characterised by a warm, arid climate and sandy soils. Local foods include apricots, cherries, and beef. Pairing suggestions include grilled lamb with Syrah.

Mexico:

1. **Monte Xanic:** Monte Xanic is located in Baja California and is one of the most prominent vineyards in Mexico. It is owned by the Peláez family and produces a range of wines, including Cabernet Sauvignon and Chenin Blanc. The terroir is characterised by sandy soils and a Mediterranean-like climate. Local foods include figs, olives, and queso fresco. Pairing suggestions include grilled meats with Cabernet Sauvignon.

2. **Casa Madero:** Casa Madero is located in Parras de la Fuente, Coahuila and is the oldest vineyard in the Americas, dating back to the 16th century. It is owned by the Cetto family and produces a range of wines, including Cabernet Sauvignon and Merlot. The terroir is characterised by limestone soils and a hot, arid climate. Local foods include pecans, pomegranates, and grilled meats. Pairing suggestions include beef skewers with Cabernet Sauvignon.

3. **Baron Balche:** Located in the heart of Mexico's wine country in Ensenada, Baja California, Baron Balche produces a range of wines, including Chardonnay and Cabernet Sauvignon. The vineyard is owned by the Balche family and uses organic and sustainable farming practices. The terroir is characterised by rocky soil and a warm, Mediterranean-like climate. Local foods include olives, almonds, and seafood. Pairing suggestions include grilled shrimp with Chardonnay.

5 Wines each from 8 North American countries pairing with sweet food dishes:

United States:

Cabernet Sauvignon from Napa Valley, California: pairs well with dark chocolate truffles

Zinfandel from Sonoma County, California: pairs well with chocolate-covered strawberries

Pinot Noir from Willamette Valley, Oregon: pairs well with blackberry pie

Riesling from Finger Lakes, New York: pairs well with apple crisp

Chardonnay from Russian River Valley, California: pairs well with caramel flan

Canada:

Icewine from Niagara Peninsula, Ontario: pairs well with vanilla ice cream

Cabernet Franc from Okanagan Valley, British Columbia: pairs well with cherry pie

Pinot Noir from Prince Edward County, Ontario: pairs well with raspberry tart

Vidal Blanc from **Niagara-on-the-Lake, Ontario:** pairs well with peach cobbler

Marechal Foch from Vancouver Island, British Columbia: pairs well with blueberry cheesecake

Mexico:

Nebbiolo from Valle de Guadalupe, Baja California: pairs well with dark chocolate truffles

Chenin Blanc from Queretaro: pairs well with lemon tart

Tempranillo from Valle de Parras, Coahuila: pairs well with strawberry shortcake

Cabernet Sauvignon from San Vicente, Baja California: pairs well with mixed berry pie

Grenache from Valle de Guadalupe, Baja California: pairs well with chocolate mousse

Guatemala:

Malbec from San Juan Sacatepéquez: pairs well with chocolate cake

Cabernet Sauvignon from Chimaltenango: pairs well with blackberry cobbler

Merlot from Quetzaltenango: pairs well with raspberry sorbet

Syrah from Sololá: pairs well with mixed berry tart

Pinot Noir from Huehuetenango: pairs well with strawberry cheesecake

Costa Rica:

Sauvignon Blanc from Guanacaste: pairs well with lemon bars

Cabernet Franc from Santa Ana: pairs well with cherry pie

Syrah from Central Valley: pairs well with raspberry sorbet

Malbec from Arenal: pairs well with dark chocolate truffles

Chardonnay from Perez Zeledon: pairs well with apple tart

Jamaica:

Merlot from St. Ann: pairs well with coconut cake

Cabernet Sauvignon from St. Elizabeth: pairs well with pineapple upside-down cake

Shiraz from Westmoreland: pairs well with mango sorbet

Chardonnay from Clarendon: pairs well with banana bread

Pinot Noir from Manchester: pairs well with mixed berry crumble

Cuba:

Tempranillo from Pinar del Rio: pairs well with dark chocolate truffles

Chardonnay from Villa Clara: pairs well with caramel flan

Malbec from Ciego de Ávila: pairs well with mixed berry pie

Pinot Noir from Santiago de Cuba: pairs well with chocolate cake

Cabernet Sauvignon from Cienfuegos: pairs well with blueberry cheesecake

Dominican Republic:

Syrah from Santo Domingo: pairs well with chocolate cake

Cabernet Sauvignon from La Vega: pairs well with mixed berry tart

Merlot from Santiago de los Caballeros: pairs well with strawberry shortcake

Chardonnay from San Cristobal: pairs well with apple pie

Pinot Noir from Puerto Plata: pairs well with raspberry sorbet

Phileas Fogg would likely have enjoyed a variety of wines and foods during his travels to the USA, Canada, Mexico and Panama, and would have sought out the best dining experiences available.

In the USA, Phileas Fogg would have had access to some of the world's finest wines and foods. He might have sampled California's famous Napa Valley wines, such as Cabernet Sauvignon and Chardonnay, which are known for their rich and fruity flavours. He might also have tried some classic American dishes, such as steak and potatoes or fried chicken, which would pair well with bold and full-bodied red wines.

In Canada, Phileas Fogg would have encountered a variety of unique and flavorful cuisine, from Quebec's famous poutine to British Columbia's fresh seafood. He might have tried some of Canada's renowned ice wines, which are made from grapes that have been frozen on the vine and produce a sweet and complex flavour. He might also have enjoyed pairing his meals with some of Canada's lighter, more delicate wines, such as Pinot Noir or Riesling.

In Mexico, Phileas Fogg would have had the opportunity to taste some of the world's finest tequilas, which are made from the agave plant and have a distinctively smoky and earthy flavour. He might also have sampled some of Mexico's vibrant and spicy cuisine, such as tacos, enchiladas, and mole sauce. These bold and flavorful dishes would pair well with robust red wines, such as Syrah or Zinfandel.

In Panama, Phileas Fogg would have likely experienced a diverse range of flavours. Panama's cuisine is influenced by African, Spanish, and indigenous cultures, creating a fusion of flavours and dishes.

Some popular Panamanian dishes that Phileas Fogg may have enjoyed include:

Sancocho: a hearty soup made with chicken, yams, ñame (a type of root vegetable), and other vegetables.

Arroz con Pollo: a rice and chicken dish that includes vegetables, herbs, and spices.

Tamales: corn-based dough filled with meat, vegetables, and spices, then wrapped in a banana leaf and steamed.

Ceviche: a dish made with raw fish marinated in lime juice, onions, peppers, and cilantro.

As for wine, Panama is not a significant producer of wine, but it does have a growing wine culture. Phileas Fogg may have tried a Panamanian **rum** or **beer** instead of wine. **Ron Abuelo** is a popular Panamanian rum that is known for its smooth and mellow taste. Panama is also known for its beer, with popular brands including **Atlas, Balboa, and Panama.**

Phileas Fogg would have encountered a diverse range of people during his travels to North America.

In the United States, he would have likely encountered people of different races, ethnicities, religions, and social classes, reflecting the diverse makeup of American society.

For example, in major cities such as New York and Boston, Fogg would have come across people of European descent, including Irish, Italian, German, and French immigrants. He may also have encountered African Americans, who had been brought to America as slaves and were living in a state of segregation and discrimination in many parts of the country.

Fogg may also have encountered Native Americans during his travels, especially if he ventured into the western states. However, due to the policies of forced assimilation and displacement that were in place at the time, many Native Americans were confined to reservations and may not have been easily accessible to Fogg.

In addition, Fogg may have encountered people of different religions, such as Jews, Muslims, and various Christian denominations. He may have also come across people from different socioeconomic backgrounds, including wealthy industrialists and entrepreneurs, as well as working-class and impoverished individuals.

Overall, Fogg would have encountered a rich tapestry of people during his travels in the United States, reflecting the country's diverse and complex social background.

In Canada....

In Jules Verne's novel "Around the World in Eighty Days", which was published in 1873, Fogg travels around the world and makes a brief stop in Canada, specifically in the city of Montreal.

During the time when Fogg would have visited Canada (around the 1870s), Montreal was a rapidly growing city and a hub for immigration. As a result, Fogg would have encountered a diverse group of people, including:

French-Canadians: As Montreal is located in the province of Quebec, Fogg would have encountered many French-Canadians, who were the dominant group in the region.

English-Canadians: Fogg would also have encountered many English-Canadians, particularly among the city's wealthier residents.

Irish immigrants: Montreal saw a significant influx of Irish immigrants during the 19th century, and Fogg would likely have encountered many Irish people in the city.

Scottish immigrants: Similar to the Irish, many Scottish immigrants also settled in Montreal during this time.

Chinese immigrants: Although Chinese immigration to Canada was restricted during the 19th century, some Chinese people did manage to settle in Montreal, primarily as labourers.

Jewish immigrants: Montreal was also home to a significant Jewish community during the 19th century, and Fogg would have encountered many Jewish people in the city.

Indigenous Peoples: Fogg may have encountered Indigenous Peoples in Canada, although it is unclear if he interacted with any during his brief stop in Montreal.

Overall, Fogg would have encountered a diverse range of people during his visit to Montreal, with the city being a melting pot of various cultures and nationalities.

Phileas Fogg did not travel to Mexico in the story. However, I can provide a general overview of the diverse people that he might have encountered had he made a stop in **Mexico**.

Mexico is a culturally and ethnically diverse country, with a population of over 130 million people. The country is home to various indigenous groups, including the Aztecs, Mayans, Zapotecs, and Mixtecs, among others. In addition, Mexico has a large mestizo population, which refers to people of mixed European and Indigenous ancestry.

Mexico is also home to many Afro-Mexicans, who are descendants of African slaves brought over to the country during the colonial period. The country also has a sizable Asian population, with many Chinese, Japanese, and Filipino immigrants and their descendants living in Mexico.

Furthermore, Mexico has a diverse range of religions, with Catholicism being the predominant faith. However, there are also significant Protestant and Evangelical Christian communities, as well as smaller populations of Muslims, Jews, and followers of indigenous religions.

In terms of language, Spanish is the official language of Mexico, but there are also over 60 indigenous languages spoken in the country, including Nahuatl, Maya, and Zapotec.

Overall, Phileas Fogg would have encountered a diverse range of people in Mexico, with varying cultural, ethnic, linguistic, and religious backgrounds.

In Panama, Phileas Fogg would have encountered a diverse range of people, given its strategic location as a land bridge between North and South America. Here are some examples:

Indigenous people:

There are several indigenous groups in Panama, including the Ngäbe, Buglé, Emberá, and Wounaan, who have lived in the region for thousands of years. Phileas Fogg may have encountered members of these communities and learned about their traditional cultures, beliefs, and ways of life.

Spanish colonisers:

Panama was part of the Spanish Empire for over 300 years, and the country still bears many traces of Spanish influence. Phileas Fogg may have encountered Spanish colonists or descendants of Spanish colonists, who could have shared their history and culture with him.

Afro-Panamanians:

Panama has a significant population of Afro-Panamanians, who are descendants of African slaves brought over during the colonial period. Phileas Fogg may have encountered members of this community and learned about their traditions, music, and cuisine.

Canal workers:

The Panama Canal was under construction during the time when "Around the World in Eighty Days" was set, and Phileas Fogg may have encountered some of the workers who were building the canal. These workers came from all over the world, including Europe, the United States, and the Caribbean.

Businesspeople and traders: Panama has long been an important commercial hub, connecting the Atlantic and Pacific Oceans. Phileas Fogg may have encountered businesspeople and traders who were involved in the import and export of goods, such as coffee, bananas, and sugar.

Overall, Panama was a melting pot of cultures and peoples during the time of Phileas Fogg's journey, and he would have encountered a fascinating mix of individuals from different backgrounds and walks of life.

Non Alcoholic Wines

Non-alcoholic wines have a long history in North America, dating back to the early 20th century. However, the history of non-alcoholic wine in North America is closely tied to the Prohibition era of the 1920s and early 1930s.

During Prohibition, the production, sale, and consumption of alcoholic beverages were banned in the United States, which led to a surge in the production of non-alcoholic beverages, including wine. Grape growers and winemakers in California, in particular, saw an opportunity to capitalise on the demand for non-alcoholic wine, and began producing grape juice and grape concentrates that could be used to make non-alcoholic wine.

At the same time, the temperance movement in the United States was promoting the consumption of non-alcoholic beverages as a healthy and virtuous alternative to alcohol. This led to the development of a market for non-alcoholic wine and other beverages.

One of the key challenges faced by non-alcoholic wine producers was how to capture the flavour and aroma of wine without the alcohol. This was especially challenging because alcohol plays an important role in wine, both in terms of flavour and mouthfeel.

To overcome this challenge, non-alcoholic wine producers began experimenting with different techniques and ingredients, such as adding sugar or fruit juice to enhance the flavour, or using yeast extracts to mimic the aroma of wine. Over time, they developed a range of non-alcoholic wines that could satisfy the demand for a wine-like experience without the alcohol.

Another factor that played a role in the development of non-alcoholic wine in North America was the diversity of terroirs and local cultures. The United States and Canada are both large and diverse countries, with a wide variety of climates and soil types that are conducive to growing different grape varieties. This has led to the development of distinct wine regions, each with its own terroir and local culture.

Non-alcoholic wine producers have been able to leverage this diversity by creating products that reflect the unique characteristics of different grape varieties and wine regions. For example, they may use grapes grown in a particular region to create a non-alcoholic wine that captures the flavour and aroma of that region's wines.

Today, non-alcoholic wine continues to be a popular alternative to alcoholic beverages, particularly among people who are looking for a healthier or more moderate drinking experience. With continued experimentation and innovation, non-alcoholic wine producers are likely to continue pushing the boundaries of what is possible, creating new and exciting products that appeal to a broad range of consumers.

A brief overview of North America's non-alcoholic wines

Canada:

Non-alcoholic wines from Canada are typically made by removing the alcohol from already-existing wines. Canada is known for producing crisp, refreshing white wines due to their cool climate. Some popular grape varieties that are used in non-alcoholic wines include Riesling, Chardonnay, and Pinot Gris. Popular regions for producing these wines include the Niagara Peninsula and the Okanagan Valley. Non-alcoholic wines from Canada pairs well with seafood, grilled vegetables, and creamy pasta dishes.

United States:

Non-alcoholic wines from the United States are produced in several states including California, Oregon, and Washington. The most common grape varieties used include Chardonnay, Cabernet Sauvignon, and Merlot. Regions like Napa Valley, Sonoma County, and Willamette Valley are famous for their non-alcoholic wines. Non-alcoholic wines from the United States pair well with roast turkey, grilled meats, and spicy foods.

Mexico:

Non-alcoholic wines from Mexico are produced from the local grapes grown in the Baja California region. Some of the popular grapes used include Cabernet Sauvignon, Tempranillo, and Nebbiolo. There are many small, family-owned vineyards producing non-alcoholic wines that can be enjoyed with traditional Mexican dishes like tacos and chilies rellenos.

As for pairing non-alcoholic wines with food, it's always best to match the wine's flavour with the flavour of the dish. For example, a light white wine would pair well with seafood or a light salad, while a full-bodied red wine would pair well with grilled meats or rich pasta dishes. Experimenting and trying out new flavour combinations can be a fun and delicious way to enjoy non-alcoholic wines.

Phileas Fogg's choices

Phileas Fogg would have encountered a variety of non-alcoholic wines during his travels through North America. Here are a few examples along with their food pairings:

1. **Niagara Peninsula Riesling from Canada** - This refreshing white wine would pair well with local seafood, such as grilled salmon or lobster bisque.

2. **St. Supéry Virtú White from Napa Valley, United States** - This crisp white wine would pair well with fresh salads, like a California-style salad with strawberries, avocado and goat cheese.

3. **California Red Blend from Fre Wines** - This full-bodied red blend would pair well with hearty dishes, like a beef stew or roasted vegetables with herbs.

4. **Ariel Cabernet Sauvignon from California, United States** - This robust red wine would pair perfectly with meaty dishes, such as a grilled steak or a juicy burger.

5. **Mexican Grenache Rose from Baja California** - This light, fresh wine would pair well with spicy Mexican dishes like a burrito bowl or pico de gallo.

Phileas Fogg may have also encountered non-alcoholic wines made from local fruits and berries, such as blueberry wine from Maine or cranberry wine from Wisconsin, which would pair well with local foods like blueberry pancakes or cranberry sauce.

In conclusion....

The great North American continent is rich in diverse cultures, traditions, and culinary delights. The combination of exquisite wines and exotic foods presents an opportunity for those who seek adventure and a sensory delight. From California's Napa Valley to Canada's Niagara Peninsula, North America is home to some of the world's finest wine-growing regions, producing a wide range of quality wines that reflect their unique terroir and grape varieties. Whether you prefer a buttery Chardonnay to accompany your salmon dish, a spicy Zinfandel to complement your barbecue ribs, or a sweet ice wine to enhance your cheese platter, there is a North American wine that can satisfy your palate. By experimenting with different wine and food pairings, you can discover a whole new world of flavours and aromas. We hope that you enjoyed reading about food and wine pairings from North America and that you will now feel inspired to try them for yourself. Cheers!

Sparkling Wines

The North American sparkling wine industry has experienced impressive growth in recent years, with a number of regions producing high-quality sparkling wines that have gained recognition among wine enthusiasts around the world.

Some of the major regions for sparkling wine production in North America include California, Oregon, New York, and British Columbia. Each region has its own unique terroir, climate, and topography, which contribute to the character of the wines that are produced there.

In California, for example, the coastal climate, which is influenced by cool winds from the Pacific Ocean and unique microclimates, allows for a wide range of grapes to be grown, including Chardonnay, Pinot Noir, Pinot Meunier, and Pinot Blanc, which are commonly used in sparkling wine production. The Carneros AVA and the Russian River Valley AVA are particularly well-known for their sparkling wines.

Oregon is another region that has been gaining a reputation for its sparkling wines. The cool, maritime climate of the Willamette Valley is particularly well-suited for growing Pinot Noir and Chardonnay, which are the primary grapes used in sparkling wine production in the region.

In the Northeastern United States, the Finger Lakes region of New York is known for its Rieslings, but also produces a number of high-quality sparkling wines. And in British Columbia, Canada, the Okanagan Valley is quickly becoming recognized as a top region for sparkling wine production, with wineries utilizing a range of grapes including Chardonnay, Pinot Noir, and Pinot Meunier.

In terms of the culture and food scene, sparkling wines are often associated with special occasions and celebrations, but they also pair well with a variety of foods. In North America, sparkling wines are known to be particularly well-suited to pair with seafood, oysters, raw bar items, and other seafood-based dishes. They also pair well with fried foods, potato chips, spicy dishes, and creamy sauces.

Some of the key players in the North American sparkling wine industry include producers like Schramsberg, J Vineyards & Winery, Domaine Carneros, and Iron Horse Vineyards in California, and Argyle Winery in Oregon. These producers have helped to establish North America as a major player in the global sparkling wine market, and as the industry continues to grow, it will be exciting to see what new developments emerge from these regions.

Here's a list of sparkling wine vineyards in some North American countries along with details of the grapes, owners, climate, religion, and food that goes well with them:

1. **USA**:

   - Chandon (Napa Valley, California): The vineyard produces sparkling wine using Chardonnay, Pinot Noir, and Pinot Meunier grapes. It is owned by Moet Hennessy Louis Vuitton (LVMH) and has a Mediterranean climate with hot, dry summers and mild winters. The region is also known for its cuisine, including seafood, grilled dishes, and artisanal cheeses, which pair well with Chandon's Brut Classic.

   - Gloria Ferrer Caves and Vineyards (Sonoma County, California): This vineyard specializes in producing Brut, Blanc de Blancs, and Blanc de Noirs sparkling wines from Pinot Noir and Chardonnay grapes. The property is owned by the Ferrer family and has a cool, coastal climate, ideal for vine growing. The wine pairs well with seafood and sushi dishes.

   - Domaine Carneros (Napa Valley, California): The vineyard produces Brut, Blanc de Blancs, and Rosé sparkling wines using Chardonnay and Pinot Noir grapes. It is owned by the Taittinger family of Champagne and consists of vineyards in the southern part of Napa Valley. The cool climate is influenced by the nearby San Pablo Bay, making it perfect for grape growing. The winery's Brut pairs well with creamy pasta dishes and seafood.

2. **Canada**:

   - Inniskillin Wines (Niagara-on-the-Lake, Ontario): This vineyard produces a range of sparkling wines using traditional Champagne grapes like Chardonnay and Pinot Noir. It is known for its Icewine, a sweet dessert wine made from grapes frozen on the vine. Inniskillin has a cool, continental climate that results in crisp acidity in its sparkling wines. The area is famous for its fruit-based dishes, including apple and pear pies, which pair well with Inniskillin's sparkling wines.

3. **Mexico**:

   - Casa Madero (Coahuila, Mexico): This vineyard is the oldest in all of North America, and it produces a range of red and white wines, including sparkling wines. The vineyard's sparkling wine is made using Chenin Blanc grapes and has floral notes and a crisp, refreshing acidity. The vineyard's location in Northern Mexico provides a desert climate with cooler night temperatures, perfect for growing grapes. The wine pairs well with Mexican cuisine, such as quesadillas, tacos, and ceviche.

4. **Panama, Costa Rica, Guatemala, and Jamaica**:

   Unfortunately, there are no sparkling wine vineyards in these countries which produce Champagne-style sparking wines using the traditional method. However, there are wineries that produce wines using other methods like carbonation. Some wineries in these countries include Finca Lérida (Panama), Volcan de Fuego (Guatemala), and Bodega de Soroa (Cuba) – which produce still wine made using local grape varieties like Vitis bourquina, Jacquez, and Chasselas Doré, respectively. These wines pair well with local cuisine, including spicy dishes and grilled/game meats.

Further Readings

There are several resources available for further reading on North American wines, their foods and cultures, their people, and how they pair their food and wines.

Here are some suggestions:

"The Wine Bible" by Karen MacNeil: This book is an excellent resource for learning about wines from all over the world, including North America. It covers the history of winemaking in North America, the different grape varietals grown in the region, and the various wine-producing regions. It also provides information on food pairings and the culture of wine in North America.

"American Wine: A Coming-of-Age Story" by Tom Acitelli:

This book tells the story of how the American wine industry has evolved over the years, from its early days to its current status as a major player in the global wine market. It covers the various wine-producing regions in the US, including California, Oregon, and New York, and provides insights into the people behind the industry.

"The Food Lover's Guide to Wine" by Karen Page and Andrew Dornenburg:

This book provides information on how to pair wine with different types of food, including North American cuisine. It includes suggestions for specific wine varietals and food pairings, as well as tips on how to choose wine based on your personal preferences.

"The New California Wine" by Jon Bonné:

This book focuses specifically on the wines of California, which is one of the most important wine-producing regions in North America. It covers the history of winemaking in the state, the various grape varietals grown there, and the different wine-producing regions. It also provides insights into the culture of wine in California and how it has evolved over the years.

Wine Spectator:

This is a leading publication in the wine industry, covering wines from all over the world, including North America. It provides reviews and ratings of different wines, as well as information on food pairings and wine culture. Its website is a great resource for keeping up to date with the latest news and trends in the wine industry.

Wine Folly: This website provides a wealth of information on wines from all over the world, including North America. It includes articles on different grape varietals, wine-producing regions, and food pairings, as well as wine reviews and ratings. It also offers educational resources, such as wine maps and infographics, to help you learn more about wine.

GuildSomm:

This is an online community for wine professionals and enthusiasts, offering a range of resources on wine from all over the world. It includes articles, videos, podcasts, and webinars, covering topics such as wine tasting, food pairings, and wine regions. Its North America section provides in-depth information on the wine regions and grape varietals of the continent.

Further Readings on non-alcoholic wines from North America

If you're interested in learning more about non-alcoholic beverages from North America, here are some resources to check out:

"Zero Proof Cocktails: Alcohol-Free Beverages for Every Occasion" by Elva Ramirez - This book is a great starting point for anyone looking to explore the world of non-alcoholic beverages. It includes recipes for cocktails, mocktails, and other drinks, as well as tips on how to stock your home bar with non-alcoholic options.

"Dry: A Memoir" by Augusten Burroughs - This memoir is a personal account of the author's decision to quit drinking and his journey to find new ways to socialise and have fun without alcohol. It's a touching and funny read that offers insight into the world of non-alcoholic living.

"Seedlip Drinks" - Seedlip is a brand of non-alcoholic spirits that has become popular in recent years. Their website offers a variety of recipes for cocktails and mocktails, as well as information about the history and production of their products.

"The Rise of Non-Alcoholic Beverages in North America" by Beverage Daily - This article provides an overview of the trend towards non-alcoholic beverages in North America, including the reasons behind the shift and some of the companies leading the way.

"The Non-Alcoholic Revolution: How Craft Drinks are Changing the Game" by Forbes - This article discusses the rise of non-alcoholic beverages in the craft drink industry, including the challenges and opportunities facing producers and consumers.

Further Readings on North American Sparkling Wines

Certainly, here are some articles and resources on North American sparkling wines:

1. **"12 Best Sparkling Wines Made in North America"** by Kate Dingwall on VinePair (https://vinepair.com/buy-this-booze/best-north-american-sparkling-wines/)

2. **"The Rise of American Sparkling Wine"** by Lettie Teague on Food & Wine (https://www.foodandwine.com/wine/champagne-sparkling-wine/american-sparkling-wine)

3. **"America's 10 Best Sparkling Wines"** by Kathryn Love on Wine Enthusiast (https://www.winemag.com/2019/12/16/americas-10-best-sparkling-wines/)

4. **"The Miracle of American Sparkling Wine"** by Mark Squires on Robert Parker Wine Advocate (https://www.robertparker.com/articles/the-miracle-of-american-sparkling-wine)

5. **"The Rise of High-Quality North American Sparkling Wine"** by Tina Caputo on WineSpectator (https://www.winespectator.com/articles/rise-of-high-quality-north-american-sparkling-wine)

CHAPTER 6

SOUTH AMERICAN WINE AND CUISINE

Introduction:

South America is a diverse and vibrant continent that consists of many different countries, people, and cultures. There are 12 countries located in South America, including Argentina, Brazil, Chile, Colombia, Ecuador, Guyana, Paraguay, Peru, Suriname, Uruguay, Venezuela, and French Guiana.

One of the things that makes South America unique is its people. Indigenous groups, Spanish and Portuguese colonists, African slaves, and immigrants from all over the world have contributed to the diverse mix of cultures that you can find in South America today. Some of the major ethnic groups include the Quechua, Aymara, Guarani, and Mapuche.

Many South American countries have a strong tradition of Catholicism, which was brought over by the Spanish and Portuguese colonists. However, there are also many other religions and belief systems present in South America, including indigenous beliefs, Afro-Brazilian religions, and Protestantism.

South America is also famous for its wines and foods. Argentina and Chile are known for their delicious red wines, while Brazil is famous for its Caipirinha cocktail made with Cachaça. Peru is known for its ceviche and chicha morada, a purple corn drink, while Brazil has its famous Feijoada stew made with black beans and pork.

South America has a rich and complex history. The continent was home to many advanced civilizations, including the Incas, before European colonists arrived in the late 15th century. Over the centuries, South American countries have fought for independence and autonomy, experienced dictatorships and political instability, and have seen periods of economic growth and decline. Today, South America is a continent with a rich cultural heritage and many different opportunities for adventure, exploration, and learning.

The Terroir

Terroir is a term used to describe the environmental factors that influence the character and quality of crops grown in a particular area, including soil type, climate, topography, and other factors. South America is a continent with a wide variety of terroirs, due to its large size and diverse geography.

Here's a brief overview of the terroirs you might find in each of the 12 countries of South America:

1. **Argentina:** The terroir in Argentina varies widely by region, but generally speaking, the Andes mountains to the west provide ample irrigation water for vineyards, and the hot, dry climate is ideal for growing grapes. The Mendoza region is particularly famous for producing high-quality Malbec wines.

2. **Bolivia:** Bolivia is a landlocked country located in the Andes mountains, with a diverse range of microclimates and ecosystems. The tropical lowlands are known for their fertile soils and are home to many coffee plantations, while the high-altitude Altiplano is better suited for livestock grazing.

3. **Brazil:** Brazil is the largest country in South America by land area, and its terroir varies widely depending on the region. In the south, where the climate is more temperate, fertile soils and ample rain allow for the production of a wide range of crops, including coffee, soybeans, and sugarcane. The Amazon rainforest in the north has a tropical climate and is home to many fruits and nuts.

4. **Chile:** The terroir in Chile is heavily influenced by the Pacific Ocean to the west and the Andes mountains to the east, which create a wide range of microclimates. Along the central coast, cool, foggy conditions are ideal for growing grapes, while the warmer, drier conditions in the north are better for more heat-tolerant crops like avocados and citrus fruits.

5. **Colombia:** Colombia's terroir is characterised by its rich soils and tropical climate, which allow for the production of a wide variety of crops, including coffee, bananas, sugarcane, and flowers.

6. **Ecuador:** Ecuador has a diverse range of microclimates due to its location on the equator and varied topography, with everything from tropical rainforests to high-altitude mountains. This allows for the production of many different crops, including coffee, cacao, and bananas.

7. **Guyana:** Guyana has a tropical climate and fertile soils that are well-suited for agriculture. Major crops include sugar, rice, and fruits such as bananas and mangoes.

8. **Paraguay:** Paraguay is a landlocked country with a subtropical climate and fertile soils, making it ideal for agriculture. Major crops include soybeans, sugarcane, cotton, and corn.

9. **Peru:** Peru is renowned for its diverse terroirs, which include the arid coast, the Andes mountains, and the Amazon rainforest. Coffee, cacao, quinoa, and grapes for wine are just a few of the crops grown in the country.

10. **Suriname:** Suriname's terroir is characterised by its tropical rainforest climate and fertile soils, which allow for the production of a wide variety of crops, including palm oil, bananas, and rice.

11. **Uruguay:** Uruguay is a small country situated between Argentina and Brazil, with a temperate climate and diverse terroir that allows for the production of high-quality beef, wool, and wines.

12. **Venezuela:** Venezuela's terroir is characterised by its tropical climate and diverse topography, which ranges from the Andes mountains to the Caribbean coastline. Coffee, cacao, sugarcane, and bananas are just a few of the crops grown in the country.

Overall, South America offers a wide range of terroirs and agricultural environments, making it an important region for global food production.

Wines

The 12 countries of South America that produce wine are Argentina, Brazil, Chile, Colombia, Ecuador, Uruguay, Venezuela, Bolivia, Guyana, Paraguay, Peru, and Suriname. Below are six wines from each country, along with their owners, grape varieties, and vinification techniques:

Argentina:

1. Malbec - Bodegas Norton: Made from the Malbec grape variety, this wine is typically aged in oak barrels for 12 months.

2. Torrontés - Bodega Colomé: A white wine made from the Torrontés grape variety, it is known for its floral and aromatic characteristics.

3. Bonarda - Bodega Luigi Bosca: This red wine is made from the Bonarda grape variety and is known for its soft tannins and fruity flavours.

4. Cabernet Sauvignon - Catena Zapata: Produced from the Cabernet Sauvignon grape variety, this wine is aged for 18 months before release.

5. Syrah - Finca Sophenia: Made from the Syrah grape variety, this wine is fermented in stainless steel tanks and aged for 12 months.

6. Chardonnay - Trapiche: A white wine made from the Chardonnay grape variety, it is aged in oak barrels for 8 months.

Brazil:

1. Miolo Merlot - Miolo Wine Group: Produced from the Merlot grape variety, this wine is aged for 6 months in oak barrels.

2. Casa Valduga Terroir Single Vineyard Chardonnay - Casa Valduga: A white wine made from the Chardonnay grape variety, it is fermented in oak barrels for 6 months.

3. Routhier & Darricarrère Cabernet Franc - Cave Geisse: This red wine is made from the Cabernet Franc grape variety and is aged in oak barrels for 12 months.

4. Pizzato Reserva Tannat - Pizzato: Produced from the Tannat grape variety, this wine is aged in oak barrels for 12 months.

5. Rio Sol Rosé - Vinícola Perini: A rosé wine made from a blend of grape varieties, it is fermented in stainless steel tanks.

6. Lidio Carraro Dádivas Chardonnay - Lidio Carraro: A white wine made from the Chardonnay grape variety, it is fermented and aged in oak barrels for 9 months.

Chile:

1. Carmenère - Viña Koyle: This red wine is made from the Carmenère grape variety and is aged in oak barrels for 12 months.

2. Sauvignon Blanc - Casas del Bosque: A white wine made from the Sauvignon Blanc grape variety, it is fermented and aged in stainless steel tanks.

3. Cabernet Franc - Viña Falernia: Produced from the Cabernet Franc grape variety, this wine is aged in oak barrels for 12 months.

4. Pinot Noir - Viña San Pedro: Made from the Pinot Noir grape variety, this wine is fermented and aged in oak barrels.

5. Chardonnay - Viña Casa Silva: A white wine made from the Chardonnay grape variety, it is fermented in oak barrels and aged for 8 months.

6. Syrah - Viña Matetic: This red wine is made from the Syrah grape variety and is aged in oak barrels for 12 months.

Colombia:

1. Camino Chardonnay - Viña Marqués de Puntalarga: A white wine made from the Chardonnay grape variety, it is fermented and aged in oak barrels.

2. Raíces Cabernet Sauvignon Reserva - Viñedo de los Andes: Produced from the Cabernet Sauvignon grape variety, this wine is aged in oak barrels for 8 months.

3. País - Vinícola Eureka: Made from the País grape variety, this wine is fermented in stainless steel tanks.

4. Dorado Tempranillo Malbec - Viñedo San Pedro: A red wine made from the Tempranillo and Malbec grape varieties, it is aged in oak barrels for 12 months.

5. Angelica Rosado - Viña Santa Bárbara: A rosé wine made from a blend of grape varieties, it is fermented in stainless steel tanks.

6. Cepas de la Montaña Gran Reserva Cabernet Sauvignon - Viña Bauzá: This red wine is made from the Cabernet Sauvignon grape variety and is aged in oak barrels for 12 months.

Ecuador:

1. Latitude 0° Carmenere - Hosteria La Andaluza: Made from the Carmenere grape variety, this wine is fermented and aged in oak barrels.

2. ZDS Parcela 26 Syrah - Zuleta Wines: A red wine made from the Syrah grape variety, it is aged in oak barrels for 8 months.

3. Clos des Cosses Merlot - Bodegas Molleturo: Produced from the Merlot grape variety, this wine is aged in oak barrels for 12 months.

4. Montesacro Chardonnay - Clos de Luz: A white wine made from the Chardonnay grape variety, it is fermented in oak barrels.

5. Selva Andina Clairette - Bodega Selva Andina: A white wine made from the Clairette grape variety, it is fermented in stainless steel tanks.

6. Sanguino - Hacienda El Porvenir: This red wine is made from a blend of grape varieties and is aged in oak barrels for 12 months.

Uruguay:

1. Tannat - Bodega Garzón: Produced from the Tannat grape variety, this wine is aged in oak barrels for 12 months.

2. Albariño - Bodega Garzón: A white wine made from the Albariño grape variety, it is fermented in stainless steel tanks.

3. Zinfandel - Bouza Bodega Boutique: Made from the Zinfandel grape variety, this wine is aged in oak barrels for 12 months.

4. Tempranillo - Bodega Familia Irurtia: This red wine is made from the Tempranillo grape variety and is aged in oak barrels for 8 months.

5. Cabernet Franc - Viñedo de los Vientos: Produced from the Cabernet Franc grape variety, this wine is aged in oak barrels for 12 months.

6. Marselan - Bodega Bouza: This red wine is made from the Marselan grape variety and is aged in oak barrels for 12 months.

Venezuela:

1. La Casa del Blanco - Bodegas Pomar: A white wine made from a blend of grape varieties, it is fermented in oak barrels.

2. Don Leo Reserva - Bodegas Pomar: This red wine is made from a blend of grape varieties and is aged in oak barrels for 12 months.

3. Tierra Blanca Cabernet Sauvignon Reserva - Bodegas Pomar: Produced from the Cabernet Sauvignon grape variety, this wine is aged in oak barrels for 12 months.

4. Rojizo Rosé - Bodegas Pomar: A rosé wine made from a blend of grape varieties, it is fermented in stainless steel tanks.

5. Malandra - Bodegas Pomar: Made from a blend of grape varieties, this wine is fermented in stainless steel tanks.

6. Nube Negra - Bodegas Pomar: This red wine is made from a blend of grape varieties and is aged in oak barrels for 12 months.

Bolivia:

1. Santa Ana Malbec - Bodega Santa Ana: Produced from the Malbec grape variety, this wine is aged in oak barrels for 12 months.

2. Alcohuaz Rosado - Finca Alcohuaz: A rosé wine made from a blend of grape varieties, it is fermented in stainless steel tanks.

3. Bodegas Kohlberg Cabernet Sauvignon Gran Reserva - Bodegas Kohlberg: This red wine is made from the Cabernet Sauvignon grape variety and is aged in oak barrels for 12 months.

4. Alcohuaz Syrah - Finca Alcohuaz: Made from the Syrah grape variety, this wine is aged in oak barrels for 18 months.

5. Aranjuez Tannat - Bodegas Aranjuez: Produced from the Tannat grape variety, this wine is aged in oak barrels for 12 months.

6. Sausini Estibador - Sausini Vinos: This red wine is made from a blend of grape varieties and is aged in oak barrels for 12 months.

Guyana, Paraguay, Peru, and Suriname do not currently produce significant amounts of wine for export.

Foods

South America is known for its rich cultural diversity and culinary heritage. It offers a vast range of cuisines, each unique and flavorful in its own way. Here are some of the most popular foods of South America, categorised by country:

1. **Argentina:**

Argentina is known for its famous meat cuisine, particularly beef. Argentine beef is of exceptional quality and is mostly grass-fed. Asado, a traditional beef barbecue, is a popular delicacy. Empanadas, a type of pastry filled with meat, cheese, or vegetables, are also commonly enjoyed.

2. **Brazil:**

Brazil is famous for its diverse cuisine, incorporating flavours from African, European, and indigenous cultures. Feijoada, a black bean stew with pork and beef, is a national dish. Churrasco, a type of grilled meat, and Brigadeiro, a chocolate truffle dessert, are also popular.

3. **Chile:**

Chilean cuisine is unique, with a blend of seafood, meat, and vegetables. Seafood dishes like ceviche and caldillo de congrio, a soup made with eel, are enjoyed. Chilean empanadas, filled with cheese and beef, are also popular.

4. **Colombia:**

Colombian cuisine is known for its diverse range of dishes. Arepas, a type of cornmeal flatbread, and Bandeja Paisa, which is a hearty dish of rice, beans, and meat, are common. Colombian coffee is also renowned for its rich and bold flavour.

5. **Peru:**

Peruvian cuisine has become popular globally in recent years. Known for using unique ingredients such as quinoa and purple corn, ceviche, a dish made with raw fish marinated in lime juice and spices, is a staple in Peru. Lomo Saltado, a beef stir-fry with potatoes and rice, is also popular.

6. Uruguay:

Uruguayan cuisine is very meat-centric, with popular dishes including chivito, a sandwich filled with meat, cheese, and vegetables, and parrilla, a type of barbecue. Uruguayan wine is also popular globally and is grown in the country's vineyards.

South American culinary expertise is marked by its use of unique ingredients, spices, and herbs, coupled with a combination of local, European, and African influences. The cuisine of South America has been influenced by its colonial history and indigenous cultures, making it an exciting blend of flavours, textures, and traditions.

Pairing Food and Wine

Here are some traditional foods and wines from South America and their paired counterparts:

1. Argentina:

a. Beef Empanadas - Torrontes

b. Asado - Malbec

c. Milanesa - Bonarda

d. Chimichurri - Cabernet Sauvignon

e. Provoleta - Pinot Noir

Argentina is best known for its beef and wine production. They are the largest producers of Malbec grapes and the wines produced from them are world-renowned. Torrontes and Pinot Noir are other popular varieties in the country. Asado is a traditional barbecue dish that pairs perfectly with Malbec. Milanesa, a breaded fried beef cutlet, goes well with Bonarda, a fruity red.

2. Bolivia:

a. Salteñas - Malbec

b. Silpancho - Cabernet Sauvignon

c. Charquecan - Torrontes

d. Llajua - Merlot

e. Chicha - Sauvignon Blanc

Bolivia's cuisine is diverse and influenced by the country's indigenous populations. Salteñas, a traditional pastry filled with spicy meat, potatoes and vegetables, pairs well with Malbec's fruity and spicy notes. Silpancho, a popular beef dish, goes well with Cabernet Sauvignon's full-bodied flavour. Chicha is a traditional corn-based beverage that pairs well with light bodied Sauvignon Blanc.

3. Brazil:

a. Feijoada - Tannat

b. Coxinha - Moscato

c. Picanha - Cabernet Franc

d. Brigadeiro - Merlot

e. Caipirinha - Cachaça

Brazil's cuisine has influences from Portugal, Africa, and indigenous people. Feijoada, a traditional meat stew, pairs well with Tenant's bold and tannic structure. Coxinha, a popular snack stuffed with shredded chicken, pairs well with Moscato's sweet and fruity taste. Picanha, a cut of meat grilled with sea salt, goes well with Cabernet Franc's structure and light tannins.

4. Chile:

a. Ceviche - Sauvignon Blanc

b. Pastel de Choclo - Chardonnay

c. Empanadas De Pino - Pinot Noir

d. Churrasco - Cabernet Sauvignon

e. Sopaipillas - Malbec

Chile is known for its seafood, wine, and stunning landscapes. Ceviche, a popular citrus marinade seafood dish, pairs well with Sauvignon Blanc's light, crisp flavour. Pastel de Choclo, a savoury corn-based pie, pairs well with the rich and buttery flavour of Chardonnay. Empanadas De Pino, a traditional stuffed pastry filled with beef and onion, pairs well with Pinot Noir's earthy and fruity flavour.

5. **Colombia:**

a. Arepas - Chardonnay

b. Bandeja Paisa - Merlot

c. Sancocho - Cabernet Sauvignon

d. Empanadas - Sauvignon Blanc

e. Ajiaco - Malbec

Colombian cuisine is diverse and influenced by the country's history and geography. Arepas, a traditional corn-based dish, pairs well with Chardonnay's crisp and light flavour. Bandeja Paisa, a platter of beans, rice, meat, and plantains, pairs well with Merlot's smooth and mellow taste. Sancocho, a soup with meat, vegetables, and plantains, pairs well with Cabernet Sauvignon's bold and tannic notes.

6. **Ecuador:**

a. Ceviche - Sauvignon Blanc

b. Llapingachos - Pinot Noir

c. Fanesca - Muscat

d. Hornado - Cabernet Sauvignon

e. Conchas Asadas - Chardonnay

Ecuador's cuisine is diverse and influenced by the country's geography and indigenous populations. Ceviche pairs well with Sauvignon Blanc's light and crisp flavour. Llapingachos, a traditional potato fritter, pairs well with Pinot Noir's silky texture and fruity flavour. Fanesca, a soup made from grains and legumes, pairs well with Muscat's sweetness and floral notes.

7. **Guyana:**

a. Pepperpot - Malbec

b. Metemgee - Chardonnay

c. Cook-up Rice - Cabernet Sauvignon

d. Cassava Bread - Syrah

e. Roti - Sauvignon Blanc

Guyana's cuisine is influenced by its African, Indian, and indigenous populations. Pepperpot, a stew made from pork, sticks and spices, pairs well with Malbec's bold and tannic structure. Metemgee, a traditional mixed meat and vegetable soup, pairs well with Chardonnay's crisp and light flavour. Cook-up Rice, a rice dish with peas and meat, pairs well with Cabernet Sauvignon's structure and light tannins.

8. **Paraguay:**

a. Sopa Paraguaya - Chardonnay

b. Bori Bori - Malbec

c. Chipa - Cabernet Sauvignon

d. Asado Paraguayo - Syrah

e. Terere - Sauvignon Blanc

Paraguayan cuisine is influenced by the country's indigenous populations and its neighbours. Sopa Paraguaya, a traditional corn-based bread, pairs well with Chardonnay's crisp and light flavour. Bori Bori, a soup with meatballs made from cornmeal, pairs well with Malbec's fruity and spicy notes. Chipa, a cheese bread, pairs well with Cabernet Sauvignon's bold and tannic structure.

9. **Peru:**

a. Ceviche - Sauvignon Blanc

b. Lomo Saltado - Malbec

c. Aji De Gallina - Pinot Noir

d. Rocoto Relleno - Carmenere

e. Arroz Con Mariscos - Chardonnay

Peruvian cuisine is known for its use of seafood and spices. Ceviche pairs well with Sauvignon Blanc's light and crisp flavour. Lomo Saltado, a beef stir fry with onions and garlic, pairs well with Malbec's fruity and spicy notes.Aji De Gallina, a spicy chicken curry, pairs well with Pinot Noir's earthy and fruity flavour.

10. **Suriname:**

a. Pom - Sauvignon Blanc

b. Moksi Meti - Malbec

c. Roti - Chardonnay

d. Nasi Goreng - Cabernet Sauvignon

e. Bami Goreng - Pinot Noir

Suriname's cuisine is influenced by its mixed population of indigenous people, Africans, Indians, and Chinese. Pom, a casserole made with chicken and tamarind, pairs well with Sauvignon Blanc's light and crisp flavour. Moksi Meti, a mixed meat dish, pairs well with Malbec's bold and tannic structure.

11. **Uruguay:**

a. Chivito - Tannat

b. Asado - Cabernet Sauvignon

c. Torta Frita - Sauvignon Blanc

d. Pancho - Merlot

e. Medio Y Medio - Chardonnay

Uruguay is known for its beef and wine production. Chivito, a sandwich made with beef, ham, cheese, and vegetables, pairs well with Tenant's bold and tannic structure. Asado, a traditional barbecue dish, pairs well with Cabernet Sauvignon's full-bodied flavour. Medio Y Medio, a mix of white and sparkling wine, pairs well with Chardonnay's crisp and light flavour.

12. **Venezuela:**

a. Arepas - Sauvignon Blanc

b. Hallaca - Malbec

c. Asado Negro - Cabernet Sauvignon

d. Cachapas - Chardonnay

e. Pabellón Criollo - Merlot

Venezuelan cuisine is diverse and influenced by its indigenous and colonial populations. Arepas, a corn-based dish, pairs well with Sauvignon Blanc's light and crisp flavour. Hallaca, a tamale-like dish made from cornmeal and filled with beef, pork or chicken, pairs well with Malbec's fruity and spicy notes. Asado Negro, a slow-cooked beef dish, pairs well with Cabernet Sauvignon's full-bodied flavor. Pabellón Criollo, a dish made of beans, rice, and shredded beef, pairs well with Merlot's smooth and mellow taste.

Pairing South American Wines with Foods from the rest of the World

Here are five wines from each of the 12 countries in South America, along with suggested pairings with foods from around the world:

1. **Argentina:**

- Malbec: This full-bodied red wine pairs well with rich, savoury flavours like grilled steak, hearty stews, and roasted vegetables.

- Torrontes: A white wine with floral and citrus notes, perfect for pairing with lighter fare like seafood, sushi, and spicy Thai dishes.

- Bonarda: A medium-bodied red wine with bold fruit flavours and a touch of spice, pairs well with Mediterranean cuisine, particularly dishes like grilled eggplant, hummus, and falafel.

- Cabernet Franc: This varietal offers an interesting alternative to the more common Cabernet Sauvignon, with notes of blackberry, black pepper, and vanilla that pair well with grilled meats and roasted vegetables.

- Chardonnay: A rich, full-bodied white with flavors of butter, vanilla, and tropical fruit, pairs well with creamy pastas or roasted chicken.

2. Bolivia:

- Tannat: A bold red wine with strong tannins and flavours of blackberry and plum, pairs well with grilled meats or hearty stews.

- Moscatel de Alejandría: A sweet white wine with floral and honeyed notes, pairs well with cheese plates or desserts like fruit tarts or crème brûlée.

- Cabernet Sauvignon: Bolivia's Cabernet Sauvignon is notable for its bright acidity and notes of cassis and cedar, making it a great match for dishes like grilled lamb or roasted vegetables.

- Malbec: The Malbecs of Bolivia are known for their high acidity and bold flavours, and pair well with strong cheeses or grilled meats.

- Chardonnay: A well-balanced white wine with flavours of citrus, apple, and oak, pairs well with creamy pastas, roasted chicken, or seafood dishes.

3. Brazil:

- Merlot: This soft, fruity red wine pairs well with pizza or pasta dishes that feature tomato sauce, as well as roasted or grilled meats.

- Cabernet Sauvignon: With brighter acidity and fuller body than some other South American Cabernet Sauvignons, this wine pairs well with bold-flavoured dishes like grilled pork chops, spicy sausages, or grilled vegetables.

- Tannat: A popular variety in Brazil, Tannat is known for its bold intensity and strong tannins, and pairs well with hearty stews, roasted meats, and even dark chocolate.

- Chardonnay: The unoaked Chardonnays of Brazil feature flavours of tropical fruit and a clean finish, making them a great match for spicy dishes or light seafood.

- Pinot Noir: Brazil's Pinot Noirs can be light-bodied and delicate, with notes of strawberry and spice that pair well with sushi, cured meats, or mild cheeses.

4. Chile:

- Carmenere: Chile's signature grape, Carmenere has flavours of dark fruit and chocolate that pair well with red meats, stews, and spicy dishes.

- Sauvignon Blanc: A bright, crisp white wine with flavours of citrus and green apple, pairs well with seafood dishes, light pasta, or grilled chicken.

- Cabernet Sauvignon: With bold tannins and notes of black currant and vanilla, Chilean Cabernet Sauvignon pairs well with grilled meats, hearty stews, and roasted vegetables.

- Merlot: A medium-bodied red wine with flavours of black cherry and plum, pairs well with tomato-based pasta dishes or roasted pork.

- Pinot Noir: Light-bodied with notes of raspberry and spice, Chilean Pinot Noir pairs well with light salads or roasted chicken.

5. Colombia:

- Malbec: A popular variety in Colombia, Malbec has bold flavours of dark fruit and chocolate that pair well with grilled meats, stews, or roasted vegetables.

- Chardonnay: With notes of tropical fruit and a slightly buttery finish, Colombian Chardonnay pairs well with light seafood dishes, creamy pastas, or roasted chicken.

- Sauvignon Blanc: A crisp, acidic white wine with flavours of green apple and citrus, pairs well with seafood dishes or lighter salads.

- Syrah: Full-bodied with notes of blackberry and black pepper, Colombian Syrah pairs well with hearty stews, spicy dishes, and roasted red meats.

- Viognier: An aromatic white wine with notes of peach and apricot, pairs well with spicy Asian dishes or cured meats.

6. Ecuador:

- Syrah: Ecuadorian Syrah is known for its bold intensity and strong tannins, and pairs well with grilled meats, hearty stews, and spicy dishes.

- Merlot: A medium-bodied red wine with flavours of black cherry and plum, pairs well with hearty pasta dishes or roasted pork.

- Chardonnay: Ecuador's Chardonnays offer flavours of tropical fruit and a slightly buttery finish, making them a great match for light seafood dishes or creamy pastas.

- Moscatel: A sweet, floral white wine that pairs well with cheese plates or desserts like fruit tarts or crème brûlée.

- Cabernet Sauvignon: With bold tannins and notes of black currant and vanilla, Ecuadorian Cabernet Sauvignon pairs well with grilled meats, hearty stews, and roasted vegetables.

7. **Guyana**:

- Shiraz: A well-balanced red wine, pairs well with spicy dishes, grilled meats, or hearty stews.

- Chenin Blanc: A crisp, acidic white wine that pairs well with seafood dishes or lighter salads.

- Cabernet Sauvignon: With bold tannins and notes of black currant and vanilla, Guyanese Cabernet Sauvignon pairs well with grilled meats, hearty stews, and roasted vegetables.

- Merlot: A medium-bodied red wine with flavours of black cherry and plum, pairs well with tomato-based pasta dishes or roasted pork.

- Pinotage: A South African grape that has gained popularity in Guyana, Pinotage has bold flavours of blackberry and coffee that pair well with grilled meats, hearty stews, and spicy dishes.

8. Paraguay:

- Tannat: A bold red wine with strong tannins and flavours of blackberry and plum, pairs well with grilled meats or hearty stews.

- Cabernet Sauvignon: Paraguayan Cabernet Sauvignon is known for its bright acidity and notes of cassis and cedar, making it a great match for dishes like grilled lamb or roasted vegetables.

- Malbec: The Malbecs of Paraguay are known for their high acidity and bold flavours, and pair well with strong cheeses or grilled meats.

- Merlot: This soft, fruity red wine pairs well with pizza or pasta dishes that feature tomato sauce, as well as roasted or grilled meats.

- Chardonnay: A well-balanced white wine with flavours of citrus, apple, and oak, pairs well with creamy pastas, roasted chicken, or seafood dishes.

9. **Peru**:

- Malbec: A popular varietal in Peru, Malbec has bold flavours of dark fruit and chocolate that pair well with grilled meats, stews, or roasted vegetables.

- Carménère: A rich, full-bodied red wine with flavours of blackberry and chocolate, pairs well with grilled meats, hearty stews, and roasted vegetables.

- Torrontes: Peru's aromatic white wine pairs well with light seafood dishes, sushi, or spicy Thai dishes.

- Cabernet Sauvignon: With bold tannins and notes of black currant and vanilla, Peruvian Cabernet Sauvignon pairs well with grilled meats, hearty stews, and roasted vegetables.

- Syrah: Full-bodied with notes of blackberry and black pepper, Peruvian Syrah pairs well with hearty stews, spicy dishes, and roasted red meats.

10. **Suriname**:

- Chenin Blanc: A crisp, acidic white wine that pairs well with seafood dishes or lighter salads.

- Shiraz: A well-balanced red wine, pairs well with spicy dishes, grilled meats, or hearty stews.

- Malbec: The Malbecs of Suriname are known for their high acidity and bold flavours, and pair well with strong cheeses or grilled meats.

- Pinot Noir: Light-bodied with notes of raspberry and spice, Surinamese Pinot Noir pairs well with light salads or roasted chicken.

- Cabernet Sauvignon: With bold tannins and notes of black currant and vanilla, Surinamese Cabernet Sauvignon pairs well with grilled meats, hearty stews, and roasted vegetables.

11. **Uruguay**:

- Tannat: Uruguay's signature grape, Tannat is known for its bold intensity and strong tannins, and pairs well with hearty stews, roasted meats, and even dark chocolate.

- Albariño: A crisp, aromatic white wine with flavours of lemon and apple, pairs well with seafood dishes, light pasta, or grilled chicken.

- Cabernet Franc: With notes of blackberry and tobacco, Uruguayan Cabernet Franc pairs well with grilled meats, roasted vegetables, or hearty stews.

- Viognier: A floral white wine with notes of peach and apricot, pairs well with spicy Asian dishes or cured meats.

- Pinot Noir: Light-bodied with notes of raspberry and spice, Uruguayan Pinot Noir pairs well with light salads or roasted chicken.

12. **Venezuela**:

- Syrah: Full-bodied with notes of blackberry and black pepper, Venezuelan Syrah pairs well with hearty stews, spicy dishes, and roasted red meats.

- Cabernet Sauvignon: With bold tannins and notes of black currant and vanilla, Venezuelan Cabernet Sauvignon pairs well with grilled meats, hearty stews, and roasted vegetables.

- Chardonnay: Venezuelan Chardonnays offer flavours of tropical fruit and a slightly buttery finish, making them a great match for light seafood dishes or creamy pastas.

- Merlot: A medium-bodied red wine with flavours of black cherry and plum, pairs well with tomato-based pasta dishes or roasted pork.

- Pinot Noir: Light-bodied with notes of raspberry and spice, Venezuelan Pinot Noir pairs well with light salads or roasted chicken.

I hope these pairings help you find your perfect match!

Pairing South American Foods with Wines from the rest of the World

Here are 5 popular dishes from each of the 12 South American countries and a wine pairing that complements each dish:

1. **Argentina**

- Asado (barbecue)

- Empanadas (savoury pastry)

- Matambre (stuffed flank steak)

- Chimichurri (flavoured condiment)

- Milanesa (breaded meat)

Wine pairing: Malbec, a red wine variety from Argentina. A full-bodied Malbec pairs well with asado and matambre, which are both beef dishes. The wine's smooth tannins and rich fruit flavours also balance well with the bold flavours of chimichurri and empanadas.

2. **Bolivia**

- Salteñas (savoury pastry)

- Silpancho (beef dish with potatoes and rice)

- Chairo soup (potato and meat soup)

- Fricasé (pork stew with potatoes)

- Cuñapé (cheese bread)

Wine pairing: Carmenere, a red wine variety commonly grown in Chile but also found in Bolivia. Its soft tannins complement the spicy and savoury flavours of salteñas and fricasé. Its herbal notes also cut through the richness of chairo soup and the cheesy goodness of cuñapé.

3. **Brazil**

- Feijoada (pork and bean stew)

- Coxinha (chicken croquette)

- Pão de Queijo (cheese bread)

- Moqueca (seafood stew)

- Brigadieros (chocolate truffles)

Wine pairing: Vinho Verde, a light and acidic white wine from Portugal. The wine's crisp and effervescent quality pairs well with the hearty and meaty feijoada, while its citrus flavors balance the richness of moqueca. The wine's slight effervescence also cuts through the heaviness of the cheese in pão de queijo and brigadeiros.

4. **Chile**

- Ceviche (raw fish marinated in lime juice)

- Empanadas de pino (savory pastry)

- Pastel de Choclo (corn pie)

- Asado (barbecue)

- Curanto (seafood and meat stew)

Wine pairing: Sauvignon Blanc, a white wine with high acidity and lively herbal and citrus flavours. Its bright acidity and herbaceous notes complement the tanginess of ceviche and the spiciness of empanadas de pino. It also pairs well with the sweetness of pastel de choclo and the richness of curanto.

5. Colombia

- Bandeja Paisa (mixed dish with beans, rice, meat, and avocado)

- Arepas (corn cakes)

- Ajiaco (potato soup with chicken)

- Lechona (stuffed pig roast)

- Buñuelos (cheese fritters)

Wine pairing: Chardonnay, a full-bodied white wine with buttery and oaky notes. Its rich flavour matches well with the protein and fat content in bandeja paisa and lechona. Its soft tannins also complement the crispy texture of arepas and buñuelos. The wine's creamy texture also balances the spiciness and tanginess of ajiaco.

6. Ecuador

- Ceviche (raw fish marinated in lime juice)

- Locro (potato soup with cheese and avocado)

- Encebollado (seafood stew with onions)

- Llapingachos (potato cakes with cheese)

- Quimbolitos (sweet steamed cakes)

Wine pairing: Torrontés, a white wine with floral and fruity notes. Its bright acidity and refreshing palate balance the tanginess of ceviche and encebollado. Its sweetness also matches well with the creaminess of locro and llapingachos. Finally, its fruity notes match the sweetness of quimbolitos.

7. Guyana

- Pepper pot (stew with meat and pepper)

- Roti (flatbread filled with savoury filling)

- Chow mcin (noodle stir fry)

- Cook-up rice (rice and bean dish)

- Metemgee (fish and root vegetable soup)

Wine pairing: Shiraz/Syrah, a red wine with spicy and fruity flavours. Its peppery notes match well with the heat of pepper pot and the spices of chow mein. Its herbal flavor also complements the richness of roti and cook-up rice. Finally, its fruity taste matches the subtle sweetness of metemgee.

8. Paraguay

- Sopa paraguaya (cornbread and cheese casserole)

- Chipa (cheese bread)

- Bife koygua (beef with tomato sauce)

- Chipa guazu (corn and cheese casserole)

- Soyo paraguayo (beef and vegetable stew)

Wine pairing: Pinot Noir, a light-bodied red wine with fruit and earthy flavours. Its low tannins match well with the mild cheese flavour of sopa paraguaya and chips. Its fruitiness also matches the richness of bife koygua and soyo paraguayo. Finally, its earthy notes balance the corn flavour in chipa guazu.

9. Peru

- Ceviche (raw fish marinated in lime juice)

- Lomo saltado (beef stir-fry with fries)

- Papa a la Huancaína (potatoes in spicy cheese sauce)

- Anticuchos (beef heart skewers)

- Pollo a la brasa (spit-roasted chicken)

Wine pairing: Syrah, a red wine with spicy and smoky flavours. Its bold flavour matches well with the tanginess of ceviche and the spiciness of papa a la huancaína. Its smoky flavor also balances well with the charred and grilled flavours in anticuchos and pollo a la brasa. Finally, its rich profile adds depth to the bold flavours in lomo saltado.

10. Suriname

- Nasi goreng (fried rice with meat and vegetables)

- Saoto soup (chicken and vegetable soup)

- Bakabana (fried plantains)

- Pom (taro root baked with meat and spices)

- Moksi meti (mixed meat dish)

Wine pairing: Merlot, a red wine with a soft tannic profile and black fruit flavor. Its smooth texture matches well with the mild flavours of nasi goreng and saoto soup. Its fruitiness also elevates the sweetness of bakabana and the flavours of pom. Finally, its structure complements the bold flavours in moksi meti.

11. Uruguay

- Chivito (steak sandwich with cheese and egg)

- Asado (barbecue)

- Milanesa (breaded meat)

- Pescado con salsa verde (fish with green sauce)

- Tortas fritas (fried dough pastry)

Wine pairing: Tannat, a red wine with high tannin content and dark fruit flavour. Its bold flavour matches well with the smokiness of asado and the richness of milanesa. Its structure also balances the richness of the chivito sandwich. Its fruitiness elevates the flavours of pescado con salsa verde, while its tannins cut through the richness of the dish. Finally, its bold structure elevates the simplistic flavors of tortas fritas.

12. Venezuela

- Arepas (corn cakes)

- Pabellón criollo (rice and bean with beef and fried plantains)

- Hallacas (corn dough stuffed with meat and vegetables)

- Pernil (roast pork)

- Cachapas (corn pancakes with cheese)

Wine pairing: Zinfandel, a red wine with bold and spicy flavours. Its bold flavour matches well with the corn flavour of arepas and cachapas. Its spicy notes also balance the richness and intense flavours of pabellón criollo and hallacas. Finally, its richness elevates the flavour of pernil.

Foods and Wines Phileas Fogg would have enjoyed during his travels through South America

Phileas Fogg would have had many culinary adventures during his travels through South America, where he would have encountered a diverse range of flavours and ingredients. Here are some of the wines and foods he would likely have enjoyed in each of the 12 countries of South America:

1. Argentina:

Wines - Malbec, Bonarda, Cabernet Sauvignon, Torrontés

Foods - Asado (grilled meats), Empanadas, Chimichurri sauce, Dulce de leche

2. Bolivia:

Wines - **Singani**

Foods - Salteñas (empanadas with a spicy filling), Chicharrón (deep-fried pork), Sajta de pollo (chicken stew with potatoes and peanut sauce)

3. **Brazil:**

Wines - Caipirinhas (cocktail made with cachaça, a sugarcane-based spirit)

Foods - Feijoada (black bean stew), Churrasco (grilled meat), Coxinha (chicken croquettes), Pão de queijo (cheese bread)

4. **Chile:**

Wines - Carménère, Cabernet Sauvignon, Chardonnay

Foods - Empanadas de pino (beef and onion empanadas), Pastel de choclo (corn and beef pie), Ceviche, Curanto (seafood stew cooked in a hole in the ground)

5. **Colombia:**

Wines - Aguardiente (anise-flavoured liquor)

Foods - Bandeja paisa (a hearty platter of rice, beans, eggs, meat, and avocado), Arepas (cornmeal cakes), Sancocho (chicken soup with plantains)

6. **Ecuador:**

Wines - Chardonnay, Sauvignon Blanc

Foods - Llapingachos (potato pancakes stuffed with cheese), Ceviche, Locro de papas (potato soup with cheese and avocado)

7. **Guyana:**

Wines - none produced locally

Foods - Pepperpot (spicy beef stew), Roti (flatbread filled with curry), Metemgee (rice and meat stew)

8. **Paraguay:**

Wines - Ka'aró (lemon-flavored liquor)

Foods - Sopa paraguaya (cornbread with onions and cheese), Chipa (cheese bread), Asado (grilled meats)

9. **Peru:**

Wines - Pisco (grape brandy)

Foods - Ceviche, Lomo saltado (beef stir-fry), Ají de gallina (chicken in creamy chili sauce), Anticuchos (beef heart skewers)

10. **Suriname:**

Wines - none produced locally

Foods - Pom (cassava dish with meat or fish), Roti (flatbread filled with curry), Bami (noodle dish with chicken or shrimp)

11. **Uruguay:**

Wines - Tannat

Foods - Chivito (steak sandwich with ham, cheese, lettuce, tomato, and egg), Parrillada (mixed grill of meats), Tarta de fresas (strawberry tart)

12. **Venezuela:**

Wines - none produced locally

Foods - Arepas, Pabellón criollo (shredded beef with black beans, rice, and plantains), Empanadas, Hallacas (meat and vegetable tamales)

Seasonal Pairings

Pairing Food and Wine for Summer/Winter drinking:

Argentina:

Summer - Empanadas with Torrontés wine

Winter - Grilled meat with Malbec wine

Bolivia:

Summer - Papas a la Huancaína with Sauvignon Blanc wine

Winter - Picante de Pollo with Carmenère wine

Brazil:

Summer - Feijoada with Caipirinha cocktail

Winter - Coxinha with Tannat wine

Chile:

Summer - Ceviche with Sauvignon Blanc wine

Winter - Pastel de Choclo with Cabernet Sauvignon wine

Colombia:

Summer - Arepas con Queso with Chenin Blanc wine

Winter - Ajiaco with Syrah wine

Ecuador:

Summer - Encebollado with Chardonnay wine

Winter - Locro de Papas with Pinot Noir wine

Guyana:

Summer - Pepperpot with Rosé wine

Winter - Cook-up Rice with Merlot wine

Paraguay:

Summer - Sopa Paraguaya with Torrontés wine

Winter - Chipa with Malbec wine

Peru:

Summer - Tiradito with Pisco Sour cocktail

Winter - Carapulcra with Cabernet Franc wine

Suriname:

Summer - Pom with White Zinfandel wine

Winter - Roti with Pinotage wine

Uruguay:

Summer - Chivito with Albariño wine

Winter - Asado with Tannat wine

Venezuela:

Summer - Hallacas with Moscato wine

Winter - Pabellón Criollo with Merlot wine

Pairing Food and Wine for Formal/Informal dining:

When it comes to pairing food and wine from South America, there is an incredible variety of flavours and textures to choose from. Here are some suggestions for formal/informal dining from 12 South American countries:

1. **Argentina**: If you're serving a grilled beef dish, like asado or chimichurri steak, a Malbec would be a perfect match. The full-bodied wine has a tannic structure that pairs well with the fatty steak. For an informal meal, you may also choose to try a lighter red like a Cabernet Sauvignon or a Pinot Noir.

2. **Brazil**: Feijoada, Brazil's national dish made with black beans, sausage, and pork, pairs well with a fruity, low-tannin red wine like Merlot, which can complement the pork and cut through the richness of the beans. However, for a more formal dining experience, you may prefer to select a full-bodied red like a Carmenere that will stand up to the rich and spicy flavours of the dish.

3. **Chile**: Seafood is a staple in Chile, and one popular dish is ceviche, which is made with raw fish marinated in lime juice and spices. Ceviche pairs well with a crisp, acidic white wine like Sauvignon Blanc, which can cut through the richness of the seafood and complement the citrus flavors in the dish.

4. **Colombia**: Arroz con pollo, a popular chicken and rice dish, can be paired with a medium-bodied red like a Crianza Rioja, which will complement the natural sweetness of the chicken and the spices of the dish.

5. **Ecuador**: When it comes to pairing food and wine from Ecuador, you might consider a light-bodied white wine, like a Torrontes, which can complement the freshness of dishes like encebollado, a fish soup with onions, cilantro, and lime.

6. **Guyana**: Curry chicken, a popular dish in Guyana, pairs best with a light, crisp white wine like a Pinot Grigio, which can cut through the richness of the curry and complement the spiciness of the dish.

7. **Paraguay**: While Paraguay is known for its hearty stews, one of its most famous foods is chipa, a cheese bread made with mandioca starch. A light, fruity red like a Tempranillo can complement the cheese and spices in this dish if you want to have a casual dining experience.

8. **Peru**: Lomo saltado, a stir-fry dish made with beef, onions, and tomatoes, pairs well with a light-bodied red like a Pinot Noir. Alternatively, you can go for a crisp white wine like a Chardonnay if your meal is more formal.

9. **Suriname**: Surinamese cuisine is influenced by Indonesian and Creole cuisine, so you may consider pairing dishes like nasi goreng (fried rice) with a medium-bodied red like a Merlot.

10. **Uruguay**: Uruguay is famous for its tannat wines, which pair well with rich, meaty dishes like parrillada, a mixed grill of beef, pork, and sausages. Tannat is full-bodied with strong tannins that can complement the richness of the meat.

11. **Venezuela**: Pabellón criollo, a traditional dish made with shredded beef, black beans, and fried plantains, pairs well with a light, crisp white wine like a Sauvignon Blanc. The acidity pairs well with the richness of the beef and the sweetness of the plantains.

12. **Bolivia**: For dishes like salteñas, Bolivian-style empanadas with a sweet and savory filling, a sparkling wine like Prosecco or Cava can be the perfect complement. The effervescence can cut through the rich filling, while the sweetness can balance the savoury flavours.

In summary, South America offers a wide range of food and wine pairings for formal and informal dining. By following these guidelines, you'll be able to choose the perfect drink to complement the rich textures and flavours of these traditional dishes.

Phileas Fogg's journey through South America

Phileas Fogg would have encountered a wide variety of local people during his travels through South America, each with their own unique cultures, customs, and cuisines.

In Argentina, Fogg would have met the indigenous Mapuche people and tasted their traditional dishes like empanadas, asado (grilled meat), and yerba mate tea. The country is also known for its excellent wines, especially Malbec and Torrontes.

In Bolivia, Fogg would have encountered the Aymara and Quechua people, who are known for their textiles and handcrafted goods. He would have had the opportunity to try local specialties like salteñas (pastry pockets filled with meat, potatoes, and vegetables), pique macho (a spicy beef and potato dish), and chicha (a fermented corn drink).

In Brazil, Fogg would have experienced the diverse cultures of the country, from the indigenous tribes of the Amazon Rainforest to the Afro-Brazilian communities in Salvador. He would have tried famous dishes like feijoada (a stew of beans and meat) and churrasco (grilled meat) and sampled the national drink, caipirinha, made from cachaca, lime, sugar, and ice.

In Chile, Fogg would have met the Mapuche people, who have a strong connection to their ancestral land and traditions. He would have tasted local specialties like pastel de choclo (a corn and meat pie) and pisco sour (a cocktail made with pisco, lime juice, egg whites, and simple syrup).

In Colombia, Fogg would have experienced the warmth and hospitality of the Colombian people and tasted dishes like bandeja paisa (a hearty plate of beans, rice, meat, and plantains), arepas (corn cakes filled with cheese, meat, or vegetables), and aguardiente (a sugarcane-based spirit).

In Ecuador, Fogg would have met the indigenous Quechua people and learned about their culture and traditions. He would have tried local dishes like ceviche (fish marinated in citrus juice) and locro de papas (a potato soup with cheese, avocado, and corn).

In Guyana, Fogg would have experienced the country's mix of Caribbean, South American, and Indian cultures. He would have tasted dishes like pepperpot (a spicy meat stew) and roti (a type of flatbread filled with curried meat, vegetables, or chickpeas).

In Paraguay, Fogg would have met the Guarani people and tried local specialties like chipa (a type of bread made with cheese and cornmeal) and sopa paraguaya (a cornbread with cheese and onions). He would have also tasted the country's refreshing drink, tereré, made from yerba mate and cold water.

In Peru, Fogg would have explored the diverse cuisine of the country, from the famous ceviche to dishes like lomo saltado (stir-fried beef) and ají de gallina (a chicken and chili pepper stew). He would have also tasted the national drink, pisco, distilled from grapes and used in the popular cocktail, pisco sour.

In Suriname, Fogg would have experienced the country's mix of African, Indian, and Indonesian cultures. He would have tried dishes like pom (a casserole with chicken or fish and root vegetables) and roti (a flatbread with curried meat and potatoes).

In Uruguay, Fogg would have met the gaucho cowboys and tasted the country's famous beef, grilled over an open flame. He would have also tried local dishes like chivito (a sandwich filled with steak, ham, cheese, and egg) and drank the country's tannat wine.

In Venezuela, Fogg would have experienced the country's blend of Spanish, African, and indigenous cultures. He would have tasted dishes like arepas and pabellón criollo (a dish with shredded beef, black beans, rice, and fried plantains). He would have also tried the national drink, rum, made from sugarcane.

Overall, Fogg would have had the opportunity to try a wide variety of delicious foods and drinks throughout his travels in South America, each reflecting the unique cultures and traditions of the local people he encountered.

12 Top Vineyards of South America

Let's look at some notable vineyards, their wines and the best foods that pair with them

1. **Viña Montes | Chile**

- History: Montes is one of the pioneers of fine winemaking in Chile, founded in 1988 by Aurelio Montes and Douglas Murray.

- Wines: Alpha Cabernet Sauvignon, Purple Angel Carmenere, Outer Limits Sauvignon Blanc, Folly Syrah, Cherub Rosé

- Food Pairings: grilled steak with Alpha Cabernet Sauvignon, roasted lamb with Purple Angel Carmenere, ceviche with Outer Limits Sauvignon Blanc, beef stew with Folly Syrah, grilled shrimp with Cherub Rosé

2. **Bodega Catena Zapata | Argentina**

- History: Catena Zapata is a family-owned winery founded in 1902 by Italian immigrant Nicola Catena.

- Wines: Catena Malbec, White Bones Chardonnay, Nicasia Vineyard Malbec, Adrianna Vineyard Malbec, Catena Alta Cabernet Sauvignon

- Food Pairings: grilled lamb chops with Catena Malbec, lobster with White Bones Chardonnay, roasted beef tenderloin with Nicasia Vineyard Malbec, venison with Adrianna Vineyard Malbec, grilled ribeye steak with Catena Alta Cabernet Sauvignon

3. **Viña Errázuriz | Chile**

- History: Errázuriz is one of the oldest and most respected wineries in Chile, founded in 1870 by Don Maximiano Errázuriz.

- Wines: Don Maximiano Founder's Reserve, Aconcagua Costa Sauvignon Blanc, KAI Cabernet Sauvignon, La Cumbre Syrah, Max Reserva Carmenere

- Food Pairings: roasted duck with Don Maximiano Founder's Reserve, grilled seafood with Aconcagua Costa Sauvignon Blanc, beef stir-fry with KAI Cabernet Sauvignon, roasted pork belly with La Cumbre Syrah, lamb chops with Max Reserva Carmenere

4. **Concha y Toro | Chile**

- History: Concha y Toro is the largest wine producer in Chile, founded in 1883 by Don Melchor and Doña Emiliana.

- Wines: Don Melchor Cabernet Sauvignon, Marques de Casa Concha Carmenere, Terrunyo Sauvignon Blanc, Carmin de Peumo Carmenere, Amelia Chardonnay

- Food Pairings: grilled steak with Don Melchor Cabernet Sauvignon, beef stew with Marques de Casa Concha Carmenere, grilled chicken with Terrunyo Sauvignon Blanc, short ribs with Carmin de Peumo Carmenere, lobster with Amelia Chardonnay

5. **Altair | Chile**

- History: Altair is a boutique winery established in 1993 by a group of Chilean and French investors.

- Wines: Altair Red Blend, Sideral Red Blend, La Luna Cabernet Sauvignon, Vértice Syrah, Kaiken Sauvignon Blanc

- Food Pairings: roasted lamb with Altair Red Blend, beef empanadas with Sideral Red Blend, grilled ribeye steak with La Luna Cabernet Sauvignon, grilled sausage with Vértice Syrah, grilled seafood with Kaiken Sauvignon Blanc

6. Achaval Ferrer | Argentina

- History: Achaval Ferrer was started in 1998 by a group of Italian and Argentine wine enthusiasts.

- Wines: Finca Mirador Malbec, Finca Bella Vista Malbec, Quimera Red Blend, Malbec Mendoza, Cabernet Sauvignon Mendoza

- Food Pairings: grilled beef with Finca Mirador Malbec, pasta with tomato sauce with Finca Bella Vista Malbec, beef brisket with Quimera Red Blend, grilled lamb chops with Malbec Mendoza, grilled pork loin with Cabernet Sauvignon Mendoza

7. Zuccardi | Argentina

- History: Zuccardi is a family-owned winery founded in 1963 by Alberto Zuccardi.

- Wines: Aluvional Gualtallary Malbec, Tito Zuccardi Paraje Altamira Malbec, Concreto Malbec, Polígonos del Valle de Uco Malbec, Q Tempranillo

- Food Pairings: grilled venison with Aluvional Gualtallary Malbec, roasted beef with Tito Zuccardi Paraje Altamira Malbec, grilled lamb with Concreto Malbec, beef stir-fry with Polígonos del Valle de Uco Malbec, roast duck with Q Tempranillo

8. Clos des Fous | Chile

- History: Clos des Fous was started in 2008 by four Chilean and French winemakers.

- Wines: Pour Ma Gueule Pais, Locura 1 Chardonnay, Grillos Cantores Cinsault, La Cima Red Blend, Aires Andinos Cabernet Sauvignon

- Food Pairings: grilled sausage with Pour Ma Gueule Pais, roasted chicken with Locura 1 Chardonnay, grilled shrimp with Grillos Cantores Cinsault, beef stew with La Cima Red Blend, grilled ribeye steak with Aires Andinos Cabernet Sauvignon

9. Viña Cono Sur | Chile

- History: Cono Sur is a winery dedicated to organic and sustainable farming, founded in 1993 by Eduardo Chadwick.

- Wines: 20 Barrels Pinot Noir, Block 23 Rulos del Alto Riesling, Bicicleta Pinot Noir, Single Vineyard Chardonnay, Pinot Noir Rosé

- Food Pairings: grilled salmon with 20 Barrels Pinot Noir, Thai green curry with Block 23 Rulos del Alto Riesling, roasted pork with Bicicleta Pinot Noir, grilled chicken with Single Vineyard Chardonnay, sushi with Pinot Noir Rosé

10. Santa Carolina | Chile

- History: Santa Carolina is one of the oldest wineries in Chile, founded in 1875 by Luis Pereira.

- Wines: Reserva de Familia Cabernet Sauvignon, Specialties Dry Farming Carignan, Herencia Carmenere, Leyda Sauvignon Blanc, Reserva de Familia Chardonnay

- Food Pairings: grilled beef skewers with Reserva de Familia Cabernet Sauvignon, beef carpaccio with Specialties Dry Farming Carignan, roasted pork belly with Herencia Carmenere, grilled seafood with Leyda Sauvignon Blanc, grilled chicken with Reserva de Familia Chardonnay

11. O. Fournier | Argentina & Chile

- History: O. Fournier is a family-owned winery founded in 2000 with vineyards in both Argentina and Chile.

- Wines: Alfa Spiga Red Blend, Urban Maule Cabernet Franc, Urban Uco Malbec, Urban Ribera del Duero Tempranillo, Urban Bio Bio Sauvignon Blanc

- Food Pairings: grilled lamb chops with Alfa Spiga Red Blend, roasted beef with Urban Maule Cabernet Franc, beef stir-fry with Urban Uco Malbec, grilled venison with Urban Ribera del Duero Tempranillo, grilled shrimp with Urban Bio Bio Sauvignon Blanc

12. Bodegas Salentein Argentina

- History: Salentein is a winery founded in 1992 by Dutch businessman Mijndert Pon.

- Wines: Salentein Reserve Malbec, Salentein Barrel Selection Cabernet Sauvignon, Killka Collection Torrontes, Portillo Malbec Rosé, Numina Gran Corte

- Food Pairings: beef lasagna with Salentein Reserve Malbec, grilled steak with Salentein Barrel Selection Cabernet Sauvignon, chicken fajitas with Killka Collection Torrontes, grilled salmon with Portillo Malbec Rosé, beef carpaccio with Numina Gran Corte.

Sweet Wines and Sweet Foods

South America boasts a rich and diverse culinary tradition, with a wide variety of sweet wines and sweet foods to indulge in. Here is a closer look at some of the most popular sweet wines and sweet foods from the region:

1. Late Harvest Malbec: Late harvest Malbec is a sweet and fruity wine that is harvested later in the season, which allows the grapes to become overripe and develop a higher concentration of sugar. Argentine Malbec is particularly known for its late harvest wines, which are often paired with chocolate desserts or strong cheeses.

2. Moscato: Moscato is a sweet, light-bodied wine that is enjoyed as a dessert wine in Argentina and Chile. Moscato is made from the Muscat grape, which produces a wine that is intensely aromatic with notes of peach, apricot and honeysuckle.

3. Port-style wines: Many winemakers in Chile and Argentina produce fortified wines that are similar in style to traditional Portuguese port. These wines are typically infused with brandy or other spirits, which stops the fermentation process and adds a subtle nutty flavour to the wine. They are often paired with rich chocolate desserts or savoury cheese plates.

Desserts of South America:

1. **Dulce de Leche**: Dulce de leche is a popular South American dessert that is made by simmering condensed milk with sugar until it caramelises into a thick, creamy sauce. This rich and indulgent sauce is often used to drizzle over cakes, pastries, and ice cream.

2. **Churros**: Churros are a beloved South American dessert that originates from the Spanish colonial period. These fried pastries are made from a simple dough that is piped into long, thin strips and then deep-fried until golden brown. They are served piping hot and sprinkled with cinnamon sugar, and can be dipped in dulce de leche or hot chocolate for added indulgence.

3. **Alfajores**: Alfajores are a popular South American sweet treat that consists of two buttery cookies that are sandwiched together with a sweet filling, typically dulce de leche. These delicate cookies are often dusted with powdered sugar or dipped in chocolate, and can also be flavoured with coconut, vanilla, or lemon zest.

Overall, South America boasts a rich and indulgent culinary tradition that is full of sweet wines, decadent desserts, and indulgent treats. From the deep, complex flavours of late harvest Malbec to the rich sweetness of dulce de leche, there is no shortage of delicious sweet foods and wines to enjoy in this vibrant and diverse region.

Pairing sweet wines with desserts:

1. **Argentina**

- **Rutini Wines, Late Harvest Malbec**: This sweet wine has notes of blackberry, plum, and spice, and pairs well with chocolate desserts or cheese plates.

- **Bodegas Salentein, Botrytis Semillon**: Made from 100% Semillon grapes affected by Botrytis cinerea, this wine has flavours of honey, peach, and apricot, and would be excellent with dulce de leche or flan.

2. **Bolivia**

- **Aranjuez, Late Harvest Torrontés**: This wine has aromas of flowers and honey, with a light sweetness that pairs well with spicy foods or salty cheeses.

- **Campos de Solana, Moscatel**: Made from 100% Moscatel grapes, this wine is light and fruity, with flavours of apricot and peach, and would be perfect with a slice of tres leches cake.

3. **Brazil**

- **Miolo, Moscato Giallo**: This wine has notes of citrus, pineapple, and honeysuckle, and pairs well with fresh fruits or light desserts.

- **Casa Valduga, Leopoldina Late Harvest**: This wine has flavours of honey, dried fruit, and toasted nuts, and would be fantastic with a slice of Brazilian-style carrot cake.

4. **Chile**

- **Viña Santa Rita, 120 Late Harvest Sauvignon Blanc**: This wine has flavours of tropical fruit and a light sweetness that would be perfect with spicy dishes or fresh fruit.

- **Concha y Toro, Late Harvest Riesling**: This wine is made from 100% Riesling grapes and has notes of honey, apricot, and jasmine; it would be great paired with crème brûlée or a fruit tart.

5. **Colombia**

- **Casa de los Dulces, Sweet White Wine**: This wine is made from Criolla grapes and has flavours of honey and tropical fruit, pairing well with sweet or spicy foods.

- **Restrepo, Late Harvest Sauvignon Blanc**: This wine has notes of passionfruit and pineapple, with a light sweetness that would be perfect with fresh fruit or a citrusy dessert.

6. Ecuador

- **Hacienda La Carriona, Sweet Muscat**: Made from Muscat of Alexandria grapes, this wine is light and floral, with notes of honey and peach, pairing well with light desserts or fresh fruit.

- **Bodegas Salas, Late Harvest Sauvignon Blanc**: This wine is made from 100% Sauvignon Blanc grapes and has flavours of honey, apricot, and citrus; it would be great paired with fresh cheeses or cheesecake.

7. Guyana

- **Black Sage Vineyard, Late Harvest Riesling:** This wine has notes of honey, apricot, and peach, with a light sweetness that pairs well with spiced foods or light desserts.

- I could not find other sweet wines produced in Guyana

8. Paraguay

- **Vinos y Bodegas del Paraguay, Sweet White Wine:** Made from local grapes, this wine is sweet and fruity, with flavours of lychee and tropical fruit.

- I could not find other sweet wines produced in Paraguay.

9. Peru

- **Tacama, Late Harvest Moscatel**: This wine has notes of honey, apricot, and peach, and pairs well with rich desserts or fresh fruit.

- **Queirolo Winery, Late Harvest Torontel**: This wine has flavours of honey, dried fruit, and spice, and would be fantastic with a slice of Peruvian-style tres leches cake.

10. Suriname

- I could not find sweet wines produced in Suriname.

- I could not find sweet foods specific to Suriname that I could pair.

11. Uruguay

- **Bodega Bouza, Albariño Dulce Naranja**: This wine has notes of honey, orange, and peach, pairing well with light desserts or fresh fruit.

- **Familia Deicas, Preludio Dolce Late Harvest**: This wine is made from 100% Gewürztraminer grapes and has flavours of honey, tropical fruit, and spice; it would be great paired with a slice of Uruguayan-style flan.

12. Venezuela

- **Bodegas Pomar, Sweet Chardonnay**: This wine has flavours of honey, caramel, and tropical fruit, pairing well with cheesy or fruity desserts.

Some popular sweet foods from South America that would pair well with these wines include dulce de leche, flan, tres leches cake, fruit tarts, and cheesecake. These desserts are typically rich and creamy, with flavours of caramel or fruit, and are a perfect complement to the light sweetness of these South American wines.

Non-alcoholic wines

Non-alcoholic wine production in South America has a relatively short history compared to other wine producing regions of the world. In fact, the vast majority of wine produced in South America is still alcoholic.

The first non-alcoholic wines in South America were likely produced in the early 2000s in response to a growing demand for non-alcoholic beverages. These early non-alcoholic wines were likely produced using methods similar to those used for dealcoholized regular wine, such as vacuum distillation or reverse osmosis.

Since then, non-alcoholic wine production in South America has grown slowly but steadily. Today, there are several wineries in Argentina and Chile that offer non-alcoholic wines, with some wineries specialising in the production of solely non-alcoholic beverages.

However, non-alcoholic wine is still a relatively niche product in South America and there is a limited market for it. Most wine drinkers in South America still prefer traditional alcoholic wine, and many wine producers in the region prioritise their alcoholic offerings.

But, let's look at some great vineyards in South America that do produce non-alcoholic wines along with some food pairing suggestions:

1. **Torres Wines** - They produce Natureo, a non-alcoholic wine made with Muscat and Gewurztraminer grapes. This wine pairs well with seafood dishes like grilled shrimp or sushi rolls.

2. **Bodega Norton** - Their Lote Negro 0.0 is a non-alcoholic blend of Cabernet Sauvignon, Merlot, and Malbec grapes. This wine can be paired with hearty dishes like grilled lamb chops or steak.

3. **Toso** - Their non-alcoholic sparkling wine is made with Torrontes and Muscat grapes. This wine pairs well with light and refreshing foods like salads or fresh fruit.

4. **Catena Zapata** - They produce an alcohol-free Chardonnay that can be paired with rich and creamy dishes like pasta with white sauce or roasted chicken.

5. **Concha y Toro** - Their Casillero del Diablo brand offers a non-alcoholic Cabernet Sauvignon that pairs well with red meats like beef or lamb.

Phileas Fogg and his choice of non-alcoholic and foods

During his travels through South America, Phileas Fogg might have enjoyed non-alcoholic wines at several places. However, since Phileas Fogg is a fictional character from the famous novel, "Around the World in Eighty Days," it is not known where exactly he would have enjoyed non-alcoholic wines or what foods he would have paired them with.

But I can recommend some non-alcoholic wines and food pairings that are popular in South America. Some non-alcoholic wine options that are commonly found in the region include Altamar del Sur Chardonnay, La Catadora Cabernet Sauvignon, and Del Bajo Chenin Blanc.

As for food pairings, typical South American cuisine consists of grilled meats, fresh seafood, rice and beans, and a variety of vegetables. Grilled meats like beef or lamb would pair well with a full-bodied non-alcoholic red wine, while seafood dishes would pair well with a lighter, citrusy white wine. Rice and bean dishes would pair well with a dry white or rosé wine.

People, Wines and Foods of South America

Phileas Fogg would have encountered a wide range of cultures, traditions, and cuisines in South American countries he visited. Here are some examples of the foods and wines he might have explored:

1. **Argentina**: Asado, a traditional barbecue method, is very common in Argentina. Malbec red wine is a great pairing for beef, and Torrontes white wine pairs well with seafood dishes.

2. **Bolivia**: Bolivian cuisine features ingredients like quinoa, potatoes, and corn. Aji de Fideo is a popular dish made with noodles, potatoes, and beef. Bolivia has several vineyards producing wine, but beer is more commonly consumed.

3. **Brazil**: Brazilian cuisine is diverse and heavily influenced by African and Portuguese flavors. Feijoada, a black bean stew with pork and sausage, is a must-try dish. Brazil produces excellent sparkling wines like Chardonnay and Pinot Noir.

4. **Chile**: Chilean cuisine features seafood, meat, and vegetables. Churrasco is a popular beef dish, while grilled salmon is another specialty. Chilean wine is famous worldwide, particularly Cabernet Sauvignon and Sauvignon Blanc.

5. **Colombia**: Colombian cuisine features rice, beans, and meat. Ajiaco, a chicken and potato soup, is a popular dish. Colombian coffee is some of the finest in the world, and fresh juices are common as well.

6. **Ecuador**: Ecuadorian cuisine is influenced by both the coastal and highland regions. Ceviche and shrimp dishes are popular along the coast, while roasted guinea pig is a delicacy in the highlands. Ecuador produces wine, but beer is the most popular alcoholic beverage.

7. **Guyana**: Guyanese cuisine is influenced by Indian and African flavors. Pepperpot, a stew made with beef, chicken, and pork, is a staple dish. Guyana produces rum, which is commonly consumed.

8. **Paraguay**: Paraguayan cuisine features soups, stews, and meat. Sopa paraguaya, a cornbread-like dish, is a must-try. Paraguay produces wine, beer, and traditional liquor made from sugarcane, called Caña.

9. **Peru**: Peruvian cuisine is diverse and heavily influenced by Incan traditions. Ceviche, grilled meats, and potato dishes are common. Pisco, a grape brandy, is the national drink.

10. **Suriname**: Surinamese cuisine features rice, saltfish, and vegetables. Roti, a flatbread filled with curry, is a popular dish. Suriname produces rum, which is commonly consumed.

11. **Uruguay**: Uruguayan cuisine features meat, particularly beef, as well as pasta, and seafood. Chivito, a sandwich filled with steak and other ingredients, is a must-try. Uruguay produces excellent wines such as Tannat and Albariño.

12. **Venezuela**: Venezuelan cuisine is diverse and features corn, plantains, and beans. Arepas, cornmeal cakes filled with cheese or meat, are a popular street food. Venezuela produces rum and beer.

I hope this gives you a taste of what Phileas Fogg might have encountered during his travels in South America!

Sparkling Wine and Food

Sparkling wine production in South America has a long and somewhat complex history. The first vines were planted in the region by the Spanish in the mid-16th century, and wine quickly became an important industry throughout colonial South America. However, it wasn't until the late 19th century - when French winemakers fleeing the phylloxera epidemic arrived in the region - that sparkling wine production began to take off.

Argentina and Chile quickly emerged as the dominant players in South American sparkling wine production. In Argentina, the Mendoza region in particular became known for its high-quality sparkling wines, with producers such as Trapiche and Chandon (a subsidiary of Moet & Chandon) leading the way. Meanwhile, Chilean producers such as Concha y Toro and Errazuriz also began to make a name for themselves in the sparkling wine world.

However, the industry was not without its challenges. Political instability in both Argentina and Chile in the mid-20th century had a negative impact on wine production in the region, and many vineyards were abandoned. In addition, competition from other wine-producing regions - particularly Europe - meant that South American sparkling wines struggled to gain recognition on the international stage.

Despite these setbacks, the South American sparkling wine industry has continued to grow and evolve. Today, many producers are experimenting with different grape varieties and production methods, and a new generation of winemakers is bringing fresh energy and innovation to the region. While they may not yet have the same level of global recognition as their counterparts in Europe, South American sparkling wines are definitely worth exploring for wine lovers looking for something different.

I cannot confirm the existence of sparkling wines produced in all 12 South American countries. However, I can share some information about sparkling wines from some of the countries in the region.

Brazil is known for its sparkling wine known as "Champagne Brasileiro" or Brazilian Champagne. This wine is made using the traditional method and is produced mainly in the region of Serra Gaucha.

Argentina is known for producing sparkling wines, known as "espumantes," primarily in the Mendoza region, which is famous for its high-altitude vineyards.

Chile is also known for producing sparkling wines, which are typically made using traditional methods, but with a unique Chilean twist. These wines may be made using grapes like Chardonnay or Pinot Noir.

Other South American countries, such as Bolivia, Ecuador, Guyana, Paraguay, and Suriname, may also produce wines, but it is not common to find sparkling wine from these regions.

Food Pairings:

Some broadly South American foods that are best paired with sparkling wines are:

1. **Ceviche**: A popular seafood dish from Peru that typically consists of raw fish cured in citrus juices, onions, cilantro, and spicy peppers. It pairs well with a crisp and refreshing sparkling wine like Argentine brut nature or Chilean brut.

2. **Empanadas**: A savory pastry that's popular throughout Latin America and typically filled with beef, chicken, or cheese. Empanadas pair well with an off-dry sparkling wine like a Brazilian demi-sec.

3. **Asado**: South America's equivalent of barbecuing, typically featuring grilled meats like beef, chicken, and chorizo. A bone-dry sparkling wine like a Chilean brut or Brazilian extra brut can complement the smoky, meaty flavours.

4. **Alfajores**: A sweet dessert sandwich cookie originating from Argentina, typically filled with dulce de leche and coated in powdered sugar. Alfajores can be paired with a sweeter sparking wine like an Argentine or Brazilian moscato.

Overall, the acidic, fruity notes of South American sparkling wines pair well with the bold flavours of South American cuisine.

A dozen examples of broad food categories that can be paired with South American sparkling wines:

1. Ceviche

2. Empanadas

3. Grilled octopus

4. Shrimp cocktail

5. Fried calamari

6. Ahi tuna tartare

7. Carpaccio

8. Charcuterie (including cured meats like prosciutto and salami)

9. Oysters

10. Seafood paella

11. Lobster

12. Fruit-based desserts (such as strawberry shortcake or peach cobbler)

Please keep in mind that the specific wine pairing can vary depending on the producer and vintage of the sparkling wine being served. It may be helpful to consult a wine professional for guidance or do some experimentation to find what works best for you.

Ah….! There's Something Special About South America

I believe that the wines and foods of South America are truly authentic and intoxicating. The combination of rich flavours, bold spices, and unique ingredients create a culinary experience unlike any other. From the robust Malbecs of Argentina to the refreshing Torrontes of Chile, each sip of South American wine is a journey through the diverse landscapes and cultures of this vibrant continent. So explore the varied cuisine of South America and savour the intoxicating flavours that embody the spirit of this region.

I am here to enlighten and inspire you on the pleasures of South American wines and food. The richness and diversity of the wines and cuisines of this region are truly intoxicating. From the robust Malbecs of Argentina to the spicy Carmenere of Chile, the bold reds of South America are a true delight to the taste buds.

In terms of food, South America boasts a variety of delicious dishes, each with its unique flavour profile. Whether you are savouring the smoky deliciousness of a perfectly cooked asado, the fresh and tangy ceviche, or the comforting warmth of a hearty stew, South American cuisine has something for every palate.

The people of South America are warm and hospitable, and their traditions are deeply ingrained in their way of life. From the vibrant music and dance of Brazil to the awe-inspiring landscapes of the Andes Mountains, South America is a captivating and enchanting place.

Pairing wine with food is an art form in South America, and it's not uncommon to see people meticulously selecting the perfect drink to accompany their meal. From the full-bodied reds of Argentina to the crisp whites of Chile, these wines are crafted to complement and enhance the flavours of their accompanying dishes.

In South America, wine and food are not just sustenance but a cultural expression. It's a celebration of life, love, and the precious moments that bring us all together. And with every sip and every bite, you too can experience the intoxicating magic of South American food and wine.

Remember, life is too short to drink bad wine and eat mediocre food!

Resources for further reading

Here are some resources for further reading on South American wines, non-alcoholic wines, sparkling wines, and food pairings:

1. **For South American wines** - Wine Folly's article on South American Wine Regions: https://winefolly.com/south-america/

2. For non-alcoholic wines - Bon Appétit's article on the best non-alcoholic wines: https://www.bonappetit.com/story/best-non-alcoholic-wines

3. **For sparkling wines** - Wine Enthusiast's Beginner's Guide to Sparkling Wine: https://www.winemag.com/buying-guide/the-beginners-guide-to-sparkling-wines/

4. **For food pairings** - Food & Wine's guide to pairing wine with food: https://www.foodandwine.com/wine-pairing

CHAPTER 7

AFRICAN WINE AND CUISINE

Introduction

Africa is the world's second-largest and second-most-populous continent, with an area of 30.2 million km² and a population of over 1.3 billion people. The continent is divided into 54 countries, each with its own unique culture and history.

Africa is known for its vast savannas, dense rainforests, and expansive deserts. It is home to some of the most iconic wildlife in the world, including lions, elephants, giraffes, and gorillas. The continent also boasts a diverse range of plant life, including baobab trees, acacias, and succulents.

Throughout history, Africa has been shaped by a range of cultural influences, including Arab, European, and indigenous African traditions. The continent is home to a variety of religions, including Christianity, Islam, and traditional African spiritual practices.

Despite its rich cultural heritage and natural beauty, Africa faces a range of challenges, including poverty, political instability, and conflict. However, the continent is also home to a growing number of thriving urban centres and emerging economies, particularly in countries such as Nigeria, South Africa, Kenya, and Ethiopia.

Overall, Africa is a diverse and complex continent with a rich history, culture, and natural environment. Whilst facing challenges, it's also making great progress and playing a vital role in the global community.

African culture is one of the most diverse and vibrant in the world. The continent is home to a wide range of unique traditions, customs, and beliefs that have been shaped by centuries of history and a rich cultural heritage. This diversity is reflected in the tourism industry, where visitors can experience an array of different cultural experiences and explore the stunning topography that Africa has to offer.

Topography:

Africa boasts some of the world's most impressive natural features, from expansive deserts and dense rainforests to towering mountains and vast savannas. Mount Kilimanjaro in Tanzania is the highest peak in Africa and one of the Seven Summits, offering a challenging climb for adventurous travellers. Similarly, the Sahara desert spanning multiple countries offers an exhilarating experience in off-road vehicles and sandboarding. The Great Rift Valley, stretching from Tanzania all the way up to Syria, is a geological phenomenon that provides stunning views and breathtaking landscapes. Also, Africa is home to numerous waterfalls, including Victoria Falls in Zimbabwe, one of the world's largest waterfalls.

Peoples:

Africa is home to a diverse range of ethnic groups, each with their unique culture and traditions. The continent has over 3,000 distinct ethnic groups, with a majority of individuals speaking one of the more than 2,000 African languages. The Bantu peoples comprise one of the largest ethnic groups, accounting for over two-thirds of the continent's population. Other significant groups include the Nilotic people, the Khoisan people, and the Nilo-Saharan people, among others.

Let's briefly overview some more of the diverse people, cultures, traditions, languages and foods in Africa:

1. **The Maasai people**: The Maasai are a semi-nomadic tribe living in Kenya and Tanzania. They are known for their distinct clothing, jewellery, and hairstyles. They speak Maa, and their diet consists mostly of cow's milk, meat, and blood.

2. **The Yoruba people**: The Yoruba are one of the largest ethnic groups in West Africa, with a population of over 40 million people. They are known for their elaborate festivals, art, and music. They speak Yoruba and their diet includes dishes such as pounded yam and Egusi soup.

3. **The Berber people**: The Berbers are an indigenous people of North Africa, with populations in Morocco, Algeria, Tunisia, Libya, Mauritania, and Mali. They speak Berber languages, and their cuisine includes dishes such as couscous, tagine, and brik.

4. **The Zulu people**: The Zulu are the largest ethnic group in South Africa, with a population of over 10 million people. They speak isiZulu, and their cuisine includes dishes such as pap (maize porridge), chakalaka (a spicy relish), and braaivleis (barbecue).

5. **The Amhara people**: The Amhara are an ethnic group in Ethiopia, and they are the second-largest ethnic group in the country. They are known for their cuisine, which includes dishes such as injera (a sourdough flatbread) and wat (a spicy stew).

6. **The Swahili people**: The Swahili are an ethnic group that spans several countries in East Africa, including Kenya, Tanzania, Uganda, and Mozambique. They speak Swahili, and their cuisine includes dishes such as pilau (rice with spices and meat or fish).

7. **The Xhosa people**: The Xhosa are an ethnic group in South Africa, with a population of over 8 million people. They speak isiXhosa, and their cuisine includes dishes such as umngqusho (maize and beans) and chakalaka.

Countries:

Africa is the world's second-largest continent, covering over 30.2 million square kilometres. The continent is home to 54 countries, with each country offering unique experiences and attractions to travellers. Some of the popular tourist destinations in Africa include Egypt, South Africa, Morocco, Kenya, and Tanzania, among others.

Wines:

Africa is rapidly becoming a thriving centre of the wine-producing industry. Countries such as South Africa, Morocco, and Tunisia are producing world-class wines that are gaining popularity in the global market. South Africa, in particular, is renowned for its quality wines, with regions such as Stellenbosch, Franschhoek, and Paarl producing some of the world's best-known wines.

Cuisine:

African cuisine is as diverse as the continent itself, with each country being known for its unique dishes and culinary traditions. In West Africa, food is heavily influenced by African, European, and Asian cultures, with popular dishes such as jollof rice, a spicy rice dish served with chicken or vegetables. East African cuisine is characterised by an extensive use of spices, herbs, and coconut milk, with dishes such as pilau and samosas. In North Africa, food is heavily influenced by Arab and Mediterranean cultures, with staple dishes such as couscous and tagine.

Culture:

African culture is steeped in tradition, history, and religion. The continent's cultural heritage is kept alive through ancient traditions such as storytelling, music, dance, and masquerade. Africa's music scene is lively and diverse, with each country having its unique style and genre, ranging from traditional folk music to modern hip-hop and pop music. Similarly, African art is renowned for its intricate designs, bold colours, and exceptional craftsmanship, with traditional artists such as sculptors and weavers continuing to create timeless pieces that are celebrated worldwide.

Tourism

African tourism offers a wide range of experiences and adventures to travellers from all over the world. From its diverse cultural heritage to its breathtaking scenery, Africa has something to offer every kind of traveller.

Adventure lovers can trek through the lush rainforests of Congo and Uganda to encounter gorillas and chimpanzees, climb the towering dunes of Namibia's Skeleton Coast, or go on a safari in the Serengeti to see the "Big Five" (lion, leopard, elephant, rhino, and buffalo).

For those interested in history and culture, Africa offers a wealth of experiences. The ancient Egyptian pyramids and temples, Zimbabwe's Great Zimbabwe ruins, and Ghana's slave castles are just a few examples of the continent's rich cultural heritage.

Beaches in Africa are some of the most beautiful in the world. From the stunning coastline of the Seychelles and Mauritius to the exotic beaches of Zanzibar and Lamu Island in Kenya, there is something for everyone.

Overall, African tourism is a unique and memorable experience, full of adventure, culture, and natural beauty.

Africa is an incredibly diverse continent with a rich cultural heritage, and vast natural resources. Its people, countries, topography, wines, cuisines, and culture create an unparalleled tourism experience that every traveller should experience at least once in their lifetime.

Wine Producers

Africa has several countries with wine-growing regions. The countries which produce wine in Africa are:

1. South Africa

2. Morocco

3. Tunisia

4. Algeria

5. Egypt

6. Zimbabwe

7. Ethiopia

8. Kenya

9. Tanzania

10. Uganda

11. Zambia

1. **South Africa**:

South Africa is the largest wine producer among African countries. The largest wine producers in South Africa include Groot Constantia, Jordan, Meerlust, and Robertson Winery. Pinotage is the country's signature grape varietal. The most common vinification technique is oak barrel ageing. Pairing suggestions include rich and spicy dishes, such as bobotie and beef curry.

2. **Algeria**:

The largest wine producers in Algeria include Château de la Pommeraie, Saint Augustin, and Coteaux d'Orie. The country cultivates indigenous grape varietals, such as Chetoui, Bouis, and Kharoubi. The vinification technique is mostly traditional and involves aging the wine in ceramic jars called "jars" or in clay amphorae. Pairing suggestions include couscous and spicy lamb meat dishes.

3. **Tunisia**:

The largest wine producers in Tunisia include Société Vinicole de Mateur, Les Vignerons de Carthage, and Domaine de Sidi Mimoun. Grapes range from local varieties to French varieties such as Syrah and Chardonnay. The vinification technique is traditional and involves the use of oak barrels. Pairing suggestions include seafood and spicy chicken dishes.

4. **Morocco**:

Morocco is famous for its unique wine, created from white Muscat grapes, L'Office des Vins, and Celliers de Meknès are among the country's biggest producers. Red wines typically consist of three grape varieties: Grenache, Syrah, and Mourvèdre. Vinification techniques involve the use of oak barrels. Pairing suggestions include tagines and lamb dishes with smoky flavours.

5. Egypt:

Egypt has an emerging wine industry, but its grapes and wine are yet to make waves in international markets. Commercial wineries include Aida, Gianaclis Vineyards, and The Saint George Vineyard. Grapes grown in Egypt include local varieties, such as Baladi, Farouki, and Karmen. Techniques employed include traditional basket pressing and aging in oak barrels. Pairing suggestions include a variety of mezze platters and grilled meats.

6. Zimbabwe:

Zimbabwe has a small wine industry, and the wines produced are mainly for the domestic market. The biggest producers include Mukuyu and Mukwa Wines. Wine varietals include Muscat of Alexandria, Chenin Blanc, and Cabernet Sauvignon. The vinification technique is traditional, and wine barrels are used for aging. Pairing suggestions include grilled meats and spicy chicken dishes.

7. Ethiopia:

Ethiopia's wine industry is still emerging. Some of the biggest producers in the country include Awash Wines and Castel Winery. The most common grape varietals grown here include Syrah, Cabernet Sauvignon, and Merlot. The vinification technique used is modern, with stainless steel fermenting tanks. Pairing suggestions include spicy stews and meat dishes.

8. Kenya:

Kenya's wine industry is small and nascent, with Leleshwa and Rift Valley Winery as the two main producers. Wine varietals grown in Kenya include Chenin Blanc, Sauvignon Blanc, and Cabernet Franc. Vinification techniques are modern and include the use of stainless steel tanks. Pairing suggestions include grilled game meats, such as ostrich and crocodile.

9. Tanzania:

Tanzania's wine industry is in its early stages, with several wineries just starting to produce commercial wines. The main wineries include Tanzania Distilleries Limited and Amani Vineyards. The grape varietals grown here include Colombard, Chardonnay, and Syrah. Traditional vinification techniques are used, and the wines are aged in barrels. Pairing suggestions include grilled and roasted meats.

10. Nigeria:

Nigeria is known for its palm tree wine, a popular regional drink made from the sap of the palm tree. The country's emerging wine industry is dominated by Le Meridien, Château de Chanté and Four Cousins. Grape varieties grown in Nigeria include Chardonnay, Sauvignon Blanc, and Cabernet Sauvignon. Vinification techniques used are mostly modern, with stainless steel vats. Pairing suggestions include spicy dishes such as jollof rice and pepper soup.

11. Mauritius:

Mauritius' wine industry is small but growing, with the biggest producers being La Vieille Cheminée Winery and Cassel & Co. Grape varieties grown here include Chenin Blanc, Sauvignon Blanc, and Shiraz. The vinification techniques employed are modern, with stainless steel tanks, and oak barrel ageing. Pairing suggestions include seafood dishes such as shrimp and fish curries.

Overall, African wines are gaining international recognition for their unique taste and character. The wine industry in Africa continues to grow, and as it does, wine lovers around the world can expect to see more exciting and delicious bottles from this continent.

Pairing wines from notable African countries with local cuisine:

1. Algeria

Wine: Medea Rosé

Cuisine: Couscous with Lamb

Culinary Culture: Algerian cuisine is rich, flavorful and heavily spiced. It is influenced by French, African, and Arab cultures.

2. Angola

Wine: Chateau Cap de Bono

Cuisine: Muamba Chicken

Culinary Culture: Angolan cuisine is characterized by its use of spices and herbs. It is influenced by Portuguese, African and Brazilian cultures.

3. Benin

Wine: Method Cap Classique

Cuisine: Maafe (peanut butter stew)

Culinary Culture: Beninese cuisine is known for its exotic ingredients and flavors. Yams, black-eyed peas, and peanuts are staples in their dishes.

4. Botswana

Wine: Douglas Green Chardonnay

Cuisine: Seswaa (beef stew)

Culinary Culture: Botswana cuisine is heavily influenced by the country's terrain and wildlife. It is known for its game meat, especially beef.

5. Burkina Faso

Wine: Henningsson & Hoehn Grenache Syrah

Cuisine: Riz Gras (fat rice)

Culinary Culture: Burkina Faso's cuisine is largely based on grains, vegetables, and meat. Millet and sorghum are common ingredients.

6. Burundi

Wine: Obikwa Pinotage

Cuisine: Ibiharage (bean stew)

Culinary Culture: Burundian cuisine is simple and wholesome. It makes use of local ingredients such as beans, bananas, and cassava.

7. Cameroon

Wine: Golden Kaan Shiraz

Cuisine: Ndole (bitterleaf stew)

Culinary Culture: Cameroon's cuisine is diverse and reflects the country's geographic and cultural diversity. It is characterized by its use of spices and herbs.

8. Cape Verde

Wine: Adega de Cantanhede Reserva Tinto

Cuisine: Cachupa (slow-cooked stew)

Culinary Culture: Cape Verdean cuisine is a fusion of African, Portuguese and Brazilian cuisine. Its dishes are characterized by its generous use of beans and corn.

9. Central African Republic

Wine: Tassenberg Shiraz

Cuisine: Kanda (pork stew)

Culinary Culture: Central African cuisine is known for its use of wild game meat such as elephant, antelope, and buffalo. It also makes use of root vegetables such as cassava and yams.

10. Chad

Wine: Armilla Blanc de Blancs

Cuisine: Boule (millet balls)

Culinary Culture: Chadian cuisine is influenced by its neighbors, Sudan and Libya. Its dishes use ingredients such as lamb, goat, and dried fish.

11. Comoros

Wine: Barton & Guestier Reserve Merlot

Cuisine: Langouste a la Vanille (lobster in vanilla sauce)

Culinary Culture: Comorian cuisine is heavily influenced by French and Indian cooking. It uses coconut, vanilla, and seafood in its dishes.

12. Congo

Wine: Leopard's Leap Cabernet Sauvignon

Cuisine: Moambé (chicken in palm nut sauce)

Culinary Culture: Congolese cuisine is heavily influenced by the country's tropical climate and abundance of natural resources. Its dishes use ingredients such as plantains, cassava, and peanuts.

Lets pair foods from 12 different African countries with some delicious wines

1. **South Africa** - Braaied meat with a bold red wine, like a Cabernet Sauvignon or a Pinotage.

2. **Morocco** - Slow-cooked tagine with a dry white wine, such as a Sauvignon Blanc.

3. **Cameroon** - Grilled fish with a crisp white wine, like a Chenin Blanc.

4. **Tunisia** - Spicy seafood gumbo with a fruity red wine, such as a Grenache.

5. **Ethiopia** - Spicy lentil stew with a dry red wine, like a Syrah or a Merlot.

6. **Zimbabwe** - Grilled game meat with a full-bodied red wine, such as a Shiraz or a Zinfandel.

7. **Egypt** - Roasted lamb with a spicy red wine, like a Malbec or a Cabernet Franc.

8. **Algeria** - Slow-roasted beef with a robust red wine, such as a Sangiovese or a Nero d'Avola.

9. **Ghana** - Jollof rice with a crisp white wine, like a Riesling or a Viognier.

10. **Kenya** - Grilled chicken with a fruity red wine, such as a Pinot Noir or a Gamay.

11. **Tanzania** - Coconut fish curry with a dry white wine, like a Chardonnay or a Vermentino.

12. **Nigeria** - Spicy beef suya with a bold red wine, like a Merlot or a Cabernet Sauvignon.

Phileas Fogg's African Experience

1. **Algeria**: Château Comtal Blanc - This crisp white wine pairs well with grilled seafood, Mediterranean salads, and spicy dishes.

2. **Angola**: Adega Mayor Reserva Tinto - A bold red wine with flavours of blackberry and currant, pairs well with meats such as grilled beef, lamb, or game.

3. **Egypt**: Obelisk Chenin Blanc & Viognier - This crisp and fruity white wine pairs well with fresh salads, grilled chicken, and seafood dishes.

4. **Ethiopia**: Rift Valley Merlot - This medium-bodied red wine with notes of cherry and plum pairs well with grilled meats and African stews.

5. **Kenya**: Leleshwa Sauvignon Blanc - This light and refreshing white wine pairs well with spicy cuisine, including seafood dishes and curries.

6. **Morocco**: Château Roslane Clos de Roslane - This elegant and fruity red wine pairs well with grilled meats, tajines, and Moroccan-style couscous.

7. **Namibia**: Neuras Grüner Veltliner - This dry white wine pairs well with lighter meals such as salads, seafood, and grilled chicken.

8. **Nigeria**: Obelisk Cabernet Sauvignon - This bold and full-bodied red wine pairs well with African stews, grilled meats, and Nigerian-style curry dishes.

9. **Rwanda**: Inzuki Vineyards Rosé - This refreshing rosé pairs well with salads, seafood dishes, and spicy cuisine.

10. **South Africa**: The Chocolate Block - This rich and complex red wine pairs well with hearty meat dishes such as beef, venison, and barbecue.

11. **Tanzania**: Rift Valley Shiraz - This full-bodied red wine with peppery notes pairs well with grilled or roasted meats, particularly lamb and beef.

12. **Zimbabwe**: Fidelitas Cabernet Sauvignon - This dry, medium-bodied red wine pairs well with grilled meats, stews, and Zimbabwean-style curries.

Overall, Phileas Fogg may certainly have enjoyed pairing these African wines with the local cuisine during his travels. The suggested food pairings for each wine include popular dishes from their respective countries, but there are likely many other options that would complement the wines equally well.

Seasonal Pairings

Wine with Local Cuisine for Summer Formal Dining

1. **South Africa** - Pinotage and Cape Malay Curry

Pinotage is a uniquely South African grape variety that produces full-bodied, fruity red wines that are perfect for summer sipping. Cape Malay Curry is a spicy, flavorful dish that combines Indian and African flavours, and is a popular dish in South Africa.

2. **Morocco** - Domaine de Sahari Rouge and Tagine

Domaine de Sahari Rouge is a bold and fruity red wine made from Grenache grapes grown in Morocco's Atlas Mountains. Tagine is a traditional Moroccan stew made with spices, vegetables, and meat or seafood, and is typically served with couscous.

3. **Nigeria** - ObiWine and Jollof Rice

ObiWine is a red wine made from grapes grown in Nigeria's Kaduna state, and is known for its fruity and earthy flavours. Jollof Rice is a spicy and savoury dish made with rice, tomatoes, onions, and a variety of meats, and is a staple of Nigerian cuisine.

4. **Ethiopia** - Tej and Doro Wat

Tej is a traditional Ethiopian honey wine that is sweet, spicy, and refreshing. Doro Wat is a spicy chicken stew made with berbere spice mix and served with injera bread.

5. **Tunisia** - Sidi Brahim and Brik

Sidi Brahim is a crisp white wine made from Sauvignon Blanc grapes grown in Tunisia's coastal region. Brik is a Tunisian pastry filled with egg, tuna, and capers and fried to crispy perfection.

6. **Kenya** - Rift Valley Wines and Nyama Choma

Rift Valley Wines are a collection of wines made from grapes grown in Kenya's Rift Valley, and are known for their fruity and floral flavours. Nyama Choma is a popular Kenyan barbecued meat dish, usually made with goat or beef.

7. **Egypt** - Omar Khayyam and Molokhia

Omar Khayyam is a full-bodied red wine made from grapes grown in Egypt's Nile Delta region. Molokhia is a green leafy vegetable often used as a base for stews or soups, and is a staple of Egyptian cuisine.

8. **Ghana** - Cape Coast Wine and Fufu

Cape Coast Wine is a red wine made from grapes grown in Ghana's Central region, and is known for its intense berry flavours. Fufu is a starchy African staple made from cassava or plantain, and is typically served with stew.

9. **Tanzania** - Dodoma Wine and Ugali

Dodoma Wine is a white wine made from grapes grown in Tanzania's central region, and is known for its light, refreshing taste. Ugali is a starchy porridge made from maize flour and is a staple of Tanzanian cuisine.

10. **Algeria** - Coteaux d'Algerie and Couscous

Coteaux d'Algerie is a crisp white wine made from grapes grown in Algeria's coastal region. Couscous is a spicy and savory dish made with semolina, vegetables, and meat or fish.

11. **Ivory Coast** - Vin de Gagnoa and Attieke

Vin de Gagnoa is a red wine made from grapes grown in Ivory Coast's Gagnoa region, and is known for its rich, fruity flavors. Attieke is a West African staple made from cassava that is grated, fermented and steamed, and is served with stews or sauces.

12. **Senegal** - Thieboudienne and Clos de Thies

Thieboudienne is a spicy and savoury rice dish made with fish or meat and vegetables, and is a staple of Senegalese cuisine. Clos de Thies is a white wine made from grapes grown in Senegal's Thies region, and is known for its crisp, citrusy flavours.

Wines with Local Cuisine for Summer Informal Dining

1. **South Africa** - Biltong and Pinotage: Biltong is dried, salted and cured meat, similar to beef jerky. Pinotage is a red wine that is a cross between Pinot Noir and Cinsaut. The salty, savoury flavours of biltong pair perfectly with the fruity notes of Pinotage.

2. **Morocco** - Tagine and Rosé: Tagine is a slow-cooked stew made with a variety of vegetables and meats. Rosé, with its light and refreshing taste, is a great way to balance out the richness of the tagine.

3. **Egypt** - Kofta and Shiraz: Kofta is a spicy meatball dish made with ground beef, lamb or chicken. Shiraz, a bold red wine with hints of pepper and spice, complements the flavours of the kofta.

4. **Tunisia** - Brik and Chardonnay: Brik is a crispy pastry filled with egg, tuna, and capers. Chardonnay, with its notes of butter and oak, balances out the salty and acidic flavours in the brik.

5. **Ethiopia** - Doro Wat and Sauvignon Blanc: Doro Wat is a spicy chicken stew made with berbere spices. Sauvignon Blanc, with its bright acidity, cuts through the heat of the spices and complements the flavours of the chicken.

6. **Ghana** - Jollof Rice and Gamay: Jollof Rice is a tomato-based dish made with rice, spices, and vegetables. Gamay, a light-bodied red wine with fruity notes, pairs well with the savoury flavours of the dish.

7. **Ivory Coast** - Attieke and Chenin Blanc: Attieke is a fermented cassava dish that is a staple in Ivorian cuisine. Chenin Blanc, with its flavors of green apple and honey, complements the light and airy texture of the attieke.

8. **Nigeria** - Suya and Malbec: Suya is a spicy grilled meat skewer made with beef or chicken. Malbec, a full-bodied red wine with bold flavours of dark fruit and spice, pairs perfectly with the spicy and smoky flavours of the suya.

9. **Algeria** - Mechoui and Tempranillo: Mechoui is a slow-roasted lamb dish that is typically served at large gatherings. Tempranillo, a medium-bodied red wine with notes of cherry and vanilla, pairs well with the tender and juicy flavours of the lamb.

10. **Kenya** - Nyama Choma and Cabernet Sauvignon: Nyama Choma is a grilled meat dish made with beef or goat. Cabernet Sauvignon, with its bold tannins and flavours of blackcurrant and vanilla, pairs well with the smoky and savoury flavours of the meat.

11. **Libya** - Couscous and Viognier: Couscous is a staple dish in North African cuisine made from steamed semolina grains. Viognier, with its light and floral aromas, complements the nutty and subtle flavours of the couscous.

12. **Zimbabwe** - Sadza and Merlot: Sadza is a mashed cornmeal dish that is a staple in Zimbabwean cuisine. Merlot, with its fruity and soft tannin flavours, pairs well with the creamy and subtle flavours of the sadza.

I hope these suggestions were helpful in creating your ideal wine and food pairings for summer informal drinking.

Wines and Local Cuisine Perfect for a Formal Winter Dining

1. **South Africa**: Pinotage and Bobotie

Pinotage is a unique red wine that is a cross between Pinot Noir and Cinsault grapes. It is known for its smoky, earthy flavours with hints of raspberries and cherries. It pairs perfectly with Bobotie, a traditional South African dish made with spiced ground meat, topped with an egg and milk custard.

2. **Egypt**: Omar Khayyam and Koshari

Omar Khayyam is a refreshing, dry white wine that pairs well with spicy foods. Koshari is a hearty Egyptian dish made with lentils, rice, chickpeas, and topped with a spicy tomato sauce and caramelised onions.

3. **Morocco**: Chardonnay and Couscous

Chardonnay, when produced in Morocco, is known for its crisp and refreshing taste. It pairs perfectly with the national dish of Morocco - couscous. It is made with steamed semolina grains, vegetables, and a variety of meats or fish.

4. **Algeria**: Coteaux and Shakshuka

Coteaux is a red wine made from the Carignan grape that has hints of cherry and plum. It pairs well with the popular Algerian dish Shakshuka, which is a warm tomato stew with poached eggs and spices.

5. **Nigeria**: Zobo and Jollof Rice

Zobo is a refreshing hibiscus tea, perfect for sipping at any event. It pairs perfectly with Jollof rice, a tomato-based rice dish with an assortment of spices and vegetables.

6. **Tunisia**: Muscat and Brik

Muscat is a sweet white wine that pairs well with the popular Tunisian dish Brik. Brik is a savoury pastry that is filled with tuna or beef, potatoes, and a soft boiled egg.

7. **Ethiopia**: Tej and Doro Wat

Tej is a sweet and spicy honey wine that is made traditionally in Ethiopia. It pairs perfectly with Doro Wat, a spicy chicken stew that is made with a variety of Ethiopian spices, served with injera, which is a sourdough flatbread.

8. **Zimbabwe**: Chenin Blanc and Sadza

Chenin Blanc is a white wine with tropical fruit aromas and a hint of apple, it pairs well with Sadza, a dish made from cornmeal that is a staple of Zimbabwean cuisine. It is typically eaten with stew, relish or soup.

9. **Ghana**: Merlot and Banku

Merlot is a red wine that is known for its soft and round finish with flavours of black cherry and currant. It pairs well with the Ghanaian dish Banku, which is a corn dough-based meal served with a soup or stew.

10. **Kenya**: Sauvignon Blanc and Nyama Choma

Sauvignon Blanc is a white wine that is known for its high acidity with flavours of citrus and green apple. It pairs perfectly with Nyama Choma, which is a popular Kenyan dish made from grilled meat, usually goat or beef.

11. **Senegal**: Cabernet Sauvignon and Thieboudienne

Cabernet Sauvignon is a rich, full-bodied red wine that has flavours of black currant and tobacco. It pairs well with the Senegalese dish Thieboudienne, which is a rice dish that is mixed with fish and vegetables typically served with a spicy tomato sauce.

12. **Cameroon**: Viognier and Ndole

Viognier is a complex white wine known for its floral and fruity undertones. It pairs well with Ndole, a dish that's made from a stew of nuts that are cooked with meat, spinach or bitter leaves, and spices.

All of these dishes and wines would be an excellent choice for a formal winter event, introducing guests to the unique and diverse culinary and wine cultures found throughout Africa.

Wines and Foods Perfect for an Informal Winter Dining

1. **South Africa**: A rich red wine like Pinotage pairs well with a hearty bowl of beef or lamb stew, called "potjiekos." This traditional South African dish is slow cooked in a potjie pot over an open fire.

2. **Morocco**: A spicy and fruity red wine like Syrah goes well with a flavorful Moroccan tagine dish. A tagine is a clay pot dish typically made with meat, vegetables, and aromatic spices such as cumin and coriander.

3. **Egypt**: A crisp and refreshing white wine like Chardonnay pairs well with koshari, a popular Egyptian street food made of rice, noodles, lentils, and spicy tomato sauce.

4. **Kenya**: A bold and complex red wine like Cabernet Sauvignon pairs well with nyama choma, a grilled meat dish eaten in Kenya. Common meats include beef or goat, served with grilled corn and vegetables.

5. **Ethiopia**: A dry and spicy red wine like Shiraz pairs well with doro wat, a chicken stew dish with a spicy and flavorful berbere sauce. Doro wat is often served with injera, a spongy bread used to scoop up the stew.

6. **Tunisia**: A full-bodied and fruity red wine like Grenache pairs well with brik, a traditional Tunisian dish that consists of a thin pastry shell filled with a savoury mixture of ingredients, such as egg, tuna, potatoes, and parsley, and then fried until crispy. The pastry shell is made from a very thin layer of Malsouka or phyllo dough, and it is folded around the filling into a triangular shape, like a samosa or empanada. The filling is usually seasoned with harissa, a spicy paste made from red peppers, garlic, and various spices. Brik is often served as an appetiser or a street food snack, and it is commonly accompanied by a side of salad and lemon wedges. It is popular in other North African countries as well and can be found with slight variations in Algeria, Morocco, and Libya.

7. **Tanzania**: A light and refreshing white wine like Sauvignon Blanc pairs well with a popular Tanzanian dish called ugali. Ugali is a kind of porridge made from maize flour served with meats and vegetables.

8. **Ghana**: A smoky and spicy red wine like Merlot pairs well with jollof rice, a popular Ghanaian rice dish cooked in a spicy tomato sauce with chicken, meat, or fish.

9. **Ivory Coast**: A spicy and fruity red wine like Zinfandel pairs well with a popular Ivory Coast dish called attiéké. Attiéké is a kind of couscous made from cassava, often served with grilled fish and vegetables.

10. **Nigeria**: A bold and tannic red wine like Malbec pairs well with suya, a popular Nigerian street food made with grilled meat rubbed with a spice blend of chilli peppers and peanuts.

11. **Senegal**: A crisp and refreshing white wine like Chenin Blanc pairs well with thieboudienne, a popular Senegalese fish and rice dish flavoured with tomato paste, garlic, and onions.

12. **Algeria**: A rich and fruity red wine like Tempranillo pairs well with couscous, a staple Algerian dish made with semolina flour and served with vegetables and meats.

I hope this helps you choose the perfect wine and food pairings for your winter informal drinking - African style!

African Sweet Dishes paired with Wines

1. **South Africa** - Malva pudding with a Chenin Blanc: Malva pudding is a sweet sponge cake topped with a creamy sauce. Chenin Blanc is a white wine that pairs well with the sweetness of the dish and brings out its fruity and nutty flavours.

2. **Nigeria** - Chin chin with a Sémillon: Chin chin is a sweet, crispy snack made with flour, sugar, and spices. Sémillon is a white wine with a honeyed flavour that complements the cinnamon and nutmeg in the chin chin.

3. **Ghana** - Kelewele with a Gewürztraminer: Kelewele is a sweet and spicy fried plantain dish seasoned with ginger and pepper. Gewürztraminer is a floral white wine with notes of lychee and spice that match the bold flavours of the kelewele.

4. **Kenya** - Mandazi with a Muscat Blanc: Mandazi is a sweet fried bread that's popular as a snack or breakfast food. Muscat Blanc is a white wine with a fruity flavour that goes well with the sweetness of the mandazi.

5. **Ethiopia** - Dabo Kolo with a Chardonnay: Dabo Kolo is a sweet and spicy snack made with crunchy chickpeas seasoned with spices like cumin and chilli powder. Chardonnay is a full-bodied white wine that pairs well with the bold flavours of the dabo kolo.

6. **Uganda** - Rolex with a Sauvignon Blanc: Rolex is a sweet and savoury omelette rolled up in a chapati bread. Sauvignon Blanc is a crisp white wine that complements the savoury notes of the omelette and the sweetness of the chapati.

7. **Morocco** - Briouat with a Malbec: Briouat is a sweet and savoury pastry filled with meats or cheeses and seasoned with honey and cinnamon. Malbec is a red wine with an earthy flavour that goes well with the spiced filling of the briouat.

8. **Egypt** - Basbousa with a Riesling: Basbousa is a sweet semolina cake soaked in a sugary syrup. Riesling is a white wine with a high acidity that balances the sweetness in the basbousa.

9. **Tanzania** - Kaimati with a Shiraz: Kaimati are sweet dumplings soaked in a syrup made with sugar and rose water. Shiraz is a red wine with a fruity flavour that pairs well with the rich flavour of the dumplings.

10. **Senegal** - Thieboudienne with a Rosé: Thieboudienne is a sweet and spicy fish and rice dish cooked in a tomato sauce. Rosé is a light, refreshing wine with a fruity flavour that goes well with the spicy and tangy notes in the thieboudienne.

11. **Liberia** - Cassava Cake with a Pinot Noir: Cassava cake is a sweet and dense cake made with cassava flour and coconut milk. Pinot Noir is a red wine with a light body that goes well with the subtle sweetness of the cake.

12. **Ivory Coast** - Attiéké with a Viognier: Attiéké is a sweet and tangy cassava couscous served with grilled chicken or fish. Viognier is a white wine with a rich flavour that pairs with the savoury and citrusy notes in the attiéké and the grilled meats.

Each wine and dish has unique flavours and characteristics that complement each other, creating a delicious taste experience for the palate.

Phileas Fogg's Sweet Pairings

I don't know what exact African desserts Phileas Fogg would have paired with African wines during his travels through Africa. However, I can give you some suggestions based on popular desserts and wines in African countries.

1. **South Africa**: Melktert (milk tart) paired with Pinotage wine

2. Morocco: Pastilla (sweet and savoury meat pie) paired with a crisp and refreshing Moroccan white wine

3. **Egypt**: Basbousa (semolina cake) paired with a sweet Egyptian dessert wine

4. **Tunisia**: Makroud (date stuffed pastry) paired with a light Tunisian red wine

5. **Algeria**: Bouza (ice cream) paired with a fruity Algerian red wine

6. **Ghana**: Kelewele (spicy plantain chips) paired with Ghanaian Tawny Port wine

7. **Nigeria**: Suya (spicy grilled meat skewers) paired with bold Nigerian red wine

8. **Kenya**: Mandazi (sweet fried dough) paired with a Kenyan sparkling wine

9. **Ethiopia**: Dabo Kolo (spiced crunchy bread) paired with a dry Ethiopian red wine

10. **Tanzania**: Uji wa Oat (oatmeal porridge) paired with a sweet Tanzanian dessert wine

11. Zimbabwe: Maheu (fermented maize drink) paired with a refreshing Zimbabwean white wine

12. Madagascar: Koba (sticky rice cake with peanuts) paired with a Madagascar semi-sweet white wine.

Please note that these are just my suggestions and my personal tastes, but I'm confident Phileas would approved.

Sparkling Wines

Sparkling wines from Africa are becoming increasingly popular, and for good reason. The continent boasts a diverse range of climates and soils, making it an ideal location for growing grapes that can be used to produce high-quality sparkling wines.

History:

The history of sparkling wine production in Africa dates back to the colonial era. During this time, the French introduced the art of winemaking to Algeria, Morocco, and Tunisia. However, it is only in recent years that African countries have begun to establish a reputation for producing some of the finest sparkling wines in the world.

Countries and Grapes:

South Africa is by far the most well-known country when it comes to sparkling wine production in Africa. Some of the most popular sparkling wines made in South Africa include Blanc de Blanc, Blanc de Noir, and Rose. The most common grape variety used to produce sparkling wines in South Africa is Chardonnay, but Pinot Noir and Pinot Meunier are also used. Other African countries that produce sparkling wines include Morocco, Algeria, and Egypt.

Owners and Culture:

In South Africa, most of the sparkling wine producers are owned by large wine estates or cooperatives. However, there are also a few smaller, boutique producers that are gaining a following. South Africa has a strong wine culture, and many people in the country are proud of their wine heritage.

Vinification Technique:

The traditional method of sparkling wine production is the most commonly used technique in Africa. This involves a secondary fermentation in the bottle, which gives the wine its characteristic bubbles. The wine is then aged on its lees for a period of time, which helps to develop its complex flavours.

Topography:

The topography of Africa is incredibly diverse, which means that there are many different areas that are well-suited to growing grapes for sparkling wine production. In South Africa, the Western Cape is the most important region for sparkling wine production. The area has a Mediterranean climate, which is ideal for growing a variety of grapes. The region's topography varies from mountains to valleys and coastal plains, providing a range of microclimates that allow for diverse production.

In conclusion, sparkling wine production in Africa is still relatively new, but the quality of the wines being produced is world-class. The continent's unique topography and diverse climates make it an ideal location for growing grapes for sparkling wine. With South Africa leading the way, it is likely that we will see many more high-quality sparkling wines coming out of Africa in the years to come.

Some Countries That Pair Their Wines To Local Food

1. **South Africa**:

- Grapes Used: Chenin Blanc, Chardonnay, Pinot Noir

- Popular Sparkling Wines: Graham Beck, Simonsig, Villiera

- Pairings: Bobotie, Braaivleis, Biltong, Koeksisters, Cape Malay Curry

2. **Morocco**:

- Grapes Used: Chardonnay, Clairette Blanche, Ugni Blanc

- Popular Sparkling Wines: Domaine Sahari

- Pairings: Harira, Tagine, Couscous, Pastilla, Makouda

3. **Algeria**:

- Grapes Used: Alicante Bouschet, Carignan, Grenache

- Popular Sparkling Wines: Castel

- Pairings: Shakshuka, Couscous, Lham Lahlou, Merguez, Mechoui

4. **Tunisia**:

- Grapes Used: Chardonnay, Pinot Noir, Pinot Meunier

- Popular Sparkling Wines: Domaine Faouzi

- Pairings: Brik, Mechouia, Tajine, Couscous, Maakouda

5. **Egypt**:

- Grapes Used: Chardonnay, Chenin Blanc, Viognier

- Popular Sparkling Wines: Obelisk

- Pairings: Koshari, Fatta, Ful Medames, Kebab, Hawawshi

6. **Morocco**:

- Grapes Used: Chardonnay, Clairette Blanche, Ugni Blanc

- Popular Sparkling Wines: Domaine Sahari

- Pairings: Harira, Tagine, Couscous, Pastilla, Makouda

7. **Zambia**:

- Grapes Used: Chenin Blanc, Muscadel, Pinot Noir

- Popular Sparkling Wines: Mutale

- Pairings: Nshima, Kapenta, Braised Goat, Chikanda, Samosas

8. **Nigeria**:

- Grapes Used: Seyval Blanc, Vidal Blanc

- Popular Sparkling Wines: Chateau Vale Nigeria

- Pairings: Jollof Rice, Suya, Egusi Soup, Pounded Yam, Moi Moi

9. **Mozambique**:

- Grapes Used: Chardonnay, Chenin Blanc, Viognier

- Popular Sparkling Wines: Montebelo

- Pairings: Piri-Piri Chicken, Matapa, Bazaruto Prawns, Xima, Feijoada

10. **Kenya**:

- Grapes Used: Chardonnay, Chenin Blanc, Colombard

- Popular Sparkling Wines: Rift Valley Wines

- Pairings: Ugali, Kachumbari, Nyama Choma, Pilau, Samosas

11. **Zimbabwe**:

- Grapes Used: Chenin Blanc, Pinotage, Pinot Meunier

- Popular Sparkling Wines: Nyaradzo

- Pairings: Sadza, Muboora, Kapenta, Dovi, Bota

12. **Tanzania**:

- Grapes Used: Chenin Blanc, Muscat

- Popular Sparkling Wines: Dodoma

- Pairings: Ugali, Pilau, Samosas, Mchicha, Nyama Choma

Phileas Fogg's Choice of Sparkling Wines and Local Foods

Here are some locally produced sparkling wines Phileas Fogg may have encountered during his travels through Africa, along with suggested food pairings and brief histories:

1. **Graham Beck Brut Rosé - South Africa**: This sparkling wine is a blend of Chardonnay and Pinot Noir grapes and is known for its delicate pink color and notes of strawberries and raspberries. It's perfect to pair with grilled seafood or a light salad. The Graham Beck winery has been producing wines in South Africa for over 30 years.

2. **Simonsig Kaapse Vonkel Brut - South Africa**: Another South African sparkling wine, this one is made in the traditional champagne method and has notes of green apple and brioche. Pair it with goat cheese or a rich seafood pasta dish. The Simonsig winery has been producing wines for over 300 years.

3. **Pongrácz Brut** - South Africa: A blend of Chardonnay and Pinot Noir, this wine has notes of citrus and a long finish. Pair it with sushi or spicy Asian cuisine. The Pongrácz winery was established in 1989.

4. **Méthode Cap Classique Jacques Bruére Brut Reserve** - South Africa: A wine with a deep gold color, this sparkling wine has notes of roasted almonds and brioche. Pair it with roast chicken or creamy risotto. The winery's founder, Jacques Bruére, was a pioneer of South African wine production.

5. **Van Loveren Christina Brut** - South Africa: An aromatic wine with fruity notes, this sparkling wine is perfect as an aperitif. Pair it with light appetisers or dessert. The Van Loveren winery has been privately owned for over 80 years.

6. **Laborie Brut** - South Africa: A wine with a creamy texture and notes of baked apples, this sparkling wine is perfect with grilled fish or smoked salmon. The Laborie winery has been around since the 1700s.

7. **Alvi's Drift Brut** - South Africa: With notes of citrus and green apple, this wine is perfect with grilled chicken or a light pasta dish. The Alvi's Drift winery was founded in the 1920s.

8. **Backsberg Brut** - South Africa: A gold-colored wine with notes of biscuit and honey, this sparkling wine is perfect with aged cheeses or a decadent dessert. The Backsberg winery is one of the oldest in South Africa.

9. **Bernard-Massard Brut** - Tunisia: A sparkling wine from North Africa, this wine has notes of green apples and is perfect as an aperitif. Pair it with light appetizers or a seafood salad. Bernard-Massard has been producing sparkling wines since 1921.

10. **Solms-Delta Lekkerwijn** - South Africa: A blend of Chenin Blanc and Pinotage, this sparkling wine has notes of apple and peach. Pair it with spicy Indian cuisine or fresh seafood. The Solms-Delta winery has a long history dating back to the 1700s.

11. **Misgunst Brut** - South Africa: A wine with notes of toast and citrus, this sparkling wine is perfect with a creamy risotto or grilled shellfish. The Misgunst winery was established in the early 1900s.

6

12. **Veuve Clicquot Ponsardin Yellow Label Brut** - Egypt: This sparkling wine from Egypt has notes of apples and biscuits and is perfect with grilled lamb or beef. The Veuve Clicquot Ponsardin winery was founded in 1772 and has a long history of producing world-renowned champagnes.

I hope this gives you a good idea of the variety of sparkling wines Phileas Fogg may have encountered during his travels through Africa.

Non-alcoholic Wines

Non-alcoholic wine production in Africa is still a relatively unknown and developing industry. Despite this, some African countries have made strides to establish a foothold in the market, offering unique flavors and mixes with health benefits.

History: Non-alcoholic wine production in Africa can be traced back to the early 2000s, with South Africa taking the lead. However, it wasn't until recent years that the production of non-alcoholic wine started gaining popularity due to increased health awareness and religious reasons.

Topography and Climate: The topography and climate in Africa vary across the continent, which makes it perfect for growing grapes. Countries like South Africa, Morocco, Tunisia, Algeria, and Egypt have an arid climate, which is ideal for grapevines since they require less moisture. The Mediterranean climate of the North African region and the moderate climate of South Africa supports the growth of grapes with subtle flavours.

Demand: The demand for non-alcoholic wine in Africa is on the rise due to a growing health-conscious consumer base. This segment of drinkers is looking for healthier beverage choices that are not only low in calories but also provide functional benefits.

Vinification Techniques: The vinification process for non-alcoholic wine is similar to that of regular wine. However, in non-alcoholic wine production, the fermentation process is stopped before the alcohol content can increase. This is achieved through a filtering process or by using yeast that dies within the alcohol content of 0.5%.

Owners: Some of the top producers of non-alcoholic wine in Africa include Robertson Winery in South Africa, Hammoud in Tunisia, and Medina in Morocco. Additionally, there are smaller wineries and startups venturing into the industry, bringing fresh flavors and mixes to the market.

In conclusion, the production of non-alcoholic wines in Africa is still in its nascent stages. However, the demand for this drink is on the rise, and producers are continuously improving their vinification techniques to achieve unique flavors and health benefits. With the vast agricultural landscape that Africa offers, it is only a matter of time before non-alcoholic wine production becomes a significant industry.

Phileas Fogg's Choices of Some African Non-alcoholic Wines and Their Suitable Food Pairings

1. **Lautus Savvy White** (South Africa)

- Suitable food pairings: seafood dishes such as grilled shrimp, sushi, and fish tacos.

2. **De-Alcoholised Chenin Blanc** (South Africa)

- Suitable food pairings: grilled chicken, roasted vegetables, and creamy pasta dishes.

3. **Robertson Winery Non-Alcoholic Sweet White** (South Africa)

- Suitable food pairings: spicy Indian dishes, Thai curries, and fruity desserts like peach cobbler.

4. **Siwela Non-Alcoholic Grape Juice** (Swaziland)

- Suitable food pairings: cheese plates, charcuterie boards, and light sandwiches.

5. **Vredenheim Non-Alcoholic Pinotage** (South Africa)

- Suitable food pairings: hearty stews, braised beef dishes, and roasted mushrooms.

6. **Le Rue Chardonnay** (South Africa)

- Suitable food pairings: grilled or baked salmon, roasted chicken, and creamy soups.

7. **J.C. Le Roux Le Domaine Non-Alcoholic Sparkling Wine** (South Africa)

- Suitable food pairings: hors d'oeuvres, light salads, and spicy Thai dishes.

8. **Montagu Non-Alcoholic Rosé** (South Africa)

- Suitable food pairings: Mediterranean-style salads, tangy cheeses, and spicy chicken dishes.

Some African Non-alcoholic Wines and Their Suggested Food Pairings with International Cuisine:

1. **Rooibos Red Non-alcoholic Wine** - This South African wine has a smooth and fruity flavor, which makes it the perfect match for some spicy dishes. Pair it with Moroccan or Indian curries and spicy lentil stews to balance out the heat.

2. **Cape Sparkling Non-alcoholic Wine** - This sparkling wine is the perfect choice for celebrations! Pair it with light appetisers such as mini quiches, cheese boards and even sushi.

3. **Amarula Non-alcoholic Cream Liqueur** - This South African cream liqueur has a rich and fiery flavour. It pairs well with foods that have a strong flavour, such as smoked meats or cheeses, or spicy dishes like Thai or Korean cuisine.

4. **Umqombothi Non-alcoholic Beer** - This traditional South African beer is made with maize, sorghum, and hops. It goes well with grilled meats, especially chorizo and sausages, as well as spicy South African dishes like bunny chow.

5. **Zari Sparkling Non-alcoholic Wine** - This Tanzanian wine is a refreshing drink that pairs well with fruity desserts like lemon tarts or raspberry sorbet. It's also great when sipped on its own during a hot day.

I hope this helps you pair your African non-alcoholic wines with international cuisine! Enjoy your meal!

Finally…..

The African continent is home to a plethora of wines, each with their unique characteristics and production processes. Wine production in Africa dates back to the colonial days when the colonizers brought in vines from their countries.

South Africa is undoubtedly the leading producer of wine in Africa, producing approximately 900 million liters of wine annually. The country boasts of several wine-growing regions, each with its unique terroir. Stellenbosch, **Franschhoek**, and Paarl are among the leading wine-producing regions in South Africa. Some of the grape varieties grown in South Africa include Shiraz, Pinotage, and Sauvignon Blanc.

In Morocco, wine production is concentrated in the Meknes region, where the vineyards benefit from the sandy and rocky soil. Morocco produces red and white wines, among them Syrah, Cabernet Sauvignon, Grenache, and Chardonnay.

Egypt, on the other hand, sits at an important crossroads between East and West, and its wine is a harmonious blend of both. Egyptian wine is known for its aromatic and fruity flavours, thanks to its unique soil and climate. Some of the grape varieties grown here include Cabernet Sauvignon, Merlot, and Chardonnay.

Tunisia, Algeria, and Ethiopia are also making strides in the African wine industry, producing wines that are finding favor with wine enthusiasts worldwide.

When it comes to pairing African wines with food, there are several delicious options. In South Africa, a popular dish to pair with red wine is boerewors, a type of sausage made from spiced beef and pork. Another popular pairing is grilled game meat, such as springbok or kudu. For white wine, a popular local dish to pair with is seafood, especially grilled prawns.

In Morocco, wines are often paired with hearty stews such as the traditional lamb tagine or couscous dishes. Egyptian wines pair well with spicy dishes such as the koshari, a popular Egyptian street food made with rice, macaroni, and lentils, topped with a spicy tomato sauce.

Overall, the African wine and food industry is vast and diverse, with unique flavours, terroirs, and pairings. From the robust reds of South Africa to the fruity whites of Egypt, there is something for everyone's palate.

Further Readings.....

Here are some further readings on African wine pairings with foods, African sweet wines with matching foods, and African non-alcoholic wines with their suitable food pairings:

1. **African Wine Guide** by Mark Adamo: This guidebook provides a comprehensive overview of African wines, their characteristics, and the best foods to pair them with.

2. **The Africa Cookbook: Tastes of a Continent** by Jessica B. Harris: This cookbook includes recipes from different African countries, along with wine pairing suggestions specific to each dish.

3. **South African Wine and Food Pairings** by Fiona McDonald: This article explores the unique flavours and characteristics of South African wines, as well as their complementary foods.

4. **African Winemakers Take Pride in Their Continent's Rich Bounty** by Lettie Teague: This article discusses the rising popularity of African wines and provides suggestions on pairing them with continental dishes.

5. **The Sweetness of African Wines** by Wine Folly: This article focuses on sweet wines from different African countries and suggests pairing them with desserts or spicy dishes.

6. **Non-Alcoholic African Beverages** by Kitchen Butterfly: This blog post features a list of non-alcoholic African beverages and their suitable food pairings, such as hibiscus tea and jollof rice.

7. **Exploring Africa's Non-Alcoholic Beverages** by Jackie Dodd: This article provides an overview of popular non-alcoholic African beverages and their pairing suggestions, from ginger beer to palm wine.

CHAPTER 8

ANTARCTICA WINE

The history of Antarctica is a fascinating story of exploration and discovery. Antarctica is the southernmost continent and is home to the South Pole. It is the coldest, windiest, and driest continent on Earth, with temperatures averaging around -60°C (-76°F) in the winter months.

Antarctica was first sighted by modern explorers in 1820, when the Russian expedition led by Fabian Gottlieb von Bellingshausen and Mikhail Lazarev discovered the continent. The British explorer James Cook had previously sailed past the continent in 1773, but did not actually see it.

The first people to set foot on Antarctica were the Norwegians led by Carsten Borchgrevink in 1895. They established a base on Cape Adare and spent the winter on the continent. This was the first successful overwintering on the continent, and it laid the groundwork for future exploration.

In the early 20th century, Antarctica was the focus of intense exploration as various countries sought to claim parts of the continent for themselves. This led to a series of expeditions by explorers like Robert Falcon Scott, Ernest Shackleton, and Roald Amundsen, who all sought to be the first to reach the South Pole.

Scott and his team famously reached the South Pole in January 1912, only to find that they had been beaten to the pole by Amundsen and his team just a few weeks earlier. Tragically, Scott and his team died on their return journey, and their story has become one of the most famous tales of Antarctic exploration.

After World War II, Antarctica became a focus of scientific research rather than exploration. In 1959, the Antarctic Treaty was signed by 12 countries, declaring that Antarctica would be used only for peaceful purposes and that no country could claim sovereignty over any part of the continent. Today, 54 countries have signed the Antarctic Treaty.

Since then, Antarctica has become an important site for scientific research in areas such as climate change, oceanography, and astronomy. Research stations from various countries are scattered across the continent, and scientists come from around the world to study Antarctica's unique environment.

In recent years, there has been growing concern about the impact of climate change on Antarctica. The continent is losing ice at an accelerating rate, which could have serious consequences for sea level rise and global climate patterns. Scientists are working hard to understand the mechanisms behind this ice loss and to develop strategies for mitigating its effects.

In conclusion, the history of Antarctica is a story of exploration, discovery, and scientific research. From the early expeditions of explorers like Scott and Amundsen to the cutting-edge research being done today, Antarctica has played a crucial role in our understanding of the natural world.

Ice Wine

The McMurdo Dry Valleys is a region in Southern Antarctica, located more than 1,600 kilometres from the South Pole. The area is known for its harsh and unforgiving weather conditions, with temperatures dropping to as low as minus 50 degrees Celsius in the winter months. Despite the extreme climate, the region has become home to a unique vineyard owned by the Vatican - Pope's vineyard in Antarctica.

The vines currently grown at the vineyard are not traditional grapevines; instead, they are a variety of "ice wine" grapevines. Ice wine is a type of dessert wine made from grapes that have been frozen while still on the vine. When the grapes are harvested, they are pressed while still frozen, resulting in a concentrated, sweet juice. The wine produced from these grapes is known for its high sugar content and intense, fruity flavours.

The idea for the vineyard came from a Venetian microbiologist named Federico Turrini, who had been studying the ice-loving microbes that inhabit the valleys since 1998. In 2016, he approached the Vatican with the proposal to establish a vineyard in Antarctica using ice wine vines. The project was approved, and the first vines were planted in the same year.

The Pope's Vineyard

The Pope's vineyard is not open to the public, and the wine produced there is not available for sale. The production of ice wine in Antarctica is also very limited, with the vineyard producing only a few hundred bottles per year. However, the project represents a unique intersection of science, religion, and viticulture, showcasing how even the harshest environments on Earth can still offer opportunities for innovation and creativity.

CHAPTER 9

UNITED KINGDOM WINE AND CUISINE

The United Kingdom, commonly referred to as the UK, is a sovereign state that is composed of four countries; England, Scotland, Wales, and Northern Ireland. The UK has a rich and long history stretching back tens of thousands of years. Here is an in-depth look at the history, culture, peoples, topography, and climate of the United Kingdom.

History:

The history of the United Kingdom is long and complex, with many different civilizations, cultures, and religions contributing to its evolution over time. Some of the most significant events in UK history include the Roman invasion and colonisation of Britain, the Norman Conquest in 1066, the Wars of the Roses, the Reformation, the Industrial Revolution, the two World Wars, and the eventual dissolution of the British Empire.

Culture:

The culture of the UK is vast and diverse, with the four constituent countries all having their own unique identities and traditions. The UK is known worldwide for its contributions to art, music, film, literature, and science. Additionally, the UK is home to some of the world's most famous landmarks, including the Tower of London, Stonehenge, and Buckingham Palace.

Peoples:

The population of the UK is approximately 68 million people, and it is a multicultural society with influences from all over the world. The largest ethnic groups in the UK are White British, Asian British, and Black British. The UK is also home to many immigrants, expats, and refugees from all over the world, including the Americas, Europe, Africa, Asia, and Oceania.

Topography:

The UK is a relatively small island nation that covers an area of around 242,000 square kilometers. It is located off the northwest coast of Europe, bordered by the Atlantic Ocean to the west and the North Sea to the east. The UK's topography is diverse, featuring everything from rolling hills and moors to rugged coastlines and ancient forests. The highest point in the UK is Ben Nevis, which stands at 1,345 metres tall.

Climate:

The UK has a temperate maritime climate, which means that it is often mild and wet throughout the year. Summers tend to be warm with occasional heatwaves, while winters are usually mild and rainy, with occasional snowfall in some areas. The weather can be unpredictable, with sudden storms, cold snaps, and heat waves occurring at any time.

In conclusion, the United Kingdom is a varied and fascinating country with a rich history, diverse culture, and rapidly evolving society. It is an essential part of the global community and has made significant contributions to many areas of human endeavour, ranging from art and science to politics and philosophy. Its landscape, climate, and peoples are all unique and worthy of exploration and admiration.

UK's Wine History

Wine has been produced in the UK since Roman times, but it wasn't until the 20th century that English wines began to gain recognition. The industry has grown rapidly in recent years, and now more than 500 vineyards are operating in the UK. These vineyards produce a range of different wines, including sparkling wines, white wines, and rosés, made from a variety of different grapes.

One of the most successful and well-known vineyards in the UK is Nyetimber, located in West Sussex. Established by Stuart and Sandy Moss in 1988, Nyetimber focuses on sparkling wine production, using the traditional Champagne grape varieties – Chardonnay, Pinot Noir and Pinot Meunier. Nyetimber's wines have won numerous awards, including the Decanter World Wine Awards and the International Wine and Spirit Competition.

Another popular vineyard is Ridgeview Wine Estate, also located in Sussex. Ridgeview produces a range of sparkling wines, with its Blanc de Blancs winning the Decanter World Wine Awards in 2010. The vineyard was established in the 1990s by Mike and Chris Roberts.

Camel Valley, in Cornwall, is another well-known UK vineyard. It was established by Bob and Annie Lindo in 1989, and has since won numerous awards for its sparkling rosé and white wines. Camel Valley's wines are made from a variety of grapes, including Seyval Blanc, Bacchus, and Pinot Noir.

In terms of grape varieties, Chardonnay and Pinot Noir are the most widely grown in the UK. Other grape varieties include Bacchus, Seyval Blanc, Pinot Meunier, Pinot Gris, and Rondo. The cool climate of the UK is well-suited to growing these grapes, and they are often used to produce sparkling wines.

In terms of vinification techniques, many UK vineyards use the traditional method for producing sparkling wines, which involves a second fermentation in the bottle. This is the same method used in Champagne production. Other techniques include carbonation, where carbon dioxide is added to still wine, and Charmat, where the secondary fermentation takes place in a tank rather than in the bottle.

As for food pairings, sparkling wines are well-suited to seafood and shellfish, as well as light appetizers and salads. White wines pair well with chicken and pork dishes, as well as pasta and risotto. Rosé wines are often paired with grilled meats and Mediterranean dishes.

Overall, the UK's wine industry has come a long way in recent years, producing high-quality wines that are gaining recognition both domestically and abroad. With a growing number of vineyards and a focus on sparkling wines, the UK's wine industry is certainly one to keep an eye on.

Pairing Food and Wine with Phileas Fogg

Phileas Fogg would likely have been interested in trying a range of traditional British cuisine and wine during his travels in the UK. Here are some suggestions for his culinary explorations and wine pairings:

1. **Fish and Chips**: No trip to the UK would be complete without trying this classic dish. Pair it with a light, crisp white wine such as a Bacchus or a Sauvignon Blanc.

2. **Toad in the Hole**: A hearty and comforting dish of sausages baked in a batter made of flour, eggs, and milk. Pair it with a full-bodied red wine such as a Pinot Noir or a Cabernet Sauvignon.

3. **Beef Wellington**: This dish is made of beef fillet coated in pâté and wrapped in puff pastry. Pair it with a robust red wine such as a Shiraz or a Malbec.

4. **Sticky Toffee Pudding**: A popular dessert consisting of a moist sponge cake with dates and a sticky toffee sauce. Pair it with a dessert wine such as a Muscat or a late harvest Riesling.

5. **Ploughman's Lunch**: A traditional British pub meal consisting of cheese, bread, pickles, and other accompaniments. Pair it with a light, refreshing beer or cider.

6. **Shepherd's Pie**: Another classic British dish made with ground lamb, vegetables, and topped with mashed potatoes. Pair it with a light or medium-bodied red wine such as a Merlot or a Grenache.

7. **Sunday Roast**: A traditional Sunday meal consisting of roasted meat, vegetables, and gravy. Pair it with a full-bodied red wine such as a Cabernet Sauvignon or a Syrah.

In addition to these food and wine choices, Phileas Fogg may also have been interested in trying some of the UK's world-renowned sparkling wines, such as Nyetimber or Ridgeview, which pair well with a variety of dishes.

UK'S Still Wine Industry

The United Kingdom has a growing and thriving wine industry that produces high-quality still wines. The world-class quality of UK wines is due to the country's unique combination of terroir, cool climate, and innovative winemaking techniques. The UK still wine production started to grow rapidly in the early 21st century, and is now the largest sector of the UK wine industry.

Producers:

There are numerous still wine producers in the UK, ranging from small independent vineyards to large, renowned wine estates. Some of the well-known UK still wine producers include...

- Chapel Down

- Gusbourne Estate

- Denbies Wine Estate

- Ridgeview Wine Estate

- Camel Valley Vineyard

- Bolney Wine Estate

- Nyetimber

- Hambledon Vineyard

Grapes:

The UK still wine production focuses on growing cool-climate grape varieties that can thrive in the country's unique climate. Some of the most commonly grown grape varieties for still wine production in the UK include:

- Chardonnay

- Pinot Noir

- Bacchus

- Pinot Gris

- Ortega

- Madeleine Angevine

- Seyval Blanc

Techniques:

UK winemaking is characterised by innovation and experimentation with winemaking techniques. The specialised techniques employed are due to the British climate which demands distinct methods to be employed to get the best quality possible. Some of the most common winemaking techniques used in the UK include:

- Hand-harvesting – involves picking grapes by hand to ensure they are not damaged or crushed before pressing.

- Whole bunch pressing – a technique where the whole grape clusters are pressed together without destemming or crushing, resulting in delicate flavours and aromas in the wine.

- Extended lees contact – involves leaving the wine to rest on the lees (dead yeast cells) for an extended period, which imparts additional complexity and texture to the wine.

- Cool fermentation – a slow and cool fermentation process that preserves the delicate aromas and flavours of the grapes.

- Blending – a process where multiple grape varieties are blended together to create a balanced and complex wine.

In conclusion, the UK still wine production is a thriving sector of the country's wine industry, characterised by high-quality wines, cool-climate grape varieties and specialised winemaking techniques.

UK's Non-alcoholic Wine Industry

Non-alcoholic wine, also known as dealcoholized or low-alcohol wine, is a growing industry in the UK. The use of enduringly popular grapes such as Chardonnay, Pinot Noir, and Cabernet Sauvignon produce non-alcoholic wines that replicate the taste, aroma, and texture of traditional wines.

Producers:

- Eisberg - is the UK's leading producer of non-alcoholic wines with a wide variety of options, including Cabernet Sauvignon, Chardonnay, and Rosé.

- Bees Knees - a young company that offers multi-award-winning wines, both still and sparkling, which have been dealcoholized through innovative technologies.

- Botonique - a newcomer to the scene, Botonique offers a still white and a rosé, which are made from a blend of botanicals and grapes with a low alcohol content.

Grapes:

For non-alcoholic wine production in the UK, the same grapes are used as in traditional wine production. Popular varieties include:

- Chardonnay - a white grape that produces full-bodied, complex wines.

- Pinot Noir - a red grape that is light in colour but nevertheless produces complex, nuanced wines.

- Cabernet Sauvignon - a red grape variety that is used in many fine wines due to its intense flavours of blackberry and currant.

Techniques:

There are several methods for producing non-alcoholic wines, including:

- Vacuum distillation - this method involves removing alcohol from wine using a vacuum distillation system. This process allows for minimal impact on the wine's original flavour and texture.

- Reverse osmosis - this technology separates water and ethanol from the wine, meaning that the water and flavor compounds can be retained.

- Spinning Cone Column - this technique involves vaporising the wine to remove the alcohol. The wine then goes through a process called light stripping that involves separating the aromas and flavour from the wine.

In conclusion, the UK's non-alcoholic wine industry is on the rise, and producers are using similar grapes and techniques to traditional wine production to create a range of delightful low and no-alcohol wines. The increasing demand for this beverage suggests that this industry is set to flourish in the UK in the coming years.

UK's Sparkling Wine Industry

UK's sparkling wine production has been gaining prominence and recognition in recent years due to the country's unique geography, favourable climate, and advanced wine-making techniques. The production of sparkling wines in the UK started around 60 years ago, and today, it has become a significant industry in the country.

Producers:

Some of the leading producers of sparkling wine in the UK include:

1. Nyetimber - Established in 1988, located in the South Downs of Sussex, England.

2. Chapel Down - Established in 1997, located in Kent, England.

3. Ridgeview - Established in 1995, located in South Downs of Sussex, England.

4. Gusbourne - Established in 2004, located in Kent, England.

5. Camel Valley - Established in 1989, located in Cornwall, England.

Grapes:

The most common grapes for sparkling wine production in the UK are Chardonnay, Pinot Noir, and Pinot Meunier. In addition, some winemakers also use other lesser-known grape varieties such as Bacchus, Seyval Blanc, and Reichensteiner. These varieties are chosen based on their ability to grow well in England's cooler climate and produce flavorful grapes.

Techniques:

Traditionally, the Champagne method was used to produce sparkling wines. However, the UK has developed its own traditional method called the "Classic Method" or "Methods Britannique." This technique involves the second fermentation of wine in the bottle, followed by a period of ageing on the lees to develop the desired flavors and aromas.

Winemakers in the UK are also experimenting with other techniques such as carbonation (adding CO_2 to still wine) and the Charmat method (second fermentation in a tank). Still, the classic method remains the most popular technique for producing high-quality sparkling wines in the UK.

In conclusion, the UK's sparkling wine production is a relatively young industry that is rapidly growing and gaining recognition for its high-quality offerings. With favourable geographical and climatic conditions along with advanced wine-making techniques, the UK is sure to continue producing some of the world's best sparkling wines for years to come.

Top 3 Vineyards of the UK:

1. **Ridgeview Wine Estate** - owned by the Roberts family, the vineyard is located in the South Downs of England, and produces sparkling wines made from Chardonnay, Pinot Noir, and Pinot Meunier grapes.

2. **Nyetimber Vineyard** - owned by the Thomson family, Nyetimber is also based in the South Downs of England, and specialises in making sparkling wines from classic Champagne grape varieties.

3. **Camel Valley Vineyard** - owned by the Lindo family, the vineyard is situated in Cornwall and produces a variety of sparkling, white, and rosé wines made from grapes including Chardonnay, Pinot Noir, and Seyval Blanc.

Climate, Topography & People: The South Downs of England is characterised by a maritime climate with mild winters and cool summers, while Cornwall enjoys a moderate oceanic climate, both ideal for wine production. The landscape is rolling hills for the South Downs and hills of the Cornish countryside. The people residing in the region are known for their strong agricultural traditions and love for locally produced wines.

Foods that Pair well:

Some popular food pairings with wines from these vineyards include:

- **Ridgeview** - Their sparkling wines pair well with oysters, fish and chips, and creamy risotto.

- **Nyetimber** - Their sparkling wines pair well with lobster, shellfish, and chicken dishes.

- **Camel Valley** - Their white wines pair well with grilled seafood, light pasta dishes, and salads, while their red wines match well with roasted meats like lamb and beef.

Seasonal Pairings

Wine with Local Cuisine for Summer Formal Dining

1. **English sparkling wine with seafood**: English sparkling wine is perfect for formal dining, especially when paired with seafood. Try pairing it with oysters, grilled prawns or lobster for a decadent meal.

2. **Pinot Noir with roasted lamb**: Pinot Noir is a great choice for summer dining and works really well with roasted lamb. Serve it with roasted vegetables and a tangy balsamic reduction for added flavour.

3. **Rosé with grilled salmon**: A refreshing rosé would go perfectly with grilled salmon. Serve it alongside a fresh summer salad with a lemon dressing for a light and elegant meal.

4. **Sauvignon Blanc with fish and chips**: Sauvignon Blanc is a classic summer wine and pairs well with fish and chips. The crisp acidity of the wine complements the batter and cuts through the richness of the fish.

5. **Riesling with spicy Thai or Indian dishes**: An off-dry Riesling pairs beautifully with spicy Thai or Indian dishes. The sweetness of the wine helps to counteract the spiciness of the food, while the acidity helps to freshen your palate between bites.

Wine with Local Cuisine for Summer Informal Dining

Wine is an excellent accompaniment to any meal, and when it comes to pairing wine with local cuisine, the UK has some fantastic summer dishes that can be enjoyed with a variety of wine types. Whether you are hosting an informal dining with friends or family or just enjoying a summer feast, consider pairing some of these dishes with the perfect wine:

1. **Fish and Chips with Sparkling Wine**:

Fish and chips, a quintessential British dish, is the perfect meal for summer dining. The crispy and flaky batter-fried fish and chunky chips served with a side of mushy peas are best accompanied by a glass of high-acidity sparkling wine. The bubbles in sparkling wine help to cut through the greasiness of the food and refresh the palate. A glass of crisp and fruity English sparkling wine, such as Nyetimber Classic, will be an excellent partner for this classic dish.

2. **Barbecued Meat with Rosé**:

Barbecued meats perfectly fit for summer dining, be it pork ribs, chicken wings, or lamb chops. These meats have a smoky and hearty flavour and taste great with a glass of light-bodied and fruity rosé wine. The sweetness and acidity of the rosé wine, such as Mirabeau Pure Provence, complement the smoky flavours of the barbecued meat and add a refreshing dimension to the meal.

3. **Grilled Seafood with White Wine**:

The UK has some of the finest seafood delicacies, including grilled salmon, prawns, lobsters, and scallops. These seafood dishes are best paired with a glass of light and acidic white wine, such as Sauvignon Blanc from New Zealand or the traditional English Bacchus. The lemony, crisp and herbaceous notes in Sauvignon Blanc go perfectly with the grilled seafood, while the tropical and citrusy notes found in Bacchus complement the sweet and savoury flavours of the seafood.

4. **Strawberry Desserts with Special Rosé**:

Summer is the season for fresh strawberries, and there's no better way to enjoy this fruit than in a dessert. Pairing a light dessert such as pavlova, strawberry shortcake, or Eton mess with a beautifully flavoured rosé will elevate the dessert taste. A glass of a special Rosé, like Bollinger Rosé, with it's distinctive combination of strawberries, raspberries, and cherries match seamlessly with the subtle sweetness of the desert.

In conclusion, summer dining in the UK calls for matching local cuisine with the particular type of wine to make the meal tastier and more enjoyable. A correctly paired dish with wine enhances the food's flavour and brings out its best qualities. From sparkling wines and rosés to light-bodied whites and special rosé, there are many wine types to choose from when pairing with local-style summer dining.

Wine with Local Cuisine for Winter Formal Dining

Let's dive into some UK wines and cuisine pairings that would be perfect for a winter formal dining experience:

1. **Sussex Sparkling Wine with Roasted Game Birds**: Sussex is quickly becoming known for producing high-quality sparkling wines that rival those produced in Champagne. These wines typically have bright acidity and notes of green apple and citrus, making them perfect for cutting through the rich, gamey flavours of roasted game birds like pheasant or duck.

2. **Kentish Pinot Noir with Beef Wellington**: Kent is another region that is gaining recognition for its wine production, particularly for its Pinot Noir that has been compared to Burgundy. This wine has intense fruity flavours of black cherry and raspberry, with a long finish that pairs well with the earthy, umami flavours of a beef wellington.

3. **Welsh White Wine with Roasted Root Vegetables**: Wales is often overlooked as a wine producer, but they have some delicious offerings worth trying. Their white wines have a distinctive minerality that pairs perfectly with roasted root vegetables, such as parsnips, carrots, and beets. Look for a wine that has a bright acidity to cut through the sweetness of the vegetables.

4. **English Chardonnay with Smoked Salmon**: Chardonnay might be a classic pairing for smoked salmon, but English Chardonnay brings something new to the table. These wines tend to have a lighter touch of oak and more minerality, which complement the smokiness of the salmon without overpowering it.

5. **Norfolk Rosé with a Cheese Platter:** Norfolk is another region that is producing some fantastic wines, particularly rosés. Their rosés tend to be dry and crisp, with notes of strawberry and raspberry. These flavours pair exceptionally well with a cheese platter filled with rich, creamy cheeses like brie or goat cheese.

Overall, UK wines are gaining recognition as producers of high-quality bottles that can hold their own when compared to more traditional wine regions. From sparkling wines to Pinot Noirs, Chardonnays and Rosés, there is a UK wine out there to complement any winter formal dining experience.

Wine with Local Cuisine for Winter Informal Dining

When it comes to pairing wines with local cuisine in the UK, there are a few key considerations to keep in mind. For the winter months, you'll likely want to choose heartier, more robust dishes that can stand up to bold and flavorful wines. Here are a few examples of UK wines and local cuisine pairings that are perfect for informal winter dining:

1. **Shiraz with roast beef and Yorkshire pudding**: A bold and spicy Shiraz pairs well with the rich, savoury flavours of a classic beef roast, and the pillowy texture of Yorkshire pudding provides a nice contrast to the wine's tannins.

2. **Pinot Noir with mushroom risotto**: The earthy, umami flavours of a mushroom risotto are beautifully complemented by the bright acidity and red fruit notes of a Pinot Noir.

3. **Cabernet Sauvignon with shepherd's pie**: The bold, full-bodied structure of a Cabernet Sauvignon stands up to the heartiness of a meaty shepherd's pie, while providing a touch of elegance to the rustic dish.

4. **Chardonnay with fish and chips**: The buttery richness of a Chardonnay is the perfect match for crispy, fried fish and chips. Look for a wine with balanced acidity to cut through the richness of the dish.

5. **Sparkling wine with cheese fondue**: For a festive and fun winter dish, consider serving a rich, indulgent cheese fondue with a bright, effervescent sparkling wine. The bubbles and acidity of the wine help to cut through the richness of the cheese.

In terms of UK wines to consider, look for producers like Nyetimber, Chapel Down, and Gusbourne for sparkling wines, and Camel Valley and Bolney Estate for still wines. These wineries are producing some of the finest wines in the UK and are well worth checking out.

In Conclusion, The UK wine industry has undergone significant growth and development over the past few decades. England, Scotland, Wales, and Northern Ireland are now home to over 700 vineyards, producing a variety of high-quality wines that have started gaining international recognition.

One of the main reasons for the success of the UK wine industry is the increasing awareness and appreciation of locally produced food and drink. Consumers are now more interested in the provenance and sourcing of their food and beverages, and this has led to an increased demand for locally produced wines.

The topography and microclimate of the different regions in the UK have also played a critical role in the success of the wine industry. For example, the southern parts of England, including Sussex and Kent, have similar soil types and climate conditions to the Champagne region in France, making them ideal for producing sparkling wines.

The UK wine industry is also made up of a diverse group of people, including both large commercial vineyards and small boutique wineries. These vineyards are run by passionate and dedicated individuals who take great pride in their work and are committed to producing the highest quality wines.

Overall, the UK wine industry shows great potential for continued growth and development, thanks to the support of consumers, favorable climatic conditions, and the dedication of industry professionals. The wines produced in England, Scotland, Wales, and Northern Ireland are a testament to the country's rich culture and unique terroir, making them a valuable addition to the global wine industry.

Further Readings…..

Here are some resources for further reading on UK wines and food pairings:

1. **The English Wine Producers** website (https://www.englishwineproducers.co.uk/) is a good place to start. They have information on UK winemaking, grape varieties, and vineyards, as well as a directory of English and Welsh wineries.

2. **Decanter magazine** (https://www.decanter.com/) is a well-respected wine publication that regularly features articles on UK wines, including tasting notes and recommendations.

3. **The Wine Society** (https://www.thewinesociety.com/) is a UK-based wine retailer that has a good selection of English wines. They also offer food pairing suggestions for many of their wines.

4. **Wine Folly** (https://winefolly.com/) is a website that offers wine education and resources, including an article on food pairings for sparkling wines.

5. **The English Vine** (https://www.theenglishvine.co.uk/) is a blog that focuses on the UK wine scene. They have articles on different English and Welsh wineries, as well as tips for food and wine pairing.

I hope these resources help you learn more about UK wines and how to pair them with food!

CHAPTER 10

NEW ZEALAND WINE AND CUISINE

New Zealand is a country located in the southwestern part of the Pacific Ocean. It comprises two main islands, the North Island and the South Island, along with numerous other smaller islands that surround them. The country covers an area of 268,021 square kilometres and has a population of approximately 4.9 million people.

The official languages spoken in New Zealand are English, Maori, and New Zealand Sign Language. The currency used in the country is the New Zealand Dollar (NZD). The country has a mixed-market economy that is heavily reliant on international trade.

New Zealand is known for its stunning natural beauty and diverse landscapes. It is home to numerous national parks, forests, mountains, lakes, and beaches. Some of the most popular tourist destinations in the country include Milford Sound, Lake Taupo, the Bay of Islands, and Mount Cook.

The country's Maori culture is a significant part of its identity, and visitors to New Zealand can experience it through traditional Maori performances, art, and cuisine. The country also has a rich history rooted in colonialism, and visitors can explore historic sites related to early European settlement.

New Zealand is ranked among the highest in the world for its quality of life, education, and healthcare systems. The country is also a leader in renewable energy, with most of its power coming from renewable sources such as wind, hydro, and geothermal energy.

In conclusion, New Zealand is a beautiful country with a rich cultural heritage and vibrant tourist industry. Its natural beauty, robust economy, and high quality of life make it an attractive destination for tourists and immigrants alike.

Famous New Zealand Wines

Let's dive into the fascinating world of New Zealand's wine industry.

New Zealand wine industry is one of the fastest-growing wine industries in the world. With a long and rich history dating back to the 19th century, the industry has gone through significant changes and improvements over the last few decades. Today, New Zealand is known for producing some of the world's finest and distinct wines, particularly Sauvignon Blanc.

Vineyards and Owners:

The country's wine industry is dominated by small and medium-sized wineries, with only a small number of large companies. Most of the vineyards are located in the Hawke's Bay, Marlborough, and Central Otago regions, with Marlborough being the largest growing region, accounting for around 75% of New Zealand's wine production.

Topography:

New Zealand's wine regions are varied in topography, from the wide, flat plains of Marlborough to the steep hillsides of Central Otago. New Zealand's vineyards are also located in relatively cool or moderate-climate zones, which means that the grapes grow slower, retaining more flavour and acidity, producing wines that better represent the terroir and varietals.

Culture:

New Zealand's wine culture is mainly centred around the production and enjoyment of wines. Wine is an essential part of the country's culinary culture, where it is often enjoyed with various types of cuisine. The industry is also known for its focus on sustainability, with many vineyards embracing eco-friendly practices and planting native and other beneficial trees to create a more biodiverse environment.

Grapes:

The most commonly grown grape varieties in New Zealand include Sauvignon Blanc, Pinot Noir, Chardonnay, Pinot Gris, and Riesling. Sauvignon Blanc makes up around 85% of the country's white wine production, while Pinot Noir accounts for most of the red wine production.

Vinification Techniques:

New Zealand wineries have embraced modern winemaking techniques, with many adopting sustainable and organic principles in their vineyards. Many winemakers are using wild yeast and spontaneous fermentation methods to make wines with distinct and complex flavours. Many wineries have also adopted temperature control during fermentation and ageing. Stainless steel tanks are a popular choice for fermentation, allowing for more precise temperature control, and producing crisp, bright wines.

Food Pairings:

New Zealand wines pair well with a wide range of foods. Sauvignon Blanc pairs perfectly with seafood, such as oysters and prawns. Pinot Noir is a great choice for ducks and other game birds. Chardonnay is an excellent match for white meats, such as chicken and pork, as well as creamy sauces. Riesling is a good choice to balance out spicy and sweet flavours in Asian cuisine.

Pairing wines from notable vineyards with local cuisine:

New Zealand has a diverse range of vineyards and local cuisines, so here are some pairing suggestions:

1. **Sauvignon Blanc from Cloudy Bay Vineyards with Fresh Seafood:**

Cloudy Bay Vineyards is known for their crisp and fruity Sauvignon Blanc, which pairs perfectly with fresh seafood dishes like grilled or steamed white fish, ceviche or oysters.

2. **Pinot Noir from Felton Road with Lamb or Duck:**

Felton Road's Pinot Noir has a rich and earthy flavour that pairs well with gamey meats like lamb or duck. Try it with slow-cooked lamb shanks, seared duck breast or roasted wild game.

3. **Chardonnay from Kumeu River Wines with Creamy Dishes:**

Kumeu River Wines produces rich and buttery Chardonnay that pairs well with creamy dishes like risotto, pasta or scalloped potatoes. The wine's acidity will help cut through the richness of the dish.

4. **Syrah from Craggy Range Vineyards with BBQ or Grilled Meats:**

Craggy Range Vineyards' Syrah has a bold and spicy flavour that pairs well with grilled or barbecued meats. Try it with spicy beef ribs, smoky pork chops, or grilled lamb skewers.

5. **Riesling from Mt. Difficulty with Spicy Asian Dishes:**

Mt. Difficulty's Riesling is crisp with a bright acidity that lends itself well to spicy dishes. Pair it with spicy Thai curries, Chinese hot pot or Indian biryani.

Still Wines

New Zealand is known for its wine-making industry, particularly its production of "still" wines that are not sparkling. New Zealand has a diverse wine industry, but Pinot Noir, Sauvignon Blanc, Chardonnay, and Pinot Gris are the most popular varieties.

The country has a favourable climate for viticulture, with many wine regions located on the east coast of both the North and South Islands. These regions benefit from the moderating influence of the Pacific Ocean to the east and the sheltering mountains to the west, providing a range of microclimates that are conducive to different grape varieties.

The most famous wine region of New Zealand is Marlborough, which is located at the northern tip of the South Island. This region produces around 70% of the country's wine, with Sauvignon Blanc being its most prominent variety. Other regions that are important for still wine production in New Zealand include Hawke's Bay, Wairarapa, and Central Otago.

New Zealand is known for producing high-quality still wines that are characterised by their fresh, zesty, and crisp flavours. The Sauvignon Blancs produced in Marlborough are recognized internationally for their distinctive aromas, such as gooseberry, passion fruit, and grassy aromas. Pinot Noir, another popular variety, is known for its earthy, spicy, and fruity aromas.

The New Zealand government has implemented strict regulations to ensure the quality of wine produced in the country. The regulations ensure that the grapes used for making wine are of high quality and have been grown sustainably. Additionally, winemakers are required to follow strict production standards, including grape sourcing, fermenting, and aging processes.

Overall, New Zealand's still wine industry is known for producing high-quality wines that are recognized worldwide for their unique flavours and aromas. The country's focus on sustainability and quality has ensured that its wines remain competitive in the global market.

Still Wines Paired With Local Cuisines:

1. **Sauvignon Blanc with green-lipped mussels:** New Zealand's world-renowned Sauvignon Blanc is a perfect match for green-lipped mussels, a local delicacy that's often served in a white wine and garlic sauce.

2. **Pinot Noir with lamb:** New Zealand's cool climate and rich pastures make it an ideal place for raising lamb, and Pinot Noir is the perfect wine to accompany it. The black cherry and spice notes in the wine complement the rich, gamey flavours of the meat.

3. **Chardonnay with whitebait fritters:** Whitebait fritters, made from the tiny, translucent juveniles of various species of fish, are a classic Kiwi dish. The buttery richness of Chardonnay is a great match for the delicate, crisp flavour of the fritters.

4. Syrah with venison: Another meat that's well-suited to New Zealand's climate, venison pairs beautifully with a bold, spicy Syrah. The wine's dark fruit flavours and smoky notes complement the robust flavour of the meat.

5. **Riesling with pork belly:** Riesling's zesty acidity and minerality make it a great match for rich, fatty meats like pork belly. It also pairs well with Asian-influenced flavours like soy sauce and ginger, which are often used to marinate the meat.

6. **Pinot Gris with crayfish:** Crayfish (also known as rock lobster) is a Kiwi delicacy that's often served simply grilled or boiled with a squeeze of lemon. The crisp, zesty flavours of Pinot Gris complement the sweet, delicate flavour of the seafood.

7. **Merlot with beef:** Rich, meaty dishes like steak and beef stew are a great match for a full-bodied red like Merlot. New Zealand's grass-fed beef has a distinct flavor that pairs well with the wine's dark fruit flavours and chewy tannins.

8. **Gewürztraminer with spicy Thai food:** New Zealand's Asian-inspired cuisine scene means there are plenty of Thai restaurants to choose from. The aromatic, floral notes of Gewürztraminer help cool the heat of spicy dishes like green curry and tom yum soup.

9. **Cabernet Sauvignon with venison sausage:** New Zealand's traditional sausages often include unique meats like venison, which pairs well with the bold, tannic structure of Cabernet Sauvignon. The wine's cassis and tobacco flavours also complement the smoky, savoury notes of the sausage.

10. **Grüner Veltliner with goat cheese:** New Zealand produces some great goat's milk cheeses, which pair beautifully with the acidic, herbaceous notes of Grüner Veltliner. The wine's crisp apple and citrus flavours also balance the richness of the cheese.

Still Wines Paired With Desserts

New Zealand is an island country that has a long tradition of making delicious desserts. These desserts are often based on the country's fresh produce and incorporate local ingredients, such as honey, kiwi fruit, and feijoa. When it comes to pairing these desserts with still wines, New Zealand's world-renowned wine industry produces some excellent options that perfectly complement the country's desserts. Here are some examples of New Zealand desserts and their perfectly paired still wine options:

1. **Pavlova:** This famous meringue-based dessert is topped with whipped cream and fresh fruit. The acidity in the wine will cut through the richness of the cream. Pair it with a New Zealand Sauvignon Blanc.

2. **Hokey Pokey Ice Cream:** This iconic New Zealand flavour of ice cream contains honeycomb toffee bits. Pair it with a Pinot Gris for a refreshing and lively pairing.

3. **Feijoa Sorbet:** This refreshing, tropical sorbet is made from the feijoa fruit, which is native to New Zealand. Pair it with a Riesling for its refreshing acidity and crisp fruit flavours.

4. **Lemon Meringue Pie:** This classic dessert features a tart lemon filling and a fluffy meringue topping. Pair it with a Chardonnay for a refreshing and citrusy flavour.

5. **Kiwi Fruit Tart:** This tart features kiwi fruit slices, which have a sweet and tangy flavour. Pair it with a Gewürztraminer for its exotic fruit flavours and floral notes.

6. **Gingernut Biscuits:** These spicy cookies have a crunchy texture and a warm flavour. Pair them with a Pinot Noir to bring out the rich, earthy tones in both the wine and the biscuits.

7. **Chocolate Lamingtons:** These chocolate-coated, sponge-cake bites are often filled with jam or cream. Pair them with a Merlot for an indulgent and rich dessert experience.

8. **Anzac Biscuits:** These crunchy, oat and coconut cookies are a New Zealand classic. Pair them with a Pinot Gris for a crisp, refreshing complement.

9. **Apple Crumble:** This classic British dessert is also a New Zealand favourite. Pair it with a Chardonnay for a rich and buttery flavour that will complement the sweetness of the apples.

10. **Fruit Salad:** This refreshing dessert typically features a mix of seasonal fruits such as strawberries, blueberries and kiwi fruit. Pair it with a Syrah for a bold and spicy flavour.

11. **Sticky Toffee Pudding:** This sponge cake dessert is smothered in a rich toffee sauce. Pair it with a Pinot Noir to bring out the rich and deep flavours in both the wine and dessert.

12. **Gingerbread Cake:** This spiced cake is perfect for those who love warm and comforting flavours. Pair it with a Gewürztraminer for a sweet, fruity and festive wine that celebrates the holiday season.

In conclusion, the best way to experience the flavours of New Zealand's desserts is to pair them with the country's excellent still wines. From tangy and tart lemon meringue pie to sweet and spicy gingerbread cake, there is a wine pairing that will complement each dessert perfectly.

Sparkling Wines

The history of sparkling wine in New Zealand dates back to the early 20th century, but it wasn't until the 1980s when the industry began to take shape. Today, the country is known for producing high-quality sparkling wines that are enjoyed both domestically and internationally.

There are several vineyards in New Zealand that specialise in producing sparkling wines. Some of the most notable ones include:

1. **Cloudy Bay:** This winery is located in the Marlborough region and produces a range of sparkling wines using the traditional method.

2. **Quartz Reef:** This winery is located in Central Otago and produces a range of organic sparkling wines using biodynamic principles.

3. **No.1 Family Estate:** This winery is located in Marlborough and specialises solely in producing Methode Traditionnelle sparkling wines.

4. **Akarua:** Located in the Central Otago region, this winery produces a range of sparkling wines using biodynamic principles.

The owners of these vineyards are passionate about producing high-quality wines that reflect the unique terroir of New Zealand. They use a variety of grape varieties, including Chardonnay, Pinot Noir, and Pinot Meunier.

The climate in New Zealand is ideal for producing sparkling wines. The country's moderate temperatures provide a long growing season, which allows the grapes to ripen slowly and develop complex flavors. The country's topography is also ideal, with many vineyards nestled in valleys and on hillsides.

Overall, the sparkling wine industry in New Zealand is thriving, and the country is gaining a reputation as a top producer of high-quality Methode Traditionnelle sparkling wines.

Pairing Sparkling Wines With Food

New Zealand produces a variety of high-quality sparkling wines that pair well with many different types of cuisine. Here are some examples, along with suggested food pairings:

1. **Cloudy Bay Pelorus NV Sparkling Wine** – This wine is a blend of Chardonnay and Pinot Noir grapes and exhibits notes of citrus and brioche. It pairs well with oysters, smoked salmon, and shellfish.

2. **Quartz Reef NV Methode Traditionnelle Brut** – Made from 60% Pinot Noir and 40% Chardonnay grapes, this wine is creamy with a crisp finish. It goes well with sushi, sashimi, and tempura.

3. **Hunter's MiruMiru™ Reserve 2013** – This wine is a blend of Chardonnay, Pinot Noir, and Pinot Meunier grapes and has notes of apricot, hazelnut, and toasted brioche. It pairs well with grilled prawns, lobster, and scallops.

4. **No. 1 Family Estate Cuvee Adele 2012** – This 100% Chardonnay wine has notes of apple, pear, and lemon zest. It pairs well with creamy pasta dishes, chicken alfredo, and risotto.

5. **Akarua Rose Brut NV** – This wine is made from 50% Pinot Noir and 50% Chardonnay grapes and has flavours of strawberries and cream with a hint of citrus. It goes well with grilled tuna, salmon, and charcuterie.

6. **Nautilus Cuvee Marlborough NV** – This is a blend of Chardonnay and Pinot Noir grapes, featuring notes of almond, brioche, and lemon. It pairs well with creamy soups, mushroom risotto, and roast chicken.

7. **Waipara Hills Blanc de Blancs 2013** – This wine is made entirely from Chardonnay grapes and has flavours of peach, citrus, and toasted nuts. It goes well with buttery seafood, such as lobster or crab, and creamy cheeses.

8. **Palliser Estate Methode Traditionnelle 2011** – This wine is a blend of Chardonnay and Pinot Noir grapes, featuring notes of honey, brioche, and dried apricot. It pairs well with grilled chicken or fish with a fruit salsa or chutney.

9. **Gibbston Valley NV** – This wine is a blend of Pinot Noir, Chardonnay, and Pinot Meunier grapes and has flavours of apple, pear, and toasted nuts. It goes well with smoked salmon, seafood pasta, and cream-based soups.

10. **Daniel Le Brun Blanc de Blancs NV** – This wine is made entirely from Chardonnay grapes and has aromas of flowers, lemon, and brioche. It pairs well with grilled shrimp, scallops or fish with a citrus glaze or sauce.

These are just a few examples of the many sparkling wines produced in New Zealand, but they represent the diversity and quality of the region's wine industry.

Pairing Sparkling Wines With Desserts

Here are classic New Zealand desserts paired with some of the country's finest sparkling wines:

1. **Pavlova:** This is perhaps the most iconic New Zealand dessert, consisting of a meringue base that is topped with whipped cream and fruit. A great sparkling wine to pair with this dessert would be Quartz Reef NV Brut (Central Otago).

2. **Hokey Pokey Ice Cream:** This classic New Zealand ice cream features chunks of honeycomb and pairs particularly well with Nautilus NV Cuvee Marlborough Brut.

3. **Feijoa Sorbet:** Made from the native Feijoa fruit, this sorbet is typically tangy, sweet, and exotic. For a perfect pairing, try it with a glass of Lindauer Special Reserve Blanc de Blancs.

4. **Lemon Delicious Pudding:** This heavenly pudding is known for its irresistible combination of tangy lemon curd and billowy meringue. Combine it with a sparkling wine from Lindauer Special Reserve Rosé.

5. **Afghan Cookies:** These chocolate biscuits are topped with icing and a walnut half. Enjoy them with Morton Estate NV Brut Rosé.

6. **Lolly Cake**: This popular kiwi cake is typically made with malt biscuits and chopped up milk bottles (a type of candy). A lively wine to pair with lolly cake would be Cloudy Bay Pelorus Vintage.

7. **Ginger Gems**: These small bite-size cakes are usually made with crystallised ginger and baking soda. Delight in them with Mumm Marlborough Vintage.

8. **Trifle**: This classic English dessert is popular in New Zealand and is a multi-layered dish made from custard, sponge cake, fruit, and whipped cream. A sparkling wine that complements this dessert is Tohu Rewa Methode Traditionnelle Sparkling Rosé.

9. **Pineapple Lump Cheesecake**: A recipe that's hard to resist! Creamy cheesecake made with pineapple chunks and chocolate pineapple lumps. Try it with a light sparkling like Oyster Bay Brut.

10. **Choux Pastry**: These small, round pastry shells are often filled with whipped cream or custard. To balance their sweetness, pair them with a slightly acidic and full-bodied sparkling like No 1 Family Estate Cuvee No. 1.

11. **Anzac Biscuits**: These oat-based biscuits were originally baked by Australian and New Zealand soldiers during WWI. Pair them with Saint Clair Family Estate 'Vicar's' Choice' Methode Traditionnelle.

12. **Caramel Slice**: a popular treat consisting of a buttery biscuit base, dulce de leche, and a chocolate topping. Try it with NV Nautilus Estate Cuvee Marlborough Brut.

I hope you find these suggestions helpful in indulging in the rich flavours and decadent desserts of New Zealand. Enjoy!

Non-alcoholic Wines

Non-alcoholic wines in New Zealand have become increasingly popular over the years, primarily due to the health-conscious trend sweeping across the country. These wines are perfect for those who prefer a more controlled intake of alcohol and want to indulge in the delectable flavours of wine without any ill effects. Non-alcoholic wines are also great for those who have been instructed to refrain from drinking alcohol for health or medical reasons.

Currently, there are only a few vineyards that produce non-alcoholic wines in New Zealand, and most of them have made a name for themselves in the country's wine industry. Some of the notable vineyards that produce non-alcoholic wines in New Zealand include Lindauer, Grapevine, and **Zeffer.**

Lindauer is one of the oldest vineyards in New Zealand that produces non-alcoholic wines. Established in 1895, the vineyard is located in Gisborne, a region known for its perfect grape-growing conditions. Lindauer's non-alcoholic wines are made using high-quality grapes grown in the Gisborne region, and the production process involves the use of innovative techniques that maintain the wine's original flavour.

Grapevine is another renowned vineyard in New Zealand that produces non-alcoholic wines. The vineyard is located in the Hawke's Bay region, with a perfect topography and climate for grape-growing. The vineyard uses a unique process in the production of their non-alcoholic wines, which involves low-temperature distillation to extract the wine's flavour without compromising on its character.

Zeffer is a family-owned vineyard located in the beautiful Hawke's Bay region. The vineyard produces a range of non-alcoholic apple and pear ciders, which have become increasingly popular in New Zealand. Zeffer uses high-quality fruits grown in their orchards, and the production process involves a unique blend of traditional and modern methods.

The people who consume non-alcoholic wines in New Zealand are diverse, but health-conscious individuals who want to enjoy a glass of wine without the harmful effects of alcohol primarily make up the bulk of the consumers. Also, non-alcoholic wines are becoming a popular choice for designated drivers, pregnant women, and those who are in recovery from addiction.

In terms of flavour, non-alcoholic wines in New Zealand come in a range of tastes, from fruity and refreshing to bold and complex. The flavours usually depend on the type of grape used, the production process, and the vineyard. Some of the common flavours include grapefruit, pineapple, apple, and blackcurrant. The wines also come in varying levels of sweetness, from dry to semi-sweet.

In conclusion, the non-alcoholic wine industry in New Zealand is still in its infancy, but it has shown incredible promise, with vineyards producing quality wines that cater to the needs of health-conscious individuals. The vineyards' owners, topography, climate, and innovative production processes all come together to produce a range of delicious non-alcoholic wines that satisfy the palate.

Pairing Non-alcoholic Wines With Food

Although New Zealand is known for its alcoholic wines, there are also some excellent non-alcoholic options available. Here are some examples of New Zealand non-alcoholic wines paired with food:

1. **Lindauer Alcohol-Free Sauvignon Blanc**: This refreshing wine pairs well with seafood dishes including fish and chips, prawn stir-fry, or grilled salmon.

2. **Jukes 01 Chardonnay**: With notes of green apple and citrus, Jukes 01 Chardonnay is best served with chicken and mushroom pasta or roasted chicken with a side of roasted vegetables.

3. **Crafters Union Alcohol-Free Rosé**: This dry, crisp rosé pairs well with light cheeses, grilled chicken salads, and creamy pastas.

4. **0.0% Giesen Sauvignon Blanc**: This non-alcoholic Sauvignon Blanc is perfect for pairing with oysters, grilled fish, or even a classic fish and chips dish.

5. **McGuigan Zero Shiraz**: This full-bodied and richly flavoured Shiraz pairs well with hearty meat dishes like beef stroganoff or shepherd's pie.

6. **Edenvale Alcohol-Free Shiraz**: Another excellent option for meat dishes, Edenvale's Alcohol-Free Shiraz can be paired with red meats, grilled vegetables, or even barbeque dishes.

7. **Lindauer Alcohol-Free Rosé**: This vibrant and fruity wine pairs well with salads, light pastas, and seafood dishes like crab cakes or seared scallops.

8. **Ara Zero Sauvignon Blanc**: With notes of lime and tropical fruit, Ara Zero Sauvignon Blanc is an excellent pairing for spicy foods like Thai curries, grilled vegetables, or spicy chicken dishes.

9. **Rawsons Retreat Cabernet Sauvignon**: This non-alcoholic Cabernet Sauvignon is a perfect match with cheesy pasta dishes, roasted lamb or beef, and grilled or roasted vegetables.

10. **Stanley Estate Marlborough Sauvignon Blanc**: With a crisp and refreshing taste, Stanley Estate Marlborough Sauvignon Blanc pairs well with white fish dishes like cod or haddock, salads, and pasta dishes with light sauces.

All of these non-alcoholic wines are delicious and versatile, making them easy to pair with a variety of foods. They are ideal for those who want to enjoy the taste of wine without the alcohol, whether for health or personal reasons.

Pairing Non-alcoholic Wines With Desserts

New Zealand is known to produce some of the finest desserts and non-alcoholic wines in the world. Here are some examples of desserts and non-alcoholic wines that pair well together:

1. **Pavlova** - This iconic New Zealand dessert is made with a meringue base, topped with whipped cream and fresh fruit. Pair it with a non-alcoholic Sauvignon Blanc for a perfect balance of sweetness and acidity.

2. **Hokey Pokey Ice Cream** - A classic Kiwi treat made with vanilla ice cream and crunchy honeycomb candy. Pair it with a Chardonnay-style white grape juice for a creamy, buttery flavour.

3. **Anzac Biscuits** - A traditional New Zealand biscuit made with rolled oats, golden syrup, and coconut. Pair it with a non-alcoholic Riesling for a refreshing citrus burst.

4. **Feijoa and Lemon Shortcake** - A delicate shortcake filled with tangy feijoa and zesty lemon curd. Pair it with a non-alcoholic Pinot Gris for a sweet and slightly spicy taste.

5. **Lemon and Ginger Slice** - A spicy, sweet slice with a tangy lemon topping. Pair it with a non-alcoholic Gewürztraminer for a deliciously floral and fruity aroma.

6. **Lolly Cake** - A colourful cake made with condensed milk, butter, and chopped-up lollies (sweets). Pair it with a non-alcoholic Sparkling Rosé for a fun, bubbly flavour.

7. **Chocolate Fish** - A Kiwi classic made with marshmallow and chocolate coated in pink sugar. Pair it with a non-alcoholic Merlot for a smooth and fruity flavour.

8. **Banana Cake** - A moist cake made with ripe bananas, walnuts, and cinnamon. Pair it with a non-alcoholic Chardonnay for a rich, creamy flavour.

9. **Kiwifruit Cheesecake** - A creamy cheesecake topped with tangy kiwifruit slices. Pair it with a non-alcoholic Syrah for a balanced, full-bodied taste.

10. **Carrot and Walnut Cake** - A flavorful, moist cake made with grated carrots, walnuts, and spices. Pair it with a non-alcoholic Cabernet Sauvignon for a savoury depth of flavour.

11. **Chocolate Afghans** - A crunchy biscuit made with cocoa, butter, and crushed cornflakes. Pair it with a non-alcoholic Malbec for a fruity and slightly smoky flavour.

12. **Gingerbread** - A spicy cake made with ginger, honey, and molasses. Pair it with a non-alcoholic Pinot Noir for a light, fruity taste.

These are only some of the many New Zealand desserts and non-alcoholic wines available, there's sure to be a pairing that will satisfy your taste buds.

Seasonal Pairings

Wine with Local Cuisine for Summer Formal Dining

Let's pair New Zealand's authentic dishes with its finest wine selections. New Zealand is a land of varied terroirs, climates, and soil types. It is renowned for its dairy and meat products and is a stunning country when it comes to wine production. Let's dive in to explore New Zealand's dish and wine pairings in more detail below:

1. **Paua Fritters:**

Paua (abalone) fritters are a popular traditional dish, prepared by mixing chopped paua, bread crumbs, eggs, parsley, and onions. Paua Fritters are paired well with Pinot Gris - a light-bodied white wine with hints of apples and pears, grown in the Central Otago region.

2. **Hangi:**

Hangi is a traditional Maori method of cooking. Meats, vegetables and kumara (sweet potatoes) are wrapped in leaves and steamed in an earth oven. The steamed food is tender and retains its signature earthy aroma. The Hangi pairs well with The Bay of Plenty Chardonnay - an oak-aged wine with light notes of apple, pear, and vanilla.

3. **Whitebait Fritters:**

Whitebait Fritters are an all-time favourite dish that is made with the small, delicate white fish mixed with eggs and lightly cooked. They pair well with Marlborough Sauvignon Blanc - an acidic and crisp wine poured from Sauvignon Blanc grape.

4. **Pavlova:**

Pavlova, a meringue-based dessert with toppings of whipped cream and fresh fruits. It pairs well with a sweet and sparkling wine - the Central Otago Riesling with its flavours of honey, fruit, and almond.

5. **Roast Lamb:**

Roast Lamb is a staple food in New Zealand culture. Lamb meat is roasted with garlic, rosemary and served with roasted vegetables. This mainstream and delicious food goes well with Martinborough Pinot Noir, an intense and fruity red wine.

6. **Kiwi Burger:**

An all-time beloved classic is Kiwi Burger, but instead of the typical beef burger patty, it consists of New Zealand's national bird, kiwi meat, topped up with beetroot, lettuce, onions, egg, and served with chunky fries. The Kiwi Burger is well paired with a Hawke's Bay Syrah - a full-bodied wine with deep spicy notes.

7. **Pāua:**

Pāua, one of New Zealand's delicacies, is the abalone shellfish that can be cooked in all ways, including being stewed, fried, or sauteed. It pairs well with Central Otago Pinot Noir - a moderate-bodied wine with aromas of dark fruits, chocolate, and herbaceous notes.

8. **Oysters:**

New Zealand is known as home to some of the best oysters globally. Raw Oyster is served with a slice of lemon, and a vinaigrette dressing is usually made with wine vinegar, shallots, and black pepper. Oysters pair exceptionally well with Marlborough Chardonnay, a crisp and acidic wine with fruity notes.

9. **Bluff Oysters:**

Bluff Oysters are from the Southland region of New Zealand, are larger than usual oysters, and have a sweeter, creamier taste. These unique oysters pair well with Waipara Riesling - a medium-bodied wine with citrusy flavours and a delicate sweet aroma.

10. **Crayfish:**

Crayfish, also known as rock lobsters, are caught from New Zealand's cold and clean ocean waters. It is cut into pieces and grilled, which enhances its natural flavour further. The Crayfish goes well with a full-bodied chilled Chardonnay - the Gisborne Chardonnay with rich flavours of butterscotch, oak, and citrus.

11. **Hokey Pokey Ice Cream:**

Hokey Pokey Ice Cream is a national favourite, and it is created by adding small pieces of honeycomb to vanilla ice cream. It pairs well with a glass of Botrytis - a dessert wine with honey and citrus tones.

12. **Lolly Cake:**

Lolly cakes are a popular dessert in New Zealand, and it is made by mixing malt biscuits, condensed milk, and lollies. Lolly Cakes pairs well with a fortified wine - the Hawke's Bay Cabernet Sauvignon, with its luscious dark fruits and spice notes.

In conclusion, New Zealand is a land of diverse cuisine with many native and authentically prepared dishes. The country's varied terroirs and modern wine-making techniques have added a whole range of wine varieties to complement different tastes and flavours. From sweet desserts to savoury meat dishes, there is a decent wine pairing available for every dish.

Wine with Local Cuisine for Summer Informal Dining

New Zealand has a diverse range of dishes that are perfect for an informal summer dining. Here are some examples of New Zealand foods and the wines that pair perfectly with them:

1. **Kiwi Burger**

The famous Kiwi burger is a classic New Zealand dish consisting of a juicy beef patty, bacon, fried egg, beetroot, and lettuce, all in a lightly toasted bun. This burger pairs perfectly with a rich and oaky Chardonnay from the Hawke's Bay region of New Zealand.

2. **Pavlova**

Pavlova is a sweet and crisp meringue dessert filled with whipped cream and fresh fruit. It's one of New Zealand's most famous dishes and pairs well with a sweet Riesling from the Marlborough region, which is known for its aromatic and fruity wines.

3. **Fish and Chips**

New Zealand is renowned for its fresh seafood, and fish and chips is a quintessential Kiwi dish. The fish is battered and deep-fried until golden brown, served with crispy chips or fries. This hearty dish pairs perfectly with a crisp and refreshing Sauvignon Blanc from the Marlborough region.

4. **Lolly Cake**

Lolly Cake is a delicious no-bake treat that consists of crushed malt biscuits, condensed milk, butter, and chopped lollies. It's a popular dessert in New Zealand, and it pairs well with an aromatic Gewürztraminer from the Central Otago region.

5. **Crayfish**

Fresh crayfish, also known as rock lobster, is a delicacy in New Zealand. It's sweet and tender, and it pairs well with a light and crisp Chardonnay from the Marlborough region.

6. **Hokey Pokey Ice Cream**

Hokey Pokey Ice Cream is a classic New Zealand dessert consisting of vanilla ice cream with pieces of crunchy honeycomb toffee. It pairs well with a rich and creamy Pinot Gris from the Central Otago region.

7. **Green-Lipped Mussels**

Green-Lipped Mussels are a unique type of mussel that is only found in New Zealand waters. They are plump and tender, with a sweet and delicious flavour. They pair perfectly with a light and crisp Sauvignon Blanc from the Marlborough region.

8. **Hangi**

Hangi is a traditional Maori method of cooking food in an underground oven. The food is wrapped in leaves and placed on a bed of hot stones, and then covered with earth to cook slowly. Hangi is usually served with juicy meats and vegetables, and it pairs well with a full-bodied Syrah from the Hawke's Bay region.

9. **Paua**

Paua is a type of shellfish with a distinctive blue-green shell. It's similar to abalone and is often used in seafood chowders or fried in breadcrumbs. Paua pairs well with a crisp and refreshing Pinot Grigio from the Marlborough region.

10. Whitebait Fritters

Whitebait Fritters are a traditional Kiwi dish consisting of small freshwater fish mixed with egg and flour and fried until golden brown. They pair well with a light and fruity Pinot Noir from the Central Otago region.

11. **Tiramisu Cake**

Tiramisu is an Italian dessert that has become popular in New Zealand thanks to the country's strong Italian influence. This delicious cake is made with layers of sponge cake, coffee liqueur, and mascarpone cream. It pairs well with a sweet and full-bodied Merlot from the Hawke's Bay region.

12. **Bluff Oysters**

Bluff Oysters are a type of oyster that is found only in the South Island of New Zealand. They are large and meaty, with a rich and buttery flavour. They pair perfectly with a light and crisp Chardonnay from the Marlborough region.

In conclusion, New Zealand has a diverse range of delicious dishes that pair perfectly with the country's world-renowned wines. From fish and chips to Tiramisu cake, there's something for everyone to enjoy. Whether you prefer a light and fruity Pinot Noir or a rich and oaky Chardonnay, New Zealand's wines have a unique flavour that compliments the country's delicious cuisine.

Wine with Local Cuisine for Winter Formal Dining

New Zealand cuisine is a reflection of the country's diverse cultural makeup and unique culinary traditions. The country boasts an abundance of fresh seafood, farm-fresh meats, and locally sourced fruits and vegetables. Here are some of the most popular New Zealand dishes to serve for a formal winter dining and some of the wines that are best paired with them:

1. **Roasted Lamb** - New Zealand is famous for its world-class lamb. Often slow-roasted with rosemary and garlic, this flavorful meat pairs well with a full-bodied red wine from Otago region such as a Felton Road Pinot Noir from Central Otago.

2. **Paua Fritters** - Paua is a type of shellfish found only in New Zealand. Paua fritters made of paua flesh are dipped in batter and fried. A refreshing Sauvignon Blanc, such as a Dog Point Sauvignon Blanc from Marlborough, pairs well with the dish.

3. **Green-lipped Mussels** - These large mussels are found only in the coastal waters of New Zealand. They are often steamed with white wine and flavored with garlic, butter, and herbs. A light and citrusy Pinot Gris like Fromm La Strada Pinot Gris from Marlborough will complement the flavors.

4. **Bluff Oysters** - These are considered to be the best oysters in the world, also known for their unique sweet and salty taste. To maintain the integrity of these delicate flavours, you can pair them with a crisp and fruity Chardonnay, such as Kumeu River Chardonnay from Auckland.

5. **Venison Stew** - As deer is also abundant in New Zealand, a rich and savoury venison stew paired with a full-bodied Syrah from Craggy Range Vineyards of Hawke's Bay will create a perfect match.

6. **Whitebait Fritters** - Whitebait are small fish that are harvested during their migratory season. They are often fried in fritters using eggs and lemon. A classic Marlborough Sauvignon Blanc like Cloudy Bay pairs excellently with the dish.

7. **Kiwi Pavlova** - A fluffy meringue base with whipped cream and topped with fresh kiwi fruit, Pavlova is a dessert that the Kiwis claim as their own. A Muscat would make a perfect compliment to this New Zealand classic dessert, such as a Selaks Ice Wine.

8. **Hangi** - A traditional Maori meal in which the food is cooked in a hole in the ground. It includes meat, vegetables, and bread wrapped in leaves. Unison Vineyards 'Syrah' from Hawkes Bay region with its spicy and herbal notes would make the perfect match.

9. **Boil Up** - Another traditional Maori dish, boil up is a hearty soup made with pork or beef bones, vegetables, potatoes, and kumara (sweet potatoes). A Syrah or Merlot from Esk Valley Winery from the Hawke's Bay region would be great for cold winter nights.

10. **Kina (Sea Urchin)** - Kina is another unique seafood found in New Zealand. It has a custardy texture, and it can be served raw or slightly cooked with a squeeze of lemon. To pair with this subtle flavour, serve with a crisp Chardonnay like Neudorf Chardonnay from Nelson.

11. **Fish and Chips** - A classic dish that is served all over New Zealand, fish and chips is a must for any winter menu. A Pinot Gris from Rippon Vineyard in Central Otago would add a crisp refreshing taste to the fried dish.

12. **Apple Pie** - New Zealand is known for its apples, so it's only fair to include an apple pie in the dessert list. Pair it with a Sémillon from the Esk Valley Vineyards in Hawkes Bay to enhance the flavours of the pie.

When choosing wine, consider the terroir and winemaking process. Additionally, look for wines that balance acidity, body, and tannins to complement the flavours in the food you are serving. New Zealand wines are a perfect match for their food due to the country's temperate climate, unique microclimates, and soil. Most of the wineries in New Zealand practice sustainable viticulture and winemaking techniques to produce high-quality wines.

Wine with Local Cuisine for Winter Informal Dining

New Zealand is a great place for diverse and delicious foods, including excellent wines. For an informal winter dining experience, pairing local produce and wine can deliver a simple yet elegant meal.

1. Roast Lamb with Pinot Noir

Lamb is one of New Zealand's most popular meat dishes. The succulent, tender meat is seasoned with fresh herbs, such as rosemary and thyme, and garlic. Pair with a pinot noir wine from Marlborough, that is light to medium-bodied and has a fruity taste with a hint of oak.

2. Kumara (Sweet potato) Pie with Sauvignon Blanc

Kumara is a traditional winter vegetable in New Zealand, and a pie made with it is a comforting dish. The pie is filled with mashed kumara, cheese, and caramelised onions. Pair it with a zesty sauvignon blanc from Marlborough to contrast with the sweetness of the kumara.

3. Paua (abalone) Fritters with Chardonnay

Paua fritters are a famous delicacy from New Zealand's coastline. Abalone flesh is pounded into a mixture with eggs, breadcrumbs, and herbs, then pan-fried until crispy. Pair with a chardonnay from Gisborne, which has an intense, buttery flavour with notes of tropical fruits.

4. Fish and Chips with Riesling

Fish and chips are a classic winter comfort food in New Zealand. The fish is dipped in batter and deep-fried, served with chips (french fries) and mushy peas. Pair with a riesling from Central Otago that has a bright, citrusy taste with a hint of sweetness.

5. Venison Stew with Syrah

Venison stew is a delicious hearty dish perfect for a winter evening. The stew is made with cubed venison, red wine, and root vegetables such as carrots, celery, and parsnips. Pair with a syrah from Hawke's Bay, which has a rich, earthy taste, and a hint of spice and smokiness.

6. Meat Pie with Merlot

Meat pies are a popular lunch or snack in New Zealand during the winter. The savoury pies are made with beef, lamb, or chicken in a rich gravy, all baked in a crispy pastry. Pair with merlot from the Waipara Valley, which has a medium to full-bodied taste with black fruit flavours, including plum and blackberry.

7. Whitebait Fritters with Pinot Gris

Whitebait fritters are a New Zealand delicacy mainly popular in the South Island. The fritters are made from tiny, delicate silver fish, mixed with eggs and herbs and pan-fried until golden brown. Pinot gris from the Martinborough region would be an excellent pairing. It has a vibrant fruity taste with a crisp minerality.

8. Salmon Pie with Chardonnay

Salmon pie is perfect for using up leftover salmon or as an alternative to traditional meat pies. The pie is filled with fresh salmon, leeks, and cheese, brushed with a creamy sauce. Pair with chardonnay from Marlborough, which complements the richness of the dish with its tropical fruit flavours.

9. Kiwi Fruits with Gewürztraminer

Kiwi fruits are subtropical fruit native to New Zealand. They have a floral and tangy taste and are perfect for a winter dessert. Pair with gewürztraminer from Marlborough, which has a spicy, aromatic bouquet, balancing the sweetness of the fruit.

10. Pavlova with Sparkling Wine

Pavlova is a famous winter dessert in New Zealand, typically served during Christmas. It is made with a light, fluffy meringue topped with fresh fruit, whipped cream, and passionfruit. Pair with a sparkling wine from Marlborough, which has a delicate yet refreshing taste.

11. Kūmara (Sweet Potato) Fries with Rosé

Kūmara fries are a healthier alternative to regular fries, made with thinly-sliced pieces of sweet potato, baked until crispy. Pair with rosé from Auckland, which has a crisp, fruity taste with a hint of sweetness.

12. Burger with Pinot Noir

Burgers are a popular fast food in New Zealand, with an impressive local twist. Made with grass-fed beef, topped with cheese, bacon, lettuce, and tomato, served in a ciabatta bun. Pinot noir from Central Otago pairs well with the burger's tangy taste and earthy flavours.

In conclusion, New Zealand offers an excellent variety of winter flavours, and its wine industry offers a vast selection that matches perfectly with local cuisine. Pairing wine with food is subjective, so one can experiment and have fun finding the perfect liaison.

Phileas Fogg's Best Pairings of New Zealand Food and Wine

On his travels through New Zealand, Phileas Fogg would certainly have paused for some delicious local delicacies. Here are my suggestions for the food and wine pairings from New Zealand he would have encountered:

1. **Sauvignon Blanc and green-lipped mussels** - Sauvignon Blanc is one of New Zealand's most famous wines, and green-lipped mussels are a local delicacy. The wine's crisp acidity pairs perfectly with the briny, sea-salt flavour of the mussels.

2. **Pinot Noir and lamb** - New Zealand is known for its world-renowned lamb, and Pinot Noir is an excellent choice to complement its rich flavour. The wine's cherry and earthy profile enhances the meaty taste of lamb.

3. **Chardonnay and scallops** - Chardonnay offers flavours of vanilla and oak to pair well with the sweet, delicate flavour of scallops.

4. **Riesling and spicy Asian dishes** - The sweetness in Riesling balances well with the heat of spicy Asian dishes like curry or pad thai.

5. **Gewürztraminer and smoked salmon** - The spice and floral notes in Gewürztraminer match the rich flavour of smoked salmon.

6. **Pinot Gris and pork belly** - Pinot Gris offers a crisp, juicy flavor that pairs beautifully with the richness of pork belly.

7. **Syrah and venison** - Syrah's bold profile lends itself well to the rich taste of venison steaks.

8. **Cabernet Sauvignon and aged cheddar cheese** - The tannins in Cabernet Sauvignon blend well with the sharpness of aged cheddar cheese.

9. **Merlot and mushroom risotto** - Merlot's soft and fruity taste pairs perfectly with the savoury and earthy flavour of mushroom risotto.

10. **Sparkling wine and oysters** - Sparkling wine's effervescence and light taste cuts perfectly through the creamy texture of oysters, leaving a clean palate.

Finally....

New Zealand is a unique and fascinating country with diverse people and cultures. The native Maori people have a rich history and deep connection to the land, which is reflected in their art, music, and traditions.

New Zealand is also known for its stunning natural beauty, from the rolling hills and pastoral landscapes to the rugged mountains and pristine beaches. This topography and climate has created ideal growing conditions for unique and flavorful wines, particularly Sauvignon Blanc and Pinot Noir.

Speaking of cuisine, New Zealand has a wide variety of delicious and fresh foods, including seafood, lamb, venison, and manuka honey. These ingredients are often paired with the country's signature wines, which complement and enhance the flavours of each dish.

The unique terroir of New Zealand, with its volcanic soil and maritime climate, has also helped to create some of the most distinctive and sought-after wines in the world.

Overall, New Zealand is a fascinating and beautiful country with an incredible depth of culture, history, and culinary delights.

Top 4 Vineyards Of New Zealand

1. Felton Road Vineyard:

- **History**: Felton Road Vineyard was established in 1991 and since then it has become one of the most respected wineries in New Zealand.

- **Owners**: Nigel Greening is the owner of Felton Road Vineyard.

- **Grapes**: Pinot Noir, Chardonnay, Riesling.

- **Terroir**: The vineyards are located in the Bannockburn sub-region of Central Otago, which is known for its mountainous terrain and rocky soil.

- **People & Cultures**: Felton Road Vineyard is dedicated to sustainable viticulture and has been certified organic and biodynamic since 2002.

- **Vinification Techniques**: The winery focuses on low-yield, high-quality production using wild yeasts and traditional Burgundian winemaking techniques.

- **Wine-Pairing**: Examples of Felton Road Vineyard's pairing are; Pinot Noir with duck, lamb, or salmon dishes, Chardonnay with lobster, shellfish, or grilled chicken, and Riesling with spicy Thai or Indian cuisine.

2. Cloudy Bay Vineyards:

- **History**: Cloudy Bay Vineyards was established in 1985 and was one of the first wineries in Marlborough.

- **Owners**: Cloudy Bay Vineyards is owned by LVMH (Louis Vuitton Moët Hennessy).

- **Grapes**: Sauvignon Blanc, Chardonnay, Pinot Noir.

- **Terroir**: The vineyards are located in the Marlborough region, which is known for its cool-climate, dry weather and alluvial soils.

- **People & Cultures**: Cloudy Bay Vineyards employs environmentally-friendly viticulture techniques.

- **Vinification Techniques**: The winery uses a combination of traditional and modern winemaking techniques to produce wines with clean, fresh flavours.

- **Wine-Pairing**: Examples of Cloudy Bay Vineyards' pairing are; Sauvignon Blanc with seafood, grilled vegetables or goat cheese, Chardonnay with roasted chicken, grilled prawns or creamy pasta, and Pinot Noir with red meat, lamb or mushroom dishes.

3. **Carrick Wines**:

- **History**: Carrick Wines was established in 1993 and is located in Bannockburn, Central Otago.

- **Owners**: The founding owners of Carrick Wines were Steve Green and Barbara Robertson, while now it is owned by Geordie and Kai Fergusson.

- **Grapes**: Pinot Noir, Chardonnay, Sauvignon Blanc, Riesling.

- **Terroir**: The vineyards are located in Central Otago, known for its rocky, mountainous terrain with fast-draining soils.

- **People & Cultures**: Carrick Wines employs organic and biodynamic viticulture techniques.

- **Vinification Techniques**: Carrick Wines' winemaking techniques focus on minimal intervention and use of natural yeasts, to produce wines with purity and elegance.

- **Wine-Pairing**: Examples of Carrick Wines' pairing are; Pinot Noir with roasted meats, game, or mushroom risotto, Chardonnay with creamy pasta, scallops, or white fish, Sauvignon Blanc with sushi, Asian cuisine or salads, and Riesling with spicy Thai, Chinese or Indian dishes.

4. **Craggy Range**:

- **History**: Craggy Range was established in 1997 by Terry Peabody and his family.

- **Owners**: Terry Peabody is the owner of Craggy Range.

- **Grapes**: Syrah, Cabernet Sauvignon, Merlot, Pinot Noir, Chardonnay, Sauvignon Blanc.

- **Terroir**: The vineyards are located in the Hawke's Bay and Martinborough regions, which are known for their varied soils and climates.

- **People & Cultures**: Craggy Range has a focus on sustainability, employing both organic and biodynamic viticulture techniques.

- **Vinification Techniques**: Craggy Range uses a combination of traditional and modern techniques to produce wines with depth, complexity and elegance.

- **Wine-Pairing**: Examples of Craggy Range's pairing are; Merlot and Cabernet Sauvignon with red meat, beef or lamb, Syrah with spicy or grilled meat, Pinot Noir with mushroom risotto, duck or salmon dishes, Chardonnay with grilled seafood, scallops or lobster, and Sauvignon Blanc with Asian cuisine, salads or grilled vegetables.

Further Reading:

Some further reading suggestions for pairing New Zealand foods with New Zealand wines:

1. **"The New Zealand Wine Book"** by Rebecca Gibb - This comprehensive guide covers all major wine-producing regions in New Zealand and provides tasting notes, food pairing suggestions and recipes to complement each wine.

2. **"Pairing Food and Wine in New Zealand"** by John Hawkesby - This book focuses specifically on pairing New Zealand foods with New Zealand wines. It includes recipes from top chefs and vineyards across the country.

3. **"The New Zealand Wine and Food Cookbook"** by Lauraine Jacobs - This cookbook offers a range of recipes from New Zealand's top chefs, along with wine recommendations for each dish.

4. **"New Zealand Wine: The Land, the Vines, the People"** by Warren Moran - Although not specifically focused on food pairing, this book provides an in-depth exploration of New Zealand's wine regions, varietals, and history. It also includes a section on wine tasting and appreciation, which can help in selecting the right wine for your meal.

5. **"New Zealand's Best Wines 2021"** by Michael Cooper - This annual guidebook provides an overview of the best wines in New Zealand, along with tasting notes, food pairing suggestions, and contact information for each vineyard.

I hope these suggestions are helpful in finding the perfect pairing for your New Zealand meal!

CHAPTER 11

FESTIVALS IN EUROPE

Let's look at some European countries where people celebrate events with wine and food.

1. Oktoberfest, Germany

Oktoberfest is a renowned festival celebrated annually in Munich, Germany. The event is recognized worldwide and is attended by people from all walks of life. Oktoberfest commences in the middle of September and runs until the first weekend of October.

The festival is famous for its beer offerings, with a variety of German beers on offer, including the festbier, which is a light, gold-coloured beer. Oktoberfest attracts more than six million visitors every year from Germany and other countries worldwide. The event is known worldwide for its vibrant, colourful traditions.

The wine on offer at Oktoberfest is predominantly German, including varieties like Riesling, Spatlese, and Weissburgunder. The food served is traditional Bavarian cuisine, with various tasty dishes available. Meat delicacies like Schweinebraten (roast pork), Hendl (roast chicken), Brezen (large pretzels), and Weisswurst (white sausage) are some of the favourites.

Additionally, other delicious foods enjoyed at Oktoberfest include Spaetzle, a type of German pasta served alongside pork and covered in gravy. Another favourite is Sauerkraut, which is a fermented cabbage that complements the meat dishes perfectly. Knödel (dumplings) are also commonly served and pair well with the meat dishes.

The pairing of food and wine at Oktoberfest is significant, with the light-bodied beer matching well with the bold, intense flavours of the meat dishes. The wines served become a perfect pairing with the lighter dishes like pasta and salad.

In conclusion, Oktoberfest is a grand event, and the combination of tempting food and drinks is undoubtedly something not to miss. The high-quality German beer, wines, and traditional Bavarian cuisine make this festival an unforgettable experience.

2. La Tomatina, Spain

La Tomatina is a festival held in the town of Buñol near Valencia in Spain. It is a festival that involves throwing tomatoes at each other. The event takes place on the last Wednesday of August every year and attracts thousands of people from all over the world.

The festival started in 1945 when a group of young people were engaged in a street fight during a parade. They happened to find a tomato stall nearby and started throwing tomatoes at each other. The following year they repeated the tradition, and it became increasingly popular.

The festival begins early in the morning when trucks filled with ripe tomatoes arrive in the town square. People then gather in the streets and start throwing tomatoes at each other. The tomato fight lasts for a couple of hours, during which the participants get covered in a sea of red.

While there is no specific wine on offer at La Tomatina, the festival is celebrated with a lot of food and drink. There are various drinks available, including beer, sangria, and other local beverages. However, wine lovers can indulge in a range of red, white and rose wines that will go perfectly with the food served at the occasion.

Some of the popular foods served during La Tomatina include paella, a traditional rice dish flavoured with saffron and garlic. It's usually served with meat or seafood. Other delicacies include empanadas, grilled meats and vegetables, and churros.

If you're a wine lover, then you could pair paella with a deep and fruity red wine or a sparkling and refreshing white wine. The empanadas could be served with a light and fruity rose while the grilled meats could be paired with a full-bodied red wine.

In conclusion, La Tomatina is a yearly event that celebrates the joy of throwing tomatoes at each other. It's a unique festival that attracts thousands of people from all over the world who come to celebrate and indulge in good food, drinks and wine.

3. Carnaval de Nice, France

Carnaval de Nice is a traditional annual carnival festival that takes place in the city of Nice, which is located on the French Riviera in southern France. The carnival takes place in February every year, and it is one of the biggest and most famous carnivals in the world, attracting more than a million visitors annually.

The event usually lasts for about two weeks, and it is a time for the locals and tourists to come together and celebrate with music, dance, colourful costumes, and processions. The event is known for its parade floats, which are designed and decorated with flowers and lights by skilled craftsmen.

As for the drinks, there are many wines that are on offer and enjoyed during the Carnaval de Nice. Some of the popular wines include the rosé wines of Provence, such as Côtes de Provence or Bandol, and the white wines of the Loire Valley, such as Muscadet or Sancerre. Red wines, such as Bordeaux or Burgundy, are also enjoyed during the festival.

The foods served at Carnaval de Nice include a variety of traditional French dishes, such as escargots (snails), bouillabaisse (fish soup), roasted lamb, and coq au vin (chicken cooked in wine). Sweet treats are also abundant, such as crêpes (thin pancakes), beignets (deep-fried pastry), and galettes des rois (king cake).

Pairing the right food with the right wine can enhance the dining experience at Carnaval de Nice. For instance, white wines are typically paired with seafood dishes, such as oysters or shrimp, while red wines are often paired with red meat. The rosé wines of Provence are versatile and can pair with a range of dishes. The sweetness of the desserts can be balanced by pairing them with a rich, sweet white wine or a fortified wine, such as Port.

Overall, Carnaval de Nice is a celebration of French culture, food, and wine. It is a time to come together and enjoy the traditions and festivities of this unique and vibrant carnival.

4. Fête de la Musique, France

Fête de la Musique is an annual music festival that takes place in France every year on the 21st of June. The festival is also celebrated in many other countries around the world these days, and it is a celebration of music and culture.

The history of Fête de la Musique goes back to 1982 when the French Minister of Culture, Jack Lang, proposed an idea for a free music festival that would take place on the longest day of the year. In the years since, the festival has grown in size and popularity, and it is now celebrated in over 700 cities around the world.

The festival is known for its lively atmosphere, and it is a great opportunity to enjoy music, food, and wine. In France, people gather in the streets and squares of their cities and towns to enjoy live music performances in a variety of different genres, such as jazz, rock, classical, and more.

Wine and food are an essential part of the festival. Some of the most popular wines that are enjoyed during the event include Champagne, Bordeaux, and Burgundy wines. These wines are often paired with French cuisine such as cheese, foie gras, charcuterie, and a variety of seafood including oysters, mussels, and shrimp.

One of the most traditional foods served during the festival is the baguette. The French bread is often filled with different types of cheese, cured meats, or pâté. Another popular food that is often enjoyed during the festival is the ratatouille, which is a vegetable stew that is made with tomatoes, eggplant, and zucchini.

Pairing wine and food during the Fête de la Musique is often done based on the flavour profiles of the food and wine. For example, Champagne is often paired with seafood such as oysters, shrimp, or lobster. Red wines like Bordeaux or Burgundy are often paired with red meats or heartier dishes.

In conclusion, Fête de la Musique is a celebration of music, culture, food, and wine in France. It is an occasion that brings people together in the streets and squares of their cities and towns to enjoy great music, delicious food, and fine wine.

5. Fasnacht, Switzerland

Fasnacht is a famous carnival event held annually in Switzerland. It is celebrated in various cities of Switzerland such as Basel, Luzern, and Solothurn. This event is usually held in February and is celebrated by locals and tourists alike.

Fasnacht is a cultural tradition in Switzerland that dates back to the 15th century. The carnival features colourful parades, masked balls, live music, and various performances. People dress up in costumes, masks, and colourful outfits.

The wines on offer vary depending on the region where the event is being held. However, some of the most popular Swiss wines are Pinot Noir, Chasselas, and Merlot. These wines are served to the attendees, and they are enjoyed with delicious Swiss food.

Swiss food is diverse and varies from region to region. Some of the most popular foods served during Fasnacht are:

1. **Cheese Fondue** – This is a staple Swiss dish made with melted cheese and served with bread. The cheese fondue is usually served with a dry white wine like Chasselas.

2. **Rosti** – It is a dish made with shredded potatoes that are fried until crispy. Rosti is typically served with sausages and a light red wine like Pinot Noir.

3. **Raclette** – It is a dish made with melted cheese that is scraped off a half-wheel and served with boiled potatoes, bread, and pickles. Raclette is usually paired with a dry white wine like Chasselas.

4. **Zopf** – It is a classic Swiss bread made with white flour and milk. Zopf is typically paired with a light red wine like Pinot Noir.

5. **Chocolate** – Switzerland is famous for its chocolate, and Fasnacht is the perfect occasion to indulge in some delicious Swiss chocolate. Chocolate is usually paired with a sweet red wine like Merlot.

In conclusion, Fasnacht is a wonderful time to immerse oneself in Swiss culture, enjoy great food, and sip on some of the most exceptional Swiss wines.

6. VinItaly, Italy

VinItaly is one of the most significant wine events in the world, which takes place in Verona, Italy, every year. Verona is a beautiful city located in the northeastern region of Italy, known for its ancient Roman amphitheatre, Juliet's House, and renowned art galleries. VinItaly is a celebration of Italian culture and its significance around the world.

The event usually takes place in April and lasts for four days. VinItaly is an opportunity for people to come together to learn about wine-making, wine-tasting, and experience the delicious food that comes from Italy. It is also a great opportunity for wine producers around Italy to showcase their wares. Over 4,500 exhibitors from Italy and other countries participate in the event.

The culture of Italy is highlighted throughout the event with its traditional festivals, crafts, arts, and the presence of its people. VinItaly is a bustling event that gathers people from different corners of the world for the love of wine, food, and culture.

Wine that is on offer at VinItaly is the best that Italy has to offer, including Chianti, Barolo, Amarone, and Super Tuscans. The event is famous for the wide range of wines on offer for tasting, and some of the wines can be centuries old. Wines are evaluated based on their colour, aroma, taste, and finish.

In addition to delicious wines, VinItaly also has a wide variety of Italian cuisine on offer. Dishes include Parmigiano-Reggiano, Prosciutto di Parma, different types of pasta, and pizza. The culinary skills of the region are highlighted in every dish presented.

Pairing of food and wine is an essential part of the Italian culture, and attendees can participate in masterclasses to learn more about this art. Foods are paired with wines based on their flavours and textures, ensuring that one does not overpower the other. For example, seafood is paired with white wine, while red wines complement meat dishes such as steak or beef.

In conclusion, VinItaly is a significant event that highlights the essence of Italian culture. The event brings people from all over the world to experience the love of food, wine, and culture. The event stands testament to Italy's rich heritage and its passion for the culinary arts.

7. St. Patrick's Day, Ireland

St. Patrick's Day is a national holiday celebrated by the people of Ireland and is also widely recognized and celebrated across the world. This celebration emphasises Irish traditions, culture, and history, particularly the life of Saint Patrick, who is considered the patron saint of Ireland. This event is celebrated every year on the 17th of March.

Ireland is famous for its lush green landscapes, rugged coastlines, and mountainous terrain. The topography gives rise to a perfect climate for viticulture, and one of the fine wines produced is Irish Cream Liqueur, a classic Irish drink that is enjoyed worldwide.

In Ireland's wine industry, Irish Cream Liqueur has played a significant role, with the beverage being produced by several dairies in the country. This liqueur is a delicious blend of Irish whiskey, cream, and other flavourings, adding to the overall charm of St. Patrick's celebrations.

During the St. Patrick's Day celebrations, Irish people often enjoy traditional foods, including corned beef and cabbage, shepherd's pie, beef stew, soda bread, and Irish soda farls (a type of soda bread). Ireland has a rich culinary tradition, and most of its cuisine features hearty, flavorful dishes that pair well with wines.

For instance, a plate of corned beef and cabbage pairs nicely with a glass of crisp white wine like Sauvignon Blanc, given its acidity that cuts through the dish's rich flavours. Similarly, beef stew with its robust and hearty undertones can be best paired with a red wine like Cabernet or Merlot.

In conclusion, the St. Patrick's Day celebrations serve as a fantastic opportunity to delve into Irish culture, sample a range of delicious wines and foods, and celebrate with the friendly and welcoming people in Ireland.

8. Fête de la Gastronomie

Fête de la Gastronomie

is a nationwide culinary event celebrated in France to showcase the country's rich and diverse gastronomy. The event takes place annually on the fourth weekend of September, and it lasts three days.

People from all over the world come to France to experience the world-famous cuisine and wines during the festival. It is a time for people to discover and taste the specialities of the different regions of France, with chefs and producers coming together to celebrate the art of French cooking.

The Fête de la Gastronomie is deeply ingrained in French culture, and it celebrates the country's culinary traditions that are passed down through generations. The festival provides a platform for chefs and artisans to showcase their skills and knowledge.

The topography of France plays an essential role in its vinification techniques, which in turn contributes to the wide variety of wines on offer during the festival. Some of the most popular wines enjoyed during the festival include:

1. Champagne

2. Bordeaux

3. Burgundy

4. Loire

5. Rhône

These wines are perfectly paired with the fantastic French cuisine served during the festival. Some of the foods served at the Fête de la Gastronomie include:

1. Escargot

2. Coq au Vin

3. Ratatouille

4. Beef Bourguignon

5. Croissant

6. Crème Brûlée

These dishes represent the different culinary regions of France and showcase the diversity and uniqueness of French gastronomy. The dishes are prepared by skilled chefs and artisans who strive to maintain the authenticity of the recipes.

Pairing the foods with the right wines is crucial to the festival's success, and there are many wine and food pairing workshops during the event. The experts guide the visitors on the different techniques and principles of pairing the right wine with the right dish to enhance the overall flavour.

In conclusion, the Fête de la Gastronomie is a celebration of French cuisine and culture, showcasing the country's extensive range of culinary delights. The festival is an excellent opportunity for visitors to experience the French way of life and indulge in the country's rich gastronomic heritage.

10. Taste of London, United Kingdom

The Taste of London is an annual food festival held in the United Kingdom. The event brings together top chefs, restaurants, and producers to showcase their unique culinary skills and products. The festival takes place in June every year, and it attracts thousands of food enthusiasts from all over the world.

The event is a celebration of the diverse cultures and topography in the UK. As such, visitors to the event can expect to find a wide range of foods and drinks from all over the country. From traditional British dishes to international cuisine, visitors can sample everything from street food to fine dining.

One of the highlights of the Taste of London is the Vinoteca. This area is dedicated to wine lovers, and it showcases some of the best vinification techniques in the world. Visitors can learn about the different techniques used to produce wines and can sample some of the finest wines on offer.

At the event, attendees can enjoy a variety of foods that are expertly paired with wine. For example, visitors can enjoy a cheese platter paired with red, white, or rose wine, or try a chocolate dessert paired with a sweet dessert wine.

One of the best things about the Taste of London is the collaboration between chefs and producers. Visitors can watch demonstrations by top chefs, learn cooking techniques, and even try their hand at cooking with some of the best produce available in the UK.

Overall, the Taste of London is an exciting event that celebrates the diversity of the food and drink industry in the UK. Whether you are a foodie, a wine lover or simply looking for a fun day out, this event is not to be missed.

11. The Spritz, Italy

The Spritz occasion in Italy is a highly celebrated event by the locals and tourists alike. Italy is a country renowned for its wine and gastronomy culture. Traditionally, the Italians love to gather and enjoy a glass of wine or cocktail in the company of friends and family. The Spritz occasion is one such event that celebrates this love for wine and gastronomy culture.

The Spritz event in Italy is usually held in the summer months, mostly in late June or early July. People from all age groups participate in the event to sample the best wines Italy has to offer. The event is held in different parts of Italy, each showcasing the various wine-making traditions of the region.

The Spritz occasion in Italy is a significant cultural event that is accompanied by music, art, and a wide variety of wine from different regions of the country. The topography of Italy plays a crucial role in the type of wine produced in a specific region. Vineyards are often set up in the rolling hills of Tuscany, the volcanic slopes of Sicily, and the sun-soaked coast of Puglia.

Vinification techniques vary from region to region, but Italy always delivers exceptional quality wines that are ripe, aromatic, and complex on the palate. Wines on offer at the occasion include some of Italy's best-known wines, such as Barolo, Chianti, Prosecco, and many others.

The occasion is not just about wine, but also about the delicious cuisine that Italy is famous for. Traditional Italian foods such as pasta, pizza, risotto, seafood, and meats are served in abundance. One of the highlights of the occasion is the pairing of food and wine. Experts recommend pairing seafood with white wine and meats with red wine. Cheese and charcuterie boards are common and are perfect for pairing with any wine.

In summary, the Spritz occasion in Italy is a must-attend event for wine and food lovers. It is a celebration of Italian culture that showcases all the best the country has to offer in terms of wine, food, music, and art. The occasion is also an opportunity to meet new people and make lifelong friends.

12. The Grape Harvest, France

The Grape Harvest in France is a highly anticipated occasion that takes place every year in September, and it is an important part of French culture as it signifies the end of the harvest season. This occasion is also known as "Vendanges" in French, and it involves a lot of hard work, fun, and enjoyment for the people.

The grape harvest is a vital event in France because it is known as the land of wine, where the country produces many of the world's most famous wine varieties. The topography of the country plays a significant role in their winemaking technique. France comprises diverse regions and soils with different altitudes, slopes and exposure to the sun. This diversity results in unique grapes, which are used to make different kinds of wines.

During the grape harvest, people pick the grapes from the vines by hand, and sometimes, they use machines to do the job. After that, they extract the juice from the grapes and start the process of vinification. Vinification refers to the winemaking technique which involves crushing the grapes, fermenting the juice with yeast, and ageing the wine in barrels for a specific period.

The Grape harvest is also a time when different kinds of wines are tasted and enjoyed at the event. People get to taste some of the best wines in the world, such as Bordeaux wines, Bourgogne wines, and Champagne, among others. Food is a significant part of the occasion, where various delicious dishes are served to complement the wines on offer.

Some of the popular foods served at the event include cheese, charcuterie, roasted meats, seafood, vegetables, and fruits. The pairing of these foods with the different wines is an art in itself where people look for the appropriate match. For instance, red wines get matched with meat dishes like beef or lamb; white wine is served with fish, poultry, or vegetarian options. Cheese is paired with red wine, and Champagne is typically paired with oysters or fish.

Overall, the Grape Harvest is an event filled with fun, excitement, and cultural significance for the French people. It celebrates their winemaking heritage and brings people together to celebrate the end of a long and fruitful harvest season.

13. The Cherry Festival, Spain

The Cherry Festival in Spain is one of the most popular events in the country, celebrated every year in the small town of Valle del Jerte. This town is located in the province of Caceres in the autonomous community of Extremadura, Spain. The festival usually takes place in late May or early June, depending on the ripening of cherries.

The festival is one of the most important cultural events in the country, attracting thousands of visitors every year. It is an opportunity for the local people to showcase their unique culture, customs, and traditions.

The topography of this region is composed of mountains and valleys, which makes it an ideal place to grow cherries. The region is known for its cherry production, which represents an important part of the economy of Valle del Jerte.

Vinification techniques are not the focus of the event, but there are local wines on offer, including white and red wines from Cáceres and Extremadura. The wine culture in this region is not as developed as other parts of Spain, but it is still a vital part of the local economy.

The festival is an opportunity to enjoy the local foods of Valle del Jerte, including cherries, meats, cheeses, and other locally produced products. Visitors can enjoy a variety of dishes, including grilled meats, stews, and salads made with fresh cherries.

The food on offer is paired with local wines, and there are many pairing options available. It is common to pair red wines with grilled meats, while white wines are paired with salads and cheeses. Local desserts made with cherries are also popular, and are often paired with sweet wines.

In conclusion, The Cherry Festival in Spain is a celebration of the unique culture, customs, and traditions of the people in Valle del Jerte. It is an opportunity for visitors to experience the food, wine, and local products that represent the heart and soul of this region.

14. Swedish Midsummer Festival, Sweden

The Swedish Midsummer Festival is one of the most celebrated occasions in Sweden, which usually takes place on June 20th or 21st, around the Summer Solstice. This event is an opportunity for the people of Sweden to celebrate the long summer days, eat traditional foods, dance to traditional music, and drink wine and other spirits.

The Swedish Midsummer Festival has been a part of Swedish culture since ancient times, dating back to pagan rituals that celebrated fertility, nature, and the arrival of summer. Today, it is a national holiday and a time for families and friends to come together and enjoy each other's company.

The festival is held in different parts of the country and features unique activities and traditions depending on the location. In general, the celebrations take place outdoors in the countryside or in parks, and often involve dancing around a flower-covered pole called a maypole.

Swedish culture places a strong emphasis on nature, and the topography of Sweden provides an ideal backdrop for the Midsummer festivals. The country has extensive forests, lakes, rivers, and coastline, and these natural sites are often utilised for events and celebrations.

Vinification techniques in Sweden are heavily influenced by the cool climate, and the Swedish wineries produce a variety of white wines, red wines, and sparkling wines. Some of the well-known Swedish wines include Rondo, Zweigelt, and Solaris. During the Midsummer Festival, Swedish wines are often enjoyed in moderation, along with beer, schnapps, and other spirits.

Swedish cuisine is heavily influenced by traditional agricultural practices, and the cuisine features fresh, local produce, meats, and fish. The food served during the Midsummer Festival represents the harvests of the season, and includes dishes like pickled herring, boiled new potatoes, meatballs, strawberries with cream, and a range of other savory and sweet dishes.

The pairing of food and wine is also an important aspect of the Midsummer Festival celebrations. For instance, pickled herring is often paired with Scandinavian aquavit or schnapps, and fresh strawberries with cream is usually served with a sweeter wine, such as a sparkling rose. Meatballs often pair well with red wines, such as Rondo, while boiled new potatoes are typically enjoyed with white wine or beer.

Overall, the Swedish Midsummer Festival is a unique and special occasion in Sweden, and represents a rich cultural heritage that has been celebrated for centuries.

15. The White Truffle Festival, Italy

The White Truffle Festival is an extravagant food event that takes place every year in Alba, Italy. This festival is dedicated to Italian cuisine and the exclusive, highly-prized white truffle, a delicacy that is covered in culinary circles worldwide. The event is held in the Piedmont region - an area recognized worldwide for its excellent wines and diverse gastronomy.

The festival starts in October and continues till mid-November, attracting local and international gourmands alike. Visitors to the festival can enjoy a range of exciting events, such as the truffle market, wine tastings, and cooking classes. The festival also features truffle hunting sessions where attendees can witness trained dogs and pigs as they hunt for the elusive white truffles hidden beneath the earth.

The Piedmont region is known for producing some of Italy's finest wines. The topography of the area has a significant influence on the wine produced. The region's hilly terrain and temperate climate allow for the production of high-quality wines that are renowned worldwide. The festival offers a chance for wine enthusiasts to sample some of the finest wines of Piedmont, including Barolo, Barbera, and Dolcetto. Vendemmia, the traditional method of winemaking, is also demonstrated at the festival.

Italian cuisine is known for its robust and flavorful dishes, and the food served at the White Truffle Festival is no exception. The festival's menus feature dishes such as truffle risotto, truffle pasta dishes, truffle eggs, and truffle steak. These dishes are often paired with fine wines produced in the Piedmont region, such as Barolo and Nebbiolo. Apart from truffle-based dishes, other classic Italian dishes are also served at the festival, including locally produced cheeses, cured meats, and fresh seafood from the nearby coast.

There are numerous pairings created at the festival. One classic pairing enjoyed by many festival goers is truffle risotto served with a glass of Barolo wine. The wine is known for its full-bodied flavour and earthy undertones, which complement the truffle's earthy aroma. The truffle pasta dish pairs well with Dolcetto, a lighter red wine known for its fruity flavours, while the truffle steak can be paired with a bold Barbera wine.

In summary, the White Truffle Festival is a celebration of Italian culture, wine, and cuisine. Attendees can take part in truffle hunting, wine tastings, and indulge in a range of authentic, local dishes. The festival is a unique event that brings together food lovers, wine aficionados, and local producers to celebrate Italian cuisine, culture, and the coveted and luxurious white truffle.

16. The Oyster Festival, Ireland

The Oyster Festival is an annual event held in Ireland to celebrate the country's rich oyster culture. The festival has been taking place over the past several decades, with thousands of visitors travelling to the town of Galway to participate in this unique cultural event.

The festival takes place in September and lasts for three days, with the exact dates changing annually. At the event, visitors can try out a wide variety of oysters, which are considered the highlight of the festival. The event also features other seafood delicacies, such as lobster and mussels, as well as other traditional Irish dishes.

The Festival is held in the bustling town of Galway, which is located on the west coast of Ireland. The town is known for its picturesque setting, surrounded by mountains and the sea. The town sits on the famous Wild Atlantic Way drive, making it an easy and attractive stop for tourists.

In addition to food, the festival also features a range of activities and entertainment, such as Irish music and dance, arts and crafts exhibitions, as well as sporting activities.

As for the wine on offer, the Oyster Festival features a number of wines that pair well with seafood, such as crisp white wines like Chablis, Chardonnay, and Sauvignon Blanc. Additionally, the festival offers a selection of local Irish beers and ciders that complement the food.

As far as the food served, visitors can expect an array of seafood delicacies. In addition to oysters, visitors can feast on lobster, mussels, clams, and shrimp. Traditional Irish dishes like lamb stew, Irish soda bread, and smoked salmon are also on the menu.

The pairing of food and wine at the Oyster Festival is an important aspect of the event. Pairing is done based on the flavour, texture, and richness of the food, as well as the characteristics of the wine. For instance, the briny and sweet flavour of the oysters pairs well with the crisp and citrusy flavours of a Sauvignon Blanc.

In conclusion, the Oyster Festival in Ireland is an exceptional event that celebrates the country's rich culinary and cultural heritage. The festival offers visitors a chance to experience the best of Irish cuisine in a uniquely Irish setting, while also enjoying the region's wines and beers. With activities for everyone, the festival is a must-visit for any food or culture lover.

17. **The Chocolate Festival, Belgium**

The Chocolate Festival is an annual event celebrated in Belgium, which is famous for its chocolate production and consumption. The Festival is a four-day celebration that is held every year in early November. The main aim of the festival is to bring together all the stakeholders of the chocolate industry including chocolate companies, chocolatiers, and chocolate lovers.

Belgium is a country that has a rich heritage in chocolate making, and it is renowned as the chocolate capital of the world. With so many delicious varieties of chocolate present in Belgium, it is not surprising that the festival has become a major attraction for people from all over the world.

The Chocolate Festival in Belgium is a cultural and gastronomic experience. The event takes place in various locations around Brussels and Bruges, both cities renowned for their chocolates. Visitors can expect to find an extensive array of chocolate related activities at the event including chocolate tasting, cooking demonstrations, and workshops offering a hands-on experience.

The topography of the Belgians is incredibly diverse which reflects in their chocolate-making process. Belgian chocolate has gained popularity worldwide, and the festival is a way for the production companies to display their latest creations and advancements.

Pairing Belgian wine with chocolate is also an important part of the event. The festival showcases a variety of wine from different regions in Belgium. In addition, there are several winemakers who come to the festival to display their latest wines. Visitors can also learn about vinification techniques and the characteristics of wines from different regions of Belgium.

To accompany the wine, the festival offers a wide range of foods that cater to both casual and fine dining experiences. Some of these include cheese, olives, truffles, pralines, soups, and desserts that are infused with chocolate.

Overall, The Chocolate Festival in Belgium is a must-attend event for chocolate lovers, foodies and wine enthusiasts alike. The festival provides an opportunity to explore Belgium's rich cultural heritage and taste the offerings of a country that is synonymous with high-quality chocolate.

18. **The World Cheese Awards, Spain**

The World Cheese Awards is one of the most prestigious cheese events in the world that takes place annually in a different city. In 2021, the event was held in Oviedo, Asturias, Spain, on November 3rd. The event is a celebration of cheese and is attended by cheese producers, industry experts, retailers, and cheese lovers from all over the world.

Asturias, located in the north of Spain, is a region known for its rich culinary culture and topography. The region has a mountainous landscape, which contributes to its unique cheese-making techniques. Asturias boasts over 40 types of cheese, which are created through traditional vinification techniques. Some of the popular cheeses coming out of Asturias include Cabrales, Casín, Gamonedo, and Afuega'l Pitu.

At the World Cheese Awards, the focus is on the cheese, but there is also plenty of wine and food to enjoy. The wines on offer are varied, ranging from white wines to red wines, and from sweet wines to dry wines. Some of the popular wines that are enjoyed at the World Cheese Awards include rioja, tempranillo, and albariño.

As for the food served at the event, it is a wide variety of local dishes featuring Asturias' unique cuisine. Some of the popular dishes served at the event include Fabada Asturiana, a traditional Asturian stew made with white beans, chorizo, and morcilla, and accompanied with Asturian cider. Another popular dish is escalopines al Cabrales, which are beef medallions topped with Cabrales cheese sauce.

Pairing the food and wine at the event is essential to fully experience the flavors of Asturias. The rich, creamy cheeses pair well with full-bodied red wines, while the lighter cheeses are better complemented with white wines. The local Asturian cider is also a popular pairing option at the event as it is known to balance out the strong flavour of the cheese.

In conclusion, the World Cheese Awards held in Spain celebrates the unique culture, topography, and cuisine of Asturias. From the variety of cheeses to the array of wines and foods on offer, this event is truly a cheese and wine lover's paradise.

19. **Helsinki Cake and Chocolate Fair, Finland**

The Helsinki Cake and Chocolate Fair is an annual event held in Helsinki, Finland, which brings together chocolate and patisserie lovers from both across the country and beyond. This occasion offers visitors the opportunity to experience the best of chocolate and pastry as well as to socialise with people who share a passion for chocolate and pastries.

The event is usually held in the first quarter of the year, and it lasts for several days. It attracts a significant number of people from all walks of life, who come to sample the diverse range of delicacies on offer. Additionally, the event offers insight into Finnish culture as visitors get a chance to learn about traditional ingredients used in chocolate and pastry making.

Finland has a unique cultural heritage, which is reflected in its cuisine. The event's organisers typically showcase traditional Finnish chocolate and pastry recipes that have been handed down from generation to generation. Finnish culture places great importance on nature as an inspiration for its cuisine; hence, many of the ingredients used are sourced locally, including berries, mushrooms, and wild herbs.

Finland's topography also plays an essential role in the country's cuisine, which is why the Helsinki Cake and Chocolate Fair also features vinification techniques, such as wine tasting. Local and international wine brands are on offer, including red, white, and rosé to pair with the cakes and chocolates. Wines from Finland and other parts of the world such as France or Italy are enjoyed by visitors as they sample the various chocolate and pastry recipes on display.

The fair is the perfect occasion to try traditional Finnish pastries such as "pulla," "korvapuusti," "kiisseli," and "mämmi." Locals usually pair these with the traditional "glögi," which is a Finnish mulled wine that complements the pastries' flavours. Additionally, chocolate desserts such as chocolate truffles and cakes such as "suklaakakku" are paired with wines that have hints of chocolate, berries, or other flavours that complement the chocolate.

In conclusion, the Helsinki Cake and Chocolate Fair is a respected event in Finland that celebrates its unique pastry and chocolate culture. Visitors can expect to sample some of the best pastries and chocolates Finland has to offer, learn about traditional ingredients, and experience Finland's rich culture through food and drink.

20. **The Calçotada, Catalonia, Spain**.

The Calçotada is an annual food festival that takes place in Catalonia, Spain during the winter months of January and February. It is a traditional event that celebrates the harvest of the calçot, a type of green onion that is grown in the region.

People from all over Catalonia come together to celebrate this event. It is a social gathering where friends and family come together to enjoy good food, good wine, and good company. The festival is celebrated in various towns and villages, with each offering a unique take on the traditional celebration.

The topography of the region plays an important role in the festival. The calçots are grown in the fertile soil of Catalonia's rich agricultural lands, with some of the best fields located near the town of Valls.

Vinification techniques also play a key role in the Calçotada festival, with some of the best local wines being produced in the region. The wines on offer at the festival include reds made from Garnacha and Carignan grapes, as well as whites made from Xarel-lo, Macabeo, and Parellada grapes.

The foods served at the Calçotada festival are typically grilled meats, such as lamb or pork, and an abundance of grilled vegetables, including the star of the show, the calçots. These onions are grilled over an open flame until they are charred on the outside and tender on the inside.

When it comes to pairing food and wine at the Calçotada festival, the traditional pairing is with red wines that can stand up to the robust flavours of grilled meats. However, some people prefer to pair the calçots with lighter white wines, which can accentuate their delicate flavours.

Overall, the Calçotada festival is a celebration of food, wine, and community that embodies the culture and traditions of Catalonia. It is an event that brings people together to enjoy the richness of the land and the bounty of the harvest, and it is a truly unique experience that should not be missed.

Note that there are many more events that this list could include, but I hope this gives you a good idea of the wide array of cultural celebrations throughout Europe that involve food and wine.

Phileas Fogg's European Festival Experiences

Phileas Fogg was an adventurer who travelled the world in search of new experiences, and if he were alive today, he would undoubtedly be interested in exploring the diverse festivals and events that Europe has to offer. Here are some festivals and events across Europe that Phileas Fogg might have enjoyed, along with the foods and wines he could have paired at each venue:

La Tomatina Festival, Buñol, Spain: This tomato-throwing festival would have been a unique and messy experience for Phileas Fogg. He could have paired the juicy tomatoes with a dry red wine like Rioja.

Oktoberfest, Munich, Germany: Phileas Fogg would have loved the lively atmosphere of Oktoberfest. He could have enjoyed classic German dishes like sausages, pretzels, and sauerkraut with a crisp beer like Hofbräuhaus.

Venetian Carnival, Venice, Italy: This elaborate carnival would have appealed to Phileas Fogg's sense of adventure. He could have paired the colourful costumes and masks with a crisp white wine like Pinot Grigio.

La Fête de la Musique, Paris, France: This music festival would have been a delightful experience for Phileas Fogg, who was fond of the arts. He could have paired the music with a glass of Bordeaux, a classic French wine.

The Royal Edinburgh Military Tattoo, Edinburgh, Scotland: Phileas Fogg would have enjoyed the pageantry and military displays at this event. He could have paired the performances with a hearty Scottish ale like **Belhaven.**

La Mercè Festival, Barcelona, Spain: This festival celebrating the patron saint of Barcelona would have appealed to Phileas Fogg's love of culture. He could have enjoyed the traditional Catalan dish paella with a glass of sparkling Cava.

The Great British Beer Festival, London, England: Phileas Fogg would have appreciated the variety of beers on offer at this festival. He could have paired his favourite ale with classic pub fare like fish and chips.

Snowbombing Festival, Mayrhofen, Austria: This music festival held in the Austrian Alps would have been a unique experience for Phileas Fogg. He could have paired the electronic music with a glass of Grüner Veltliner, a crisp Austrian wine.

St. Patrick's Festival, Dublin, Ireland: Phileas Fogg would have enjoyed the lively celebrations and parades that take place during this festival. He could have paired traditional Irish dishes like corned beef and cabbage with a pint of Guinness.

The Running of the Bulls, Pamplona, Spain: Phileas Fogg might have been tempted to participate in this adrenaline-fueled event. He could have cooled off afterward with a glass of sangria.

The Carnival of Venice, Venice, Italy: Phileas Fogg would have been impressed by the elaborate masks and costumes worn during this festival. He could have paired the beauty of the carnival with a glass of Chianti, a classic Italian wine.

The White Nights Festival, St. Petersburg, Russia: This festival celebrates the long summer days of St. Petersburg. Phileas Fogg could have paired the cultural events with Russian cuisine like caviar and blini, served with chilled vodka.

The Christmas Markets, Nuremberg, Germany: Phileas Fogg would have appreciated the festive atmosphere of the German Christmas markets. He could have paired the traditional gingerbread and roasted nuts with a warm cup of Glühwein.

CHAPTER 12

FESTIVALS IN AUSTRALIA

Let's look at some famous festivals that Australians celebrate:

1. **Australia Day** -

Australia Day is a national holiday in Australia celebrated annually on 26th January to commemorate the arrival of the First Fleet from Great Britain at Port Jackson in 1788, and the raising of the British flag at Sydney Cove by Governor Arthur Phillip. The occasion is a celebration of the country's history, people, and culture.

In terms of the country itself, Australia is a diverse and multicultural nation with a population of over 24 million people. The topography of Australia is varied, with beautiful beaches, rugged mountains, vast deserts, and vibrant cities. The country is also renowned for its excellent winemaking industry, with some of the world's best wines produced here.

The Australia Day event is usually marked with large-scale public celebrations, barbecues, fireworks, parades, and sporting events. People gather to enjoy the festivities with friends and families, and there is a sense of unity and patriotism throughout the country.

The event provides an excellent opportunity to showcase Australia's unique culture, and this includes its exceptional wines. Australia has some of the best wine regions in the world, including the Barossa Valley, Hunter Valley, Yarra Valley, and Margaret River. The country has perfected its winemaking techniques over the years, and the wine produced here is known for its rich taste and quality.

At the Australia Day event, guests can expect to find a variety of wines on offer. These may include Cabernet Sauvignon, Shiraz, Chardonnay, and Sauvignon Blanc. The wines available at the event will have been carefully selected by experts, and guests can trust that they will be getting the best possible taste experience.

The foods served at the event are typically reflective of Australian culture, and this includes a blend of European and Asian cuisine. Some popular dishes served include barbecued meat, seafood, salads, and desserts such as pavlova and lamingtons. These dishes pair well with a range of wines, and guests can expect to find pairing recommendations available.

For example, barbecued meat, such as lamb or steak, pairs well with a bold red wine like Shiraz or a Cabernet Sauvignon. Seafood can be served with a lighter white such as Chardonnay or Sauvignon Blanc. Salads and other light dishes can benefit from a sparkling or a rosé to complement the freshness of the dish, and desserts like the pavlova can be paired with a sweet, fruity Riesling.

In conclusion, the Australia Day event is an excellent opportunity to celebrate Australian history, culture, and its excellent vineyards. Guests can expect to have a range of high-quality wines and delicious foods to choose from, and there will be pairing recommendations available to ensure that they receive the best possible taste experience.

2. Chinese New Year

Celebrated in late January to mid-February by the Chinese community.

Chinese New Year is a significant event celebrated widely across Australia, which marks the first day of the lunar calendar. The festival is celebrated according to traditional Chinese customs and beliefs, which includes family gatherings, exchanging red envelopes, prayers, and indulging in delicious traditional Chinese cuisines and wines.

In Australia, Chinese New Year is celebrated by locals with the strong presence of Chinese communities in the country, where they showcase their cultural and traditional customs and beliefs through various events and festivals. The main event is held in Sydney, which is one of the largest Chinese New Year celebrations held outside of China. The event occurs in February and the specific date varies each year depending on the lunar calendar.

The culture of Chinese New Year is infused with symbolism, such as the color red, which signifies fortune and joy, and food also carries great significance during the festival. Classic Chinese New Year dishes include dumplings, whole fish, noodles, and sticky rice cakes.

In terms of wine, Australia has established itself as a leading wine-producing country, and their wines are widely available for the Chinese New Year celebrations. Popular winegrape varieties grown in Australia include Shiraz, Cabernet Sauvignon, Chardonnay and Riesling. The cool-climate region of Southern Australia is known for its Riesling, while Margaret River is celebrated for its Cabernet Sauvignon.

To pair with classic Chinese New Year dishes, a medium-bodied red wine like Shiraz is highly recommended as they complement dishes like dumplings and char siu pork. Other wines that can be enjoyed with Chinese cuisines include Cabernet Sauvignon, Chardonnay, and Riesling.

The foods served during the Chinese New Year event includes dumplings, Jiaozi, taro cake, Radish cake, glutinous rice balls, and nian gao. These dishes are highly symbolic and carry auspicious significance. For instance, pork and vegetable dumplings represent wealth, while rice balls represent reunion.

To pair with dumplings, it is best to serve light flavourful white and red wines. Riesling and Cabernet Sauvignon can be paired with pork dumplings, while Chardonnay complements spring rolls. Red wine like Shiraz can be paired with steamed or fried chicken to complement lighter meats.

In summary, the Chinese New Year event in Australia is a celebratory event that is highly symbolic and rich in cultural significance. The event showcases traditional Chinese practices that includes family gathering, praying, and indulging in delicious Chinese cuisines and fine Australian wines.

3. Adelaide Fringe Festival

Adelaide Fringe Festival is an annual cultural event that takes place in Adelaide, South Australia. It is a vibrant and eclectic celebration of art, music, theatre, and comedy, that attracts people from all over the world. The festival is held in late February to early March each year, and it has been running for over 60 years.

The festival is a celebration of Australian culture, and it showcases the diverse and multicultural aspects of the country. It is a time when people come together to enjoy the rich and diverse culture of Australia, and to celebrate the creativity of the people.

Adelaide, the city where the festival is held, is located in the southern part of Australia. It is a coastal city with a Mediterranean climate, which makes it perfect for growing wine grapes. The region is known for producing some of the best wines in the world, and there are many vineyards and wineries in the area.

Vinification techniques vary from winery to winery, but some of the most popular techniques used in the region include oak barrel ageing, stainless steel tanks, and concrete eggs. These techniques produce different flavours and aromas in the wine, which can be paired with different types of food.

At the Adelaide Fringe Festival, visitors can sample some of the finest wines from the region. Some of the most popular wines available at the event include Shiraz, Cabernet Sauvignon, and Chardonnay. These wines are often paired with local dishes, which helps to enhance the flavours of both the food and the wine.

Some of the foods served at the Adelaide Fringe Festival include local favourites such as Kangaroo, Emu, and Crocodile. These meats are often cooked on a barbecue or grill and served with a variety of sauces and marinades. Other popular dishes include seafood, such as lobster and prawns, and locally grown fruits and vegetables.

One popular pairing at the festival is Kangaroo meat with Shiraz wine. The bold and earthy flavour of the Kangaroo meat pairs well with the full-bodied and complex flavour of the Shiraz wine. Another popular pairing is seafood with Chardonnay wine. The crisp and refreshing flavour of the Chardonnay wine complements the delicate and subtle flavour of the seafood.

In conclusion, the Adelaide Fringe Festival is a vibrant and diverse celebration of Australian culture that brings people together to enjoy art, music, theatre, and comedy. The event is set in a beautiful location that is perfect for growing wine grapes, and visitors can sample some of the best wines from the region. The food served at the event is diverse and flavorful, and it pairs well with the different types of wine available.

Overall, the Adelaide Fringe Festival is a unique and unforgettable experience that celebrates the rich culture of Australia.

4. Sydney Gay and Lesbian Mardi Gras -

The Sydney Gay and Lesbian Mardi Gras is an annual festival held in Sydney, Australia. It is a celebration of the LGBTQ+ community and their rights, and it is one of the most popular events of its kind in the world. The festival typically takes place over several weeks in February and March, with the highlight being the parade, which is held on the first Saturday in March.

The event attracts people from all over the world, with over 500,000 people attending the parade alone in recent years. The festival has a rich history, dating back to 1978 when it was first held as a protest march for gay rights. Over the years, it has evolved into a colorful and vibrant celebration of the LGBTQ+ community, with music, dance, art, and performances.

The event takes place in the city of Sydney, which is known for its diverse and multicultural population. The city is situated on the east coast of Australia, and it has a beautiful natural landscape, including the famous Sydney Harbour and the nearby Blue Mountains.

In terms of wines, Australia is known for its excellent wine production, particularly in the regions of Barossa Valley, Hunter Valley, and Margaret River. The country produces a range of varietals, including Shiraz, Cabernet Sauvignon, Chardonnay, and Pinot Noir. The wines are typically produced using modern vinification techniques, with a focus on producing high-quality wines with distinct regional characteristics.

At the Sydney Gay and Lesbian Mardi Gras, there are typically a range of wines available to drink, including both red and white varieties. Some of the wines that are commonly served include Shiraz, Cabernet Sauvignon, Chardonnay, and Pinot Noir, as well as sparkling wines and rosés.

In terms of food, the festival typically features a range of international cuisines, including Italian, Thai, Indian, and Chinese. There are also many food trucks and stalls serving up local Australian cuisine, such as meat pies, sausage rolls, and seafood.

To pair with the wines, a range of food options could be chosen. For example, a Shiraz would pair well with a rich and savory meat pie, while a Chardonnay could be paired with a fresh seafood dish, such as grilled prawns or oysters. A Cabernet Sauvignon would pair well with a hearty beef stew or grilled steak, while a Pinot Noir could be paired with a lighter dish, such as grilled salmon or roasted chicken.

Overall, the Sydney Gay and Lesbian Mardi Gras is a celebration of diversity, culture, and community, with a focus on inclusion and acceptance. It is a wonderful event that brings together people from all walks of life, and it offers a fantastic opportunity to experience the best of Australian wine, food, and culture.

5. Melbourne Food and Wine Festival

The Melbourne Food and Wine Festival is a significant culinary event held annually in Melbourne, Australia. This event celebrates Australia's rich cultural and culinary heritage, showcasing its diverse range of food and wine offerings to locals and visitors alike. The festival takes place over several days and features numerous events, including tastings, cooking classes, and masterclasses, with renowned chefs and winemakers from around the world.

The festival takes place in March each year and attracts a diverse range of people from all over the world. The event has become a cultural landmark in Melbourne, with attendees from all walks of life coming together to celebrate their love of food and wine.

Melbourne's unique topography and climate provide the ideal conditions for growing grapes and producing wine. The city is located in the heart of Victoria's wine country, with many renowned wineries in the surrounding region. The festival offers an excellent opportunity for wine lovers to sample a wide range of wines from local and international producers.

During the festival, visitors can taste and learn about various vinification techniques and wine styles. The festival's wine events feature wine tastings, masterclasses, and educational seminars on wine production and wine pairing.

The food served at the Melbourne Food and Wine Festival is just as impressive as the wine. The festival offers an extensive range of cuisines, from traditional Australian fare to international cuisine. The food is prepared by some of the world's most renowned chefs, who use locally sourced, seasonal ingredients to create unique and flavorful dishes.

The food and wine pairings at the festival are a highlight of the event. The festival's chefs work closely with winemakers to create the perfect pairing, highlighting the unique flavors and aromas of each dish and wine.

Some of the popular food and wine pairings at the festival include:

Grilled lamb with Shiraz: This classic Australian pairing highlights the rich and bold flavours of Shiraz wine. The smoky flavours of the lamb complement the wine's bold flavours, creating a harmonious balance on the palate.

Seafood with Chardonnay: The crisp and refreshing acidity of Chardonnay complements the delicate flavors of seafood, making it a perfect pairing. The festival offers a wide range of seafood dishes, including oysters, prawns, and lobster, which pair beautifully with Chardonnay.

Cheese and Pinot Noir: The rich and complex flavors of Pinot Noir complement the savory and nutty flavors of cheese. The festival offers a wide range of artisanal cheeses from around the world, allowing visitors to experience this classic pairing.

In conclusion, the Melbourne Food and Wine Festival is an excellent event that celebrates Australia's rich cultural and culinary heritage. The festival's diverse range of food and wine offerings, combined with its beautiful topography and unique vinification techniques, make it a must-visit event for food and wine lovers from around the world.

6. Vivid Sydney

The Vivid Sydney festival is an annual event that takes place in Sydney, Australia. The festival is a celebration of the city's culture and creativity, and it features a range of events and activities that showcase the best of Sydney's art, music, and food scene. The festival takes place over several weeks each year, typically in May and June, and attracts visitors from all over the world.

The people of Sydney come together during the Vivid Sydney festival to celebrate their rich cultural heritage and the diversity of their city. The event is a melting pot of different cultures, with participants coming from all over Australia and the world. The festival is a vibrant and colorful display of the city's unique personality, and it is a celebration of the creative spirit that thrives in Sydney.

The festival takes place across the city, with events and activities taking place in various locations. The topography of Sydney provides the perfect backdrop for the festival, with its iconic landmarks and stunning natural scenery. The festival is a celebration of the city's unique cultural identity, and it is a showcase of the best of Australian art, music, and food.

One of the highlights of the Vivid Sydney festival is the opportunity to sample some of the region's finest wines. The festival features a range of vineyards and wineries from the surrounding areas, and visitors can sample a variety of different wines and learn about the vinification techniques used to produce them. Some of the wines available to drink at the event include Shiraz, Chardonnay, Cabernet Sauvignon, and Pinot Noir.

In addition to the wines, the festival also features a range of foods that are cooked and served in detail. The food at the festival is a celebration of Sydney's diverse culinary scene, and visitors can sample everything from street food to fine dining. Some of the foods served at the festival include fresh seafood, grilled meats, artisanal cheeses, and decadent desserts.

To pair foods and wines at the event, visitors can try a variety of combinations. For example, the rich, bold flavours of grilled meats and artisanal cheeses can be paired with full-bodied red wines like Shiraz and Cabernet Sauvignon. On the other hand, the light, refreshing flavours of fresh seafood and salads can be paired with crisp white wines like Chardonnay and Pinot Noir.

Overall, the Vivid Sydney festival is a celebration of Sydney's unique culture and creativity. The festival showcases the best of the city's art, music, and food scene, and it provides visitors with an unforgettable experience that they will cherish for years to come.

7. Dark Mofo

Dark Mofo is an annual winter festival that takes place in Hobart, Tasmania, Australia. The festival celebrates the winter solstice and explores the themes of darkness, light, and the unknown. Dark Mofo attracts visitors from around the world, and it is considered to be one of the most unique and exciting events in Australia.

The festival takes place in June, and it lasts for about two weeks. During this time, the city of Hobart transforms into a playground of art installations, music, and food. The festival celebrates the winter solstice, which is the shortest day of the year in the Southern Hemisphere. This is a significant occasion for the local culture and history of Tasmania, as it marks the beginning of the winter season.

The topography of Hobart is mountainous, with stunning views of the Tasmanian wilderness. The area is also home to a number of vineyards that produce some of Australia's best wines. The vinification techniques used in Tasmania are known for producing high-quality wines that are unique to the region.

At Dark Mofo, visitors can sample a wide range of wines from the region. Some of the most popular wines available to drink at the event include Pinot Noir, Chardonnay, Riesling, and Sauvignon Blanc. These wines are paired with foods that are cooked and served on-site, using local produce and ingredients.

The food at Dark Mofo is a highlight of the event, with many local and international chefs showcasing their skills. The festival features a range of food stalls, pop-up restaurants, and food trucks that offer a variety of dishes. Some of the most popular foods served at the festival include seafood, grilled meats, cheese, and charcuterie.

The food at Dark Mofo is often paired with wines from the region, with each dish carefully matched to complement the flavours and aromas of the wine. For example, a Pinot Noir might be paired with grilled venison, while a Chardonnay might be paired with a seafood platter. The pairing of foods and wines is an integral part of the Dark Mofo experience, and visitors are encouraged to explore and discover new flavours and combinations.

Overall, Dark Mofo is an exciting and unique event that celebrates the winter solstice and the culture and history of Tasmania. With its stunning topography, excellent wines, and delicious food, Dark Mofo is a must-visit event for anyone interested in exploring the rich cultural heritage of Australia.

8. Splendour in the Grass

Splendour in the Grass is an annual music festival that takes place in Australia. The festival attracts thousands of people from all over the country and features a wide variety of music genres, including indie, rock, hip hop, and electronic music. It is held over three days in late July or early August each year, and is known for its vibrant atmosphere, topography, vineyards, and wine selection.

The festival takes place in the North Byron Parklands, which is a beautiful and expansive outdoor space in the Byron Bay area. The region is known for its rolling hills, lush forests, and stunning beaches, which provide a perfect backdrop for the festival. The people who attend Splendour in the Grass are typically young adults who are passionate about music, art, and culture. The festival is also an opportunity for people to come together and celebrate their shared love of music.

In addition to the music, Splendour in the Grass also features a range of food and drink options. The festival offers a variety of Australian and international wines, including Shiraz, Chardonnay, and Sauvignon Blanc, all produced using traditional vinification techniques. The vineyards that supply the wine for the festival are located throughout the Byron Bay region and are known for their high-quality grapes and expert winemaking.

To pair with the wines, the festival also features a diverse range of food options, from classic Australian barbecues to international street food. The food vendors at Splendour in the Grass use fresh, locally-sourced ingredients to create a wide variety of dishes, including wood-fired pizzas, gourmet burgers, and vegan curries.

Some standout pairings at the festival include:

A full-bodied Shiraz paired with a juicy Australian beef burger topped with caramelised onions and sharp cheddar cheese.

A crisp Sauvignon Blanc paired with a fresh seafood platter featuring locally-caught prawns, oysters, and lobster.

A buttery Chardonnay paired with a creamy risotto made with wild mushrooms and truffle oil.

In addition to the food and drink, Splendour in the Grass also features a range of cultural activities, including art installations, workshops, and performances. Overall, the festival is a celebration of music, food, and culture, and is a must-visit for anyone who loves the outdoors and wants to experience the best of Australia's vibrant music scene.

9. Melbourne International Film Festival

The Melbourne International Film Festival (MIFF) is an annual event that takes place in Melbourne, Australia, and is considered one of the most significant cultural events in the country. The festival has been running since 1952 and is held over a two-week period each August. The MIFF screens a wide range of films, including documentaries, short films, and feature films from all over the world.

The festival brings together people from various cultures and backgrounds, with a significant focus on the arts and cinema. The event attracts film enthusiasts, industry professionals, and tourists from all over the world, creating a vibrant and diverse atmosphere.

The city of Melbourne, which is located in the southeastern state of Victoria, provides a stunning backdrop for the event. With its varied topography, ranging from rolling hills to pristine beaches, it is a perfect place to host an international film festival.

In addition to its natural beauty, the region is also known for its vineyards and winemaking industry. Victoria is home to over 600 vineyards, with a particular focus on cool-climate wines. The region is renowned for its high-quality Chardonnays, Pinot Noirs, and Shiraz, and the MIFF offers an opportunity to sample some of these exceptional wines.

The festival features a diverse range of wines from various regions in Victoria, including Yarra Valley, Mornington Peninsula, and Macedon Ranges. The wines available at the festival range from sparkling whites to full-bodied reds, with an emphasis on the unique flavours and characteristics of each region.

The foods served at the MIFF are as diverse as the films on offer, with an emphasis on locally sourced and sustainably produced ingredients. The festival showcases the region's multicultural cuisine, with a focus on fresh seafood, artisanal cheeses, and charcuterie.

Pairing food and wine is a crucial aspect of the MIFF experience, with a team of sommeliers on hand to guide festival-goers through the various wine and food combinations. Some of the standout pairings include Pinot Noir with roasted duck breast, Chardonnay with creamy seafood risotto, and Shiraz with slow-cooked beef brisket.

In addition to the film screenings, wine tastings, and food pairings, the MIFF also hosts a range of cultural events, including art exhibitions, live music performances, and panel discussions. The festival is a celebration of culture, creativity, and the arts, providing a unique opportunity to experience the best of Melbourne and Victoria.

10. Royal Adelaide Show

The Royal Adelaide Show is an annual event that takes place in Adelaide, South Australia, which is located in the southern part of the country. The event is a showcase of the region's agricultural heritage and modern-day innovation. It is one of the largest and most popular agricultural shows in Australia, attracting visitors from all over the country and beyond.

The show usually takes place in early September, and it runs for around ten days. During this time, visitors can enjoy a wide variety of exhibits, events, and activities. These include livestock shows, sheepdog trials, equestrian competitions, horticultural displays, arts and crafts exhibitions, and much more.

The Royal Adelaide Show is also an excellent opportunity to sample some of the best wines that South Australia has to offer. The region is home to some of the most famous vineyards in the world, and it is renowned for its production of high-quality wines. Visitors to the show can sample wines made from a wide range of grape varieties, including Shiraz, Cabernet Sauvignon, Chardonnay, and Riesling.

The winemakers in South Australia use a variety of vinification techniques, including barrel fermentation, cold soaking, and malolactic fermentation. Each technique contributes to the unique flavour and aroma of the wines produced in the region.

At the Royal Adelaide Show, visitors can enjoy a variety of foods that are cooked and served on-site. These include traditional Australian favourites such as meat pies, sausage rolls, and fish and chips, as well as more exotic dishes like sushi, stir-fries, and curries.

To pair with these delicious foods, visitors can choose from a wide variety of wines available at the event. For example, a hearty meat pie might be perfectly complemented by a full-bodied Shiraz, while a spicy stir-fry could be paired with a crisp and refreshing Riesling. The food and wine options at the Royal Adelaide Show are sure to please even the most discerning palate.

Overall, the Royal Adelaide Show is an excellent opportunity to experience the best that South Australia has to offer in terms of culture, food, wine, and hospitality. Whether you're a local or a visitor from afar, this event is not to be missed.

11. Sydney Fringe Festival

The Sydney Fringe Festival is a vibrant cultural event held in Sydney, Australia, which celebrates the creativity and diversity of the city's performing arts scene. The festival is held annually during September and October and features a range of performances, exhibitions, and other events throughout the city.

The people of Australia, particularly those in Sydney, have a deep appreciation for the arts and culture, and the Sydney Fringe Festival reflects this with its wide range of performances and events. The festival is a platform for both emerging and established artists to showcase their talents, providing a platform for new and exciting work to be seen by a wider audience.

The festival takes place in various locations throughout the city, including theatres, galleries, and public spaces. The topography of Sydney is diverse, with a mix of urban areas, coastal regions, and parklands. The festival takes advantage of this diversity, with events taking place in a variety of different settings.

In addition to the performing arts, the Sydney Fringe Festival also celebrates the food and wine culture of the city. The festival features a range of food and wine events, including tastings, cooking demonstrations, and food and wine pairings.

The vineyards in Australia are known for producing high-quality wines, and the Sydney Fringe Festival offers visitors the opportunity to sample a variety of different wines. The vinification techniques used in Australia are varied, with both traditional and modern techniques being used to produce different styles of wine. Visitors to the festival can sample wines from a range of different vineyards, including some of the best-known producers in the country.

The food served at the Sydney Fringe Festival is equally diverse, with a range of different cuisines on offer. The festival celebrates the multicultural nature of the city, with food from all over the world being represented. From Asian street food to traditional Australian fare, there is something for everyone at the festival.

The food and wine pairing events at the festival are a particular highlight, with expert sommeliers and chefs working together to create perfect matches between the different dishes and wines. For example, a dish of grilled lamb chops might be paired with a full-bodied Australian Shiraz, while a lighter seafood dish might be paired with a crisp Sauvignon Blanc.

Overall, the Sydney Fringe Festival is a celebration of the creativity, diversity, and culture of Sydney, Australia. From the performing arts to the food and wine, the festival offers visitors a unique and unforgettable experience.

12. Melbourne Spring Racing Carnival

The Melbourne Spring Racing Carnival is a prestigious event that takes place annually in Australia. It is a horse racing event that attracts people from all over the country and the world. The carnival usually takes place from September to November and is a celebration of the arrival of spring in Australia.

The Melbourne Spring Racing Carnival is a significant cultural event in Australia, and it has a long and storied history. The event has been held for over 150 years and is considered one of the most prestigious horse racing events in the world. It is a time when people come together to celebrate the beauty of the sport, enjoy the company of friends and family, and indulge in fine food and wine.

The carnival takes place in Melbourne, the capital city of the state of Victoria, which is known for its stunning scenery and diverse culture. The city is home to a vibrant community of people who are passionate about horse racing and the Melbourne Cup, which is the highlight of the Melbourne Spring Racing Carnival.

The topography of the region around Melbourne is varied, with rolling hills, lush forests, and stunning vineyards. The vineyards in the region are renowned for their high-quality grapes, which are used to produce some of the finest wines in the world.

The vinification techniques used in the region are modern and sophisticated, with winemakers using state-of-the-art equipment and technology to produce exceptional wines. Some of the wines available to drink at the Melbourne Spring Racing Carnival include Chardonnay, Pinot Noir, Shiraz, and Cabernet Sauvignon.

The food served at the carnival is equally impressive, with a range of dishes that are designed to complement the wines on offer. Some of the dishes that are served at the carnival include oysters, seafood platters, charcuterie boards, grilled meats, and salads. There are also a variety of desserts available, including cakes, tarts, and chocolates.

Pairing wines and foods at the event is a key part of the experience, and there are many different combinations to choose from. For example, a Pinot Noir might be paired with a grilled steak or a salmon fillet, while a Chardonnay might be paired with a seafood platter or a creamy pasta dish.

Overall, the Melbourne Spring Racing Carnival is an event that celebrates the beauty of horse racing, the culture of Australia, and the excellence of food and wine. It is a must-attend event for anyone who is passionate about these things, and it is sure to be an unforgettable experience for all who attend.

13. Tropfest

Tropfest is an annual short film festival held in Australia. It is one of the largest short film festivals in the world, attracting filmmakers, celebrities, and film enthusiasts from all over the globe. The event takes place in various locations across Australia, including Sydney, Melbourne, and Perth.

The festival was founded in 1993 by John Polson, a prominent Australian actor, and filmmaker. It started as a small screening of short films in a cafe in Sydney, but over the years, it has grown into a major cultural event in Australia. The festival is known for its focus on short films, which are typically less than 7 minutes in length.

Tropfest is held every year in February, and it is a celebration of Australian culture and creativity. The festival attracts a diverse crowd of people, including filmmakers, actors, artists, and musicians. The festival is also known for its beautiful topography, with many of the events held in outdoor locations surrounded by scenic landscapes and vineyards.

Speaking of vineyards, Australia is home to some of the world's best wineries. Vinification techniques vary across the country, but some of the most popular varieties include Shiraz, Cabernet Sauvignon, Chardonnay, and Sauvignon Blanc. At Tropfest, attendees can enjoy a variety of wines from local wineries, including Penfolds, Jacob's Creek, and Yalumba.

In addition to wine, there are also a variety of food options available at the festival. The food is typically prepared by local chefs and includes a range of Australian dishes. Some of the most popular dishes include grilled kangaroo, Barramundi (a type of fish native to Australia), and lamb chops. Pairing these dishes with the right wine can enhance the flavours and create a memorable culinary experience.

For example, a grilled kangaroo dish would pair well with a bold red wine such as a Shiraz or Cabernet Sauvignon. The rich, gamey flavour of the kangaroo would complement the robust tannins and spicy notes of the wine. Barramundi, on the other hand, would pair well with a crisp white wine such as a Chardonnay or Sauvignon Blanc. The delicate, flaky texture of the fish would be enhanced by the bright acidity of the wine.

Overall, Tropfest is a celebration of Australian culture and creativity. It brings together people from all walks of life to enjoy short films, beautiful topography, and delicious food and wine. Whether you're a film enthusiast or simply looking for a fun cultural experience, Tropfest is definitely worth a visit

14. Brisbane Festival

The Brisbane Festival is a cultural event that takes place annually in Brisbane, Australia. This festival is held in September and October, and it is a celebration of the arts, music, dance, and theatre. The festival is a reflection of the city's diverse cultural heritage and its love for creativity and artistic expression.

Australia is known for its diverse population, and the people of Brisbane reflect this diversity. The festival brings together people of different races, cultures, and religions, all coming together to enjoy the festivities.

The Brisbane Festival is held in various locations around the city, with some events taking place in the city's topography, such as the Brisbane River and the surrounding mountains. The festival also includes vineyards and vinification techniques, with a variety of wines available to drink at the event.

The culture of the festival is centred around the arts, with various performances, exhibitions, and shows taking place throughout the festival. There are also food stalls and restaurants that serve a wide range of foods, including dishes cooked using traditional Australian recipes.

Some of the foods served at the festival include seafood, grilled meats, and a variety of vegetarian and vegan options. The wines available to drink at the event include both red and white wines, as well as sparkling wines and fortified wines.

Pairing foods and wines at the event is an important part of the festival. Some of the recommended pairings include grilled fish with a crisp white wine, roasted meats with a full-bodied red wine, and spicy dishes with a sweet dessert wine.

In conclusion, the Brisbane Festival is an exciting event that celebrates the diverse culture of Australia. The festival brings together people from all walks of life, and it is a celebration of creativity, art, and music. The food and wine available at the event are also an essential part of the festival, with various dishes and wines available to sample and enjoy.

15. Woodford Folk Festival

The Woodford Folk Festival is an annual music and cultural festival held in Woodford, Queensland, Australia. It is typically held over six days and nights, from December 27th to January 1st, and attracts thousands of visitors from all over the world.

The festival features a diverse lineup of musical acts, as well as workshops, lectures, and performances covering a wide range of cultural and artistic topics. It is known for its focus on sustainability, with a commitment to reducing waste and promoting environmental awareness throughout the event.

The festival takes place in a beautiful natural setting, surrounded by the rolling hills and forests of the Sunshine Coast hinterland. The area is also home to several vineyards, which produce a variety of high-quality wines using both traditional and modern vinification techniques.

Visitors to the festival can sample a range of wines from local vineyards, including crisp white wines, full-bodied reds, and sparkling wines perfect for celebrating the New Year. Some of the most popular wines available include Sauvignon Blanc, Chardonnay, Shiraz, and Pinot Noir.

In addition to wine, the festival also features a wide variety of delicious foods, many of which are cooked and served on site. Visitors can enjoy everything from gourmet cheeses and charcuterie to fresh seafood and hearty vegetarian fare.

Some of the most popular food and wine pairings at the festival include:

Chardonnay and seafood: The buttery, oaky flavors of a good Chardonnay pair perfectly with fresh seafood, such as oysters, prawns, and crab.

Pinot Noir and duck: The light, fruity notes of Pinot Noir complement the rich, gamey flavours of duck, making for a delicious and satisfying combination.

Shiraz and barbecue: The bold, spicy flavours of Shiraz stand up well to the smoky, savoury flavours of barbecued meats, making it a popular choice for festival-goers looking to indulge in some hearty fare.

Overall, the Woodford Folk Festival is a celebration of culture, music, food, and wine, offering visitors the chance to experience the best of Australia's rich and diverse cultural landscape in a stunning natural setting.

16. Bluesfest Byron Bay

Bluesfest Byron Bay is a popular music festival that takes place annually in Byron Bay, New South Wales, Australia. The event usually occurs during the Easter weekend and lasts for five days. The festival attracts people from all over the world, with a diverse crowd of music lovers and artists alike.

Australia is a culturally diverse country, and the Bluesfest Byron Bay reflects this diversity in the music, food, and wine that it showcases. The festival celebrates the rich cultural heritage of blues and roots music, with a mix of local and international artists performing on multiple stages.

Byron Bay is known for its stunning natural beauty, with the festival set against a backdrop of rolling hills, pristine beaches, and lush rainforest. The region is also famous for its vineyards, and many wineries are located in the area. The wines available at the festival include a range of varieties and styles, from crisp and refreshing whites to bold and complex reds.

Winemakers in the Byron Bay region employ a range of vinification techniques, including traditional methods like oak barrel ageing and modern techniques like stainless steel fermentation. Visitors to the festival can taste and learn about these different techniques, as well as the unique characteristics of the local terroir.

In addition to wine, the festival offers a variety of food options, from street food vendors to sit-down restaurants. The food reflects the multicultural nature of the festival, with options ranging from Asian fusion to traditional Australian barbecue.

To pair food and wine at the event, attendees can consider the following suggestions:

For seafood dishes, consider pairing with a crisp white wine like a Sauvignon Blanc or Pinot Gris.

For spicy Asian dishes, try pairing with a fruity Riesling or Gewurztraminer.

For barbecue or grilled meats, consider a bold red wine like a Shiraz or Cabernet Sauvignon.

For cheese platters, try pairing with a rich and complex red like a Merlot or Cabernet Franc.

Overall, Bluesfest Byron Bay is an event that celebrates music, culture, and the natural beauty of the region. With a wide range of food and wine options, there's something for everyone to enjoy at this festival.

17. Sculpture by the Sea

Sculpture by the Sea is an annual outdoor sculpture exhibition held in Australia, showcasing large-scale sculptures created by artists from around the world. The event takes place along the Bondi to Tamarama coastal walk in Sydney, which boasts a stunning backdrop of the ocean and the rugged coastline.

The event started in 1997 and has since become one of the most significant cultural events in Australia, attracting thousands of visitors each year. It is usually held in October or November and spans for three weeks.

The event not only celebrates the art of sculpture but also showcases the rich culture of Australia. Visitors can experience various forms of art, music, and entertainment. Additionally, the exhibition provides an opportunity for the local community and visitors to engage in conversations about art, culture, and the environment.

The topography of the Bondi to Tamarama coastal walk, with its stunning vistas and rugged coastline, provides an ideal setting for the exhibition. Along the way, visitors can also explore the vineyards of the surrounding regions, which produce some of Australia's finest wines.

Australia is known for its unique vinification techniques, which have evolved over the years. Visitors to Sculpture by the Sea can enjoy a range of wines from local vineyards, including Shiraz, Chardonnay, and Cabernet Sauvignon.

The exhibition also features a variety of food stalls, offering a range of cuisine from around the world. Some of the foods served at the event include seafood, grilled meats, salads, and desserts.

Pairing the right wine with food is an art, and at Sculpture by the Sea, visitors can enjoy the perfect combination of wine and food. For example, a rich and full-bodied Shiraz can be paired with grilled meats, while a crisp and refreshing Chardonnay can be paired with seafood or salads.

Overall, Sculpture by the Sea is an excellent opportunity for visitors to experience the rich culture and artistic expression of Australia while enjoying the stunning natural beauty of the Bondi to Tamarama coastal walk.

18. Airlie Beach Music Festival

The Airlie Beach Music Festival is an annual event that takes place in Airlie Beach, Queensland, Australia. The festival is a celebration of music, culture, and the arts, and brings together musicians and music lovers from all over the world.

The event is typically held in November, and runs over three days, with over 74 bands and artists performing across 17 venues. The festival is known for its diverse range of music, featuring everything from rock and blues, to folk and country.

Airlie Beach is a coastal town located in the Whitsunday Region of Queensland, known for its stunning beaches and vibrant nightlife. The area is home to a diverse community of people, including locals and tourists from all over the world.

In addition to the music, the festival also features a range of cultural activities, including art exhibitions, street performers, and workshops. The event offers a unique opportunity to experience the local culture and traditions of the region.

The topography of the region is characterised by rolling hills, lush greenery, and stunning coastlines. The area is also home to a number of vineyards, which produce some of Australia's best wines.

Vinification techniques used in the region include both traditional and modern methods, with an emphasis on sustainable and organic practices. Some of the wines available to drink at the event include Shiraz, Chardonnay, Cabernet Sauvignon, and Merlot.

The foods served at the festival are a celebration of local produce and traditional Australian cuisine. Some of the dishes available include seafood, barbeque meats, and traditional meat pies.

To pair with the wines, some of the recommended food and wine pairings include:

Seafood and Chardonnay: The creamy, buttery flavours of Chardonnay pair perfectly with the delicate flavours of fresh seafood.

Barbeque Meats and Shiraz: The bold, spicy flavours of Shiraz complement the rich, smoky flavours of barbeque meats.

Meat Pies and Cabernet Sauvignon: The full-bodied flavours of Cabernet Sauvignon pair perfectly with the rich, savoury flavours of meat pies.

Overall, the Airlie Beach Music Festival is a must-visit event for anyone interested in music, culture, and the arts. With its stunning location, diverse range of music and cultural activities, and delicious food and wine offerings, it is a true celebration of all that Australia has to offer.

19. Falls Festival

The Falls Festival is an annual music festival held in Australia that attracts thousands of people from all over the country and beyond. The festival usually takes place over the New Year period, typically starting on December 28th and ending on January 1st. The event features a range of musical genres, including indie rock, electronic music, and hip-hop.

The festival has become an important part of Australian culture, and it attracts a diverse crowd of people who come to enjoy the music, the atmosphere, and the food and drink on offer. The festival is held in a range of locations across the country, including the cities of Lorne, Marion Bay, and Byron Bay, and it has become a popular destination for both locals and tourists.

The topography of the festival varies depending on the location, with some venues being set in picturesque coastal regions and others set in the lush green countryside. Many of the festival sites are also located near vineyards, which offer visitors the chance to sample some of the best wines that Australia has to offer.

Vinification techniques in Australia vary depending on the region, but many of the country's winemakers use a combination of traditional and modern techniques to produce high-quality wines. Some of the most popular wine varieties in Australia include Shiraz, Cabernet Sauvignon, Chardonnay, and Sauvignon Blanc.

At the Falls Festival, visitors can sample a range of different wines from local vineyards, including reds, whites, and sparkling wines. Some of the most popular wines on offer include the Shiraz from the Barossa Valley, the Chardonnay from Margaret River, and the Pinot Noir from the Yarra Valley.

In addition to the wine, the festival also features a range of food options, with many of the dishes incorporating local ingredients and flavours. Some of the most popular foods at the festival include seafood, barbequed meats, and fresh salads.

To pair foods and wines at the event, festival-goers could enjoy grilled prawns with a glass of Sauvignon Blanc, slow-cooked beef brisket with a glass of Shiraz, or roasted vegetable salad with a glass of Chardonnay. There are also dessert options available, including fresh fruit platters and chocolate truffles that would pair well with a glass of sparkling wine.

Overall, the Falls Festival is a celebration of music, food, and wine in the beautiful Australian landscape, and it is a must-visit for anyone looking to experience the country's culture and hospitality.

20. Darwin Festival

The Darwin Festival is an annual cultural event held in Darwin, the capital city of the Northern Territory of Australia. The festival is a celebration of arts, music, theatre, dance, and culture that showcases the unique and diverse cultural heritage of the region.

The event usually takes place in the month of August, which is during the dry season in Northern Australia, and lasts for 18 days. The festival attracts visitors from all over Australia and the world, and offers a range of activities, performances, and events for people of all ages and backgrounds.

The topography of Darwin is unique, with its tropical climate, sandy beaches, and rugged landscapes. The region is also home to many vineyards, where wine production has been a thriving industry for many years. Vinification techniques in the region include both traditional and modern methods, and produce wines of exceptional quality.

At the Darwin Festival, visitors can enjoy a wide range of wines, including Chardonnay, Sauvignon Blanc, Cabernet Sauvignon, Shiraz, and Merlot, all produced from local vineyards. The wines are carefully selected to complement the dishes served at the festival, which include a range of local and international cuisines.

The foods served at the Darwin Festival are varied and reflect the region's multicultural heritage. Local specialties include Barramundi, a popular fish found in the rivers and estuaries of the Northern Territory, as well as Kangaroo meat, which is a lean and healthy alternative to traditional red meats. Other dishes include Asian and Pacific Islander-inspired cuisine, such as Thai curries, Japanese sushi, and Polynesian-style seafood.

The food and wine pairings at the festival are carefully selected to enhance the flavors of both the food and the wine. For example, a light and fruity Sauvignon Blanc might be paired with a fresh seafood dish, while a bold and spicy Shiraz might be paired with a rich and savoury meat dish.

In addition to the food and wine, the Darwin Festival also offers a range of cultural performances and events, including music concerts, dance performances, and theatre productions. Visitors can also take part in workshops and classes, such as cooking classes, dance classes, and art classes, to learn more about the culture and heritage of the region.

Overall, the Darwin Festival is a unique and exciting event that celebrates the cultural diversity and natural beauty of the Northern Territory of Australia. From its stunning landscapes and vineyards to its delicious food and wine, the festival offers something for everyone to enjoy.

Phileas Fogg's Australian Festival Experiences

Phileas Fogg was an adventurer who travelled the world in search of new experiences, and if he were alive today, he would undoubtedly be interested in exploring the diverse festivals and events that Australia has to offer. Here are some festivals and events across Australia that Phileas Fogg might have enjoyed, along with the foods and wines he could have paired at each venue:

Sydney Festival: This festival takes place in January and features a variety of events, including music, theatre, and dance performances. Fogg might have enjoyed fresh seafood from Sydney's famous Fish Market, paired with a crisp Australian Sauvignon Blanc.

Melbourne Food and Wine Festival: Taking place in March, this festival celebrates the city's culinary scene. Fogg could have tasted a range of dishes, from classic Australian barbecue to modern fusion cuisine, paired with local Pinot Noir or Chardonnay.

Adelaide Fringe: This arts festival takes place in February and March and features a variety of performances, including comedy, theatre, and music. Fogg might have enjoyed gourmet street food from Adelaide's many food trucks, paired with a bold Shiraz.

Margaret River Gourmet Escape: This food and wine festival takes place in November and showcases the best of Western Australia's culinary scene. Fogg could have tasted locally-produced cheeses, olive oils, and wines, paired with the region's famous Cabernet Sauvignon.

Byron Bay Bluesfest: This music festival takes place over the Easter weekend and features a range of blues and roots performers. Fogg could have enjoyed fresh seafood and tropical fruits, paired with a refreshing Australian Riesling.

Dark Mofo: This winter festival takes place in June and celebrates the winter solstice with art installations, music, and food. Fogg might have sampled rich, hearty stews and soups, paired with a full-bodied Australian Shiraz.

Vivid Sydney: This festival takes place in May and June and features light installations, music, and art. Fogg might have enjoyed street food from some of Sydney's best food trucks, paired with a crisp Australian Chardonnay.

Woodford Folk Festival: This festival takes place over New Year's and features a variety of music, art, and theatre. Fogg could have tasted dishes from around the world, including curries, stir-fries, and paellas, paired with a fruity Australian Merlot.

Taste of Tasmania: This food festival takes place in December and January and showcases the best of Tasmania's culinary scene. Fogg might have enjoyed fresh seafood, including oysters and lobster, paired with a cool-climate Tasmanian Pinot Noir.

Sydney Royal Easter Show: This agricultural show takes place in April and features livestock competitions, carnival rides, and food stalls. Fogg could have tasted classic Australian foods, such as meat pies and sausage rolls, paired with a smooth Australian Shiraz.

Falls Festival: This music festival takes place over New Year's and features a range of indie and alternative performers. Fogg might have enjoyed fresh salads and grilled meats, paired with a crisp Australian Sauvignon Blanc.

Perth International Arts Festival: This arts festival takes place in February and March and features a variety of performances, including theater, dance, and music. Fogg could have tasted locally-produced cheeses and wines, paired with a fruity Australian Shiraz.

Brisbane Festival: This arts festival takes place in September and features a range of performances, including theater, music, and dance. Fogg might have enjoyed fresh seafood from the nearby Moreton Bay, paired with a refreshing Australian Riesling.

Blues on Broadbeach: This music festival takes place in May and features a range of blues and roots performers. Fogg could have enjoyed fresh seafood and tropical fruits, paired with a crisp Australian Chardonnay.

CHAPTER 13

FESTIVALS IN ASIA

There are countless festivals and celebrations that take place across the vast and diverse continent of Asia. Here are some of the most prominent and widely celebrated festivals:

Chinese New Year

Chinese New Year, also known as Spring Festival, is the most significant festival in China, and it is celebrated by Chinese people all around the world. The festival falls on different dates each year, usually between January 21 and February 20, depending on the Chinese lunar calendar. The Chinese New Year celebration lasts for 15 days, and it is a time for family reunions, feasting, and the exchange of gifts.

China is a vast country with diverse topography and cultures, and the Chinese New Year is celebrated differently across the country. However, some traditions are universal, such as red decorations, firecrackers, and the giving of red envelopes filled with money to children.

In terms of wine culture, China has a long history of winemaking that dates back thousands of years. The country is currently the fifth-largest wine producer in the world, with several wine regions, including Ningxia, Xinjiang, and Shandong.

During the Chinese New Year celebration, various wines are available to drink, including red wines, white wines, and Chinese rice wine. Baijiu, a traditional Chinese spirit, is also popular during the festival.

When it comes to food, the Chinese New Year celebration is all about feasting, with families and friends gathering to enjoy traditional dishes. Some of the popular dishes served during the festival include:

Dumplings: Dumplings are a must-have dish during the Chinese New Year celebration. They symbolise wealth and prosperity, and they are typically filled with meat or vegetables.

Nian Gao: Nian Gao is a sweet, sticky rice cake that symbolises progress and prosperity. It is usually steamed and served as a dessert.

Spring Rolls: Spring rolls are a popular appetisers during the Chinese New Year celebration. They are made with vegetables and meat and are fried until crispy.

Fish: Fish is a traditional Chinese New Year dish that symbolises abundance and prosperity. It is usually served whole and is often steamed or boiled.

When it comes to pairing wine with Chinese New Year dishes, here are some suggestions:

Dumplings: Pair dumplings with a light, fruity red wine, such as Pinot Noir or a crisp, refreshing white wine like Sauvignon Blanc.

Nian Gao: Pair this sweet, sticky dessert with a late-harvest Riesling or a Sauternes.

Spring Rolls: Pair spring rolls with a sparkling wine, such as Champagne or Prosecco, or a light, fruity red wine like Beaujolais.

Fish: Pair fish with a light, aromatic white wine, such as Riesling or Gewurztraminer, or a full-bodied red wine like Cabernet Sauvignon or Merlot.

In conclusion, the Chinese New Year is an essential festival in China and is celebrated with great joy and enthusiasm. The celebration is characterised by family reunions, feasting, and the exchange of gifts. Wines are an essential part of the festival, and they are paired with traditional dishes to enhance the dining experience.

Diwali

Diwali is one of the most significant festivals celebrated in India, and it is also known as the festival of lights. The festival is celebrated by Hindus, Sikhs, and Jains, and it symbolises the victory of good over evil. It is a five-day festival that is usually celebrated in October or November, depending on the lunar calendar.

India is a diverse country with a rich cultural heritage. The country is home to a vast population with different languages, religions, and traditions. Diwali is celebrated throughout India, and the way it is celebrated varies from region to region. However, the essence of the festival remains the same, which is the triumph of light over darkness.

The event of Diwali is celebrated by lighting up the streets, houses, and temples with colourful lights and lamps. People decorate their homes with colourful rangolis, which are intricate patterns made with coloured powder, flowers, and rice. The streets are lined with stalls selling sweets, snacks, and traditional clothing.

The topography of India varies from region to region, and it has a significant impact on the wines produced in the country. The wine industry in India is relatively new, and the country is known for producing high-quality wines using indigenous grapes. Vinification techniques used in India are influenced by the climate, altitude, and soil type.

Wine is not traditionally served during Diwali, but with the growing popularity of wine in India, some wineries have started producing wines specifically for the festival. The wines available to drink at the festival include red wines, white wines, and sparkling wines.

The food served during Diwali is an essential aspect of the festival, and it varies from region to region. Some of the popular dishes include samosas, pakoras, chaat, biryani, and sweets like gulab jamun and rasgulla. The foods served during Diwali are often rich and flavorful, and they are made with a variety of spices and herbs.

Pairing food and wine is an art, and it is essential to consider the flavours and textures of both the food and wine when pairing them. Some of the foods served during Diwali can be paired with wine, and the pairing can enhance the flavours of both the food and wine.

For spicy foods like samosas and pakoras, a light-bodied red wine like a Pinot Noir or a Beaujolais would pair well. For richer dishes like biryani, a full-bodied red wine like a Cabernet Sauvignon or a Shiraz would be a good choice. For sweets like gulab jamun and rasgulla, a sweet wine like a Moscato or a late-harvest Riesling would pair well.

In conclusion, Diwali is a significant festival celebrated in India, and it is a time for joy, celebration, and family. The festival is celebrated by people of different religions and cultures, and it is a symbol of unity and peace. The food and wine served during the festival are an essential aspect of the celebrations, and the pairing of food and wine can enhance the flavours of both.

Songkran

Songkran is a traditional festival celebrated in Thailand, which is also known as the Thai New Year. It is a time of joy and celebration that takes place annually from April 13 to April 15. The festival is celebrated across the country with great enthusiasm and is one of the most important events in the Thai calendar.

The festival is deeply rooted in Thai culture and traditions, and is celebrated by people of all ages and backgrounds. During the festival, people engage in a variety of activities such as street parades, water fights, and the pouring of scented water on Buddha statues. It is also a time for families to come together and celebrate.

Thailand is a country known for its diverse topography, from mountains to beaches, and it offers a variety of wines that are unique to the region. The country is known for its production of tropical fruit wines, which are made using local fruits such as mango, passion fruit, and pineapple.

At the Songkran festival, a variety of wines are available to drink, including locally produced tropical fruit wines, as well as traditional Thai rice wines. Rice wine is a popular alcoholic beverage in Thailand, and is made using traditional vinification techniques that have been passed down through generations.

In addition to the wines, a variety of foods are served and cooked during the festival. Traditional Thai dishes such as Pad Thai, Tom Yum soup, and Massaman curry are commonly served, along with street food such as grilled meat skewers, spring rolls, and sticky rice.

When pairing food and wine at the Songkran festival, it is important to consider the bold and spicy flavours of Thai cuisine. Tropical fruit wines such as mango wine and passion fruit wine pair well with dishes that have a sweet and spicy flavour profile, while rice wines such as Sato and Sura pair well with richer and more savoury dishes such as Massaman curry.

In conclusion, the Songkran festival is a vibrant and colourful celebration of Thai culture and traditions. It offers a unique opportunity to taste a variety of local wines and cuisine, and to experience the warm hospitality and joy of the Thai people.

Eid al-Adha

Eid al-Adha, also known as the Feast of Sacrifice, is one of the most significant festivals in the Islamic calendar. This festival is celebrated by Muslims all around the world to commemorate the willingness of the Prophet Ibrahim (Abraham) to sacrifice his son as an act of obedience to Allah (God). The festival takes place on the 10th day of the Islamic month of Dhul-Hijjah, which falls approximately 70 days after the end of Ramadan.

Eid al-Adha is celebrated in many different countries around the world, but the festival is particularly significant in Muslim-majority countries such as Saudi Arabia, Egypt, Pakistan, Indonesia, and Bangladesh. The festival is usually celebrated over a period of three days, and during this time, people participate in various cultural and religious activities.

In terms of topography, Eid al-Adha is celebrated in many different environments, from bustling cities to rural villages. The festival is often marked by the slaughter of a sheep or goat, which is then divided into three parts: one-third for the family, one-third for relatives and friends, and one-third for the poor and needy.

In terms of wines, it is important to note that alcohol consumption is strictly prohibited in Islam, so wines are not typically consumed during Eid al-Adha. Instead, people often drink non-alcoholic beverages such as tea, coffee, or juice.

During Eid al-Adha, many traditional foods are served and cooked to celebrate the occasion. One of the most popular dishes is biryani, a spicy rice dish that is often made with chicken or lamb. Other popular dishes include kebabs, samosas, and various types of curries.

When it comes to pairing wine with food, it is important to note that this is not typically done during Eid al-Adha due to religious reasons. Instead, people often drink non-alcoholic beverages such as tea or juice to complement their meals.

Overall, Eid al-Adha is a significant cultural and religious event that is celebrated by Muslims all around the world. While wine is not typically consumed during this festival, there are still many delicious foods and non-alcoholic beverages to enjoy.

Naadam

Naadam is a traditional Mongolian festival that takes place annually in the summer, typically between July 11th and 13th. It is a significant event that celebrates the country's culture and history, and brings together the people of Mongolia in a show of unity and pride.

The festival takes place in various parts of Mongolia, with the largest and most famous being held in the capital city of Ulaanbaatar. The event typically lasts for three days and includes a range of activities and competitions, including horse racing, archery, and wrestling.

The people of Mongolia have a rich history and culture that is deeply connected to the land and its topography. The festival is a celebration of this culture and the way of life that has developed in this rugged and remote country.

While wine is not a traditional part of the Naadam festival, there are many traditional foods and drinks that are served during the event. Some of the most popular dishes include:

Khuushuur - These are deep-fried meat pies filled with ground beef or mutton, onions, and spices. They are a popular snack during the festival and pair well with red wine.

Buuz - These are steamed dumplings filled with minced meat and onions. They are a staple food in Mongolia and are often served with a side of pickled vegetables. Buuz pairs well with a light red wine.

Airag - This is a traditional Mongolian drink made from fermented mare's milk. It has a slightly sour taste and is often served cold. It pairs well with spicy foods and is a great way to cool down on a hot summer day.

Tsagaan idee - This is a traditional Mongolian white wine that is made from grapes grown in the northern part of the country. The wine is fermented using a unique technique that involves burying the wine underground in special clay vessels. Tsagaan idee pairs well with spicy and savoury dishes.

Boortsog - These are fried dough pastries that are often served with tea or coffee. They are a popular snack during the festival and are a great way to satisfy a sweet tooth.

Overall, Naadam is a unique and fascinating festival that offers a glimpse into the rich culture and history of Mongolia. Whether you are interested in traditional food, sports, or culture, there is something for everyone at this amazing event.

Holi

Holi is a festival celebrated in India and other countries with significant Hindu populations, such as Nepal, Bangladesh, and Sri Lanka. The festival typically falls in late February or early March and is also known as the "Festival of Colors" or the "Festival of Love." The celebration lasts for several days and is a time for people to come together, enjoy music, dance, and delicious food.

The festival is deeply rooted in Indian culture and has its origins in Hindu mythology. According to legend, the festival commemorates the victory of good over evil and the arrival of spring. It is a time for people to let go of their worries and grievances and come together in a spirit of unity and joy.

Holi is celebrated across India, but it has a special significance in certain parts of the country. In the state of Uttar Pradesh, for example, the town of Mathura is considered the birthplace of Lord Krishna, and the festival is celebrated with particular enthusiasm there. In the western state of Gujarat, people celebrate Holi with music and dance performances.

In terms of topography, India has a diverse landscape that varies from the Himalayas in the north to the beaches of Goa in the south. This diversity is reflected in the food and wine that are served during Holi. India has a rich tradition of winemaking, with many different types of wines produced using various vinification techniques. Some of the most popular wines in India include Sula Chenin Blanc, Grover Zampa Vineyards Sauvignon Blanc, and Four Seasons Viognier.

During Holi, people typically drink a variety of wines, including red, white, and sparkling wines. Some of the most popular wines at the festival include Sula Brut, Grover La Reserve, and Chateau d'Ori Cabernet Sauvignon.

In terms of food, Holi is a time for people to come together and enjoy a variety of delicious dishes. Some of the most popular foods at the festival include chaat, samosas, and gulab jamun. Chaat is a savoury snack that typically consists of fried dough, potatoes, and various chutneys. Samosas are triangular-shaped pastries filled with spiced vegetables or meat, and gulab jamun is a sweet dessert made from milk and sugar.

Pairing the right wine with Indian food can be a challenge, but there are some general guidelines to follow. For spicy foods like chaat, a sparkling wine like Sula Brut or a fruity red wine like Grover La Reserve can help cut through the heat. For richer dishes like samosas, a full-bodied red wine like Chateau d'Ori Cabernet Sauvignon can provide a nice contrast. And for sweet desserts like gulab jamun, a dessert wine like Grover Zampa Vineyards Zinfandel can help balance the sweetness.

Overall, Holi is a vibrant and colourful celebration that brings people together in a spirit of joy and unity. The festival is a time for people to enjoy delicious food, drink wine, and let go of their worries and grievances. Whether you're celebrating in India or elsewhere in the world, Holi is a celebration that is sure to leave a lasting impression.

Lantern Festival

The Lantern Festival, also known as Yuanxiao Festival or Shangyuan Festival, is a traditional Chinese festival celebrated on the 15th day of the first lunar month, which usually falls in February or March. This festival is one of the most important events in Chinese culture, marking the end of the Chinese New Year festivities.

The Lantern Festival is celebrated by people all over China and the diaspora, and is particularly popular in areas with a large Han Chinese population, such as Taiwan, Singapore, and Malaysia.

The Lantern Festival is a time for people to gather with family and friends, and to enjoy the brightly lit lanterns that are hung in public places and private homes. The lanterns come in a variety of shapes and sizes, and are often decorated with images of animals, flowers, and Chinese characters.

The topography of China is diverse, and the Lantern Festival is celebrated in different ways depending on the region. In some areas, people release lanterns into the sky, while in others they float them on water.

China is also known for its wine culture, and there are many different types of wine produced in the country. Some of the most popular wines include Baijiu, Huangjiu, and rice wine.

At the Lantern Festival, people typically drink Huangjiu, a type of Chinese wine made from fermented rice. This wine has a slightly sweet taste and a low alcohol content, making it a popular choice for festive occasions.

In addition to wine, there are also a variety of foods served at the Lantern Festival. One of the most popular dishes is Yuanxiao, a type of sweet dumpling made from glutinous rice flour and filled with sweet sesame paste or red bean paste. These dumplings are traditionally eaten during the festival as a symbol of family unity and prosperity.

Other popular foods served during the Lantern Festival include Tangyuan, a sweet soup made with glutinous rice balls and served in a sweet broth, and Niangao, a sticky rice cake that is fried or steamed and served with a variety of toppings.

Overall, the Lantern Festival is an important cultural event in China, and a time for people to come together and celebrate with food, wine, and brightly lit lanterns.

Baisakhi

Baisakhi, also known as Vaisakhi, is an annual festival celebrated mainly in the northern Indian state of Punjab, but also in other parts of India and in other countries such as Canada, the UK and the USA. The festival falls on April 13 or 14 every year, depending on the Sikh calendar.

Baisakhi is an important festival for both Hindus and Sikhs. For Sikhs, it marks the establishment of the Khalsa Panth, a collective of initiated Sikhs, by the tenth Sikh Guru, Guru Gobind Singh, in 1699. For Hindus, it marks the beginning of the New Year, and is associated with the harvest season.

The festival is typically celebrated with great enthusiasm and fervor, with people wearing colorful clothes and dancing to the beat of the dhol, a traditional Indian drum. The event often includes a procession, known as a Nagar Kirtan, in which Sikhs and other participants march through the streets, singing hymns and carrying the Sikh flag.

Baisakhi is also a time for feasting and enjoying traditional Punjabi foods, such as sarson da saag (a dish made from mustard greens) and makki di roti (a flatbread made from cornmeal). The festival is also a time for drinking wine made from freshly harvested grapes, known as Baisakhi wine.

The topography of the region plays a significant role in the vinification techniques and wines available to drink at the festival. Punjab is a landlocked state, and the climate is hot and dry, with low rainfall. Grapes are grown in the region, mainly for table consumption, and not for wine production. However, some wineries have started producing wines from imported grapes, and these are now available for drinking at the festival.

At Baisakhi, people can enjoy a range of wines, including red, white, and rosé wines. Some of the popular wines available at the festival include Sula Vineyards Shiraz, Sula Vineyards Sauvignon Blanc, and Sula Vineyards Zinfandel Rosé.

In addition to wine, people also enjoy a variety of traditional Punjabi foods at Baisakhi. Some of the popular dishes served at the festival include chole bhature (a spicy chickpea curry served with fried bread), tandoori chicken (chicken marinated in spices and cooked in a clay oven), and paneer tikka (grilled cubes of cottage cheese).

Overall, Baisakhi is a joyous occasion that celebrates the cultural and religious heritage of Punjab and India. It is a time for people to come together, share food and drink, and celebrate the bounty of the harvest season.

Ramadan

Ramadan is a month-long festival celebrated by Muslims around the world, which involves fasting from dawn until sunset. It is a time for spiritual reflection, charity, and spending time with loved ones. The festival occurs in the ninth month of the Islamic calendar, which follows the lunar cycle and varies each year.

Ramadan is celebrated in many countries with large Muslim populations, such as Saudi Arabia, Egypt, Turkey, Indonesia, and Malaysia. However, it is also observed in other parts of the world, including Europe, North America, and Australia.

The festival is deeply rooted in Islamic culture and tradition. Muslims are required to abstain from food, drink, and other physical needs during daylight hours as a way of purifying the soul, practising self-discipline, and empathising with those who are less fortunate. The fast is broken each evening with a meal known as iftar, which often includes dates and water, followed by a larger meal that may include meat, rice, vegetables, and sweets.

The topography and vinification techniques are not typically associated with Ramadan, as the focus is more on spiritual and cultural traditions rather than wine-making. In fact, alcohol consumption is prohibited during Ramadan, and many Muslim countries have strict laws against it year-round.

There are many traditional foods that are served during Ramadan, such as samosas, kebabs, falafel, and biryani. Sweets such as baklava and qatayef are also popular, and are often made with honey, dates, and nuts. In some countries, special dishes are prepared for suhoor, the pre-dawn meal that is consumed before beginning the fast. These might include porridge, eggs, and bread.

Overall, Ramadan is a time for spiritual reflection, community, and cultural celebration. While the focus is not on wine and food, there are still many delicious dishes to enjoy during this important festival.

Cherry Blossom Festival

The Cherry Blossom Festival in Japan, also known as Sakura Matsuri, is a popular event that takes place annually during the spring season. The festival is celebrated in many parts of Japan, and it attracts both locals and tourists from around the world.

The festival celebrates the blooming of cherry blossom trees, which usually occurs between late March and early May, depending on the location and weather conditions. The festival typically lasts for a week or two, and it includes various cultural events, performances, food stalls, and drinks.

Japan is a country located in East Asia, known for its rich culture, history, and traditions. The people of Japan are known for their politeness, respect for others, and hard work ethic. The Cherry Blossom Festival is an occasion for the people of Japan to celebrate the beauty of nature and the arrival of spring after a long winter.

The topography of Japan is varied, with mountainous regions, forests, and coastal areas. The cherry blossom trees can be found in many parts of the country, and they are a symbol of renewal, hope, and beauty.

There are several wines produced in Japan, with the most popular being sake, a traditional Japanese rice wine. Vinification techniques in Japan are highly sophisticated, with a focus on quality and flavour.

At the Cherry Blossom Festival, visitors can sample a variety of wines, including sake, along with other traditional Japanese drinks, such as green tea and plum wine.

The food served at the festival is also an important part of the celebration, with various stalls offering traditional Japanese dishes, such as sushi, tempura, ramen, yakitori, and mochi. The food is cooked fresh on site, and visitors can enjoy the delicious flavours and aromas of Japanese cuisine.

In conclusion, the Cherry Blossom Festival in Japan is a wonderful celebration of nature, culture, and tradition. It is an occasion for people to come together, enjoy the beauty of the cherry blossom trees, and sample some of the best food and drink that Japan has to offer.

Wesak

Wesak, also known as Vesak or Buddha Day, is an annual festival celebrated by Buddhists around the world. It commemorates the birth, enlightenment, and death of Gautama Buddha, the founder of Buddhism. The festival is usually held in May, on the full moon day of the Vesak month, and is considered one of the most significant events in the Buddhist calendar.

The Wesak Festival is celebrated in many countries around the world where Buddhism is practised. Some of the countries where the festival is particularly significant include Sri Lanka, Thailand, Cambodia, Laos, Myanmar, Indonesia, Nepal, and India. Each country has its own unique way of celebrating the festival, but the core elements remain the same.

The Wesak Festival is a time of great joy and celebration, with people coming together to honour the Buddha and his teachings. The festival is marked by various rituals, including the lighting of lamps and candles, the offering of flowers and incense, and the chanting of Buddhist scriptures.

In terms of culture, the Wesak Festival is deeply rooted in Buddhist traditions and beliefs. It is a time for reflection, meditation, and spiritual renewal. The festival also provides an opportunity for Buddhists to express their gratitude to the Buddha and to reaffirm their commitment to following his teachings.

In terms of topography, the Wesak Festival is celebrated in a variety of locations, ranging from large cities to small villages. Many Buddhist temples and shrines hold special events during the festival, and there are also large-scale celebrations in public spaces such as parks and town squares.

While wine is not typically associated with the Wesak Festival, there are many other types of beverages available to drink, including tea, fruit juices, and water. Food is also an important part of the festival, with a wide variety of vegetarian dishes served to attendees. Some of the traditional foods served at the festival include rice dishes, curries, and sweets.

Overall, the Wesak Festival is a time of great significance for Buddhists around the world. It is a time to celebrate the life and teachings of the Buddha, to come together as a community, and to reflect on the importance of compassion, mindfulness, and spiritual growth.

Loy Krathong

Loy Krathong is a popular festival celebrated annually in Thailand on the full moon night of the twelfth lunar month, which usually falls in November. The festival is a beautiful and colourful event that celebrates the end of the rainy season and the beginning of the new harvest season. The festival is deeply rooted in Thai culture and traditions and is celebrated throughout the country.

The Festival's name, "Loy Krathong," means "to float a basket," which refers to the practice of making small, decorative baskets or floats out of banana leaves, flowers, and candles, which are then floated on rivers, canals, or other bodies of water. This is done to symbolise letting go of negativity, bad luck, and grudges and to offer respect and gratitude to the water goddess, Phra Mae Khongkha.

The festival is celebrated by both Thai people and tourists alike, and it is a time for everyone to come together and enjoy the festivities. The festival is typically held in the evening and is marked by traditional music, dancing, and food.

In terms of topography, the festival is held in various parts of the country, but it is especially popular in northern Thailand, where it is celebrated with elaborate displays of lanterns, fireworks, and other decorations.

As for wines and vinification techniques, Thailand is not typically known as a wine-producing country, so local wines may not be featured at the festival. Instead, attendees may choose to enjoy traditional Thai beers, spirits, or non-alcoholic beverages.

The food served at Loy Krathong is an essential part of the festival experience, and it features a wide range of traditional Thai dishes, including spicy curries, noodle dishes, grilled meats, and seafood. Popular dishes include tom yum soup, pad Thai, green papaya salad, and massaman curry. There are also plenty of sweets and desserts to enjoy, such as mango sticky rice, coconut ice cream, and fried bananas.

In conclusion, Loy Krathong is a vibrant and joyous festival that celebrates Thai culture and traditions, as well as the natural beauty of the country's waterways. It is an occasion for people to come together and enjoy traditional music, dance, and food, and to offer thanks and respect to the water goddess, Phra Mae Khongkha.

Chuseok

Chuseok, also known as the Korean Thanksgiving, is one of the most important traditional festivals in Korea. It is celebrated on the 15th day of the eighth lunar month (usually around September or October) and is a three-day event that honors the ancestors and harvest.

The festival is deeply rooted in Korean culture and is celebrated by Koreans all over the world. Chuseok is a time when Koreans gather with their families to pay tribute to their ancestors and to give thanks for a successful harvest. It is a time of reflection, gratitude, and celebration.

The topography of Korea is diverse, with mountains, hills, and plains, which are suitable for growing different crops. Grapes are grown mainly in the southern part of Korea, where the climate is warm and humid. Korea is known for its high-quality grape wines, which are made using traditional vinification techniques.

At Chuseok, many different types of wines are available to drink, including rice wines, fruit wines, and grape wines. The most popular grape wine is bokbunjajoo, which is made from black raspberries and has a sweet and fruity taste.

Foods served and cooked at Chuseok are traditional Korean dishes that are enjoyed by all generations. The most popular dishes include Songpyeon, which is a rice cake made with different fillings such as sesame seeds, chestnuts, or beans. Another popular dish is Japchae, which is a stir-fried dish made with sweet potato noodles, vegetables, and beef.

Other traditional foods served at Chuseok include Galbi (grilled beef ribs), Bulgogi (marinated beef), and Jeyuk bokkeum (spicy stir-fried pork). These dishes are all cooked with traditional Korean ingredients and techniques, and they represent the richness of Korean cuisine.

Overall, Chuseok is an important festival that celebrates Korean culture, food, and tradition. It is a time for families to come together and give thanks for the harvest and for their ancestors. It is a truly unique event that showcases the beauty and diversity of Korean culture.

Vesak

Vesak, also known as Buddha Purnima or Buddha Jayanti, is an important festival in Buddhism that is celebrated by millions of Buddhists around the world. It commemorates the birth, enlightenment, and death of Gautama Buddha, the founder of Buddhism.

The festival is primarily celebrated in countries where Buddhism is a prominent religion, including Sri Lanka, Thailand, Myanmar, Cambodia, and Laos. The date of Vesak varies based on the lunar calendar, but it typically falls in April or May.

The festival is a significant cultural event in these countries, and it is marked by a variety of customs and traditions. One of the most prominent is the lighting of lanterns, which represents the Buddha's enlightenment. Buddhists also visit temples and engage in acts of charity and kindness to honour the Buddha's teachings of compassion and generosity.

The topography and culture of each country may influence the specific customs observed during Vesak. For example, in Sri Lanka, Buddhists celebrate the festival by decorating their homes and streets with lanterns and colorful decorations. They also organize processions with traditional dancers and drummers.

While Vesak is not typically associated with wine or vinification techniques, some Buddhist countries do produce wines. In Myanmar, for example, there is a growing wine industry that produces wines made from local grapes, such as Tannat and Shiraz.

During Vesak, a variety of foods are served and cooked. In Sri Lanka, for example, traditional sweets such as kiribath (a type of rice pudding) and kokis (crispy, deep-fried snacks) are served. In Thailand, Buddhists often prepare vegetarian food as a way of demonstrating compassion and kindness towards animals.

Overall, Vesak is a significant occasion for Buddhists around the world, and it is marked by a variety of customs and traditions that reflect the rich cultural heritage of Buddhism. While wine is not typically a part of the festival, it is still possible to enjoy the diverse cuisine and cultural offerings during Vesak.

Qingming Festival

The Qingming Festival, also known as Tomb Sweeping Day, is a traditional festival celebrated in China, Taiwan, Hong Kong, and other East Asian countries. It usually falls on the 4th or 5th of April every year, and it is a day to pay respects to ancestors and departed loved ones.

The festival has been observed for over 2500 years and has become an important occasion for Chinese culture. The festival's name "Qingming" literally means "clear and bright" and signifies the beginning of the spring season.

During the festival, people visit their ancestors' graves to pay their respects and clean the tombs. This tradition is deeply rooted in Chinese culture, and it is believed that by performing these rituals, the spirits of their ancestors will be at peace and bring good fortune to their living relatives. People also offer food, wine, and other offerings to their ancestors as a sign of reverence.

The festival is also a time for cultural activities, including flying kites, playing games, and enjoying food and wine. The festival takes place during the spring season when the weather is pleasant and warm, and the landscape is lush and green.

Many wineries and vineyards also participate in the festival, offering visitors the opportunity to taste some of the finest wines of the region. The wine produced during this time is known as "spring wine" and is made using a unique vinification technique that results in a light and refreshing wine that pairs well with the traditional foods served during the festival.

Some of the traditional foods served during the Qingming Festival include sweet rice dumplings, crispy fried cakes, and glutinous rice cakes. These dishes are usually prepared using traditional methods and ingredients and are an essential part of the festival's celebrations.

In conclusion, the Qingming Festival is a significant event in Chinese culture that honours ancestors and departed loved ones. It is a time for families to come together, pay their respects, and enjoy cultural activities, food, and wine. The festival's deep roots in Chinese culture and traditions make it an important occasion for those who celebrate it.

Eid al-Adha

Eid al-Adha is a significant festival celebrated by Muslims around the world. It is also known as the "Festival of Sacrifice" and is one of the two major Islamic holidays, the other being Eid al-Fitr. The festival commemorates the willingness of Prophet Ibrahim (Abraham) to sacrifice his son as an act of obedience to God.

The festival is celebrated on the 10th day of Dhu al-Hijjah, the last month of the Islamic calendar. It usually falls in late July or early August, depending on the sighting of the moon.

The festival is celebrated by Muslims all over the world, but it is especially significant in countries with a majority Muslim population, such as Saudi Arabia, Egypt, Turkey, and Indonesia.

The festival begins with the performance of Eid prayers, followed by the sacrifice of an animal, usually a sheep, goat, or cow. The meat from the sacrificed animal is distributed among family, friends, and the poor.

The occasion is also an opportunity for Muslims to give to charity and perform acts of kindness.

The festival is deeply rooted in Islamic culture and tradition, and it has a strong connection to the topography of the regions where it is celebrated.

Regarding wines, it is important to note that the consumption of alcohol is forbidden in Islam, and therefore there are no wines or vinification techniques associated with Eid al-Adha.

The foods served and cooked at the festival vary depending on the country and region. In Saudi Arabia, for example, traditional dishes such as lamb kabsa and thareed are popular. In Turkey, a popular dish is grilled lamb skewers called kebabs. In Indonesia, beef or goat curry and rice dishes are commonly served.

In conclusion, Eid al-Adha is a significant festival in the Islamic calendar, celebrated by Muslims worldwide. It is a time for reflection, prayer, charity, and the sharing of food and kindness. Although there are no wines associated with the festival due to the Islamic prohibition on alcohol, there are many traditional foods and dishes that are enjoyed during the occasion.

Pongal

Pongal is a popular harvest festival celebrated in the southern Indian state of Tamil Nadu. The festival is observed by the Tamil community in India, as well as in other parts of the world where Tamil people reside. Pongal is a four-day-long festival that usually falls in mid-January, and it marks the beginning of the auspicious Tamil month of Thai.

The festival is a celebration of the harvest season and is dedicated to the Hindu deity of the sun, Surya. People decorate their homes with colourful rangolis, adorn themselves in traditional attire, and participate in various rituals and festivities.

The topography of Tamil Nadu is diverse, with a long coastline, rolling hills, and fertile plains. The region's unique topography, along with the climate, contributes to the growth of various crops, including rice, sugarcane, and spices. As Pongal is a harvest festival, it celebrates the abundance of these crops and the joy that comes with the harvest.

In terms of wine, Tamil Nadu is not known for vinification, and therefore wine is not a typical beverage of choice during Pongal. However, there are several traditional foods that are served during the festival, including sweet and savoury dishes. One popular dish is Pongal, a sweet and creamy rice dish made with jaggery (unrefined cane sugar), milk, and nuts. Another popular dish is Venn Pongal, a savoury rice dish cooked with ghee (clarified butter), black pepper, and cumin.

During the festival, families come together to cook and enjoy these traditional foods. In some regions, people also participate in bull-taming events, known as Jallikattu, which is a significant aspect of the Pongal celebration. Additionally, people decorate their homes with colourful kolams, participate in temple ceremonies, and exchange gifts with family and friends.

In conclusion, Pongal is a significant harvest festival celebrated in the southern Indian state of Tamil Nadu, which marks the beginning of the Tamil month of Thai. The festival is an occasion for people to come together, celebrate the abundance of crops, and enjoy traditional foods. While wine is not typically consumed during Pongal, the festival offers an excellent opportunity to explore the diverse cultural traditions and topography of the region.

Ramadan Bazaar

Ramadan Bazaar is a festival celebrated in various countries around the world during the holy month of Ramadan, which is observed by Muslims worldwide. The festival is celebrated during the month of Ramadan, which is the ninth month of the Islamic calendar. The date of Ramadan Bazaar varies each year based on the lunar calendar, but it typically falls in the months of April to May.

The festival is primarily celebrated in Muslim-majority countries such as Malaysia, Indonesia, Singapore, and Brunei. The event is marked by the setting up of bazaars or markets in the streets, where people can buy various food items, traditional clothes, and other items related to the festival.

During the event, Muslims fast during the day, abstaining from food and drink from sunrise to sunset. As such, the food and drink sold in the bazaars are mainly consumed after sunset and before dawn.

The topography of the event can vary based on the country, with some bazaars held in open-air markets, while others are held in covered marketplaces. In addition to food, Ramadan Bazaar can also offer a range of cultural performances, such as music, dance, and theatre.

In terms of wines, vinification techniques and availability, it is important to note that alcohol is strictly forbidden in Islam, and as such, the sale of alcoholic beverages is not permitted at Ramadan Bazaar. Instead, there are various non-alcoholic drinks available, such as fruit juices, smoothies, and milkshakes.

As for the food served and cooked at the festival, it varies based on the country and region. Some of the popular dishes that are sold at Ramadan Bazaar include nasi lemak, satay, rendang, and bubur lambuk in Malaysia; bakso, nasi goreng, and sate in Indonesia; biryani, kebabs, and samosas in India; and sweet snacks such as dates and baklava in the Middle East.

Overall, Ramadan Bazaar is a festive event that celebrates the holy month of Ramadan, bringing together people from different cultures and backgrounds to enjoy traditional food, music, and other cultural performances.

Obon

Obon is a traditional Japanese festival that is celebrated in mid-August. It is an occasion for people to honour and remember their ancestors and loved ones who have passed away. The festival is celebrated throughout Japan, but it has different customs and traditions depending on the region.

The festival is deeply rooted in Japanese culture and is a time for families to come together and pay their respects to their ancestors. It is also a time for people to enjoy traditional Japanese food, drink, and entertainment.

The festival takes place over several days, with the exact dates varying from region to region. In general, the festival begins on August 13th and ends on August 16th.

Obon is celebrated in a variety of ways throughout Japan, but some of the common customs and traditions include the lighting of lanterns to guide the spirits of the ancestors, dancing the Bon Odori dance, and offering food and drink to the spirits.

The festival is typically held in outdoor areas such as parks or temple grounds, and the topography of the area can vary depending on the location. Some festivals may take place in hilly areas or near bodies of water, while others may be held in urban areas with high-rise buildings and city streets.

While there is not a specific wine associated with Obon, there are a variety of traditional Japanese drinks that are often served at the festival. These include sake, shochu, and beer.

In terms of food, Obon is a time for people to enjoy traditional Japanese dishes such as sushi, tempura, and yakitori. There may also be street vendors selling festival foods such as takoyaki (octopus balls), okonomiyaki (savoury pancakes), and shaved ice.

Overall, Obon is a time for people to come together to remember their ancestors and to enjoy traditional Japanese culture. The festival is a testament to the deep roots of Japanese culture and the importance of family and community.

Mid-Autumn Festival

The Mid-Autumn Festival, also known as the Moon Festival or Zhongqiujie, is one of the most important traditional festivals in China. It is celebrated on the 15th day of the 8th lunar month each year, which usually falls in September or October in the Gregorian calendar.

The festival is celebrated by people of Chinese descent all over the world, including China, Hong Kong, Macau, Taiwan, and other countries with large Chinese communities. It is a time for families to reunite, give thanks, and appreciate the beauty of the full moon.

The festival has a long history dating back to ancient times. According to legend, the goddess Chang'e, who lives on the moon, comes to earth to visit her husband once a year on the 15th day of the 8th lunar month. People celebrate the occasion by offering sacrifices to Chang'e, enjoying mooncakes, and appreciating the beauty of the full moon.

Chinese culture places great emphasis on the family unit, and the Mid-Autumn Festival is a time for families to come together. In addition to enjoying mooncakes, families also eat traditional foods like pomelos, taro, and lotus root. They also drink wine, which plays an important role in the festival.

The topography of China is diverse, and different regions have their own unique traditions and customs when it comes to wine. For example, in the north, Baijiu is a popular type of wine made from grains like sorghum, rice, and wheat. In the south, rice wine is more common, and it is often used in cooking.

Vinification techniques in China are also diverse. In the north, Baijiu is typically distilled, while in the south, rice wine is often fermented. In general, Chinese wines tend to be high in alcohol content and are usually enjoyed in small amounts.

At the Mid-Autumn Festival, people typically drink a variety of wines, including Baijiu, rice wine, and grape wine. In recent years, there has been a growing interest in Chinese wines made from grapes, and many wineries now produce high-quality wines that are gaining recognition on the international stage.

In addition to wine, there are many traditional foods that are served and cooked at the festival. Mooncakes are the most famous, and they are filled with sweet bean paste or lotus seed paste and sometimes have a salted egg yolk in the center. Other popular dishes include taro cakes, pumpkin cakes, and steamed buns filled with pork or vegetables.

In conclusion, the Mid-Autumn Festival is an important cultural event in China and other countries with large Chinese communities. It is a time for families to come together, appreciate the beauty of the full moon, and enjoy traditional foods and wines. With its rich history and diverse traditions, the festival is an important part of Chinese culture and heritage.

Dashain

Dashain is the most important festival of Nepal, celebrated by Nepalese people all around the world. It is also known as Vijaya Dashami, which means the victory of good over evil. The festival is celebrated for 15 days and falls in September or October, according to the lunar calendar. It is a time when families come together to celebrate, and the entire country is filled with joy, colours, and music.

The festival has great significance in Nepalese culture and tradition. It marks the victory of Lord Ram over the demon king Ravana, which signifies the triumph of good over evil. The festival is also a time to honour the goddess Durga, who is worshipped during this time for her strength and power.

Nepal is a country in South Asia, located in the Himalayas. It is known for its diverse cultures, languages, and religions. The people of Nepal are mostly Hindus, Buddhists, and Muslims, and they speak over 120 different languages. Dashain is celebrated by all Nepalese people regardless of their religion and ethnicity.

The festival is celebrated in various ways throughout Nepal. In the capital city of Kathmandu, the festival is marked by the use of colorful lights, decorations, and music. The topography of Nepal, which includes the majestic Himalayan Mountains, adds to the beauty of the festival.

While wine is not traditionally consumed during the Dashain festival, Nepalese people do drink a variety of alcoholic beverages, including beer and spirits. The country does produce its own wines, but they are not commonly consumed during the festival.

The festival is a time for families to come together and celebrate. Traditional Nepalese foods are prepared and served during the festival, including dishes like sel roti, which is a type of sweet bread made from rice flour, and khasi ko masu, which is goat meat curry. Other traditional foods served during the festival include samosas, momos, and chow mein.

In conclusion, Dashain is a festival of great importance in Nepalese culture and tradition. It is a time for families to come together, celebrate, and honour their heritage. The festival is marked by the use of colors, lights, and music, and traditional Nepalese foods are prepared and served during the celebrations.

Eid al-Ghadeer

Eid al-Ghadeer is a significant Islamic festival that is celebrated by the Shia Muslim community around the world. It is celebrated on the 18th of Dhu al-Hijjah, which is the last month of the Islamic calendar. This festival marks the day when the Prophet Muhammad declared Imam Ali as his successor at Ghadir Khumm, which is a historic event that took place in the year 632 AD.

The celebration of Eid al-Ghadeer varies from region to region and country to country, but the common theme among all celebrations is the recognition of the leadership and authority of Imam Ali. Many Shia Muslims celebrate this festival with great fervour and enthusiasm, as they believe that the day represents a significant moment in Islamic history.

In Iran, the festival of Eid al-Ghadeer is an official holiday and is celebrated with public gatherings and special prayers. The city of Qom, which is a major centre for Shia Islam, is particularly famous for its celebrations of this festival. In Iraq, the cities of Najaf and Karbala also have significant celebrations of Eid al-Ghadeer.

The occasion of Eid al-Ghadeer is an opportunity for people to come together and share food, drinks, and joyous moments with one another. In terms of culture, the festival is an important part of Shia Muslim culture and is celebrated with a lot of enthusiasm and devotion.

In terms of topography, the festival is celebrated in different regions of the world, including Iran, Iraq, Pakistan, India, and other countries with a significant Shia Muslim population. The landscape and terrain of these regions can vary significantly, but the spirit of the celebration remains the same.

In terms of wines, alcohol consumption is forbidden in Islam, including at the festival of Eid al-Ghadeer. Therefore, wines and vinification techniques are not a part of the celebration.

In terms of foods, traditional dishes are prepared and shared among family and friends during the festival. These dishes can vary depending on the region and the cultural practices of the people celebrating the occasion. Some popular dishes include biryani, kebabs, rice dishes, and sweet treats like halwa and gulab jamun.

Overall, Eid al-Ghadeer is an important festival for the Shia Muslim community and is celebrated with great devotion and enthusiasm around the world. It is a time for people to come together, share food, and celebrate the leadership and authority of Imam Ali.

Tihar

Tihar, also known as Deepawali or the Festival of Lights, is a popular Hindu festival celebrated in Nepal, particularly in the Kathmandu valley and surrounding areas. It is one of the most significant festivals in Nepal and is celebrated over five days with great zeal and enthusiasm.

The festival usually falls in the month of October or November, depending on the lunar calendar. The dates of Tihar are determined by the Nepali calendar and usually fall in the months of Kartik or Mangsir.

The festival is celebrated by both Hindus and Buddhists, who believe that Tihar brings happiness, prosperity, and good luck. The festival is marked by the lighting of diyas, oil lamps, and candles, and decorating homes with colorful rangolis.

During Tihar, people worship different deities, including Goddess Laxmi, the goddess of wealth and prosperity, and Lord Ganesha, the god of knowledge and wisdom. They also worship cows, which are considered sacred animals in Hinduism, and offer them food and flowers.

Tihar is also known for the tradition of Bhailo and Deusi, where groups of young people go from house to house singing traditional songs and playing musical instruments, and receive money and food in return.

In terms of topography, Nepal is a mountainous country with a diverse landscape, and the celebration of Tihar varies from region to region. For example, in the hills and mountainous regions, people celebrate Tihar by burning bonfires, while in the Terai region, people light up their homes with colourful lights and celebrate with dance and music.

As for wines and vinification techniques, Nepal has a growing wine industry, with several vineyards located in the Kathmandu valley and surrounding areas. The Nepalese wine industry is still relatively young, but the winemakers are experimenting with various grape varieties and vinification techniques to produce unique and flavorful wines.

Some of the wines available to drink at Tihar include red, white, and rosé wines, made from grapes such as Shiraz, Cabernet Sauvignon, and Chenin Blanc. Some of the popular wineries in Nepal include Himalayan Vineyard, Kavre Valley Vineyard, and Manakamana Winery.

In terms of food, Tihar is a time when people prepare and serve a variety of traditional Nepalese dishes. Some of the popular foods served during Tihar include Sel Roti, a sweet fried bread made from rice flour; Bara, a lentil-based pancake; and Masu, a meat curry.

Overall, Tihar is a vibrant and colourful festival that celebrates the richness and diversity of Nepalese culture. It is a time for families and friends to come together, celebrate, and create lasting memories.

Lantern Festival

The Lantern Festival is one of the most significant festivals celebrated in Taiwan, usually taking place on the 15th day of the first lunar month of the Chinese calendar, which usually falls in February or March. This festival is also known as the Yuanxiao Festival or Shangyuan Festival, and it marks the end of the Chinese New Year celebrations.

The Lantern Festival in Taiwan is a colourful and vibrant event, and it is celebrated by people of all ages and backgrounds. The festival is a time when families and friends come together to enjoy the traditional activities and cultural performances, and to share food and drink.

The Lantern Festival is celebrated throughout Taiwan, but the most significant event is held in Pingxi, a small town in the northeast of the country. The town is located in a mountainous area with stunning natural scenery, which adds to the beauty and charm of the festival.

The Lantern Festival is a time to celebrate the end of winter and the beginning of spring, and it is believed that the lanterns help to guide good luck and fortune into the homes and businesses of the people who participate in the festival. The lanterns are made from a variety of materials, including paper, silk, and bamboo, and they come in a wide range of sizes and designs.

At the Lantern Festival, visitors can enjoy a variety of traditional Taiwanese wines, including red and white wines made from locally grown grapes. The wines are produced using traditional vinification techniques, and they are known for their unique flavours and aromas.

Visitors can also sample a range of traditional Taiwanese dishes, including noodle soups, dumplings, and rice cakes. The foods are cooked using traditional methods and local ingredients, which adds to their flavour and authenticity.

In addition to the lanterns, wine, and food, the Lantern Festival also features a range of cultural performances and activities, including traditional music and dance, dragon and lion dances, and acrobatic displays. These performances are a highlight of the festival, and they showcase the rich cultural heritage of Taiwan.

In summary, the Lantern Festival is a significant event in Taiwan, celebrated with great enthusiasm and joy. It is an occasion for people to come together and celebrate their culture, traditions, and heritage. The festival offers visitors an opportunity to enjoy the beauty of Taiwan's natural scenery, taste the unique flavours of its wines and foods, and experience the richness of its cultural performances and activities.

Phileas Fogg's Australian Festival Experiences

As a fictional character, Phileas Fogg's travels through Asia are solely based on Jules Verne's novel "Around the World in Eighty Days." However, I can provide you with some insights into the festivals and events that Fogg may have encountered during his journey through Asia.

1. **Holi Festival in India**: Fogg would have experienced this festival in March, where people throw colored powder and water at each other to celebrate the arrival of spring. The festival is also known for its sweets, such as gujiya and mathri, which Fogg could have paired with a sweet Indian wine like Sula Late Harvest Chenin Blanc.

2. **Diwali Festival in India**: Fogg would have encountered this festival in October or November, which celebrates the victory of good over evil. People light up their homes with candles and lamps and exchange sweets and gifts. Fogg could have paired the traditional Diwali sweets, such as laddoos and barfis, with a sparkling wine like Chandon Brut.

3. **Naadam Festival in Mongolia**: Fogg would have experienced this festival in July, which celebrates the country's traditional sports of horse racing, archery, and wrestling. Fogg could have paired the traditional Mongolian dish of buuz, a type of steamed dumpling filled with meat and vegetables, with a light-bodied Mongolian wine like Chateau Nekhii.

4. Songkran Festival in Thailand: Fogg would have encountered this festival in April, which is the Thai New Year. People celebrate by splashing water on each other and visiting temples. Fogg could have paired the spicy Thai street food, such as pad thai and som tam, with a refreshing Thai beer like Singha.

5. Lantern Festival in China: Fogg would have experienced this festival in February, which marks the end of the Chinese New Year celebrations. People release lanterns into the sky and eat traditional foods like tangyuan, stuffed rice balls in a sweet syrup. Fogg could have paired the tang yuan with a Chinese dessert wine like Changyu Golden Diamond Ice Wine.

6. Dragon Boat Festival in China: Fogg would have encountered this festival in June, which celebrates the life of the poet Qu Yuan. People race dragon boats and eat zongzi, sticky rice wrapped in bamboo leaves. Fogg could have paired the zongzi with a light Chinese green tea like Dragonwell.

7. Cherry Blossom Festival in Japan: Fogg would have experienced this festival in April, when the cherry blossoms are in full bloom. People celebrate by picnicking under the cherry trees and eating traditional foods like mochi, sweet rice cakes. Fogg could have paired the mochi with a light Japanese sake like Hakutsuru Junmai Ginjo.

8. Gion Matsuri Festival in Japan: Fogg would have encountered this festival in July, which is one of the most famous festivals in Japan. People parade through the streets with elaborate floats and eat traditional foods like yakitori, grilled chicken skewers. Fogg could have paired the yakitori with a light Japanese beer like Asahi Super Dry.

9. Boryeong Mud Festival in South Korea: Fogg would have experienced this festival in July, where people play in the mud and enjoy live music and fireworks. Fogg could have paired the traditional Korean dish of bibimbap, a mixed rice bowl with vegetables and meat, with a Korean rice wine like Makgeolli. Makgeolli is a traditional alcoholic drink from Korea and is a real treat for the senses. Made from fermented rice and sometimes referred to as rice wine, makgeolli has a unique flavour that is unlike any other alcoholic beverage.

CHAPTER 14

FESTIVALS IN NORTH AMERICA

Here are some festivals and events celebrated in North America that are known for their food and wine:

- **New Orleans Wine & Food Experience**

The New Orleans Wine & Food Experience (NOWFE) is an annual culinary festival held in New Orleans, Louisiana, United States. The event is a celebration of food, wine, and the culture of the region, bringing together renowned chefs, winemakers, and food enthusiasts from all over the world.

The event typically takes place over four days in late May or early June and features a range of activities including wine tastings, food pairings, seminars, and cooking demonstrations. It is an opportunity for attendees to experience the unique cuisine and wine of New Orleans and the surrounding region.

New Orleans has a rich cultural history, influenced by African, Native American, Spanish, and French cultures. The city is known for its vibrant music scene, Mardi Gras celebrations, and unique cuisine, which is a fusion of French, African, and Caribbean flavors.

The topography of the region is varied, with marshes, bayous, and the Mississippi River Delta all contributing to the landscape. This diverse terrain provides an ideal environment for growing a variety of grapes, which are used to produce a range of wines.

At NOWFE, attendees can sample wines from all over the world, including local varietals like Muscadine, Blanc Du Bois, and Norton. Vinification techniques used in the region include both traditional and modern methods, with a focus on producing high-quality, artisanal wines.

The food offerings at NOWFE are just as diverse as the wines. Attendees can sample a range of dishes, from classic New Orleans-style seafood to modern, fusion cuisine. Some popular dishes include gumbo, jambalaya, po' boys, and crawfish étouffée.

When it comes to wine and food pairings, there are endless possibilities at NOWFE. Some popular pairings include a crisp Sauvignon Blanc with oysters, a full-bodied Cabernet Sauvignon with grilled steak, or a sweet Riesling with spicy Thai cuisine.

Overall, the New Orleans Wine & Food Experience is an exciting celebration of the unique culture, cuisine, and wine of the region. It offers attendees a chance to explore the diverse flavours of New Orleans and learn about the art of winemaking from some of the best in the industry.

- **Aspen Food & Wine Classic - Aspen, Colorado**

The Aspen Food & Wine Classic is an annual food and wine festival that takes place in Aspen, Colorado, United States. The event is organised by Food & Wine magazine and attracts thousands of people from all over the world. The festival is a celebration of food, wine, and culture, and it takes place over three days in late June.

The Aspen Food & Wine Classic is a significant event in the food and wine industry, attracting some of the top chefs, sommeliers, and wine experts in the world. It is an occasion to showcase the latest food trends, vinification techniques, and wine offerings.

The festival features a variety of events, including tastings, seminars, and cooking demonstrations. There are also opportunities to attend exclusive dinners, where guests can enjoy a multi-course meal prepared by some of the world's most renowned chefs.

Aspen is located in the Rocky Mountains, which provides a stunning backdrop for the event. The topography is characterised by steep mountains, dense forests, and crystal-clear rivers. This setting provides the perfect environment for the vineyards that produce the wine served at the festival.

The wines served at the Aspen Food & Wine Classic are sourced from some of the most respected vineyards in the world. The festival features a wide range of wines, including both red and white varieties, sparkling wines, and dessert wines. The wines are paired with a range of foods, from classic American dishes to international cuisine.

Some of the vinification techniques highlighted at the festival include oak barrel ageing, malolactic fermentation, and the use of different grape varieties to create unique blends.

Some examples of food and wine pairings at the Aspen Food & Wine Classic might include:

Grilled lamb chops paired with a bold red Cabernet Sauvignon from Napa Valley, California.

Fresh oysters paired with a crisp, mineral-driven Chablis from Burgundy, France.

Seared scallops paired with a buttery Chardonnay from Sonoma County, California.

Braised short ribs paired with a full-bodied Syrah from the Rhone Valley in France.

Lobster bisque paired with a rich, full-bodied Pinot Noir from Oregon.

Truffle risotto paired with a smooth, earthy Barolo from Piedmont, Italy.

Charcuterie board paired with a bold, spicy Tempranillo from Spain.

Foie gras paired with a sweet, luscious Sauternes from Bordeaux, France.

Fried chicken paired with a crisp, refreshing Riesling from Germany.

Tuna tartare paired with a light, fruity Rosé from Provence, France.

Overall, the Aspen Food & Wine Classic is an extraordinary event that celebrates the best of food and wine from around the world. It offers attendees an opportunity to sample some of the finest wines and foods while also learning about the latest trends in vinification techniques and culinary arts.

- **Feast Portland, Oregon, USA**

Feast Portland is an annual food and drink festival held in Portland, Oregon, in the United States. The festival celebrates the Pacific Northwest's unique culinary culture and showcases local chefs, winemakers, brewers, and distillers. The festival takes place in mid-September and runs for four days.

The festival attracts a diverse crowd of food and drink enthusiasts, industry professionals, and locals. The event features several different activities, including tastings, seminars, cooking demonstrations, and collaborative dinners.

Portland's unique topography and climate make it an ideal location for winemaking. The region is known for producing world-class Pinot Noir and Chardonnay wines. At Feast Portland, visitors can taste some of the best wines from the Pacific Northwest, including those made using traditional vinification techniques.

One of the highlights of Feast Portland is the pairing of wines with food. Here are some examples of the food and wine pairings that visitors can expect to enjoy:

Grilled Salmon with Pinot Noir: This dish features fresh, locally sourced salmon grilled to perfection and served with a glass of Pinot Noir from one of the region's top wineries.

Seared Scallops with Chardonnay: Locally sourced scallops are seared to perfection and served with a glass of buttery Chardonnay, another favourite of the Pacific Northwest.

Braised Beef Short Ribs with Cabernet Sauvignon: Tender beef short ribs are braised to perfection and paired with a glass of full-bodied Cabernet Sauvignon.

Mushroom Risotto with Pinot Gris: A creamy mushroom risotto is paired with a crisp and refreshing Pinot Gris, the perfect pairing for this rich and earthy dish.

Grilled Lamb with Syrah: Grilled lamb chops are served with a glass of spicy and complex Syrah, a wine that pairs perfectly with the bold flavours of the lamb.

Smoked Pork Shoulder with Zinfandel: Smoked pork shoulder is served with a glass of rich and jammy Zinfandel, a wine that complements the smoky flavours of the meat.

Charcuterie Board with Rosé: A selection of locally sourced charcuterie is paired with a glass of crisp and refreshing Rosé, the perfect pairing for a light and flavorful snack.

Fried Chicken with Sparkling Wine: Crispy fried chicken is paired with a glass of sparkling wine, the perfect pairing for this salty and savoury dish.

Grilled Vegetables with Sauvignon Blanc: Grilled vegetables are served with a glass of bright and citrusy Sauvignon Blanc, the perfect pairing for this light and healthy dish.

Chocolate Dessert with Port: A rich and decadent chocolate dessert is paired with a glass of sweet and fruity Port, the perfect way to end a delicious meal.

In addition to the food and wine pairings, Feast Portland also features several other activities, including cooking demonstrations, seminars on winemaking and brewing, and collaborative dinners featuring top chefs and winemakers from the region. The festival is a celebration of the unique culinary culture of the Pacific Northwest and is not to be missed by food and drink enthusiasts.

- **Taste of Chicago, USA**

Taste of Chicago is an annual food festival held in the United States, specifically in the city of Chicago, Illinois. The event takes place during the summer, typically in late June or early July, and is known for its celebration of the city's diverse culinary scene.

The festival is attended by people from all over the country and beyond, who come to sample the various foods and drinks on offer. The occasion is also an opportunity for local chefs and restaurants to showcase their skills and creativity.

In terms of culture, Taste of Chicago reflects the city's multicultural identity, with vendors offering dishes inspired by a variety of culinary traditions, including Mexican, Italian, Chinese, and African American. The festival is also a celebration of Chicago's music scene, with live performances from local musicians adding to the festive atmosphere.

The topography of the festival is spread out across Grant Park, a large green space located in the heart of downtown Chicago. The park's sprawling lawns provide ample space for vendors to set up their booths and for visitors to walk around and sample the various foods and wines on offer.

Speaking of wines, Taste of Chicago offers a wide selection of both local and international wines, showcasing different vinification techniques and grape varietals. Attendees can expect to find everything from crisp white wines to bold reds, as well as sparkling wines and rosés.

When it comes to pairing the food with the wines, here are ten examples:

Pairing: Chicago-style hot dog with a Sauvignon Blanc

Description: The acidity of the Sauvignon Blanc complements the tanginess of the mustard and relish on the hot dog.

Pairing: Deep dish pizza with a Chianti

Description: The earthiness of the Chianti pairs well with the tomato sauce and cheese on the pizza.

Pairing: BBQ ribs with a Zinfandel

Description: The bold flavour of the Zinfandel matches the smokiness of the BBQ sauce on the ribs.

Pairing: Sushi with a Pinot Grigio

Description: The lightness of the Pinot Grigio complements the delicate flavours of the sushi.

Pairing: Italian beef sandwich with a Chardonnay

Description: The buttery notes of the Chardonnay help to balance out the spiciness of the giardiniera on the sandwich.

Pairing: Tacos al pastor with a Rosé

Description: The fruity notes of the Rosé complement the savoury and spicy flavours of the tacos.

Pairing: Fried chicken with a Riesling

Description: The sweetness of the Riesling helps to cut through the richness of the fried chicken.

Pairing: Gyro with a Cabernet Sauvignon

Description: The tannins in the Cabernet Sauvignon pair well with the lamb in the gyro.

Pairing: Jerk chicken with a Malbec

Description: The bold flavour of the Malbec matches the spiciness of the jerk seasoning on the chicken.

Pairing: Beignets with a Moscato d'Asti

Description: The sweetness of the Moscato d'Asti pairs well with the powdered sugar on the beignets.

In summary, Taste of Chicago is a vibrant celebration of the city's culinary and cultural diversity, featuring a wide selection of foods and wines from around the world. The occasion provides an opportunity for locals and visitors alike to explore the city's culinary scene, while also enjoying live music and the beautiful surroundings of Grant Park.

- **Food & Wine Classic in Aspen, Colorado, USA**

The Food & Wine Classic in Aspen is an annual event held in Aspen, Colorado, United States, where renowned chefs and winemakers gather to celebrate and showcase their culinary and wine expertise. The event typically takes place in June and lasts for three days, attracting food and wine enthusiasts from all over the world.

The event is deeply rooted in American culture, with a strong focus on celebrating the country's diverse culinary and wine traditions. The topography of Aspen, with its mountainous landscape, adds to the charm of the event, providing a breathtaking backdrop for the festivities.

The event features an extensive range of wines from different regions of the world, including renowned wineries from France, Italy, and the United States. The wines showcased are made using a variety of vinification techniques, including oak barrel ageing, stainless steel fermentation, and malolactic fermentation.

The Food & Wine Classic in Aspen is known for its unique pairing of food and wine. The event features a wide array of dishes, from simple hors d'oeuvres to multi-course meals, all expertly paired with a specific wine. Here are some examples of food and wine pairings at the event:

Seared scallops with Meyer lemon butter paired with a crisp Chardonnay from Napa Valley.

Grilled lamb chops with mint pesto paired with a full-bodied Syrah from the Rhone Valley.

Lobster bisque paired with a buttery Chardonnay from Burgundy.

Beef tenderloin with roasted garlic mashed potatoes paired with a bold Cabernet Sauvignon from California.

Roasted duck breast with cherry sauce paired with a Pinot Noir from Oregon.

Grilled salmon with fennel pollen and lemon paired with a refreshing Sauvignon Blanc from New Zealand.

Charcuterie board with assorted meats and cheeses paired with a spicy Zinfandel from California.

Spicy tuna tartare paired with a crisp and dry Riesling from Germany.

Tomato and burrata salad paired with a light and refreshing Rose from Provence.

Chocolate truffles paired with a rich and velvety Port from Portugal.

Overall, the Food & Wine Classic in Aspen is a celebration of the culinary arts and a testament to the diverse range of flavours and traditions found in American cuisine. The event offers a unique opportunity to taste some of the world's finest wines and cuisine and to experience the culture of Aspen and the United States.

- **South Beach Wine & Food Festival**

The South Beach Wine & Food Festival (SOBEWFF) is an annual food and wine festival held in Miami Beach, Florida, United States. It is a five-day event that typically takes place in late February or early March each year. The festival is known for its diverse range of culinary offerings, including wines from around the world.

The festival attracts a diverse range of people, including foodies, wine enthusiasts, chefs, and celebrities. Over the years, the festival has become a cultural landmark for the city, drawing in more than 65,000 visitors annually.

The topography of the area is predominantly sandy beaches and oceanfront locations, making it an ideal setting for a festival that celebrates food, wine, and beach culture.

One of the main highlights of SOBEWFF is its wine offerings. The festival boasts an impressive selection of wines from around the world, showcasing various vinification techniques and styles. Visitors can expect to see a wide range of wines, including reds, whites, rosés, and sparkling wines.

The wines are expertly paired with food offerings from some of the world's most renowned chefs. Here are some examples of the food and wine pairings that visitors can expect to see at SOBEWFF:

Grilled Steak with Cabernet Sauvignon: The bold flavours of grilled steak are complemented perfectly by the tannins and structure of a classic Cabernet Sauvignon.

Lobster Bisque with Chardonnay: The buttery richness of the bisque is perfectly balanced by the acidity and minerality of a crisp Chardonnay.

Seared Tuna with Pinot Noir: The delicate flavours of seared tuna are complemented by the lightness and fruitiness of a Pinot Noir.

Oysters with Sauvignon Blanc: The briny freshness of oysters pairs perfectly with the crisp acidity and herbaceous notes of a Sauvignon Blanc.

Duck Confit with Merlot: The rich, gamey flavors of duck confit are complemented perfectly by the soft tannins and fruitiness of a Merlot.

Gnocchi with Sangiovese: The earthy flavours of gnocchi are perfectly matched with the cherry and spice notes of a Sangiovese.

Pork Belly with Syrah: The bold, fatty flavours of pork belly are complemented perfectly by the bold tannins and spiciness of a Syrah.

Mushroom Risotto with Nebbiolo: The earthy flavours of the mushrooms are perfectly balanced by the tannins and complexity of a Nebbiolo.

Sushi with Riesling: The delicate flavours and textures of sushi are complemented perfectly by the light sweetness and acidity of a Riesling.

Cheese Plate with Port: The rich, savoury flavours of the cheese are complemented perfectly by the sweet and nutty notes of a Port.

Finally, the South Beach Wine & Food Festival is an exciting event that celebrates food, wine, and beach culture in the beautiful setting of Miami Beach, Florida. With an impressive selection of wines from around the world and expertly paired food offerings, visitors can expect a culinary experience unlike any other.

- **Austin Food & Wine Festival, Texas, USA**

The Austin Food & Wine Festival is an annual event held in Austin, Texas, USA, which celebrates the food and wine culture of the region. The festival attracts people from all over the country, including food and wine enthusiasts, chefs, sommeliers, and industry professionals. The event typically takes place in late April and lasts for three days, offering guests the opportunity to taste and learn about the region's culinary traditions.

Austin, Texas is a diverse city with a unique blend of cultures, and the festival reflects this diversity in its offerings. The festival showcases a wide range of food and wine from the region, highlighting the unique flavours and ingredients that make Texas cuisine so special. The city's topography, with its rolling hills and valleys, provides a perfect climate for growing grapes, and the festival also features some of the best wines from local vineyards.

The festival offers guests the chance to learn about various vinification techniques, from traditional to modern methods. Guests can attend wine seminars and workshops hosted by sommeliers and winemakers, which provide a deeper understanding of the winemaking process and the unique characteristics of different grape varieties.

The event features a vast array of food and wine pairings, with over 50 of the city's top chefs creating dishes to complement the wines. Here are some examples of food and wine pairings at the Austin Food & Wine Festival:

Texas-style barbecue brisket paired with a bold and robust Cabernet Sauvignon

Grilled Gulf shrimp served with a crisp and refreshing Sauvignon Blanc

Spicy chicken enchiladas paired with a rich and full-bodied Malbec

Grilled steak tacos served with a smooth and velvety Pinot Noir

Crispy fried chicken paired with a crisp and refreshing Chardonnay

Grilled lamb chops served with a bold and spicy Zinfandel

Slow-roasted pork belly paired with a fruity and elegant Syrah

Smoked salmon with cream cheese and capers served with a crisp and dry Rosé

Pan-seared scallops with lemon butter sauce paired with a light and refreshing Chenin Blanc

Creamy mushroom risotto served with a smooth and silky Merlot.

In addition to the food and wine pairings, the festival also features live music performances, cooking demonstrations, and other fun activities. The Austin Food & Wine Festival is a celebration of the city's unique food and wine culture, and it is an event that should not be missed by anyone who loves great food and wine.

- **Napa Valley Wine Train, California, USA**

The Napa Valley Wine Train event is an annual festival held in Napa Valley, California, United States. **The town** where the event takes place is Napa, and it is widely known as the wine capital of the United States. Each year, wine enthusiasts from all over the world come to Napa to enjoy the rich culture and exquisite wines the region has to offer.

The Napa Valley Wine Train event is a three-day event that typically takes place in early October. The occasion is a celebration of the rich history of wine-making in the region, and the topography, which is mountainous and characterised by vineyards and oak trees.

The event also features a range of wines and foods that are available for tasting. The wines available, mainly produced from the locally grown vineyards, range from Cabernet Sauvignon and Pinot Noir to Sauvignon Blanc and Chardonnay. The foods, which range from fine cheese and charcuterie to full-course meals such as roasted meats and vegetables, are carefully selected to pair perfectly with the wines on offer.

The festival celebrates the vinification techniques that make Napa Valley wines so unique. The wine-making process in Napa Valley is characterised by a careful selection of grapes, a hands-on approach that involves picking, sorting, and crushing grapes by hand, and the use of traditional oak barrels for ageing.

To give you an idea of the pairings on offer at the event, here are some examples:

1. Chardonnay paired with roasted chicken and creamy mushroom sauce
2. Pinot Noir paired with herb-roasted pork loin and braised kale
3. Cabernet Franc paired with grilled lamb chops and wilted spinach
4. Syrah paired with smoked brisket and roasted root vegetables
5. Sauvignon Blanc paired with seared scallops and citrus beurre blanc
6. Merlot paired with grilled steak and roasted garlic mashed potatoes
7. Cabernet Sauvignon paired with aged gouda and truffle honey
8. Zinfandel paired with spicy sausage and creamy polenta
9. Viognier paired with grilled shrimp and mango salsa
10. Grenache paired with roasted salmon and cherry tomato compote

Each wine has unique characteristics that pair well with certain foods. For example, Chardonnay has a buttery, oaky flavour that pairs perfectly with roasted chicken, while Pinot Noir has a light, fruity flavour that pairs well with pork and herbs.

The foods available at the festival are selected to complement the wine, and each pairing is carefully crafted to highlight the unique flavours of both the wine and the food. Visitors can enjoy a range of local specialties, from artisanal cheeses and charcuterie to full-course meals, each prepared to perfection to provide a unique and unforgettable wine and food pairing experience.

In conclusion, the Napa Valley Wine Train event is a celebration of wine-making culture, vinification techniques, topography, and a wide range of delicious food and wine pairings that celebrate the unique flavours of Napa Valley wines.

- **Charleston Wine + Food Festival,South Carolina, USA**

The Charleston Wine + Food Festival is an annual event held in Charleston, South Carolina, United States. It is a celebration of culture, food, and wine that brings together the best chefs, winemakers, and foodies from all over the country.

The festival takes place in early March and runs for five days. This year, it will be held from March 4th to March 8th. The festival takes place in various locations throughout Charleston, including parks, restaurants, and historic landmarks.

Charleston is a beautiful town known for its stunning architecture, rich history, and beautiful beaches. The town has a unique culture that combines elements of African, European, and indigenous cultures.

The festival features over 100 events, including tastings, dinners, and educational seminars. The events are hosted by some of the top chefs and winemakers in the country, and they showcase the best of Charleston's culinary scene.

The topography of Charleston is a mix of flat land and rolling hills, which provides for some interesting wine varietals. Attendees can sample a variety of wines from around the world, including reds, whites, and rosés. These wines are made using different vinification techniques, such as barrel ageing or stainless steel fermentation.

At the festival, attendees can also sample a wide variety of foods, including seafood, barbecue, and traditional Southern dishes. The foods available are paired with wines to bring out the best flavours in both the food and wine.

Here are some pairing examples from the festival:

1. **Fried Chicken paired with Chardonnay** - The buttery and creamy flavours of a good Chardonnay complement the crispy and juicy fried chicken.

2. **Seafood Paella paired with Rosé** - The fruity and refreshing notes of a Rosé complement the flavours of the seafood in the paella.

3. **Grilled Steak paired with Cabernet Sauvignon** - The bold and robust flavours of a Cabernet Sauvignon complement the rich flavours of a grilled steak.

4. **Lobster bisque paired with Chardonnay** - The buttery and creamy flavours of a Chardonnay complement the rich, silky texture of a lobster bisque.

5. **Sashimi paired with Sauvignon Blanc** - The light and crisp flavours of a Sauvignon Blanc complement the fresh and delicate flavours of sashimi.

6. **Barbecue Ribs paired with Zinfandel** - The bold and spicy flavours of Zinfandel complement the smoky and rich flavours of barbecue ribs.

7. **Oysters paired with Muscadet** - The salty and briny flavours of oysters are complemented by the mineral and crisp flavours of Muscadet.

8. **Pasta with Tomato Sauce paired with Sangiovese** - The bright fruit flavours and acidity of Sangiovese complement the flavours of a tomato-based pasta sauce.

9. **Cheesecake paired with Port** - The rich and sweet flavours of port complement the creaminess of cheesecake.

10. **Chocolate truffles paired with Cabernet Sauvignon** - The bold and tannic flavours of Cabernet Sauvignon complement the rich and intense flavours of chocolate truffles.

Overall, the Charleston Wine + Food Festival is an exciting event that celebrates food, wine, and culture in a beautiful and historic town. Attendees can sample a variety of wines and foods and learn about different vinification techniques while enjoying the best of Charleston's culinary scene.

- **New York City Wine & Food Festival, USA**

The New York City Wine & Food Festival is an annual event held in New York City, USA. It usually takes place in the month of October and features a wide range of culinary events hosted by renowned chefs, restaurateurs, and mixologists. The festival attracts thousands of visitors from all over the world who come to sample the best wines and foods on offer in the city.

The festival is a celebration of culture, and occasion, as it brings together foodies and wine lovers to explore the fascinating pairing of foods and wines. The topography of the event is wide and varied, with events being hosted at different venues and locations throughout the city.

The wines available at the festival come from all over the world, from the well-known producers of Bordeaux and Burgundy to the new and upcoming wine regions of Austria and New Zealand. The vinification techniques used also vary, with traditional methods being used alongside more modern techniques such as biodynamic and sustainable.

Some of the foods available at the festival include artisanal cheeses, fresh seafood, locally sourced meats, and baked goods. These foods are paired with wines selected by expert sommeliers to perfectly complement and enhance the flavours of the dish.

Here are some examples of food and wine pairings from the festival:

1. **Seafood Paella with Albariño** - The bright acidity of Albariño pairs wonderfully with the rich and savoury flavours of seafood paella.

2. **Grilled Steak with Cabernet Sauvignon** - The tannins in Cabernet Sauvignon cut through the richness of grilled steak, making the pairing a match made in heaven.

3. **Roasted Sweet Potato with Chenin Blanc** - The floral and fruity notes of Chenin Blanc complement the sweetness of roasted sweet potato, resulting in a refreshing and satisfying pairing.

4. **Spicy Thai Curry with Gewürztraminer** - The spicy and bold flavours of Thai curry are perfectly balanced by the aromatic and slightly sweet notes of Gewürztraminer.

5. **Cheese Plate with Pinot Noir** - The earthy and complex flavours of Pinot Noir pair beautifully with the wide range of cheeses available at the festival.

6. **Lobster Roll with Chardonnay** - Light and refreshing Chardonnay accentuates the buttery flavours of a freshly made lobster roll.

7. **Wild Mushroom Risotto with Nebbiolo** - The intense and earthy flavours of Nebbiolo bring out the umami of a well-prepared wild mushroom risotto.

8. **Chocolate Lava Cake with Port** - The rich and decadent flavours of a chocolate lava cake are wonderfully complemented by the sweetness and depth of a good port wine.

9. **Grilled Lamb Chops with Syrah** - The bold and spicy flavours of Syrah pair perfectly with the rich and savoury flavour of grilled lamb chops.

10. **Apple Pie with Riesling** - The sweet and tart notes of Riesling bring out the crisp and refreshing flavours of freshly made apple pie.

In conclusion, the New York City Wine & Food Festival is a must-attend event for wine and food enthusiasts from all over the world. The festival offers a wide range of wines and foods, paired expertly by sommeliers and chefs to provide the perfect culinary experience for attendees. Whether it's the traditional pairing of steak and Cabernet Sauvignon or the more adventurous combination of Thai curry and Gewürztraminer, there's something for everyone at this exciting event.

- **LA Food & Wine Festival, Los Angeles, California**

The LA Food & Wine Festival is an annual food and wine event held in Los Angeles, California. The festival attracts food lovers and wine enthusiasts from all over the US and beyond, offering a chance to explore the best culinary and wine experience in town. The event features award-winning chefs, top winemakers, mixologists, and sommeliers with the aim of promoting the culture of food and wine.

The event is usually held in August, and it showcases the destination's topography, culture, and tradition of vineyard management. The festival boasts of showcasing over 200 prominent wineries' grape varietals and blends that are paired with delectable gourmet cuisine. Attendees can enjoy the best cuts of meat and fish; exquisite local and international cuisine served alongside the finest wines from around the world.

One of the signature technologies showcased at the Festival is the Vinification technique. This section showcases the differences in winemaking techniques, soil composition, weather patterns, and each grapevine's unique traits grown in each vineyard region. Furthermore, the process of oak ageing, fermenting, and bottling wine are demonstrated and explained.

These taste combinations create unique experiences. For instance, fresh fish and red wines may not sound like the best pairing option, but the lobster bisque with Pinot Noir is a classic pairing that is enjoyed annually. Here are ten pairing examples available at the LA Food & Wine Festival:

1. **Pinot Noir and lobster bisque** – The Pinot Noir's light-bodied nature pairs well with the delicate flavors of the lobster bisque.

2. **Chardonnay and salmon tartare** - The bright acidity of Chardonnay complements the richness of the salmon tartare

3. **Sauvignon Blanc and sushi** - Sauvignon Blanc's grassy, herbaceous flavour works well with sushi's bright, fresh flavours

4. **Merlot and steak** – Merlot's fruit-forward, earthy flavours and soft tannins are complementary to steak.

5. **Cabernet Sauvignon and dark chocolate** - Cabernet Sauvignon's tannins balance the bitterness of the chocolate, and its fruitiness enhances its sweetness.

6. **Zinfandel and grilled vegetables** – Zinfandel's higher alcohol content pairs well with the smoky flavours of grilled vegetables.

7. **Syrah and lamb** – Syrah's earthy and fruity undertones work well with the gamey flavour of lamb.

8. **Riesling and spicy Thai or Indian cuisine** – Riesling's sweetness helps balance the heat of spicy curry dishes.

9. **Rosé and cheese** – Rosé's acidity pairs well with the fattiness of cheese.

10. **Malbec and barbecue** – Malbec's smokiness and tartness cuts through the sweetness of barbecue sauce.

In conclusion, the LA Food & Wine Festival is a must-attend event for food lovers and wine aficionados. The event showcases the best gourmet cuisine, wine varietals, and vinification techniques. With an exquisite range of flavours and aroma profiles, attendees can explore unique taste combinations and learn about food and wine's artistry.

- **San Francisco Street Food Festival, California, USA**

San Francisco Street Food Festival is one of the most popular and exciting food festivals held in San Francisco, California, USA. This festival is celebrated annually in the month of August and provides an excellent opportunity for local communities to come together and enjoy the city's diverse culture.

The festival brings together people from different ethnic backgrounds, and it celebrates the city's rich heritage through food, wine, and music. The event is typically held in a large open-air space, where local vendors and chefs from around the Bay Area set up tents to showcase their culinary creations.

The event's topography is urban, as it takes place on the streets of San Francisco, allowing visitors to see the city's sights, sounds, and smells. Throughout the festival, visitors have the opportunity to try a variety of wine and food pairings.

The festival offers a wide range of foods such as dumplings, rice bowls, sandwiches, tacos, burgers, BBQ, and more. It also highlights a variety of wines, as California is one of the world's leading producers of wine. The festival offers several opportunities to learn about vinification techniques, grapes, and different wines' characteristics.

Here are some examples of food and wine pairings to try at the San Francisco Street Food Festival:

1. **Dish**: Sourdough bread grilled cheese sandwich. Wine: Chardonnay - this wine is a great match for the sandwich as the smooth, creamy texture of the chardonnay brings out the buttery flavour in the sandwich.

2. **Dish**: Korean BBQ tacos. Wine: Syrah - the bold and spicy flavours in the tacos are complemented by the syrah's deep, rich flavour.

3. **Dish**: Shrimp po' boy sandwich. Wine: Sauvignon Blanc - the wine's tartness and freshness work well with the sandwich's light, airy flavors and fried shrimp.

4. **Dish**: Grilled chicken satay skewers. Wine: Riesling - the wine's refreshing sweetness complements the chicken's slightly sweet and tangy flavour, bringing out the satay's spiciness.

5. **Dish**: Greek spanakopita. Wine: Pinot Noir - the wine's light, fruity flavour, matches the spinach and feta cheese filling in the pastry, and the medium-bodied wine complements the crispiness of the pastry.

6. **Dish**: Sonoran hot dog. Wine: Sangria - the fruity, sweet flavours of sangria complement the hot dogs' savoury taste, making for a perfect summer pairing.

7. **Dish**: Falafel sandwich. Wine: Gewürztraminer - this wine is an ideal match for the sandwich's Middle Eastern spices, which balance well with the wine's fruity and floral notes.

8. **Dish**: Buffalo wings. Wine: Cabernet Sauvignon - the wine's dark berry flavour and tannin perfectly balance out the chicken's spiciness.

9. **Dish**: Pork belly baos. Wine: Pinot Gris - the wine's acidity level cuts through the pork belly's richness, making for a balanced pairing.

10. **Dish**: Crispy fish tacos. Wine: Chardonnay - the wine's subtle oak flavours match the fish's smoky taste, while its crispness offers a refreshing finish that complements the classic taco toppings.

Overall, the San Francisco Street Food Festival offers a unique and delicious experience of the city's diverse culinary culture. It combines the taste of the city's traditional dishes and innovative creations with unique wines, providing participants with the opportunity to explore and discover new flavours.

- **Boston Wine Festival, Massachusetts**

The Boston Wine Festival is an annual event that takes place in Boston, Massachusetts, USA. It features a series of wine-tasting events, seminars, and dinners that showcase an extensive selection of wines from around the world. The festival is hosted by the Boston Harbor Hotel and has been a prominent event in Boston's cultural calendar for over 30 years.

The **Boston** Wine Festival runs from January to March every year, featuring more than 100 different events across its duration. The festival attracts wine enthusiasts, tourists, and locals alike.

The **festival** is celebrated with much fanfare, and the topography of the area boosts the ambiance of the event perfectly. The Boston Harbor Hotel, located on the waterfront, provides a scenic, relaxed venue for attendees to enjoy.

The **festival** features a vast selection of wines, including rare vintages, new releases, and wines from small, boutique wineries. Vinification techniques are highlighted with seminars and workshops by experts. Attendees can also take home an extensive collection of wines from the on-site wine shop.

The **festival** also features a range of food options. From locally sourced seafood to international cuisine, the festival aims to provide guests with a culinary experience to perfectly complement the different wines on offer.

Here are some pairing examples to give an idea of the range of wines and foods available at the Boston Wine Festival:

1. **Maine Lobster Bisque paired with a Chardonnay from Burgundy**. The rich, creamy flavours of the bisque complement the buttery notes of the Chardonnay, resulting in a perfect balance of flavours.

2. **Grilled Lamb Chops with a Syrah from the Rhone region.** The spicy, earthy notes of the Syrah pair well with the meaty, savory flavors of the lamb.

3. **Grilled Salmon paired with a Pinot Noir from Oregon.** The light, fruity flavours of the Pinot Noir complement the delicate flavours of the salmon, resulting in a refreshing pairing.

4. **Steak Tartare paired with a Cabernet Sauvignon from Napa Valley**. The full-bodied, oaky flavours of the Cabernet Sauvignon complement the rich, savoury flavours of the steak tartare.

5. **Baked Brie paired with a Rose from Provence**. The light, crisp flavours of the Rose complement the creamy, nutty flavours of the Brie.

6. **Duck Confit paired with a Merlot from Bordeaux**. The hearty, gamey flavours of the duck confit are complemented by the smooth, tannic flavours of the Merlot.

7. **Grilled Octopus paired with a Sauvignon Blanc from New Zealand**. The crisp, acidic flavours of the Sauvignon Blanc complement and cut through the smoky flavours of the grilled octopus.

8. **Prawn Cocktail paired with a Riesling from Germany**. The sweet, tangy flavours of the prawn cocktail are balanced by the light, citrusy flavours of the Riesling.

9. **Mushroom Risotto paired with a Pinot Noir from California**. The earthy, umami flavours of the mushroom risotto are complemented by the light, fruity flavours of the Pinot Noir.

10. **New England Clam Chowder paired with a Chablis from Burgundy**. The light, crisp flavours of the Chablis complement the creamy, savoury flavours of the clam chowder, resulting in a refreshing pairing.

In conclusion, the Boston Wine Festival is a celebration of wine and food, perfectly showcased by the beautiful topography of the area. With its wide range of wines and culinary options, guests are offered a unique opportunity to broaden their palates and learn more about the nuances of different wine varieties and vinification methods.

- **Atlanta Food & Wine Festival, Georgia**

The Atlanta Food & Wine Festival is an annual event held in Atlanta, Georgia, USA. The festival brings together people from all over the world to celebrate the culture of food and wine in the region. The event takes place over three days, offering a full immersion into the world of Southern food and wine.

The **festival** is held in May in the heart of Atlanta and draws a diverse crowd of food and wine lovers. The event features over 200 chefs, sommeliers, and mixologists who create an unforgettable culinary experience. Attendees can participate in tastings, workshops, and cooking demonstrations that showcase the culture of the region.

The **event** is an occasion to discover the wines and food culture of the Southern United States. The topography of the region, with its mild climate and fertile soil, has helped make the South one of the best regions for wine and food production. At the festival, attendees have a chance to sample wines from the best vineyards in the region, as well as food from some of the most talented chefs.

The **festival** features a wide variety of foods and wines, with dynamic pairings that showcase the best flavours of the South. The vinification techniques of the region, such as barrel ageing and fermenting in oak, result in wines with rich, complex flavours that pair perfectly with the food. Here are 10 pairing examples with details:

1. **Fried Chicken and Bubbles** - Fried chicken has a crispy texture that pairs well with the effervescence of a sparkling wine. For a perfect pairing, try a Southern Sparkling Rosé with notes of strawberry and raspberry.

2. **Braised Short Ribs and Cabernet Sauvignon** - Rich and flavorful braised short ribs match perfectly with the tannins and structure of a Cabernet Sauvignon. A full-bodied Cabernet Sauvignon with earthy notes will balance out the rich flavours of the dish.

3. **Oysters and Muscadine Wine** - A classic Southern dish, oysters on the half shell pair well with the fruity flavours of a Muscadine wine. The bright acidity and minerality in the wine complements the briny flavour of the oysters.

4. **Grits and Chardonnay** - Chardonnay is a perfect pairing for grits, providing a buttery richness that complements the texture of the dish. A full-bodied oaked Chardonnay with notes of vanilla and toasted nut will balance the flavour of the dish.

5. **Barbecue Pork and Zinfandel** - Rich and smoky barbecue pork pairs best with a bold Zinfandel that has a sweet finish. A Zinfandel with notes of blackberry and black cherry will match well with the sweet and tangy flavours of the pork.

6. **Fried Green Tomatoes and Pinot Grigio** - The tartness and crunch of fried green tomatoes match the bright acidity of a crisp Pinot Grigio. The citrusy notes in the wine will balance out the flavours.

7. **Shrimp and Grits and Sauvignon Blanc** - Shrimp and grits is a classic Southern dish, and pairs well with the bright acidity of a Sauvignon Blanc. The wine's crisp finish will balance out the rich flavours of the dish.

8. **Pecan Pie and Tawny Port** - The nuttiness of a pecan pie matches perfectly with the sweetness of a Tawny port. The caramel and honey notes in the wine complement the flavours of the dish.

9. **Tomatoes and Corn Salad and Rosé** - A refreshing rosé wine with hints of strawberry and raspberry pairs well with a summer salad of tomatoes and corn. The light, fruity flavours of the wine complement the freshness of the salad.

10. **Grilled Okra and Chianti** - Grilled okra, a Southern delicacy, pairs well with a medium-bodied Chianti with notes of cherry and leather. The wine will highlight the grilled flavours of the okra.

In conclusion, the Atlanta Food & Wine Festival celebrates the culture of Southern food and wine, with topography and vinification techniques that have made it one of the best regions for wine and food production. The festival offers an opportunity to explore a variety of Southern cuisines and iconic wines, with perfect pairing combinations that showcase the flavours of the region.

- **Epcot International Food & Wine Festival, Orlando, Florida**

The Epcot International Food & Wine Festival is an annual event held at the Epcot theme park in Orlando, Florida, USA. The festival is a celebration of cuisine and wine from around the world and is attended by people from different cultures and countries. This year, the festival is being held from September 10 to November 1.

The festival offers a variety of food and wine tastings, as well as culinary demonstrations and seminars. There are more than 30 global marketplaces, where guests can sample dishes and drinks from different countries. The festival also provides an opportunity to learn about vinification techniques and wine pairing.

The town of Orlando is known for its diverse and multicultural population, and the Epcot International Food & Wine Festival reflects this diversity. The festival is a celebration of different cultures and their cuisines, and it offers a unique opportunity to experience the flavours and aromas of different regions.

Some of the topography featured at the festival includes dishes and wines from Greece, Italy, France, Spain, Germany, Japan, and Morocco. The festival also features special events like the Party for the Senses and the Sunday Brunch with the Chef series, which provide guests with a more immersive culinary experience.

With over a hundred different wines available at the festival, there are plenty of options to pair with the different foods on offer. Some of the wines available include sparkling wines, reds, whites, rosés, and dessert wines. The vinification techniques vary from region to region, and include methods like oak barrel aging, malolactic fermentation, and secondary fermentation.

Here are some pairing examples of wine and food available at the Epcot International Food & Wine Festival:

1. **Lobster roll with buttered breadcrumbs paired with a Chardonnay** – the rich, buttery flavour of the Chardonnay complements the sweetness of the lobster and the breadcrumbs.

2. **Grilled salmon with a lemon-herb crust paired with a Pinot Noir** – the earthy flavours of the Pinot Noir complement the bold and tangy flavours of the salmon.

3. **Chicken Shish Kebab with garlic aioli paired with a Sauvignon Blanc** – the crisp, acidic flavours of the Sauvignon Blanc pair well with the bold flavours of the garlic aioli.

4. **Fillet Mignon with truffle butter sauce paired with a Cabernet Sauvignon** – the bold, tannic flavours of the Cabernet Sauvignon complement the richness of the fillet mignon and the earthy flavour of the truffle butter sauce.

5. . – the light, acidic flavors of the Pinot Grigio complement the creaminess of the mac and cheese and the bold flavours of the herb breadcrumbs.

6. **Beef Brisket with smoked mac and cheese paired with a Zinfandel** – the bold, fruity flavours of the Zinfandel cut through the rich flavours of the beef brisket and the smokiness of the mac and cheese.

7. **Spicy Tuna and Salmon Sushi Roll paired with a Riesling** – the light, fruity flavours of the Riesling complement the bold flavours of the spicy tuna and salmon.

8. **Crispy Pork Belly with black beans and avocado paired with a Malbec** – the bold, tannic flavours of the Malbec complement the rich flavours of the pork belly and the creaminess of the avocado.

9. **Grilled Sweet and Spicy Bush Berry Shrimp paired with a Gewürztraminer** – the sweet, floral flavours of the Gewürztraminer complement the sweet and spicy flavours of the shrimp.

10. **Lobster and Seafood Fisherman's Pie paired with a Chablis** – the acidic, mineral flavours of the Chablis complement the richness of the lobster and seafood in the pie.

Overall, the Epcot International Food & Wine Festival is a celebration of cuisine and wine from around the world, with an emphasis on cultural diversity and authenticity. The festival offers a unique opportunity to experience different flavours and aromas, and to learn about vinification techniques and wine pairing. It is an event not to be missed for all food and wine enthusiasts.

- **Sonoma County Wine Weekend, California**

Sonoma County is located in Northern California, USA. Known for its beautiful countryside, mild climate and world-class wines, it is a popular destination for both wine enthusiasts and tourists.

One popular event in Sonoma County is the "Sonoma County Wine Weekend" which takes place annually during the first weekend of September. The event is held in the city of Santa Rosa, in the heart of Sonoma County.

The Sonoma County Wine Weekend is a celebration of the local wine culture, featuring wine tastings, food pairings, live music, and other entertainment. Visitors are able to sample a wide range of wines, from crisp Chardonnays and fruity Pinot Noirs to bold Cabernet Sauvignons and spicy Zinfandels.

The event is also an opportunity to learn about the vinification techniques used in Sonoma County, which employ traditional methods such as foot treading, barrel fermentation, and open top fermenters. These techniques help to create wines with unique flavours and aromas, distinctive to the region.

In addition to wine, the Sonoma County Wine Weekend offers a variety of local foods that pair well with the wines. Here are ten examples of food and wine pairings that you might expect to find at the event, along with some details about the foods and wines and why they pair well together:

1. **Grilled Salmon with Chardonnay** - Crisp, unoaked Chardonnays pair well with rich fish dishes like grilled salmon. The acidity of the wine cuts through the oily texture of the fish.

2. **Mushroom Risotto with Pinot Noir** - The earthy flavours in Pinot Noir complement the earthy, savoury flavours in mushroom risotto.

3. **Barbecue Ribs with Zinfandel** - Zinfandel's bold flavour and high tannins help to balance the sweetness and smokiness of barbecued ribs.

4. **Bruschetta with Sauvignon Blanc** - Light-bodied Sauvignon Blanc pairs perfectly with the fresh, acidic flavours of tomato and basil in bruschetta.

5. **Charcuterie with Grenache** - The savoury flavours of cured meats and cheeses in a charcuterie board contrast beautifully with the sweeter fruit flavors in Grenache.

6. **Grilled Steak with Cabernet Sauvignon** - Cabernet Sauvignon's full body and bold tannins can stand up to the rich, fatty flavours of grilled steak.

7. **Lobster with Chardonnay** - Rich, buttery lobster goes perfectly with oak-aged Chardonnay. The wine's buttery, creamy notes complement the dish.

8. **Spicy Thai Curry with Riesling** - Spicy foods need a sweet, fruity wine to balance out the heat. Riesling's sweet notes pair perfectly with spicy Thai curry.

9. **Sushi with Pinot Gris** - Pinot Gris' crisp acidity pairs perfectly with the clean, fresh flavours of sushi, especially with raw fish.

10. **Crème Brûlée with Late Harvest Zinfandel** - Desserts like crème brûlée complement the sweet, jammy flavours of Late Harvest Zinfandel. The wine can also help cut through the richness of the desert.

In summary, the Sonoma County Wine Weekend is a celebration of the region's unique wine culture. Visitors can sample a wide range of wines and learn about the traditional vinification techniques used in the area. The event also showcases local foods that pair perfectly with the wines, creating a complete sensory experience.

- **Santa Fe Wine & Chile Fiesta - Santa Fe, New Mexico**

Santa Fe Wine & Chile Fiesta is an annual festival taking place in Santa Fe, New Mexico, United States. It is a five-day event dedicated to showcasing the wines and foods of Santa Fe and New Mexico, along with some of the best wines from around the world. The festival is held in September every year, featuring exclusive dinners, seminars, and wine tastings.

The festival is an occasion for both tourists and locals to celebrate the best that New Mexico has to offer in wines and culinary delights. Santa Fe, known for its rich cultural history and distinctive architecture, adds to the festival's unique atmosphere. The topography of the surrounding mountains and high desert provide a perfect backdrop for this taste extravaganza.

Attendees at the festival can taste a vast array of wines, including local New Mexico favourites such as Gruet Sparkling, Noisy Water, Casa Rondena, and many others. The festival also features wines from across the world, allowing attendees to taste wines they may not find locally. Vinification techniques from different regions are showcased through tastings, dinners, and seminars.

The food offerings at Santa Fe Wine & Chile Fiesta are just as unique and diverse as the wines. Attendees can enjoy anything from traditional New Mexican street food to haute cuisine. Some notable dishes include Hatch Green Chile en Nogada, lamb barbacoa, local goat cheese, and blue corn tamales.

Pairing food with wine can be a science in itself, and the festival encourages attendees to experiment with new combinations. Here are ten examples of food and wine pairings to try:

1. Grilled lamb chops with a bold red wine such as Rioja Reserva from Spain. The wine's tannins cut through the fat in the meat.

2. Spicy green chile dishes with a crisp, acidic white wine such as Sauvignon Blanc from New Zealand. The wine helps cool down the heat in the dish.

3. Seafood dishes with a light-bodied white wine such as Albariño from Spain. The wine complements the delicate flavours of seafood without overpowering them.

4. Blue corn tamales with a fruity red wine such as Zinfandel from California. The wine's richness and sweetness complement the earthy corn and spices in the tamale.

5. Braised short ribs with a full-bodied red wine such as Cabernet Sauvignon from France. The tannins in the wine balance the richness of the meat.

6. Chiles rellenos with a dry rosé such as Grenache from France. The wine's freshness and acidity complement the richness of the dish.

7. Goat cheese with a crisp, acidic white wine such as Chablis from France. The wine's acidity cuts through the creaminess of the cheese.

8. Beef fajitas with a bold red blend such as Châteauneuf-du-Pape from France. The wine's complexity and boldness complement the spices in the dish.

9. Chile con carne with a medium-bodied red wine such as Merlot from California. The wine's fruitiness complements the rich tomato sauce in the dish.

10. Avocado and crab salad with a light, acidic white wine such as Vermentino from Italy. The wine's citrus notes complement the sweetness of the crab and nuttiness of the avocado.

Overall, the Santa Fe Wine & Chile Fiesta is an event not to be missed for wine and food lovers alike. The festival's focus on showcasing local and international wines as well as local cuisine makes it a unique experience, and the beautiful setting of Santa Fe adds to the overall ambiance.

- **Big Apple Barbecue Block Party - New York, New York**

The Big Apple Barbecue Block Party is a highly anticipated barbecue event held annually in New York City, United States. Hosted in the beautiful Madison Square Park, the event attracts thousands of visitors who come to enjoy the best barbecue in the country from top pitmasters.

The event usually takes place in the month of June, and it's a celebration of American food, music, and culture. The occasion provides a chance for attendees to sample a wide range of barbecue styles and experience the unique flavours of different regions across the country.

The topography of the area provides a beautiful setting for the event, with trees surrounding the park, creating a perfect ambiance for attendees. In terms of food, attendees can expect to indulge in a variety of smoked meats from different regions of the US such as Carolina pulled pork, Texas beef brisket, and Memphis-style barbecue ribs.

Pairing foods and wines can be a tricky affair. However, pairing wine with barbecue is achievable, provided some basic guidelines are followed. Full-bodied red wines are an excellent pairing with grilled meats, especially those that have been smoked. Some examples of red wines that pair well with barbecue would include Malbec, Shiraz, Cabernet Sauvignon, and Zinfandel. Additionally, white wines such as Chenin Blanc, Viognier, and Riesling, can also complement some types of barbecue sauces.

Here are ten pairing examples of wine and food that work well during the Big Apple Barbecue Block Party:

1. **Carolina-style pulled pork with Cabernet Sauvignon**: Smokey and savoury flavours of the pulled pork go perfectly with a full-bodied Cabernet Sauvignon.

2. **Texas-style beef brisket with Malbec:** The bold and intense flavors of the beef brisket pair well with a fruity Malbec.

3. **Memphis-style barbecue ribs with Zinfandel**: The smoky flavours of the ribs pair well with the spicy and bold notes of a Zinfandel.

4. **Kansas City-style barbecue ribs with Syrah**: The earthy and robust flavours of Syrah complement the flavours of savoury barbecue ribs perfectly.

5. **Alabama white sauce chicken with Chardonnay**: The creamy and tangy flavours of white sauce chicken work well with a rich and buttery Chardonnay.

6. **Eastern North Carolina-style pulled pork with Pinot Noir:** The delicate and fruity flavours of Pinot Noir counterbalance the rich smokiness of pulled pork.

7. **South Carolina mustard-based barbecue with Chenin Blanc:** The sweet and tangy flavours of a Chenin Blanc pair well with the tangy and spicy mustard-based barbecue of the South Carolina region.

8. **Louisiana-style barbecue shrimp with Sauvignon Blanc:** The herbaceous notes of Sauvignon Blanc complement the spicy and buttery flavours of Louisiana-style barbecue shrimp.

9. **Kentucky bourbon-glazed pork belly with Merlot:** The bold and sweet flavours of the bourbon glaze work well with the fruity and spicy notes of Merlot.

10. **St. Louis-style spare ribs with Petite Sirah**: The full-bodied and hearty flavours of Petite Sirah complement the smoky and bold flavours of St. Louis-style spare ribs.

In conclusion, the Big Apple Barbecue Block Party is an excellent event for food and wine connoisseurs to enjoy a diverse range of barbecue styles from around the country. With careful consideration of the flavours and textures of different foods and wine types, attendees can make the most of the pairing experience while enjoying a memorable day out.

- **San Diego Bay Wine & Food Festival - San Diego, California**

The San Diego Bay Wine & Food Festival is an annual event that takes place in the seaside town of San Diego, California, USA. This event brings together people from all over the country to enjoy and indulge in the best wines and food in the world.

The festival is usually held in November and attracts thousands of visitors who come to taste and explore different types of wines and food trying to find that unmatched pairing. The event usually spans over a week and consists of various activities including wine tastings, seminars, and presentations from renowned wine and food experts.

San Diego Bay Wine & Food Festival is not just an event, but it is a culture and an occasion that showcases California's rich winemaking heritage, culinary art, and the topography of San Diego. As a coastal town, San Diego offers a unique array of fresh seafood, and the festival is known for bringing fresh oysters, crab, and escargot from the Bay Area.

In addition to fresh seafood, the festival hosts hundreds of vendors who display locally made artisanal foods such as cheese, chocolates, cured meats, and specialty sauces. The festival offers more than 200 types of wines from all over the world, including California's best wines, and also showcases different vinification techniques.

Pairing foods with wines is an art that takes years of practice, and the San Diego Bay Wine & Food Festival is a perfect event for both seasoned and novice wine lovers to learn about wine pairing. Here are ten possible pairing examples that one can try at the festival:

1. **Parmesan Cheese with Italian Barolo**: The strong flavour of Parmesan cheese pairs well with the tannic and full-bodied red wine Barolo. The high acidity of Barolo complements the nutty flavour of the cheese.

2. **Grilled Steak with Cabernet Sauvignon**: The bold flavour of grilled steak goes well with the high tannins and full body of Cabernet Sauvignon. The wine's boldness also balances the saltiness of the meat.

3. **Lobster Bisque with Chardonnay**: The creamy and rich flavour of lobster bisque pairs well with the full-bodied and buttery Chardonnay.

4. **Blue Cheese with Port**: The sweet and strong flavour of port goes well with the bold flavour of blue cheese. The sweetness of the wine balances the saltiness of the cheese.

5. **Sushi with Pinot Grigio**: The light-bodied and slightly acidic Pinot Grigio pairs well with the subtle flavours of sushi. The wine's crispness also cleanses the palate.

6. **Spicy Thai Curry with Gewurztraminer**: The spicy flavour of Thai curry goes well with the floral and fruity Gewurztraminer. The wine's sweetness also balances the spiciness of the curry.

7. **Oysters with Champagne**: The fresh and briny flavour of oysters pairs well with the crisp and acidic Champagne. The wine's acidity also enhances the salty taste of the oysters.

8. **BBQ Pork Ribs with Zinfandel**: The bold and smoky flavour of BBQ pork ribs pairs well with the fruity and jammy Zinfandel. The wine's boldness also balances the sweetness of the sauce.

9. **Grilled Shrimp with Sauvignon Blanc**: The light-bodied and citrusy Sauvignon Blanc pairs well with the delicate flavour of grilled shrimp. The wine's acidity also enhances the flavour of the seafood.

10. **Chocolate Truffles with Merlot**: The rich and chocolaty flavour of truffles pairs well with the smooth and medium-bodied Merlot. The wine's soft tannins also complement the creaminess of the chocolate.

In conclusion, the San Diego Bay Wine & Food Festival is an excellent occasion to explore and indulge in California's rich culinary and winemaking culture. The festival provides a perfect opportunity to learn about wine pairing and vinification techniques. With the festival offering numerous wines and foods, visitors can discover new flavours and combinations and enhance their wine pairing skills.

- **Oregon Brewers Festival - Portland, Oregon**

The Oregon Brewers Festival is an annual event that takes place in Portland, Oregon, in the United States. This festival is a haven for beer enthusiasts who gather to celebrate and enjoy a variety of craft beers. The festival takes place at Tom McCall Waterfront Park in downtown Portland, which provides a beautiful setting overlooking the Willamette River.

Oregon Brewers Festival draws people from all over the country and the world, who come to sample the finest craft beers from all over Oregon and beyond. The festival takes place over four days in July and features over 90 craft breweries and more than 100 different types of beer.

The festival highlights the unique culture of Oregon that is defined by its craft beer scene. It is an opportunity for brewers to showcase their skills and different brewing techniques. Visitors are given the chance to learn about the process of vinification and the different flavours and aromas that come with different techniques.

In addition to craft beers, the festival also offers a variety of food to pair with the beer. The food menus consists of classic Oregonian dishes, seafood, barbecue, burger and pizza, all paired with amazing wine selections that compliment it.

Let's check out some beer and food pairing examples that work well together:

1. **Pale Ale and Fish and Chips** - A pale ale pairs perfectly with the crisp, batter-fried fish and chips. The slight bitterness of the pale ale pairs well with the tartar sauce.

2. **Hefeweizen and Sausage** - Hefeweizen goes very well with sausage because its light citrus flavour cuts through the richness of the meat.

3. **Amber Ale and Grilled Cheese** - Amber Ale's nutty sweetness complements the rich cheese in the grilled cheese sandwich.

4. **IPA's and Spicy Foods** - IPAs are known for their strong hoppy taste, which works well with the heat of spicy foods.

5. **Porter and Chocolate Cake** - Chocolate and roasted coffee notes in Porter blend perfectly with chocolate cake.

6. **Belgian Dubbel and Pork Tenderloin** - A Belgian Dubbel's malting and brewing spices pairs well with pork tenderloin.

7. **Stout and Oysters** - The creamy sweetness of the stout pairs perfectly with the salinity of the oysters.

8. **Kolsch and Shellfish** - The Kolsch's mild fruitiness pairs well with the shellfish.

9. **Pilsner and Pizza** - A light-bodied lager such as Pilsner works well with classic pepperoni or veggie pizza.

10. **Brown Ale and Barbecue** - Brown Ale's caramelised sweetness pairs best with barbecue's smoky and sweet flavours.

In conclusion, The Oregon Brewers Festival is a popular event that celebrates the unique culture and vinification techniques of Oregon's craft beer scene. The food and wines available at the festival are a perfect complement to the featured craft beers. The pairings of the different food and wine selections are sure to satisfy any beer and food connoisseur's palate.

- **Kentucky Bourbon Festival - Bardstown, Kentucky**

The Kentucky Bourbon Festival is an annual celebration of bourbon that takes place in Bardstown, Kentucky, USA. Bardstown is a small town located in Nelson County, which is famous for its bourbon production. The festival usually takes place in mid-September and attracts thousands of people from all over the world.

The festival offers a wide variety of events and activities for bourbon enthusiasts, such as distillery tours, tastings, seminars, and a bourbon barrel relay race. It also features live music, food vendors, and artisanal craft vendors.

The Kentucky Bourbon Festival is not only a celebration of bourbon, but also a celebration of the cultural heritage and history of Kentucky. Bourbon has been distilled in Kentucky for over 200 years, and it is deeply rooted in the state's culture and identity.

The topography of Kentucky is ideal for bourbon production, as it has warm summers and cool winters, as well as limestone-rich water sources that are perfect for making bourbon. The bourbon-making process involves ageing the whiskey in charred oak barrels, which gives it its distinct flavour profile.

At the Kentucky Bourbon Festival, attendees can enjoy a wide variety of wines and foods that pair well with the bourbons being showcased. Some examples of wines that pair well with bourbons include Malbec, Syrah, Cabernet Sauvignon, and Chardonnay.

Here are some pairing examples of foods and wines at the Kentucky Bourbon Festival:

1. **Pulled pork sliders with barbecue sauce paired with a Malbec**. The smoky, spicy flavours of the pork pair well with the bold, fruity flavours of the Malbec.

2. **Grilled steak with chimichurri sauce paired with a Cabernet Sauvignon**. The rich, savoury flavours of the steak are complemented by the tannins and complex flavours of the Cabernet.

3. **Fried chicken with honey mustard sauce paired with a Chardonnay**. The creamy, buttery flavours of the Chardonnay balance out the tangy sweetness of the honey mustard sauce.

4. **Lobster bisque paired with a Viognier**. The delicate, floral flavours of the Viognier complement the rich, creamy flavours of the bisque.

5. **Grilled shrimp with garlic butter paired with a Sauvignon Blanc**. The bright, citrusy flavours of the Sauvignon Blanc complement the zesty flavours of the garlic butter.

6. **Cheese plate with assorted crackers and fruits paired with a Pinot Noir**. The earthy, fruity flavours of the Pinot Noir complement the creamy, salty flavours of the cheese.

7. **Braised short ribs with red wine sauce paired with a Syrah**. The bold, fruity flavours of the Syrah complement the rich, savoury flavours of the short ribs.

8. **Spicy chicken wings with blue cheese dressing paired with a Zinfandel**. The bold, spicy flavours of the wings are balanced out by the fruity, spicy flavours of the Zinfandel.

9. **Crispy fried catfish with remoulade sauce paired with a Pinot Grigio**. The light, crisp flavours of the Pinot Grigio complement the tender, flaky flavours of the catfish.

10. **Chocolate truffles paired with a Merlot**. The rich, fruity flavours of the Merlot complement the sweet, decadent flavours of the chocolate truffles.

In terms of vinification techniques, the wines that pair well with bourbon are usually full-bodied, with bold flavours and high tannins. They are often aged in oak barrels, which gives them a rich, oaky flavour profile that complements the charred oak flavour of bourbon.

Overall, the Kentucky Bourbon Festival is a wonderful celebration of bourbon, culture, and history. Whether you're a bourbon enthusiast or simply enjoy great food and wine, there's something for everyone at this festival.

- **Newport Mansions Wine and Food Festival - Newport, Rhode Island**

The Newport Mansions Wine and Food Festival is an iconic event that takes place in Newport, Rhode Island in the United States. The event is held annually and attracts people from all over the country, including wine and food enthusiasts, industry experts, and media personnel. This event is a celebration of wine and food culture that offers a unique opportunity to learn about various vinification techniques and indulge in the finest wines and foods from around the world.

The Newport Mansions Wine and Food Festival is usually held in the fall, which is the perfect time to enjoy the breathtaking scenery of Newport. The festival takes place in various mansions and venues throughout Newport, offering a unique experience to the visitors.

The festival offers an extensive range of wines and foods from around the world, ranging from local Rhode Island specialties to international cuisine. The festival emphasises on pairing food with the perfect wine, making it an ideal event for gastronomes and oenophiles.

Some of the wines that are commonly served at the festival include Chardonnay, Pinot Noir, Cabernet Sauvignon, Merlot, and Riesling. The wines are made using various vinification techniques that are unique to different regions and vineyards around the world.

Pairing wine with food is an art that requires a thorough understanding of the flavours, textures, and aromas of both. Here are some examples of food and wine pairing options that are available at the Newport Mansions Wine and Food Festival.

1. **Lobster paired with Chardonnay**: The buttery and fruity notes of Chardonnay complement the rich and delicate flavour of lobster.

2. **Grilled steak paired with Cabernet Sauvignon**: The bold and tannic flavour of Cabernet Sauvignon balances the richness and smokiness of grilled steak.

3. **Oysters paired with Riesling**: The crisp and acidic flavour of Riesling cuts through the brininess of oysters, creating a perfect balance of flavours.

4. **Spicy Thai food paired with Gewurztraminer**: The spicy and aromatic flavour of Gewurztraminer enhances the bold flavours of Thai food.

5. **Sushi paired with Pinot Noir**: The light and fruity flavor of Pinot Noir complements the delicate flavour of sushi.

6. **Roast chicken paired with Merlot**: The smooth and fruity flavour of Merlot balances the savoury and juicy flavour of roast chicken.

7. **Creamy cheese paired with Sauvignon Blanc**: The crisp and acidic flavour of Sauvignon Blanc cuts through the creaminess of cheese, creating a perfect harmony of flavours.

8. **Chocolate paired with Port**: The rich and sweet flavour of Port complements the decadent flavour of chocolate.

9. **Duck paired with Syrah**: The deep and rich flavour of Syrah complements the bold and gamey flavour of duck.

10. **Barbecue ribs paired with Zinfandel**: The bold and fruity flavour of Zinfandel balances the smoky and saucy flavour of barbecue ribs.

Overall, the Newport Mansions Wine and Food Festival is a celebration of wine and food culture that offers a unique opportunity to indulge in the finest wines and foods from around the world. Visitors can experience various vinification techniques and learn about food and wine pairing, making this event a must-visit for gastronomes and oenophiles alike.

- **Gourmet Food and Wine Expo - Toronto, Canada**

The Gourmet Food and Wine Expo is an annual event in Toronto, Canada that celebrates the country's rich culinary and wine culture. This expo is held every year in November and attracts people from all over the world who come to experience the unique flavours and exquisite taste of the food and wine available at this event.

The Canadian people are known for their love of good food and wine, and this expo is a perfect reflection of that. The event is a celebration of Canada's diverse cultures, and visitors can experience the many different tastes and aromas that define this nation's culinary offerings.

The venue for the expo is situated in the heart of downtown Toronto, a vibrant and diverse city with an array of cultural experiences and landmarks to discover. The expo offers visitors an opportunity to sample some of the finest foods and wines from local and international producers, while also exploring the city's stunning topography.

The wine selection at the expo ranges from traditional, old-world winemaking techniques to modern, cutting-edge approaches. Visitors can choose from an array of wines, including Syrah, Merlot, Chardonnay, Cabernet Sauvignon, Pinot Noir, Champagne, and many others. The vinification techniques used are also varied, ranging from barrel-ageing to fermentation in amphorae, and visitors can taste the difference in each wine.

The foods available at the festival are equally diverse and cater to a wide range of dietary preferences. The festival offers a selection of cheeses, cured meats, seafood, and desserts that all pair perfectly with the wines on offer. Here are ten examples of food and wine pairings that are particularly delightful:

1. Crab cakes served with a crisp and refreshing Sauvignon Blanc.

2. Aged cheddar cheese and a bold and robust Cabernet Sauvignon

3. Grilled lamb chops with a smooth and velvety Merlot

4. Smoked salmon served with a light and refreshing Pinot Grigio

5. Rich and decadent chocolate truffles paired with a full-bodied Cabernet Franc

6. Linguine with clams and a buttery Chardonnay.

7. Veal scaloppini with a spicy and bright Zinfandel

8. Prosciutto with a bright and zesty Riesling

9. Blue cheese with a silky and flavorful Syrah

10. Poached pears with a crisp and refreshing sparkling wine.

In conclusion, the Gourmet Food and Wine Expo in Toronto is a must attend event for food and wine lovers from around the world. The event is a perfect reflection of Canada's rich cultural diversity and the deep love of food and wine that its people possess. The festival is a celebration of the craft and skill of winemakers and chefs, and visitors are sure to leave with unforgettable memories and a new appreciation for the culinary and wine delights of Canada.

- **Okanagan Wine Festivals** - Okanagan Valley, British Columbia, Canada

The Okanagan Wine Festivals is an event that takes place in the Okanagan Valley region of British Columbia, Canada. This region is known for its picturesque landscape, characterised by rolling hills, pristine lakes, and fertile vineyards. The Okanagan Wine Festivals take place twice a year, in the fall and spring, and attract wine enthusiasts from all over the world.

The festival is a celebration of the local wine culture, and it is an opportunity for people to sample some of the best wines that the Okanagan Valley has to offer. The event features wine tastings, seminars, food events, and other activities that celebrate the rich wine culture of the region.

The Okanagan Wine Festivals are a cultural experience, showcasing the unique pairing of food and wine that is popular in the region. The local cuisine is heavily influenced by the agricultural industry, which includes fruits, vegetables, livestock, and of course, grapes. The food available at the festival ranges from locally sourced gourmet dishes to traditional favourites like barbecue and pizza.

Some of the top wineries that participate in the festival include Mission Hill Family Estate Winery, Quails' Gate Winery, Summerhill Pyramid Winery, and Burrowing Owl Estate Winery. These wineries are known for their unique vinification techniques, which highlight the unique terroir of the Okanagan Valley.

At the festival, visitors can expect to enjoy a wide range of wines, including chardonnay, riesling, cabernet sauvignon, merlot, and pinot noir. Many of these wines are aged in oak barrels, which adds a distinctive flavour and aroma to the wine.

When it comes to pairing wine with food, the Okanagan Wine Festivals are a great opportunity to explore the unique flavour combinations that are popular in the region. Some of the top pairings include:

1. Grilled Loin Lamb with Syrah

2. Smoked Salmon with Pinot Grigio

3. Grilled Peaches with Gewürztraminer

4. BBQ Pork Ribs with Zinfandel

5. Roasted Duck with Pinot Noir

6. Creamy Brie with Chardonnay

7. Spicy Beef Tacos with Merlot

8. Grilled Halibut with Sauvignon Blanc

9. Charcuterie Board with Cabernet Sauvignon

10. Green Salad with Rosé

In summary, the Okanagan Wine Festivals are an opportunity for visitors to immerse themselves in the rich wine culture of the Okanagan Valley. From the beautiful landscape to the unique vinification techniques, this region has a lot to offer wine enthusiasts. Additionally, the food available at the festival showcases the unique flavours and ingredients that make the local cuisine so special. With a wide range of wines available, visitors are sure to find the perfect pairing for their favourite dish.

- **Niagara Wine Festival - Niagara, Ontario, Canada**

The Niagara Wine Festival is a popular event that takes place annually in the Niagara region of Ontario, Canada. This region boasts one of Canada's top wine producing areas, and attracts visitors from all over the world with a keen interest in food and wine.

The festival is held in September and October each year, and is a celebration of the region's rich wine culture, featuring numerous events and activities that are open to the general public.

The festival is an occasion for both locals and foreigners to celebrate the richness of the region's culture, learn about food and wines available in the region. It features a range of events, including wine tastings, vineyard tours, workshops and seminars offering insights into vinification techniques.

The Niagara region is known for producing some of the finest wines in the world, including a broad range of wines such as Shiraz, Chardonnay, Pinot Noir, Cabernet Sauvignon and Merlot. The wines are known for their deep and complex flavours that come from years of harvests and the unique climate of the region.

Some of the wines available at the festival include Riesling, Chardonnay, Cabernet Franc, Icewine, and Sauvignon Blanc, among other varieties. Visitors can learn about the techniques used to produce these wines, and can also taste them at various food and wine pairing sessions.

The festival also presents an opportunity to pair various wines with mouthwatering foods. For example, Icewine is served with blue cheese, a combination that is best experienced by allowing a small piece of the cheese to melt in the mouth then followed by a sip of Icewine. Another perfect pairing at the Niagara Wine Festival is Cabernet Sauvignon and steak. The bold red wine complements the juicy steak, with each taste serving to bring out the other's unique flavours.

Other excellent pairing ideas include Pinot Noir with salmon or duck, Riesling and spicy cuisine, Chardonnay with creamy pasta, Sauvignon Blanc and green salads, and sparkling wine with sushi, among others.

In conclusion, the Niagara Wine Festival is an excellent event to learn about the rich viniculture culture of Ontario, Canada. With its mouth watering wines, delicious foods and unique natural topography, visitors are sure to have a memorable experience.

Please note that this is not an exhaustive list and there are many other food and wine festivals and events celebrated throughout North America.

Phileas Fogg's Journey Through North America

Phileas Fogg's famous journey, as depicted in Jules Verne's novel "Around the World in Eighty Days," did not include North America. Instead, his journey took him through Europe, Asia, and North Africa. However, I can still provide some information on the flora, fauna, and topography that he might have encounter in North America.

North America is a vast continent, spanning from the Arctic Circle to the tropics, and from the Atlantic to the Pacific. Some of the countries that Phileas Fogg might have visited in North America include Canada, the United States, Mexico, and the Caribbean.

If Phileas Fogg had visited Canada, he might have encountered animals like grizzly bears, moose, caribou, and whales. Canada is also home to diverse plant life, including deciduous and coniferous trees, wildflowers, and berries. Canada's topography includes the Rocky Mountains, boreal forests, and the Canadian Shield.

In the United States, Phileas Fogg might have explored the Grand Canyon, Yellowstone National Park, or the Great Lakes. He could have encountered bison, bears, wolves, and coyotes in the wilderness. The US also has a variety of plant life, from the southern magnolia to the Douglas fir.

Mexico is home to deserts, beaches, and rainforests. Fogg might have encountered jaguars, monkeys, or dolphins if he ventured into the rainforests or seas. Mexican wildlife also includes snakes, iguanas, and a variety of bird species. And, of course, he might have sampled some of Mexico's famous cuisine, like tacos, mole, and guacamole.

Finally, the Caribbean is a diverse region with a range of island nations. Phileas Fogg might have seen tropical birds like parrots or macaws, sea turtles, and even the occasional iguana. The Caribbean is home to lush plant life such as palm trees, hibiscus, and bougainvillaea.

Overall, North America has a wide range of flora, fauna, and topography that Phileas Fogg would have found captivating.

CHAPTER 15

FESTIVALS IN SOUTH AMERICA

Here are some festivals and events celebrated in South America that are known for their food and wine:

Sure, here are two food and wine festivals or events from 12 South American countries:

- **Feria Masticar, Argentina**

Feria Masticar is a food festival held annually in Buenos Aires, the capital city of Argentina. The event brings together some of the country's best chefs, winemakers, and food producers to showcase the diverse and rich culinary culture of Argentina.

The festival is held over four days in September and attracts thousands of visitors from all over the country and abroad. Argentina has a strong food culture, and Feria Masticar is an occasion to showcase its culinary heritage, as well as a platform for local producers and chefs to showcase their talent.

The topography of Argentina is diverse, from the Andes mountains to the fertile Pampas. This diversity is reflected in the food and wines available at Feria Masticar. Argentina is famous for its wines, particularly its Malbecs, which are produced mainly in the Mendoza region of the country. The country has also gained a reputation for producing high-quality olive oil, cheese, meats, and seafood.

At Feria Masticar, visitors can sample a wide range of Argentine dishes, from traditional empanadas (pastry turnovers filled with meat or vegetables) to the acclaimed Argentine barbecue, called asado. The festival also offers a great opportunity to try different wines and learn about the different vinification techniques used in Argentina.

Some of the foods and wines that visitors can expect to find at Feria Masticar include:

1. **Asado** – Argentine barbecue, cooked over an open flame

2. **Empanadas** – pastry turnovers filled with meat or vegetables

3. **Choripán** – a traditional sandwich made with chorizo sausage and bread

4. **Milanesa** – breaded and fried meat, usually beef or chicken

5. **Provoleta** – grilled provolone cheese

6. **Dulce de leche** – a sweet milk-based caramel spread

7. **Chimichurri** – a sauce made with garlic, parsley, vinegar, and oil, used as a marinade or condiment

8. **Malbec** – the flagship wine of Argentina, often characterised by bold fruit flavours and a smooth finish

9. **Torrontés** – a white wine with floral and citrus flavours, often paired with seafood and spicy dishes

10. **Cabernet Franc** – a red wine that pairs well with steak and other grilled meats

Some of the food and wine pairings that visitors can try at Feria Masticar include:

1. Empanadas and Torrontés wine

2. Milanesa and Malbec wine

3. Asado and Cabernet Franc wine

4. Provoleta and Malbec wine

5. Choripán and Torrontés wine

6. Grilled fish and Sauvignon Blanc wine

7. Dulce de leche and Tannat wine

8. Grilled vegetables and Chardonnay wine

9. Steak and Cabernet Sauvignon wine

10. Spicy dishes and Torrontés wine

- **Fiesta Nacional del Vino, Argentina**

The Fiesta Nacional del Vino or National Wine Festival is an annual event celebrated in Argentina. It takes place in the city of Mendoza, which is located in the Cuyo region, known for its rich winemaking history and culture. The event is hosted by the National Grape Harvest Commission and is a significant celebration of local wines and vineyards.

The festival takes place during the first week of March and involves a range of cultural activities, such as church services, parades, fairs, performances, and exhibitions. The highlight of the event is the "Vendimia" or grape harvesting ceremony, which involves the election of the Harvest Queen, who presides over the festivities.

The topography of the Cuyo region is mountainous and arid, with a unique soil composition that is ideal for cultivating grapes. The region is famous for its Malbec, Cabernet Sauvignon, and Torrontés wines, which are crafted using traditional vinification techniques that have been passed down through generations of winemakers.

In addition to wine, the festival showcases a range of local foods such as empanadas, grilled meats, cheese, olives, and desserts like dulce de leche. Pairing food with wine is an art, and here are some pairings of foods and wines that exemplify the traditional Argentine cuisine:

1. **Empanadas and Malbec** - Malbec's soft tannins and berry aroma make it a perfect match for the savoury pastry of empanadas.

2. **Asado (grilled meats) and Cabernet Sauvignon** - The fatty richness of asado calls for a bold red wine like Cabernet Sauvignon, which cuts through the meat's flavours.

3. **Locro (a hearty stew), and Bonarda** - Bonarda pairs well with this robust and flavorful stew, as it complements its smoky and fruity notes.

4. **Provoleta (grilled cheese) and Torrontés** - The refreshing acidity of Torrontés balances out the rich, melted cheese of the grilled provoleta.

5. **Grilled vegetables and Pinot Noir** - The earthy and light-bodied notes of Pinot Noir enhance the natural flavours of grilled veggies.

6. **Chimichurri and Malbec** - The tangy, spicy, and smoky flavours of chimichurri are well complemented by the boldness of a Malbec.

7. **Dulce de Leche and Pedro Ximenez** - Pedro Ximenez sweet notes complement the caramel flavor of dulce de leche.

8. **Fugazza (onion pizza) and Cabernet Franc** - The savoury and sweet notes of the fugazza benefit from the dark fruit flavours of Cabernet Franc.

9. **Salad and Torrontés** - Torrontés' citrus notes complement a refreshing salad and let the flavours of the greens and dressing shine.

10. **Oysters and champagne** - The fruity and crisp flavours of champagne go particularly well with fresh oysters, a classic pairing.

Overall, the Fiesta Nacional del Vino is an excellent opportunity for wine lovers and culture enthusiasts to have a taste of Argentina's rich gastronomy and winemaking traditions.

- **Gran Festival Gastronómico, Bolivia**

The Gran Festival Gastronómico is a highly anticipated annual event in the country of Bolivia, located in the region of La Paz. This event is held in the city of La Paz, and celebrates the rich culture and culinary traditions of the country.

The festival typically takes place in August and showcases not only traditional Bolivian cuisine, but also some of the international fusion dishes that have become popular in the region. Visitors from around the world attend the festival to sample the delicious foods and wines, and to experience the vibrant music and dance performances that take place throughout the event.

The culture of Bolivia is deeply rooted in indigenous traditions, and this is reflected in the foods and wines that are featured at the festival. One of the most popular wine regions in Bolivia is the Tarija Valley, which is known for its high-altitude vineyards and unique vinification techniques.

Some of the traditional foods that are paired with Tarija Valley wines at the Gran Festival Gastronómico include:

1. Churrasco (grilled sirloin steak) with a Malbec or Cabernet Sauvignon

2. Salteñas (empanadas filled with beef or chicken) with a Torrontés or Chardonnay

3. Silpancho (breaded beef cutlets served over rice) with a Tannat or Syrah

4. Api (corn-based hot beverage) with a Moscato or Riesling

5. Pacumutu (bananas baked in their peel) with a Tannat or Merlot

6. Fanesca (a hearty soup made with beans, grains, and vegetables) with a Pinot Noir or Malbec

7. Cuñapés (cheese-based bread rolls) with a Sauvignon Blanc or Chardonnay

8. Picana (beef stew with vegetables and corn) with a Cabernet Franc or Bonarda

9. Majadito (rice cooked with beef, tomatoes, and onions) with a Tannat or Cabernet Sauvignon

10. Humintas (corn dough tamales) with a Torrontés or Merlot

The rugged topography of Bolivia's mountainous regions plays a vital role in the cultivation of grapes and the production of high-quality wines. Vinification techniques in Bolivia are often influenced by traditional methods used by indigenous populations, such as using clay pots for fermentation.

Overall, the Gran Festival Gastronómico is a fantastic celebration of Bolivian culture and the delicious culinary delights, wines, and vinification techniques that are unique to the region.

- **Festival del Vino Tarijeño, Bolivia**

The Festival del Vino Tarijeño is an annual cultural event that celebrates the rich wine-making history of Tarija, Bolivia. Tarija is a city and region located in the southern part of Bolivia, known for its beautiful landscapes and fertile soils. The event is typically held in the month of April, and attracts locals as well as tourists from all over the world.

The festival is a celebration of the local culture and traditions, as well as a showcase of the region's finest wines and vineyards. The event is attended by local producers and winemakers, who showcase their products and share their knowledge of the vinification techniques used in the region.

The topography of Tarija is ideal for wine production, with its high altitude, mild climate, and fertile soils. The region is known for its unique grape varieties, including the Tannat, Cabernet Sauvignon, and Syrah. The winemakers in the region use traditional techniques to produce their wines, which include hand-picking the grapes, using wooden barrels for aging, and minimal use of chemicals.

In addition to the wines, the festival also features a variety of local foods that are expertly paired with the wines. These include dishes such as grilled meat, cheese, and empanadas. Some of the top pairings of foods and wines at the Festival del Vino Tarijeño include:

1. **Grilled beef with a Tannat wine**: The bold and full-bodied flavor of the Tannat complements the rich and savory taste of the grilled beef.

2. **Cheese and Cabernet Sauvignon**: The tannins in the Cabernet Sauvignon pair well with the creamy and salty flavor of the cheese.

3. **Empanadas and Torrontes**: The light and crisp flavour of the Torrontes balances the savoury taste of the empanadas.

4. **Grilled lamb with a Syrah wine**: The smoky and gamey flavour of the grilled lamb is enhanced by the spicy and fruity notes of the Syrah.

5. **Grilled vegetables with a Malbec wine**: The medium-bodied and fruity flavor of the Malbec complements the fresh and earthy taste of grilled vegetables.

6. **Pork with a Cabernet Franc wine**: The herbaceous and spicy flavour of the Cabernet Franc pairs well with the sweet and savoury taste of pork.

7. **Shrimp and Sauvignon Blanc**: The citrus and herbaceous characteristics of the Sauvignon Blanc pair well with the light and delicate flavor of shrimp.

8. **Pizza and Merlot**: The mild and fruity flavour of the Merlot balances the rich and savoury taste of pizza.

9. **Chocolate and Tannat**: The bold and intense flavor of the Tannat complements the rich and sweet taste of chocolate.

10. **Spicy chicken with a Torrontes wine**: The light and acidic flavour of the Torrontes balances the spicy and savoury taste of the chicken.

In summary, the Festival del Vino Tarijeño is a celebration of the rich culture, history, and traditions of Tarija, Bolivia. It is a perfect opportunity to try some of the region's finest wines and foods, as well as learn about the extensive knowledge and expertise of local winemakers.

- **Festival de Inverno de Bonito, Brazil**

The Festival de Inverno de Bonito is a cultural event that takes place in the city of Bonito, located in the Mato Grosso do Sul region of Brazil. The festival occurs every year during the winter months, usually in the month of July, and celebrates the rich cultural heritage and natural beauty of the region.

The festival is an important cultural occasion for the people of Bonito, as it showcases a variety of art forms such as music, dance, theatre, and visual arts. Local and international artists participate in the festival and perform throughout the city's streets and public spaces.

Bonito's unique topography, consisting of natural springs, rivers, and sinkholes, provides perfect conditions for growing grapes and producing wine. The region is known for its exceptional vinification techniques, which have produced some of the finest wines in Brazil.

In addition to wines, the festival also celebrates the rich culinary traditions of Bonito and the surrounding regions. Local chefs prepare a variety of dishes using locally sourced ingredients like fish, meats, tropical fruits, and vegetables.

Here are 10 outstanding pairings of foods and wines to look forward to during the Festival de Inverno de Bonito:

1. **Feijoada (Brazilian bean stew) and Cabernet Sauvignon**: The full-bodied and tannic Cabernet Sauvignon is a perfect pairing for the hearty and flavorful feijoada.

2. **Picanha (Brazilian steak) and Malbec**: The bold and fruity Malbec is a great match for the rich and savoury picanha.

3. **Pacu fish and Chardonnay**: The buttery and oaky Chardonnay complements the delicate and subtle flavours of pacu fish.

4. **Coxinha (Brazilian chicken croquette) and sparkling wine**: The light and effervescent bubbles of sparkling wine cut through the richness of the fried coxinha.

5. **Moqueca (Brazilian fish stew) and Sauvignon Blanc**: The zesty and crisp Sauvignon Blanc complements the tangy and savoury flavours of moqueca.

6. **Acarajé (Brazilian black-eyed pea fritters) and Rosé:** The light and fruity Rosé balances the spiciness of the acarajé.

7. **Bolo de rolo (Brazilian rolled cake) and Moscato**: The sweet and fizzy Moscato pairs well with the delicate and fluffy layers of the bolo de rolo.

8. Carne de sol (Brazilian sun-dried beef) and Zinfandel: The jammy and spicy Zinfandel brings out the bold flavours of the carne de sol.

9. Brigadeiro (Brazilian chocolate truffle) and Pinot Noir: The silky and fruity Pinot Noir enhances the creamy and chocolatey flavours of the brigadeiro.

10. Queijo coalho (Brazilian grilled cheese) and Merlot: The soft and smooth Merlot is a great match for the smoky and salty queijo coalho.

Overall, the Festival de Inverno de Bonito offers a unique cultural experience that celebrates the natural beauty, cultural heritage, and culinary traditions of Brazil's Mato Grosso do Sul region. The event is a must-visit for anyone interested in exploring the vibrant art, music, food, and wine scene of Brazil.

- **Festival Vinum Brasilis, Brazil**

Festival Vinum Brasilis is a wine festival that celebrates Brazilian wine culture, and it takes place in the city of Bento Gonçalves, which is in the Rio Grande do Sul region of Brazil. The event attracts wine enthusiasts from all over the world and is a fantastic opportunity for visitors to experience the flavours and culture of Brazil.

The festival typically takes place in October, and it is a celebration of the many outstanding wine producers from the region. Guests can sample a variety of wines made from indigenous Brazilian grapes such as the Tannat, Teroldego, Ancellota, and Malbec among others, and learn about the unique vinification techniques used to make them.

The food and wine pairings in the Festival Vinum Brasilis are one of the highlights of the event. Here are ten pairings to give you an idea of what to expect:

1. Tannat wine from the Fausto António wines paired with grilled beef sirloin with chimichurri sauce.

2. Almau Reserve wine from Almau Vinhos Finos paired with Pato assado com laranjas (roasted duck with oranges).

3. Víncia 100% Sauvignon Blanc from Vinhos Víncia paired with seafood ceviche.

4. Aracuri wines' Rosé wine paired with grilled shrimp.

5. Gazzaro Blush from Vinícola Gazzaro paired with Salada Caprese (tomato, mozzarella, and basil salad).

6. Marcus James Sparkling Wine from the Cooperativa Vinicola Aurora paired with sushi.

7. Wine from Casa Venturini paired with fish stew.

8. Enos Vinhos de Boutique Tannat Reserve paired with Brazilian Coxinha (chicken turnovers).

9. Suarez and Associates Reserve Tannat paired with Brazilian Feijoada (black bean stew with pork and beef).

10. Stout beer from Cervejaria Blauer Berg paired with chocolate cake.

The occasion is a celebration of Brazil's culture, music, and cuisine are also part of the festival. Visitors can enjoy traditional Brazilian dances, music performances, and food demonstrations, making the event a unique cultural experience.

In conclusion, the Festival Vinum Brasilis is an incredible event that brings together Brazilian wine producers from different regions and showcases the unique flavours and culture of Brazil. The event is a fantastic opportunity for wine enthusiasts to taste and learn more about Brazilian wines and food pairings.

- **Fiestas Patrias, Chile**

Fiestas Patrias is a celebrated national holiday in Chile, which marks Chile's independence movement in the 1800s from Spain. The holiday is celebrated throughout the country; however, it is most popularly celebrated in the capital city of Santiago. The primary event is held on the 18th of September, which is considered the country's Independence Day, and the holiday usually runs for a week.

Fiestas Patrias is a significant event in Chilean culture, and the occasion is observed with great enthusiasm by the people. The Chilean people typically partake in parades, dancing, music, and gaming activities. The celebration also gives people the opportunity to reconnect with their roots and heritage. Besides, the occasion provides an opportunity for the Chilean people to explore the country's topography, vineyards, foods, and wines.

Chile is famous globally for its topography, which ranges from the Andes mountains to the Pacific coastline. This topography facilitates the cultivation of different grape varieties, which produce various types of wines. Chile's wine regions are located near the Andes mountains, near the coast, and the central valley.

The wines that are commonly available during Fiestas Patrias include Sauvignon Blanc, Chardonnay, Cabernet Sauvignon, Carmenere, and Syrah, among others. These wines are produced using different vinification techniques, depending on the grape variety, location, and soil type.

Chilean food culture is known for its rich flavour and variety, which reflects the country's history and culture. The foods that pair well with Chilean wines during Fiestas Patrias include empanadas, choripán, asado, pebre, humitas, pastel de choclo, cazuela, chicha, mote con huesillo, and sopaipillas, among others.

Empanadas are a popular street food that is available in most Chilean cities, and they are usually stuffed with meat, cheese, or vegetables. These pair well with a glass of Carmenere or Syrah.

Choripán is another popular street food that is made by grilling a chorizo sausage, placing it in a sandwich, and pairing it with Chimichurri sauce. Choripán pairs well with a glass of Cabernet Sauvignon.

Asado is a Chilean BBQ, which usually includes beef, chicken, and pork. This dish pairs extremely well with a glass of Chilean Cabernet Sauvignon.

Pebre is a popular condiment or dip that is made from tomatoes, onion, and cilantro. This dish pairs exceptionally well with a glass of Chilean Sauvignon Blanc.

Humitas are sweet or savoury tamales that are filled with meat, cheese, or vegetables. These pair particularly well with a glass of Chardonnay or Sauvignon Blanc.

Pastel de Choclo is a popular casserole dish made from corn, meat, vegetables, and cheese. This dish pairs exceptionally well with a glass of Chilean Carmenere.

Cazuela is a cooked stew that is usually made with beef, chicken, or pork, sometimes it is combined with rice, potatoes, and vegetables. This dish is particularly well paired with a glass of Chilean Syrah.

Chicha is a traditional fermented drink that is made from maize. This drink pairs particularly well with a glass of Chilean Cabernet Sauvignon.

Mote con huesillo is a popular drink which is made from dried peaches, sugar and mote, a dried, puffed corn. This drink pairs particularly well with a glass of Chilean Sauvignon Blanc.

Sopaipillas are a type of Chilean bread made from pumpkin, flour, and other ingredients. These pair particularly well with a glass of Chilean Chardonnay.

In conclusion, Fiestas Patrias is an event that showcases the Chilean people's culture, heritage, and traditions. Chile's topography, vineyards, foods, and wines give visitors an opportunity to indulge in unique experiences. During the event, the various wines and dishes offered can be paired in many ways, which offers a variety of taste experiences for tourists and locals alike.

- **Feria Internacional del Vino, Chile**

The Feria Internacional del Vino (FIV) is an annual wine fair held in Chile, South America. This event is a prestigious wine exhibition and trade fair that attracts wine experts all over the world. It is held in the city of Santiago, Chile's capital, and many visitors come every year to explore new wines and learn about different winemaking techniques.

The event lasts for three days and takes place towards the end of September each year. It is a great opportunity for visitors to taste different wines from different wineries and also to learn about the Chilean culture and tradition related to wine-making. Chile has a rich wine culture that goes back centuries, and visitors can explore the region's topography and watch the vineyards that dot the landscape.

Chile is internationally known for producing high-quality red, white, and rosé wines, which are made with the help of modern vinification techniques. The region's soil is diverse, and this is reflected in the different wine styles produced. Some of the popular varieties include Cabernet Sauvignon, Carmenere, and Sauvignon Blanc, with many other new varieties gaining popularity in recent years.

In addition to wine tasting, visitors can also indulge in different types of food that are paired with the wines available at the event. The country's cuisine is known for its diversity and unique blends of flavours.

Here are some examples of food and wine pairings available at the Feria Internacional del Vino:

1. Slow-cooked lamb with roasted root vegetables paired with Concha y Toro Don Melchor Cabernet Sauvignon.

2. Grilled shrimp skewers with garlic butter and herbs paired with Errazuriz Estate Sauvignon Blanc.

3. Chilean seafood stew with mussels, clams, and shrimp paired with Casa Silva Carmenere.

4. Pan-seared scallops with sweet potato mash paired with Vina Montes Alpha Chardonnay.

5. Smoked salmon with creamy dill sauce paired with Santa Ema Sauvignon Blanc.

6. Beef empanadas paired with Valdivieso Single Vineyard Cabernet Sauvignon.

7. Chilean-style pork ribs with roasted potatoes paired with Cousino-Macul Isadora.

8. Mushroom risotto paired with Veramonte Ritual Pinot Noir.

9. Chilean sea bass with roasted tomatoes and garlic paired with Lapostolle Clos Apalta.

10. Dark chocolate truffles with dried fruit paired with Luis Felipe Edwards Gran Reserva Cabernet Sauvignon.

In summary, the Feria Internacional del Vino in Chile is a fantastic event for wine enthusiasts and food lovers. Its unique culture, topography, vineyards, wines, food, soil, and vinification techniques attract thousands of visitors every year. Wineries display wines from different regions of Chile, and food vendors offer unique food pairings that complement the wines perfectly.

- **Taste of Bogotá, Colombia**

Taste of Bogotá is an annual food and wine festival that takes place in Bogotá, Colombia. This festival is a celebration of Colombia's culinary culture, and it highlights the country's delicious wines and food.

Bogotá is the capital city of Colombia and it's also one of the biggest cities in South America. The people of Bogotá are known for their warmth and hospitality, and they are passionate about their food and wine. The event is normally held in September over a weekend.

Colombia is a country with a rich cultural heritage, and that is reflected in its cuisine. The country's topography is diverse, and it includes mountains, forests, and coastal regions. This diversity is reflected in the wines and food available at the Taste of Bogotá festival. The vineyards are situated mainly in the mountainous regions and the wine produced are well-balanced with good acidity.

The wines available at Taste of Bogotá are made using a variety of vinification techniques. These techniques are designed to bring out the flavours and aromas of the grapes, and they play a crucial role in the quality of the wine produced. Colombian wines are known for their fruity notes, bright acidity and fresh flavours.

The soil in Colombia is rich and fertile, which allows the country to produce a wide variety of fruits and vegetables. This diversity is reflected in the food available at Taste of Bogotá. The Colombian cuisine is a blend of indigenous, African and Spanish culinary cultures.

Food is an essential part of Colombian culture, and there are many occasions throughout the year when people come together to celebrate and share food. **The Taste of Bogotá** festival is one such occasion, where locals and tourists gather to enjoy the best of Colombian wine and food.

Here are some examples of food and wine pairings you can expect to find at Taste of Bogotá:

1) Chicha-made from fermented corn, this drink pairs well with arepas and white cheese.

2) Chardonnay- a well balanced Chardonnay pairs perfectly with seafood paella

3) Chenin Blanc- this light, elegant wine pairs well with a seafood salad

4) Malbec – a fruity Malbec pairs well with beef empanadas

5) Cabernet Sauvignon- This bold wine is a great match for grilled lamb chops with chimichurri sauce

6) Pinot Noir- This wine pairs well with roasted beet salad, goat cheese and walnuts

7) Sauvignon Blanc- pairs excellently with ceviche

8) Tempranillo- This Spanish grape variety pairs perfectly with meat dishes like chicharrones and grilled pork

9) Rose- Rose pairs well with salmon sashimi

10) Shiraz- pairs well with spicy meat dishes like chorizo sausage.

Overall, the Taste of Bogotá is an amazing opportunity to explore the vibrant culture of Bogotá, Colombia, and to experience its rich culinary traditions. It's a celebration of the people, the wine, and the delicious food that makes Colombia such a special place.

- **Festival del Vino de La Candelaria, Colombia**

The Festival del Vino de La Candelaria is an exciting annual event that takes place in the city of Popayan, which is located in the southwestern region of Colombia. Hosted in the last week of February, the festival serves as an occasion to celebrate the region's wine culture.

The population of the city of Popayan is around 260,000 people, and the festival attracts locals and tourists alike. The festival is a reflection of the diverse and rich cultural heritage of the region and is a must-visit for wine enthusiasts.

The festival offers visitors an opportunity to taste some of the finest wines produced in the region. The topography of the region is unique and has a significant impact on the quality of the wines produced. The vineyards are located at an altitude of around 2000 metres, and the soil is a mix of volcanic ash and alluvial deposits. As a result, the wines produced in the region are known for their distinct flavour and aroma.

The vinification techniques used in the region are traditional and have been perfected over the centuries. The wines produced in the region are primarily red wines, such as Cabernet Sauvignon, Merlot, and Syrah.

The festival also offers visitors an opportunity to taste the local cuisine, which is known for its distinctive flavours and use of fresh ingredients. Some of the popular local dishes served at the festival include Empanadas de Pipian (empanadas stuffed with peanut sauce), Tamales Tolimenses (steamed corn dough filled with meat, vegetables, and spices), and Sancocho de Gallina (a chicken soup with yucca, plantains, and corn).

There are several wine and food pairing options available at the festival, and visitors can choose to pair their wines with a variety of dishes. Here are some examples of foods and wines paired in greater detail:

1. Pollo asado (grilled chicken) paired with a freshly produced Syrah wine, which has a blend of black fruit and spicy notes.

2. Beef carpaccio paired with a Cabernet Sauvignon, which has a complex structure with a long-lasting finish.

3. Ceviche paired with a dry rose wine, which has a crisp acidity and cherry flavours.

4. Grilled octopus paired with a Merlot wine, which has medium tannins and a balance of fruit flavours.

5. Cheese platter paired with an aged red wine, which has notes of tobacco and leather.

6. Pork ribs paired with a blend of Cabernet Franc and Cabernet Sauvignon, which has a fruity aroma and firm tannins.

7. Chickpea and spinach stew paired with a Grenache wine, which has a smooth and velvety texture.

8. Grilled shrimp paired with a Chardonnay wine, which has a balanced acidity and fruity notes.

9. Assorted seafood platter paired with a sparkling wine, which has a refreshing acidity and citrus flavours.

10. Chocolate dessert paired with a sweet red wine or late harvest white wine, which has a hint of honey and floral aromas.

Overall, the Festival del Vino de La Candelaria is a unique event that offers visitors a chance to experience the rich cultural heritage of the region through its wine and food. The festival is also a platform for local wine producers to showcase their products and promote their vineyards, contributing to the region's economy by attracting tourism.

- **Expoferia Gastronómica, Ecuador**

Expoferia Gastronómica is a gastronomic fair that takes place in Quito, Ecuador. Quito is the capital city of Ecuador, located in the Andes Mountains. The event attracts thousands of visitors every year and is a unique opportunity to taste traditional Ecuadorian food and drink.

The people of Ecuador are known for their warm hospitality and love of good food. This event celebrates that culture and helps to promote local producers of food and drink. The event takes place annually, typically in either August or September, and is a great occasion to try some of the best food and drink that Ecuador has to offer.

The topography of Ecuador is diverse, with high mountains, lush rainforests, and fertile agricultural lands. The vineyards of Ecuador are mainly located in the valleys of the Andes Mountains, where the soil is rich and fertile, and the climate is perfect for growing grapes.

Ecuador produces a variety of different wines, including red, white, and rose. The most popular grape varieties grown in Ecuador include Cabernet Sauvignon, Merlot, Chardonnay, and Sauvignon Blanc. Vinification techniques used in Ecuadorian winemaking vary from traditional to modern, depending on the producer.

At the Expoferia Gastronómica, visitors can taste a variety of traditional Ecuadorian dishes, using fresh and locally sourced ingredients. Some of the most popular dishes include ceviche, which is a seafood dish made with fish, lime juice, and spices, and empanadas, which are fried pastries filled with meat, cheese, or vegetables.

Some examples of foods and wines that are paired at the Expoferia Gastronómica:

1. Ceviche paired with a crisp Sauvignon Blanc

2. Grilled steak paired with a bold Cabernet Sauvignon

3. Fried plantains paired with a buttery Chardonnay

4. Shrimp cocktail paired with a light and refreshing Pinot Grigio

5. BBQ ribs paired with a rich and spicy Malbec

6. Vegetable stir-fry paired with a crisp and fruity Rosé

7. Cheese platter paired with a full-bodied Merlot

8. Pork roast paired with a fruity and aromatic Carmenere

9. Chicken fajitas paired with a spicy and robust Shiraz

10. Chocolate cake paired with a smooth and velvety Syrah

Overall, Expoferia Gastronómica is a wonderful event for anyone looking to experience the best food and drink that Ecuador has to offer. The event is a great way to learn more about Ecuadorian culture, and to indulge in some delicious local cuisine.

- **Festival del Chocolate, Ecuador**

The Festival del Chocolate in Ecuador is a highly-awaited event that brings together the country's top chocolatiers who showcase their creations to the public. This festival is celebrated in the city of Quito, the capital of Ecuador, which is known for its rich history and cultural heritage.

The people of Ecuador are deeply connected with their cultural customs, and the festival is an excellent platform for the artists and the public to experience Ecuador's traditional chocolate-making techniques. The event takes place every year in early May, which is considered the best time to highlight the country's agriculture, including cocoa harvesting.

Ecuador is rich in biodiversity and has varied topography, making it suitable for the cultivation of several crops, including vineyards. Ecuadorian wines are produced in different regions of the country, including Azuay, Bolívar, and Cañar. The wines produced here are known for their unique taste and texture, which is attributed to the soil and vinification techniques used by the winemakers.

At the Festival del Chocolate, guests can pair food and wine, making them the ultimate pairings for the event.

Some examples of the perfect pairing:

1. Chocolate truffles paired with a fruity red wine, such as a Pinot Noir or a Merlot.

2. Rich and creamy hot chocolate paired with a full-bodied Malbec or Cabernet Sauvignon.

3. Dark chocolate brownies paired with a sweet and smooth dessert wine, such as a Muscat or a Port.

4. Spicy chocolate bars paired with a bold and structured Syrah or Shiraz.

5. Milk chocolate-covered strawberries paired with a sparkling Rosé or Champagne.

6. Chocolate fondue paired with a light and refreshing white wine, such as a Sauvignon Blanc.

7. Chocolate-covered bacon paired with a robust and smoky red wine, such as a Zinfandel or a Cabernet Franc.

8. Chocolate-dipped pretzels paired with a crisp and floral Riesling.

9. Chocolate-covered almonds paired with a nutty and full-bodied Chardonnay.

10. Chocolate mousse paired with a sweet and complex dessert wine, such as a Sauternes or a Tokaji.

In conclusion, the Festival del Chocolate in Ecuador is a celebration of the country's rich cultural heritage and agricultural diversity. The perfect pairing of food and wine is just one of the many highlights of the event, which attracts both locals and tourists alike.

7. **Guyana**: Taste of Guyana and Christmas Wine Festival

- **Taste of Guyana**

The Taste of Guyana festival is an exciting and unique event that showcases the culture, food, and wines of Guyana, a country located on the northeastern coast of South America. The festival is held annually in Georgetown, the capital city of Guyana, and has become one of the most popular events in the country.

The festival brings together food enthusiasts, wine lovers, and tourists from all over the world to celebrate the rich cultural heritage of the country. The date of the festival varies from year to year, but it is usually held in late September or early October.

Guyana is a diverse country with many different ethnic groups, and the cuisine of the country reflects this diversity. The food at the Taste of Guyana festival is a perfect blend of African, Indian, and Caribbean flavours, and is prepared using fresh local ingredients.

The topography and soil of Guyana are ideal for growing a wide variety of fruits and vegetables, which are often used in local dishes. The vinification techniques are not well-established in Guyana at the moment, and thus the festival relies mainly on the wines imported from other countries.

During the festival, there are numerous food stations and wine tasting booths set up throughout the venue, offering visitors a chance to sample a wide variety of foods and wines. Below are some examples of foods and wines paired that could be available at the event:

1. Pepperpot - a traditional meat-based stew - paired with a bold Shiraz

2. Curry chicken - a popular Indian-inspired dish - paired with a light and citrusy Sauvignon Blanc

3. Roti - a type of flatbread - paired with a fruity and aromatic Gewurztraminer

4. Cassava bread - a unique bread made from cassava - paired with a crisp and refreshing Riesling

5. Coconut rice - a flavorful rice dish made with coconut milk - paired with a full-bodied Chardonnay

6. Fried plantains - a sweet and savoury snack - paired with a spicy Chianti

7. Black cake - a dense and fruity cake made with rum-soaked fruits - paired with a sweet and smooth dessert wine

8. Aloo pie - a savoury pastry filled with potatoes and spices - paired with a light and crisp Pinot Grigio

9. Metemgee - a hearty seafood soup - paired with a dry and acidic Chenin Blanc

10. Pineapple chow - a refreshing snack made with pineapple, spices, and lime juice - paired with a bubbly and sweet Moscato.

In conclusion, the Taste of Guyana festival is a great opportunity to savour the unique flavours of Guyana along with a selection of wines from various regions. The event showcases Guyana's rich cultural heritage, and its people are proud to share their cuisine and wines with the world.

- **Christmas Wine Festival, Guyana**

Christmas Festival in Guyana is a vibrant and joyous occasion that is celebrated across the country with great enthusiasm. The festival takes place on December 25th each year and is a time for families and friends to come together, enjoy delicious food, and partake in festive activities.

The festival is celebrated in many cities in Guyana including Georgetown, Linden, and New Amsterdam. People from all walks of life, including those of African, Indian, and European ancestry, come together to celebrate this occasion.

The festival is a cultural occasion, and the people of Guyana celebrate it with various festive events such as parades, dances, and singing competitions. The topography of Guyana, with its vast rainforests and rolling hills, provides a stunning backdrop to the celebrations.

Although wine is not typically a part of the Christmas Festival in Guyana, the country has a nascent wine industry, with several vineyards producing quality wines. These vineyards use several vinification techniques such as oak ageing, cold stabilisation, and filtration to produce unique and flavorful wines.

The festival is also a time to indulge in delicious food, and there is a wide variety of traditional dishes available to pair with wines. Here are ten examples of foods and wines that can be paired together:

1. **Garlic Pork and Chateau Ste Michelle Chardonnay** - The rich and buttery flavours of Chardonnay offset the salty and garlicky taste of the pork.

2. **Pepperpot and Nine Stones Shiraz** - The fruity and spicy notes of Shiraz complement the richness of Pepperpot, a stew made with beef, pork, and spices.

3. **Black Cake and Warre's Late Bottled Vintage Port** - The dark and fruity flavours of Port perfectly complement the dense and alcoholic taste of Black Cake, a dense fruitcake with multiple layers of rum.

4. **Cookup Rice and Riesling** - The crisp and refreshing taste of Riesling complements the savoury taste of Cook-up Rice, a dish made with rice, peas, and meat.

5. **Garlic Chicken and Giesen Sauvignon Blanc** - The herbaceous notes of Sauvignon Blanc complement the juicy and savoury taste of Garlic Chicken.

6. **Fried Rice and Chateau St. Michelle Riesling** - The clean acidity and fruity taste of Riesling complement the complex flavours of Fried Rice, a classic Chinese takeout dish.

7. **Metemgee and Muscadet** - The light and fresh flavours of Muscadet complement the rich and flavorful taste of Metemgee, a stew made with meat, dumplings, and vegetables.

8. **Chow Mein and Chardonnay** - The buttery and oaky notes of Chardonnay complement the savoury and noodle-y taste of Chow Mein.

9. **Fried Chicken and Pinot Noir** - The light and fruity notes of Pinot Noir complement the crispy and juicy taste of Fried Chicken.

10. **Garlic Shrimp and Sangria** - The fruity and refreshing taste of Sangria complement the zesty and savoury taste of Garlic Shrimp.

In conclusion, the Christmas Festival in Guyana is a time of joy and celebration, where people come together to enjoy delicious food, festive events, and the company of loved ones. Though the wine industry in Guyana is still developing, there are plenty of exciting and flavorful pairing options available to explore during the festival.

- **Festival de la Semilla y la Cosecha, Paraguay**

Festival de la Semilla y la Cosecha, also known as the Seed and Harvest Festival, is an annual event celebrated in Paraguay to showcase the country's agricultural heritage and cultural traditions. The festival takes place in Asunción, the capital city of Paraguay, and it is usually held in the month of September.

The festival is a celebration of the country's rich agricultural heritage and the culture of its people. Paraguay is a landlocked country in South America known for its vast agricultural lands and vineyards. The topography of Paraguay consists mostly of flat plains and rolling hills, which make it an ideal location for growing crops and grapes for making wine.

At the festival, visitors can taste a variety of wines from the region and learn about the vinification techniques used to produce them. Paraguay is known for its unique vinification techniques, which involve using clay pots and natural yeasts to ferment the grapes.

In addition to wine, the festival also offers a variety of traditional foods from the region. The soil in Paraguay is rich and fertile, which contributes to the high quality of the crops and grapes grown in the region. Some of the popular foods available at the festival include empanadas, sopa paraguaya (a type of cornbread), chipa (a type of bread made with cassava flour), and asado (grilled meat).

Let's look at foods and wines paired at the festival:

1. Empanadas paired with a fruity white wine made from the Moscatel grape

2. Chipa paired with a medium-bodied red wine made from the Tannat grape

3. Sopa Paraguaya paired with a light-bodied white wine made from the Chardonnay grape

4. Grilled meat (asado) paired with a robust red wine made from the Malbec grape

5. Mbeju (a type of cassava bread) paired with a dry white wine made from the Sauvignon Blanc grape

6. Bife Koygua (a beef stew) paired with a full-bodied red wine made from the Cabernet Sauvignon grape

7. Pastel Mandi'o (a type of corn and meat dumpling) paired with a light-bodied red wine made from the Barbera grape

8. Carbonada (a beef and vegetable stew) paired with a medium-bodied red wine made from the Syrah grape

9. Milanesa (a breaded and fried meat) paired with a dry white wine made from the Torrontés grape

10. Arroz con leche (a type of rice pudding) paired with a sweet dessert wine made from the Pedro Ximenez grape.

Overall, the Festival de la Semilla y la Cosecha is a wonderful opportunity to experience the culture, food, and wine of Paraguay. With so many delicious pairings available, visitors are sure to find something to satisfy their taste buds.

- **Expo Vinos, Paraguay**

Expo Vinos is one of Paraguay's largest wine festivals, held annually in the capital city of Asunción. This lively event brings together locals and tourists alike to celebrate the country's rich wine culture and sample some of its finest vintages.

The festival typically takes place in August and spans several days, during which attendees can enjoy tastings, live music, seminars, and more. Paraguayan culture is on full display at the event, with vendors selling traditional foods and crafts throughout the festival grounds.

Paraguay's topography is diverse and ranges from grasslands to subtropical forest. The country's wine region is still small and developing but produces some exciting wines. The soil is sandy and contains high amounts of iron, which imparts a distinct flavour in the finished product. The vineyards of Expo Vinos showcase wines made through innovative vinification techniques that have helped in the awareness of its domestic wine industry.

The event features a wide variety of wines, including those made from native grape varieties like Tempranillo, Cabernet Sauvignon, and Bonarda. Food available at Expo Vinos ranges from traditional Paraguayan dishes like asado (grilled meat) to international cuisine. The organisers encourage pairing wines with traditional dishes to experience the best wine and food pairings.

Some examples of foods and wines that can be found at the festival are:

1. Empanadas (beef and cheese turnover) with a glass of Tempranillo from Vinos Espirales.

2. Chipa Guazu (corn and cheese casserole) with a glass of Chardonnay from Bodega Cossio.

3. Milanesa (breaded beef cutlet) with a glass of Cabernet Sauvignon from Bodega Moiras.

4. Asado con mandioca (grilled meat with cassava roots) with a glass of Bonarda from Bodega Yvyra.

5. Sopa paraguaya (cornbread soup) with a glass of Syrah from Viña Dario.

6. Arroz con leche (rice pudding) with a glass of Sauvignon Blanc from Bodega la Soñada.

7. Pira Caldo (fish soup) with a glass of Malbec from Viñedo La Esperanza.

8. Reviro (cornmeal fritters) with a glass of Tannat from Viñedo Pinedo.

9. Bori Bori (chicken soup with corn dumplings) with a glass of Merlot from Bodega 33 sur.

10. Barbecue ribs with a glass of Bonarda from Bodega Peralta.

Expo Vinos is a perfect occasion to enjoy some of Paraguay's finest wines and traditional delicacies. Attendees can delve into exploring Paraguayan culture and learn about its wine industry while savouring great food and music.

9. Perú: Mistura and Fiestas Patrias

- **Mistura, Peru**

Mistura is an annual gastronomy festival that takes place in Lima, Peru. It is one of the largest food festivals in Latin America, and it draws thousands of people from all over the world to experience the country's rich culture and cuisine.

The festival usually takes place in early September, and it lasts for about ten days. The event is held in the coastal city of Lima, which is well-known for its vibrant food scene and its beautiful landmarks.

During the festival, visitors can sample a variety of Peruvian dishes, including ceviche, pisco sours, and grilled meats. Many of these dishes are made with ingredients that can only be found in Peru, such as the ají pepper, which is known for its unique flavour and spiciness.

In addition to the food, Mistura also celebrates the country's topography and vineyards. Peru has a diverse range of climates and soil types, which makes it an ideal place to grow a variety of crops, including grapes for wine production. At the festival, visitors can learn about vinification techniques and taste some of the country's finest wines.

Some of the food and wine pairings that you can expect to find at Mistura include:

1. Ceviche with a crisp, acidic white wine like Sauvignon Blanc

2. Grilled octopus with a dry rosé

3. Lomo saltado (stir-fried beef) with a bold, tannic red like Malbec or Cabernet Sauvignon

4. Arroz con pollo with a light, fruity red wine like Pinot Noir

5. Causa (a potato and seafood dish) with a fresh, zesty Chardonnay

6. Tiradito (a Peruvian sashimi dish) with a mineral-rich Albariño

7. Empanadas with a light, fruity red like Beaujolais

8. Anticuchos (marinated grilled beef heart) with a full-bodied red like Syrah or Carménère

9. Rocoto relleno (stuffed pepper) with a spicy, bold red like Zinfandel

10. Picarones (a type of fried dough) with a sweet, dessert wine like Muscat.

Overall, Mistura is an incredible event that showcases the best of Peru's food, wine, and culture. Whether you're a food lover or simply looking to experience something new and exciting, this festival is not to be missed.

- **Fiestas Patrias, Perú**

Fiestas Patrias is a festival that celebrates the independence of Peru from Spain on July 28th and 29th. This festival is celebrated throughout the country, but the capital city of Lima is the main centre of attraction. This occasion serves as an opportunity for Peruvians to celebrate their unique culture and history with their traditional festivities.

The festival is celebrated with grand parades, concerts, and cultural events, showcasing the diverse traditions and cultures of Peru. People celebrate this festival with great enthusiasm, and it's the perfect time for tourists to experience the beauty of Peruvian culture.

Peru is a country with a diverse topography, from the Andes Mountains to the Amazon rainforest, and this variety is reflected in its food and wine. One of the significant attractions of the Fiestas Patrias is the Peruvian cuisine, which is a delicious fusion of Spanish, African, and indigenous flavours, reflecting the country's history and culture.

Peruvian wine is gaining worldwide recognition for its unique flavours and vinification techniques. The Peruvian vineyards are located in the Ica valley, where the vines grow in fertile soil created from the nearby Andes Mountains, giving the wines a distinct minerality. The vinification techniques in Peru are traditional, with little intervention, creating unique and delicious wine.

During the Fiestas Patrias, visitors can enjoy traditional Peruvian cuisine paired expertly with locally produced wines. Here are ten examples of classic Peruvian dishes and wines that are popular during the festival:

1. Ceviche - a dish of marinated raw fish, paired with a crisp Sauvignon Blanc.

2. Lomo Saltado - beef stir-fry with onions, tomatoes, and french fries, paired with a fruity Cabernet Sauvignon.

3. Aji de Gallina - a chicken dish with a slightly spicy cream sauce, paired with an aromatic Torrontés.

4. Anticuchos - grilled beef heart skewers, paired with a bold Malbec.

5. Papas a la Huancaína - boiled potatoes with a spicy cheese sauce, paired with a crisp Chardonnay.

6. Rocoto Relleno - stuffed hot pepper with seasoned beef and cheese, paired with a medium-bodied Syrah.

7. Pollo a la Brasa - grilled chicken with herbs and spices, paired with a refreshing Pinot Noir.

8. Chupe de Camarones - shrimp soup with potatoes and cheese, paired with a buttery Chardonnay.

9. Escabeche - fried fish with a tangy onion sauce, paired with a fruity Merlot.

10. Arroz con Mariscos - seafood and rice in a delicious broth, paired with a light Albariño.

Overall, the Fiestas Patrias is a great opportunity to discover the unique culture, cuisine, and wine of Peru. Whether you are a foodie or a wine enthusiast, this festival is sure to satisfy your senses and leave you with an unforgettable experience.

Surifesta, Suriname

Surifesta is an annual cultural festival that takes place in Suriname, a small country located in South America. The festival is held in the capital city of Paramaribo and lasts for approximately two weeks, usually held in November. The festival is a celebration of Surinamese culture and diversity, showcasing the country's music, art, cuisine, and traditions.

Suriname is a culturally diverse country, with a mix of Indigenous, African, Indian, Chinese, and European cultures. Surifesta brings together people from all of these backgrounds to celebrate their shared history and traditions. The festival is an occasion for locals and tourists alike to enjoy the cultural richness of Suriname.

Suriname has a varied topography and climate, with highlands in the south and coastal plains in the north. Although Suriname is not known for its vineyards or wines, the country's rich soil and climate provide an ideal environment for a variety of fruits, vegetables, and spices that are used in the local cuisine.

Surinamese cuisine is a fusion of European, African, and Asian flavours, with a particular emphasis on seafood and exotic fruits. The local cuisine also features spicy marinades and slow-cooked meats. Some of the most popular dishes in Suriname include roti, which is a flatbread filled with curried vegetables, and bakabana, which is a fried plantain dish.

Although Suriname is not known for its wine production, there are a variety of wines available at Surifesta that are carefully selected to pair with the local cuisine. The wines are typically imported from Europe and South America and are chosen for their ability to complement the bold flavours and spices found in Surinamese dishes. Some of the most popular wine varietals at Surifesta include Cabernet Sauvignon, Chardonnay, and Merlot.

Some examples of foods and wines that are commonly paired at Surifesta:

1. **Roti and Chardonnay** - The rich, buttery flavour of Chardonnay complements the spicy flavours of curried vegetables in roti.

2. **Bakabana and Sangria** - The fruity sweetness of Sangria pairs well with the caramelised sweetness of fried plantains.

3. **Pom and Merlot** - The bold, full-bodied flavour of Merlot pairs well with the rich, meaty flavours of pom, which is a traditional Surinamese stew.

4. **Pepperpot and Cabernet Sauvignon** - The bold, peppery flavours of Cabernet Sauvignon complement the rich, slow-cooked flavours of Surinamese pepperpot.

5. **Suriname-style** Fried Rice and Sauvignon Blanc - The light, crisp flavour of Sauvignon Blanc complements the bold flavours of Surinamese-style fried rice.

6. **Sate and Pinot Noir** - The light, fruity flavour of Pinot Noir complements the bold, savoury flavours of Surinamese-style sate, which is a grilled meat dish.

7. **Moksi Meti and Malbec** - The bold, full-bodied flavour of Malbec complements the rich, meaty flavours of Moksi Meti, which is a Surinamese dish made with chicken and pork.

8. **Telo and Riesling** - The light, fruity flavour of Riesling complements the bold, starchy flavours of Telo, which is a Surinamese dish made with boiled taro root.

9. **Saoto Soup and Gewürztraminer** - The light, floral flavour of Gewürztraminer complements the bold, savoury flavours of Surinamese-style Saoto soup.

10. **Bojo Cake and Moscato** - The light, fruity flavour of Moscato pairs well with the sweet, sticky flavours of Surinamese-style Bojo cake, which is made with grated cassava and coconut.

- **Uruguayan Wine Festival**

Country: Uruguay

City: Montevideo

People: The Uruguayan Wine Festival is attended by wine lovers, industry professionals, local producers, and tourists.

Event Date: The Uruguayan Wine Festival is held annually in Montevideo during the first or second week of April.

Culture & Occasion: The Uruguayan Wine Festival is a cultural and social event that celebrates the country's excellent wines and helps promote its wine industry. The occasion is a great way for locals and visitors to explore and appreciate Uruguay's unique wines, food, and culture.

Topography and Vineyards: Uruguay is a small country in South America, and its wine regions are predominantly located in the southern and central areas. The topography is mostly flat, and the climate is temperate with cool Atlantic breezes.

Uruguay is home to several vineyards known for their high-quality wines. Some of the most famous include Bodega Garzón, Bouza Bodega Boutique, and Juanicó Bodegas Familiares.

Wines: Uruguay is known for producing some of the best red wines in the world, particularly Tannat, which is the country's signature grape variety. The wines are characterised by their deep, rich flavours, and complexity. Other grape varieties grown in Uruguay include Cabernet Sauvignon, Merlot, Tempranillo, and Pinot Noir.

Foods: Uruguay's cuisine is largely influenced by Spanish and Italian traditions, known for its grilling and barbecue or asado culture. Meat is a key element in many Uruguayan dishes, such as beef, lamb, and pork. Uruguay's gastronomy also features a wide range of seafood, grains, and cheeses.

Pairing Wines with Foods:

Here are some examples of wine and food pairings that work well together:

1. Tannat with grilled beef steak

2. Cabernet Sauvignon with hearty stews

3. Merlot with mushroom risotto

4. Chardonnay with grilled fish

5. Sauvignon Blanc with ceviche

6. Pinot Noir with roast pork

7. Tempranillo with grilled lamb chops

8. Rosé with shrimp cocktail

9. Albariño with grilled octopus

10. Viognier with quinoa salad.

I hope this helps provide a better understanding of the Uruguayan Wine Festival and the country's excellent wines and cuisine!

- **Punta del Este Food & Wine Festival**

The Punta del Este Food & Wine Festival is an annual event held in Punta del Este, Uruguay, a city located on the coast of the South Atlantic Ocean. The festival is a celebration of the rich culture and variety of wines and foods that come from this part of the world.

The festival is usually held in January, when the weather is warm and sunny, and the city is filled with tourists and locals alike. It is a chance for people to come together and enjoy some of the best wine and food pairings that Uruguay has to offer.

The festival is attended by food and wine lovers from all over the world, and it features a variety of events and activities, including wine tastings, cooking classes, and food and wine pairings. Attendees can sample some of the most delicious foods and wines from local vineyards and restaurants while learning about the culture and history of the region.

The topography of Uruguay is characterised by rolling hills, grasslands, and plateaus, which provide the perfect conditions for growing grapes. The country is home to a variety of vineyards that produce some of the best wines in the region, including reds, whites, and rosés.

Some of the best food and wine pairings that you might find at the Punta del Este Food & Wine Festival include:

1. **Beef empanadas with Tannat wine** - Tannat is the signature wine of Uruguay, and it pairs perfectly with beef empanadas, a traditional dish in the country.

2. **Grilled octopus with Albariño wine** - The crisp acidity of Albariño wine pairs perfectly with the salty and smoky flavours of grilled octopus.

3. **Spaghetti with clams and Sauvignon Blanc** - The lightness and acidity of Sauvignon Blanc complements the briny flavours of the clams in this dish.

4. **Roasted chicken with Chardonnay** - The buttery richness of Chardonnay complements the subtle flavour of roasted chicken.

5. **Grilled ribeye steak with Malbec** - Malbec is a bold and full-bodied wine that pairs perfectly with the rich flavours of a grilled ribeye steak.

6. **Seafood paella with Viognier** - The floral and fruity notes of Viognier complement the subtle flavours of seafood in a paella.

7. **Smoked salmon with Pinot Noir** - The smoky flavours of smoked salmon are perfectly balanced by the light and fruity flavours of Pinot Noir.

8. **Grilled shrimp with Rosé** - The lightness and acidity of Rosé wine pairs perfectly with the delicate flavours of grilled shrimp.

9. **Vegetable risotto with Chianti** - The earthy flavours of vegetable risotto are complemented by the robust flavours of Chianti.

10. **Artichoke and spinach dip with Cabernet Sauvignon** - The bold and tannic flavours of Cabernet Sauvignon pair perfectly with the rich and creamy flavours of an artichoke and spinach dip.

Overall, the Punta del Este Food & Wine Festival is a must-attend event for food and wine enthusiasts who are looking to experience the unique flavours and culture of Uruguay.

12. **Venezuela**: Feria Internacional de la Arepa and Feria del Chocolate y Café.

- **Feria Internacional de la Arepa, Venezuela**

The Feria Internacional de la Arepa is a significant event in Venezuela that attracts food lovers from all over the world.

Country: Venezuela

City: Caracas

Date: Typically held in the month of October

People: Venezuelans and visitors from all around the world

Event: Feria Internacional de la Arepa

Occasion: An annual celebration of the iconic Venezuelan dish, Arepa.

The Feria Internacional de la Arepa is a cultural celebration that takes place in the heart of Caracas, the capital of Venezuela. It is a festival that celebrates the beloved corn flour bread, which is a staple dish in the cuisine of Venezuela. The topography of Caracas is such that it is located within a valley that is surrounded by mountains. This provides an amazing view for attendees at the festival.

The festival showcases different vineyards and wines that pair perfectly with the arepa, which is considered the star of the event. The food at the festival is a combination of Venezuelan and international cuisines. Attendees can enjoy a variety of dishes such as grilled meats, street food, vegan and vegetarian options, and of course, the traditional arepas.

Some of the pairing examples of wines and foods at the Feria Internacional de la Arepa include:

1. Arepa stuffed with smoked salmon paired with a crisp white wine such as Sauvignon Blanc.

2. Arepa stuffed with roasted pork paired with a full-bodied red wine like Cabernet Sauvignon.

3. Arepa stuffed with black beans and fried plantains paired with a medium-bodied red wine such as Merlot.

4. Arepa stuffed with cream cheese and avocado paired with a dry Rosé wine.

5. Arepa stuffed with shrimp and spicy salsa paired with a chilled Chardonnay.

6. Arepa stuffed with chicken and vegetables paired with a Pinot Grigio.

7. Arepa stuffed with pork rinds paired with a sweet Moscato wine.

8. Arepa stuffed with beef and cheese paired with a bold Malbec.

9. Arepa stuffed with Venezuelan cheese paired with a light Chablis wine.

10. Arepa stuffed with scrambled eggs and bacon paired with a sparkling wine like Champagne.

In addition to the food and wine pairings, visitors can also enjoy live music, dancing, and cultural performances at the Feria Internacional de la Arepa. Overall, the Feria Internacional de la Arepa is a celebration of Venezuelan culture and its cuisine, and it is an event that food lovers should not miss.

- **Feria del Chocolate y Café, Venezuela**

Feria del Chocolate y Café is a vibrant event that takes place in Venezuela, specifically in the city of Caracas, the capital of the country. Venezuela is situated in the northern region of South America and is known for its rich biodiversity and varied topography, including jungles, mountains, and sandy beaches. The Feria del Chocolate y Café is a popular event that takes place annually, with the most recent event being held in November 2019.

The occasion of the Feria del Chocolate y Café is to celebrate the national production of coffee and chocolate in Venezuela in a fun and engaging way. The Feria offers visitors an opportunity to sample the finest chocolates and coffees the country has to offer. The event is widely attended by locals and tourists alike, with the festival being an ideal opportunity to learn more about the national culture and traditional foods.

The Feria del Chocolate y Café features a variety of exhibitors representing farmers and artisan chocolatiers from across the country. Topography and vineyards are significant aspects of this event. Venezuela's varied topography allows for diverse agricultural practices, including coffee and cocoa cultivation. The country's vineyards are known to produce high-quality red, white, and sparkling wines.

Visitors to the Feria del Chocolate y Café are treated to a culinary spectacle, with some of the country's finest foods served. Venezuelan cuisine is rich in flavours and ingredients, such as plantains, corn, beef, chicken, and seafood. Pairing these local dishes with fine wine is a delightful experience.

To illustrate, here are ten pairing examples:

1. **Polvorosas** (shortbread cookies with powdered sugar) go great with a glass of rose wine.

2. **Arepas** (masa-based dough filled with cheese or meat) are well-suited to serve with a tannic red wine like Merlot.

3. **Tequeños** (fried pastries filled with cheese) pairs nicely with a dry white wine like Sauvignon Blanc.

4. **Empanadas** (pastry shells filled with ground beef, chicken or cheese) goes well with a light-bodied red wine like Pinot Noir.

5. **Hallacas** (tamales stuffed with beef, chicken or pork, and seasonings) is best matched with a full-bodied red wine like Chianti.

6. **Mandocas** (corn-based fried with anise seed) pairs deliciously with a sparkling wine like Prosecco.

7. **Cocada** (coconut milk sweets) is an excellent dessert to enjoy with a glass of sweet wine like moscato.

8. **Tizana** (fruit cocktail with rum) makes the perfect partner to pair with a fruity wine like Zinfandel.

9. **Parrilla** (mixed grill meat) goes well with robust red wines like Merlot.

10. **Pabellón Criollo** (traditional Venezuelan dish consisting of rice, black beans, shredded beef, and plantains) is paired well with a full-bodied red wine like Zinfandel.

The Feria del Chocolate y Café is an event that showcases the best of coffee and chocolate grown locally in Venezuela, and the wine and food pairings are one of the highlights of the festival. It is a time to celebrate the country's rich culture, diverse agriculture, and culinary artistry.

Please note that this is not an exhaustive list and there are many other food and wine festivals and events celebrated throughout South America.

Phileas Fogg's Adventures Through South America

Phileas Fogg did not go to South America during his journey. However, if he did, here are some of the people, places, and animals he might have encountered:

1. **Brazil**: In Brazil, Fogg would have encountered the bustling city of Rio de Janeiro, where he could have taken a cable car to the top of Sugarloaf Mountain for a panoramic view of the city. He may have also visited the Amazon rainforest, where he could have seen giant otters, jaguars, and anacondas.

2. **Peru**: Fogg would have visited the ancient Incan city of Machu Picchu and hiked through the Andes Mountains. He may have also seen llamas, alpacas, and vicuñas along the way.

3. **Ecuador**: In Ecuador, Fogg may have visited the Galapagos Islands and encountered giant tortoises, blue-footed boobies, and marine iguanas. He could have also explored the Amazon rainforest, where he may have come across pink river dolphins and piranhas.

4. **Venezuela**: Fogg may have visited Angel Falls, the highest waterfall in the world, located in Venezuela's Canaima National Park. He could have also encountered jaguars, capybaras, and anacondas in the park.

5. **Uruguay**: In Uruguay, Fogg would have visited the capital city of Montevideo and explored the historic Old City. He may have also seen penguins and sea lions on Isla de Lobos.

6. **Argentina**: In Argentina, Fogg would have visited Buenos Aires, known for its vibrant tango scene and delicious steak. He may have also explored the Patagonia region, where he could have seen glaciers, penguins, and guanacos.

Overall, Phileas Fogg would have encountered diverse landscapes, from the lush rainforests of the Amazon to the towering Andes mountains, and a variety of unique flora and fauna in his travels through South America.

CHAPTER 16

FESTIVALS IN AFRICA

Sure, here are 25 festivals and events celebrated in Africa:

- **Cape Town International Jazz Festival - South Africa**

Cape Town International Jazz Festival is an annual event that takes place in South Africa's beautiful coastal city of Cape Town. The festival is usually held in March of each year and is a celebration of jazz music and culture from around the world.

The festival attracts thousands of people from across South Africa and the world, making it one of the biggest jazz festivals on the continent. The event features a line-up of world-renowned jazz musicians, as well as emerging artists from South Africa and the rest of the continent.

The festival takes place over two days, with multiple stages and venues throughout the city. In addition to the music, there are also food and beverage stalls offering a variety of local and international cuisine, wine and spirits.

South Africa is a country with a rich cultural history, and this is reflected in the diverse range of people and music that are featured at the festival. The topography of the city of Cape Town also plays a role in shaping the festival experience, with the stunning coastline and nearby vineyards providing a unique backdrop for the event.

In terms of wine, the Cape Town International Jazz Festival offers a unique opportunity to sample some of the best wines from the region's famous vineyards. South Africa is known for its exceptional vinification techniques, and the local wines are some of the best in the world.

Food and wine pairing is a popular trend in South Africa, and at the festival, you'll find a range of delicious food options that pair perfectly with local wines. Here are 10 examples of food and wine pairings that you might find at the Cape Town International Jazz Festival:

1. **Chardonnay and grilled prawns**: The buttery texture of the Chardonnay complements the smoky flavour of the prawns.

2. **Pinot Noir and lamb chops**: The earthy flavours of the Pinot Noir complement the richness of the lamb.

3. **Chenin Blanc and fish tacos**: The crisp acidity of the Chenin Blanc pairs perfectly with the spicy flavours of the fish tacos.

4. **Riesling and chicken curry**: The sweetness of the Riesling helps to balance the spicy heat of the curry.

5. **Sauvignon Blanc and grilled vegetables**: The bright flavours of the Sauvignon Blanc pair well with the smoky flavours of grilled vegetables.

6. **Merlot and beef sliders**: The fruity flavours of the Merlot complement the richness of the beef sliders.

7. **Shiraz and pulled pork**: The bold flavours of the Shiraz pair perfectly with the smoky, sweet flavours of pulled pork.

8. **Cabernet Sauvignon and steak**: The tannins in the Cabernet Sauvignon help to cut through the richness of the steak.

9. **Pinotage and biltong**: The intense flavours of the Pinotage pair perfectly with the salty, smoky flavours of biltong.

10. **Rose and seafood**: The light, crisp flavours of Rose pair perfectly with the delicate flavours of seafood.

Overall, the Cape Town International Jazz Festival is a celebration of the rich cultural heritage of South Africa, and the unique flavours and experiences that can be found in this beautiful part of the world. If you're a lover of jazz music, food, wine, and culture, this festival is not to be missed!

- **Carthage International Festival - Tunisia**

The Carthage International Festival is a prominent art and cultural event held annually in the city of Carthage, Tunisia. The festival is one of the largest and most popular cultural festivals in North Africa, attracting people from all over the world. The festival combines a mix of contemporary and traditional art, music, and dance, along with the cultural richness of the region.

The festival typically runs during the summer months, usually starting in late July and ending in mid-August. The event is hosted in the historic site of the ancient city of Carthage that showcases Tunisia's rich cultural heritage. The city's topography offers a spectacular view of the Mediterranean coastline and offers an atmosphere of freshness and exhilaration.

The festival is an occasion to bring together people from different backgrounds, cultures and traditions, all celebrating and sharing in the rich artistic and cultural heritage of the region. Tunisia has a very diverse culture, influenced by Berbers, Phoenicians, Arab Muslims, and French colonialists, making the festival a melting pot of artistic and cultural expression.

Moreover, Tunisia is also popular for its vineyards and production of wines. The country's history in winemaking dates back to the time of Carthage, where it was well-known for its vinification techniques. The festival offers visitors a chance to taste wines from local vineyards that showcase the unique terroirs.

Food is also a significant aspect of the festival, with vendors offering a rich variety of cuisines from around the region. Tunisian cuisine is a fusion of Mediterranean, Middle Eastern, and African influences that provide a delicious array of dishes. Some of the foods that can be found at the festival include:

1. **Brik** - A popular Tunisian food consisting of a thin pastry shell stuffed with eggs, tuna, parsley and optionally other ingredients like capers and harissa.

2. **Couscous** - A classic Tunisian dish made of semolina grains with steamed vegetables and meat.

3. **Shakshuka** -A Tunisian dish made up of eggs cooked lightly in tomato sauce and served with bread.

4. **Red Snapper** - Fresh fish seasoned and grilled with a variety of herbs and spices.

5. **Merguez** - Spicy sausage made from lamb or beef, often served with a side of French fries.

6. **Mechouia** - A salad made of roasted vegetables, tomatoes, onions, and peppers.

7. **Harissa** - Red chilli paste, often used as a condiment or added to dishes for flavour.

8. **Tagine** - A hearty stew often served with vegetables and meat, cooked in a clay pot on an open flame.

9. **Ojja** - A dish with eggs, cheese, meat, and vegetables, often served with bread.

10. **Makroudh** - A Tunisian dessert made from semolina dough and filled with dates.

These foods can be paired with a variety of Tunisian wines that showcase the unique terroirs of the region, some of which include:

1. **Sidi Salem Chardonnay** - A dry white wine, with hints of tropical fruits and a lingering finish.

2. **Mornag Tannat** - A rich and full-bodied red wine with notes of dark fruit and spices.

3. **Sidi Dhaher Rosé** - A refreshing and crisp rosé, with hints of berries and citrus.

4. **La Marsa Muscat** - A sweet white wine, best paired with desserts like makroud.

5. **Kairouan Syrah** - A complex and elegant red wine, perfect for pairing with spicy foods like merguez.

6. **Chenini Chardonnay** - A buttery and oaky white wine, perfect for pairing with rich dishes like couscous.

7. **Carthage Rosé** - A fresh and fruity rosé, perfect for pairing with light salads and sandwiches.

8. **Mornag Pinot Noir** - A medium-bodied red wine, ideal for pairing with grilled fish like red snapper.

9. **Tibhar Grenache** - A smooth and spicy red wine, perfect for pairing with hearty stews like tagine.

10. **Cap Bon Gris** - A dry white wine, with hints of herbs and spices, best paired with grilled vegetables and meats.

Overall, the Carthage International Festival provides an excellent opportunity for visitors to celebrate the artistic, cultural, and culinary richness of Tunisia. The festival's combination of music, dance, cuisine, and wine makes it a unique cultural event, bringing together people from all walks of life to celebrate and connect with each other.

- **Ouidah International Voodoo Festival - Benin**

The Ouidah International Voodoo Festival is a unique celebration that takes place in Benin, particularly in the city of Ouidah, every year on January 10. This festival is a major event in the West African country, and it attracts a large number of tourists from all over the world.

The festival is a celebration of the country's culture and the traditional religion of Voodoo. Voodoo is an animistic religion, and it is an important part of the Beninese culture. During the festival, people gather to worship, dance, and pay homage to their ancestors and the spirits that they believe permeate the world.

The topography of Ouidah is characterised by sandy beaches and coastal plains, and this region of Benin is home to several vineyards that produce wines. However, wine is not a typical drink during this festival.

Food and drink are an integral part of the Ouidah International Voodoo Festival, and visitors can indulge in a variety of local cuisines. Some popular dishes include:

1. **Akoumé** - a type of cornmeal served with fish or meat.

2. **Moin moin** - a bean cake served with vegetables.

3. **Pâte** - a type of stew made with vegetables and meat.

4. **Yovo Doko** - a spicy fish dish.

5. **Agouti** - a type of bush meat soup.

6. **Aloko** - fried plantains.

7. **Attieké** - a type of couscous made from cassava.

8. **Atassi** - a type of bean cake.

9. **Kepala** - fried fish

10. **Gumbo sauce** - a soup-like dish often served with rice.

As for wine, Benin's vineyards are relatively small and unknown, and not much is known about their vinification techniques. Thus, wine is not typically paired with the foods available at the festival. Instead, visitors can enjoy a variety of local drinks. Some popular choices include:

1. **Palm wine** - a drink extracted from the sap of palm trees.

2. **Zobo drink** - a drink made from the hibiscus flower.

3. **Ginger drink** - a drink made from ginger root.

4. **Soy milk** - a drink made from soybeans.

5. **Soda** - locally produced soda.

Overall, the Ouidah International Voodoo Festival is an exciting celebration of Beninese culture, tradition, and religion. Visitors can expect a variety of local foods and drinks, all served against a backdrop of colourful costumes, music, and dance.

- **Festival au Desert - Mali**

Festival au Desert is an annual music festival held in Essakane, Mali. Essakane is a small town in the Sahara Desert, located approximately 65 km northwest of Timbuktu, Mali. The festival started in 2001 and featured various traditional and contemporary styles of music, including Sahrawi, Tuareg, and traditional Malian music. The festival is a celebration of the nomadic culture of the Saharan regions, and it brings together different ethnic groups from Mali, Niger, and Algeria.

The festival is usually held in January, and it lasts for three days. It attracts thousands of tourists and music lovers from all over the world. The event is a platform for showcasing traditional and contemporary styles of music, dance, and art. It is aimed at promoting peace, tolerance, and understanding between different ethnic groups and cultures.

The festival is not only about music, but it's also a celebration of nomadic life, culture, and tradition. The event offers visitors the opportunity to explore the Saharan region and its unique topography, which includes sand dunes, rocky hills, and desert plains. Along with its diverse landscapes, the region is known for its vineyards, which produce a range of wines using traditional vinification techniques.

The food available at the Festival au Desert is just as diverse and unique as the music and culture it represents. Here are some food and wine pairings that visitors can enjoy at the event:

1. Tagine with lamb and prunes (paired with Moroccan Syrah)

2. Couscous with vegetables and chicken (paired with Algerian Chardonnay)

3. Spicy grilled goat kebab (paired with Moroccan Grenache)

4. Chicken and vegetable tagine (paired with Algerian Cabernet Sauvignon)

5. Spicy lentil stew (paired with Moroccan Tempranillo)

6. Beef and vegetable stew (paired with Moroccan Carignan)

7. Grilled lamb chops (paired with Algerian Merlot)

8. Chickpea and vegetable stew (paired with Moroccan Pinot Noir)

9. Grilled chicken breast (paired with Algerian Shiraz)

10. Roasted eggplant and tomato salad (paired with Moroccan Mourvedre)

11. Grilled beef skewers (paired with Algerian Syrah)

12. Tomato and onion salad (paired with Moroccan Sauvignon Blanc)

13. Grilled fish (paired with Algerian Chardonnay)

14. Fried potato cakes (paired with Moroccan Viognier)

15. Vegetable and chickpea tagine (paired with Algerian Pinot Gris)

The wines produced in the Saharan region are unique, with a distinct flavour profile. They are typically full-bodied and complex, with notes of dark fruit, spice, and earthiness. Some of the most popular varieties include Syrah, Grenache, and Mourvedre.

In conclusion, Festival au Desert is a celebration of music, culture, and tradition, and it provides visitors with a unique opportunity to experience the Saharan region and its diverse landscapes, food, and wine. Whether you're a lover of music, food, or wine, there's something for everyone at this event.

- **Fes Festival of World Sacred Music - Morocco**

The Fes Festival of World Sacred Music is a renowned cultural event that is held every year in the city of Fes, which is situated in Morocco. This event is celebrated with great enthusiasm and zeal by people from around the world. The festival is a magnificent celebration of world cultures and spirituality, bringing together thousands of visitors from all over the globe.

The Fes Festival of World Sacred Music was first held in 1994 and has been celebrated annually since then. The festival is organised by the city of Fes and the Moroccan Ministry of Culture. The event takes place in the month of June or July and lasts for a period of 10 days.

The city of Fes is known for its rich cultural heritage, and the festival is a reflection of this. The city has many historical sites such as the Fes Medina, which is a UNESCO World Heritage Site. Fes is also known for its vineyards, which produce some of the best wines in the world. The topography of the city is ideal for wine production, and vinification techniques used here are very unique.

The festival is a celebration of culture and spirituality. The occasion is marked by the presence of many renowned musicians, artists, and performers from different parts of the world. The festival showcases various musical genres such as classical, traditional, and contemporary music. The festival is a celebration of the world's cultural diversity and brings together people from different cultures and religions.

The foods and wines available at the festival are a highlight of the event. Some of the top food and wine pairings available at the festival include:

1. **Grilled meats and red wine** - The richness of the red wine complements the smoky flavour of the grilled meats perfectly.

2. **Moroccan salads and white wine** - The light and refreshing taste of white wine pairs perfectly with the flavorful and spicy Moroccan salads.

3. **Spiced rice and rosé wine** - The delicate flavours of rosé wine pair beautifully with the fragrant and flavorful spiced rice.

4. **Seafood and white wine** - The light and refreshing taste of white wine complements the delicate flavours of seafood perfectly.

5. **Grilled vegetables and red wine** - The richness of the red wine complements the smoky flavour of grilled vegetables perfectly.

6. **Tagine and red wine** - The rich and spicy flavours of tagine pair perfectly with the full-bodied richness of red wine.

7. **Couscous and white wine** - The light and refreshing taste of white wine pairs beautifully with the fragrant and flavorful couscous.

8. **Spicy kebabs and rosé wine** - The delicate flavours of rosé wine complement the spiciness of the kebab perfectly.

9. **Grilled fish and white wine** - The light and refreshing taste of white wine complements the delicate flavours of grilled fish perfectly.

10. **Lamb and red wine** - The rich and full-bodied flavours of red wine complement the rich and flavorful lamb perfectly.

11. **Fattoush salad and rosé wine** - The delicate flavours of rosé wine complement the flavorful and slightly spicy fattoush salad perfectly.

12. **Stuffed peppers and white wine** - The light and refreshing taste of white wine pairs beautifully with the flavorful stuffed peppers.

13. **Chicken and red wine** - The richness and full-bodied flavours of red wine pair perfectly with the tender and juicy chicken.

14. **Lamb chops and rosé wine** - The delicate flavours of rosé wine complement the richness of the tender lamb chops perfectly.

15. **Grilled vegetables and rosé wine** - The delicate flavours of rosé wine pair beautifully with the smoky flavour of grilled vegetables.

In conclusion, the Fes Festival of World Sacred Music is a celebration of cultures and spirituality that brings together people from all over the world. The festival is a tribute to Morocco's rich cultural heritage and showcases its unique topography, vineyards, vinification techniques, foods, and wines. The food and wine pairings available at the festival are a highlight of the event, and visitors can savour the delicious flavours of Moroccan cuisine while enjoying the festival's musical performances and cultural activities.

- **Lake of Stars Festival - Malawi**

The Lake of Stars Festival is a vibrant, multidisciplinary celebration of arts and culture, held annually in Malawi, a landlocked country situated in southeastern Africa. The festival takes place on the shores of Lake Malawi, in the city of Mangochi, and welcomes people from all over the world to experience a unique blend of music, dance, film, art, and cultural exchange.

The festival, which dates back to 2003, is a great opportunity to embrace Malawi's rich cultural heritage, characterised by its diverse ethnic groups and colourful traditions. It is an occasion to showcase the dynamic creativity and innovation of Malawi's emerging artists and musicians, as well as the warm hospitality of its people.

The country's topography comprises mountains, plateau, and savannah, making it suitable for grape cultivation. Malawi has a relatively new and small wine industry, but it is growing fast, and some wine producers in the country produce good quality wine. The grapes are harvested from mainly mountainous areas, and vinification techniques are modern.

At the festival, guests can enjoy a wide range of food and wines. There are food and wine pairings available at the event, and here are some of them:

1. **Grilled fish paired with Chenin Blanc** – the fish is prepared with spices and served with lemon seasoning, making it a perfect match for a light, crisp white wine like Chenin Blanc.

2. **Roast pork paired with a Shiraz** – the pork is marinated with a blend of spices and paired with a bold red wine like Shiraz, which has a full-bodied flavour that complements the richness of the pork.

3. **Vegetable curry paired with a Riesling** – the sweetness of the vegetables and the spiciness of the curry make a perfect match for a refreshing, fruity Riesling.

4. **Beef stew paired with a Merlot** – the beef is slowly cooked with aromatic spices, and a Merlot's mellow tannins and soft fruit flavours provide an excellent complement to the complex flavours of the stew.

5. **Roast chicken paired with Sauvignon Blanc** – the chicken is roasted to perfection and paired with a light, refreshing Sauvignon Blanc, which has a zesty, citrusy flavour that balances out the richness of the chicken.

6. **Samosas with Chardonnay** – Samosas are a popular snack in Malawi, and the buttery texture and savoury flavour make them an excellent match for an oaked Chardonnay, which has a buttery flavour that complements the samosas well.

7. **Fried rice with Viognier** – this pairing is perfect as the nuttiness of the rice and the spice of the sauce match well with the floral and peachy notes of a Viognier.

8. **Beef burgers and Cabernet Sauvignon**- burgers are a popular food item, so pairing them with a bold red such as Cabernet Sauvignon makes an excellent combination.

9. **Grilled Chicken and Pinot Grigio** – Pairing grilled chicken with a light and crisp Pinot Grigio is great as the wine brings out the nuances in the grilled chicken.

10. **Spaghetti Bolognese and Cabernet Franc**- The acidity of the tomato sauce pairs perfectly with the cherry flavours of the Cabernet Franc.

11. **Stuffed Jalapenos and Zinfandel** – These pairings work great as the velvety Zinfandel harmonises with the spicy stuffed jalapenos.

12. **Tacos and Garnacha** – The sweet notes of the Garnacha coupled with the Mexican spices in the taco create an excellent pairing

13. **Fruit Salad with Moscato** – the sweetness of the fruit salad matches well with the caramel and fruity notes in a Moscato.

14. **Chocolate cake and Port** – The intense flavours of the chocolate are best complemented by the richness of an aged Port.

15. **Cheese platter with Malbec** – the acidic punch from the cheese paired with the Malbec's tannins makes for an excellent pairing.

In conclusion, the Lake of Stars Festival is a must-attend cultural event that offers a unique opportunity to enjoy delicious food and quality wine while celebrating the diverse cultural heritage of Malawi. The festival's location by the lake, Malawi's topography, and the dynamic viticulture industry, sets the stage for an excellent culinary experience.

- **Mawazine Festival - Morocco**

Mawazine Festival is one of the largest and most popular music festivals in Africa and the Arab world. The festival takes place annually during the month of June in Rabat, the capital city of Morocco. Mawazine Festival brings together renowned artists and music lovers from different parts of the world.

The festival includes a variety of music genres such as Pop, Hip Hop, African Music, and Electronic Music. The event aims to promote cultural diversity and enhance cultural exchanges between artists and attendees. It is an excellent opportunity for music lovers to experience Moroccan culture and traditions.

Morocco is known for its rich cultural heritage and diverse geography, which makes it an ideal destination for wine tourism. The country has a range of vineyards spread across different regions, each with a unique topography and vinification technique that produces distinct wines.

Morocco has a rich culture of food, with a blend of influences from Berber, Arab, Andalusian and French cuisines. The Mawazine festival provides an excellent opportunity for visitors to experience Moroccan gastronomy and wine culture.

Some foods and wines to try at Mawazine Festival in Morocco:

1. **Pastilla** – a traditional Moroccan dish made of layered phyllo pastry with chicken, almonds, and spices. Pair it with a crisp and dry white wine like Thalvin – Sables d'Ocre.

2. **Harira** – a hearty soup made with tomatoes, lentils, chickpeas, and spices. Enjoy it with a rich and full-bodied red wine like Celliers de Meknes – Guerrouane.

3. **Couscous** – a traditional Moroccan dish made of small steamed balls of semolina served with vegetables and meat. Pair it with a fruity and spicy red wine like Domaine de Sahari – Syrah/Grenache.

4. **Tagine** – a slow-cooked stew of meat, vegetables, and spices. It is best paired with a full-bodied and earthy red wine like Les Trois Domaines – Guerrouane.

5. **Zaalouk** – a delicious salad made of roasted eggplant, tomatoes, and spices. Enjoy it with a crisp and refreshing white wine like Volubilia – Sauvignon Blanc.

6. **Kefta** – a traditional Moroccan dish made of spiced ground beef or lamb, served with tomato sauce and eggs. Pair it with a bold and tannic red wine like Domaine Beni M'tir – Syrah.

7. **Mechoui** – a roasted lamb dish cooked slowly over an open fire. Enjoy it with a medium-bodied and smooth red wine like Ouled Thaleb – Signature Rouge.

8. **Briwat** – a sweet or savoury pastry made of phyllo dough filled with meat, cheese, or almond paste. Pair it with a sweet and fruity dessert wine like Les Celliers de Meknes – Chaabi.

9. **Khobz** - Traditional Moroccan bread. Enjoy it with a medium-bodied red wine like Les Trois Domaines – Cabernet Sauvignon.

10. Batbout – a flatbread that is cooked over low heat and served hot. Pair it with a medium-bodied and flavorful white wine like Château Roslane – Chardonnay.

11. **Baghrir** – a fluffy and spongy pancake, commonly regarded as Moroccan crepes. Enjoy it with a sweet and aromatic dessert wine like Les Celliers de Meknes – Paille.

12. **Makouda** – a fried potato patty filled with minced meat and spices. Pair it with a medium-bodied and fruity red wine like Domaine Ouled Thaleb – Syrah.

13. **Chebakia** – a popular Moroccan sesame and honey cookie. Enjoy it with a sweet and velvety dessert wine like Domaine de Sahari – Muscat.

14. **Gazelle Horns** – crescent-shaped almond cookie dough. Pair it with a citrus and floral white wine like Domaine Val d'Argan – Sauvignon Blanc.

15. **Mint tea** – Moroccan's iconic beverage. It is perfect on a hot day, and it pairs especially well with a sweet and aromatic dessert wine like Terres Rouges – Sémillon.

In conclusion, the Mawazine Festival in Morocco is truly an epitome of cultural diversity, enriched with exquisite wines and an abundance of culinary delights.

- **Nyege Nyege Festival - Uganda**

The Nyege Nyege Festival is a unique cultural and music event that takes place annually in Uganda. The event is held in the city of Jinja, Uganda, and attracts thousands of music enthusiasts, culture lovers, and travellers from all over the world. The festival is not only about music, but it also aims to promote Ugandan culture, food, wine and tourism.

The festival takes place towards the end of the year, usually in September or early October. It is a four-day event that features a range of activities including music performances, cultural exhibitions, art installations, workshops, and food and wine tastings.

Uganda, located in East Africa, is known for its diverse cultures and landscapes. The country is home to over 50 different tribes, each with their own unique customs, beliefs, and traditions. This diversity is reflected in the Nyege Nyege Festival, which showcases music and performances from various Ugandan communities.

Jinja, which hosts the festival, is a city located in southern Uganda, on the shores of Lake Victoria. The city is known for its beautiful tourism sites, including Bujagali Falls and the source of the Nile. The festival is held at the Nile Discovery Beach, a stunning location that has become famous for its scenic views, sandy beaches, and soothing waters.

Although vineyards and vinification techniques are not particularly prevalent in Uganda, the festival has become a platform to showcase Ugandan food and wine. Attendees can enjoy a variety of Ugandan dishes, including popular street foods such as Rolex (a chapati wrapped around an omelette with vegetables), matoke (steamed green bananas), and samosas (fried pastries filled with potatoes or meat).

There are several Ugandan wines, and while some of them are made with grapes, most are made from other fruits, such as pineapples, passion fruits, and mangoes. The wines are sweet and refreshing, making them an excellent pairing for spicy foods, which are prevalent in Ugandan cuisine. The top 15 wine and food pairing options at the festival include:

1. Chapati and pineapple wine

2. Goat stew and passion fruit wine

3. Samosas and mango wine

4. Fried plantains and guava wine

5. Matoke and pomegranate wine

6. Simsim (sesame) balls and orange wine

7. Groundnut sauce and grape wine

8. Chicken curry and tangerine wine

9. Cassava chips and banana wine

10. Fish stew and kiwi wine

11. Beans and beetroot wine

12. Fried chicken and lemon wine

13. Beef stew and grapefruit wine

14. Fried shrimp and lime wine

15. Rice and mixed fruit wine

These pairings work well for several reasons. First, most Ugandan dishes are spicy, and the sweetness of the wines helps to balance out the heat. Additionally, the fruitiness of the wines complements the bold flavors of the dishes. Lastly, the acidity in the wines helps to cleanse the palate and prepare it for the next bite.

In conclusion, the Nyege Nyege Festival is a celebration of music, culture, food, and wine in Uganda. The four-day event offers a unique opportunity to experience Ugandan culture and enjoy its diverse cuisine and wines. The festival gives attendees the chance to unwind, connect with new people, and immerse themselves in a vibrant, welcoming culture.

- **Timkat Festival - Ethiopia**

The Timkat Festival, also known as the Ethiopian Epiphany Festival, is one of the most prominent cultural events in Ethiopia. It takes place every year on January 19th (or January 20th in leap years) in the city of Lalibela. This stunning highland town is located in the northern region of Ethiopia, nestled in the ruggedly beautiful Ethiopian Highlands. The Timkat Festival is a joyous celebration of the baptism of Jesus and is considered one of the most important religious holidays in Ethiopia.

The Timkat Festival begins with a colourful procession of religious leaders, priests, and laymen carrying holy relics and icons from the various churches in the city. The procession leads to a nearby body of water, where a replica of the Ark of the Covenant is ceremonially bathed. Participants immerse themselves in the water, symbolically renewing their baptismal vows.

The festival is an opportunity for Ethiopians from all walks of life to come together and celebrate their cultural heritage. The region is known for its unique culture, language, and traditions. The rugged terrain of the area makes it difficult to grow many crops, but the highlands are known for producing some of the best coffee in the world.

Some of the most well-known foods from the region include spicy stews, flatbreads, and a variety of vegetarian dishes made with lentils, vegetables, and spices. The food is hearty and flavorful, with many dishes featuring a spicy kick. Wines from Ethiopia are not as well-known as other African countries, but they are gaining in popularity. The region is ideal for vineyards due to its high altitude, fertile soils, and cool temperatures.

Here are some Ethiopian foods and wines that can be enjoyed at the Timkat Festival:

1. Doro Wat (spicy chicken stew) paired with a full-bodied red wine

2. Injera (sour flatbread) paired with a light, fruity red wine

3. Tibs (grilled meat) paired with a medium-bodied red wine

4. Kitfo (spicy beef tartare) paired with a dry white wine

5. Gomen (collard greens) paired with a light, crisp white wine

6. Shiro (curried chickpeas) paired with a medium-bodied red wine

7. Kik Alicha (mild yellow split pea stew) paired with a dry white wine

8. Misir (spicy red lentil stew) paired with a full-bodied red wine

9. Ayib (fresh cheese) paired with a light, crisp white wine

10. Tofu (soybean curd) paired with a dry rosé wine

11. Berbere (spice blend) paired with a spicy, full-bodied red wine

12. Teff (ancient grain) paired with a light, fruity red wine

13. Shrimp & avocado salad paired with a dry white wine

14. Spiced beef skewers paired with a medium-bodied red wine

15. Ethiopian coffee paired with a sweet, dessert wine

The pairing of foods and wines is an art form, and it is important to consider the flavours and textures of both to create a harmonious experience. For example, the spicy Doro Wat pairs well with a full-bodied red wine because the bold flavours of the wine can complement the dish, while the light, fruity red wine pairs well with Injera because the wine can stand up to the sourness of the bread. Similarly, Teff pairs well with a light, fruity red wine because the mild flavour of the grain can be enhanced by the wine's subtle fruitiness.

Overall, the Timkat Festival is a vibrant celebration of Ethiopian culture, tradition, and religion. The region's unique geography, cultural heritage, and delicious food and wine make it a fascinating and diverse destination for travellers and locals alike.

- **Zanzibar International Film Festival - Tanzania**

The Zanzibar International Film Festival (ZIFF) is one of the oldest and most well-regarded film festivals in East Africa, held annually on the island of Zanzibar which is a semi-autonomous part of Tanzania. The festival brings filmmakers and cinema enthusiasts from all over the world together for a week of screenings, workshops, exhibitions, and cultural events. This event is organised in Stone Town, a city in Zanzibar, and attracts visitors from all over the world.

The festival hosts a diverse range of films, including world premieres, classic films, and documentaries. It also showcases African and international films of different genres such as short, feature, and animation films. The festival creates an opportunity for filmmakers to showcase their talents in front of a diverse audience and to promote African and international cultures.

The event generally takes place in July, which is the low season in Zanzibar due to the hot weather. However, the Film festival provides a more exciting and vibrant atmosphere for the city and its people. The occasion is an opportunity for the people of Zanzibar to enjoy the diversity of films, arts and cultures.

Zanzibar has a rich cultural heritage due to its unique location at the crossroads of African, Indian, and Arab cultures. The city boasts of beautiful topography with stunning beaches, coral reefs, forests and mountains. Zanzibar is famous for its unique foods such as biriyani, samosas, pilau, and a host of seafood dishes like grilled fish and coconut curry.

In terms of wines, Zanzibar has no domestic wine production as the country is located in a tropical climate with hot and humid temperatures, which are not always suitable for grape cultivation. However, the festival does not lack in alcoholic beverages as it features local and imported wines from countries such as South Africa and Italy.

We can pair foods and wines available at the ZIFF event, with some of the notable ones including:

1. Biryani with a South African Chardonnay

2. Grilled fish with an Italian Pinot Grigio

3. Pilau with a South African Merlot

4. Samosas with a South African Shiraz

5. Coconut Curry with an Italian Chardonnay

6. Lobster with a South African Sauvignon Blanc

7. Octopus with an Italian Prosecco

8. Fried chicken with a South African Cabernet Sauvignon

9. Chapati with an Italian Pinot Noir

10. Chicken Biryani with a South African Chenin Blanc

11. Jollof Rice with an Italian Montepulciano d'Abruzzo

12. Beef Shawarma with a South African Pinotage

13. Zanzibar Pizza with an Italian Sangiovese

14. Grilled Prawns with a South African Chardonnay

15. French Fries with a South African Chenin Blanc

The wines have been paired based on their ability to complement the flavors and spices of the food. For instance, the spicy Biryani and the creamy Coconut Curry are paired with a South African Chardonnay for its buttery and tropical fruit flavours.

The event provides an opportunity for visitors to experience the rich cultural heritage of the city through its various culinary delights and wine tasting. Visitors can have a taste of Zanzibar's unique cuisine while washing it down with a glass of wine. Overall, ZIFF is not just a film festival, but an iconic occasion that is a gateway to immerse oneself in the unique culture, food, wine, and cinema of Zanzibar.

- **Lagos Fashion Week - Nigeria**

Lagos Fashion Week is an annual fashion event held in Lagos, Nigeria. Lagos is the largest city in Nigeria, situated in the south-western region of the country. The fashion week event features some of the top fashion designers and models in Nigeria as well as other African countries. The event is usually held in October, showcasing different collections from various designers, and is a significant part of Nigerian culture.

The Nigerian culture is diverse and colourful, making it an exciting destination for tourists. The city of Lagos has a rich history and culture, and the people are welcoming and hospitable. The topography of Lagos is a coastal plain and has some scenic spots, including beaches, parks, and gardens.

In terms of cuisine, Lagos has an array of local and international cuisines to offer. Some of the popular Nigerian dishes include Jollof rice, Egusi soup, Efo Riro, Pounded Yam, and Suya. Lagos also has plenty of street food vendors, including Akara, Boli, Shawarma, and Puff Puff. The city also has a vibrant nightlife scene, with bars, clubs, and lounges where people can enjoy music, drinks, and socialise.

When it comes to wine pairing, Lagos Fashion Week features different wine vendors, offering a variety of red, white, and sparkling wines from around the world. Here are some foods and wines available at the event:

1. **Jollof Rice** – This is a popular Nigerian dish that comprises rice cooked in a rich tomato-based sauce with various spices, served with grilled chicken. It pairs well with a red wine, such as South African Pinotage.

2. **Egusi Soup** – A delicious traditional Nigerian soup made with melon seeds and spinach, served with pounded yam or rice. It pairs well with a white wine, such as Sauvignon Blanc from New Zealand.

3. **Efo Riro** – This is another delicious Nigerian soup made with assorted meat, fish, and vegetables. It pairs well with a Merlot from Chile.

4. **Pounded Yam** – A Nigerian cuisine staple served with soup or stew. It pairs well with South African Chenin Blanc.

5. **Suya** – A popular Nigerian street food, made of skewered meat spiced with ground peanuts and spices. It pairs well with a light-bodied red wine, such as Beaujolais from France.

6. **Fried Rice** – This is a common dish in Nigeria that features fried rice, mixed vegetables, and chicken. It pairs well with a Chardonnay from Australia.

7. **Shawarma** – An Arabian fast-food delicacy, well-loved in Nigeria. It pairs well with a white wine, such as Riesling from Germany.

8. **Puff Puff** – A West African snack made from deep-fried dough, eaten as a sweet treat. It pairs well with a sweet sparkling wine, such as Moscato from Italy.

9. **Akara** – A Nigerian street food snack made from black-eyed beans. It pairs well with a light and fruity Spanish Rose.

10. **Boli** – A popular street food made from roasted plantains, eaten with pepper sauce or groundnut sauce. It pairs well with a Zinfandel from California.

11. **Grilled Fish** – A common Nigerian dish consisting of grilled fish seasoned with spices. It pairs well with a Chenin Blanc from South Africa.

12. **Ewa Agoyin** – A popular Nigerian beans dish, served with sauce and fried plantain. It pairs well with a full-bodied Cabernet Sauvignon from Argentina.

13. **Fried Plantain** – A staple snack in Nigeria, eaten alone, or as an accompaniment to other dishes. It pairs well with a dry white wine, such as Chablis from France.

14. **Pepper Soup** – A spicy Nigerian soup found across many of the country's cultures, usually served with rice. It pairs well with a Malbec from Argentina.

15. **Pounded Yam with Egusi Soup** – A favourite Nigerian food combo, consisting of Pounded Yam and Egusi Soup. It pairs well with Californian Merlot.

In conclusion, Lagos Fashion Week is not only about fashion, but it is also a celebration of Nigeria's diverse culture and cuisine. The event features an array of food and drink options, showcasing the best flavours the country has to offer. With its mix of traditional and contemporary attractions, Lagos is an ideal destination for culture enthusiasts and food and wine lovers.

- **Pan-African Festival of Algiers (Festival Panafricain d'Alger) - Algeria**

The Pan-African Festival of Algiers, also known as the Festival Panafricain d'Alger, is a cultural event that takes place in the capital city of Algeria. It is a celebration of African cultural heritage, designed to bring together people from across the continent to participate in music, dance, theatre, and other artistic displays.

The Festival Panafricain d'Alger usually takes place in July, with events and activities taking place over several days. The festival first took place in 1969 and has been held periodically since then, with the most recent iteration taking place in 2019.

The festival has been regarded as an important cultural event in Africa, promoting the diversity of African culture while simultaneously giving attendees an opportunity to learn more about different African countries and their cultures.

One of the most prominent features of the Pan-African Festival of Algiers is the food and wine available at the event. The festival offers a wide range of foods from various African countries, paired with wines that complement the flavors of the dishes.

Here are some food and wine pairings that are often available at the festival:

1. South African Bobotie with a Chenin Blanc wine

2. Egyptian Tameya with a Pinot Gris wine

3. Moroccan Tagine with a Syrah wine

4. Nigerian Jollof Rice with a Shiraz wine

5. Tunisian Brik with a Chardonnay wine

6. Ethiopian Injera with a Malbec wine

7. Algerian Couscous with a Cabernet Sauvignon wine

8. Ghanaian Waakye with a Sauvignon Blanc wine

9. Rwandan Matoke with a Merlot wine

10. Libyan Shakshuka with a Grenache wine

11. Senegalese Thieboudienne with a Zinfandel wine

12. Kenyan Ugali with a Pinot Noir wine

13. Cameroonian Ndole with a Pinot Grigio wine

14. Malian Yassa Poulet with a Gamay wine

15. Congolese Fufu with a Cabernet Franc wine

Each of these dishes has a unique taste profile that is enhanced by the accompanying wine. For example, the South African Bobotie is a savoury, slightly spicy dish that pairs well with a Chenin Blanc wine, which has a fruity flavour with hints of spice.

Similarly, the Tunisian Brik, a crispy, deep-fried pastry filled with a savoury mixture of tuna, egg, and harissa, is complemented by the rich, buttery flavour of a Chardonnay wine.

Overall, the Pan-African Festival of Algiers is an exciting event that celebrates the rich cultural heritage of Africa, offering a diverse range of food, wine, and entertainment from different African countries.

- **Sauti za Busara - Tanzania**

Sauti za Busara is an annual music festival that takes place in Stone Town, Zanzibar, Tanzania. The festival was first held in 2004 and has become a significant cultural event in East Africa. It usually takes place over four days in February and attracts thousands of music enthusiasts from around the world.

The festival is a celebration of African music, culture, and traditions. The event showcases different African music genres like Taarab, Mchiriku, Kidumbak, and Hiphop. The festival brings together musicians, dancers, and artists from all over Africa and beyond. It is a melting pot of cultures where people come together to share in the experience of African music, art, and culture.

Stone Town is a UNESCO World Heritage Site and is famous for its narrow streets, historic architecture, and vibrant culture. The topography is mostly flat, with beautiful beaches and coral reefs that attract many tourists. The temperatures are relatively high, with an average of 30°C in February.

When it comes to foods and wines, the festival offers a wide range of traditional African dishes and wines. Here are some of the foods and wines that you can expect to find at the festival:

1. Zanzibar pizza paired with a sweet white wine

2. Grilled seafood paired with a dry white wine

3. Pilau rice paired with a red wine

4. Chapati paired with a fruity red wine

5. Ugali paired with a dry white wine

6. Coconut rice paired with a sweet white wine

7. Mshikaki (grilled meat skewers) paired with a dry red wine

8. Zanzibar mix (a mix of local snacks) paired with a rosé wine

9. Kachumbari salad paired with a fruity white wine

10. Nyama Choma (grilled meat) paired with a full-bodied red wine

11. Samosas paired with a rosé wine

12. Vitumbua (sweet pancakes) paired with a sweet white wine

13. Makande (beans and maize stew) paired with a dry white wine

14. Chips Mayai (omelet with french fries) paired with a crisp white wine

15. Mangoes paired with a sweet white wine.

The food and wine pairing is essential because it enhances the flavours of both the food and wine. For example, a sweet white wine pairs well with Zanzibar pizza because it balances the salty and savoury flavours. Grilled seafood pairs well with a dry white wine because the wine's acidity cuts through the richness of the seafood. Pilau rice pairs well with a red wine because the wine's tannins complement the spices in the rice.

In conclusion, Sauti za Busara is not only a music festival but also a celebration of African culture, food, and wine. The festival provides an opportunity for people to experience the rich traditions of Africa and to enjoy excellent food and wine pairings. If you plan to attend the festival, make sure to try some of the dishes and wines mentioned above, and you will not be disappointed.

- **Marrakech International Film Festival - Morocco**

The Marrakech International Film Festival is an annual event held in Morocco's famously colourful city, Marrakech. The people of Marrakech are very proud of the Festival and it is one of the most important events on the city's cultural calendar. The Festival celebrates international cinema, as well as the best in Moroccan cinema, and draws celebrities and industry professionals from around the world.

The event takes place every year for nine days in December, often around the first weekend of the month. This year (2021), the festival will take place from December 3rd to 11th. The festival was first launched in 2001, making it quite a recent addition to the international film festival circuit, but it has already established itself as a significant event and an excellent platform for the promotion of global cinema.

The culture of Morocco is rich and varied, with influences coming from Berber, Arab, and European cultures. The festival is an excellent opportunity to experience and learn more about Moroccan culture, as it brings together people and films from all over the world. Marrakech is an exceptional city, known for its stunning architecture, bustling souks, and delicious cuisines.

The topography of Marrakech offers various settings for the film festival, including the iconic Jemaa el-Fnaa square, which is the starting point of Morocco's traditional story-telling scene. Attendees can explore the city's traditional markets, wander the historic medina, or visit the stunning Koutoubia Mosque. Visitors can also take a trip to the Atlas Mountains, which provide an awe-inspiring backdrop to the city and provide an excellent opportunity to go on excursions.

Food and wine are a vital part of Marrakech's culture, and the festival offers an exceptional selection of delicious Moroccan cuisine and wines. Here are 15 recommended pairings:

1. Tagine with couscous and a glass of Moroccan red wine

2. Spiced chicken skewers with Moroccan white wine

3. Harira soup with a glass of red wine

4. Moroccan lamb kebabs with spicy tomato salsa and a glass of red wine

5. Moroccan seafood platter with a glass of dry white wine

6. Mechoui (slow-roasted lamb) with a glass of sparkling wine

7. Moroccan spices chicken with a glass of rosé wine

8. Moroccan meatball soup with a glass of red wine

9. Molokhia (leafy green stew) with a glass of Moroccan red wine

10. Grilled beef with Ras-el-hanout (Moroccan spice mix) with a glass of red wine

11. Chicken Bastilla (savoury pie) with a glass of sweet white wine

12. Cherries stuffed with goat cheese with a glass of rosé wine

13. Almonds with a glass of sweet Moroccan wine

14. Fresh mint tea with Moroccan pastry with a glass of Moroccan white wine

15. Moroccan orange salad with a glass of Moroccan rosé wine

Moroccan cuisine is influenced by Berber, Arab, and Moorish cultures, and many of the dishes are tagines, spicy stews that are cooked and served in traditional clay pots. The wine culture in Morocco is just as prominent, with a wide range of wines produced locally. Morocco has some of the best wine regions in Africa, and many of the wineries are located close to Marrakech, making it easy to pair the Moroccan cuisine with the perfect wines.

In conclusion, the Marrakech International Film Festival is an excellent event to experience the beautiful city of Marrakech, learn more about Moroccan culture, and discover excellent Moroccan cuisine and wines. With its beautiful setting, exceptional cultural offerings, and delectable food and wine, the Festival has become one of the most exciting and dynamic events in the film festival calendar.

- **Aké Arts and Book Festival - Nigeria**

The Aké Arts and Book Festival is a highly anticipated annual event in Nigeria that takes place in the city of Abeokuta. The festival was founded in 2013 by the Nigerian author, Lola Shoneyin, with the aim of promoting literacy and showcasing the diverse cultures of Nigeria and Africa as a whole.

The festival typically takes place in November and attracts visitors from all over the world, including writers, poets, scholars, and literary enthusiasts. In addition to literary events, the festival also includes music concerts, art exhibitions, film screenings, and cultural performances.

Nigeria is a highly diverse country with over 500 different ethnic groups, and the Aké Arts and Book Festival provides a platform for people from different cultures to come together and celebrate their differences. The occasion is especially significant because it takes place in Abeokuta, which is the capital city of Ogun State and the birthplace of several prominent Nigerian writers, including Wole Soyinka and Chinua Achebe.

Nigeria's topography is characterised by a mix of forests, grasslands, and savannas, and this diversity is reflected in the food and wine available at the festival. Some of the most popular traditional dishes served at the event include jollof rice, egusi soup, pounded yam, and suya, which is a spicy grilled meat dish.

For wine drinkers, there are several options available, including several local Nigerian wines. Nigeria is not traditionally known as a wine-producing country, but there are several local wineries that have recently started producing high-quality wines using a variety of vinification techniques.

Pairing foods and wines is often a matter of personal taste, but here are some recommendations of Nigerian dishes and wines that could be paired together at the Aké Arts and Book Festival:

1. Jollof rice and a fruity red wine such as a Cabernet Sauvignon – the ripe fruit flavours in the wine complement the spices in the dish.

2. Egusi soup and a crisp, unoaked white wine such as a Sauvignon Blanc – the acidity in the wine balances the richness of the soup.

3. Pounded yam and a full-bodied red wine such as a Shiraz – the bold flavours of the wine stand up to the earthy flavours of the yam.

4. Suya and a dry white wine such as a Chardonnay – the wine's crispness helps to cut through the spiciness of the dish.

5. Jollof spaghetti and a light-bodied red wine such as a Pinot Noir – the wine's delicate flavours work well with the subtle spices in the dish.

6. Pepper soup and a medium-bodied red wine such as a Merlot – the wine's smoothness complements the rich flavours of the soup.

7. Fried rice and a sweet white wine such as a Gewürztraminer – the wine's sweetness helps to balance the salty flavours of the dish.

8. Moi moi and a sparkling wine – the wine's effervescence provides a refreshing contrast to the dense texture of the dish.

9. Pounded yam and vegetable soup and a rosé wine – the wine's lightness and acidity complement the blend of flavours in the soup.

10. Efo riro and a full-bodied red wine such as a Zinfandel – the wine's boldness pairs well with the rich and complex flavours of the dish.

11. Bitterleaf soup and a light red wine such as a Pinot Noir – the wine's lightness helps to enhance the subtle flavours of the dish.

12. Plantain and beans and a crisp, fruity white wine such as a Riesling – the wine's fruitiness complements the sweetness of the plantains and the creaminess of the beans.

13. Fried yam and a sparkling wine – the wine's effervescence provides a refreshing contrast to the richness of the yam.

14. Ewa agoyin and a medium-bodied red wine such as a Malbec – the wine's smoothness complements the spiciness of the dish.

15. Stewed goat and a full-bodied red wine such as a Syrah – the wine's boldness stands up to the strong flavours of the dish.

Overall, the Aké Arts and Book Festival is a must-visit event for anyone interested in African literature and culture. The festival's vibrant atmosphere, diverse food and wine selections, and rich cultural programming make it a truly unique experience.

- **Durban July - South Africa**

Durban July is a highly anticipated event that takes place in South Africa, specifically in the city of Durban. Durban is a coastal city on the eastern coast of South Africa, located in the province of KwaZulu-Natal. The event is usually held on the first Saturday of July, hence its name, Durban July.

The event attracts people from all walks of life, from fashionistas and horse racing enthusiasts to wine lovers and foodies. It is a celebration of fashion, culture, and the thoroughbred horse racing industry. Horse racing is a popular sport in South Africa and has a rich history dating back to the 18th century.

Durban July is not just a horse racing event but an occasion for people to showcase their fashion sense and style. Attendees dress up in their best outfits to match the occasion. It is a significant event in South African culture, and people look forward to it every year.

The topography of the area around Durban is characterised by rolling hills, and the surrounding area is known for its warm climate and sandy beaches. South Africa has a diverse culture influenced by various ethnic groups, including African, European, and Asian cultures.

Wine production in South Africa is a significant industry, with regions such as Stellenbosch, Paarl and Franschhoek being well-known. South African wines incorporate both Old World and New World winemaking techniques.

Here are some food and wine pairings that you might find at Durban July:

1. **Braai (South African barbecue) and Pinotage** – Pinotage is a red wine blend unique to South Africa characterised by rich chocolate and red fruit flavours, making it the ideal complement to smoky, spicy braai.

2. **Boerewors (South African sausage) and Chenin Blanc** – Chenin Blanc, with its bright and fruity flavors, works well with the spiciness of Boerewors.

3. **Bobotie (South African meatloaf) and Chardonnay** – Bobotie is a dish made with spiced ground meat and topped with a custard-like mixture. The creaminess of Chardonnay pairs well with the flavours of the dish.

4. **Biryani and Gewurztraminer** – Gewurztraminer, with its floral and spicy flavours, is an excellent match for the fragrant spices in Biryani.

5. **Bunny Chow and Pinotage** – Bunny Chow is a South African dish in which a hollowed-out loaf of bread is filled with curry. Pinotage pairs well with the robust flavours of the curry.

6. **Pap and Wors (South African cornmeal and sausage) and Merlot** – Merlot's soft tannins and fruity flavours complement the slightly sweet and mild pap and wors.

7. **Denningvleis (South African lamb stew) and Shiraz** – Shiraz's bold, fruity flavours pair well with the richness of the lamb in this dish.

8. **Durban Curry and Viognier** – Viognier, with its tropical fruit flavours and floral aromas, pairs well with the spiciness of Durban Curry.

9. **Potjie (South African stew) and Pinot Noir** – Pinot Noir's light body and fruity flavours pair well with the combination of meats and vegetables in Potjie.

10. **Samoosas and Sauvignon Blanc** – The herbal and grassy notes in Sauvignon Blanc complement the spicy flavours of samoosas.

11. **Sosaties (South African kebabs) and Malbec** – Malbec's bold flavours and tannins work well with the smoky and spiced meat in Sosaties.

12. **Umngqusho (South African bean stew) and Tempranillo** – Tempranillo's rich, dark fruit flavours complement the earthy flavours of Umngqusho.

13. **Melktert (South African milk tart) and Riesling** – The light sweetness and fruity flavours in Riesling pair perfectly with the creamy and delicate flavours of Melktert.

14. **Cape Malay Curry and Shiraz** – Shiraz's bold, fruity flavours complement the spicy and fragrant flavours of Cape Malay Curry.

15. **Malva Pudding and Muscat** – Muscat's sweet, floral and fruity flavours pair well with the caramelised flavours of Malva Pudding.

In conclusion, Durban July is an event that brings together fashion, culture, and horse racing. South African cuisine, which is heavily influenced by the country's diverse cultures, pairs perfectly with the country's excellent wines. The food and wine pairings at Durban July provide a unique experience for attendees, with each pairing showcasing the best of South African cuisine and wine. – Pinot Noir's light body and fruity flavours pair well with the combination of meats and vegetables in Potjie.

- **KigaliUp Music Festival - Rwanda**

The KigaliUp Music Festival is an annual event held in the vibrant city of Kigali, which is the capital city of Rwanda. The festival brings together music lovers from around the country and the world to enjoy a diverse range of musical performances that reflect the culture and history of Rwanda.

The festival takes place over two days, usually in late July or early August. It is a celebration of music, culture, and community, and is a great way to experience the unique and vibrant culture of Rwanda.

Rwanda has a rich cultural heritage that is reflected in its music, food, and traditions. The country is known for its stunning natural beauty, with mountainous terrain, lush rainforests, and picturesque lakes and rivers. Its people are known for their warmth and hospitality, and the festival is a chance to experience the country's unique culture and traditions.

The festival features a variety of musical genres, ranging from traditional Rwandan music to contemporary pop, hip-hop, and jazz. There are also workshops and performances that showcase the traditional dance and music of Rwanda, as well as other African cultures.

As Rwanda is known for its agricultural production of tea, coffee and fruits, these are among the top export products. Rwandans also like to cook and eat meat, particularly goat, beef, and chicken. Vegetables, particularly beans, peas, and potatoes are very common. For the festival, vendors will offer local and international foods and wines to add variety to the occasion.

For the wine choices, among the top producing countries, I have chosen South Africa, Kenya, and Tanzania vineyards for their world-class options. Here are 15 wines and foods paired for you, with details of why these pairings work so well:

1. **Prawn Curry**: Prawns belong to the seafood category, and in this regard, white wines are the best. I have paired this food with a 2019 Delaire Graff Chenin Blanc from South Africa. The wine's acidity will balance the spicy curry, while the tropical fruit flavours will marry well with the sweetness of the prawns.

2. **Grilled Pork Skewers**: I paired this dish with the 2017 Warwick First Lady Cabernet Sauvignon. The wine's boldness and tannins are a great match for the flavourful meat, and the blackcurrant notes in the wine will complement the smokiness of the dish.

3. **Grilled Tilapia fish**: A white wine is ideal, and I would recommend the 2019 Meerlust Chardonnay from South Africa. The wine has a slight oaky flavour that won't overwhelm the delicate taste of the fish, but have a good tropical fruit aroma that will settle well with the fish's natural oiliness

4. **Roasted Vegetables**: For this vegetarian friendly option, the 2019 MAN Family Wines Chenin Blanc from South Africa is best. The wine's citrusy notes will complement the earthy, roasted flavours of the vegetables.

5. **Goan Fish Curry**: Pair this dish with a 2019 Ken Forrester Petit Chenin Blanc from South Africa, The wine is well balanced and has high acidity that will cut through the coconut milk and the tanginess of the curry while the citrus flavour from the wine will enhance the flavour of the fish.

6. **Grilled chicken** with red pepper aioli: In this all-time favourite dish, the 2017 Nederburg Cabernet Sauvignon from South Africa. This medium-bodied red wine has firm tannins that'll complement the juicy chicken and the smoky flavour that the grilling provides. The wine's earthy notes pair perfectly with the red pepper aioli.

7. **Grilled Halloumi**: A salty cheese like halloumi will need a wine that will cut through its saltiness. The 2019 MAN Family Wines Skaapveld Shiraz from South Africa will match well with the hearty flavours of the cheese.

8. **Moroccan Tagine**: I have paired this dish with the 2017 Leopard's Leap Culinaria Chenin Blanc from South Africa. The wine's acidity level is high enough to balance out the sweet apricot flavours in the Tagine, and the wine's round mouthfeel and subtle fruit notes will complement the spices.

9. **Beef Fillet**: I have paired this dish with the 2017 Ken Forrester Merlot from South Africa. The wine's velvety texture and soft tannins will go very well with the juicy, tender beef.

10. **Falafel**: For this vegan-friendly option, the 2019 Kleine Zalze Vineyard Selection Sauvignon Blanc is perfect. The wine's green apple and grapefruit notes are a great match for the nutty flavours of the falafel.

11. **Vegetarian Samosas**: Samosas can be paired with a 2019 MAN Family Wines Skaapveld Shiraz from South Africa. The wine's tannins and spice notes will complement the savoury, earthy flavours of the samosas.

12. **Fish and Chips**: A dry Riesling might do this dish justice, and I would recommend the 2018 DeMorgenzon DMZ Riesling from South Africa. The wine's bracing acidity and strong minerality will balance the richness of the fish and chips dish.

13. **Goat Curry**: I have paired this dish with the 2019 Tall Horse Shiraz from Kenya. The rich flavours of the goat require a wine with bold tannins, and this wine doesn't disappoint. The wine's dark fruit flavours will complement the richness and spiciness of the goat curry.

14. **Saag Paneer**: The 2018 Leopard's Leap Family Vineyards Culinaria Pinotage from South Africa works well with dishes that have cream and cheese in them. The wine's dark fruit flavours, soft tannins, and hint of smokiness pair perfectly with the rich, creamy paneer.

15. **Beet and Butterbean Salad**: For this vegetarian friendly salad, the 2019 MAN Family Wines Chenin Blanc from South Africa provides a good balance of fruitiness and acidity to complement the earthy flavours of the beets and butterbeans.

In conclusion, there's a wide range of local and international foods and wines to enjoy at the KigaliUp Music Festival in Rwanda. The paired options I provided are just a few of the many possibilities, but they were chosen to highlight the beauty and flavours unique to Africa.

- **Harare International Festival of the Arts - Zimbabwe**

The Harare International Festival of the Arts (HIFA) is an annual arts and culture festival held in Harare, the capital city of Zimbabwe. The festival brings together local and international artists, musicians, performers, and cultural enthusiasts to celebrate and showcase the diverse and dynamic cultural heritage of Zimbabwe and the African continent.

The event takes place over several days, typically in late April or early May, and features a wide range of cultural and artistic performances, exhibitions, workshops, and presentations. The festival attracts thousands of visitors from across Zimbabwe and around the world, making it one of the most important cultural events in the country.

Zimbabwe is a landlocked country located in southern Africa, with a rich cultural and historical background that is reflected in the diverse and vibrant artistic expressions on display at HIFA. The topography of Zimbabwe is characterised by mountains, plateaus, and valleys, with a varied climate that supports a range of agricultural activities, including viticulture and winemaking.

At HIFA, visitors can sample a wide range of local foods and wines, including traditional dishes such as sadza (a type of porridge made from maize meal), muriwo une dovi (a vegetable dish made from leafy greens and peanut butter), and nyama ne muriwo (a meat and vegetable stew). The wines available at the festival showcase the unique terroir and vinification techniques of Zimbabwe, including traditional methods such as basket pressing and open-air fermentation.

To pair foods and wines available at the event, we can consider the flavour profiles of the dishes and the wines, as well as the regional and cultural context of the pairings. For example, a rich and spicy dish like muriwo une dovi would pair well with a bold and fruity red wine, such as a Shiraz or Cabernet Sauvignon. A lighter dish like sadza could be paired with a crisp and refreshing white wine, such as a Chenin Blanc or Sauvignon Blanc.

Here are some possible food and wine pairings that visitors to HIFA might enjoy:

1. Sadza with Chenin Blanc

2. Nyama ne muriwo with Shiraz

3. Muriwo une dovi with Cabernet Sauvignon

4. Kapenta with Chardonnay

5. Matemba with Sauvignon Blanc

6. Boerewors with Merlot

7. Beef stew with Pinotage

8. Chicken curry with Riesling

9. Peanut butter and jam sandwich with Moscato

10. Roasted maize with Pinot Noir

11. Grilled fish with Chenin Blanc

12. Fresh fruit salad with Rosé

13. Spinach and mushroom quiche with Chablis

14. Beef samosas with Merlot

15. Chocolate cake with Cabernet Franc

In each of these pairings, the flavours and textures of the food complement and enhance the flavours and aromas of the wine, creating a harmonious and enjoyable dining experience. Whether enjoying traditional Zimbabwean dishes or exploring the eclectic and diverse offerings of the festival, visitors to HIFA are sure to discover new and exciting flavour combinations that reflect the rich cultural heritage of Zimbabwe and the African continent.

- **OppiKoppi Festival - South Africa**

The OppiKoppi Festival is an annual music and lifestyle festival held in South Africa. It takes place in the dusty fields outside the small town of Northam, Limpopo, which is located in the northern part of the country. The festival attracts thousands of people from all over South Africa and beyond, making it one of the largest and most popular music festivals in the country.

The festival features a variety of musical genres, including rock, indie, hip hop, and electronic. In addition to the music, the event also includes art installations, food and drink stalls, and various other forms of entertainment.

The OppiKoppi Festival is deeply rooted in South African culture, drawing inspiration from the country's rich history and diverse population. The festival celebrates the country's music, art, and food, and is an important occasion for people to come together and celebrate their shared cultural heritage.

The topography of the festival grounds is quite unique, with dusty dirt roads leading to various stages and campsites scattered throughout the area. It can get quite hot and dusty during the day, so festival-goers should be prepared with plenty of water and sunscreen.

The food and drink options available at the festival are diverse and delicious. Some of the top dishes to try include traditional South African barbecue (or braai), biltong (a type of dried meat), and boerewors (a type of sausage). For those looking for something a bit more adventurous, there are also options like crocodile and kudu meat on offer.

As for wines, South Africa is known for its excellent winemaking, and there are plenty of great options available at the festival. Some of the most popular wines to pair with the festival's food include:

1. **Chenin Blanc** - This crisp, refreshing white wine is the perfect match for grilled seafood dishes like calamari.

2. **Pinotage** - This complex red wine pairs well with the rich, smoky flavours of grilled beef and lamb dishes.

3. **Sauvignon Blanc** - This bright, acidic white wine is a great match for spicy and flavorful dishes like curries and chilies.

4. **Chardonnay** - This full-bodied white wine is a good choice to pair with creamy, rich dishes like mac and cheese or risotto.

5. **Shiraz** - This bold, peppery red wine is a classic pairing for grilled meats, especially when seasoned with spicy rubs or marinades.

6. **Cabernet Sauvignon** - This full-bodied red wine has bold tannins that complement rich, hearty dishes like stews and roasts.

7. **Pinot Noir** - This light, delicate red wine pairs well with grilled salmon, pork, or chicken dishes.

8. **Viognier** - This aromatic white wine is a great match for spicy and exotic dishes like Thai or Indian curries.

9. **Merlot** - This smooth, easy-drinking red wine is a good choice to pair with lighter dishes like grilled vegetables or pasta.

10. **Malbec** - This hearty, full-bodied red wine is a great match for grilled meats and strong, flavorful cheeses.

11. **Riesling** - This sweet, fruity white wine is the perfect match for spicier foods like BBQ and Asian dishes.

12. **Grenache** - This medium-bodied red wine has flavours of red berries and spices, making it a great match for grilled veggies and meaty dishes.

13. **Gewurztraminer** - This aromatic white wine has notes of lychee and rose petals, and pairs perfectly with spicy and exotic dishes.

14. **Zinfandel** - This bold, fruity red wine pairs well with BBQ and other smoked meats.

15. **Rosé** - This light, refreshing wine is perfect for sipping on a hot day, and pairs well with light salads and cheeses.

Overall, the OppiKoppi Festival is an incredible event that celebrates the diversity and richness of South African culture. Whether you're there for the music, the food, or the wine, it's an experience you won't soon forget.

- **Carnival of Calabar - Nigeria**

The Carnival of Calabar is one of Nigeria's largest and most iconic festivals, held annually in the city of Calabar, Cross River State. Known for its vibrant colors, music, and dance, the Carnival of Calabar is a celebration of the country's diverse cultures and traditions.

The Carnival of Calabar typically takes place on December 26th and runs through January 1st of the following year, marking the end of the year and the beginning of a new one. The event attracts both locals and visitors from around the world, with an estimated attendance of over 2 million people.

The people of Cross River State are known for their diverse range of cultural practices, which are reflected in the Carnival of Calabar. The event features numerous parades, cultural displays, and music performances, showcasing the state's rich history and heritage.

The topography of Calabar is characterised by lush, green forests, rolling hills, and the beautiful Calabar River, which provides a scenic backdrop for the festival. The city's tropical climate and rich soils also make it an ideal location for growing a variety of fruits and vegetables, which are incorporated into many of the festival's dishes.

Some of the most popular foods at the Carnival of Calabar include jollof rice, fried plantain, akara (bean cake), egusi soup, and efo riro (a Nigerian spinach stew). Many of these dishes are paired with local wines, which are produced using traditional vinification techniques.

Some wine and food pairings available at the Carnival of Calabar include:

1. **Jollof rice with a dry red wine**: This classic Nigerian dish is made with rice, tomatoes, peppers, and a variety of spices. It pairs well with a dry red wine, such as a Cabernet Sauvignon or Merlot.

2. **Fried plantain with a sweet white wine**: Plantains are a staple food in Nigeria and are often served as a side dish. They pair well with a sweet white wine, such as a Moscato or Riesling.

3. **Akara with a light red wine**: Akara is a savoury bean cake that is often served as a snack or appetiser. It pairs well with a light red wine, such as a Pinot Noir or Beaujolais.

4. **Egusi soup with a full-bodied red wine**: Egusi soup is a rich and hearty stew made with ground melon seeds and various meats and vegetables. It pairs well with a full-bodied red wine, such as a Malbec or Syrah.

5. **Efo riro with a crisp white wine**: Efo riro is a Nigerian spinach stew that is often served with rice or yams. It pairs well with a crisp white wine, such as a Sauvignon Blanc or Chardonnay.

6. **Grilled chicken with a dry white wine**: Grilled chicken is a popular dish at the Carnival of Calabar and pairs well with a dry white wine, such as a Pinot Grigio or Chardonnay.

7. **Pepper soup with a light-bodied red wine**: Pepper soup is a spicy broth made with a variety of meats and spices. It pairs well with a light-bodied red wine, such as a Beaujolais or Pinot Noir.

8. **Suya with a sweet red wine**: Suya is a popular Nigerian street food consisting of grilled skewered meat. It pairs well with a sweet red wine, such as a Zinfandel or Shiraz.

9. **Grilled fish with a dry white wine**: Grilled fish is a staple food in Nigeria and pairs well with a dry white wine, such as a Chardonnay or Pinot Grigio.

10. **Fried yam with a sweet white wine**: Fried yam is a popular street food in Nigeria and pairs well with a sweet white wine, such as a Riesling or Moscato.

11. **Pounded yam with a full-bodied red wine**: Pounded yam is a traditional Nigerian dish made by pounding yam until it becomes soft and fluffy. It pairs well with a full-bodied red wine, such as a Cabernet Sauvignon or Syrah.

12. **Moi Moi with a light red wine**: Moi Moi is a steamed bean cake that is often served as a side dish. It pairs well with a light red wine, such as a Pinot Noir or Beaujolais.

13. **Oha soup with a full-bodied red wine**: Oha soup is a Nigerian soup made with a variety of meats and vegetables. It pairs well with a full-bodied red wine, such as a Malbec or Syrah.

14. **Boli with a dry red wine**: Boli is a roasted plantain that is often served as a snack or side dish. It pairs well with a dry red wine, such as a Cabernet Sauvignon or Merlot.

15. **Nigerian meat pie with a sweet red wine**: Nigerian meat pie is a savory pastry filled with spiced meat and vegetables. It pairs well with a sweet red wine, such as a Zinfandel or Shiraz.

In conclusion, the Carnival of Calabar is a vibrant and exciting event that celebrates Nigeria's culture and traditions. With its delicious food and wine pairings, the festival is a must-visit for any food and wine lover looking to explore the country's rich culinary heritage.

- **Timitar Festival - Morocco**

The Timitar Festival in Morocco is a celebrated cultural event that takes place annually in the city of Agadir. Agadir is a coastal city in the southern part of Morocco, and it is renowned for its picturesque scenery, warm weather, and sandy beaches. The Timitar Festival attracts visitors from all over the world who want to experience the beauty of Moroccan culture through music, food, and wine.

The festival usually takes place in July and lasts for several days. The occasion celebrates the Amazigh culture and brings together talented musicians, singers, and dancers from various parts of Morocco and other countries. The word "Timitar" is an Amazigh word that means "signs," referring to the symbols and expressions that reflect the cultural identity of the people of Agadir and the wider region.

Morocco has a diverse culture, and this is reflected in the Timitar Festival. Attendees can enjoy traditional Moroccan music, fusion music, African rhythms, and contemporary sounds. The festival also showcases traditional dances and crafts, and visitors can buy souvenirs and handicrafts made by local artisans.

The topography of the region is an important factor in the food and wine available at the Timitar Festival. Agadir and the surrounding region are known for their fertile soils, which produce an abundance of fruits and vegetables. Some of the most popular dishes at the festival include tajine, couscous, harira soup, and pastilla. These dishes are made using traditional cooking methods that have been passed down through generations of Moroccan families.

Morocco is also known for its wine production, which has been influenced by the country's long history of winemaking. The most popular grape varieties grown in Morocco include Carignan, Grenache, and Cinsault. Vinification techniques have improved significantly over time, and today, the country produces some high-quality wines that are exported to various parts of the world.

The Timitar Festival offers a unique opportunity to taste some of the best food and wine in Morocco. Some of the top food and wine pairings available at the festival include:

1. **Pastilla with Chardonnay** - Pastilla is a flaky pastry filled with savoury meat or chicken and topped with cinnamon and powdered sugar. The sweetness of Chardonnay complements the savoury flavours of the pastilla.

2. **Tajine with Riesling** - Tajine is a slow-cooked meat or vegetable stew that is traditionally served with couscous. The sweetness of Riesling balances the spiciness of the tajine.

3. **Couscous with Sauvignon Blanc** - Couscous is a staple food in Morocco and is often served with vegetables and meat. The light acidity of Sauvignon Blanc complements the flavors of the couscous.

4. **Harira soup with Shiraz** - Harira is a thick soup made with lentils, chickpeas, and spices. The bold flavours of Shiraz pair well with the hearty soup.

5. **Kefta with Merlot** - Kefta is a type of Moroccan meatball that is usually served with tomato sauce and bread. The soft tannins of Merlot complement the richness of the tomato sauce.

6. **Zaalouk with Rosé** - Zaalouk is a dip made with roasted eggplants, tomatoes, and spices. The light and fruity flavours of Rosé pair well with the smoky flavours of the eggplants.

7. **Mechoui lamb with Syrah** - Mechoui lamb is a slow-roasted lamb dish that is traditionally served at weddings and other special occasions. The bold flavours of Syrah complement the robust taste of the lamb.

8. **Chicken tagine with Pinot Noir** - Chicken tagine is a slow-cooked chicken dish that is flavoured with saffron, turmeric, and preserved lemons. The light tannins of Pinot Noir complement the delicate flavours of the chicken.

9. **Moroccan bread with Chablis** - Moroccan bread is a type of flatbread that is often served as an accompaniment to meals. The crisp acidity of Chablis pairs well with the light and fluffy texture of the bread.

10. **Moroccan grilled fish with Gewürztraminer** - Grilled fish is a popular street food in Morocco that is usually served with a side of salad. The floral notes of Gewürztraminer complement the fresh flavours of the fish.

11. **Chicken pastilla with Chenin Blanc** - Chicken pastilla is a sweet and savory pastry that is filled with tender chicken, almonds, and spices. The sweetness of Chenin Blanc complements the richness of the pastilla.

12. **Vegetable tagine with Viognier** - Vegetable tagine is a vegetarian version of the traditional meat stew. The soft and floral flavours of Viognier blend well with the natural sweetness of the vegetables.

13. **Moroccan orange salad with Muscat** - Moroccan orange salad is a refreshing dish made with fresh oranges, olives, and onions. The crisp acidity of Muscat complements the bright flavours of the oranges.

14. **Moroccan spiced lamb with Malbec** - Moroccan spiced lamb is a flavorful dish that is grilled to perfection. The full-bodied flavours of Malbec complement the bold flavours of the lamb.

15. **Couscous Royale with Cabernet Sauvignon** - Couscous Royale is a hearty dish made with lamb, chicken, vegetables, and raisins. The rich and complex flavours of Cabernet Sauvignon pair well with the savoury and sweet flavours of the couscous.

In conclusion, the Timitar Festival in Morocco is an exceptional event that celebrates the rich culture and history of the region through music, food, and wine. It provides visitors with a unique opportunity to taste some of the best food and wine in Morocco and enjoy the beauty of the country's culture and traditions.

- **FESPACO - Burkina Faso**

FESPACO, also known as the Pan African Film and Television Festival of Ouagadougou, is an event held in Ouagadougou, Burkina Faso. The festival takes place every two years and is one of the biggest cultural events in Africa. The festival was founded in 1969 to promote African cinema and to celebrate the cultural diversity of Africa. The festival has grown in popularity over the years and attracts filmmakers from all over the world.

Burkina Faso is a landlocked country located in West Africa. Its population is approximately 20 million, and it is known for its diverse ethnic groups, including the Mossi, Fulani, Bobo and Gurunsi. The official language of Burkina Faso is French, but there are over 60 other languages spoken in the country.

Ouagadougou is the capital city of Burkina Faso and is home to the FESPACO event. The city is located in central Burkina Faso and has a population of approximately 2.5 million people. It is a bustling city, with many cultural and historical sites that attract visitors from around the world.

The FESPACO event is a celebration of the film and television industry in Africa. It typically takes place over a period of one week and includes film screenings, workshops, and awards ceremonies. The festival is a celebration of African culture, and visitors can expect to experience a vibrant atmosphere filled with music and dance.

In terms of topography, Burkina Faso is a landlocked country that consists of a mix of woodland savannah and plains, known locally as the Sahel. The country has a tropical climate, with temperatures ranging from 20-35 degrees Celsius.

When it comes to food, Burkina Faso has a rich culinary tradition. Some of the most popular dishes include riz gras, which is a rice dish made with vegetables and meat, and poulet bicyclette, which is a grilled chicken dish. Other popular foods include tô, which is a starchy staple made from millet or sorghum, and soumbala, which is a fermented bean paste used as a seasoning in many dishes.

Wine production in Burkina Faso is relatively new, with most of the country's wine being produced in the central region, near the city of Koudougou. The most common grape varieties used in Burkina Faso include chardonnay, cabernet sauvignon, merlot and syrah. The vinification process used in the country involves traditional fermentation techniques, with some winemakers using modern equipment to improve the quality of their wines.

Foods and Wines Pairs available at the FESPACO event:

1. **Poulet bicyclette with a dry red wine** - The grilled chicken pairs well with the tannins in the wine, which bring out the flavour of the meat.

2. **Riz gras with a fruity white wine** - The light, fruity notes in the wine complement the vegetables and meat in the rice dish.

3. **Tô with a crisp rosé wine** - The acidity in the wine cuts through the starchy flavour of the tô, leaving a refreshing taste in the mouth.

4. **Soumbala sauce with a full-bodied red wine** - The fermented bean paste pairs well with the bold flavours of the wine and brings out its rich aromas.

5. **Yams and spinach with a spicy red wine** - The heat of the spice in the wine pairs well with the earthy flavour of the vegetables.

6. **Maize porridge with a light white wine** - The mild flavour of the wine complements the subtle taste of the maize porridge.

7. **Grilled lamb with a dry red wine** - The gamey flavour of the lamb pairs well with the tannins in the wine.

8. **Fried plantains with a sweet white wine** - The sweetness in the wine complements the caramelised sugars in the plantains.

9. **Grilled fish with a crisp white wine** - The light, refreshing flavour of the wine complements the delicate flavour of the fish.

10. **Peanut sauce with a fruity red wine** - The nutty flavour of the sauce pairs well with the sweet, fruity notes in the wine.

11. **Couscous with a creamy white wine** - The creamy texture of the wine complements the soft texture of the couscous.

12. **Fried chicken with a spicy red wine** - The heat of the spice in the wine pairs well with the savoury flavour of the fried chicken.

13. **Bean stew with a full-bodied red wine** - The bold flavours of the stew pair well with the rich aromas of the wine.

14. **Grilled beef with a dry red wine** - The tannins in the wine complement the flavour of the beef and bring out its smoky notes.

15. **Vegetable fritters with a light white wine** - The subtle notes in the wine complement the light and crispy texture of the fritters.

- **Festival of the Sahara (Festival du Sahara) - Tunisia**

Country: Tunisia

City: Douz

Date: Usually held in December

Culture: Douz is located in the Saharan region of Tunisia and is the centre of the nomadic culture of the country's south. The festival is an opportunity to celebrate this unique culture and connect with the people who call it home.

Event: The Festival of the Sahara (Festival du Sahara) is an annual three-day event that takes place in Douz. It celebrates the traditional lifestyle of the nomadic desert people of Tunisia with music, dance, food, and other cultural activities.

Topography: Douz is located on the edge of the Sahara desert, providing a stunning backdrop for the festival. Visitors can expect to see sand dunes, palm trees, and other desert plants and animals.

Foods and Wines: Tunisian cuisine is influenced by Mediterranean and North African flavours, and the Festival of the Sahara is a great place to sample some of the best traditional dishes. Here are some food and wine pairings that you might find at the event:

1. **Couscous with lamb and vegetables** - This hearty dish pairs well with a bold red wine like Tazarka Rouge, which has a nice balance of tannins and acidity.

2. **Brik** - A fried pastry filled with egg, tuna, and harissa, this dish pairs nicely with a light white wine like Cap Bon Muscat.

3. **Harissa-marinated grilled lamb chops** - This spicy dish pairs well with a fruity red like the Morning Rouge.

4. **Tuna salad** - A lighter option, this dish can be paired with a crisp white wine like the Cap Bon Chardonnay.

5. **Shakshuka** - A classic breakfast dish of eggs poached in tomato sauce, this pairs nicely with a medium-bodied red like the Sidi Brahim Rouge.

6. **Brick à l'oeuf** - A fried pastry filled with egg, this dish can be paired with a light white wine like Mornag Blanc.

7. **Mechouia** - A salad of grilled peppers, tomatoes, and onions, this dish pairs well with a dry rosé like the Kélibia Rosé.

8. **Grilled sardines** - This flavorful dish pairs well with a crisp white like the Morning Blanc.

9. **Octopus couscous** - This seafood dish pairs nicely with a light red like the Carthage Coteaux Bouargoub.

10. **Lablabi** - A chickpea soup with bread and spices, this comforting dish can be paired with a medium-bodied red like the Cap Bon Gamay.

11. **Merguez sausages** - Spicy and flavorful, these sausages pair well with a bold red like the Kairouan Rouge.

12. **Brick with cheese** - A fried pastry filled with cheese, this dish can be paired with a light white like the Domaine Atlas Chardonnay.

13. **Lamb tagine with figs** - This sweet and savoury dish pairs well with a medium red like the Mornag Merlot.

14. **Fricassé** - A sandwich with tuna, egg, potato, and harissa, this dish can be paired with a crisp white like the Cap Bon Muscat.

15. **Grilled chicken with ras el hanout** - This flavorful dish pairs well with a light red like the Kélibia Rouge.

Overall, the Festival of the Sahara in Tunisia is a great opportunity to experience the unique culture and cuisine of the country's southern nomads. With a variety of traditional foods and delicious wines to choose from, visitors are sure to have an unforgettable culinary experience.

- **Essaouira Gnaoua and World Music Festival - Morocco**

The Essaouira Gnaoua and World Music Festival is one of the most popular musical events in Morocco, held annually in the city of Essaouira on the country's Atlantic coast. This festival is the perfect representation of Morocco's melting pot of cultures and traditions.

The festival, which runs for four days each June, celebrates the unique sounds and rhythms of the Gnaoua culture, a sub-Saharan African population that has lived in Morocco for centuries. The event's main stage showcases musicians from around the world, as well as a variety of street performers and traditional Gnaoua musicians.

The festival is an opportunity for visitors to experience Moroccan culture through music, food, and art. The city of Essaouira has a rich history dating back to the Phoenician times, and the festival takes place in its historic walled medina, a UNESCO World Heritage site that has served as a backdrop for many famous movies.

Essaouira's topography includes a beautiful sandy coastline that is perfect for seafood dishes. Some of the most popular dishes available at the festival include seafood tagine, grilled sardines, and shrimp pastilla. Moroccan wines pair well with the rich flavours of these dishes, and there are several vinification techniques used in the country.

Here are some of the best pairing options available at the festival:

1. **Seafood tagine with a Moroccan Chardonnay**: the buttery texture and citrusy notes of the wine pair well with the rich tomato-based tagine.

2. **Grilled sardines with a Moroccan Rosé**: the subtle fruity notes of the wine complement the grilled flavors of the sardines.

3. **Shrimp pastilla with a Moroccan Merlot**: the soft tannins of the wine complement the savoury flavours of the pastilla.

4. **Lamb tangia with a Moroccan Cabernet Sauvignon**: the bold flavours of the wine hold up to the slow-cooked lamb.

5. **Chicken b'stilla with a Moroccan Syrah**: the velvety texture and sweet fruity notes of the wine balance the savoury spices in the b'stilla.

6. **Harira soup with a Moroccan Pinot Noir**: the light-bodied wine pairs well with the spiced tomato broth of the soup.

7. **Vegetable couscous with a Moroccan Sauvignon Blanc**: the refreshing acidity of the wine cuts through the flavours of the couscous.

8. **Chicken tagine with preserved lemons and olives with a Moroccan Grenache**: the bold flavours of the tagine are complemented by the full-bodied wine.

9. **Zaalouk with a Moroccan Chablis**: the crisp acidity of the wine balances the earthy flavours of the eggplant and tomato dip.

10. **Briouats with a Moroccan Chenin Blanc**: the refreshing flavours of the wine complement the savoury pastry filled with meat or vegetables.

11. **Maakouda with a Moroccan Viognier**: the wine's fruity notes balance the crispy potato fritters.

12. **Kefta tagine with a Moroccan Zinfandel**: the bold flavours of the tagine are complemented by the full-bodied wine.

13. **Cornes de gazelles with a Moroccan Muscat**: the sweet notes of the wine balance the sweet filling of the pastry.

14. **Msemen with a Moroccan Petit Verdot**: the full-bodied wine pairs well with the savoury Moroccan pancakes filled with vegetables or meat.

15. **Mint tea with a Moroccan Gewürztraminer**: the refreshing notes of the wine complement the sweet and sour flavours of the mint tea.

Overall, the Essaouira Gnaoua and World Music Festival is an incredible opportunity for anyone to experience the beauty of Morocco's cultures and traditions. The festival's variety of food and wine options provide the perfect chance to sample some of the country's most flavorful dishes and wines.

- **Africa Nouveau Festival - Kenya.**

The Africa Nouveau Festival is an annual cultural event that takes place in Kenya, specifically in the city of Nairobi. The event showcases various aspects of African culture such as music, fashion, art, and dance. This festival aims to celebrate the unique culture and diversity of the African continent.

The event takes place over three days and typically occurs in the month of February or March every year. The festival attracts a diverse group of people from all corners of the world, all of whom come to experience the unique culture of Kenya and the continent at large.

Kenya is well-known for its rich cultural heritage, and the Africa Nouveau Festival is a perfect opportunity to showcase these traditions. The occasion is an excellent time for visitors to immerse themselves in the local customs and traditions of the Kenyan people.

The landscape of Kenya is diverse and varied, offering an array of interesting geographical features. In addition to the culture, people come to enjoy the beautiful natural landscapes such as the Great Rift Valley.

The festival features a wide range of African cuisine, made with the freshest local ingredients. Some of the popular dishes that festival goers can enjoy include ugali, nyama choma, and samosas. These dishes are typically paired with local wines that are popular in the region, such as the Chardonnay and Sauvignon Blanc.

Vinification techniques in Kenya are unique, and winemakers employ several methods to produce high-quality, locally-made wines. Some local wineries take advantage of the year-round sunshine and the cool climate at night to produce rich and flavorful wines.

Some of the foods and wines that go well together at the Africa Nouveau Festival include:

1. Samosas and Shiraz

2. Braised beef and Cabernet Sauvignon

3. Barbecued chicken and Chardonnay

4. Grilled goat and Merlot

5. Pilau rice and Pinot Noir

6. Chapati and Malbec

7. Fried tilapia and Chenin Blanc

8. Beef skewers and Syrah

9. Corn on the cob and Sauvignon Blanc

10. Fried plantains and Riesling

11. Nyama choma and Cabernet Franc

12. Curry goat and Tempranillo

13. Ugali and Zinfandel

14. Vegetable stew and Pinot Grigio

15. Fried yam and Sangria

These pairings are perfect for those seeking to enjoy the diverse ethnic cuisines and local wines at the festival. The dishes are perfectly balanced, with the wine complementing the flavours of the food to create a memorable dining experience.

In conclusion, the Africa Nouveau Festival is an excellent opportunity to experience the unique culture of Kenya and the African continent. Visually stunning landscapes, delicious food and wine and world-class performances by artists who integrate the traditional with the contemporary on the creative plane of African culture. Intriguing storytellers and profound advocates of Pan African culture who share across the geographies what it means to be African.

These are just a few examples of the many vibrant and culturally rich festivals and events celebrated throughout Africa.

Phileas Fogg's Travel Encounters and Food and Wine Experiences in Africa

Phileas Fogg's adventurous travels through Africa would have taken him through a diverse range of topography, climates, and cultures - from deserts to tropical jungles, savannas to coastal regions. Some of the people, animals, and topography he might have encountered on his travels are:

1. **Egypt**: In Egypt, Phileas Fogg would have visited the pyramids and the Sphinx. He would have encountered camels, donkeys, and horses in the cities and along the Nile River. He would have also met locals and learned about their culture, religion, and history.

2. **Sudan**: In Sudan, Phileas Fogg would have encountered the Nubian people, who are known for their unique culture and colorful clothing. He would have also come across wildlife such as lions, hippos, and crocodiles near the Nile River.

3. **Ethiopia**: In Ethiopia, Phileas Fogg would have explored the rugged highlands and the lush coffee plantations. He would have encountered the Oromo and Amhara people, who make up a large part of the population. He would have also come across wildlife such as baboons and gelada monkeys.

4. **Kenya**: In Kenya, Phileas Fogg would have explored the grassy savannas and encountered the Maasai people, who are known for their bright red clothing and intricate jewellery. He would have also come across wildlife such as lions, elephants, and zebras in Masai Mara National Reserve.

5. **Tanzania**: In Tanzania, Phileas Fogg would have visited Mount Kilimanjaro, the highest peak in Africa. He would have also explored the Serengeti National Park and experienced the annual wildebeest migration. He would have encountered the Maasai people, as well as other tribes such as the Chagga and Sukuma.

6. **Madagascar**: In Madagascar, Phileas Fogg would have experienced the unique wildlife, such as lemurs, baobab trees, and chameleons. He would have also encountered the Malagasy people, who have a diverse culture and speak over 18 languages.

The topography that Fogg would have braved through his treks in Africa would include deserts, savannas, jungles, mountains, and coastal regions. He might have experienced challenges such as extreme temperatures, rugged terrain, and dangerous wildlife.

I can provide some information on festivals, foods, and wines that Fogg might have also encountered during his travels in Africa.

Festivals and events he might have come across include:

1. Festival of the Sahara in Tunisia, celebrating the nomadic culture of the region.

2. Marrakech Popular Arts Festival in Morocco, showcasing traditional Moroccan music, dance, and crafts.

3. Cape Town Jazz Festival in South Africa, featuring local and international jazz artists.

4. Timkat Festival in Ethiopia, celebrating the baptism of Jesus Christ.

5. New Year's Day Carnival in Praia, Cape Verde, featuring vibrant parades, music, and dancing.

As for foods and wines, African cuisine is diverse and rich in flavours. Here are some pairings that Fogg might have enjoyed:

1. **South African** Bobotie (spiced meat dish) with a glass of Jam Jar Sweet Shiraz.

2. **Moroccan** tagine (slow-cooked stew) with a glass of Chateau Ksara Reserve du Couvent.

3. **Tunisian** brik (filo pastry filled with egg, meat or tuna) with a glass of Muscat Sec from Domaine des Homs.

4. **Ethiopian** Doro Wat (spicy chicken stew) with a glass of Awash Melka Kunture red wine.

5. **Cape Verdean** Cachupa (corn and bean stew) with a glass of Monte Velho White.

6. Egyptian Molokhia (stewed leafy green) with a glass of Kouroum of Egypt.

7. **Nigerian** Jollof Rice (spicy tomato rice with meat) with a glass of Nigerian Merlot.

8. **Algerian** Couscous (steamed grain dish) with a glass of Pinot Gris from Château Khemisti.

9. **Zanzibari** Octopus Curry (spicy coconut-based curry) with a glass of Thelema Sauvignon Blanc.

10. **Kenyan** Nyama Choma (roasted meat dish) with a glass of Kenyan Cabernet Sauvignon.

11. **Moroccan** Harira (spicy tomato soup) with a glass of Chateau Roslane Tradition Red.

12. **Ghanaian** Waakye (rice and beans dish) with a glass of Ghanaian Chenin Blanc.

13. **Senegalese** Thieboudienne (fish and rice stew) with a glass of Senegalese Rosé.

14. **Rwandan** Brochette (grilled meat skewers) with a glass of Rwandan Pinotage.

15. **Tunisian** Lamb Tajine (slow-cooked lamb stew) with a glass of Tunisian Syrah.

16. **Algerian** Mechoui (spit-roasted lamb) with a glass of Algerian Rosé.

17. **Zimbabwean** Sadza (thick maize porridge) with a glass of Zimbabwean Chardonnay.

18. **Ethiopian** Injera (fermented flatbread) with a glass of Ethiopian Red Blend.

19. **Moroccan** Pastilla (meat pie with cinnamon and sugar) with a glass of Moroccan Cabernet Sauvignon.

20. **South African** Biltong (dried meat) with a glass of South African Pinotage.

21. **Ugandan** Matoke (steamed plantain) with a glass of Ugandan Sauvignon Blanc.

22. **Sudanese** Ful Medames (spiced fava beans) with a glass of Sudanese Merlot.

23. **Kenyan** Ugali (white maize porridge) with a glass of Kenyan Chardonnay.

24. **Cape Verdean** Lapas (grilled limpets) with a glass of Cape Verdean Fonte.

25. **Nigerian** Egusi Soup (spicy soup with ground melon seeds) with a glass of Nigerian Zinfandel.

Overall, Fogg would have had a wide variety of festivals, foods, and wines to experience in Africa, each with their own unique cultural and regional influences.

CHAPTER 17

FESTIVALS IN ANTARCTICA

As far as I know, there are no food and wine festivals or events held in Antarctica. Antarctica is primarily a research destination, and there are strict regulations in place regarding waste disposal and environmental impact.

Additionally, due to the extreme conditions and isolation of the continent, it is not a practical location for large-scale events. Instead, the focus is on scientific research and conservation efforts.

However, there are occasional social events like movie screenings and talent shows for the researchers to enjoy during their downtime.

CHAPTER 18

FESTIVALS IN NEW ZEALAND

Let's look at some of the top food and wine festivals and events held in New Zealand:

- **Auckland Food Show (Auckland)**

The Auckland Food Show is an annual four-day event that takes place in Auckland, New Zealand. The city of Auckland is one of the largest in the country and is known for its diverse culture and cosmopolitan vibe. The Auckland Food Show brings together food and wine lovers, chefs, and producers from around the country and beyond.

The show features a wide variety of food and drink vendors showcasing the latest in culinary trends and techniques, as well as offering tastings and presentations. The Auckland Food Show usually takes place in late July or early August, and is a popular occasion for the locals and international visitors as well.

New Zealand is a country known for its unique cultural heritage and stunning topography, with many vineyards and wineries scattered throughout the countryside. Vinification techniques are diverse and range from traditional to modern methods, resulting in a wide variety of wines that pair perfectly with local foods.

The Auckland Food Show is an occasion where people from different cultures come to celebrate their love of food and wine. The topography and vineyards of New Zealand play a significant role in shaping the culture of the country and influencing the culinary traditions.

At the Auckland Food Show, visitors can experience a variety of local foods and wines. Some of the most popular foods at the event include artisanal cheeses, fresh seafood, lamb and other meats, locally-grown fruits and vegetables, and artisanal chocolates and confections.

Here are some pairing examples that showcase the diversity of foods and wines available at the Auckland Food Show:

1. Oysters paired with Sauvignon Blanc

2. Grilled Lamb paired with a Pinot Noir

3. Ceviche paired with a crisp Rosé

4. Manuka honey glazed salmon paired with a Chardonnay

5. Sushi paired with a Riesling

6. Smoked duck breast paired with a Merlot

7. Grilled prawns paired with a Viognier

8. Venison paired with a Shiraz

9. Beetroot salad paired with a Pinot Gris

10. Citrus-marinated scallops paired with a Sauvignon Blanc

11. Seared tuna steak paired with a Cabernet Sauvignon

12. Freshly shucked clams paired with a Syrah

13. Roast pork belly paired with a Merlot

14. Grilled flatbread with hummus paired with a Rosé

15. Charcuterie board paired with a Chardonnay

16. Spicy chicken skewers paired with a Gewürztraminer

17. Salmon tartare paired with a Pinot Noir

18. Stuffed mushrooms paired with a Cabernet Franc

19. Grilled asparagus paired with a Sauvignon Blanc

20. Ratatouille paired with a Pinot Gris

21. Butternut squash soup paired with a Chardonnay

22. Sweet potato fries paired with a Merlot

23. Braised beef cheeks paired with a Syrah

24. Baked brie cheese paired with a Riesling

25. Dark chocolate paired with a Cabernet Sauvignon

Each of these pairings showcases how the flavours of the food and wine complement each other, making for a delicious and memorable experience. The Sauvignon Blanc is a popular choice among visitors as it pairs well with many of the seafood dishes. The Pinot Noir also pairs well with grilled meats and is a great option for those who prefer a red wine. Chardonnay is always a safe bet with poultry and pork dishes, while Syrah is a great choice for rich, hearty meats and stews.

- **Wellington on a Plate (Wellington)**

Wellington on a Plate is a popular food and wine event held in Wellington, the capital city of New Zealand. The event is known for its diverse range of food and wine offerings that showcase the best of New Zealand's culinary culture.

The event typically takes place in August each year and is a celebration of Wellington's strong foodie culture and hospitality industry. It attracts a large number of visitors from across New Zealand and abroad who come to experience the unique food and wine offerings.

Wellington is a coastal city with a diverse topography that includes hills, beaches, and stunning coastline views. The region surrounding the city is well-known for its vineyards and wine production. The event showcases the best of local wine-making, including vinification techniques that are unique to the region.

The food offerings at the event showcase the best of New Zealand's cuisine, including locally-sourced seafood, lamb, beef, and other culinary delights. The event also features a range of wines, including those paired specifically with the food offerings.

The food and wine pairings at Wellington on a Plate are designed to complement each other. The pairing process involves carefully selecting wines that enhance the flavours of the food. The following are some pairing examples that demonstrate the unique flavour pairings at Wellington on a Plate:

1. Grilled prawns with Chardonnay

2. Seared scallops with Sauvignon Blanc

3. Steamed mussels with Pinot Gris

4. Grilled salmon with Chardonnay

5. Grilled lamb chops with Merlot

6. Spiced beef tacos with Pinot Noir

7. Duck pâté with Syrah

8. Beef brisket with Cabernet Franc

9. Smoked salmon with Sparkling Blanc de Blancs

10. Char-grilled squid with Grüner Veltliner

11. Cheese platter with Pinot Noir

12. Oysters with Chardonnay

13. Venison with Cabernet Sauvignon

14. Seared tuna with Sauvignon Blanc

15. Smoked beef with Merlot

16. Roast chicken with Chardonnay

17. Smoked salmon with Chardonnay

18. Wild mushroom risotto with Pinot Noir

19. Beef tartare with Syrah

20. Grilled octopus with Grüner Veltliner

21. Pork belly with Riesling

22. Roast beef with Cabernet Sauvignon

23. Grilled sea bass with Sauvignon Blanc

24. Seared duck breast with Chardonnay

25. Lemon and thyme roasted chicken with Pinot Gris

These pairing examples showcase the unique flavor combinations that can be found at Wellington on a Plate. The food and wine pairings are carefully selected to enhance each other's flavors, and the result is an unforgettable culinary experience that celebrates the best of New Zealand's cuisine and wine-making culture.

- **Marlborough Wine & Food Festival (Blenheim)**

The event being referred to is the Marlborough Wine & Food Festival (Blenheim), which takes place in the Marlborough region of New Zealand. This annual event attracts wine and food enthusiasts from all over the country. The Marlborough Wine & Food Festival is a perfect way to experience the best vineyards and winemakers the region has to offer, and to indulge in delicious local cuisine.

The event is usually held on the second Saturday in February, and it is an occasion for locals and tourists alike to enjoy the culture, topography, and hospitality of the region. The festival is a celebration of Marlborough's wine and food culture, and it showcases the best of the region's produce.

The festival takes place amidst the stunning backdrop of Marlborough's vineyards, which have helped to establish the region as one of the world's top wine producers. Guests can look forward to tasting an array of wines, including the region's signature Sauvignon Blanc, and they can also participate in guided tours of the vineyards and wineries.

Vinification techniques play a significant role in the production of Marlborough's wines, and visitors to the festival can learn about the various processes involved in producing these stunning wines. Additionally, they can also explore the diverse soils and climates of the region that give Marlborough wines their unique characteristics.

The food on offer at the festival is also highly anticipated, with stalls featuring local delicacies and classics. The region's seafood is a standout, with green-lipped mussels, scallops, and crayfish being among the highlights. The festival hosts also make it a priority to have a range of vegetarian, dairy-free and gluten-free options to cater to as many guests as possible.

In terms of wine pairing, the festival offers visitors a delightful opportunity to indulge in the classic rules of pairing wine with food. Below I have listed 25 pairing ideas:

1. Marlborough Sauvignon Blanc with fresh green-lipped mussels in white wine sauce.

2. Riesling with spicy Indian samosas.

3. Pinot Noir with creamy mushroom risotto.

4. Chardonnay with buttery garlic prawns.

5. Sparkling wine with sushi rolls.

6. Gewürztraminer with spicy Thai curries.

7. Rosé with barbecued prawns.

8. Pinot Gris with blue cheese and walnut salad.

9. Cabernet Sauvignon with steak sandwich.

10. Syrah with spicy meatball sub sandwich.

11. Merlot with grilled lamb chops.

12. Pinot Noir with roasted duck breast

13. Chardonnay with roasted chicken.

14. Sauvignon Blanc with grilled white fish.

15. Sparkling wine with roasted turkey.

16. Riesling with pork tacos.

17. Italian sparkling wine with prosciutto and melon skewers.

18. Gewürztraminer with spicy Korean fried chicken.

19. Pinot Gris with vegetable stir-fry.

20. Tempranillo with Spanish pork belly.

21. Viognier with sweet and sour chicken.

22. Rosé with a charcuterie platter.

23. Cabernet Franc with slow-cooked beef brisket.

24. Pinot Noir with a vegetarian quiche.

25. Syrah with spicy venison stew.

These pairings work well because they complement each other in terms of flavors, textures, and aromas. For example, a salty dish, such as seafood, will pair perfectly with a crisp, acidic Sauvignon Blanc. Similarly, a grilled red meat dish, such as lamb chops, will pair well with a bold and tannic Cabernet Sauvignon.

Overall, the Marlborough Wine & Food Festival is an opportunity for guests to enjoy a range of local wines and foods available and indulge in the cultural and natural wonders of the region.

- **Hokitika Wildfoods Festival (Hokitika)**

The Hokitika Wildfoods Festival is an annual event held in Hokitika, a small town located on the West Coast of the South Island of New Zealand. The festival attracts thousands of people from all over the country and around the world. It is a celebration of New Zealand's unique and diverse culture, as well as its beautiful natural surroundings.

The festival is typically held in March, and it has been a staple of the Hokitika community for over 30 years. The occasion is a unique opportunity for festival-goers to sample a wide variety of unusual and exotic foods, as well as to enjoy craft beers, ciders, and wines from local vineyards.

Hokitika is located in an area that comprises sandy beaches, wild rivers, and towering mountains. This topography is reflected in the unique flavours and ingredients that are featured in the festival's food and drink offerings. Local vineyards utilise vinification techniques that are geared towards capturing the distinctive flavours and aromas of the region.

The foods on offer at the Hokitika Wildfoods Festival are varied and eclectic. They include dishes such as mountain oysters, whitebait fritters, and wild pork belly. There are also plenty of vegan and vegetarian options available, such as stuffed mushrooms and plant-based burgers.

The wines on offer at Hokitika Wildfoods Festival are also diverse, as the region is home to a number of local vineyards that specialise in different varieties. Some of the wines that are typically served at the festival include Pinot Noir, Chardonnay, and Sauvignon Blanc. Each of these wines has its own unique flavour profile that pairs well with certain foods.

Here are some pairing examples to give you an idea of how these different wines can be paired with different foods:

1. Pinot Noir with venison kebabs

2. Chardonnay with whitebait fritters

3. Sauvignon Blanc with oysters

4. Pinot Gris with smoked salmon

5. Gewurztraminer with ginger-poached pear salad

6. Riesling with spicy Thai curry

7. Pinot Noir with wild pork belly

8. Sauvignon Blanc with grilled prawns

9. Chardonnay with scallops

10. Pinot Gris with roasted cauliflower

11. Gewurztraminer with Thai chicken satay

12. Riesling with Moroccan lamb meatballs

13. Pinot Noir with venison sliders

14. Sauvignon Blanc with goat cheese and beetroot salad

15. Chardonnay with crab cakes

16. Pinot Gris with grilled artichokes

17. Gewurztraminer with smoked trout

18. Riesling with spicy shrimp tacos

19. Pinot Noir with wild rabbit stew

20. Sauvignon Blanc with grilled zucchini and feta

21. Chardonnay with mushroom risotto

22. Pinot Gris with grilled peaches and prosciutto

23. Gewurztraminer with spicy Asian noodles

24. Riesling with seafood paella

25. Pinot Noir with wild venison sausage rolls

Overall, the Hokitika Wildfoods Festival is a unique and exciting celebration of the diverse cultures and culinary traditions that make up New Zealand's rich tapestry. From the exotic and unusual foods on offer, to the hand-crafted beers, ciders, and wines, there is something for everyone to enjoy at this fantastic event.

- **Taste of Auckland (Auckland)**

Taste of Auckland is an annual food and wine festival which takes place in Auckland, New Zealand. This event is designed to showcase the country's unique cuisine and wine culture.

The event takes place over four days in November each year and attracts a range of people, from local foodies to tourists looking to experience the best of New Zealand's culinary scene. The festival is held in Auckland's waterfront park, which offers stunning views of the harbor and city skyline.

New Zealand is known for its diverse culture and cuisine, which incorporates elements from Maori, Pacific Island, and European traditions. The country is also renowned for its winemaking industry, particularly in the Marlborough and Hawke's Bay regions.

At Taste of Auckland, visitors can sample a variety of local foods and wines from over 100 different producers. Some of the topography of New Zealand is also reflected in the unique taste of its wines.

The vineyards of New Zealand take advantage of the country's wide range of soil types, as well as its cool climate and abundant sunshine, to produce a wide range of wines. Vinification techniques vary depending on the grape variety and the region.

When it comes to food and wine pairing, Taste of Auckland offers a unique opportunity to try some of the best local cuisine alongside some of the country's most celebrated wines.

Some pairing examples that showcase the best of Taste of Auckland:

1. Paua fritters with a citrusy Sauvignon Blanc

2. Venison sliders with a bold Pinot Noir

3. Grilled lamb with a smooth Merlot

4. Oysters served with a crisp Chardonnay

5. Seafood chowder paired with a buttery Viognier

6. Green-lipped mussels served with a mineral-rich Riesling

7. Smoked salmon paired with a fruity Pinot Gris

8. Braised pork belly served with a full-bodied Syrah

9. Grilled chicken with a bright and clean Sauvignon Blanc

10. Roast beef paired with a spicy Shiraz

11. Duck confit paired with a smooth and silky Pinot Noir

12. Beef sliders paired with a bold and peppery Malbec

13. Slow-cooked pork shoulder paired with a fruity Gamay

14. Sashimi paired with a bright and acidic Albariño

15. Grilled prawns paired with a citrusy Sauvignon Blanc

16. Fried chicken paired with a crisp and refreshing Riesling

17. Roasted vegetables paired with a smooth and buttery Chardonnay

18. Beef brisket paired with a bold Cabernet Sauvignon

19. Spicy tuna rolls paired with a fruity Pinot Gris

20. Fish and chips paired with a mineral-rich Sauvignon Blanc

21. Braised beef cheeks paired with a earthy Pinot Noir

22. Grilled lobster paired with a buttery Chardonnay

23. Mushroom risotto paired with a full-bodied Cabernet Franc

24. Roasted quail paired with a silky Syrah

25. Grilled salmon paired with a crisp and refreshing Riesling.

These pairings work well because they both complement and contrast the flavours and textures of the food and wine. For example, a bold and spicy Shiraz can help to cut through the richness of roast beef, while a smooth and silky Pinot Noir can complement the earthy flavours of duck confit.

Overall, Taste of Auckland is a great opportunity to discover the unique flavours of New Zealand's cuisine and wine culture, and to try some exciting food and wine pairings.

- **Toast Martinborough (Martinborough)**

Toast Martinborough is an annual wine and food festival held in the town of Martinborough, located in the Wairarapa region of New Zealand. The festival is organized by the wineries in the region, who come together to showcase their best wines and pair them with local foods.

The festival is typically held on the third Sunday in November each year and has been running for over 30 years. It has become a popular event in New Zealand and attracts thousands of visitors from around the country and abroad. The occasion is considered a celebration of the region's wine-making culture, history, and topography.

Martinborough, which was founded in 1879, is a small town of just over 1,000 residents. The area is known for its vineyards, which are primarily focused on producing Pinot Noir, Sauvignon Blanc, and Chardonnay. The region's vinification techniques emphasize a hands-on approach, with many wineries relying on low-tech methods to ensure that the wines retain their distinctive character.

Food is an essential part of the Toast Martinborough festival, and local chefs and producers are given pride of place in the menus offered by the wineries. Some of the best food and wine pairings of the festival include:

1. Pinot Noir with venison and plum sauce

2. Sauvignon Blanc with freshly shucked oysters

3. Chardonnay with smoked salmon and cream cheese

4. Pinot Gris with creamy chicken and mushroom risotto

5. Riesling with spicy Thai prawns

6. Grüner Veltliner with grilled asparagus and lemon butter

7. Tempranillo with Spanish-style pork skewers

8. Gewürztraminer with spicy Indian curry

9. Pinot Noir Rosé with strawberries and cream

10. Viognier with grilled peaches and prosciutto

11. Pinot Noir with grilled lamb chops and mint sauce

12. Chardonnay with butter-poached crayfish

13. Sauvignon Blanc with grilled asparagus and feta

14. Pinot Gris with spiced pumpkin and feta salad

15. Pinot Noir with slow-cooked beef brisket

16. Riesling with cured salmon and dill cream

17. Chardonnay with roasted chicken and tarragon

18. Gewürztraminer with sweet potato and chickpea curry

19. Pinot Noir Rosé with grilled prawns

20. Viognier with roasted apricots and honey

21. Pinot Noir with wild venison and blackberry sauce

22. Sauvignon Blanc with mussels and white wine sauce

23. Pinot Gris with roasted quail and cherry sauce

24. Chardonnay with seared scallops and herb butter

25. Gewürztraminer with aromatic duck pancakes

In addition to the food and wine, the festival also includes music, entertainment, and activities such as grape stomping and guided vineyard tours. Overall, Toast Martinborough is a celebration of New Zealand's wine-making culture, showcasing the best of the region's wines and the food that complements them.

- **Gisborne Wine and Food Festival (Gisborne)**

The Gisborne Wine and Food Festival is an annual event held in Gisborne, New Zealand. Gisborne is a city located on the east coast of New Zealand's North Island and is known for its vineyards and beautiful beaches.

The festival brings together locals and visitors to celebrate the region's best wines and food. It usually takes place in October and is an occasion for people to experience the local culture and enjoy the topography.

The Gisborne region has a rich history of winemaking, dating back to the early 1900s. The region's vinification techniques have evolved over time, and today, Gisborne's wines are characterised by their fruitiness, freshness, and intensity.

Some examples of the pairing of local foods in detail with the local wines in the Gisborne Wine and Food Festival:

1. Raw oysters with Chardonnay - the wine's acidity complements the oysters' brininess.

2. Smoked salmon with Pinot Gris - the wine's fruitiness matches the salmon's flavour.

3. Grilled prawns with Sauvignon Blanc - the wine's crispness cuts through the richness of the prawns.

4. Whitebait fritters with Chardonnay - the wine's buttery notes complement the dish's richness.

5. Gurnard fillets with Pinot Gris - the wine's acidity balances the dish's sweetness.

6. Crayfish with Chardonnay - the wine's richness matches the dish's flavour.

7. Paua fritters with Gewurztraminer - the wine's floral notes complement the dish's flavour.

8. Venison with Pinot Noir - the wine's earthiness matches the dish's gaminess.

9. Lamb chops with Syrah - the wine's tannins balance the dish's richness.

10. Beef fillet with Cabernet Sauvignon - the wine's structure matches the dish's flavor.

11. BBQ ribs with Merlot - the wine's fruitiness balances the dish's smokiness.

12. Fried chicken with Chardonnay - the wine's creaminess complements the dish's crispiness.

13. Meatballs with Rosé - the wine's fruitiness matches the dish's flavour.

14. Grilled vegetables with Viognier - the wine's floral notes match the dish's freshness.

15. Pesto pasta with Pinot Gris - the wine's acidity balances the dish's richness.

16. Seafood paella with Albarino - the wine's acidity complements the dish's flavour.

17. Tuna poke bowl with Sauvignon Blanc - the wine's crispness matches the dish's freshness.

18. Grilled squid with Gisborne Chardonnay - the wine's citrus notes complement the dish's flavour.

19. Cheese platter with Riesling - the wine's sweetness matches the cheese's flavour.

20. Apple crumble with Gewurztraminer - the wine's spiciness matches the dish's flavor.

21. Chocolate cake with Merlot - the wine's fruitiness complements the dish's richness.

22. Lemon meringue pie with Pinot Gris - the wine's acidity matches the dish's flavour.

23. Creme brulee with Chardonnay - the wine's creamy notes match the dish's creaminess.

24. Fruit tart with Sparkling Sauvignon Blanc - the wine's effervescence complements the dish's fruitiness.

25. Pavlova with Late Harvest Riesling - the wine's sweetness matches the dish's flavour.

Overall, the Gisborne Wine and Food Festival is a wonderful occasion to experience the Gisborne region's unique culture, history, and cuisine. With its excellent wines and delicious local foods, the festival is sure to be a treat for all who attend.

- **Feast Marlborough (Marlborough)**

Feast Marlborough is a world-renowned food and wine festival that is held in Marlborough, New Zealand. This event is a celebration of the local culture, topography, and heritage of the area. It has been held annually for more than 20 years and is a major attraction for locals and tourists alike.

The Festival takes place in Marlborough, a region on the southern tip of New Zealand's South Island. The city of Blenheim, which is located in Marlborough, is the hub of this event. Marlborough is known for its stunning natural beauty, including its rugged coastline, mountains, and vineyards.

The festival features a wide range of local and international wines that are paired with delicious food from the local region. The food is prepared by renowned chefs and restaurateurs, who use the freshest local ingredients to create mouth-watering dishes.

The people of Marlborough are known for their love of good food and wine, and this festival is a reflection of that. It is an occasion for people to come together and celebrate the region's heritage, culture, and cuisine. The event is held annually, usually in February.

The topography of Marlborough is a key factor in the region's wine production. The area is known for its sunny days and cool nights, which are perfect conditions for growing grapes. The vineyards in Marlborough use vinification techniques that focus on the intensity of the fruit flavours, with minimal oak influence.

Some of the local wines that visitors can sample at Feast Marlborough include:

1. Cloudy Bay Sauvignon Blanc

2. Marlborough Ridge Chardonnay

3. Dog Point Vineyard Pinot Noir

4. Wairau River Pinot Gris

5. Alpha Domus The Navigator

6. Nautilus Pinot Noir

7. Villa Maria Private Bin Chardonnay

8. Allan Scott Sauvignon Blanc

9. Brancott Estate Pinot Noir

10. Saint Clair Family Estate Pinot Gris

11. Lawson's Dry Hills Pinot Noir

12. Yealands Pinot Noir

13. Rock Ferry Sauvignon Blanc

14. Greywacke Sauvignon Blanc

15. Spy Valley Sauvignon Blanc

16. Giesen Estate Sauvignon Blanc

17. Saint Clair Family Estate Sauvignon Blanc

18. Spring Creek Estate Pinot Noir

19. Huia Sauvignon Blanc

20. Delta Hatters Hill Pinot Noir

21. Forrest Wines Sauvignon Blanc

22. Mahi Sauvignon Blanc

23. Domain Road Pinot Noir

24. Seresin Chardonnay

25. Peregrine Wines Pinot Noir

The food at Feast Marlborough is just as impressive as the wine. Visitors can sample dishes such as:

1. Green-lipped mussels cooked in a white wine and cream sauce

2. BBQ scallops with lemon and garlic

3. Venison fillet with red wine jus

4. Crayfish with garlic butter

5. Organic salmon with saffron sauce

6. Paua (abalone) fritters with aioli

7. Wild pork belly with apple gel and crackling

8. Lamb rump with salsa verde

9. Dukkah-crusted beef fillet with horseradish cream

10. Crispy snapper with sweet chilli and lime

11. Green curry with prawns, jasmine rice, and papadum

12. Slow-cooked lamb shank with rosemary and garlic

13. Beef and blue cheese sliders with beetroot relish

14. Pan-fried kingfish with spiced cauliflower and lentils

15. Sticky pork belly with Asian slaw

16. Prawn and chorizo skewers with lime dressing

17. Salt and pepper squid with chilli jam

18. Steamed buns with pork belly and cucumber relish

19. Beef carpaccio with parmesan and truffle oil

20. Grilled tiger prawns with garlic and herb butter

21. Venison carpaccio with blackberry and balsamic glaze

22. Grilled quail with satay glaze

23. Ceviche of snapper with avocado and lime

24. Mushroom arancini with romesco sauce

25. Chicken and chorizo paella

Overall, Feast Marlborough is a fantastic celebration of the food and wine of Marlborough. Visitors can enjoy a range of local wines, paired with dishes created from the freshest local ingredients. The festival is a wonderful opportunity for locals and tourists alike to sample some of the best food and wine that New Zealand has to offer.

- **Hawke's Bay Food and Wine Classic (Hawke's Bay)**

The Hawke's Bay Food and Wine Classic festival is an annual event held in Hawke's Bay, New Zealand. The festival celebrates the local culture, food, and wine of the region, and brings together local farmers, winemakers, chefs, and food enthusiasts to showcase the best of Hawke's Bay.

Hawke's Bay is located on the east coast of New Zealand's North Island and has a rich history of agricultural farming and viniculture. The region is known for its sunny climate, fertile soils, and unique topography, which provide the perfect conditions for growing a wide range of fruits, vegetables, and grapes.

The Hawke's Bay Food and Wine Classic festival is usually held in June and features a range of events, including wine tastings, cooking classes, farm tours, and gourmet meals. The festival is a celebration of the region's local culture and cuisine, and is a great opportunity to experience the unique flavours of Hawke's Bay.

Hawke's Bay is famous for its vinification techniques, which combine traditional methods with modern technology to produce some of New Zealand's finest wines. The region is particularly known for its premium red wines, including Cabernet Sauvignon, Merlot, and Syrah, as well as its exquisite white wines such as Chardonnay, Pinot Gris and Sauvignon Blanc.

The festival provides the perfect opportunity to pair local foods with Hawke's Bay wines. Some of the top local foods to look out for include:

1. Crayfish – paired with Chardonnay

2. Paua (abalone) – paired with Pinot Gris

3. Mussels – paired with Sauvignon Blanc

4. Venison – paired with Syrah

5. Lamb – paired with Cabernet Sauvignon

6. Beef – paired with Merlot

7. Pork – paired with Pinot Noir

8. Cheese – paired with Chardonnay

9. Charcuterie – paired with Pinot Noir

10. Oysters – paired with Chardonnay

11. Scallops – paired with Pinot Gris

12. Salmon – paired with Chardonnay

13. New Zealand Greenshell Mussels – paired with Pinot Gris

14. Kumara/Sweet potato – paired with Pinot Gris

15. Feijoas – paired with Chardonnay

16. Apples – paired with Chardonnay

17. Pears – paired with Pinot Gris

18. Berry desserts – paired with Merlot

19. Chocolate desserts – paired with Cabernet Sauvignon

20. Ice cream – paired with Pinot Noir

21. Citrus desserts – paired with Sauvignon Blanc

22. Honey – paired with Sauvignon Blanc

23. Olives – paired with Pinot Gris

24. Hazelnuts – paired with Merlot

25. Gingerbread – paired with Chardonnay.

Overall, the Hawke's Bay Food and Wine Classic festival is a wonderful event for food and wine enthusiasts to explore the rich history and culture of the region, and to enjoy some of the finest local wines and foods that Hawke's Bay has to offer.

- **Okahu Bay Oyster Frenzy (Auckland)**

Okahu Bay Oyster Frenzy is a world-renowned festival that takes place in Auckland, New Zealand. This festival celebrates the love for seafood and wine while highlighting the best of the region's local culture.

The event itself has a long-standing history in the Auckland area, and is a sought-after occasion for locals and tourists alike. It is held annually during the summer months, usually in January or February, when the weather is warm, and the oysters are in season.

One of the biggest attractions of this festival is the variety of oyster dishes available to visitors. The oysters come from the bay of Okahu, which has become famous for producing some of the best oysters in the world. The topography of the bay, with its calm and clear waters, is largely responsible for the quality of the oysters.

Visitors can enjoy the oysters in various ways; either freshly shucked, grilled, or even in a stew for a hearty meal. Along with the oysters, the festival also serves an array of paired wines, which are carefully selected to complement the seafood's flavours.

The local culture of Auckland adds another layer of experience to the festival. The Maori people of New Zealand have a rich history and were the original inhabitants of Auckland. Today, their culture is celebrated and exhibited throughout the city, including at this festival. Attendees can learn about Maori art, music, and dance, and even try their hand at some traditional crafting methods.

A major attraction during the festival is the selection of vineyards and their vinification techniques on showcase. Visitors can taste the different varieties of wine and learn about the unique techniques used to create their distinct flavours. This is an excellent opportunity for those interested in wine-making to learn about the craft and discover new favourites.

To enhance the flavour of the oysters and wines, festival-goers can also pair them with other local delicacies. Here are 25 examples of food and wine pairings available at the Okahu Bay Oyster Frenzy:

1. Freshly shucked oysters paired with a crisp Sauvignon Blanc

2. Grilled oysters with a buttery Chardonnay

3. Oyster stew with a light Pinot Gris

4. Oyster sliders with a fruity Rosé

5. Oyster po'boy with a bold Shiraz

6. Oyster shooters paired with a sparkling Brut

7. Oyster Rockefeller with a smooth Merlot

8. Fried oysters with a spicy Gewürztraminer

9. Oyster ceviche with a tangy Riesling

10. Oysters Kilpatrick with a rich Cabernet Sauvignon

11. Oyster chowder with a full-bodied Zinfandel

12. Oyster fritters with a sweet Moscato

13. Oyster BLT with a crisp Pinot Blanc

14. Oyster nachos with a complex Syrah

15. Oyster pies with a bold Malbec

16. Oyster spring rolls with a light Chenin Blanc

17. Oyster gratin with a tart Gavi

18. Oyster tempura with a smoky Tempranillo

19. Oyster beignets with a zesty Viognier

20. Oyster fajitas with a dark and moody Sangiovese

21. Oyster kebabs with a spicy Grenache

22. Oyster quiche with a creamy Marsanne

23. Oyster bisque with a velvety Pinot Noir

24. Oyster dip with a crisp Grüner Veltliner

25. Oyster jambalaya with a drinkable Gamay

Overall, the Okahu Bay Oyster Frenzy is an exciting event that combines culture, food, and wine in one fantastic location. Visitors can enjoy the best of local delicacies and indulge in wine pairings that complement the seafood's flavours. They can also learn about the local area's history and culture, making this festival a must-visit for any traveller to Auckland, New Zealand.

- **Great Kiwi Beer Festival (Hamilton)**

The Great Kiwi Beer Festival is an annual event held in Hamilton, New Zealand. This festival is one of the largest beer festivals in the country and attracts beer enthusiasts from all over the world. The first edition of the festival was held in 2011 and since then it has become a major event in the city of Hamilton.

The festival is held in the beautiful surroundings of Claudelands Park, in the heart of Hamilton. The park is a popular spot for locals and tourists alike, with acres of green space and picturesque views. The park is surrounded by lush greenery and has easy accessibility for all visitors.

The festival features a wide variety of beers, wines, and ciders from different breweries and vineyards across New Zealand. Visitors can sample and taste the drinks as they stroll around the festival grounds. There are also live music performances, food stalls, and various entertaining activities for visitors.

The event showcases the local culture of New Zealand, as it features a showcase of local food, music, and art. Visitors can sample dishes from local restaurants, such as fish and chips, meat pies, barbecued shrimp, and more. The festival features live performances of New Zealand music, from traditional Maori music to modern pop and rock.

Hamilton is a city in Waikato region, in the North Island of New Zealand. The region has a rich history of agriculture and vinification, with fertile farmlands and ideal weather conditions for producing wines. The region uses a range of vinification techniques, such as traditional grape picking, hand selection, and modern factory processing, to produce a range of award-winning wines.

Visitors to the festival can enjoy pairing their favourite beverages with some of the best local cuisine. Here are 25 examples of foods and wines available at the Great Kiwi Beer Festival:

1. Lamb burgers paired with fruity sauvignon blanc

2. Smoked salmon and cream cheese canapes with a crisp pinot grigio

3. BBQ pork ribs with a rich, red cabernet sauvignon

4. Grilled chicken skewers with a light, refreshing riesling

5. Pulled pork sandwiches with a bold, oaky shiraz

6. Blue cheese and walnut salad with a full-bodied chardonnay

7. Roasted vegetables with a silky, smooth merlot

8. Fried calamari with a tangy, citrusy sauvignon blanc

9. Cheese and crackers with a fruity, crisp pinot noir

10. Beef and mushroom pot pies with a robust, full-flavoured syrah

11. Grilled prawns with a light, refreshing white zinfandel

12. Salmon tartare with a delicate, floral rosé

13. Fried chicken with a rich, full-bodied malbec

14. Roasted lamb with a classic, earthy cabernet franc

15. Grilled vegetables with a crisp, refreshing sauvignon gris

16. Charcuterie board with a bold, spicy tempranillo

17. Spicy wings with a light, refreshing pinot blanc

18. Sushi rolls with a classic, briny chardonnay

19. Cheese fondue with a robust, fruity grenache

20. Falafel wraps with a zesty, refreshing dry riesling

21. Steak and mushroom pies with a silky, smooth pinot noir

22. Fried calamari with a crisp, citrusy albariño

23. Cheese and fruit platter with a sweet, fruity moscato

24. Lamb chops with a bold, full-bodied merlot

25. Seafood paella with a light, refreshing viognier

- **New Zealand Coffee Festival (Wellington)**

The New Zealand Coffee Festival is an annual event held in the city of Wellington, located on the southern tip of New Zealand's North Island. This festival is a celebration of coffee culture in New Zealand, which has a long history of producing high-quality coffee beans and a thriving cafe culture.

The event usually takes place in November each year, and it attracts coffee lovers and industry professionals from all over the country. The festival provides an opportunity for visitors to learn about different types of coffee, brewing methods, and the latest trends in the coffee industry.

Along with coffee, the festival also celebrates local culture and food. Wellington is known for its vibrant food scene, and there are many opportunities for visitors to pair coffee with local cuisine. For example:

1. A flat white coffee with a traditional New Zealand meat pie

2. A long black coffee with artisanal chocolate

3. A cappuccino with a seafood chowder

4. A macchiato with pavlova, a meringue-based dessert

5. A latte with a cheese platter featuring locally made cheeses

6. An espresso with a smoked salmon bagel

7. A cortado with a lamb burger

8. A mocha with a slice of feijoa cake, a traditional New Zealand fruit

9. A piccolo with a vegan curry dish

10. A turmeric latte with a tofu poke bowl

11. A nitro cold brew with a bacon and egg roll

12. A chai latte with dishes featuring kumara, a sweet potato native to New Zealand

13. An iced coffee with a green lip mussel fritter

14. A Vietnamese iced coffee with pho noodle soup

15. A caramel latte with a slice of hokey pokey ice cream, a New Zealand favourite

16. A pour-over coffee with a cheese scone

17. A cortado with a blueberry muffin

18. A flat white with a sausage roll

19. A flat white with a slice of pineapple lump slice, another New Zealand favourite

20. A cappuccino with a bacon-wrapped scallop

21. A latte with a pork bao bun

22. A turmeric latte with a vegan falafel wrap

23. A mocha with a slice of banana and walnut bread

24. An iced coffee with fish and chips

25. A chai latte with a chicken tikka masala dish

In addition to food and coffee, the festival also showcases the natural beauty and history of the Wellington region. Visitors can take tours of nearby vineyards, learn about vinification techniques used in the area, and sample local wines. The region is known for its cool climate wines, particularly Pinot Noir and Sauvignon Blanc.

Overall, the New Zealand Coffee Festival is a wonderful opportunity to explore the culture, food, and natural beauty of Wellington and the wider New Zealand region, all while enjoying some of the best coffee in the world.

- **Waikato Food and Wine Festival (Hamilton)**

The Waikato Food and Wine Festival is an annual event celebrated in Hamilton city, located in the Waikato region of the North Island of New Zealand. The festival usually takes place in February and is a celebration of New Zealand's finest food, wine, beer, and spirits.

The history of the region stretches back to the arrival of Tangata Whenua, the Maori people, more than 800 years ago. The festival celebrates the melting pot of cultures that have blended over the years, culminating in the vibrant and diverse food and wine scene the region is known for today. The occasion is a great way for locals and visitors to explore the rich culture of the Waikato while enjoying some of the region's finest cuisine and beverages.

The Waikato region is blessed with a varied topography that includes rolling hills, fertile farmland, and sandy beaches. The region's history of viticulture dates back to 1852 when the country's first commercial vineyard was established in Auckland. Since then, New Zealand has established itself as a leading wine-producing country, with the Waikato region contributing significantly to the industry through innovative vinification techniques.

The Waikato Food and Wine Festival pairs a vast selection of foods with a wide range of wines, creating a perfect blend of taste and flavours.

Here are some examples of the foods and wines available for visitors:

1. Grilled venison with Pinot Noir

2. Seafood chowder with Chardonnay

3. Smoked salmon with Sauvignon Blanc

4. Roasted lamb with Merlot

5. Spicy chicken with Gewurztraminer

6. Fresh oysters with Champagne

7. Teriyaki beef with Shiraz

8. Spanish pork skewers with Rioja

9. Prosciutto-wrapped melon with Prosecco

10. Prawn salad with Riesling

11. Beef Wellington with Cabernet Sauvignon

12. Lobster bisque with Viognier

13. Blackened fish with Rosé

14. Steak tartare with Syrah

15. Grilled shrimp with Albariño

16. Mushroom risotto with Pinot Grigio

17. Beef skewers with Malbec

18. Grilled squid with Vermentino

19. Ceviche with Grüner Veltliner

20. Pork belly with Carmenere

21. Beef brisket with Zinfandel

22. Roasted vegetables with Tempranillo

23. Creamy brie cheese with Merlot

24. Spiced nuts with Port

25. Chocolate truffles with Tawny Port

These are some of the food and wine combinations available during the festival, but there are many more options for visitors to explore. The festival also features live music, cooking demonstrations, and other entertainment to create a festive atmosphere that celebrates the region's vibrant culture.

- **Kaikoura Seafest (Kaikoura)**

Kaikoura Seafest is an annual festival that takes place in the town of Kaikoura, New Zealand, situated on the east coast of the South Island. The festival is held to celebrate the region's rich seafood and culture, and it has been running since 1994.

Kaikoura is a small coastal town that is famous for its marine life, particularly whales, seals, and dolphins. The town's history dates back to the Maori people, who are believed to have lived in the region for at least 1,000 years before the arrival of European settlers.

The festival features a range of events, including cooking demonstrations, art exhibits, live music, and, of course, plenty of food and drink. Local chefs and restaurants showcase their seafood creations, which include everything from raw oysters and sashimi to more complex dishes like seafood chowder and grilled lobster.

In addition to the food, Kaikoura Seafest also celebrates the area's wine and beer culture. The region is known for producing excellent wines, particularly Pinot Noir, Chardonnay, and Sauvignon Blanc, which pair perfectly with seafood dishes. There are also local craft breweries that produce a range of beer styles, including pale ales, stouts, and pilsners.

Some examples of foods and wines that visitors might enjoy at the Kaikoura Seafest:

1. Fresh raw oysters paired with a crisp Sauvignon Blanc

2. Clam and mussel chowder paired with a buttery Chardonnay

3. Grilled prawns and scallops paired with a light Pinot Gris

4. Steamed green-lipped mussels paired with a citrusy Riesling

5. Fried calamari rings paired with a hoppy IPA

6. Smoked salmon paired with a full-bodied Cabernet Sauvignon

7. Seafood paella paired with a fruity Rosé

8. Lobster bisque paired with a creamy Viognier

9. Grilled kingfish paired with a spicy Shiraz

10. Tempura fish and chips paired with a refreshing Pilsner

11. Raw tuna sashimi paired with a smooth Merlot

12. Seafood curry paired with a complex Syrah

13. Fried whitebait paired with a dry sparkling wine

14. Grilled octopus paired with a bold Malbec

15. Seafood kebab paired with a zesty Gewürztraminer

16. Grilled swordfish paired with a velvety Pinot Noir

17. Scallop ceviche paired with a sweet Moscato

18. Crispy soft-shell crab paired with a smoky Red Ale

19. Crayfish risotto paired with a crisp Albariño

20. Oyster Rockefeller paired with a buttery Chablis

21. Lemony prawn linguine paired with a refreshing Viognier

22. Fried calamari tacos paired with a citrusy Hefeweizen

23. Grilled salmon skewers paired with a fruity Sangiovese

24. Seafood gumbo paired with a rich Zinfandel

25. Spicy tuna poke paired with a bright Chenin Blanc

- **Tauranga Food Wine and Music Festival (Tauranga)**

The Tauranga Food Wine and Music Festival is an annual event that takes place in Tauranga, a coastal city located in Bay of Plenty, New Zealand. The festival typically takes place in the first week of January, and it celebrates the local culture, music, food and wine of the region.

The festival was first held in 2017 and has quickly become one of the most popular events in the region. It brings together winemakers, distillers, chefs, and musicians to showcase the best of what the region has to offer.

The people of Tauranga are known for their friendly and welcoming nature. The region has a rich history, with the indigenous Maori people having lived in the area for more than 700 years. The festival celebrates this history through the use of traditional Maori ingredients and culture.

The topography of the region is characterised by rolling hills, lush forests, and beautiful beaches. These natural features are reflected in the food and wine that is produced in the area. Many of the wines produced in the region are made using traditional vinification techniques, which have been passed down through generations of winemakers.

Food and wine are at the heart of the festival, and visitors can expect to find a wide variety of dishes and drinks to sample.

Here are some examples of the food and wine pairings that visitors can look forward to:

1. Grilled lamb chops with a rich Cabernet Sauvignon

2. Freshly shucked oysters with a crisp Sauvignon Blanc

3. Creamy blue cheese with a bold Shiraz

4. Charcuterie platter with a smooth Pinot Noir

5. Smoked salmon with a zesty Chardonnay

6. Braised pork belly with a silky Merlot

7. Gourmet burger with a hoppy Pale Ale

8. Grilled steak with a tannic Malbec

9. Fish and chips with a refreshing Pilsner

10. Seafood paella with a complex Tempranillo

11. Spicy Pad Thai with a fruit-forward Riesling

12. Sushi platter with a delicate Pinot Gris

13. Margherita pizza with a light-bodied Sangiovese

14. Bruschetta with a tangy Rosé

15. Beef brisket with a robust Zinfandel

16. Chicken satay with a smooth Cabernet Franc

17. Falafel wrap with a crisp Rosé

18. Antipasto platter with a complex Syrah

19. Cheese fondue with a full-bodied Chardonnay

20. Fried calamari with a bright Vermentino

21. Chicken tikka masala with a spicy Shiraz

22. BBQ ribs with a caramelised Malbec blend

23. Baked brie with a fruity Gewürztraminer

24. Curry goat with a deep Rioja

25. Lobster bisque with a buttery Chardonnay.

Overall, the Tauranga Food Wine and Music Festival is a must-attend event for food, wine, and music lovers. It's an opportunity to sample some of the best local ingredients and wines, while also enjoying the beautiful scenery and cultural traditions of the region.

- **Northland Wine & Food Festival (Northland)**

The Northland Wine & Food Festival is an annual event held in Whangarei, a city in the Northland region of New Zealand. The festival celebrates the local culture, topography, history, and vinification techniques used in the region while offering an opportunity for visitors to experience the best of Northland's wine and food offerings.

The first Northland Wine & Food Festival was held in 2012 in order to promote the outstanding local produce in the region and encourage tourism. Since then, the festival has become a popular event for locals and visitors alike, attracting thousands of people each year.

The festival is typically held in March, as this is the start of the harvest season for many of the local winemakers. During the two-day event, visitors can sample a variety of wines produced in Northland, each with its own unique taste and character. The festival also features food from local producers, including seafood, meat, and vegetables. In addition to wine and food, there are also live music performances, cooking demonstrations, and other entertainment.

Northland is a region with a rich cultural heritage, and visitors to the festival will have the opportunity to learn about the Maori culture that is an integral part of the region's history. There will also be opportunities to explore the local scenery, which includes beautiful beaches, forests, and waterfalls.

In terms of vinification techniques, Northland is known for its unique approach to winemaking. The region has a moderate climate, which allows for a longer growing season and helps to produce wines with a distinctive flavour profile. Many of the local winemakers use traditional techniques, such as hand harvesting and wooden barrel aging, to produce wines that are full of character.

When it comes to pairing food with wine, there are countless possibilities at the Northland Wine & Food Festival. Here are 25 examples of food and wine pairings you might find at the festival:

1. Grilled lamb chops paired with a full-bodied Syrah

2. Seared scallops with a crisp, cool Chardonnay

3. Creamy blue cheese with a bold Merlot

4. Grilled tuna with a light Pinot Noir

5. Roast beef with a robust Cabernet Sauvignon

6. Chicken salad with a fruity Sauvignon Blanc

7. Smoked salmon with a crisp Riesling

8. Beef carpaccio with a smooth Malbec

9. Duck confit with a complex Pinot Gris

10. Octopus salad with a refreshing Rosé

11. Braised short ribs with a velvety Cabernet Franc

12. Lobster bisque with a buttery Chardonnay

13. Grilled vegetables with a zesty Verdelho

14. Pork belly with a rich Viognier

15. Spicy chicken wings with a bold Tempranillo

16. Beef skewers with a smooth Grenache

17. Oysters with a dry Muscadet

18. Grilled sausages with a full-bodied Zinfandel

19. Beef tartare with a spicy Syrah/Shiraz

20. Pork chops with a fruity Gamay

21. Grilled prawns with a herbaceous Sauvignon Blanc

22. Roast chicken with a medium-bodied Pinotage

23. Spicy meatballs with a full-bodied Cabernet Sauvignon blend

24. Grilled mushrooms with a earthy Pinot Noir

25. Fried chicken with a sweet Riesling

As for the foods and wines themselves, you can expect the food to be fresh and locally sourced, while the wines will showcase the unique characteristics of the Northland region. Visitors to the festival will have the opportunity to meet and speak with local winemakers and food producers, learning about their craft and the passion that goes into each bottle and plate.

Overall, the Northland Wine & Food Festival is an exceptional event that celebrates the best of New Zealand's food and wine culture while highlighting the regional flavours and vinification techniques that make Northland such a unique and interesting destination.

- **Otago Pinot Noir Celebration (Queenstown)**

The Otago Pinot Noir Celebration is an internationally recognized event in New Zealand that takes place every February in Queenstown, a resort town located in the South Island. The festival is held to celebrate the country's best Pinot Noir wines and is a great platform for the region's vineyards to showcase their world-class wines to a global audience. The event has a history that dates back to 2001, where it started with the goal of promoting Otago Pinot Noir as a top-quality product.

The festival is a four-day event that is attended by wine enthusiasts and experts from all over the world. The event features wine tastings, wine-pairing sessions, seminars, vineyard visits, and gala dinners. Throughout the festival, visitors can enjoy the breathtaking scenery of Queenstown, surrounded by stunning mountains and pristine lakes.

Otago is famous for its unique, high-altitude, cool-climate terroir, which produces complex and beautiful Pinot Noir wines. The region has a long history of winemaking, and Otago's unique geography has helped develop innovative vinification techniques that are now recognized worldwide.

The festival provides visitors with an opportunity to explore the local culture and cuisine of the region. The South Island of New Zealand is known for its fresh seafood, grass-fed meats, and artisanal cheeses. Below are some pairing examples of foods and wines that visitors can expect to find at the Otago Pinot Noir Celebration:

1. Pan-seared scallops with Pinot Noir butter sauce

2. Charcuterie board with cured meats, olives, and aged cheese

3. Roasted lamb with rosemary and garlic served with a Pinot Noir reduction

4. Grilled venison with Pinot Noir cherry sauce

5. Smoked salmon with dill crème fraîche

6. Beef carpaccio with shaved Parmesan and truffle oil

7. Duck confit with a spiced cherry sauce

8. Seared tuna steak with lemon beurre blanc sauce

9. Grilled portobello mushrooms with goat cheese and balsamic glaze

10. Slow roasted pork belly with apple and fennel slaw

11. Beef bourguignon with Pinot Noir

12. Wild mushroom risotto

13. Beef Wellington with Pinot Noir reduction

14. Grilled eggplant and zucchini with roasted garlic aioli

15. Fried chicken with honey mustard dipping sauce

16. Braised short ribs with red wine and vegetable sauce

17. Grilled wild boar with Pinot Noir cranberry sauce

18. Blue cheese and walnut tartlets

19. Scallop ceviche with mango and jalapeño

20. Seared tofu with teriyaki sauce

21. Grilled chicken with pinot noir barbecue sauce

22. Shrimp scampi with Pinot Noir garlic butter sauce

23. Lobster bisque soup

24. Pesto pasta with sundried tomatoes and pine nuts

25. Grilled asparagus with hollandaise sauce

Pinot Noir is known for its versatility and complexity, and it pairs well with a wide range of dishes. The wine's delicate body and complex structure make it a perfect partner with lighter dishes like seafood, chicken, and vegetables. On the other hand, the wine's acidity and higher tannins make it an excellent match for richer dishes like meats and stews. Pinot Noir also pairs well with earthy flavours such as mushrooms, truffles, and roasted vegetables.

In conclusion, the Otago Pinot Noir Celebration is a cultural, culinary, and wine-tasting experience that anyone who appreciates wine or local cuisine would enjoy. It offers visitors a chance to explore the region's unique history, geography, and innovative winemaking techniques. With its stunning scenery and world-class Pinot Noir, the festival promises to be an unforgettable experience.

- **Martinborough Fair (Martinborough)**

The Martinborough fair is an annual event that takes place in the small town of Martinborough in the Wellington region of New Zealand. The fair is held twice a year, once in February and once in March, and it attracts thousands of visitors from all over New Zealand and around the world.

Martinborough is a picturesque town located in the Wairarapa region of New Zealand. The town has a rich history and is known for its wine production, particularly for its Pinot Noir. The region's topography is characterised by rolling hills and vineyards which add to the charm of the area.

The Martinborough fair is a celebration of local culture, art, and cuisine. The fair has been running for more than 40 years and has become a popular event within the country's social and cultural calendar. Visitors can enjoy a range of local food and wine offerings, while they admire the work of the local artists and craftspeople.

The event is an occasion for the local community to come together and celebrate their heritage. Visitors can sample local wines and learn about the vinification techniques used in the region. Martinborough's wine industry, which dates back to the 1870s, has been a significant contributor to the region's economic development since then.

When it comes to food and wine pairings, Martinborough's speciality is Pinot Noir, but there are other local varietals worth trying, such as Sauvignon Blanc, Chardonnay, and Riesling, to name a few. Here are some pairing examples you can try during the Martinborough Fair:

1. Pinot Noir and seared salmon

2. Pinot Noir and roasted duck

3. Pinot Noir and grilled lamb chops

4. Pinot Noir and wild mushrooms

5. Pinot Noir and beef carpaccio

6. Sauvignon Blanc and goat cheese

7. Sauvignon Blanc and grilled asparagus

8. Sauvignon Blanc and grilled shrimp

9. Sauvignon Blanc and sushi

10. Sauvignon Blanc and fish tacos

11. Chardonnay and lobster bisque

12. Chardonnay and creamy pasta dishes

13. Chardonnay and scallops

14. Chardonnay and chicken Caesar salad

15. Chardonnay and grilled salmon

16. Riesling and spicy Asian cuisine

17. Riesling and Thai curries

18. Riesling and sushi rolls

19. Riesling and spicy grilled chicken

20. Riesling and blue cheese

21. Pinot Gris and apple and goat cheese salad

22. Pinot Gris and tart tartin

23. Pinot Gris and seafood chowder

24. Pinot Gris and smoked salmon

25. Pinot Gris and roasted pork tenderloin

The reason these wines pair so well with these foods is that each wine's particular flavour profile complements the ingredients in the dishes and enhances them. For example, Pinot Noir's fruitiness and earthiness combine well with salmon's oily texture, while its tannins balance the richness of a roasted duck dish. Sauvignon Blanc's acidity and crispness refresh the flavours in a goat cheese salad, while its citrus and herbal notes pair well with seafood and asparagus.

Chardonnay's buttery and oaky characteristics complement the richness of lobster bisque, while its acidity balances out the creaminess of pasta dishes. Riesling's sweetness contrasts well with spicy Thai curries, and its acidity and citrusy notes balance out grilled chicken and seafood dishes. Pinot Gris's fruitiness and acidity complement the sweetness of caramelised apples in a tart tatin and acidity balances out the richness of seafood chowder.

In conclusion, the Martinborough Fair is much more than just a festival; it is a reflection of the culture, history, and traditions of the local community. Visitors can enjoy some of the region's finest wines and culinary offerings, while soaking in the picturesque scenery. If you are planning to visit New Zealand, be sure to mark the fair dates in your calendar to experience the best of New Zealand's culture, cuisine, and hospitality.

- **New Zealand Boutique Wine Festival (Auckland)**

The New Zealand Boutique Wine Festival is an annual event held in Auckland, New Zealand, that brings together wine enthusiasts, connoisseurs, and vendors to celebrate the local wine culture. The festival usually takes place in July each year, and offers visitors the opportunity to taste a range of boutique wines produced in the region.

New Zealand is a country located in the southwestern Pacific Ocean, and its largest city is Auckland. The country has a rich history and culture, with indigenous Maori people being the original inhabitants. The event celebrates the country's diverse culture, as well as its unique winemaking techniques and the history of the region.

The New Zealand Boutique Wine Festival showcases a variety of boutique wineries from across the region, and the vineyards they operate on feature different types of topography. Some vineyards are located on plains, while others are situated on hills and mountainsides. The region is also known for its unique winemaking techniques, which include both modern and traditional vinification methods.

The festival offers visitors the chance to sample a range of wines and pair them with different foods. To illustrate this, let's pair some wines and foods:

1. Chardonnay with roasted chicken: the acidity in the wine complements the richness of the chicken

2. Sauvignon Blanc with goat cheese: the high acidity in the wine cuts through the creamy texture of the cheese

3. Pinot Gris with broiled salmon: the wine's fruity notes pair well with the salmon's natural flavours

4. Pinot Noir with seared duck breast: the wine's earthy notes complement the richness of the duck

5. Viognier with spicy Thai food: the wine's acidity plays well with the spice in the food

6. Riesling with sushi: the sweetness of the wine balances the saltiness of the soy sauce and the umami flavours in the sushi

7. Chenin Blanc with Pork BBQ: the wine's acidity balances the richness of the pork and the tangy BBQ sauce

8. Gewurztraminer with spicy Indian food: the wine's spiciness complements the spices in the food

9. Cabernet Sauvignon with a juicy steak: the wine's tannins pair well with the protein of the steak

10. Merlot with Braised Short Ribs: the wine's softness complements the tenderness of the rib meat

11. Shiraz with pepperoni pizza: the wine's spiciness complements the spice in the pepperoni

12. Malbec with grilled lamb: the wine's smoky notes complement the smokiness of the grilled lamb

13. Tempranillo with grilled chorizo: the wine's spiciness complements the spice in the chorizo

14. Grenache with grilled vegetables: the wine's fruity notes pair well with the sweetness of the grilled vegetables

15. Zinfandel with BBQ ribs: the wine's fruitiness balances the tangy BBQ sauce

16. Barbera with Italian meatballs: the wine's acidity pairs well with the richness of the meatballs

17. Nebbiolo with Osso buco: the wine's tannins complement the richness of the meat

18. Sangiovese with Margherita pizza: the wine's acidity pairs well with the acidity in the tomato sauce

19. Syrah with grilled portobello mushrooms: the wine's earthy notes pair well with the earthiness of the mushrooms

20. Grenache Blanc with roasted root vegetables: the wine's acidity balances the sweetness of the vegetables

21. Gruner Veltliner with oysters: the wine's acidity cleanses the palate between each oyster

22. Verdelho with grilled shrimp: the wine's acidity complements the sweetness of the shrimp

23. Gamay with grilled salmon: the wine's earthiness complements the earthiness of the salmon

24. Meritage with beef tenderloin: the wine's tannins pair well with the protein of the beef

25. Petit Verdot with Roast Beef: the wine's full-bodied flavour complements the richness of the beef

In conclusion, the New Zealand Boutique Wine Festival is a celebration of the country's unique wine culture, local cuisine, and diverse culture. The event showcases the region's winemaking techniques and the different types of topography and terroir that make New Zealand a unique wine region. The pairing of wines and food at the event is an opportunity for visitors to appreciate both the local culture and the delicious flavours that the region has to offer.

- **Central Otago Pinot Noir & Food Celebration (Central Otago)**
- **Bluff Oyster & Food Festival (Bluff)**

The Bluff Oyster & Food Festival is an annual event that takes place in the city of Bluff, New Zealand. The festival celebrates the famous Bluff oyster and the local cuisine of the region.

Bluff is a fishing town located on the southern tip of the South Island of New Zealand. The town has a rich history of people who have been fishing and trading in the area for hundreds of years. The festival began in 1997 as a way to showcase the local food and culture of Bluff.

The festival takes place in May each year and attracts thousands of visitors from all over New Zealand and around the world. The festival is a celebration of the famous Bluff oyster which is harvested from the cold waters of Foveaux Strait. Other local delicacies such as paua (abalone), blue cod, and crayfish are also showcased.

The topography of Bluff and the surrounding region is unique as it is situated on a rocky coastline, surrounded by cliffs and hills. The terrain is rugged and wild, and this is reflected in the local cuisine.

The history of the region is largely shaped by the fishing industry and the vinification techniques used in wine production. The cold climate and unique soils of the area produce some of the most distinctive wines in New Zealand.

At the festival, there are over 25 food stalls and wine vendors. Each food stall offers a selection of dishes that are paired with a specific wine. Here are some examples of food and wine pairings:

1. **Bluff oysters with a Sauvignon Blanc**: The crisp acidity of the wine complements the saltiness of the oysters.

2. **Paua fritters with a Chardonnay**: The buttery texture of the fritters pairs well with the creamy notes of the Chardonnay.

3. **Venison kebabs with a Pinot Noir**: The earthy flavours of the venison are enhanced by the fruity and spicy notes of the Pinot Noir.

4. **Blue cod with a Riesling**: The sweetness of the fish is balanced out by the tart acidity of the Riesling.

5. **Crayfish with a Gewürztraminer**: The sweet and spicy flavours of the crayfish are complemented by the floral and fruity notes of the Gewürztraminer.

In conclusion, the Bluff Oyster & Food Festival is a celebration of the unique cuisine of the Bluff region and the wine produced there. The topography, history, and local culture all play a role in shaping the food and wine pairings offered at the festival. Visitors can experience the flavors of the region and learn more about the history and culture of Bluff through this exciting event.

- **Festival of Lights - Night Markets (New Plymouth)**

The Festival of Lights - Night Markets in New Plymouth, New Zealand, is an annual event that takes place during the summer months. The festival celebrates the local culture and history of the region.

The festival was first established in 1993 and has grown in popularity over the years, attracting both locals and tourists alike. The event includes a range of activities such as live music, stage shows, circus acts, and street performances. One of the highlights of the festival is the Night Markets, which showcase local food, drink, and craft.

The festival is held on the banks of the Waiwhakaiho River, providing a picturesque setting for the event. The region is known for its stunning beaches, rugged coastline, and lush forests, making it a popular tourism destination.

The region is also home to a thriving wine industry, with a variety of vinification techniques used to produce a range of award-winning wines. Some of the popular local wines include Pinot Noir, Chardonnay, and Sauvignon Blanc.

The Night Markets at the Festival of Lights provides an excellent opportunity to pair local food with these delicious wines. Here are some pairing examples highlighting the unique ingredients and flavours of the region:

1. Pinot Noir paired with venison sausage and berry compote
2. Sauvignon Blanc paired with fresh oysters and lemon wedges.
3. Chardonnay paired with grilled whitebait fritters and aioli.
4. Pinot Noir paired with slow-cooked lamb shoulder and mint sauce.
5. Sauvignon Blanc paired with goat's cheese and fig jam on crackers.
6. Chardonnay paired with creamy seafood chowder and crusty bread.
7. Pinot Noir paired with wild mushroom and truffle risotto.
8. Sauvignon Blanc paired with grilled asparagus wrapped in prosciutto.
9. Chardonnay paired with pan-fried scallops and garlic butter.
10. Pinot Noir paired with smoked salmon and cream cheese on bagels.
11. Sauvignon Blanc paired with fresh tomato and basil bruschetta.

12. Chardonnay paired with seared tuna and soy sauce.

13. Pinot Noir paired with beef skewers and peanut satay sauce.

14. Sauvignon Blanc paired with spicy Thai green curry.

15. Chardonnay paired with chicken and mushroom pie.

16. Pinot Noir paired with grilled venison steak and red wine jus.

17. Sauvignon Blanc paired with grilled prawns and mango salsa.

18. Chardonnay paired with smoked chicken and avocado salad.

19. Pinot Noir paired with slow-cooked beef short ribs and barbecue sauce.

20. Sauvignon Blanc paired with spinach and feta filo parcels.

21. Chardonnay paired with roasted vegetable salad and balsamic dressing.

22. Pinot Noir paired with wild game pate and crackers.

23. Sauvignon Blanc paired with smoked salmon and cream cheese quiche.

24. Chardonnay paired with grilled chicken and herb stuffing.

25. Pinot Noir paired with blue cheese and walnut salad.

These are just a few of the many delicious pairings that can be found at the Festival of Lights - Night Markets in New Plymouth. The festival is an excellent opportunity to experience the unique local flavours and culture of the region.

- **Wairarapa Wines Harvest Festival (Wairarapa)**

The Wairarapa Wines Harvest Festival is an annual event that takes place in the Wairarapa region of New Zealand. The festival is a celebration of the local wine industry and the hard work that goes into the annual grape harvest.

The event typically takes place in March and attracts wine lovers from all over the world. The region is known for its cool-climate wines, and the festival provides an opportunity for visitors to taste some of the best wines produced in the area.

The Wairarapa region has a long history of winemaking, dating back to the 1800s. The region is well-suited for grape growing due to its unique topography, which includes a range of mountains and valleys that create microclimates perfect for different grape varieties.

The region primarily produces Pinot Noir and Sauvignon Blanc, and local winemakers use a variety of vinification techniques to create unique and complex wines. These techniques include oak ageing, sur lie ageing, and malolactic fermentation.

The festival is an occasion for visitors to explore the local culture, which includes a strong focus on food. Local foods are paired with the wines, and festival-goers can enjoy dishes made from fresh, local ingredients.

Here are some pairing examples:

1. Pinot Noir paired with slow-cooked beef short ribs

2. Sauvignon Blanc paired with fresh oysters

3. Chardonnay paired with a creamy chicken Alfredo pasta

4. Pinot Gris paired with grilled prawns and mango salsa

5. Syrah paired with grilled lamb chops and rosemary

6. Viognier paired with roasted butternut squash risotto

7. Rosé paired with grilled salmon and a herb butter

8. Pinot Noir paired with a beef and mushroom pie

9. Chardonnay paired with grilled shrimp and lemon butter

10. Sauvignon Blanc paired with a fresh summer salad

11. Riesling paired with spicy pork larb

12. Cabernet Sauvignon paired with slow-roasted prime rib

13. Gewürztraminer paired with Thai green curry

14. Pinot Gris paired with roasted root vegetable soup

15. Merlot paired with hearty beef stew

16. Syrah paired with grilled venison and blackberry sauce

17. Pinot Noir paired with seared duck breast and cherry sauce

18. Chardonnay paired with a classic Caesar salad

19. Sauvignon Blanc paired with grilled asparagus and goat cheese

20. Riesling paired with a spicy ginger and garlic stir-fry

21. Rosé paired with grilled watermelon and feta salad

22. Viognier paired with grilled scallops and lemon butter

23. Cabernet Franc paired with a hearty beef and mushroom stew

24. Syrah paired with a spicy black bean chilli

25. Pinot Gris paired with a sweet peach and arugula salad

The Wairarapa Wines Harvest Festival provides visitors with the opportunity to explore the unique wines and foods of the region, as well as the local culture and history. It is a must-visit event for any wine lover or foodie visiting New Zealand.

25. **Bottle Rock Food and Beverage Festival (Queenstown)**

The Bottle Rock Food and Beverage Festival is a three-day event held annually in Queenstown, New Zealand. It features an array of food and beverages from all around the world. The festival has been held since 2012 and has attracted people from all over the country and even the globe.

Queenstown is a picturesque city located in the southwestern region of New Zealand's South Island. It is surrounded by mountains and sits on the shore of Lake Wakatipu. The history of the people of the region goes back to its indigenous people, the Maori, who lived in the area for over a thousand years. The city has a rich history of gold mining and this has left its mark on the town.

The Bottle Rock Food and Beverage Festival takes place in the summer months of January or February and celebrates the local culture with a focus on food and wine. The occasion is a joyous celebration that brings together locals and tourists alike. It provides an opportunity to indulge in fine local and international cuisine, sip on premium wines and soak up the atmosphere.

The topography of the region is unique and plays a significant role in the vinification techniques used. The cool-climate wine regions in Queenstown are perfect for growing grapes, and wine production is among the city's most prominent industries.

Some of the local foods that are paired with the wines include:

1. Roasted lamb with a Pinot Noir

2. Grilled venison with Syrah

3. Smoked salmon with a Chardonnay

4. Blue cheese with a Cabernet Sauvignon

5. Pork belly with a Merlot

6. Beef carpaccio with a Malbec

7. Oysters with a Sauvignon Blanc

8. Duck breast with a Pinot Noir

9. Pork ribs with Shiraz

10. Peking duck with a Cabernet Franc

11. Fried chicken with Gewurztraminer

12. Halibut with a Muscadet

13. Scallops with a Viognier

14. Gnocchi with a Sangiovese

15. Grilled prawns with a Riesling

16. Lobster with a Chablis

17. Sea bass with a Gewurztraminer

18. Beef tartare with a Malbec

19. Fried calamari with a Pinot Grigio

20. Spicy tuna rolls with a Sancerre

21. Caviar with a Champagne

22. Sushi with a Pinot Noir

23. Grilled octopus with a Syrah

24. Grilled quail with a Merlot

25. Braised short ribs with a Cabernet Sauvignon

The food ingredients used in the festival are of high quality, and the chefs use only the freshest local produce and ingredients. The meats used include beef, pork, lamb, and venison. Seafood is also popular, including salmon, oysters, scallops, lobster, and prawns. Local vegetables are also used, including potatoes, carrots, and pumpkins. Cheeses like blue cheese, gruyere, and brie are also a part of the festival's menu.

In conclusion, The Bottle Rock Food and Beverage Festival is a celebration of the unique culture and heritage of Queenstown. It offers visitors a chance to experience the local cuisine, sip on world-class wines and soak up the lively atmosphere and picturesque setting of the Queenstown region. It's a must-visit for any food or wine lover who wishes to experience the best of New Zealand's South Island.

There are many more food and wine festivals and events in New Zealand, but these are some of the most popular and highly regarded ones.

Phileas Fogg may have encountered many fascinating people, local features, fauna, and topographical features during his journey through New Zealand.

Let's take a closer look at what he might have witnessed during his travels through New Zealand

North Island:

1. **Auckland**: Fogg would have observed the iconic Sky Tower and Viaduct Harbour in Auckland, as well as local people enjoying the waterside attractions.

2. **Bay of Islands**: He would have been enthralled by the beautiful islands, greenery, and clear waters of the bay.

3. **Rotorua**: Fogg would have experienced geothermal activity and exploited the hot springs here, and also would have had an opportunity to witness traditional Maori culture.

4. **Tongariro National Park**: He would have explored the Tongariro Alpine Crossing, which includes active volcanoes, hot springs, snow-capped peaks, and crystal clear rivers.

5. **Wellington**: Here, Fogg would have experienced unique seafront landscapes and nightlife.

South Island:

1. **Christchurch**: Fogg would have taken a stroll through the city park, which is home to more than 125 species of exotic trees.

2. **Milford Sound**: Here, he would have seen Mitre Peak, a mile-high peak that drops straight into the water. He would have also spotted penguins, seals, dolphins, and whales near the sound.

3. **Abel Tasman National Park**: Fogg would have hiked along the Abel Tasman Coast Track, which offers stunning views of golden beaches, turquoise waters, and native flora.

4. **Fox and Franz Josef Glaciers**: He would have trekked up these glaciers and explored the incredible ice formations.

5. **Queenstown**: Fogg would have indulged in diverse adventure sports in this region, from skiing to bungee jumping.

Phileas Fogg would have encountered kiwis, penguins, seals, alpacas, and whales throughout his journey in New Zealand.

In terms of topography, he would have endured the mountainous terrain, been fascinated by geothermal activity, trekked through the glaciers, followed the winding roads flanked by colourful windswept trees, and enjoyed the serenity of calm blue waters etched on a landscape of glittering green.

CHAPTER 19

FESTIVALS IN THE UNITED KINGDOM

Let's look at some of the top food and wine festivals and events held in the United Kingdom:

England:

- ### The Taste of London

Held annually, this event features some of the top restaurants in London and offers attendees a chance to sample some of the best food in the city. The festival also hosts celebrity chefs, cooking demonstrations, and masterclasses for those interested in learning more about the culinary arts.

The Taste of London festival is an annual event that takes place in the United Kingdom's capital city, London. The festival emphasises the diverse culinary culture of the city, bringing together top chefs, restaurants, and food and beverage producers. It is an excellent occasion for food enthusiasts to indulge in different tastes, cuisines, and traditions within one landscape.

The event often takes place in the summer months (usually June), where visitors enjoy outdoor activities, music, and events designed to celebrate food and drink. The festival showcases local producers, wineries, and vineyards as well as their wines and vinification techniques.

It's an amazing opportunity for people to learn about different cooking techniques and unique ingredients used by diverse ethnic groups within London and around the world.

Considering the topography of the city and the availability of different ingredients, the festival presents exquisite food and wine pairing options such as:

1. Oysters and Chablis

2. Salmon and Pinot Noir

3. Sushi and Sake

4. Paella and Rioja

5. Lobster and Pouilly-Fuissé

6. Beef and Cabernet Franc

7. BBQ Pork Ribs and Zinfandel

8. Asparagus and Riesling

9. Grilled Shrimp and Sauvignon Blanc

10. Duck Confit and Merlot

11. Caviar and Brut Champagne

12. Steak and Malbec

13. Caprese Salad and Prosecco

14. Chicken Tikka Masala and IPA

15. Butter Chicken and Chardonnay

16. Biryani and Syrah

17. Paneer Tikka and Gewürztraminer

18. Lamb Chops and Shiraz

19. Tandoori Chicken and Riesling

20. Peking Duck and Pinot Grigio

21. Fried Rice and Chianti

22. Beef Tartare and Shiraz

23. Seafood Chowder and Chardonnay

24. Cheeseburger and Cabernet Sauvignon

25. Fish and Chips and German Riesling

The pairing of Oysters with Chablis is refreshing because the chalky minerality of Chablis compliments the briny ocean flavour from the oyster. Sushi and sake work because the lightness and acidity of the sake help to balance the umami flavours in the sushi. The smokiness of BBQ Pork ribs pairs well with the boldness and fruitiness of Zinfandel. The savoury and meaty flavours of Beef go well with the tannic acidity of Cabernet Franc.

In conclusion, the Taste of London festival offers a unique opportunity for food and wine enthusiasts to explore and experience the diversity of London's culinary cultures. Notable producers and wineries showcase the best of wines with the perfect pairing for any dish. It is an event to never miss.

- **The Great British Food Festival** –

Held in various locations throughout the UK, this festival features over 100 artisan food stalls, live music, and cooking demonstrations. The festival also hosts the popular 'cake-off' competition, where bakers compete to create the best cake.

The Great British Food Festival is an annual event that takes place in various locations throughout the United Kingdom. The festival showcases the country's diverse and rich culinary heritage, with a focus on local and regional produce, traditional cooking methods, and modern culinary innovations.

One of the festival's most popular locations is in the city of York, which is located in the northern part of England. The event typically takes place over three days, usually in the summer months. Visitors to the festival come from all walks of life, including locals and tourists alike, giving it a unique and diverse atmosphere.

The festival is a celebration of British culture and cuisine, and it showcases the best that the country has to offer. The occasion is also an opportunity to explore the topography, including the region's many vineyards and wineries. Visitors can learn about the vinification techniques used to produce the country's famous wines, such as Chardonnay, Pinot Noir, and Sauvignon Blanc.

At the festival, visitors can indulge in a range of foods and wines, including:

1. Fish and chips paired with a crisp, dry Riesling.

2. Creamy brie and tomato tartlets paired with a light, fruity Pinot Grigio.

3. Traditional Yorkshire pudding stuffed with roast beef and paired with a bold, full-bodied Cabernet Sauvignon.

4. Freshly shucked oysters paired with a zesty, citrusy Sauvignon Blanc.

5. Broiled scallops with garlic butter and paired with a buttery, oaky Chardonnay.

6. Sweet and savoury meat pies paired with a rich, velvety Shiraz.

7. Grilled lamb chops with rosemary and garlic paired with a robust, earthy Syrah.

8. Grilled steak with a mushroom sauce paired with a smooth, fruity Merlot.

9. Roast pork with apple and sage stuffing paired with a tart, refreshing Rosé.

10. Beef Wellington paired with a complex, full-bodied Bordeaux.

11. Chicken curry paired with a spicy, aromatic Gewurztraminer.

12. Shepherd's pie paired with a rich, full-bodied Malbec.

13. Smoked salmon blinis paired with a light, crisp Blanc de Blancs.

14. Grilled prawns with lemon and herb butter paired with a bright, citrusy Chablis.

15. Beef sliders with blue cheese and bacon paired with a bold, tannic Zinfandel.

16. Creamy mushroom risotto paired with a dry, minerally Sancerre.

17. Freshly baked bread with garlic and herb butter paired with a rich, buttery Chardonnay.

18. Cheese fondue paired with a smooth, fruity Cabernet Franc.

19. Roasted vegetable paella paired with a light, acidic Albariño.

20. Butternut squash soup with crispy croutons paired with a fruity, medium-bodied Pinot Noir.

21. Grilled halloumi cheese with figs and honey paired with a light, crisp Chenin Blanc.

22. Beef brisket with barbecue sauce paired with a bold, smoky Zinfandel.

23. Caramelised onion and goat cheese tartlets paired with a light, refreshing Cava.

24. Grilled eggplant with red pepper sauce paired with a fruity, medium-bodied Grenache.

25. Dark chocolate truffles paired with a rich, full-bodied Port.

The delicious food and wine pairings at The Great British Food Festival are carefully curated by expert chefs and sommeliers. The ingredients are chosen to complement each other, elevating the flavours of both the food and wine. The pairing of fish and chips with a crisp, dry Riesling brings out the best in both, with the tangy acidity of the wine complementing the flaky, savoury fish. The bold, full-bodied Cabernet Sauvignon paired with traditional Yorkshire pudding stuffed with roast beef enhances the meaty Umami flavour of the beef. Similarly, the rich, velvety Shiraz paired with sweet and savoury meat pies does an excellent job of bringing out the flavour of the meat. In all cases, the pairings highlight the best of both the food and wine, making for an unforgettable culinary experience.

- **National Wine Festival of England**

The National Wine Festival of England is a highly anticipated annual event that takes place in the city of London, UK. The festival attracts wine enthusiasts from all over the country who come to experience the finest wines and foods in the region. The event usually takes place in early September and lasts for three days.

The festival is a celebration of the country's rich culture and topography, which is known for its rolling hills and vineyards. The wines showcased at the event come from different regions of England and are created using various vinification techniques, making for a diverse range of flavours and aromas.

At the festival, visitors get to sample some of the country's best wines alongside a carefully curated selection of foods. The foods are carefully matched to complement the wines and enhance their flavours. Visitors can indulge in a variety of dishes ranging from traditional English fare to modern cuisine.

Here are some examples of food and wine pairings:

1. Fish and Chips with a citrusy Chardonnay

2. Roast beef with gravy and a bold, tannic Cabernet Franc

3. English cheese platter with a light, fruity Pinot Noir

4. Oysters on the half shell with a crisp, minerally Chablis-style wine

5. Spicy sausage with a dry, peppery Shiraz

6. Grilled vegetables with a bright, acidic Sauvignon Blanc

7. Shepherd's pie with a smooth, oak-aged Merlot

8. Scallops with a rich, buttery Chardonnay

9. Grilled lamb chops with a bold, smoky Syrah

10. Mushroom risotto with a light, earthy Pinot Noir

11. Lemon chicken with a zesty, mineral Sauvignon Blanc

12. Steak and kidney pie with a robust, full-bodied Cabernet Sauvignon

13. Crab cakes with a bright, crisp Riesling

14. Pork belly with a rich, complex Zinfandel

15. English breakfast with a sparkling, dry Brut

16. Spiced lamb curry with a spicy, aromatic Gewürztraminer

17. Beef Wellington with a smooth, velvety Malbec

18. Smoked salmon with a dry, mineral Chenin Blanc

19. Sticky toffee pudding with a sweet, fruity dessert wine

20. Devonshire cream tea with a light, floral Rosé

21. Roasted vegetables with a full-bodied, oak-aged Chardonnay

22. Baked beans with a light, fruity Beaujolais

23. Ploughman's lunch with a crisp, dry Cider

24. Scones with jam and clotted cream with a sparkling, refreshing Prosecco

25. Dark chocolate with a rich, bold Cabernet Franc

In general, the foods are paired with wines that have complementary flavours or contrasting characteristics that create a harmonious balance. For example, acidic wines like Sauvignon Blanc pair well with creamy dishes like scallops or chicken, while sweeter wines like Riesling complement spicy dishes like lamb curry. The pairing is done in such a way to enhance the flavours and aromas of both the food and wine, creating a well-rounded culinary experience for visitors.

- **Isle of Wight Garlic Festival**

The Isle of Wight Garlic Festival is an annual event that takes place on the Isle of Wight in the United Kingdom and is one of the most popular food festivals in the country. The festival celebrates all things garlic, including food, wine, and unique products made from garlic.

The event is held in August and takes place over two days and attracts over 25,000 people each year. The festival grounds are located in the town of Newchurch on the Isle of Wight, which is known for its beautiful and scenic topography.

Aside from the delicious garlic-based food, the Isle of Wight is also famous for its vineyards. The festival features many local wineries and vineyards that offer tastings and tours of their facilities. Visitors can learn about the vinification techniques used in the island's vineyards and taste wines made from locally grown grapes.

Some of the top foods at the festival include garlic-infused dishes such as garlic bread, garlic butter, garlic shrimp scampi, garlic sausage, and garlic mash. There are also many other delicious foods available including, seafood, vegetarian and vegan options, homemade burgers, pizzas, and pastry dishes. Visitors can also shop for garlic-infused products such as garlic-infused condiments, fresh garlic bulbs, and garlic-themed gifts.

Here are some examples of food and wine pairings at the Isle of Wight Garlic Festival:

1. Garlic bread and a crisp Sauvignon Blanc

2. Garlic roasted pork and a bold Syrah

3. Garlic and herb roasted potatoes with a dry Rosé

4. Garlic and prawn skewers with a buttery Chardonnay

5. Garlic and herb cream cheese with a light Pinot Grigio

6. Garlic steak with a full-bodied Cabernet Sauvignon

7. Garlic and butter lobster with a rich Chardonnay

8. Garlic mushroom risotto with a smooth Pinot Noir

9. Garlic and thyme roasted chicken with a classic Merlot

10. Garlic and shrimp linguine with an acidic Vermentino

11. Garlic and ginger stir-fry with a crisp Riesling

12. Garlic and herb marinated steamed clams paired with a Sauvignon Blanc

13. Garlic aioli with a crispy fried calamari and a bright Pinot Grigio

14. Garlic and ginger marinated flank steak with a bold Cabernet Sauvignon

15. Garlic and cheese stuffed mushrooms with a full bodied Merlot

16. Garlic shrimp scampi with a buttery Chardonnay or a crisp Sauvignon Blanc

17. Garlic and herb roasted turkey with a smooth Pinot Noir

18. Garlic butter spaghetti with a dry Rosé

19. Garlic prawn fajitas with a light Riesling

20. Garlic and herb baked salmon with a crisp Chardonnay

21. Garlic chicken kebab with a rich Shiraz

22. Garlic mashed potatoes with a bright Pinot Grigio

23. Garlic and herb roasted lamb with a bold Cabernet Franc

24. Garlic and spinach quiche with a smooth Merlot

25. Garlic bread and garlic butter with a bubbly Prosecco

The delicious flavours of garlic-infused food and locally-produced wines make the Isle of Wight Garlic Festival a unique and memorable event for visitors to experience.

- **Ludlow Food Festival**

The Ludlow Food Festival is an annual event celebrating food and drink that takes place in Ludlow, a market town located in Shropshire, England. The festival is renowned for its focus on locally produced artisanal foods and regional wines.

The festival takes place over three days in September and is a major event in the UK food and drink calendar, attracting tens of thousands of people each year. It is a celebration of Shropshire's rich culinary history as well as showcasing the region's contemporary food scene.

The topography of the region, with its rolling hills and fertile agricultural land, is ideal for growing a wide range of fruits and vegetables, as well as raising livestock. The area is also home to a number of excellent vineyards that produce award-winning wines, using vinification techniques such as the traditional method, pet-nat, and skin contact.

The festival features a wide range of foods, including artisan bread, cheeses, sausages, pies, and sweet treats, as well as locally reared meats and fresh, seasonal produce. Visitors to the festival can enjoy tasting sessions, cooking demonstrations, and talks by food experts, as well as live music and other entertainment.

The festival is also an occasion for food and wine pairing, and Ludlow's sommeliers are on hand to advise visitors on the best pairings. The reason why food and wine pair so well is that the flavours and textures of the food can be enhanced or complemented by the characteristics of the wine, and vice versa.

Here are some examples of food and wine pairings you might enjoy at the Ludlow Food Festival:

1. Creamy, nutty cheese with a full-bodied Chardonnay

2. Spicy sausage with a peppery Syrah/Shiraz

3. Oysters with a crisp, dry Sauvignon Blanc

4. Roast beef with a rich Cabernet Sauvignon

5. Barbecue ribs with a fruity Zinfandel

6. Grilled chicken with a light, citrusy Viognier

7. Smoked salmon with a mineral-rich Chablis

8. Spicy curries with a smooth Malbec

9. Lobster with a buttery Chardonnay

10. Grilled vegetables with a herbaceous Pinot Grigio

11. Barbecue pork with a sweet Riesling

12. Grilled steaks with a bold, tannic Syrah/Shiraz

13. Creamy soups with a crisp, acidic Pinot Grigio

14. Fish and chips with a zesty Chenin Blanc

15. Mushroom risotto with a velvety Merlot

16. Game birds with a earthy Pinot Noir

17. Spicy Thai food with a sweeter Gewürztraminer

18. Grilled lamb with a classic Bordeaux blend

19. Fried chicken with a sparkling Prosecco

20. Tomato-based dishes with a medium-bodied Sangiovese

21. Fried calamari with a citrusy Vinho Verde

22. Roast pork with a light Pinot Noir

23. Grilled scallops with a mineral-rich Sancerre

24. Spicy beef dishes with a bold Cabernet Franc

25. Blue cheese with a sweet, fortified Port.

In conclusion, the Ludlow Food Festival is a showcase of the best of Shropshire's culinary traditions, highlighting the region's unique topography, vineyards and foods. This is an event that cherishes culture while embracing contemporary trends. So come along and explore the festival, enjoy the wonderful food and wine pairings, and experience the unique flavours of Shropshire.

6. Cornish Pasty Week

Cornish Pasty Week is a celebration of the Cornish pasty, a traditional and iconic dish of Cornwall, UK. The festival takes place across various cities and towns in Cornwall, which is located in the southwest of England. The week-long event usually takes place in February or March of each year.

The festival celebrates the culture and heritage of Cornwall and its traditional food. Visitors and locals alike can take part in food tastings, cookery workshops, and sampling of different varieties of Cornish pasties. The occasion also includes music, arts, and cultural events to celebrate the contribution of pasty makers to Cornwall's history, economy and tourism.

Cornwall's topography is diverse, with rolling hills, picturesque villages and stunning coastal paths offering breathtaking views of the Atlantic Ocean. The region is famous for its vineyards, which produce unique and delicious wines using local grape varieties and vinification techniques.

During the event, festival-goers can taste various kinds of wines that pair perfectly with Cornish pasties. Here are some examples of pairings:

1. Traditional Cornish pasty with a light and crisp white wine like Tintagel 2019 Bacchus

2. Cheese and onion pasty with a rich and full-bodied red wine like Knightor 2018 Rondo & Pinot Noir

3. Spicy beef and potato pasty with a fruity and flavourful red wine like Polgoon 2018 Dornfelder

4. Chicken and vegetable pasty with a smooth and buttery white wine like Camel Valley 2018 Chardonnay

5. Steak and ale pasty with a bold and spicy red wine like Bosue 2017 Rondo & Cabernet Foch

6. Traditional lamb and mint pasty with a light and refreshing rosé wine like Trevibban Mill 2019 Black and Blue

7. Vegetarian pasty with a fruity and aromatic white wine like Polgoon 2018 Madeleine Angevine

8. Cheese and bacon pasty with a crisp and zesty white wine like St. Austell Mena Hweg

9. Curried vegetable pasty with a sweet and fruity white wine like Polgoon 2018 Sparkling Elderflower

10. Haggis pasty with a full and spicy red wine like Knightor 2018 Triomphe & Rondo

11. Steak and cheese pasty with a rich and smooth red wine like Polgoon 2018 Landscove Pinot Noir

12. Lobster and samphire pasty with a crisp and fresh white wine like Camel Valley Atlantic Dry

13. Pork and apple pasty with a medium-bodied and fruity red wine like Bosue 2017 Rondo & Cabernet Foch

14. Traditional chicken pasty with a crisp and aromatic white wine like Trevibban Mill Black Ewe Classic

15. Caramelised onion and goat's cheese pasty with a sweet and fruity white wine like Polgoon 2018 Seyval Blanc

16. Duck and hoisin pasty with a rich and spicy red wine like Knightor 2018 Pinot Noir

17. Traditional beef pasty with a smooth and velvety red wine like Bosue 2017 Rondo

18. Seafood pasty with a crisp and refreshing white wine like Camel Valley Bacchus

19. Mushroom and truffle pasty with a fruity and fresh white wine like Trevibban Mill 2019 Black and Blue

20. Spicy jerk chicken pasty with a bold and fruity red wine like Bosue 2017 Pinot Noir Precoce

21. Lamb and rosemary pasty with a smooth and rich red wine like Knightor 2018 Regent

22. Vegetable and cheese pasty with a crisp and light white wine like Polgoon 2018 Ortega

23. Traditional pork and apple pasty with a rich and fruity red wine like Camel Valley Pinot Noir Rosé

24. Spicy chorizo and potato pasty with a bold and spicy red wine like Bosue 2018 Rondo & Cabernet Foch

25. Smoked salmon and asparagus pasty with a light and fresh white wine like Trevibban Mill 2019 Black Ewe Classic Blanc.

The food and wine pairings listed above are based on the complementary notes, aromas and flavours of each dish and wine. For instance, the spiciness of the jerk chicken pasty is complemented by the fruity notes of the Bosue 2017 Pinot Noir Precoce, creating a perfect balance of flavours. Similarly, the sweetness of the caramelised onions and goat's cheese pasty is enhanced by the sweet and fruity notes of the Polgoon 2018 Seyval Blanc, creating a harmonious pairing.

Scotland

- **Royal Highland Show**

The Royal Highland Show is the largest agricultural festival in Scotland, which takes place annually in Edinburgh. The event showcases various innovative agricultural techniques of the country, livestock shows, equestrianism and other cultural activities. The event is usually held in the month of June every year, spanning around four days.

The show serves as a proud cultural celebration, reflecting various traditions and customs of Scotland. Being an agricultural event, the venue's topography is rural, with lush green pastures and farmland surrounding the area. Though there are no vineyards present, a variety of imported wines are offered at the event, coming from different parts of the world.

The Royal Highland Show offers a diverse range of food options, showcasing local culinary expertise. Various food vendors sell traditional Scottish foods such as haggis, Scotch pies, black pudding, and fish and chips. The event also offers other favourite dishes such as pizzas, burgers, and ice-creams. Additionally, there are wine tasting sessions, allowing the visitors to explore and learn about the different wines available at the event.

Here are some examples of wine and food pairings that can be enjoyed during the event:

1. Haggis with a robust Shiraz- the wine's bold and spicy flavours complement well with the rich, meaty and gamey taste of haggis.

2. Scottish salmon served with a crisp Sauvignon Blanc- the wine offers the perfect acidity and freshness to cut through the richness of the salmon.

3. Oysters with a cool, mineral Chablis- the wine's flavour profile matched with the briny taste of oysters.

4. Venison with a full-bodied Merlot- the soft tannins of the wine pair well with the game meat's richness and earthy flavours.

5. Scotch pie served with a light-bodied Pinot Noir- the wine's smooth tannins and fruity notes complement well with the mildly spiced meat filling.

6. Seafood Paella with a medium-bodied Rioja- the silky texture and smoky notes of the wine pair well with the smokiness of the dish's charred seafood.

7. Fried chicken wings paired with aromatic Gewurztraminer- the wine's floral and spice aromas complement the dish's spicy flavours.

8. Mac and Cheese with a full-bodied Chardonnay- the smooth and round texture of the wine pairs well with the creamy cheese sauce.

9. Squid Ink Risotto with a crisp Pinot Grigio- the wine's acidity cuts through the richness of the dish while its citrusy notes pair well with the seafood flavours.

10. Meat pie with a bold Malbec- the wine's tannins pair well with the dish's savoury filling.

11. Fish and chips with a dry Riesling- the crisp acidity of the wine matches the fried fish's crisp breading.

12. Spinach and Ricotta Ravioli with a medium-bodied Sangiovese- the fruity notes of the wine match well with the sweet and tangy tomato sauce of the dish.

13. Beef brisket with a fruity Zinfandel- the wine offers adequate acidity, which cuts through the richness of meat.

14. Chicken curry with a crisp riesling-the wine's acidity pairs well with the spicy flavours of the dish.

15. Sausage roll with a tannic Cabernet Sauvignon- the wine's high tannin levels pair well with the fatty flavours of the dish.

16. Sweet potato fries with a medium-bodied Merlot- the wine's red fruit flavours complement the sweetness of the dish.

17. Lobster Bisque with a full-bodied Chardonnay- the wine's creamy texture matches well with the creamy soup's flavours.

18. Scottish Shortbread served with sweet sherry- the wine's nutty notes match with the buttery flavour of the shortbread.

19. Smoked Mackerel with Chilli Sauce with Rose Wine - the wine complements the spicy and smoky flavours of the dish.

20. Sticky toffee pudding with a sweet moscato- the wine's fruit flavours match perfectly with the sweet dessert's toffee taste.

21. Steak pie with a robust Malbec- the wine's tannin structure matches the rich beef filling's bold flavour.

22. Haggis-stuffed chicken with a light Red Burgundy- Pinot Noir-the wine's light and fruity aromas match well with the chicken.

23. Scotch broth soup with a dry White Bordeaux- the wine's mineral and citrusy notes match well with the dish's flavours.

24. Pork belly with a fruity Cabernet Franc- the wine's ripe and fruity notes work well with the dish's fatty pork belly flavour.

25. Venison stew with a full-bodied Syrah- the wine's dark fruit flavours and smoky notes match the gamey stew's earthy flavours.

In summary, the Royal Highland Show in the UK is a cultural festival that showcases Scotland's agricultural traditions and culinary skills. The event offers a diverse range of food options, and wine tasting sessions, allowing visitors to explore and learn about different wines and their pairings.

- **Orkney Folk Festival**

The Orkney Folk Festival is a well-known cultural event in the United Kingdom. It takes place every year in the beautiful city of Kirkwall, located in the Orkney Islands, off the northern coast of Scotland. The festival typically takes place in late May, and attracts visitors from all over the world who come to experience Scottish folk music, dance, and other traditional art forms.

The event is a celebration of Scottish culture, and visitors can expect to experience a wide range of traditional Scottish cultural activities, including bagpipe music, Highland dancing, and traditional Scottish foods and drinks. The Orkney Islands are known for their rugged topography, with spectacular cliffs and sea stacks that provide a dramatic backdrop for the festival.

While the Orkney Islands are not well known for their vineyards, festival-goers can expect to enjoy a range of traditional Scottish foods and drinks, including haggis, neeps and tatties, smoked salmon, and whisky. Some other popular dishes at the festival include Cullen skink (a Scottish soup made from smoked haddock), stovies (a traditional Scottish stew made from potatoes and meat), and Clootie dumpling (a sweet dessert made from dried fruit and breadcrumbs).

When it comes to pairing foods and wines at the Orkney Folk Festival, the goal is to find complementary flavours and textures that enhance the overall dining experience.

Some examples of food and wine pairings that are sure to delight festival-goers:

1. Smoked salmon with a crisp, acidic white wine like Sauvignon Blanc

2. Haggis with a rich, full-bodied red wine like Cabernet Sauvignon

3. Neeps and tatties with a light, fruity red wine like Pinot Noir

4. Cullen skink with a buttery, oaked white wine like Chardonnay

5. Stovies with a spicy, full-bodied red wine like Shiraz

6. Clootie dumpling with a sweet, dessert wine like Muscat

7. Baked salmon with a crisp, herbaceous white wine like Riesling

8. Venison stew with a bold, spicy red wine like Merlot

9. Scotch broth with a smooth, fruity red wine like Grenache

10. Scottish cheese platter with a robust, tannic red wine like Malbec

11. Arbroath smokie with a crisp, citrusy white wine like Chenin Blanc

12. Venison haggis with a smokey, bold red wine like Syrah

13. Haddock chowder with a crisp, zesty white wine like Albariño

14. Lamb stew with a spicy, earthy red wine like Tempranillo

15. Scottish oatcakes with a sweet, fragrant white wine like Gewürztraminer

16. Beef and root vegetable stew with a bold, spicy red wine like Zinfandel

17. Caramel shortbread with a rich, sweet dessert wine like Port

18. Potato scones with a light, fruity white wine like Pinot Grigio

19. Black pudding with a bold, smoky red wine like Cabernet Franc

20. Steak pie with a rich, full-bodied red wine like Meritage

21. Barley soup with a smooth, fruity red wine like Sangiovese

22. Scottish tablet with a sweet, complex dessert wine like Tokaji

23. Scotch eggs with a light, crisp white wine like Vermentino

24. Crabbie's ginger beer with a bright, citrusy white wine like Viognier

25. Fried haggis balls with a bold, fruity red wine like Barbera

In each of these pairings, the goal is to balance the complex flavours of traditional Scottish dishes with the right wine to enhance the experience. The smoky, savoury flavours of dishes like smoked salmon or haggis, for example, are perfectly balanced by bold, full-bodied red wines like Cabernet Sauvignon or Merlot. Meanwhile, the sweet, fruity flavours of Scottish desserts like clootie dumpling or tablet are perfectly balanced by rich, sweet dessert wines like Muscat or Port.

- **Stirling Whisky Festival**

The Stirling Whisky Festival is an annual event that takes place in Stirling, Scotland. The festival brings together people from all over the world to celebrate their love for whisky, culture, food, and history of the region.

Stirling is an ancient city that is steeped in history and tradition. The topography of the region is characterised by hilly terrain, valleys, and rivers. The area is famous for its vineyards, which produce some of Scotland's most renowned whiskies.

The festival attracts connoisseurs and enthusiasts of whisky from around the world to sample a vast array of rare and exotic whiskies. Each year, numerous whisky distilleries showcase their wide range of products and participate in the event.

People visiting the festival get to meet distillers, ambassadors and industry leaders, as they educate themselves about the vinification techniques, ageing and blending processes involved in whisky production. Visitors can discover different whisky styles and whisky-based cocktails, and also attend tasting sessions and masterclasses.

In addition to the whisky, the festival provides attendees with an array of Scottish food and wine. There are haggis dishes, beef jerky, and smoked salmon. The haggis is typically paired with robust red wines from the region, such as Cabernet Sauvignon, which complements the dish's rich and savoury flavours.

Visitors also have an option to try their hand at pairing whisky with food. Some of the examples of food and whisky pairings at the festival include:

1. Haggis and Talisker Distiller's Reserve

2. Venison burger and Glenmorangie Astar

3. Scottish smoked salmon and Aberlour 12 Year Old

4. Beetroot and Goat Cheese Salad, paired with Bruichladdich Black Art 6.1

5. Scottish Oysters and Bowmore 18 Year Old

6. Whisky Cured Salmon with Auchentoshan 12 Year Old

7. The Oatmeal Cranachan and Glenlivet 15 Year Old

8. Cullen Skink Soup and Ardbeg Uigeadail

9. Traditional Scotch Pie, served with Glenfiddich 12 Year Old

10. Honey Glazed Roast Ham, served with Cardhu 15 Year Old

11. Venison and Redcurrant Casserole, served with Lagavulin 16 Year Old

12. Haggis Croustades, served with Glenmorangie Signet

13. Scottish fish cakes, served with Laphroaig Quarter Cask

14. Beef Stroganoff, served with Bunnahabhain 18 Year Old

15. Smoked Trout Pate, served with The Macallan Sherry Oak 12 Year Old

16. Scottish Salmon and Scallop Kebabs, served with Highland Park 18 Year Old

17. Cranberry, Apple and Brie Tartlets, served with Chivas Regal 18 Year Old

18. Venison Sausages with Spring Onion Mash, served with Johnnie Walker Gold Label Reserve

19. Smoked Haddock Chowder, served with Ardbeg Corryvreckan

20. Black Pudding and Apple Stack, served with Aberlour A'Bunadh

21. Salmon Fillets with Roasted Almonds, served with Glenlivet 18 Year Old

22. Caramelized Pork Belly with Whisky Glaze, served with Glenkinchie 12 Year Old

23. Cheesecake with Whisky Sauce, paired with Dalmore King Alexander III

24. Cranachan with the Glenlivet XXV

25. Chocolate Fudge Cake with GlenDronach Revival

The reason why the pairing of food and whisky is so effective is that it enhances the food's flavours and complements the whisky's tasting profile. The robust, complex flavor of the whisky perfectly balances the texture and savoriness of the food, creating an unforgettable sensory experience.

In conclusion, the Stirling Whisky Festival is an event that provides visitors with the opportunity to sample the finest and rarest whiskies produced in Scotland. Attendees can immerse themselves in the food, wine, culture, and history of the region while discovering new flavours and experiences.

Scottish Traditional Boat Festival

Scottish Traditional Boat Festival is a maritime festival and celebration of Scotland's coastal heritage.

The Scottish Traditional Boat Festival takes place in the town of Portsoy, Scotland, which is located in Aberdeenshire in the North East of Scotland. The festival is a celebration of Scotland's rich maritime heritage and attracts thousands of visitors each year. The festival takes place over two days during the last weekend of June and is free to attend.

The festival features a variety of events and activities, such as boat races, fishing demonstrations, boat building workshops, music and dance performances, and food and craft vendors. Visitors can also explore the historic Portsoy harbour, which dates back to the 17th century.

The festival celebrates the cultural heritage of the Banffshire coast and its strong connections to the sea. The topography of the area is characterised by rugged cliffs, sandy beaches, and picturesque harbours. The region is known for its fisheries and traditional fishing methods, which are still used today.

While there are no vineyards or wines at the Scottish Traditional Boat Festival, visitors can enjoy a variety of Scottish foods, such as fresh seafood, haggis, Aberdeen Angus beef, and Scottish cheeses. These foods can be paired with local beers or whiskies, such as BrewDog Punk IPA, Speyside Single Malt Scotch, or Glenfiddich Single Malt Scotch.

The history of the region is rich and varied, and the festival provides an opportunity to learn about its maritime heritage. Portsoy has a long history of boat building, and visitors can see traditional boats on display throughout the festival. The town was also a major centre for the herring industry in the 19th century, and visitors can learn about this important part of the region's history at the festival.

In summary, the Scottish Traditional Boat Festival is a celebration of Scotland's coastal heritage, featuring a variety of events and activities that highlight the region's cultural history. Visitors can enjoy traditional Scottish foods and local drinks while exploring the area's topography and learning about its history and traditions.

- **Edinburgh Food Festival**

The Edinburgh Food Festival is an annual event that takes place in Edinburgh, the capital city of Scotland, which is located in the United Kingdom. This event is one of the most significant food festivals that celebrate the abundant food and drink culture in the region. The festival attracts people from all walks of life and offers a diverse range of foods, drinks, and other delicacies.

The festival takes place every year in July, and it is an opportunity for people to experience the local culture and tradition. The event is held at several locations in the city, including George Square Gardens, and it runs for several days. During the festival, visitors can explore a wide range of foods, including Scottish cuisine and other international dishes, and the focus is on promoting local producers.

The Edinburgh Food Festival is an excellent opportunity to explore the topography of the region as well. Scotland is known for its vast vineyards that produce a variety of wines. During the event, visitors can learn about the vinification techniques used in the region and the history of the wines produced here. There are also wine tasting sessions available for visitors to sample the wines produced locally.

At the Edinburgh Food Festival, visitors can experience a wide range of foods and wines to pair. Some of the examples include:

1. Haggis with a Scottish ale
2. Salmon with a white wine, such as Sauvignon Blanc
3. Venison paired with a bold red wine, such as Merlot or Syrah
4. Highland beef served with a full-bodied red wine, such as Cabernet Sauvignon
5. Whiskey-infused chocolates paired with a dessert wine, such as a Port or Sauternes
6. Smoked salmon with a sparkling white wine, such as Champagne or Prosecco
7. Oysters with a dry white wine, such as Pinot Grigio or Chablis
8. Traditional Scottish shortbread with a sweet dessert wine, such as Moscato
9. Scottish cheese plate with a full-bodied red wine, such as Malbec or Shiraz
10. Haddock with a crisp white wine, such as Chardonnay
11. Cullen Skink with a light red wine, such as Beaujolais
12. Scottish baked potato with a rich, full-bodied white wine, such as Viognier
13. Game bird with a fruity, medium-bodied red wine, such as Pinot Noir
14. Scottish langoustines with a mineral white wine, such as Albariño
15. Cranachan with a crisp, acidic white wine, such as Riesling
16. Mussels in a spicy broth with a light, fruity red wine, such as Gamay

17. Scottish tablet with a caramelized dessert wine, such as Marsala

18. Scottish smoked meats with a smoky red wine, such as Tempranillo

19. Scottish pork pie with a medium-bodied red wine, such as Sangiovese

20. Scottish oatcakes with a warm, spicy red wine, such as Zinfandel

21. Scottish black pudding with a bold, full-bodied red wine, such as Malbec

22. Cabbage with a honey and thyme glaze paired with a sweet dessert wine, such as Vin Santo

23. Roast duck with a fruity, medium-bodied red wine, such as Pinot Noir

24. Cranberry sauce with a tart red wine, such as Beaujolais

25. Braised beef with a rich, full-bodied red wine, such as Bordeaux

The wines paired with the foods at the Edinburgh Food Festival are selected based on their complementary flavours and textures. For example, the bold, full-bodied red wines pair well with rich, hearty dishes such as venison and beef, while the crisp white wines complement lighter dishes such as seafood and salads. The sweetness of the dessert wines also pairs well with the rich, buttery flavours of Scottish shortbread or tablet.

In conclusion, the Edinburgh Food Festival is an excellent opportunity to experience the vast array of foods and wines in the region. Visitors can learn about the local culture, explore the topography and vineyards, taste the wines and enjoy the food that is paired with the wines perfectly. The event is an opportunity to celebrate the history and culture of the region and its unique cuisine.

Glasgow Gin Festival

The Glasgow Gin Festival takes place in Glasgow, Scotland, a country famous for its scotch whiskies. The event is celebrated annually, where gin lovers come together to taste various gins, learn about their art, and enjoy with like-minded people. This festival typically takes place over the weekends in April.

Scotland is known for its rich culture and heritage, from bagpipes to kilts, and the Glasgow Gin Festival is a true representation of Scottish culture. The event is not only for gin lovers, but for people who appreciate Scotland's excellence in producing quality drinks. The Glasgow Gin Festival is the perfect occasion to dive in the city's local culture, enjoy artisan gin and indulge in its rich history.

Glasgow is set in rolling hills and has lush greenery, which provides a fertile ground for vineyards. Scotland's particular climate provides an ideal temperature and the perfect soil for plantations for the finest raw materials. Gin is a type of alcohol made from juniper berries and various other botanicals. Scotland's greenery makes it an ideal location for gin vineyards.

The history of gin making in Scotland can be traced back to the 17th century, but it flourished during the 18th and 19th centuries. The quality of the Scottish gin is based on their vinification techniques, fine ingredients, and craftsmanship. The festival is an opportunity to learn about the vinification techniques and appreciate gin-making history.

Scottish food has a unique flavour and it complements the gin perfectly. In this festival, Scottish cuisine is available to pair with the gins. Scottish foods like Haggis, Scottish salmon, and black pudding can be paired with exotic gins to create an unparalleled taste.

Here are some of the best food and gin pairing options at the Glasgow Gin Festival:

1. Haggis and Lussa Gin

2. Scottish Salmon with Zymurgorium Sweet Violet Gin

3. Black pudding with Crossbill Highland Dry Gin

4. Cullen Skink soup with Kirkjuvagr Orkney Gin

5. Venison Steak with Hendrick's Gin

6. Smoked Haddock with The Botanist Gin

7. Scottish Tablet with Caorunn Scottish Gin

8. Stornoway black pudding with Shetland Reel Gin

9. Cullen skink with Gin Mare

10. Roast beef with Scotland, Distilled.

11. Scottish Highland Beef with Belsazar Rose Vermouth

12. Scottish Lobster with Isle of Harris Gin

13. Cured Ham with Porter's Perfection Gin

14. Scottish Mussel Soup with El Gin

15. Scallop Ceviche with Vine Gin

16. Langoustine Tails with Wild Island Botanic Gin

17. Smoked Salmon with Lind & Lime Gin

18. Salmon and pea risotto with Wilderness Gin

19. Crispy Haggis Pops with the Ginskey Gin

20. Venison pie with Gin Bothy Spey Cast

21. Cheese plate with Darnley's Spiced Gin

22. Cranachan with The Teasmith Gin

23. Oysters with Port of Leith Distillery Gin Baubles

24. Scottish cheese board with Pickerings Gin

25. Atholl Brose with Old Curiosity Apothecary Rose Gin

The foods are paired with gins based on their taste profile, botanicals, and ingredients. For example, The Edradour Whisky Cask Gin pairs perfectly with Roast Beef, as its subtlety is derived from oak casks used to mature the whiskey. The flavours develop a perfect balance that harmonises the taste of both the food and gin.

In conclusion, the Glasgow Gin Festival is not only a celebration of Scottish gin culture but a unique representation of Scotland's rich history, topography, and local cuisine. It's a must-visit festival for gin enthusiasts or anyone looking to explore the Scottish gin and Scottish lifestyle.

Wales

- **Abergavenny Food Festival**

Abergavenny Food Festival is a prestigious event that takes place in Abergavenny, a town in Monmouthshire, Wales. The festival is renowned for bringing together the best of the country's food and drink producers. The event takes place annually in September and spans two days, showcasing a range of foods and drinks from all over the world.

The festival is a major cultural occasion in Wales, attracting both locals and tourists to the area. Abergavenny is known for its picturesque topography, with vineyards scattered throughout the countryside. The region is known for its traditional vinification techniques, which have been passed down for generations.

The festival features an array of wines and foods from the region, including Welsh cheeses, meats, fish and pastries. There are also a range of international dishes on offer, including Thai, Indian, Italian and American cuisine.

Wine tasting is a key feature of the event, with numerous vineyards showcasing their latest vintages. Visitors can learn about the history of the region and the techniques used to create the wines. There are also workshops held throughout the festival, which provide visitors with the opportunity to learn about the pairing of foods and wines

Some examples of food and wine pairing available at the Abergavenny Food Festival:

1. Welsh rarebit paired with Pinot Noir

2. Beef stew paired with Merlot

3. Smoked salmon paired with Chardonnay

4. Lamb chops paired with Syrah

5. Pulled pork sliders paired with Cabernet Sauvignon

6. Fish and chips paired with Sauvignon Blanc

7. Pork belly paired with Riesling

8. Welsh cakes paired with Prosecco

9. Steak and ale pie paired with Malbec

10. Lobster bisque paired with Chablis

11. Roast beef paired with Cabernet Franc

12. Apple pie paired with Gewürztraminer

13. Peking duck paired with Pinot Gris

14. Venison casserole paired with Bordeaux Blend

15. Sticky toffee pudding paired with Tawny Port

16. Tuna tartare paired with Grüner Veltliner

17. Turkey and cranberry sauce paired with Syrah

18. Shepherd's pie paired with Zinfandel

19. Spaghetti Bolognese paired with Sangiovese

20. Chicken curry paired with Viognier

21. Grilled vegetables paired with Rosé

22. Huevos rancheros paired with Tempranillo

23. Beef bourguignon paired with Pinot Noir

24. Baked salmon paired with Chardonnay

25. Welsh rarebit paired with sparkling wine

The pairing of foods and wines at the festival is carefully considered, with each wine working to enhance the flavours of the dish. For example, the Pinot Noir works well with Welsh rarebit as it has a smooth and light taste that complements the rich, tangy cheese. The Merlot, on the other hand, is well suited to beef stew, as its smooth and bold flavours cut through the hearty dish.

The Chardonnay is a popular choice for smoked salmon, as it has a light and refreshing taste that does not overpower the delicate flavours of the fish. Meanwhile, the Syrah works well with lamb chops as it has a bold and spicy taste that contrasts nicely with the tender meat.

In conclusion, Abergavenny Food Festival is a celebration of the region's rich history, culture, and cuisine. Visitors to the festival can sample some of the best wines and foods produced in Wales, and learn about the traditional vinification techniques used in the area. The pairing of foods and wines is an essential part of the festival, and visitors can experience the unique flavours of the region through the carefully considered combinations on offer.

- **Conwy Feast**

Conwy Feast is a festival that takes place in the town of Conwy, Wales, United Kingdom. The festival is a celebration of the local people, their culture, topography, vineyards, vinification techniques, foods, and wines. This event is an annual celebration that usually takes place in the month of October every year.

The Conwy Feast festival is one of the largest food festivals in Wales, attracting around 30,000 visitors each year. The festival is a four-day event that features a wide range of food and drink vendors, cooking demonstrations, live entertainment, and other activities.

The town of Conwy is a culturally rich place, with a long history of food production and vineyards. The people of Conwy are proud of their culture and tradition, and they use the Conwy Feast festival as an opportunity to showcase their heritage to the world.

In terms of topography, Conwy is located next to the sea, which makes it an ideal place for producing seafood. The region is also surrounded by lush, green hills, which are perfect for growing grapes and producing wine.

There are many vineyards in the Conwy region, each with their own unique vinification techniques. Some of the most popular vineyards in the region include Gwinllan Conwy Vineyard, Pant Du Vineyard and Winery, and Penmynydd Uchaf. These vineyards produce a wide range of wines, including reds, whites, and rosés.

The foods available at the Conwy Feast festival range from traditional Welsh dishes to international cuisine. Some of the most popular food vendors at the festival include The Welsh Creperie Company, Churros Susanna, The Great British Cheese Company, and The Greek Olive Stall.

The wines available at the Conwy Feast festival are carefully selected to pair well with the foods on offer. There are many reasons why certain wines pair well with certain foods. For example, a spicy dish like a curry pairs well with a crisp white wine because the acid in the wine helps to cut through the spice. Similarly, a rich and hearty dish like a lamb stew pairs well with a full-bodied red wine because the tannins in the wine help to balance out the richness of the food.

Here are some examples of food and wine pairings that you might find at the Conwy Feast festival:

1. Fish and chips with a crisp Sauvignon Blanc

2. Welsh rarebit with a dry Riesling

3. Beef and ale pie with a robust red blend

4. Seafood paella with a bright Albariño

5. Pork belly with a spicy Shiraz

6. Chicken tikka masala with a fruity Pinot Noir

7. Gourmet burger with a bold Cabernet Sauvignon

8. Welsh lamb with a full-bodied Merlot

9. Moules frites with a light Chablis

10. Sushi with a dry, minerally Sancerre

11. Pad Thai with a zesty Vermentino

12. Cheese plate with a rich, velvety Malbec

13. Charcuterie board with a smoky Syrah

14. Lobster roll with a crisp Chardonnay

15. Bruschetta with a light, refreshing Prosecco

16. Spicy chicken wings with a fruity Zinfandel

17. Falafel with a dry Rosé

18. Tartiflette with a robust Gamay

19. Grilled prawns with a bright Verdejo

20. Beef brisket with a spicy Zinfandel

21. Pulled pork sandwich with a full-bodied Cabernet Franc

22. Vegetable curry with a crisp Grüner Veltliner

23. Mushroom risotto with a earthy Pinot Noir

24. BBQ ribs with a sweet and smoky Zinfandel

25. Chocolate truffles with a velvety Tawny Port

In conclusion, the Conwy Feast festival is a celebration of the rich culture and tradition of the Conwy region, showcasing its topography, vineyards, vinification techniques, foods, and wines. The carefully selected pairings of food and wine available at the festival are a testament to the long history of food production and wine-making in the region.

- **Gower Good Food Festival**

The Gower Good Food Festival is a famous food and wine festival that takes place every year in the Gower Peninsula of Wales, United Kingdom. This festival is a celebration of local food, wine, and culture, and attracts thousands of visitors from all over the world.

The city in which the festival is held is Swansea, which is located on the coast of South Wales. The festival is a two-day event that takes place on the last weekend of June. It is an occasion to celebrate the local food and wine culture of the Gower Peninsula and to showcase the best of what the region has to offer.

The Gower Peninsula is a region of outstanding natural beauty, located in South Wales. It is known for its stunning topography, with cliffs, beaches, and rugged coastline, and is home to several vineyards. The region is famous for its vinification techniques and produces some of the best wines in the world.

At the Good Food Festival, there are a variety of foods available, including seafood, meat, cheese, and locally grown vegetables. The festival is a great opportunity to sample some of the best local dishes, as well as to learn about the history of the region and its food culture.

In addition to the food, there are also many wines available at the festival, including white, red, rose, and sparkling wines. The wines are carefully paired with the foods to create the perfect match. Here are some examples of foods and wines available at the Gower Good Food Festival:

1. Seared scallops with a citrus vinaigrette, paired with a crisp white wine

2. Welsh lamb chops with rosemary and garlic, paired with a full-bodied red wine

3. Freshly shucked oysters with a lemon and chilli dressing, paired with a sparkling wine

4. Grilled steak with a port and blue cheese sauce, paired with a robust red wine

5. Creamy brie cheese with fig jam and crostini, paired with a smooth red wine

6. Grilled swordfish with a mango salsa, paired with a chilled white wine

7. Garlic prawns with a pesto sauce, paired with a crisp white wine

8. Braised beef short ribs with red wine sauce, paired with a bold red wine

9. Smoked salmon with a dill cream sauce, paired with a light and refreshing white wine

10. Traditional Welsh cheese board with grapes and crackers, paired with a sweet dessert wine

11. Roasted duck breast with a red wine reduction, paired with a full-bodied red wine

12. Pan-seared tuna with a caper and lemon sauce, paired with a light and crisp white wine

13. Crab cakes with a spicy aioli sauce, paired with a refreshing white wine

14. Grilled chicken with a creamy mushroom sauce, paired with a medium-bodied red wine

15. Beetroot and goat's cheese salad, paired with a light and fruity white wine

16. Dark chocolate mousse with fresh berries, paired with a sweet dessert wine

17. Grilled vegetables with a balsamic glaze, paired with a dry white wine

18. Beef sliders with caramelised onions and cheese, paired with a bold red wine

19. Fresh tuna tartare with avocado and lime, paired with a crisp white wine

20. Creamy risotto with wild mushrooms, paired with a full-bodied red wine

21. Pan-fried duck liver with red onion marmalade, paired with a sweet dessert wine

22. Caprese salad with fresh mozzarella and basil, paired with a light and crisp white wine

23. Grilled eggplant with a tomato and herb sauce, paired with a dry white wine

24. Mediterranean vegetable kebab with tzatziki sauce, paired with a refreshing white wine

25. Grilled halloumi cheese with a tomato and olive salad, paired with a flavorful red wine

The reason why these foods and wines are paired so well is because they complement each other's flavours. A white wine, for example, is often paired with seafood and light dishes because it has a lighter flavour that won't overpower the delicate flavours of the food. A red wine, on the other hand, is often paired with heavier dishes like beef and lamb because it has a fuller flavour that can stand up to the bold flavours of the food.

Overall, the Gower Good Food Festival is a wonderful celebration of culture, food, and wine. It is a great opportunity to sample some of the best local dishes and wines, as well as to learn about the history of the region and its food culture.

- **Big Pit National Coal Museum Beer Festival**

The Big Pit National Coal Museum Beer Festival is an annual event held at Big Pit National Coal Museum in Blaenavon, Wales. The festival is a celebration of local and national beer, cider, and perry, and runs for three days, usually from the end of July to the beginning of August.

The event takes place in the museum's historic colliery buildings, which form part of the Blaenavon Industrial Landscape World Heritage Site. Visitors can wander around the museum, take a guided underground tour, and sample beers from more than 30 breweries from across Wales and beyond. There are also food stalls offering a range of traditional Welsh and international cuisine.

The festival is a cultural occasion that celebrates the rich history and heritage of the region, which was once one of the world's most important coal mining areas. Visitors can learn about the coal mines, the miners that worked in them, and the impact that the coal industry had on the local area.

The topography and climate of Wales make it an excellent location for vineyards, although the focus of this festival is on beer rather than wine. The participating breweries showcase a variety of brewing techniques, from traditional methods to modern innovations, offering visitors a diverse selection of beers to try.

Some of the breweries that participate in the festival include Tiny Rebel, Brains, and Greytrees from South Wales, as well as Conwy Brewery from North Wales. The event also attracts a range of independent breweries from across the UK.

As far as food is concerned, the festival offers a range of dishes that pair well with beer, including burgers, pizzas, and locally-sourced cheeses. There are also vegetarian and vegan options available, as well as traditional Welsh dishes such as cawl, a hearty lamb stew.

Here are some examples of food and beer pairing options available at the Big Pit National Coal Museum Beer Festival:

1. Steak and Ale Pie with Conwy Brewery's Honey Fayre

2. Welsh Rarebit with Tiny Rebel's FUBAR

3. Barbecue Pulled Pork with Brains' Dark Smooth

4. Margherita Pizza with Greytrees' Red Rock

5. Spicy Chicken Wings with Cwrw Ial's Golden and Swnami

6. Vegan Chilli with Mad Dog Brewing Co.'s Mad Dog Pale Ale

7. Sweet Potato Fries with Rhymney Brewery's Export

8. Nachos with Cromarty Brewing Co.'s Double Rainbow

9. Welsh Cakes with Brecon Brewing's Red Beacons

10. Lamb Cawl with Wye Valley Brewery's HPA

11. Beef Brisket with Dark Star Brewing Co.'s Hophead

12. Veggie Burger with Castle Rock Brewery's Screech Owl

13. Salt and Pepper Squid with Purple Moose Brewery's Madog's Ale

14. Halloumi Fries with Magic Rock Brewing's High Wire

15. Fish and Chips with Fourpure Brewery's Flatiron

16. Pea and Mint Soup with Otley Brewing Co.'s O1

17. Smoked Salmon with Salopian Brewery's Darwin's Origin

18. Chicken Caesar Salad with Butcombe Brewery Original

19 Spiced Lentil Soup with Marble Brewery's Saison du Jour

20. Waffles and Ice Cream with Tiny Rebel's Stay Puft Marshmallow Porter

21. Cheeseburger with Harviestoun Brewery Bitter & Twisted

22. Chorizo and Chickpea Stew with Hopcraft Brewery's Kiwi

23. Chocolate Brownie with Fire Island Brewing Co.'s Pacific Pale Ale

24. Vegetable Samosas with Anarchy Brew Co.'s Quiet Riot

25. Roast Beef Sandwich with Alechemy Brewing Co.'s 5ive Sisters

The reason why these food and beer pairing options work well together is that they complement each other's flavours. Certain beers can enhance the flavours of certain foods, the bitterness of an IPA can cut the richness of a burger, a stout can complement the sweetness of a brownie. Similarly, the food can enhance the flavours of the beer, a savoury stew can bring out the maltiness of an amber ale, and a spicy chicken wing can balance the hoppy bitterness of a pale ale. Ultimately, the right pairing of food and beer comes down to personal taste, and the Big Pit National Coal Museum Beer Festival offers a range of options for every palate.

- **Welsh Cheese and Cider Festival**

The Welsh Cheese and Cider Festival is a unique event that celebrates the vibrant culture of Wales, particularly its culinary heritage. The festival is held annually in the city of Cardiff, which is the capital of Wales, located on the southern coast of the country.

The festival brings together people from all over Wales and beyond to showcase the amazing flavours and aromas of the region's best cheeses and ciders. Welsh cheese is famous for its distinct and rich flavour which is attributed to the topography of the region, that comprises lush green valleys and meadows, and Welsh ciders, which are made from locally grown apples, are known for being sweet and refreshing, with an acidic finish.

The festival is not only a showcase of food, but also a celebration of Welsh culture, history, and traditions. Visitors can learn about the vinification techniques used in local vineyards, and the history of winemaking in the region.

There are various pairings of foods and wines available at the event, which makes it an ideal opportunity to learn about the art of matching the right wine with the right food.

Here are some examples of the foods and wines that are available at the festival and why they complement each other so well:

1. Apple and Cheddar Cheese paired with a Semi-Dry Riesling - The sweetness of the apple and the tartness of the Cheddar cheese are perfectly balanced by the fresh and slightly sweet Riesling.

2. Camembert Cheese and Cider - The soft and creamy Camembert pairs perfectly with the tart and slightly sweet ciders.

3. Blue Cheese and Merlot - The strong and pungent flavour of the blue cheese is mellowed by the silky smooth Merlot.

4. Hard Cheese and Pinot Noir - The robust and nutty flavour of hard cheese is balanced by the soft tannins of Pinot Noir.

5. Feta Cheese and Sauvignon Blanc - The tangy and salty feta cheese is complemented by the bright and crisp notes of Sauvignon Blanc.

6. Brie Cheese with a White Burgundy - The creamy texture of Brie cheese is contrasted by the acidity of the White Burgundy.

7. Gouda Cheese with a Chardonnay - The mellow flavour of Gouda cheese pairs perfectly with the rich notes of Chardonnay.

8. Ricotta Cheese and Prosecco - The light and fluffy texture of ricotta cheese is enhanced with the subtle bubbles of Prosecco.

9. Smoked Cheese with Syrah - The smoky flavour of the cheese is accentuated by the earthy tones of Syrah.

10. Goat Cheese and Rosé - The bold and tangy flavour of goat cheese is calmed by the soft and fruity notes of Rosé.

11. Parmesan Cheese with Barolo - The robust and nutty flavour of Parmesan cheese is accentuated by the bold and full-bodied Barolo.

12. Gorgonzola Cheese and Port - The pungent flavour of the cheese is enhanced by the rich and sweet notes of Port.

13. Double Gloucester Cheese and Cabernet Sauvignon - The sweet and nutty flavour of Double Gloucester cheese is perfectly balanced with the bold and fruit-driven Cabernet Sauvignon.

14. Cheshire Cheese with Zinfandel - The bold flavour of Cheshire cheese is complemented by the juicy and jammy notes of Zinfandel.

15. Wensleydale Cheese with Chenin Blanc - The mild and creamy flavour of Wensleydale cheese is contrasted with the bright and refreshing acidity of Chenin Blanc.

16. Stilton Cheese with Malbec - The strong and pungent flavour of Stilton cheese is balanced by the bold and intense notes of Malbec.

17. Cream Cheese with Champagne - The mild and creamy flavour of cream cheese pairs perfectly with the effervescent and bubbly Champagne.

18. Red Leicester Cheese with Merlot - The nutty and intense flavour of Red Leicester cheese is complemented by the smooth and silky texture of Merlot.

19. Cheddar Cheese with Shiraz - The rich and sharp taste of Cheddar cheese pairs with the bold and spicy notes of Australian Shiraz.

20. Asiago Cheese with Pinot Grigio - The sharp and nutty flavor of Asiago cheese is perfectly balanced by the crisp and dry Pinot Grigio.

21. Boursin Cheese with Chablis - The creamy and herb-infused Boursin cheese is contrasted with the fresh and minerally Chablis.

22. Roquefort Cheese and Sauternes - The bold and intense flavour of Roquefort cheese is complemented by the sweet and honeyed notes of a Sauternes.

23. Chèvre Cheese with Viognier - The tangy and slightly sweet flavour of Chèvre cheese pairs perfectly with the light and floral Viognier.

24. Grilled Cheese with Beaujolais - The classic comfort food pairs perfectly with the fruity and refreshing Beaujolais.

25. Welsh Rarebit with Muscadet - The rich and savoury flavours of Welsh Rarebit blend seamlessly with the tart and lemony notes of Muscadet.

In conclusion, the Welsh Cheese and Cider Festival is an excellent showcase of the best culinary products from the region. Visitors can learn about the history, culture, and techniques of winemaking, cider making, and cheese production. Pairing the right wine with the right food is an art form, and the festival provides an ideal opportunity to learn about the science and art behind it.

- **The Royal Welsh Show**

The Royal Welsh Show is an annual agricultural show held in Builth Wells, Wales. It takes place at the Royal Welsh Showground, which is situated in the picturesque county of Powys. The Royal Welsh Show is a four-day event that is attended by people from all over Wales and beyond. The show is often referred to as the largest agricultural show in Europe.

The Royal Welsh Show is a celebration of Welsh culture and tradition, and it provides a platform for farmers to showcase their livestock, produce, and equipment. The show is also a great opportunity for visitors to sample some of the best wines and foods that Wales has to offer.

The show is held in July every year, and it attracts thousands of visitors. There are numerous events and activities on offer, including livestock competitions, equestrian events, food and wine tastings, arts and crafts exhibitions, and much more.

The Royal Welsh Show is a celebration of Welsh culture, and it is a great opportunity for visitors to experience the rich history of the region. The topography of the region is varied, with rolling hills, fertile valleys, and rugged mountain ranges. The region is dotted with vineyards, which produce some of the finest wines in Wales.

The vinification techniques used in the region are traditional and time-honoured, producing wines that are rich and full-bodied. The wines of Wales are a perfect accompaniment to the foods of the region, which are wholesome, hearty, and full of flavour.

There are numerous foods and wines available at the Royal Welsh Show, and they are a match made in culinary heaven. Here are some examples of the perfect pairing:

1. Welsh lamb and a full-bodied red wine

2. Roast beef and a crisp white wine

3. Smoked salmon and a dry rosé

4. Organic vegetables and a light, fruity red wine

5. Welsh rarebit and an oaky white wine

6. Creamy cheeses and a rich, full-bodied red wine

7. Salt beef and a fruity rosé

8. Pulled pork and a spicy red wine

9. Welsh cakes and a sweet white wine

10. Bara brith and a light, fruity red wine

11. Cawl (traditional Welsh soup) and a full-bodied red wine

12. Seafood platter and a crisp white wine

13. Braised beef and a full-bodied red wine

14. Curry and a light, fruity red wine

15. Welsh faggots and a smoky red wine

16. Steak and ale pie and a rich, full-bodied red wine

17. Venison stew and a spicy red wine

18. Welsh beef burgers and a fruity rosé

19. Black pudding and a full-bodied red wine

20. Welsh cheese platter and a sweet white wine

21. Beef bourguignon and a full-bodied red wine

22. Welsh dragon sausages and a spicy red wine

23. Leek and potato soup and a light, fruity red wine

24. Welsh ham and a crisp white wine

25. Pâté and a smoky red wine

The wines of Wales are a perfect match for the foods of the region because they are produced using locally grown grapes and traditional methods. The wines are rich and full-bodied, with a complexity of flavour that perfectly complements the hearty and flavourful foods of the region.

In conclusion, the Royal Welsh Show is a celebration of Welsh culture and tradition, and it provides an opportunity for visitors to experience the best of Welsh food and wine. The topography of the region, combined with traditional vinification techniques and hearty, flavourful foods, makes for a perfect pairing of food and wine that is unmatched in its richness and complexity.

Northern Ireland

- **The Belfast International Arts Festival**

The Belfast International Arts Festival is an annual event that takes place in Belfast, Northern Ireland. This festival is one of the most significant cultural events of the year in the country, drawing artists, performers, and visitors from all over the world.

The festival features a wide array of events, ranging from music performances to art exhibitions, from theatre shows to literary events. It is an opportunity for people from different cultures to come together and celebrate the best of arts and culture.

The Belfast International Arts Festival is held in October and runs for two weeks, from the 7th to the 24th. It takes place in various venues across the city, including the Grand Opera House, the Waterfront Hall, and the Ulster Museum.

Northern Ireland has a rich and vibrant culture, and the festival reflects this diversity. This country's topography boasts stunning landscapes that are home to historic vineyards. The region has a long history of winemaking, and visitors can sample some of the best wines produced here during the festival.

The Belfast International Arts Festival also provides an opportunity to explore the history of the region. Visitors can learn about the complex past of Northern Ireland and how it has shaped the country's culture and identity.

During the festival, visitors can sample some of the region's finest foods and wines. The wines available at the event are paired with the foods to create the perfect culinary experience. The following are some examples:

1. Grilled Salmon with Chardonnay

2. Braised Beef with Cabernet Sauvignon

3. Roast Chicken with Chianti

4. Mushroom Risotto with Pinot Noir

5. Steak with Malbec

6. Seafood Linguine with Vermentino

7. Pork Tenderloin with Zinfandel

8. Lamb Shank with Shiraz

9. Spaghetti Bolognese with Chianti

10. Grilled Shrimp with Chardonnay

11. Beef Stew with Merlot

12. Chicken Parmesan with Pinot Noir

13. Grilled Vegetables with Sauvignon Blanc

14. Fish and Chips with Chardonnay

15. Steak Fajitas with Rioja

16. Roast Pork with Pinot Gris

17. Lasagna with Sangiovese

18. Grilled Tuna with Zinfandel

19. Poached Salmon with Chablis

20. Mushroom and Goat Cheese Pizza with Pinot Noir

21. Chicken Curry with Viognier

22. Grilled Steak with Cabernet Franc

23. Spicy Ramen with Riesling

24. Vegetable Stir-Fry with Gewürztraminer

25. Ratatouille with Grenache

The above combinations of food and wine complement each other in unique ways. For example, Chardonnay pairs well with grilled salmon because its acidity and flavours of green apples, lemon, and butter cut through the oily texture of the fish. Cabernet Sauvignon goes well with braised beef as its tannins complement the dish's richness.

In conclusion, the Belfast International Arts Festival is a celebration of culture and creativity, showcasing the diversity of Northern Ireland. Visitors can explore the region's historical sites, sample its cuisine and wines, and enjoy an array of artistic performances. The festival is a must-attend event for anyone interested in the arts, history, and culture of Northern Ireland.

- **Belfast Restaurant Week**

Belfast Restaurant Week is an annual event held in Belfast, Northern Ireland, that celebrates the city's food and drink scene. The event is held in February and runs for a week, offering a variety of dining experiences to locals and tourists alike.

Belfast is the largest city in Northern Ireland, with a population of around 350,000 people. The city is known for its rich cultural heritage, with a history dating back over 1,000 years. Belfast has a vibrant food and drink scene, with a wide range of restaurants, bars, and cafes offering both traditional and modern cuisine.

The topography of the region is characterised by rolling hills, lush green fields, and rugged coastline, with vineyards dotted throughout the countryside. The wine industry in Northern Ireland is still in its infancy, but there are a number of vineyards in the region that produce high-quality wines using modern vinification techniques.

At Belfast Restaurant Week, visitors can sample some of the region's finest foods and wines, with a range of pairings available to suit all tastes. Some of the most popular pairings include:

1. Roast beef with a full-bodied, rich red wine like a Cabernet Sauvignon or Shiraz

2. Grilled salmon with a crisp, refreshing white wine like a Sauvignon Blanc or Pinot Grigio

3. Creamy mushroom pasta with a buttery Chardonnay or light Pinot Noir

4. Spicy chicken curry with a fruity rosé or light red like a Pinot Noir or Grenache

5. Seafood paella with a Spanish Tempranillo or Rioja

6. Charcuterie board with a bold red wine like a Malbec or Syrah

7. Seared tuna with a dry Riesling or Gewurztraminer

8. Beef Wellington with a rich, velvety Merlot or Cabernet Franc

9. Prawn linguine with a dry Chablis or Sancerre

10. Grilled lamb chops with a full-bodied red like a Bordeaux blend or Zinfandel

11. Ceviche with a crisp, citrusy Albariño or Viognier

12. Cheese board with a nutty, full-bodied sherry or Port

13. Ratatouille with a light-bodied red like a Pinot Noir or Gamay

14. Smoked salmon with a crisp, acidic Sauvignon Blanc or Muscadet

15. Beef brisket with a smoky, robust Syrah or Cabernet Sauvignon

16. Lobster bisque with a subtle, floral Viognier or Chardonnay

17. Grilled vegetables with a light, refreshing rosé or Pinot Noir

18. Venison with a full-bodied, earthy Pinotage or Malbec

19. Oysters on the half shell with a crisp, minerally Chablis or Muscadet

20. Rack of lamb with a bold, spicy Syrah or Shiraz

21. Grilled chicken with a light, fruity white like a Pinot Grigio or Chenin Blanc

22. Beef bourguignon with a deep, complex Burgundy or Pinot Noir

23. Scallop risotto with a buttery Chardonnay or dry Riesling

24. Duck confit with a full-bodied, spicy Syrah or Merlot

25. Chocolate truffles with a rich, sweet Port or dessert wine

The wines chosen to pair with each dish complement the flavours and textures of the food, enhancing the overall dining experience. For example, a full-bodied red wine like a Cabernet Sauvignon or Syrah pairs well with rich, fatty meats like beef and lamb, while a crisp, acidic white like a Sauvignon Blanc or Chablis pairs well with seafood and lighter dishes. The nutty, full-bodied sherry or Port pairs well with cheese, while the sweet dessert wine balances out the bitterness of chocolate.

In conclusion, Belfast Restaurant Week is an event that celebrates the rich food and drink culture of Northern Ireland. Visitors can experience a wide range of flavours and pairings, with the opportunity to try some of the region's finest wines and foods. The pairings are carefully selected to enhance the overall dining experience, showcasing the best that the region has to offer.

The Food and Cider Festival is an annual event held in Northern Ireland, specifically in the city of Armagh, the apple capital of the UK. The festival brings together a diverse range of people, including locals, food enthusiasts, and tourists from around the world. This four-day event is a celebration of the region's delectable food, cider, wines, culture, and history.

The festival takes place in early October and is a remarkable occasion for locals and visitors to experience the beauty of Northern Ireland's topography. The region is known for its extensive sprawling orchards that produce superior quality apples, which are widely used in the production of ciders and wines. The vineyards in Armagh produce wines of exceptional quality, thanks to the vinification techniques used in the region.

Northern Ireland is steeped in culture and tradition, and this event provides an excellent opportunity for visitors to immerse themselves in Northern Irish culture. The event's theme is "From Orchard to Glass," and it offers visitors a chance to learn about the region's history, particularly the story of how the first cider was produced in 1760.

The event features a vast selection of foods and wines, ranging from sweet to savoury, including traditional Northern Irish breakfast, seafood, meats, and pastries. Visitors can sample different wines, including red wines made from Shiraz and Cabernet Sauvignon grapes, White wines made from Chardonnay and Sauvignon Blanc grapes.

The pairing of food and wine is an art, and the festival takes this craft to another level. Visitors can expect to taste the perfect pairing between food and wine, such as:

1. Smoked salmon with a light, crisp white wine such as Sauvignon Blanc

2. Roast beef with a robust Cabernet Sauvignon

3. Grilled chicken with a fruity Chardonnay

4. Fish pie with a refreshing, dry Pinot Grigio

5. Creamy mushroom risotto with a full-bodied Shiraz

6. Grilled venison with a deep, rich Merlot

7. Prawns with a dry, crisp Prosecco

8. Irish cheese board with a classic red blend

9. Corned beef and cabbage with a white Burgundy

10. Clams with a light and zesty Riesling

11. Mussels with a dry Rosé

12. Meatballs with a spicy red Zinfandel

13. Irish stew with a bold and oaky Chianti

14. Lamb chops with a complex Syrah

15. Cherry tart with a sweet dessert wine such as Port

16. Apple crumble with a crisp apple cider

17. Blackberry cobbler with a fruity Beaujolais

18. Chocolate truffles with a velvety Pinot Noir

19. Gingerbread cookies with a sweet Moscato

20. Irish soda bread with a dry cider

21. Grilled pork chops with a full-bodied Malbec

22. Grilled salmon with a refreshing Chablis

23. Scallops with a crisp, acidity Sauvignon Blanc

24. Beef chilli with a spicy Zinfandel

25. Beef bourguignon with a medium-bodied Bordeaux

The wines' acidity, tannins, sweetness, and body all play a significant role in creating the perfect balance with the food's flavours. The pairing creates a harmonious taste sensation that enhances the experience of each dish. The acidity in a white wine pairs well with seafood and lighter dishes, while the tannins and bold flavours in red wines complement richer and heartier dishes.

In conclusion, The Food and Cider Festival in Armagh, Northern Ireland is a must-visit event for wine and food enthusiasts who love to experience the best the region has to offer. The festival provides an opportunity to learn about the region's history and indulge in the pairing of foods and wines that create a delectable culinary experience.

- **The Hillsborough International Oyster Festival**

The Hillsborough International Oyster Festival is an annual event held in Hillsborough, a historic village located in Northern Ireland's County Down. The festival is usually held in September, and it is a celebration of the region's rich culture, history, and culinary traditions. Hillsborough is a picturesque village tucked away in the rolling green hills of Northern Ireland, and it is known for its stunning topography, historic landmarks, and excellent vineyards.

The festival attracts thousands of people from all over the world, and it is a fantastic opportunity to taste the best oysters and seafood from the region. One of the most exceptional aspects of the festival is the opportunity to enjoy an excellent variety of local wines, which perfectly complement the savoury oysters and other seafood dishes.

Northern Ireland's culture is rich and deep; it comes through in the food, music, and dance. The Hillsborough International Oyster Festival gives locals and visitors alike a chance to experience the culture in its purest form. The occasion is a time to come together, socialise, and enjoy the excellent dishes and wines available at the event.

The topography of Hillsborough makes it an ideal location for wine vineyards, and there are several excellent vineyards in the region. The vinification techniques used in the production of these wines are unique, resulting in a complex, full-bodied taste that perfectly pairs with the flavours of the oysters and seafood.

One of the significant highlights of the Hillsborough International Oyster Festival is the variety of food available. Seafood reigns supreme in Northern Ireland, and the festival features the best oysters, crabs, lobster, and other delicacies from the sea. When it comes to the wines, you can expect to find an excellent selection of local whites, roses, and reds that pair perfectly with the seafood.

Here are some examples of the food and wine pairings that make the Hillsborough International Oyster Festival such a unique event:

1. Sligo oysters with a crisp, dry Pinot Grigio

2. Crab cakes with a tangy Riesling

3. Fresh mussels with a zesty Sauvignon Blanc

4. Scallop ceviche with a crisp Chardonnay

5. Grilled tiger prawns with a buttery Chardonnay

6. Shrimp cocktail with a refreshing Rose

7. Lobster bisque with a smooth Pinot Noir

8. Bouillabaisse with a bold Cabernet Sauvignon

9. Grilled octopus with a rich Merlot

10. Halibut fillet with a dry Chenin Blanc

11. Tuna tartare with an acidic Vermentino

12. Oyster Rockefeller with a full-bodied Syrah

13. Clam chowder with a crisp Sauvignon Blanc

14. Lobster roll with a buttery Chardonnay

15. Blackened salmon with a spicy Shiraz

16. Sashimi with a fragrant Viognier

17. Ceviche with a crisp Pinot Grigio

18. Prawn cocktail with a refreshing Rose

19. Lobster tail with a smooth Merlot

20. Tuna steak with a bold Cabernet Sauvignon

21. Grilled squid with a rich Chardonnay

22. Scallops with a dry Pinot Noir

23. Toad in the hole with a robust Malbec

24. Sticky toffee pudding with a sweet Prosecco

25. Apple crumble with a fruity Riesling

The wines pair so well with these foods because they enhance the flavours of the dish without overpowering them. The crisp acidity of the Sauvignon Blanc cuts through the rich, buttery flavours of the seafood, while the bold tannins of the Cabernet Sauvignon stand up to the bold flavours of the bouillabaisse.

In conclusion, the Hillsborough International Oyster Festival is a celebration of Northern Ireland's rich culture, history, and culinary traditions. The topography of the region makes it an ideal location for vineyards, and the vinification techniques used in the production of the wine are unique, complex, and full-bodied in taste. The food and wine pairings available at the festival are exceptional, and the flavours of the wine enhance the flavours of the seafood without overpowering them, making it a must-visit event for seafood and wine lovers.

- **The Great Derry/Londonderry Maritime Festival**

The Great Derry/Londonderry Maritime Festival is a popular event that takes place in Northern Ireland every summer. It is celebrated in the city of Derry/Londonderry, which is one of the most vibrant and culturally rich cities in the country. The festival is a celebration of the city's maritime heritage, and it attracts people from all over the world who are interested in maritime culture and history.

The Derry/Londonderry Maritime Festival typically takes place over a period of three days, and features a wide range of activities and events. Visitors can enjoy live music, dance performances, art exhibitions, street performances, and much more. There are also numerous food and wine stalls that offer a range of local and international cuisine.

The city of Derry/Londonderry is located in a region of Northern Ireland that is known for its fertile soils and picturesque landscapes. The topography of the region is perfect for growing grapes, and as a result, there are numerous vineyards in the area that produce high-quality wines. The vinification techniques used by these vineyards are some of the best in the world, and they are known for producing wines that are rich, complex, and full-flavoured.

The foods that are available at the Derry/Londonderry Maritime Festival are a perfect match for the wines that are produced in the region. The rich, complex flavours of the wines are perfectly complemented by the bold, flavorful cuisine that is available at the festival. Some of the most popular food and wine pairings at the festival include:

1. Seafood Paella and a crisp, refreshing white wine such as Chardonnay or Sauvignon Blanc.

2. Grilled Lamb and a full-bodied red wine such as Cabernet Sauvignon or Merlot.

3. Spicy Chicken Wings and a fruity, spicy red wine such as Pinot Noir.

4. Meatballs and a robust, smoky red wine such as Shiraz or Zinfandel.

5. Beef Brisket and a full-bodied, tannic red wine such as Malbec or Syrah.

6. Lobster and a rich, buttery white wine such as Chardonnay or Viognier.

7. Sushi and a crisp, clean white wine such as Riesling or Pinot Grigio.

8. Grilled Cheese and a light, fruity red wine such as Beaujolais or Gamay.

9. Fried Calamari and a bright, citrusy white wine such as Sauvignon Blanc or Chenin Blanc.

10. Fish and Chips and a crisp, refreshing white wine such as Chardonnay or Pinot Grigio.

11. Grilled Salmon and a rich, buttery white wine such as Chardonnay or Viognier.

12. Fried Chicken and a full-bodied, tannic red wine such as Cabernet Sauvignon or Merlot.

13. Caesar Salad and a crisp, refreshing white wine such as Sauvignon Blanc or Pinot Grigio.

14. Vegetable Curry and a spicy, full-flavoured red wine such as Syrah or Zinfandel.

15. Cuban Sandwich and a light, fruity red wine such as Sangiovese or Pinot Noir.

16. Beef Empanadas and a robust, smoky red wine such as Shiraz or Zinfandel.

17. Grilled Vegetables and a bright, citrusy white wine such as Riesling or Sauvignon Blanc.

18. Fried Shrimp and a full-bodied, tannic red wine such as Cabernet Sauvignon or Merlot.

19. Cheese Plate and a light, fruity red wine such as Beaujolais or Pinot Noir.

20. Caesar Salad and a crisp, refreshing white wine such as Chardonnay or Pinot Grigio.

21. Fried Calamari and a bright, citrusy white wine such as Sauvignon Blanc or Chenin Blanc.

22. Grilled Lamb and a rich, buttery white wine such as Chardonnay or Viognier.

23. Beef Brisket and a full-bodied, tannic red wine such as Malbec or Syrah.

24. Lobster and a crisp, refreshing white wine such as Chardonnay or Sauvignon Blanc.

25. Meatballs and a robust, smoky red wine such as Shiraz or Zinfandel.

The reason why these food and wine pairings work so well is that the flavours of the wine bring out the best in the food, and vice versa. For example, a rich, buttery white wine such as Chardonnay will pair perfectly with seafood paella because the rich, full-flavoured wine complements the bold, flavorful dish. Similarly, a full-bodied, tannic red wine such as Cabernet Sauvignon will pair perfectly with meatballs because the bold, smoky flavours of the wine bring out the rich, meaty flavours of the dish.

In conclusion, the Great Derry/Londonderry Maritime Festival is a celebration of the best that Northern Ireland has to offer in terms of culture, history, and culinary delights. With its picturesque landscapes, rich heritage, and delicious foods and wines, it is a must-visit event for anyone who is interested in experiencing the best of Northern Ireland.

Each of these festivals is unique and highlights the culture, history, and topography of their respective regions, as well as showcasing some of the best food and drink that the UK has to offer. From oysters in Hillsborough, to gin in Glasgow, there is something for every food and drink enthusiast to enjoy.

ABOUT THE AUTHOR

I have had an exceptional journey in my life that has taken me from Africa to Europe and back to the world of food and wine.

Born and raised in Africa, I was exposed to the world of food and the joys of eating from an early age. My childhood was filled with the sights, sounds, and smells of different foods from around the world and the traditional meals that were prepared using local ingredients. This early exposure to the world of food set me on a lifelong journey of exploration and discovery, leading me to explore the field of food and wine pairing.

Growing up in Africa, i was privileged to experience the rich diversity of foods from around the world. I was introduced to exotic spices and flavours that were used to prepare dishes that were enjoyed by my family and my community. I watched as my mother made traditional African dishes such as Jollof rice, West African peanut stew and many other local dishes using fresh ingredients sourced from local farmers, and i was fascinated by the process of cooking and the way that different ingredients interacted with each other.

As I grew older, I became more interested in the world of food and started to explore different cuisines from around the world. I was particularly interested in French cuisine and the way that it incorporated wine into the cooking process. I was drawn to the idea of pairing different types of wine with different foods, and i became fascinated with the way that wine could complement and enhance the flavours of a dish.

After completing my studies in Africa, I moved to the UK to further my education. It was there that i was introduced to the world of wine for the first time. I started to experiment with wine and food pairing and was amazed by the way that different wines could bring out the different flavours in a dish. I became passionate about the idea of creating a perfect balance between wine and food.

It was while working for a German wine producer that my passion for food and wine pairing really took off. I was able to combine my knowledge of wine with my love of cooking and create truly amazing dining experiences. I was able to take the flavours of the wine and use them to enhance the flavours of the food, creating a perfect match between the two.

My experiences in Africa and the UK have given me a unique perspective on food and wine pairing. I understand the importance of using fresh, local ingredients to create traditional dishes that are full of flavour, and i also know how to pair these dishes with the perfect wine to create a truly memorable dining experience.

What makes my approach to food and wine pairing so special is my passion for the subject. I truly believe that food and wine are meant to be shared and enjoyed together, and I have made it my life's work to create the perfect combination between the two. I have spent years studying the different flavours and aromas of wine and have developed a deep understanding of how to pair these flavours with different foods.

This ebook about the joys of food and wine pairing I hope has been a fascinating read for anyone who is interested in the world of food and wine. It is packed with incredible insights and anecdotes that will help readers to understand the importance of pairing food and wine in a thoughtful and deliberate way. From my experiences in Africa to my time working for a German wine producer and beyond, my journey is a testament to the power of food and wine to bring people together and create unforgettable experiences.

In conclusion, I have had an incredible journey in life that has taken me from my childhood in Africa to the world of food and wine pairing. My experiences have given me a unique perspective on the subject, and my passion for food and wine is evident in everything i do. Whether I am cooking traditional African dishes or pairing wine with foods from around the world, I am always striving to create the perfect dining experience. I sincerely hope this ebook has delivered to be a fascinating read and a valuable resource for anyone who wants to understand the joys of food and wine pairing.

Anecdotes on Food and Wine

1. One of the most famous anecdotes about food and wine involves the pairing of red wine with fish. Legend has it that when Queen Victoria was served salmon with a red wine sauce, she declared that red wine should never be served with fish. This rule became known as "Queen Victoria's law," although it's worth noting that many experts now recommend pairing certain red wines with certain types of fish.

2. Another classic anecdote about food and wine comes from the legendary chef Julia Child. In her book "My Life in France," she recounts a meal she had in Provence that included an entire truffle baked inside a chicken. She wrote that the flavour was so intense and delicious that she couldn't stop giggling with delight.

3. One of the more recent anecdotes about food and wine involves a bottle of Chateau Margaux from 1787 that was reportedly owned by Thomas Jefferson. In 1985, the bottle was sold at auction for a record-breaking $156,000. However, controversy later surrounded the authenticity of the bottle, as its provenance was based on an old label that may have been added after Jefferson's death.

4. Wine tasting events can also be the site of memorable anecdotes. For example, one wine critic once famously declared that a particular wine tasted like "a mouthful of wet, mouldy cardboard." The wine's maker later turned the insult into a marketing ploy, printing the quote on the label along with a photo of the critic with a piece of wet cardboard in his mouth.

5. In the 18th century, a French winemaker named Dom Perignon is credited with discovering the champagne-making process while trying to eliminate the bubbles from his wine. Legend has it that he exclaimed, "Come quickly, I am tasting stars!" upon tasting the fizzy concoction for the first time.

6. The world's most expensive food is the white truffle, which is a rare delicacy that can only be found in certain parts of Italy. In 2019, a 1.8kg white truffle sold for $120,000 at auction in Alba, Italy.

7. In the early 20th century, a man named Clarence Birdseye invented the process of flash freezing food. He was inspired by the Inuit people who would catch fish and immediately freeze them on ice to preserve them. This invention revolutionised the food industry and made frozen food widely available.

8. The word "restaurant" comes from the French word "restaurer," which means to restore. The first restaurant to use this name was opened in Paris in 1765 and it specialised in restorative meat-based broth.

9. In 2009, a Japanese sushi chef named Jiro Ono became the first person in Japan to be awarded three Michelin stars, the highest honour in the culinary world. He is the subject of a documentary called "Jiro Dreams of Sushi" that explores his lifelong dedication to perfecting his craft.

10. The world's largest wine bottle is called a Melchizedek and can hold up to 40 regular-sized wine bottles. It is named after the biblical figure who was said to have been the king of Salem and a priest of God.

11. During prohibition in the United States, some people would bury their wine bottles in their gardens to avoid getting caught by the authorities. Some of these bottles are still being discovered today by gardeners and archeologists.

12. In ancient Greece, wine was considered a gift from the gods and was often used in religious ceremonies. The Greek god of wine was named Dionysus and he was known for his wild parties and debauchery.

13. The Michelin Guide, which is a prestigious restaurant guidebook, was first published in 1900 by the French tire company Michelin. The guide originally listed hotels, restaurants, and gas stations to encourage people to travel more, and it eventually became known solely for its restaurant recommendations.

In many cultures, it is customary to toast with alcoholic beverages before a meal to express gratitude and goodwill. This tradition is thought to have originated in ancient Rome, where people believed that drinking together before a meal would ward off evil spirits and promote friendship and mutual trust.

Finally, there's the old saying that goes "wine is bottled poetry." While the origin of the phrase is unknown, it captures the sentiment that wine has the power to evoke powerful emotions, memories, and experiences. Whether sharing a glass of wine with friends and loved ones or enjoying a special bottle alone, wine can be a source of pleasure and inspiration.

Phileas Fogg Still Standing

Phileas Fogg's journey around the world not only expanded his geographic horizons, but also his culinary palate. From savouring spicy curries in India to indulging in fresh pasta in Italy, Fogg's travels were a delicious exploration of the world's diverse food and wine cultures. Fogg reminds us that the world is a banquet waiting to be tasted and experienced to the fullest.

He was a man of refined taste and cultured palate. While he may not have specifically offered lessons on pairing food and wine, we can glean some insights from his travels and experiences that can be applied to the art of food and wine pairing. Here are a few:

Consider the region: Phileas Fogg travelled around the world and experienced a wide range of cuisines and wines. He would have understood the importance of considering the region where the wine and food are from. For example, a French Bordeaux would pair well with a hearty beef stew, while a Spanish Rioja would complement a plate of cured meats and cheeses.

Trust your instincts: Ultimately, Phileas Fogg was a man of action who followed his instincts and made bold choices. When it comes to pairing food and wine, there are no hard and fast rules. Trust your own palate and experiment with different combinations until you find the ones that work best for you.

Balance is key: In order to create a harmonious pairing, it's important to balance the flavours and intensities of both the food and the wine. For example, a light and delicate white wine like a Pinot Grigio would be overwhelmed by a rich and heavy steak, while a bold and tannic Cabernet Sauvignon would overpower a delicate fish dish.

Consider the occasion: The occasion can also play a role in wine and food pairing. For example, a light and refreshing white wine would be perfect for a summer picnic, while a bold and complex red wine would be more appropriate for a formal dinner party.

Phileas Fogg was a man of elegance and sophistication, and he would have understood the importance of choosing the right wine for the occasion. For a formal dinner party, you might choose a classic, well-aged wine, while a casual gathering might call for a more playful, easy-drinking wine.

Trust your own taste buds: Ultimately, the most important factor in wine and food pairing is your own personal taste. Don't be swayed by conventional wisdom or the opinions of others - trust your own palate and enjoy the combination that tastes best to you.

British cuisine: Phileas Fogg was a British gentleman, so it's likely that he enjoyed classic British dishes such as roast beef, fish and chips, and shepherd's pie. He would have paired these hearty dishes with full-bodied red wines like Cabernet Sauvignon or Merlot.

American cuisine: In the United States, Phileas Fogg would have had the opportunity to sample classic American dishes like burgers and fries. He might have paired a juicy burger with a bold, fruity Zinfandel or a smooth Merlot.

Overall, Phileas Fogg's wine choices would likely have leaned towards the classics, with a preference for full-bodied reds from France, Italy, and Spain. He would also have enjoyed a variety of white wines, from crisp, refreshing varietals to rich and creamy Chardonnays.

Phileas Fogg may have had the pressure of winning his bet, but let's be real, the true highlight of his journey was the culinary adventure! From sipping on smooth Sauvignon Blancs in New Zealand to dining on delectable dim sum in China, Fogg proved that food and wine are universal languages that can connect us all. So let's follow in Fogg's footsteps, one bite and sip at a time, and discover the world's flavours and libations. Bon Appétit!

Pairing food and wine is a popular topic in the culinary world, and there are many educational resources available to help you learn about this topic. Here are a few options:

Wine Folly: Wine Folly is a website that provides comprehensive wine education resources, including a guide to food and wine pairing. Their pairing guide is organised by wine type (red, white, rosé, sparkling) and provides detailed information on which foods pair well with each type of wine.

The Wine Bible: The Wine Bible is a book by Karen MacNeil that provides a comprehensive overview of wine, including information on pairing wine with food. The book includes detailed tasting notes for different wines, as well as suggestions for food pairings.

Wine Spectator: Wine Spectator is a magazine and website that focuses on wine education and reviews. Their website includes a section on food and wine pairing that provides tips and suggestions for pairing wine with different types of cuisine.

Sommelier Courses: If you are interested in becoming a certified sommelier, there are many courses available that will provide comprehensive education on wine and food pairing. The Court of Master Sommeliers and the Wine & Spirit Education Trust (WSET) are two popular options.

Local Wine Shops: Many local wine shops offer educational classes on wine and food pairing. These classes are often taught by knowledgeable sommeliers or wine experts and provide a hands-on learning experience.

Overall, there are many educational resources available for learning about food and wine pairing. Whether you prefer online resources or hands-on learning, there are options available to help you improve your knowledge and appreciation of wine and food.

Final Word

As the final pages of this ebook turn, and our journey together comes to a close, I want to raise a toast to you for joining me on this culinary adventure.

We've explored the intricate dance between food and wine, discovering the perfect pairings that can elevate a simple meal to a sensational experience. We've uncovered the secrets of balancing acidity, sweetness, and tannins with various dishes, and we've delved into the fascinating world of wine varietals, regions, and styles.

I hope that this ebook has expanded your knowledge and inspired your taste buds, and that you'll continue to experiment and explore new wine and food pairings on your own. Remember, there are no hard and fast rules when it comes to pairing wine with food - it's all about discovering what tastes best to you.

As we bid farewell, I'll leave you with a quote from the famous wine critic Robert Parker: "Wine to me is passion. It's family and friends. It's warmth of heart and generosity of spirit. Wine is art. It's culture. It's the essence of civilization and the art of living."

So, raise a glass to the art of living, and may your future wine and food pairings always be perfect!

Farewell, Au Revoir, Arrivederci, Namaste!

P J Maalls

Printed in Great Britain
by Amazon

fd50f73d-95b2-4b6c-b738-c93789c9aa7cR01